JEREMIAH

Volume II

JEREMIAH

Volume II

Robert P. Carroll

SHEFFIELD PHOENIX PRESS

2006

First published in paperback in 1986 by SCM Press
This edition published in 2006 by arrangement with SCM-Canterbury Press Ltd

Sheffield Phoenix Press
Department of Biblical Studies, University of Sheffield
Sheffield S10 2TN

www.sheffieldphoenix.com

A CIP catalogue record for this book
is available from the British Library

Printed on acid-free paper by Lightning Source

ISBN 1-905048-64-5

PART TWO

Oracles against the Nations

25.15–38; 46–51

The tripartite structure of the three major prophetic anthologies consists of judgment material, oracles against the nations (OAN), and salvation elements (cf. Isa. 1–12; 13–23; 40–55; Ezek. 1–24; 25–32; 34–39). In spite of significant differences the Jeremiah tradition retains this structure, but there are marked variations between MT and G. In the developments between the two editions the OAN (i.e. Part II) have been separated from their beginnings in 25 and appear in MT after Part IV in 46–51. In G everything concerning the nations is in the one place, but the order of the nations is different (G 25.14–19; 26–32 = MT 46–51; 25.15–38 with minor variations and a distinctive sequence of the nations listed in MT).

The existence of many discrete and disparate strands, books and traditions within the larger Jeremiah tradition points to the diverse forms which originally gave rise to the construction of the book. If these all existed in earlier independent forms, then the OAN also would have circulated in separate form. When they were added to the developing tradition they were probably attached to 25.13a in conformity to the tripartite pattern reflected in Isaiah and Ezekiel. The extent to which they were *added* to or *inserted* into existing manuscripts will have depended upon the state and scope of such manuscripts. The differences between MT and G testify to the flexibility of development and suggest the circulation of manuscripts of both kinds once the OAN were attached to the tradition (i.e. the OAN after 25.13a or appended after 45.5). Between the two editions the order of the oracles has been brought into conformity to the listing in MT 25.15–26 (to some extent) and this points to the originality of G's order (cf. Janzen 1973, 116). For lack of firm information it is only possible to speculate about the different placings of the OAN and such speculations may be consulted in the standard commentaries. (On the shape, substance and interpretation of the OAN see the introduction to 46–51 after Part IV.)

25.15–29

15 Thus the LORD, the God of Israel, said to me: 'Take from my hand this
cup of the wine of wrath, and make all the nations to whom I send you drink
it. 16 They shall drink and stagger and be crazed because of the sword
which I am sending among them.'

17 So I took the cup from the LORD's hand, and made all the nations to
whom the LORD sent me drink it: 18 Jerusalem and the cities of Judah, its
kings and princes, to make them a desolation and a waste, a hissing and a
curse, as at this day; 19 Pharaoh king of Egypt, his servants, his princes, all
his people, 20 and all the foreign folk among them; all the kings of the land
of Uz and all the kings of the land of the Philistines (Ashkelon, Gaza, Ekron,
and the remnant of Ashdod); 21 Edom, Moab, and the sons of Ammon; 22
all the kings of Tyre, all the kings of Sidon, and the kings of the coastland
across the sea; 23 Dedan, Tema, Buz, and all who cut the corners of their
hair; 24 all the kings of Arabia and all the kings of the mixed tribes that
dwell in the desert; 25 all the kings of Zimri, all the kings of Elam, and all
the kings of Media; 26 all the kings of the north, far and near, one after
another, and all the kingdoms of the world which are on the face of the
earth. And after them the king of Babylon shall drink.

27 'Then you shall say to them, "Thus says the LORD of hosts, the God
of Israel: Drink, be drunk and vomit, fall and rise no more, because of the
sword which I am sending among you." '

28 'And if they refuse to accept the cup from your hand to drink, then
you shall say to them, "Thus says the LORD of hosts: You must drink! 29
For behold, I begin to work evil at the city which is called by my name, and
shall you go unpunished? You shall not go unpunished, for I am summoning
a sword against all the inhabitants of the earth, says the LORD of hosts." '

[25.15–29] = G 32.1–24. G prefaces the section with 25.13b as a title: *hosa eprophēteusen Ieremias epi panta ta ethnā*, 'which Jeremiah prophesied against all the nations'. Rudolph, 164, uses 25.13b as a preface to vv. 15–29. **[15]** MT *kī*, 'for . . .': a secondary linking of vv. 14, 15 (JPSB translates it but not RSV, NEB); lacking in G. MT *'ēlay*, 'to me': lacking in G and some Vrs. MT *qaḥ 'et-kōs hayyayin haḥēmāh hazzō't miyyādī*, 'take the cup of wine, this wrath from my hand': lit. '. . . the cup of the wine, the wrath this . . .'.

G *tou oinou tou akratou*, 'of unmixed wine' = *yayin haḥemer*, cf. Ps. 75.9; Driver 1937–38, 119, reads *hayyain haḥōmeh*, 'strong wine'. MT 'this cup of wine, wrath' may represent variants (Bright, 158); Rudolph deletes 'of wrath', cf. BHS. MT *wᵉhišᵉqītāh 'ōtō*, 'and cause to drink *it*': *kōs*, 'cup' is fem., *yayin*, 'wine', is masc., so 'it' must refer to the wine rather than the cup; *'ōtō* lacking in G. **[16]** MT *wᵉšātu wᵉhitgōᶜᵃšu*, 'and they shall drink and stagger': G *kai piontai kai exemountai*, 'and they shall drink and vomit', cf. NEB 'When they have drunk it they will vomit'; *yitgōᶜᵃšū* is used of the waters of the Nile in 46.8 'like rivers whose waters surge', an image better conveyed by the term 'vomit' than 'reel to and fro' (?), cf. 5.22b for similar images. McKane 1980b, 491, regards 'vomiting' as the meaning of *htgᶜšw* rather than 'reeling'. 16b (from 'because of the sword . . .') is omitted by Rudolph as an addition from v. 27b; it spoils the image created by 16a (Duhm, 203): the wine makes them dizzy, crazed, not the sword. **[17]** MT *wā'ašᵉqeh*, 'and I made drink': EVV '. . . drink it' imply *wā'ašᵉqehā* (cf. Duhm, 204). **[18]** G lacks 'and a curse, as at this day'. What does *'ōtām*, 'them', refer to in v. 18? Only cities, not kings or princes, can be a ruin or a desolation; but the context requires officials (to drink the wine), not places. As the unit is directed against foreign nations, v. 18 should be deleted as an addition derived from vv. 1–14 (cf. Bright, 161). Rudolph treats it as an addition reflecting vv. 9b, 11a; 44.6, 22; cf. BHS. **[20]** MT *wᵉ'ēt kol-hāᶜereb*, 'and all the mixed company': NEB 'and all his rabble of followers'; G *kai pantas tous summeiktous autou*, 'and all *his* mixed (people)', understanding it as a continuation of v. 19 and referring to those under the Pharaoh's control (cf. Ex. 12.38). G lacks 'and all the kings of the land of Uz', cf. Lam. 4.21 for the association of Uz and Edom (the phrase may belong to v. 21). Rudolph deletes also 'and all the kings of the land of the Philistines'. The absence of Gath from the formal listing of the Philistine Pentapolis (also absent in 47) is curious; the reference to 'the remnant of Ashdod' may reflect the Egyptian campaign of Psammetichus I against the town which destroyed it after a long siege (cf. Herodotus II, 157 which refers to a twenty-nine year siege). G lacks 'and' before the towns (MT *wᵉ'et*), thus making them a new set for visiting with the cup (cf. v. 19 *'et-parᶜōh*). **[22]** MT *malᵉkē hā'ī*, 'kings of the coast, islands': NEB 'kings of the coasts and islands'; the coasts which are across the sea, i.e. the regions beyond the sea, are the Phoenician colonies and islands. G *basileis tous en tō peran tes thalassēs*, 'kings in (the region) beyond the sea'. Rudolph treats v. 22 as secondary in his translation. **[23]** MT *būz*, 'Buz': G *rōs*, 'Ros'. MT *wᵉ'ēt kol-qᵉṣūṣē pē'āh*, 'and all who cut the edge (of their hair)'; cf. 9.25 (EV 26), a reference to the desert tribes (G 'all who shave round their face'). **[24]** MT *wᵉ'ēt kol-malᵉkē ᶜᵃrāb*, 'and all the kings of Arabia': cf. v. 20a; lacking in G. MT repeats the phrase (vocalizing *ᶜrb* as *ᶜᵃrāb*, 'Arabia', in the first instance and *ᶜereb*, 'mixed company', in the second); G lacks the dittography and reads *ᶜrb* as 'mixed (people)'. Both phrases in MT are probably glosses on v. 23b (cf. Bright, 158); Rudolph retains only 'who dwell in the desert' of v. 24 which he reads with v. 23. **[25]** MT *zimrī*, 'Zimri': the place or territory is unknown; G lacks the phrase 'all the kings of Zimri'. Rudolph reads Zimki as an athbash (see on v. 26) for *'ēlām*, 'Elam' (*zmk* for *'lm*), so that the following clause is a gloss on it ('all the kings of Zimki'). An athbash followed by its decoded form may be possible but is unlikely. Volz, 387–8, reads the name as Simri, in the neighbourhood of Elam and Media. **[26]** MT *kol-hammamᵉlᵉkōt hā'āreṣ*, 'all the kingdoms of the earth': G lacks 'earth'; MT *hā'āreṣ*, a variant of 'upon the face of the earth'; one version is sufficient. BHS repoints MT as *hammamᵉlākōt*. MT *ūmelek šēšak*, 'and the king of Sheshak': *šēšak* is an athbash – a cryptographic device whereby letters of the alphabet in reverse order are substituted for letters in the proper order (' becomes *t*, *b š* etc. in Hebrew). Hence MT *ššk* = *bbl* (Babylon). Sheshak may have been a genuine name for Babylon used by the Babylonians (cf. Nicholson, II, 222–3; see on 51.1, 41). As a cipher athbash need not imply secrecy or contribute to dating v. 26 before 539 (cf. Bright, 161), but in the context of vv. 15–29 (and OAN) may be an echo of magical rituals of an incantatory nature. G lacks the phrase; T has 'Babylon'. G also lacks 'shall drink after them' (i.e. all of MT after '. . . on the face of the earth'). Rudolph treats vv. 25–26 as secondary. **[27]** MT *ūqᵉyū* (K[Mss] *wqww*): Rudolph vocalizes as *wᵉqīyyū* (= *wᵉqī'ū*, stem *qy'*, 'vomit, disgorge, spew up'), '(drink and be drunk) and vomit'. **[29]** G lacks 'says Yahweh of hosts'.

Brongers 1969; McKane 1980b, 487–92

Three stages form this unit: a trial by ordeal procedure contributes an image introducing the motif of the judgment of the nations, a list of the kings of the nations provides the victims of this judgment, and the drinking image is developed to give a justification for the destruction of the nations. The three elements do not form an original unity but are used to build up an attack on the nations. Even though the drinking metaphor appears in vv. 15–17 and vv. 27–28, the two pieces are quite distinct. They encapsulate the list of kings and peoples within a context of ritual magic which guarantees the downfall of all those named in the list. The present position of the unit is linked to vv. 8–11, 12–14 by the parallel motifs of 'sending' and 'taking' (*šlḥ*, *lqḥ*, vv. 9, 15): in the word of judgment against Judah Yahweh sends for and takes a family (MT 'families' makes a better parallel with the nations of vv. 18–26) from the north, in the cup metaphor Jeremiah (assuming the continuity of vv. 1, 2, 15) takes from Yahweh's hand the fatal cup and is sent to all the nations. Thus in the redaction of 25 a certain symmetry is obtained and the commonalty of all the nations, including Judah, stressed.

The action of vv. 15–17 is not easily understood. The divine command and the response to it of the speaker suggest the magical action category encountered in 13.1–7; 19.1–2, 10–11. But whereas obtaining a girdle or a ceramic flask and travelling to a specific place with either are coherent ideas with quite feasible possibilities of execution, taking a cup *from Yahweh's hand* and making *the nations* drink are far from clear notions. Rudolph treats the unit as a vision (this approach is used by him for 13.1–8 as well and doubles the amount of visionary material in the tradition) and thereby resolves the problem of staging the action. Interpreting the images as part of a literary production would also avoid the difficulties entailed by envisaging a literal event. Clearly no literal meaning can be posited of vv. 15–17: a cup handed by Yahweh to Jeremiah and then taken around the nations, from Egypt to Babylon and from the bedouins of Arabia to the islands beyond the sea, cannot be interpreted literally. A dramatic performance with various individuals playing the parts of the kings of the nations is possible (cf. Carroll 1981, 133), but unlikely. It is unlikely because part of the problem is caused by the addition of the list of nations to the image of the cup and also because the development of the unit has turned a metaphor into a dramatic representation of magical significance. If an original poem has been reworked here into a more complicated literary piece (cf. DeRoche 1978) or the original image has been extended by the list (cf. Isa. 3.16–24 where simple transformations of beauty into ugliness have been extended by a lengthy list of garments and ornaments), then it is futile seeking to reconstruct an original setting for a hypothesized action. As a unit vv. 15–17, 19–26 may give the appearance of a sustained action (magical or symbolic), but that is the effect of reading the different elements as a coherent whole. The action only takes place in the redacted material; in its constituent parts there are only discrete images.

The image of the cup of wine, identified as Yahweh's anger, is a common metaphor (cf. 51.7; Obad. 16; Ezek. 23.31–4; Isa. 51.17, 22; Hab. 2.16; Zech. 12.2; Lam. 4.21; Ps. 75.9; analysis in Brongers). Drinking from this cup is a way of expressing the view that somebody or something is the recipient of divine wrath. Behind the metaphor may be one of two background settings: a banquet or a trial by ordeal (cf. McKane). In the trial by ordeal (Num. 5.11–31) the wife suspected of adultery must submit to a magical ritual operated by the priest: in the sacred precincts she must drink the water of bitterness containing holy water, dust from the sacred floor, and the curses washed from the book in which they have been written. This act of drinking is the final element in a series of ritual gestures, and its outcome determines her state (i.e. whether she has committed adultery or not) and therefore her fate. It is an ordeal which may demonstrate her guilt or her innocence. In so far as the images of vv. 15–17 portray judgment, elicit a verdict, prove guilt and impose a penalty, they may be said to reflect the trial by ordeal (McKane, 490–1). But that ceremony only provides the metaphor of the cup: the nations are not on trial but are already guilty and the wine is their execution (hence the addition of v. 16b explaining the meaning of the images of drunkenness). The woman's fate in the ritual drinking of the curse-laden water is not predetermined but may be settled either way depending upon whether her guilt or innocence is established (cf. Brongers, 183). The fate of the nations is determined and when they drink from the cup they vomit. Hence they are doomed. The cup divines their future (cf. Volz, 389; Gen. 44.5 for the divining cup).

The banquet imagery may also contribute to the understanding of the metaphors in vv. 15–16. In 8.14; 9.15; 23.15 Yahweh is represented as supplying a banquet of poisonous substances for the people and prophets of Judah. The same idea may be behind the giving of the cup to the nations (what McKane, 491, calls a 'banquet of death'), only wine rather than poison is the drink served. The great wine feasts, drunken orgies associated with funerary cults (cf. 16.5, 7; Amos 6.7), may be the setting here. On this occasion of the feast, however, it is Yahweh who serves (via his messenger) the wine, and the terrible drunkenness and vomiting which follow represent the divine judgment against the nations. Those who have caused Judah such appalling suffering must now take their turn at drinking the wine of Yahweh's wrath. This reversal is better expressed in Hab. 2.15–16, where the sense of reciprocation is plainly asserted. Both the trial by ordeal and the wine banquet settings may provide elements of the images used in vv. 15–17.

The various secondary features of vv. 18–26 (details in Rudolph, 164; see Notes) indicate how the second stage of the unit has been built up to include all the nations, the mighty enemies of Judah and the lesser tribes which had never had any contact with it. The presence of v. 18 makes the whole sequence a movement of the divine wrath from original target (vv. 8–11) to original instrument (vv. 9, 26). Such a universalization of Yahweh's anger is evidence of an apocalyptic development in the unit and confirms the lateness of the redaction. This apocalyptic feast for the nations reverses the image of a divine wine feast for them in Isa. 25.6 but can hardly include v. 18 (cf. Isa. 51.22–3 for the necessary adjustment of the image of Yahweh's bowl of wrath). The listing of the nations in vv. 19–26 is much more comprehensive than in the oracles against the nations of 46–51 and the order, although quite similar, is not the same (closer in MT than G). That the final point of the list is Babylon may be deduced from the oracles against the nations, but the use of Sheshak in v. 26 (cf. 51.41) may indicate a cipher for whatever the great power of the period may have been (e.g. Greek or Roman; cf. Duhm, 206). In 51.41 the cipher has no concealment force but the manipulation of letters may be a trace of the ritual magic inherent in the OAN. Its occurrence in 25.26 within a context of magical rituals and curses is evidence for reading it as an incantatory device – whether against Babylon or Babylon's successor (cf. Rev. 18.2, 10, 21) is a moot point.

The third stage returns to the cup image but develops it in terms of an explanation of why the nations must suffer. The presentation of the cup to the nations is not an invitation to drink but a command. No option is offered them. Thus the image is developed by means of a discussion between messenger and nations. The lack of choice provides an explanation in v. 29. The nations must consume the wine because Jerusalem has suffered Yahweh's wrath already and the nations can be no exception to that movement of anger. There is a transformation here which turns the destruction of Jerusalem (the theme of 2.5 – 25.11, 13a) from being Yahweh's punishment for its long history of oppression and offences against Yahweh into the first act (i.e. 'I am beginning . . .') of Yahweh's doing evil against *all* the inhabitants of the earth. A quite radical reinterpretation of the tradition appears here and the apocalyptic character of the unit is quite marked (cf. Peake's view of the cipher as an apocalyptic fondness for mysterious designations). A hint of this reinterpretation is to be found in v. 12 where the Babylonians are to be punished 'for their iniquity', presumably because they had attacked Jerusalem (cf. 51.49, 'Babylon must fall for the slain of Israel'). However, in

v. 29 it is not only Babylon but all the nations who must suffer – if Jerusalem is punished, why should any nation go unpunished? Yet there is no hint of this idea in the first part of the tradition (cf. 30. 7; 45.5). Jerusalem and its people suffer for many reasons, but never as an instalment of a universalized divine wrath (a motif more at home in the later apocalyptic movements). The development of the cup metaphor may reflect the images associated with the divine day of vengeance in Isa. 63.1–6, where the deity tramples down the people in his anger just as he has trodden the wine press. The transference of the deity's bowl of wrath from Jerusalem to its tormentors (Isa. 51.21–23) is part of this imagery but is not used in the unit here. With the incorporation of the different units into the redaction of 25, the word of judgment dominates the whole chapter and therefore there is no place for such a transference motif. But if judgment begins at Jerusalem it will most certainly not end there.

25.30–38

30 'You, therefore, shall prophesy against them all these words, and
say to them:
"The LORD will roar from on high,
and from his holy habitation utter his voice;
he will roar mightily against his fold,
and shout, like those who tread grapes,
against all the inhabitants of the earth.
31 The clamour will resound to the ends of the earth,
for the LORD has an indictment against the nations;
he is entering into judgment with all flesh,
and the wicked he will put to the sword,
says the LORD."
32 Thus says the LORD of hosts:
Behold, evil is going forth
from nation to nation,
and a great tempest is stirring
from the farthest parts of the earth!
33 And those slain by the LORD on that day shall extend from one
end of the earth to the other. They shall not be lamented, or
gathered, or buried; they shall be dung on the surface of the ground.
34 Wail, you shepherds, and cry,
and roll in ashes, you lords of the flock,

for the days of your slaughter and dispersion have come,
and you shall fall like choice rams.
35 No refuge will remain for the shepherds,
nor escape for the lords of the flock.
36 Hark, the cry of the shepherds,
and the wail of the lords of the flock!
For the LORD is despoiling their pasture,
37 and the peaceful folds are devastated,
because of the fierce anger of the LORD.
38 Like a lion he has left his covert,
for their land has become a waste
because of the sword of the oppressor,
and because of his fierce anger.'

[MT 25.30–38] = G 32.30–38. **[30]** MT *ūmimm^{e}'ōn qod^{e}šō*, 'and from his holy habitation': G *apo tou hagiou autou*, 'from his sanctuary' = *miqqod^{e}šō*. The motif of Yahweh roaring from his sanctuary (in Zion) also appears in Amos 1.2; Joel 3.16 (MT 4.16); cf. Isa 66.6. MT *hēdād k^{e}dōr^{e}kīm ya'^{a}neh*, 'a shout like treaders will answer': cf. NEB 'an echo comes back like the shout of men treading grapes'; for the imagery cf. 48.33; 51.14; Isa. 16.9f. Rudolph, 166, reads the final clause 'against all the inhabitants of the earth' with v. 31 (cf. BHS; G); Bright, 162, takes 'the clamour will resound' of v. 31 with v. 30. Rudolph regards vv. 30–31, 33 as secondary. **[31]** MT *n^{e}tānām*, 'he will give them (to the sword)': G *edothēsan*, 'are given' = *nitt^{e}nū*; V *tradidi* = *nātatti*, 'I have given'. For the motif of a quarrel between Yahweh and the nations (*kī rīb layhwh baggōyim*, 'for Yahweh has a dispute with the nations') cf. 2.9; Isa. 3.13, where the quarrel is with Judah (reversed in 50.33–34). Both motifs are metaphors and have no necessary connections with a covenant lawsuit. **[33]** MT *bayyōm hahū'*, 'on that day': G *en hēmera kuriou*, 'in the day of the lord' = *b^{e}yōm yhwh*. G lacks 'they shall not be lamented, or gathered'. The verse is a prose expansion using motifs to be found elsewhere in the tradition (cf. 8.2b; 12.12; 16.4) but here reapplied to the nations; it interrupts the connection between vv. 32, 34. **[34]** MT *w^{e}hitpall^{e}šū*: an act of mourning – 'roll in ashes' (RSV), 'sprinkle yourselves with ashes' (NEB), 'strew (dust) on yourselves' (JPSB); cf. 6.26 ('ashes' expressed); Micah 1.10; Ezek. 27.30; G *koptesthe* 'mourn, lament', by striking oneself as a sign of grief. MT *ūt^{e}pōṣōtīkem*, 'and your dispersal': lacking in G; exegetes regard the word as unintelligible (e.g. Weiser, Rudolph, Bright). Weiser, 222 n. 1, suggests *w^{e}nippaṣtīkem*, 'and I shatter you' (*npṣ*, 'shatter'; cf. *pṣṣ*, 'shatter'). MT *kik^{e}lī ḥemdāh*, 'like choice vessel': the two verbs *pūṣ*, 'scatter'; *npl*, 'fall', may be variants, one referring to sheep (the dominant metaphor of vv. 34–7), the other to vessels; G *hōsper hoi krioi hoi eklektoi*, 'like choice rams' = *k^{e}'ēlē ḥemdāh* (?). Ehrlich 1912, 309, reads as *bib^{e}lī ḥem^{e}lāh*, 'without mercy'. **[37]**

Bright, 160, omits the phrase 'because of the fierce anger of Yahweh' as it duplicates the last clause of v. 38 (where G lacks it). **[38]** MT *kakk^epîr . . . kî*, 'like a lion . . . for': BHS deletes *k . . . kî* as dittographies. MT *mipp^enê ḥ^arôn hayyônāh ûmipp^enê ḥ^arôn 'appô*, 'because of the anger of the oppressor(s) and because of his fierce anger': G *apo prosōpou tēs machairas tēs megalēs*, 'before the great sword'. EVV read 'sword' with G (cf. Vrs), treating 'anger' as a dittography from the final clause; cf. 46.16, where *mipp^enê ḥereb hayyônāh*, 'because of the sword of the oppressor', may represent what MT should be here (but see on 46.16).

Whatever the taking of the cup of wine around the listed nations sequence may refer to, it is provided with a commentary (Rudolph) in vv. 30–38. A series of poetic sayings grouped together is presented as a prophetic statement ('and *you* shall prophesy against them', v. 30). The words of this statement spell out the message of the cup and conclude the introduction to the oracles against the nations. These poems would fit anywhere in the tradition because they are about the fierce wrath of Yahweh destroying the nations of the earth, the wicked and the leaders of the peoples. Nothing precise or particular is to be found in vv. 30–38, but images of destruction and anger (already pervasive throughout 2–20). The dominant metaphors are drawn from the language of sheep-herding: shepherds, sheep, pastures and sheep-folds (cf. 6.1–3; 23.1–4). The repeated references to 'shepherds' and 'lords of the flock' parallel the subject of 'kings' in vv. 19–26. It is the leaders of the nations who are addressed, but the devastation will include their peoples. If the language of the poems repeats images found throughout Part I and the rest of the tradition (e.g. v. 32, 'the farthest parts of the earth', cf. 6.22; 32.8; 50.41), it would be unwise to attribute it to any one particular speaker (e.g. Jeremiah; to whom Rudolph attributes vv. 32, 34–8). It is a dominant feature of the book of Jeremiah that many of its strands (metaphors and poetry) are shifted around throughout the tradition without any firm location within a specific section. Such shifts point to redactional influences rather than indicate authentic Jeremiah speeches. The metaphors which describe Yahweh's destruction of the nations do double service in the tradition; they refer as much to Judah as to the nations (which direction the influence goes is a moot point).

The commentary or, better, appendix is a prophetic utterance (reflecting the late strand of Jeremiah *as* prophet implicitly if not explicitly) introduced by the announcement of Yahweh's war against the inhabitants of the earth. This is the language of apocalyptic doom rather than of military campaigns. Although v. 30 is similar to Amos 1.2 and Joel 3.16 (the nations are the context of all three occurrences), there are subtle differences between them. Zion is the stated centre of divine action in Amos and Joel but is only implied in v. 30 (but NEB 'roars from Zion on high' makes it explicit). The transcendental atmosphere of apocalyptic language is more direct here because it allows for the divine roaring (the lion of v. 38) to be done from the heavens in contradistinction to its effects being felt to the ends of the earth (MT 31). The sanctuary (G) may well refer to the temple (cf. Ex. 15.17), so the interpretation of v. 30 should allow for a dual reference to heavenly and earthly sanctuaries. But the judgment of Yahweh against the nations starts from the holy place and spreads out across the earth (note the similar images of temple and destruction of the nations enclosing the work of Haggai). Only the Joel reference counterbalances the divine roaring with a statement about the protected status of the people of Israel, but there is nothing in vv. 30–38 which militates against reading such a notion as being implicit in all the material directed against the nations. In v. 27 there is the beginning of a reversal of Judah's fate (cf. vv. 12, 14); the oracles which follow (G ends the collection with vv. 15–38) in 46–51 contain further statements to this effect.

Yahweh's roar is like the shout of those who tread the grapes (cf. Isa. 16.9–10), i.e. the riotous pleasure of those who enjoy what they are doing and anticipate the consumption of their labours. It has about it a furious strength, a full-blooded engagement in the task at hand, that is well characterized by the reference to treading the grapes in the winepress (cf. 48.33). The roar of those who trample the grapes and stain their garments red easily becomes a metaphor for the appalling slaughter of war (Isa. 63.1–3). Commotion, confusion, enthusiasm, liquefaction processes and social encounter are the common elements shared by making wine or waging war. But the deity's form of wine-making is blood-letting. The noise will be heard throughout the earth because Yahweh has a quarrel (*rīb*) with the nations (cf. 2.9). The divine quarrel with which Part I begins has been transferred from Judah to the nations by Part II, but in neither case is it necessary to construct a complex theology of covenantal forms to explain such a quarrel. There is no covenant between Yahweh and the nations, yet he has a *rīb* against them. Why, then, should a *rīb* against Judah necessarily entail a covenant? Yahweh's evil (cf. v. 29), i.e. his storm (cf. 23.19; 30.23), goes forth from nation to nation (just like the cup in v. 17), and disaster befalls all. The leaders of the nations are commanded to go into mourning because there can be no escape from this disaster. It is like a lion leaving its lair and going among the sheep – terrible destruction follows. The metaphors of sheep-herding dominate vv. 34–38. Hence the shepherds fall like choice rams and what they should be protecting, namely the sheep-folds, are devastated. Yahweh's anger wipes out the nations.

PART THREE

Miscellaneous Narratives and Cycles

26–36

The second half of the book of Jeremiah poses serious problems of division and classification. The long stretch of chapters from 26 to 45 is broken into smaller collections and discrete narratives, but commentators differ on how they should be grouped. No central organizing theme can be detected in the twenty chapters which would allow them to be treated as a unity or give them a unifying title. Bright's 'Incidents from the life of Jeremiah' as a title is only a loosely accurate description which requires the extraction of 30–33 from the collection and incorporates into it units from other parts (e.g. 19.1–2, 10–11, 14–15; 20.1–6; 21.1–10; 24; 32.1–15; 51.59–64b). It also ignores the absence of Jeremiah from 40.7–41.18. If the word of judgment dominates 2.5–25.11 as an overarching concept (with only a few fragments of salvation material), there is no equivalent organizing principle for 26–45. The closest element to such a unifying feature is the notion of the word of Yahweh proclaimed by Jeremiah (26–36) and its fulfilment in the destruction of Jerusalem and the fate of those who survived that catastrophe (37–45; cf. Ackroyd 1968b). Jeremiah as the servant of the word holds together most of the narratives (with the exception of 39.1–10; 40.7–41.18) rather than incidents from his life and this theme may be used to organize the material in a number of ways (cf. Kessler 1968, 83–7).

The precise division of 26–45 into two parts (i.e. Parts III and IV in this commentary) is equally a matter for disagreement among exegetes. 26.1 ('the reign of Jehoiakim') and 37.1 (Zedekiah as replacement of Jehoiakim) indicate the most natural division of 26–45 into two blocks. If 26–45 are not divided up into parts, decisions of this kind may be avoided, but the subtle shifts of emphasis which appear in the redaction will be missed. Commentators organize the sections of the book in many different ways (e.g. Volz, Hyatt, Thompson), but the scheme followed here is essentially the four-part division proposed by Rudolph, with minor variations (cf. Rudolph, 1). The variations include the classification of 1 and 52 as prologue and epilogue and the precise division of 26–45. Rudolph divides parts C and D into 26–35 and 36–45 (cf. Rietzschel 1966, who also follows this division). Rudolph's title for part C is 'prophecies of salvation for Israel' (Rudolph, 168). The presence of doom material in 26–29; 32.26–35; 34.8–22 hardly justifies Rudolph's title, and a less one-sided category is required to describe the contents of Part III. A further disagreement with Rudolph concerns the actual division of the two parts. A better case can be made for dividing the collection at 36 than at 35 (cf. Kessler 1968). 36 functions in relation to 26–35 in the same way as 25.1–11 relates to 2–20: it summarizes and acts as a closure of the section. It concludes what is begun by 26. It therefore belongs with 26–35 much more than it does with 37–45 (see on 37.1–2).

In Part III 26 and 36 act as preface and conclusion: 26 raises the question of turning, but 36 demonstrates the rejection of that possibility. Two distinctive cycles are included in Part III: an independent treatment of prophetic conflict (27–29), with its own peculiar features, and a book of salvation oracles (30–31), with prosaic appendices (32–33). Two independent narratives (34–35) complete the collection in III.

26.1–24

26[1] In the beginning of the reign of Jehoiakim the son of Josiah, king of
Judah, this word came from the LORD, 2 'Thus says the LORD: Stand in the
court of the LORD's house, and speak to all the cities of Judah which come
to worship in the house of the LORD all the words that I command you to
speak to them; do not hold back a word. 3 It may be they will listen, and
every one turn from his evil way, that I may repent of the evil which I intend
to do to them because of their evil doings. 4 You shall say to them, "Thus
says the LORD: If you will not listen to me, to walk in my law which I have
set before you, 5 and to heed the words of my servants the prophets whom
I send to you urgently, though you have not heeded, 6 then I will make this
house like Shiloh, and I will make this city a curse for all the nations of the
earth." '

7 The priests and the prophets and all the people heard Jeremiah speaking
these words in the house of the LORD. 8 And when Jeremiah had finished
speaking all that the LORD had commanded him to speak to all the people,
then the priests and the prophets and all the people laid hold of him, saying,
'You shall die! 9 Why have you prophesied in the name of the LORD, saying,
"This house shall be like Shiloh, and this city shall be desolate, without
inhabitant?" ' And all the people gathered about Jeremiah in the house of
the LORD.

10 When the princes of Judah heard these things, they came up from the
king's house to the house of the LORD and took their seat in the entry of the
New Gate of the house of the LORD. 11 Then the priests and the prophets
said to the princes and to all the people, 'This man deserves the sentence of
death, because he has prophesied against this city, as you have heard with
your own ears.'

12 Then Jeremiah spoke to all the princes and all the people, saying, 'The
LORD sent me to prophesy against this house and this city all the words you
have heard. 13 Now therefore amend your ways and your doings, and obey
the voice of the LORD your God, and the LORD will repent of the evil which
he has pronounced against you. 14 But as for me, behold, I am in your
hands. Do with me as seems good and right to you. 15 Only know for certain
that if you put me to death, you will bring innocent blood upon yourselves
and upon this city and its inhabitants, for in truth the LORD sent me to you
to speak all these words in your ears.'

16 Then the princes and all the people said to the priests and the prophets,
'This man does not deserve the sentence of death, for he has spoken to us
in the name of the LORD our God.' 17 And certain of the elders of the land
arose and spoke to all the assembled people, saying, 18 'Micah of Moresheth
prophesied in the days of Hezekiah king of Judah, and said to all the people
of Judah: "Thus says the LORD of hosts,

Zion shall be ploughed as a field;
 Jerusalem shall become a heap of ruins,
 and the mountain of the house a wooded height."

19 Did Hezekiah king of Judah and all Judah put him to death? Did he not
fear the LORD and entreat the favour of the LORD, and did not the LORD
repent of the evil which he had pronounced against them? But we are about
to bring great evil upon ourselves.'

20 There was another man who prophesied in the name of the LORD,
Uriah the son of Shemaiah from Kiriath-jearim. He prophesied against this
city and against this land in words like those of Jeremiah. 21 And when
King Jehoiakim, with all his warriors and all the princes, heard his words,
the king sought to put him to death; but when Uriah heard of it, he was
afraid and fled and escaped to Egypt. 22 Then King Jehoiakim sent to
Egypt certain men, Elnathan the son of Achbor and others with him, 23

and they fetched Uriah from Egypt and brought him to King Jehoiakim, who slew him with the sword and cast his dead body into the burial place of the common people.

24 But the hand of Ahikam the son of Shaphan was with Jeremiah so that he was not given over to the people to be put to death.

[MT 26] = G 33. **[1]** MT *hāyāh haddābār hazzeh*, 'this word came . . .': S adds *'l 'rmy'*, 'to Jeremiah', cf. 27.1; Rudolph inserts it into the text (cf. BHS), also Volz, 92. MT *b^erē'šît mam^el^ekût y^ehôyāqîm*, 'in the beginning of the reign of Jehoiakim': cf. 27.1; 28.1, which both start with the same formulaic 'in the beginning of the reign of . . .' (with the variation *mam^eleket*, 'reign'). Such stereotypical introductions to 26.1; 27.1; 28.1 are indicative of redactional activity rather than accurate historical datings (see on 27.1). The accession year (cf. Akk. *rēš šarrūti*) of Jehoiakim refers to the period between the king's accession and the following new year, i.e. c. Sept 609 – April 608 (Bright, 169). **[2]** Cf. 7.2. MT *'al-tigra' dābār*, 'do not withhold a word': cf. Deut. 4.2; 13.1 (EV 12.32); Janzen 1981 for the concept of withholding the word (i.e. diminishing it). Cf. 50.2 for the sense of hiding the message (also 38.25). **[5]** MT *w^ehaškēm w^ešālōaḥ*, 'and rising early and sending': cf. 7.25; 25.4; 29.19; 44.4 (variations in 7.13; 11.7; 35.15); delete first 'and' with many mss and Vrs. MT *w^elō' š^ema'tem*, 'but you did not listen': the phrase is virtually a Leitmotif in Part III (cf. the variations on it in 27.9, 14, 16, 17; 29.19; 32.33; 34.17; 35.14, 15, 16, 17; 36.31). **[6]** K *hz'th*; Q *hazzō't*, 'this': K a scribal error, but Driver 1951, 244–5, regards the rare pronominal form as a remnant of colloquial or local idiom; G lacks 'this (city)'. For the city as a curse (*q^elālāh*) cf. 25.18; more often used of remnants who survive the defeat of the city (24.9; 42.18; 44.8, 12). Used of the land (44.22), Bozrah (49.13), and a general curse (29.22). **[8]** MT *kol-'^ašer-ṣiwwāh yhwh*, 'all which Yahweh had commanded': Vrs read . . . *ṣiwwāhū* . . . '. . . commanded *him* . . .', cf. BHS. MT *w^ekol-hā'ām*, 'and all the people': BHS regards the phrase as an addition from v. 7a; Rudolph, 170, deletes it because only the priests and prophets are prosecutors, whereas the people belong with the judges in vv. 11, 16. The fluctuating role of the people is one of the problems of the interpretation of 26 (Bright, 170, takes it to mean 'various of the people' rather than literally). MT *mōt tāmūt*, 'you will surely die': a variation of the formal legal ruling *mōt yūmat*, 'he will surely die' (cf. Schulz 1969, 71–83, on the legal terminology and its sacral background and 118–23 on 26.7–19). **[9]** MT *nibbētā*, 'you have prophesied': some mss have the more usual form *nibbē'tā*. MT *wayyiqqāhēl kol-hā'ām 'el-yirm^eyāhū*, 'and all the people gathered to Jeremiah': some mss, Vrs have *'al*, 'against', for *'el*, 'to', cf. NEB; see BHS for the *'el*/*'al* variations in 26. The use of *qhl* may reflect a formal religious assembly (cf. v. 17b), which would suit the sacral language used in the story (cf. Schulz, 122). **[10]** MT *wayyu'^alū*, 'and they came up':

cf. 22.1; the temple was at a higher level than the royal residences. MT *b^epetaḥ ša'ar-yhwh heḥādāš*, 'at the door of the gate of Yahweh, the new one': many mss, Vrs read *bēt*, 'house of' before 'Yahweh', cf. 36.10. **[12]** G lacks 'all' before princes; cf. v. 16. **[13]** Cf. 7.5; the notion of Yahweh's repentance (cf. v. 19) is mooted as a general principle in 18.7–10. **[17]** MT *wayyāqumū 'anāšīm mizziq^enē hā'āreṣ*, 'and *men* from the elders of the land stood up'. **[18]** K *mykyh*; Q *mīkāh*, 'Micah'; cf. Micah 1.1. The citation in v. 18b is from Micah 3.12. G lacks *hāyāh nibbā'*, 'was prophesying'. MT *'iyyīm*, 'ruins' (*'iyyīn* in Micah 3.12), cf. Ps. 79.1; EVV 'heap of ruins' is justified as a parallel to *l^ebāmōt yā'ar*, 'forest heights', lit. 'high places of a wood, forest', cf. NEB 'rough heath'; JPSB 'a shrine in the woods' (G *alsos drumou*, 'a grove [sacred] of oaks', i.e. 'a thicket grove'). Rudolph, 172, reads *l^ebah^amōt*, 'for beasts of (the forest)', as in Micah 5.7 (EV 8), fulfilled in Lam. 5.18 (cf. BHS); cf. Janssen 1956, 89. **[19]** MT has '*they* put to death . . . *he* feared . . . *he* appeased . . .', Vrs sing . . . plur . . . plur. MT *way^eḥal*, 'and he appeased (the face of Yahweh)': *ḥillāh*, 'appease, mollify, entreat the favour of, pacify'; NEB 'seek to placate'. The anthropomorphism ('soften the face') is a vestige of ancient rituals relating to the idol of the god in the cult (cf. Bright). **[20]** G lacks 'against this city and'. Kiriath-jearim: about six miles north-west of Jerusalem. **[21]** G lacks 'and all his warriors . . . and he was afraid and fled'. MT *way^ebaqqēš hammelek*, 'and the king sought': G *kai ezētoun*, 'and they sought'. **[22]** MT *'anāšīm miṣrāyim*, 'men Egypt': cf. v. 17; an unnecessary addition (cf. BHS) in view of 22b (lacking in G); cf. 36.12 for Elnathan. **[23]** MT *qib^erē b^enē hā'ām*, 'the graves of the sons of the people': i.e. the common burial ground (probably in the Kidron valley, cf. II Kings 23.6). G *to mnēma huiōn laou autou*, 'the memorial of the sons of his people': i.e. his family grave.

Hossfeld und Meyer 1974; Reventlow 1969

The second half of the book of Jeremiah opens with a story which attempts to present Jeremiah as the speaker of the authentic word of Yahweh, a role which is recognized and acknowledged by important social strata in the community. Part III will end with a story in which very powerful strata of society will reject that role and seek his execution (36). If in the first story he escapes for reasons which are far from clear (see on v. 24), in the second he escapes because he has gone into hiding (36.26). In 26 he openly proclaims his message of doom against temple and city, in 36 he does it by sending a deputy speaker to read a written account of his oracles. Both proclamations (in person and delegated) take place in the temple precincts. Between the two stories subtle shifts in Jeremiah's temerity may be imagined to have taken place but the text allows no insight into them (see on 36.5). In point of fact, the two stories should be read as parallel and paradigmatic. In 26 Jeremiah is fully present and Jehoiakim completely absent (the redaction in vv. 1a, 20–23 makes that absence palpable); in 36 Jeremiah absents himself while Jehoiakim is very much present. The tradition knows of no encounter between Jeremiah and Jehoiakim. A few incidents are dated to the reign of Jehoiakim but Jeremiah never confronts him nor addresses him directly. The only contact between Jeremiah and a king allowed by the tradition is that in which Jeremiah and Zedekiah meet or that king consults Jeremiah. Even the formal dating of certain speeches to the time of Jehoiakim (e.g. 25.1; 26.1; 36.1) may be questioned as to historical accuracy and these passages are probably to be treated as redactional notes making connections between the tradition and 605, the date of Carchemish and Nebuchadrezzar's rise to supreme power (see on 1.2–3). The two formidable characters, Jehoiakim and Jeremiah, never meet because they only belong together as elements in the structured narratives. It is in the redaction of the tradition and the creation of the story in 36 that the two approach, but only as shadows. The absence of the one is the presence of the other – both cannot occupy the stage at the same time.

In the original story of 26 there is no place for Jehoiakim and the absence of the king from matters of sacral law is to be expected. Some Deuteronomistic influence may be detected in 26 (e.g. vv. 3–5, 12–15 show traces of Deuteronomistic reflection, cf. Thiel 1981, 3–4; Nicholson 1970, 52–6), especially in the presentation of what looks like a formal trial without any recourse to the king (Deut. 16.18; 17.8–12 allow no place for the king in relation to the dispensation of justice; cf. Boecker 1980, 40–9; de Vaux 1965, 150–2). Given the nature of the debate in 26 there is no role for the king to play and, although it may well be asked how the princes became involved without the king knowing about it (especially in view of vv. 20–23), therefore he is absent. Yet his absence may be accounted for also on the grounds that the narrative is a story constructed to make certain points and not an account of a historical incident in the life of Jeremiah (cf. Hossfeld und Meyer; Schulz 1969, 122–3). As a fictional story the narrative cannot be expected to answer questions asked about historical matters. Questions such as 'Why is the king absent throughout the trial?', 'Why are vv. 20–23 included in the story?', 'Why should there be such a reaction to Jeremiah's preaching in 609 when, according to 2–20, he has been saying such things for decades?', 'What coherent role do the people play in the story?', 'If the princes and *all* the people acquitted him (v. 16) what does v. 24 mean?', 'If Jeremiah was acquitted as one who genuinely spoke in Yahweh's name, in what sense may the people be said to have rejected the divine message?', and many others cannot be asked because they all presuppose that 26 is about a real event. The story is not the record of what happened to Jeremiah as a result of his preaching vv. 4–6 in the temple precincts. It is a complex of different strands of redaction which has developed an original story about a public procedure for establishing Jeremiah's authenticity in a number of different ways (cf. Hossfeld und Meyer; Reventlow, 341–51). As a result of these diverse interferences the final form of the story mystifies the modern reader as to its meaning. The redactional levels provide a surfeit of meaning without clarifying their aim by ending the narrative at v. 16.

Many commentators treat 26 as a real event in the life of Jeremiah and their work may be consulted for an alternative handling of the text (e.g. Bright, Thompson). There are similarities between the edited version of 26 and the temple sermon as presented in 7.1–15 (cf. vv. 2, 4–6, 13), but these represent strands added to 26 rather than another version of 7.1–15 giving occasion and response. The tensions between conditional and absolute elements in the sermon (e.g. 7.3–7, 8–15) are not so apparent in 26 but may be discerned in vv. 3–6, 13 (contingent word) and vv. 9, 11–12 (absolute word). But the editing of the story makes it impossible to separate out conditional from absolute elements because the Deuteronomistic schema of the sending of the prophets, and their rejection seals the fate of the city whatever the response of one particular generation. Jerusalem's fate is inevitable, not only because it happened but as a result of a long history of the rejection of the prophetic word (v. 5). This is such a dogma of the tradition that it skews any presentation of Jeremiah as a preacher of repentance (the radical nature of 18.7–10 is post-Deuteronomistic and late). A call to repentance would hardly have sparked off the riot of a lynching mob (cf. vv. 8–9, 24), nor would it have led to Uriah's extradition and execution (vv. 20–3).

The formal structures of the story should be noted. Jeremiah stands in the temple courtyard and announces the word to all the cities of Judah as they congregate there. He utters a curse against the city – in the environment of the temple an uttered curse is a most powerful and fateful act. It releases aweful forces against its object. Small wonder then that those who heard it should seize (v. 8 *tpś*, 'lay hold of, arrest', cf. 2.8; 34.3; 38.23) the speaker of it. Priests, prophets and people arrest Jeremiah and charge him with a capital offence. The crowd milling around him (v. 9b) may give the impression of a near riot, but there may be an element of a formal religious gathering against him (*qahal*, v. 17; cf. v. 9, may refer to the sacred congregation). Temple precincts, destruction of a sanctuary (Shiloh), curse, cultic officials, and the sacred congregation all point in the direction of a sacral procedure in which the accused is liable to face the penalty for blasphemy. Temple and city have been cursed and the charges of blasphemy against god and people (king?, cf. I Kings 21.10, 13) are implicit in the demand for the death penalty. The story does not explain why this should be so, but the reaction of priests, prophets and people clearly indicates that cursing the temple (vv. 6, 9, 12) or the city (vv. 6.9, 11, 12, 20) warrants such punishment. This can only be explained on the grounds that an ideology of the sacred site and city existed which made both the property of the deity (e.g. Ps. 46; 48; Lam. 4.12). So to speak against either was to blaspheme Yahweh of hosts, *the* god of Israel. What justification can there ever be for such blasphemy?

The story changes in v. 10 with the introduction of the princes. What are they doing in a case involving sacral matters? They have no jurisdiction here. This is a matter for priests. The Deuteronomic regulations allow for cases which are too difficult for local judgments to be taken to the divinely chosen place and there to be heard by the priests (Deut. 17.8–12; cf. Mayes 1979, 268–9). Difficult decisions are to be determined not by the royal house and certainly not by the king but by sacral means. Now the king is rightly absent from the story, but what are the princes doing here? They are introduced into the story to turn the proceedings into a kind of trial. Sufficient evidence is already available to convict Jeremiah of blasphemy, but the shaping of the story by the redaction is in a different direction from that charge. The commotion or a report brings the princes up from the royal residences to the temple gate, where they take their seat (thus combining the ancient village practice of judgment in the gate with the sacral proceedings in the temple; on the old practice cf. Köhler 1956, 149–75). There are now five parties to the dispute; Jeremiah, priests, prophets, people and the princes: accused (Jeremiah), accusers (priests, prophets, people) and judges (princes).

But another switch is introduced in v. 11, when the people appear to become part of the judges (so Rudolph), or certainly cease to be among the accusers (contrast v. 24). A symmetrical structure is developing here: priests and prophets on one side, princes and people on the other side, and Jeremiah in the middle. The charge is repeated in v. 11, though the claim 'as you have heard with your own ears' can only loosely include the princes in view of v. 10.

Now Jeremiah speaks in his own defence (cf. Ramsey 1977, 51). This self-defence speech contains a number of elements: he claims as his warrant for what has been said Yahweh's sending – a formal claim to the right to prophesy (cf. Amos 7.15) – a call to the amendment of life, thus rendering the judgment a contingent one and raising the possibility of Yahweh's repentance – the city is not yet doomed – a complete submission of the speaker to his judges' power – a magnificent gesture of self-humbling which indicates a lack of arrogance – and a warning that a death sentence executed against him will bring innocent blood upon the city. These elements constitute a formidable set of claims which is summed up in v. 15b: 'for in truth Yahweh sent me to you to speak in your ears all these words'. It is an impressive performance by a man facing death at the hands of a mob screaming for his blood and, even more dangerous, a tribunal with the power to execute him. The editors have penned the portrait of a very brave man.

Having duly considered his defence (vv. 12–15), the princes and the people answer his accusers with what appears to be the verdict: 'this man does not warrant the sentence of death (*mišpaṭ-māwet*) because he has spoken to us in the name of Yahweh our god' (v. 16). The story should end here with everybody returning to their homes. Jeremiah has been vindicated by the 'court' on his own testimony and has neutralized the power of the priests and prophets by gaining the sympathy of the princes and the people. He has also acquired public recognition of his authenticity as one who speaks the words of Yahweh (the verdict emphasizes that point '*in the name of Yahweh our god* he has spoken to us'). The decision of the princes and the people has affirmed his innocence and he has escaped from death.

The narrative should end at v. 16 because Jeremiah has been vindicated and had his claim to be sent by Yahweh accepted by the nation. If the purpose of the story is to present Jeremiah before the tribunal and its outcome, then it has been achieved. However, in vv. 17–19 a further element is added to the story: men from the senior representatives of the rural areas (i.e. elders, cf. 19.1) arise and address the sacred congregation. In a most unusual fashion they cite another prophetic saying from a previous century. The citation from Micah of Moresheth-gath (cf. Micah 1.14; Mays 1976, 37), a countryman from the area south-west of Jerusalem, provides a precedent for Jeremiah's attack on the city and the temple-hill (cf. Micah 3.12). It also indicates a history of attacks on the city from non-residents (cf. 1.1, which locates the family home of Jeremiah at Anathoth, a town to the north of Jerusalem). The introduction of Micah's prediction about the destruction of Jerusalem, city and temple, may afford a precedent but the real concern of the elders' speech is with the community's response to it. In the light of Micah's terrible words what was the response of king and nation? Did they put Micah on trial and execute him? No! they most certainly did not. They listened to him, took him seriously, feared Yahweh, and appeased the deity. In turn the deity repented and the evil predicted against the city was withdrawn from it (cf. 18.7–8). The final element of their appeal relates to the trial of Jeremiah: if the community proceeds to execute Jeremiah (after v. 16!), then it will bring upon itself even greater evil (cf. v. 15).

There are a number of strange features in vv. 17–19. The direct citation of another speaker's work and its use as an argument are unique in the prophetic traditions. The availability of such a quotation suggests a collection of Micah's oracles (at least those which may be regarded as authentic in Micah 1–3) and therefore a period when such a record had some authority (i.e. after the fall of Jerusalem in 587). The conclusions drawn from Micah's utterance (the citation in v. 18 is prefaced by the oracular 'thus says Yahweh of hosts', whereas Micah 1.2–3.12 hardly ever use such indicators) are most unusual. The modern reader of Micah 3.12 would conclude that Micah had been unduly pessimistic and wrong (cf. von Rad 1965, 150 n. 5). But an entirely different conclusion is taken from the failure of his prediction in the eighth century. The elders see in its non-fulfilment the rescinding of the threat by Yahweh because king and people respond in the proper fashion to such threats. There is no evidence for such a view in Micah 1–3 because the charges levelled against the community are not the kind that ritual gestures (e.g. the appeasement of Yahweh referred to in v. 19) can dissipate. The context of Micah's prediction is an attack on the leaders of Zion (rulers, priests, prophets cf Micah 3.9–11) and the city's fate is caused by those leaders (Micah's 'therefore because of *you*' is notably absent in v. 18). Having built Zion in blood, how could they change that past? But Micah 3.12 is only inappropriate in the context of 26.7–16 because of the argument based on it in v. 19. It does provide a precedent for Jeremiah's preaching, but it does not warrant the use made of it in v. 19 by the redactors.

The function of the Micah citation in v. 19 belongs to the editorial strand which presents the story as a call to change (vv. 3, 13). There is no evidence for Hezekiah's change of heart, and in the Deuteronomistic history he is presented as an incomparable king: 'there was none like him among all the kings of Judah after him, nor among those who were before him' (II Kings 18.5; Hezekiah's piety and rectitude are unimpeachable, cf. II Kings 18–20; only the Chronicler hints at a blemish in terms of his pride after his illness [II Chron. 32.24–26. cf. II Kings 20.12–19], and that reflects the fact of the Babylonian exile [cf. Williamson 1982, 386]). Yet if Micah was a genuine speaker of the divine word, and his utterance of 3.12 did not come to pass (cf. the regulation in Deut. 18.20–22), then some account must be provided which will justify his status. That justification is amply supplied in v. 19 and any dissonance arising from a falsified prediction is avoided (cf. Carroll 1976b). However that is but an incidental by-product of v. 19. A more important feature of v. 19 is the implicitly prescriptive nature of its description of Hezekiah's response to the word of absolute doom. Reference to Hezekiah (whether it reflects a memory of Micah playing a role similar to Isaiah's in II Kings 19.1, 14–28 [cf. Mays 1976, 92] is a moot point) inevitably transforms 26 into a statement for king and people. Hence the editorial allusions to Jehoiakim in vv. 1, 20–23 in spite of his complete absence from the story.

The story in vv. 20–23 has nothing to do with the structured confrontation of vv. 7–16 but is a response to v. 19. It also functions as background information on the situation facing Jeremiah, but lacks cogency here because, even if it represented an accurate historical account of a particular event rather than a further editorial creation, it neither reflects a trial nor the beginning of Jehoiakim's reign (v. 1). Some exegetes read it as an illustration of what might have happened to Jeremiah (e.g. Bright, 172; Thompson, 528), but the absence of Jehoiakim from the story of Jeremiah renders that less than likely. Jehoiakim and his court are introduced to make a formal contrast with Hezekiah and his people. Both are represented as hearing the prophetic word proclaimed against the city: Micah in the time of Hezekiah and Uriah ben Shemaiah (also from outside Jerusalem) in the time of Jehoiakim (see on 36 for further paradigmatic parallels). Hezekiah and his people responded by appealing to and appeasing Yahweh, thereby changing the deity's mind (thus confirming the principle expressed in v. 13). Jehoiakim and his people, on the contrary, responded to Uriah by seeking to kill him (just like priests, prophets, people in v. 8). Like a fool Uriah fled to Egypt, where (could he have not known?) the authorities supported Jehoiakim because he was their vassal. Uriah was extradited from Egypt (as he must have known he would be, unless he was an exceptionally ignorant prophet!), returned to the court and was there executed. His burial may have been ignominious (but cf. G; is this the origin of the application of 22.18–19 to Jehoiakim by way of revenge for Uriah?). Jehoiakim's response to Uriah could not be more different from Hezekiah's reaction to Micah. Thus vv. 19–23 provide two paradigms of response to the word of absolute judgment: the prescriptive nature of v. 19 and the disapproved of behaviour of vv. 20–23 are implicit features of the narrative.

What about Jeremiah? What happened to him? His absence in vv. 17–23 is noteworthy, though his implied presence may cast a shadow over the material here. In v. 24 the editors return to him and observe that he escaped death at the hands of the people because Ahikam ben Shaphan enabled him to do so. How odd! In v. 16 the people, as well as the princes, acquit Jeremiah of the charge of blasphemy (or treason as vv. 20–23 seem to imply). So why should he be given to them for stoning? (For stoning as the penalty cf. Deut. 13.6–11; 21.18–21; I Kings 21.13–15.) Have the people changed sides yet again? What power did they have that could override that of the princes? These questions, like so many other questions raised by the editing of this chapter, cannot be answered because we are not dealing with a historical account which provides accurate information. Too many discrete strands make up the story for a coherent account to be derived from it. The theological shaping of Part III (cf. 36) is such that the word proclaimed by Jeremiah must be heard by all (e.g. 26.2, 7; 36.6, 10), yet also rejected (36.31; cf. 37.1–2). Jeremiah must be acquitted of blasphemy or else his authenticity will not be established (hence v. 16), but if he is acknowledged as being sent by Yahweh the people will have to pay attention to him and believe his words. How to achieve both his legitimation *and* his rejection is the real problem for the editors. It cannot be achieved because it involves a logical contradiction, but the editing of the story using many discrete strands allows the contradiction to be glossed over by separating the verdict from the conclusion. 26 may be heard now as if it were a coherent story rather than an amalgam of very different elements all doing quite separate things in the narrative. 587 and the theology of some of the redactors are responsible for that state of affairs.

This analysis of 26 represents an attempt to allow each separate strand to contribute to the story without ignoring the way so many discrete elements have ruined whatever may have been the original story. The fate of Jeremiah is hardly an interest of the editors (cf. Hossfeld und Meyer, 48), but as the introduction to the second half of the book the story points to opposition between Jeremiah and different strata of society. As the bearer of the divine word his social role is important, but his own personal fate lacks all significance for the editors (e.g. the tradition lacks both birth and death notices for him). Conflict with the prophets (27–29) and the upper classes (36, 38) will characterize many of the narratives, and all these elements are in 26. The passing references to Micah and Uriah are strange, but exemplify the diverse elements forming the narrative. The switches and shifts in the narrative underline the discrete nature of much of the material but also frustrate the interpretative task of making sense of the whole text.

The transformation of Micah into a preacher of doom leading to repentance is one of the most remarkable features of 26. Such a reversal indicates the distance the tradition has travelled from Micah of Moresheth-gath in the direction of Jonah ben Amittai. Jonah is the paradigmatic figure of the prophet preaching a message of absolute doom and achieving repentance by it. The people of Nineveh repent by means of ritual gestures and appease the deity by fasting, dressing in sackcloth, crying to God, and turning from their evil ways (both man *and beast*, cf. Jonah 3.5–10). Thus their imminent doom is averted. King Hezekiah and his people are presented as responding to Micah's proclamation of imminent catastrophe in a similar way and with equal success. Elements of the prophet as the preacher of repentance by means of the absolute word of destruction appear in 26. But whereas Micah and Jonah are successful transformations of doom into salvation, Jeremiah remains as an example of an unsuccessful reversal. Real disasters (e.g. 587) cannot be so averted.

In point of fact the reversals of Micah and Jonah were but holding actions, because Jerusalem and Nineveh later were destroyed. However, that is hardly the point of the stories. The reversal of Micah in 26.17–19 is of a piece with the many reversals of material within the Jeremiah tradition itself (see on 27.16–22; 32.36–41; 33.10–11; 52.31–4) and illustrates just how radically elements could be handled and transformed in relation to their original meanings.

Another late element in 26 is the notice about the pursuit and execution of Uriah ben Shemaiah (vv. 20–3). Apart from its contribution to doing down Jehoiakim (cf. 22.17, which is associated with Jehoiakim by virtue of the redactional note in 22.18a), it is one of only two such notices in the Bible (cf. II Chron. 24.20–22 where Zechariah ben Jehoiada, in whom the divine spirit clothes itself, speaks out against the people in an oracular fashion and is stoned for his moment of inspiration) where the prophetic activity is punished by execution. The traditions earlier than the Chronicler's know nothing of the killing of prophets. The people of ancient Israel were not in the habit of executing their prophets (the legendary Jezebel may have tried to introduce the practice into Israelite culture but such 'folly in Israel' never caught on) – the motif of the persecuted and murdered prophet is a dogma of a later time (cf. Steck 1965) and its appearance in 26.20–23 reflects that late belief. If the later dogma had any truth in it, Jeremiah would not have lived as long as the tradition (cf. 1.1–3) represents him as having done so. He would quickly have met the fate said to have befallen Uriah (in post-biblical literature he is stoned by the people in Egypt!). That he lived such an active life for so long undermines the dogma and exposes it as a later romantic glossing of the prophets as so many Ishmaels (i.e. 'his hand against every man and every man's hand against him', Gen. 16.12). Yet the editing of the Jeremiah tradition contributed to the making of that dogma, and the midrash of Uriah ben Shemaiah especially reflects its development. However, the people of ancient Israel are maligned enough in 2–20, and should be spared this further libel against their collective memory. They may not have listened to their prophets: they certainly did not refuse to listen to the point of killing them.

Jeremiah against the prophets: an independent cycle 27–29

A series of stories about Jeremiah is set in and around 597 in a cycle of narratives. These stories portray Jeremiah's attitudes to all the other prophets, whether Judaean or foreign, Jerusalem-based or active in Babylon, and to Babylon. He is against *all* the prophets and for Babylon. The cycle is an independent one in the tradition, as its distinctive style demonstrates (cf. Rudolph, 172). In it Jeremiah is described as *the* prophet (28.1, 5, 6, 10, 11, 12, 15; 29.1; lacking in G), and some of his prophetic opponents are named (e.g. Hananiah, Shemaiah; cf. Ahab and Zedekiah 29.21–23). The theoretical nature of the attack on the prophets in 23.13–32 is replaced in this cycle by specific situations in which the prophets are presented as opponents of Jeremiah. Distinctive features of the cycle are the spelling variations which indicate its discrete origins and circulation. The regular spelling of Jeremiah is *yirmᵉyāhū* (e.g. 1.1, 11; 7.1; 11.1), but in the cycle it is the variant form *yirmᵉyāh* (27.1; 28.5, 6, 10, 11, 12, 15; 29.1; reverting to regular spelling in 29.27, 31). A similar variation is to be found for Zedekiah's name: *ṣidᵉqiyyāhū* is the regular form (e.g. 21.1, 4, 7; 32.1; 37.1; 39.1), but it is *ṣidᵉqiyyāh* in the cycle (27.12; 28.1; 29.3; cf. 49.34). The proper form of the Babylonian emperor's name is Nebuchad*r*ezzar (e.g. 25.9; 32.1; 34.1; 37.1), but it appears as Nebuchad*n*ezzar in the cycle (27.6, 8, 20; 28.3, 11, 14; 29.1, 3; except for 29.21), a form to be found in other biblical traditions (e.g. II Kings 24.1, 10, 11; 25.1, 8, 22; Ezra 1.7; Dan. 1.1; 2.1). Such spelling variations are only minor matters, but they indicate the independent origins of the cycle.

The three chapters of the cycle share a number of motifs, and 28 may be considered a variant story of 27.16, 18–22. The treatment of Shemaiah in 29.31–32 parallels that of Hananiah in 28.15–16, and the denunciation of the Judaean prophets in Babylon (29.8–9) is a variant of the attack on the foreign prophets (27.9–10). Such shifts of motifs point to the literary origins of the cycle. The cycle is a literary creation rather than historical records or reflections. The legendary role of Jeremiah is quite apparent and, although dating the cycle is not possible, there are a number of similarities between the way he behaves and the Chronicler's portrayal of prophets. Furthermore, the discussion about the fate of the temple furnishings (27.16–28.4) is akin to views held about them in Chronicles, Ezra and Daniel. The Nebuchadrezzar of the cycle is very much the Nebuchadrezzar of the legends of Daniel. All these connections *suggest* a provenance in the fifth century (if not later) for the cycle. The expansion of 29 with material about the restoration of the people from exile (vv. 10–14) spoils the force of the cycle as a statement about life under Babylonian rule and 29 as a strategy for *permanent* community life in Babylonia. As such, the cycle probably represents the legitimation of life outside Palestine, though it has been glossed by a Judaean redactor at some point.

The cycle is tied into the larger tradition by means of redactional introductions at the beginning of each chapter. These are similar to the introductory note in 26.1, except for 29.1–3 where a more complicated preface introduces the story. Nothing in the stories which follow these redactional notes is necessarily dependent upon the dating or setting, and the stories may be regarded as quite independent of their present presentations. They are in this way similar to the stories of Daniel and his companions in Babylon, which are set in the period immediately after Jeconiah's deportation by Nebuchadrezzar. Although the cycle is stitched into the tradition by various means, its distinctive character and outlook cannot be overlooked. It is pro-Babylonian in a fundamental way and rejects the belief that there would be a return of the temple furnishings to the shrine in Jerusalem (MT 27.22 modifies this attitude). In the light of the campaign to return the furnishings to Jerusalem in the book of Ezra it is possible that the cycle retains traces of a particular controversy about the temple of which 27–28 represent an anti-Ezra movement. Analogous to this reading of the cycles is the one offered on 22.24–30, where it is suggested that the categorical rejection of Coniah in the oracles there is directed against the Haggai-Zechariah campaign to make one of his descendants the new Davidic leader of the community. The stress on the theme of Jeremiah against all the other prophets overshadows this other strand but it may still be discerned in the cycle. The balance to the view that Babylon is now the centre of Yahwistic life is to be found in the next cycle (30–31) and other elements throughout the tradition.

27.1–22

27 1 In the beginning of the reign of Zedekiah the son of Josiah, king of
Judah, this word came to Jeremiah from the Lord. 2 Thus the Lord said
to me: 'Make yourself thongs and yoke-bars, and put them on your neck. 3
Send word to the king of Edom, the king of Moab, the king of the sons of
Ammon, the king of Tyre, and the king of Sidon by the hand of the envoys
who have come to Jerusalem to Zedekiah king of Judah. 4 Give them this
charge for their masters: "Thus says the Lord of hosts, the God of Israel:
This is what you shall say to your masters: 5 'It is I who by my great power
and my outstretched arm have made the earth, with the men and animals
that are on the earth, and I give it to whomever it seems right to me. 6 Now
I have given all these lands into the hand of Nebuchadnezzar, the king of
Babylon, my servant, and I have given him also the beasts of the field to
serve him. 7 All the nations shall serve him and his son and his grandson,
until the time of his own land comes; then many nations and great kings
shall make him their slave.'

' "8 But if any nation or kingdom will not serve this Nebuchadnezzar
king of Babylon, and put its neck under the yoke of the king of Babylon, I
will punish that nation with the sword, with famine, and with pestilence,
says the Lord, until I have consumed it by his hand. 9 So do not listen to
your prophets, your diviners, your dreamers, your soothsayers, or your
sorcerers, who are saying to you, "You shall not serve the king of Babylon."
10 For it is a lie which they are prophesying to you, with the result that you
will be removed far from your land, and I will drive you out, and you will
perish. 11 But any nation which will bring its neck under the yoke of the
king of Babylon and serve him, I will leave on its own land, to till it and
dwell there, says the Lord." '

12 To Zedekiah king of Judah I spoke in like manner: 'Bring your necks under the yoke of the king of Babylon, and serve him and his people, and live.
13 Why will you and your people die by the sword, by famine, and by pestilence, as the Lord has spoken concerning any nation which will not serve
the king of Babylon? 14 Do not listen to the words of the prophets who are
saying to you, "You shall not serve the king of Babylon," for it is a lie which
they are prophesying to you. 15 I have not sent them, says the Lord, but
they are prophesying falsely in my name, with the result that I will drive you
out and you will perish, you and the prophets who are prophesying to you.'

16 Then I spoke to the priests and to all this people, saying, 'Thus says
the Lord: Do not listen to the words of your prophets who are prophesying
to you, saying, "Behold, the vessels of the Lord's house will now shortly be
brought back from Babylon," for it is a lie which they are prophesying to
you. 17 Do not listen to them; serve the king of Babylon and live. Why
should this city become a desolation? 18 If they are prophets, and if the

word of the LORD is with them, then let them intercede with the LORD of hosts, that the vessels which are left in the house of the LORD, in the house of the king of Judah, and in Jerusalem may not go to Babylon. 19 For thus says the LORD of hosts concerning the pillars, the sea, the stands, and the rest of the vessels which are left in this city, 20 which Nebuchadnezzar king of Babylon did not take away, when he took into exile from Jerusalem to Babylon Jeconiah the son of Jehoiakim, king of Judah, and all the nobles of Judah and Jerusalem – 21 thus says the LORD of hosts, the God of Israel, concerning the vessels which are left in the house of the LORD, in the house of the king of Judah, and in Jerusalem: 22 They shall be carried to Babylon and remain there until the day when I give attention to them, says the LORD. Then I will bring them back and restore them to this place.'

[MT 27] = G 34. G is considerably shorter than MT and illustrates well how the second edition (MT) developed from a shorter text by way of many expansions as well as a different recension (analysis and exegesis of differences in Tov 1979). **[1]** G lacks this redactional introduction; MT is presumably modelled on 26.1 (cf. 28.1). MT *bᵉrē'šīt mamᵉleket yᵉhōyāqim*, 'in the beginning of the reign of *Jehoiakim*': a few mss, S have 'Zedekiah' for 'Jehoiakim'. The inaugural year of Jehoiakim (see on 26.1) is wrong for what follows (e.g. Zedekiah is mentioned in vv. 3, 12 and implied in vv. 16–22). The mistaken MT raises the question of the extent to which 26.1 may not also be wrong. 26.1; 27.1; 28.1 all appear in MT as stories set in the inaugural years of kings (see on 28.1), but their errors and redactional nature suggest that they are most unreliable guides. BHS reconstructs the dating as 'in the fourth year' following 28.1 (cf. Rudolph, 176, where it is mooted that this may be the heading for 27–29; perhaps 26.1 has influenced 27.1); cf. 28.1 'in that year', i.e. the same year (Zedekiah's fourth year). The formulaic reception of the divine word phrase is the same here as in 26.1 *hāyāh haddābār hazzeh . . . mē'ēt yhwh*, '*this* word came . . . from Yahweh' (cf. Neumann 1973 for the formulaic variations in 1–25); both occurrences of '*this* word' indicate the redactional influence linking the two chapters. **[2]** MT *kōh-'āmar yhwh 'ēlay*, 'thus said Yahweh to me': the formula also occurs in 13.1; 19.1, where Jeremiah is ordered to go and purchase items; cf. 25.15 (expanded divine title), where the item acquired by Jeremiah is that with which he is sent to the nations (as here). **[3]** MT *wᵉšillaḥtām*, 'and send them': this is the logic of such magical-symbolical acts (cf. 25.15–17); EVV delete 'them' (cf. JPSB margin), BHS reads *wᵉšālaḥtā*, 'and you send', cf. G^L. 28.10 shows Jeremiah to be wearing the yoke-bars, hence he could hardly have sent them to the nations (cf. Rudolph), but as 28 is a variant story, such logic may not apply in this case. MT *mal'ākīm*, 'messengers': G *aggelōn autōn*, 'their messengers' = *mal'ᵃkēhem* (so BHS); Tov, 81, regards *autōn* as an addition rather than a variant reading. G *eis apantēsin autōn* '(who have come) to meet them (at Jerusalem)' = *liqrā'ōtām* (cf. BHS). Tov, 82, treats the shorter MT as more original here than G. **[4]** MT *yhwh ṣᵉbā'ōt 'ᵉlōhē yiśrā'ēl*, 'Yahweh of hosts, the god of Israel': G lacks 'of hosts', as it frequently does in Jeremiah. Out of nineteen occurrences of the phrase 'of hosts' in 'thus says Yahweh of hosts', G lacks fifteen; it never registers *ṣᵉbā'ōt* in the thirty-two instances of the longer phrase 'Yahweh of hosts, the god of Israel'; *ṣᵉbā'ōt* is therefore a divine epithet almost entirely added in the second edition (cf. Tov, 82; Janzen 1973, 75–80). **[5]** G lacks 'with man and beast on the face of the earth' due to homoioteleuton (i.e. the scribe's eye may have jumped from the first *hā'āreṣ*, 'the earth', to the second *hā'āreṣ*). MT *yāšar bᵉ'ēnāy*, 'right in my eyes': cf. 26.14 *wᵉkayyāšār bᵉ'ēnēkem*, 'and as right in your eyes'. The phrase 'by my great power and my outstretched arm' may reflect Deuteronomistic influence (cf. Thiel 1981, 7); it occurs in a similar form in 32.17; Deut. 9.29 ('your' for 'my'); II Kings 17.36 but is not to be confused with the Deuteronomistic cliché 'with mighty hand and outstretched arm' (and its variations). **[6]** G lacks the introductory phrase *wᵉ'attāh 'ānōkī*, 'but now I . . .'; cf. Tov, 82–3 for discussion of the textual fluidity of the two editions here. MT *'et-kol-ha'ᵃrāṣōt hā'ēlleh bᵉyad nᵉbūkadne'ṣṣar melek-bābel 'abdī*, 'all these lands into the hand of Nebuchadnezzar, the king of Babylon, my servant': G *tēn gēn tō Nabouchodonosor basilei Babulōnos douleuein autōn*, 'the earth to Nebuchadnezzar, the king of Babylon, to serve him'. G^{S} lacks 'Nebuchadnezzar' and 'to serve him'. The spelling Nebuchad*n*ezzar is peculiar to the cycle 27–29 in the Jeremiah tradition (normal spelling in 29.21). The phrase 'Nebuchadnezzar, my servant' also occurs in 25.9; 43.10 (lacking in G but see on 43.10); there are some problems in establishing whether the first edition knew this phrase or not (*'abdī*, 'my servant', is conspicuously absent in G 25.9; 50.10 [MT 43.10]), cf. Tov, 83–4; Lemke 1966; Overholt 1968; Zevit 1969. Tov, 84, concludes that MT here reflects the original text rather than G; but G is the original text in the other two references. Nebuchadrezzar's oversight of the beasts of the field is ironic in view of the legend about Nebuchadrezzar's vision, the meaning of which entailed his being driven from among men to have his dwelling *with the beasts of the field* (Dan. 4.25 [MT 22]). 'Yahweh gives and Yahweh takes away' (Job 1.21); but there are times when he gives – he *really* gives! **[7]** G lacks v. 7 (discussion of speculations as to why in Tov, 84–5). The fact that Nebuchadrezzar did not have a grandson who ruled over the empire need not count against MT, as the biblical writers were not historians and did not necessarily have access to such historical knowledge. Nebuchadrezzar's line was superseded in 560 (Bright, 200, thinks it possible that G dropped it in view of this fact and that v. 7 is conceivably original). The triple stages of the phrase 'N . . . son . . . grandson' may refer to three generations or may be an idiomatic way of referring to 'many generations', i.e. 'an indeterminable period of time' (Weinfeld 1972a, 144 n. 5. cf. Tov, 85). If this latter view is taken, then the question of historical inaccuracy does not arise. MT may have developed the time factor by adding '. . . and his son . . . and the son of his son . . .' retrospectively, after 539 (cf. Tov). As in the interpretation of the 'seventy years' of 25.11; 29.10, there is a wide range of possible meanings for v. 7 (whether it is original or secondary). MT *bō*, 'him': this must refer to Nebuchadrezzar, hardly his grandson (cf. *w*ᵉ*'ābᵉdū 'ōtō*, 'they will serve *him*': *w*ᵉ*'ābᵉdū bō*), cf. 25.14. The reversal of the fate of the Babylonians requires a different sense for *bō* which does not fit 'many nations and great kings'; BHS reads *bāh* '(they will make) it (serve)', i.e. the country of Babylon, rather than Nebuchadrezzar (or his descendants, if they are not a further addition to v. 7). MT *gam-hū'*, 'even he': this phrase suggests that the first form of v. 7 applied only to Nebuchadrezzar and envisaged his defeat (cf 28.2–4). **[8]** For 'nation or kingdom' regulations cf. 18.7–10. MT *'ᵃšer lō'-ya'abᵉdū . . . w*ᵉ*'et 'ᵃšer lō'-yittēn 'et-ṣawwā'rō*, 'which will not serve . . . and which will not yield its neck . . .': the two phrases are variants: G lacks the whole sentence up to '. . . king of Babylon' (due to homoioteleuton according to BHS). MT *'ad-tummī 'ōtām b*ᵉ*yādō*, 'until I have consumed them by his hand': *tmm*, 'complete, finish', is seldom used as a transitive verb, so commentators emend to *tittī*, 'I will give (into his hand)', cf. S, T; if MT is retained a word may have fallen out (cf. Bright, 200). The familiar triad 'sword, famine, pestilence' (cf. v. 13; 14.12; 21.7, 9; 24.10; 29.17–18; 32.24, 36; 34.17; 38.2; 42.17, 22) also appears in 44.13 in combination with the verb *pqd*, 'punish, visit upon'. **[9]** MT *ḥᵃlōmōtēkem*, 'your dreams': the list is of agents rather than instruments, so *ḥōlᵉmēkem*, 'your dreamers', is read with Vrs; NEB 'your wise women' suggests a reading of *ḥᵃkamōtēkem* (but cf. Brockington 1973, 208). **[10]** G lacks 'and I will drive you out, and you will perish': the phrase appears in v. 15. It is out of place here because the activity of the agents of v. 9 is distancing (*harḥīq*) the people from their land, rather than Yahweh. **[11]** G lacks *n*ᵉ*'um-yhwh*, 'says Yahweh'. **[12]** MT *b*ᵉ*'ōl melek-bābel*, 'under the yoke of the king of Babylon': repeated from vv. 8, 11; lacking in G. Cf. Neh. 3.5 for the idiom 'bringing the neck under', i.e. 'submitting to'. **[13–14]** G lacks v. 13 and part of v. 14, including the ending of v. 12 (homoioteleuton due to *w*ᵉ*'ibᵉdū 'ōtō . . . ta'abᵉdū 'et-melek bābel*, 'and serve him . . . do [not] serve the king of Babylon', 12b–14a); cf. the discussion in Tov, 87. Rudolph, 177, treats v. 13 as an addition from v. 8. **[15]** MT *lᵉma'an hiddīḥī 'etkem*, 'in order that I might drive you out': cf. v. 10; suffix lacking in G and deleted by BHS 'to drive you out'. Bright here and v. 10 translates 'which will only serve to . . .' as the force of *lᵉma'an*. G reflects a doublet at end of v. 15 ('and your prophets who are prophesying to you, false lies', where *adikō pseudē* represents *šeqer* twice and in a different sequence). **[16]** MT *w*ᵉ*'el-hakkōhᵃnīm*, 'and to the priests': G *humin*, 'to you' (*lākem* from v. 15 in doublet), with reversal of order of people and priests. 16b can hardly be a divine speech in view of

v. 18, where Yahweh is referred to in the third person. Heb. *kᵉlī*, 'articles, vessels, utensils, objects, implements, apparatus, instruments, equipment': 'vessels' does not quite fit the furnishings and equipment of temples and palaces which include furniture and appliances, i.e. any and all movable objects (cf. Bright, 200, 'furnishings'). MT *'attāh mᵉhērāh*, 'now quickly': lacking in G; in 28.3, 11 'within two years' is the expected return period (lacking in G but G^A has it in 28.3). The first edition (G) is concerned with the general question of *whether* the furnishings will be returned, whereas the second edition debates *when* (cf. Tov, 88). Bar. 1.1–3.8 deals, at length, with the story (cf. Tov 1976). MT *kī šeqer hēmmāh nibbᵉ'īm lākem*, 'for it is falsehood which they are prophesying to you': G + *ouk apesteila autous*, 'I did not send them', cf. end of v. 15; Tov, 88. G lacks v. 17. **[17]** BHS treats v. 17 as an addition as G lacks it; it disrupts the flow of vv. 16, 18 on the subject of the (temple) furnishings. **[18]** MT *bayhwh ṣᵉbā'ōt*, 'with Yahweh of hosts': G *moi*, 'me' = *bī*, 'with me' (*bī* may represent an abbreviation of the tetragrammaton, cf. Driver 1960, 119–21). G ends v. 18 at this point, MT continues with an expanded account of the fate of the furnishings. G knows of temple furnishings, but MT includes palace materials as well, cf. 52.13. **[19–22]** A much shorter text appears in G: 'For thus says the lord – and as for the remaining implements which the king of Babylon did not take, when he carried Iechonias from Jerusalem, they shall go to Babylon, says the lord.' Cf. Tov, 89–90, on MT expansions. **[22]** Cf. Ezra 1.7–11; Dan. 5.2–3; discussion of 'vessels' theme in Ackroyd 1972, 176–7.

Tov 1979

The linking motif between the three chapters of the cycle 27–29 is the prophets and their relationship to Babylon. The failure of their position on Babylon is reflected in 29 where the material concentrates on the community of exiles there and only in passing touches on a further example of prophets behaving in a false way. The triple strata of 26, priests, prophets and people, are present in all three chapters of the cycle and allow 26 to be considered as a preface to 27–29. Yet the difference in the roles of the priests in 26 and 27–29 should be noted. They are not the hostile figures of 26 but an important element in the organization of the community, whether in Jerusalem or Babylon.

Differences between MT and G not only point to developmental variations between the two editions but also indicate independent treatments of particular motifs (e.g. the fate of the vessels in 27.16–22; the use of the term *pseudoprophetēs* in G to describe the prophets in 26.7, 8, 11, 16; 27.9; 28.1; 29.1, 8; cf. 6.13; Zech. 13.2). Among the themes of 27 is a general rejection of the prophets and their preaching against the Babylonians (vv. 9, 14, 16, 17, 'Do not listen to your prophets'). In view of this central theme its instantiation in 28 is odd in that a specific conflict between two individual named prophets over the issue is unnecessary. However, in the interests of the story in 28 the general ruling 'do not listen to your prophets' is suspended so that a debate between Jeremiah and Hananiah may be presented. 27, 28, therefore, are doublets rather than two historical incidents and should be treated as variations on a theme.

In 27 a number of elements are combined in relation to the central theme of 27–29, 'reaction to Babylon'. The redactional dating at the beginning of each chapter is questionable, but the MT focus on 597/3 is understandable as an attempt to locate the material in some historical context. But the difficulties of demonstrating a specific set of events which would account for a coalition against Babylon *after* 597 (Driver 1963, 83–8; cf. Wiseman 1956, 32–7) must raise questions about the historicity of 27–28. That Zedekiah, a vassal of Neubchadrezzar and presumably also pro-Babylonian in outlook and policy, should even entertain the idea of a rebellion against his overlord *and* at the beginning of his reign (corrected MT 27.1) is too unlikely to be realistic. The already noted phenomenon of the tradition's blending together of 597 and 587 (see on 24.1) may account for the confusion here, but even that cannot resolve all the difficulties. These are created by the editing of the different themes together so that the impression is given that Zedekiah may be contemplating revolt or that he is under pressure from his prophets (where did they come from after the deportation of 597?) to join in a coalition of rebellion represented by the embassy of five kings and their representatives (cf. Driver 1963, 87–8, who dates this visitation to 596). The historical problems may be put to one side in order to pursue the exegesis of 27 as they only bear on the question of the redaction of the text and the genre of the material presented.

Chapter 27 consists of a magical act performed by Jeremiah with reference to the messengers of the five kings of neighbouring countries, an attack on their soothsayers, diviners and prophets who are preaching resistance to Babylon, a statement along similar lines to king Zedekiah, and a denunciation of the Judaean prophets over the matter of the fate of the temple furnishings (cf. the analysis in Seebass 1970 for different emphases). These thematic elements include a number of features which are to be found throughout the tradition (on Deuteronomistic factors cf. Thiel 1981, 5–10; for others cf. Wanke 1971, 19–36, 73–7). The combination of a magical act with direct reference to a list of foreign powers makes vv. 2–11 similar to the cup of wine given to the nations material in 25.15–27. However, here the performance of the divine command is intended to persuade certain nations not to resist Babylon, whereas the wine cup act refers to their destruction (most likely by Babylon). The delegated nature of the message in v. 4 is parallel to the delegated word sent to Babylon in 51.59–64 (on prophetic delegation cf. Schmidt 1982). The one distinctive feature of vv. 2–11 is the fact that the five nations are appealed to rather than informed of their destruction. It is an illustration of the late motif of Jeremiah as a 'prophet to the nations' (1.5) and reflects a somewhat more positive attitude to other nations, characteristic of the cycle 27–29 (cf. 29.7). The making and wearing of the yoke-bars are part of the strand of performative behaviour in the tradition (cf. 19.1–2, 10–11; Wanke 1971, 75; also 13.1–7; 25.15–17; 43.8–13; 51.59–64) but in 28.10–12 the motif has a variable function. If in 27.2–3 the yoke-bars are a message to the foreign nations, in 28.10–12 they are treated as a statement about the fate of Judah (cf. 28.13–14).

The focus on Babylon, one of the distinctive features of the whole cycle, in MT 27 includes the phrase 'Nebuchad*n*ezzar, my servant' (*'abdī*, v. 6, cf. 25.9; 43.10). This expression 'my servant', in which Yahweh is represented as acknowledging the pagan emperor to be his devotee, has occasioned debate. Very different views have been taken of the phrase: it is an accidental error in the textual transmission of the book and represents an addition from a later period when, according to Dan. 2.47; 3.28–4.3, 34–37, 'the famous pagan king has now become a conscious worshipper of the only true God' (so Lemke 1966, 50). Overholt disagrees with Lemke's instrument – servant distinction, argues that 'the basic perception of Nebuchadnezzar is a theological one' (1968, 45) and attributes the phrase to Jeremiah as a statement about Yahweh's instrumental use of the foreign power (cf 50.17; Isa. 10.5). Another approach treats *'ebed*, 'servant', as a diplomatic term meaning 'vassal', so that Jeremiah in using this phrase asserts that the king of Babylon is Yahweh's vassal (Zevit 1969, 77). Various exegetes regard the term as Jeremiah's own invention (e.g. Weiser, Rudolph, Hyatt), even allowing that it is a 'bold thought' (Hyatt, 1011). Comparisons with the designation of the Persian emperor Cyrus as *māšîaḥ*, 'anointed one' (Isa. 45.1), are also made.

The instrumental view of other nations as the deity's way of punishing Israel is a feature of the tradition (e.g. 25.9) and is clearly represented by the metaphors of 50.17 where Assyria and Babylon form an enclosure of such activity. But 'my servant' goes beyond the notion of instrumentality (cf. Assyria as the *rod*, not the servant, in Isa. 10.5) to a level of relationship between deity and emperor more characteristic of Second Isaiah's view of Cyrus. The Jeremiah tradition knows a formal servant-Yahweh relationship but only of the prophets (e.g. 7.25; 25.4; 26.5), and that is a late Deuteronomistic strand. Chapters 27–29 have distinctive features as a cycle, but the phrase is found outside it (25.9; 43.10), so its genuineness cannot be argued for on the grounds of its appearance in a special cycle (though all three references may reflect a common strand or addition to such a strand). G is ambiguous in 27.6 (cf. Tov, 83–4), though it lacks the phrase in 25.9; 43.10. The presentation of Babylon in 27, 29 points to a pro-Babylonian strand (especially 29.7) and reflects the interests of a particular party. For the exiles in Babylon are presented as Yahweh's special concern in 24.4–7; 29.4–7, 10–14 and all the other communities (e.g. Zedekiah's people, the refugees in Egypt) are dismissed from being recipients of Yahweh's favour. The hidden agenda of this strand is to bolster the claims of the *gālût yᵉhûdāh* (the exile party), and the representation of Nebuchadrezzar as the servant of the living god, who carried them into exile, would contribute to those claims. This argument works whether the epithet reflects the later development of Nebuchadrezzar into a pious worshipper of Yahweh or a theology of him as Yahweh's vassal. The treatment of Cyrus in Second Isaiah points to a similar development and suggests a post-exilic date for the cycle. It should be read not so much as a claim for those in Babylon as one on behalf of the few who have returned from Babylon and who wish to gain power in the reconstructed Jerusalem (cf. Ezra-Nehemiah). Nebuchadrezzar and Jeremiah, *both* servants of Yahweh, underwrite that claim. Part of the Babylonian contribution to Judaean theology may be seen in 27.5 where the designation of Nebuchadrezzar is set in the context of Yahweh as the creator of the earth (the exiles learned much about the creator gods in Babylon, cf. Saggs 1978, 41–52; note how the material on Cyrus in Isa. 44.24–45.1, 12–13 is structured by references to Yahweh the creator god). The singling out of the animals in vv. 5, 6 as part of Yahweh's creation and also his gift to Nebuchadrezzar allows for reflection on the irony of Nebuchadrezzar's dream in Dan. 4.4–37 (MT 1–34).

The report of the command to make and wear yoke-bars is not developed to the point where Jeremiah's act of carrying out the command is reported (contrast 13.2, 5, 7; 25.17; cf. 19.14), but the variant in 28.10 implies that he did so. The yoke-bars are thought to symbolize the sovereignty given to Nebuchadrezzar by Yahweh, though such performances carry a much stronger force than that. Hananiah's breaking of them is more than a symbol of their reversal, it is an act designed to reverse their significance. By wearing the yoke-bars Jeremiah *asserts* (by doing) the domination of Babylon. Although the act would have more direct relevance to Judah it is presented in 27.3 as a message for the five nations (listed in the same order as in 25.21–2) and therefore resembles the reading of the scroll in 36 in having a delegated status. Two strands appear to be mixed here: the magical act which destroys Judah (cf. 36.23, where the king tries to prevent it) and the delegated message against the nations (cf. 51.59–64). In v. 8 the message is universalized as a principle of national action in relation to Babylon in a manner similar to the disruption of the visit to the potter's house by the regulations of 18.7–10. The five nations' prophets, diviners, dreamers, soothsayers and sorcerers are dismissed as telling lies with their programme of 'you shall not serve the king of Babylon' (a strange reversal of Jeremiah's message, cf. 28.14; 36.29). The application of so many elements from the tradition to foreign nations is part of the peculiarity of the cycle and is indicative of a secondary usage of conventional motifs quite distinctive in the book of Jeremiah. It may display the logic of the creator god who rules over all the nations (as in 18.7–10 which is a very late element), but it looks more like the misapplication of terms due to the redactional history of the unit.

In vv. 12–15 the same message is proclaimed to Zedekiah (hence the tendency of EVV to substitute his name for Jehoiakim's in v. 1). The essence of the yoke-bars performance is 'submit to Babylon and live' (vv. 12, 17). How very different a view is taken of Zedekiah's kingdom in 24.1–3, 8–10 where no such option is offered to it but it is written off as worthless and doomed! Now it is the Judaean prophets who are described as prophesying 'you shall not serve the king of Babylon' (in v. 14 the plural form of address makes the community rather than Zedekiah the recipient of the message, though it is formulaic in 27). These prophets are dismissed in the language of 23.25, 26, 32 and are blamed for the potential expulsion of the people. The vagueness of the material in 27.2–15 (even allowing for considerable editorial activity cf. Thiel 1981, 7–8) does not permit the exegete sufficient, clear information to determine whether any particular historical occasion is part of the background to the story (e.g. 605, 597, 587). What appears to be the case is the fact that the cycle uses conventional motifs (e.g. the triad in vv. 8, 13; the attack on prophets) drawn from the larger tradition to construct a very distinctive view of Babylon and the causes of the destruction of the nation(s). There is in 27 a radical handling of traditional material which cannot be squared with other parts of the tradition and which therefore points to the independent origin and development of the whole cycle.

In vv. 16–22 the subject matter changes and the speaker addresses the priests and the people (no longer the king). They are not to listen to the prophets (the combination 'priests and prophets' so frequent in the tradition, e.g. 2.8, 26b; 5.31; 6.13b; 8.10b; 26.7, 8, 11, 16 is here broken). This time the falsehood being prophesied by the prophets is different, though it may be regarded as a variation on the previous ie (this is unlikely). What is *šeqer* on this occasion is the proclamation that the temple vessels (i.e. furnishings) will be returned to Jerusalem from Babylon. So the temple has been raided and the Babylonians are in control. That at least means that the attack on Jerusalem of 597 is in the past (implied by MT v. 1). The parallel story in 28.2–4 (with 27.20) sets the temple furnishings motif in the period following the first attack on Jerusalem. But why prophetic activity about the temple furnishings? Why not a more direct claim for the return of the king and the deportees (as in 28.4, but note order of precedence)?

The reference to the temple furnishings (extended in vv. 18, 21 to include palace and other furnishings in Jerusalem) signals the discussion of a topic of controversy at some stage in the rebuilding of Jerusalem (cf. Ezra 1.5–11; 5.14–16; 6.5; analysis of all the relevant texts in Ackroyd 1972). The subject is controversial because according to 52.17–23 and II Kings 25.13–17, when Nebuchadrezzar took Jerusalem in 587 the large furnishings were all broken up and therefore were not in a fit condition to be restored. The matter is more complicated than that because in II Kings 24.11–17 when Nebuchadrezzar captured Jerusalem in 597 he deported Jehoiachin, the leading strata of society, and *all* the treasures of the *temple* and the king's *palace*. The temple vessels were cut in pieces (for transportation purposes and as a ruination of their sacral functions because the god of that temple cult had been defeated). That there are problems with these double accounts of the same event can hardly be doubted, and the temple-furnishings motif is an excellent illustration of the view that the biblical traditions regularly confuse and conflate the invasions, defeats and deportations of 597 and 587. In 27.18–21 there is a recognition that the furnishings in the temple and palaces are those which Nebuchadrezzar *left* after the first penetration of the city. II Kings 24.13 leaves no room for any such residue, and the account of the fall of Jerusalem in 587 in 39.2–10 makes no reference to any temple or palace treasures being taken. There is therefore a variety of very different traditions about the fate of the city's treasures, a multiplicity of viewpoints which cannot be harmonized (cf. Ackroyd 1972, 175). The variety of disparate positions includes the views that in 597 the temple furnishings were destroyed and taken to Babylon as loot, that some were left behind and taken in 587 as loot, that the sacral objects were taken to Babylon and housed in a Babylonian shrine (Ezra 1.7) and therefore were available for transportation back to Jerusalem. The Chronicler's view agrees with that found in Ezra 1: the furnishings were taken in 597 and housed in Nebuchadrezzar's palace; other furnishings were taken to Babylon in 587 (II Chron. 36.7, 10, 18; cf. Dan. 1.2; 5.2–4), and there is no knowledge of their being cut up and rendered useless by the Babylonians (the legend of Belshazzar's feast in Dan. 5 would be spoiled by such a knowledge).

27.16–22 as a discussion of the fate of the temple furnishings belongs to the world of Ezra and the Chronicler. It bears on the social controversy behind the rebuilt temple and the rebuilding of Jerusalem relating to power in the community and the right to reorganize the cult. When will the furnishings return from Babylon and whose party is in the right with reference to them? The struggle to answer such questions is reflected in the conflict between prophets in 27.16–28.9. The importance of the cultic furnishings, their survival in Babylon and their return to Jerusalem *after* having been preserved for a long time in exile are the central issues in the dispute. Those traditions which know an end to the temple and the breaking up of the valuable sacral furnishings (e.g. Micah 3.12; II Kings 24.13; 25.13; Jer. 52.17) are an alternative approach to the debate, but are essentially irrelevant to it. Only the stories which claim that the furnishings went intact to Babylon, survived there but not as loot, and therefore were available for return (e.g. 27–28; II Chron. 36; Ezra 1; Dan. 1; 5) are germane to the discussion about power and legitimation in the second temple period. The key feature of the furnishings motif is continuity with the past – the sacral vessels and temple furniture provide the only link with the first temple (note the disappearance of the ark in 3.16). Those who possess them and bring them back from Babylon have strong claims to a legitimacy other claims lack. The furnishings confer on the new temple power and an identification with the old temple. 'Clearly restoration of the vessels implies re-establishment of that continuity of the cultus which was in some measure interrupted by the disaster of 597.' (Ackroyd 1972, 175).

Verses 16, 18–22 should be read against this background. The two deportations are recognized: implicitly in the preaching of the prophets about the return of the furnishings and in v. 18, where the remaining vessels are mentioned. The listing of furnishings left behind by Nebuchadrezzar reflects the list of sacral objects taken to Babylon in 587 (v. 19; cf. 52.17; II Kings 25.13), but ignores the fact that they were broken up (this is in keeping with the presentation of the story as an event taking place before 587). There is an element of irony in v. 18, where it is suggested that evidence of being prophets who possess the divine word would be for the prophets to intercede with Yahweh on behalf of the furnishings which are left in the temple and palaces. 'Never mind the furnishings which were taken away to Babylon, pray for what the Babylonians left behind!' (cf. 22.10). The notion of residual furnishings allows for two deportations rather than there being the need to assume the acquisition of new furnishings after 597 in order that there might be furnishings available for capture in 587 (even though such a notion does conflict with the plain meaning of II Kings 24.13).

The very repetitive MT vv. 19–22 (in contrast to the brevity of G) reveals a development of the tradition in a quite different direction from G. In the first edition the attack on the prophets is a straightforward reversal of their message. Instead of the furnishings returning from Babylon, those which were left behind will go to Babylon. The second edition of the story hints at the possibility that the furnishings need not be deported (v. 19), then repeatedly asserts that furnishings from the temple, the royal palace and the city will be taken to Babylon, and ends on a note of restoration to 'this place' (v. 22). G is a doom oracle, but MT introduces the notion of restoration. The furnishings are now a symbol of restoration and therefore of continuity: 'we have a theme of restoration built into a theme of exile; the idea of continuity with the previous temple is maintained by the promise of the restoration of the temple vessels.' (Ackroyd 1972, 177). The viewpoint of G is continued in 28, but the effect of this restoration theme in 27.22 is to reverse that note of doom. In a subtle way v. 22 vindicates Hananiah, but because 27 and 28 are independent variations on a theme, there is no conscious acknowledgment of that vindication (see on 29.10). In MT v. 22 Yahweh's attention (*pqd* is a frequently used motif in the tradition, even though its use with reference to objects here is unusual) in the future will be on the furnishings and he will bring them up (*'lh* indicates a sacral procession, but is not used in the allusions to the restoration of the furnishings in Ezra) and restore them to the temple. So the prophets of v. 16 were right after all but were wrong about the timing! MT's expansion of the material produces a programme of deportation and restoration which allows for the passage of time between the destruction of Jerusalem and the events of Ezra's period.

28.1–17

28[1] In that same year, at the beginning of the reign of Zedekiah king of Judah, in the fifth month of the fourth year, Hananiah the son of Azzur, the prophet from Gibeon, spoke to me in the house of the LORD, in the presence of the priests and all the people, saying, 2 'Thus says the LORD of hosts, the God of Israel: I have broken the yoke of the king of Babylon. 3 Within two years I will bring back to this place all the vessels of the LORD's house, which Nebuchadnezzar king of Babylon took away from this place and carried to Babylon. 4 I will also bring back to this place Jeconiah the son of Jehoiakim, king of Judah, and all the exiles from Judah who went to Babylon, says the LORD, for I will break the yoke of the king of Babylon.'

5 Then the prophet Jeremiah spoke to Hananiah the prophet in the presence of the priests and all the people who were standing in the house of the LORD; 6 and the prophet Jeremiah said, 'Amen! May the LORD do so; may the LORD make the words which you have prophesied come true, and bring back to this place from Babylon the vessels of the house of the LORD, and all the exiles. 7 Yet hear now this word which I speak in your hearing and in the hearing of all the people. 8 The prophets who preceded you and me from ancient times prophesied war, famine, and pestilence against many countries and great kingdoms. 9 As for the prophet who prophesies peace, when the word of that prophet comes to pass, then it will be known that the LORD has truly sent the prophet.'

10 Then the prophet Hananiah took the yoke-bars from the neck of Jeremiah the prophet, and broke them. 11 And Hananiah spoke in the presence of all the people, saying, 'Thus says the LORD: Even so will I break the yoke of Nebuchadnezzar king of Babylon from the neck of all the nations within two years.' But Jeremiah the prophet went his way.

12 Sometime after the prophet Hananiah had broken the yoke-bars from off the neck of Jeremiah the prophet, the word of the LORD came to Jeremiah: 13 'Go, tell Hananiah, "Thus says the LORD: You have broken wooden bars, but I will make in their place bars of iron. 14 For thus says the LORD of hosts, the God of Israel: I have put upon the neck of all these nations an iron yoke of servitude to Nebuchadnezzar king of Babylon, and they shall serve him, for I have given to him even the beasts of the field." ' 15 And Jeremiah the prophet said to the prophet Hananiah, 'Listen, Hananiah, the LORD has not sent you, and you have made this people trust in a lie. 16 Therefore thus says the LORD: "Behold, I will remove you from the face of the earth. This very year you shall die, because you have uttered rebellion against the LORD." '

17 In that same year, in the seventh month, the prophet Hananiah died.

[MT 28] = G 35. Lys 1979 provides a structural analysis of the chapter which permits the various inner relations between the elements of the story to be seen clearly. **[1]** MT *baššānāh hahīʾ*, 'in that year': i.e. the same year as 27; lacking in G. MT encloses the whole story between two occurrences of the phrase. MT has two dates for the story: 1. in the beginning of Zedekiah's reign (cf. 26.1; 27.1 for formal structure); 2. in the fifth month of the fourth year. Both cannot be right and exegetes vary in the options exercised: e.g. BHS (i.e. Rudolph, 178) reads 'in the fourth year, in the fifth month' (cf. Oded 1977, 472); Driver 1963, 84–7, dismisses the fourth year as impossible and opts for the fifth month of the first year (the textual fourth year he explains as being due to an erroneous reading of an abbreviated text); Bright, 200, appears to accept the fourth year following G's 'in the fourth year', but his argument about the factual correctness of 'in the same year' is confused because only MT has that phrase and it refers back to 27.1, which Bright recognizes as not original (Bright's echo Thompson, 537 n. 1, uses the same confused argument). Some such note as 'in the same year' is required in order to point out that Jeremiah did not spend years wearing the yoke-bars! Part of the confusion is caused by the redactional fondness in 26–28 for using the same formulaic introductions; the rest is supplied by 28 being a variant of 27 (28.1 has the seams showing). K *bšnt*, 'in the year of'; Q *baššānāh*, 'in the (fourth) year'. MT *ʾēlay*, 'to me': in 28 Jeremiah is a third-person character (e.g. v. 5), so this first-person reference is either an error or an abbreviation for *ʾel-yirmᵉyāh* (cf. BHS). As in 27.9; 29.1, 8 G uses *pseudoprophetēs* to describe a prophet other than Jeremiah, hence Hananiah 'the false prophet' (G). This is not consistently carried out in 28 because G lacks MT's persistent contrasting of the two as 'Hananiah the prophet' (vv. 1, 5, 10, 12, 17) and 'Jeremiah the prophet' (vv. 5, 6, 10, 11, 12, 15). The location of Gibeon is disputed cf. 41.12, 16; Blenkinsopp 1972, 98–100. It would be ironic if the Gibeon from which Hananiah came were the Benjaminite Gibeon (cf. Volz, 260); for the purposes of the story Gibeon might be the great high place used by Solomon (I Kings 3.4–5) where sacrifices were offered and dreams received. **[3]** MT *bᵉʿôd šᵉnātayim yāmîm*, lit. 'in yet two years days', i.e. 'within two years time'. G has a shorter text of vv. 3–4: 'In two years time (*hēmerōn*, 'days') I will bring back to this place the vessels of the house of the lord and Iechonias and the colony of Judah, for I will break the yoke of the king of Babylon.' MT demonstrates how the second edition expanded the text in many small ways. **[5]** G has an inverted order of 'priests . . . people'. Throughout the story MT presents the two characters as 'Hananiah *the prophet*' and 'Jeremiah *the prophet*'; apart from the formal aspect of the redaction the phrase is indicative of the later second edition. **[6]** MT *yāqēm yhwh 'et-dᵉbārekā*, 'may Yahweh establish your words': i.e. fulfil them; some mss, G, T, read 'your word'. **[7]** MT *haddābār hazzeh*, 'this word': G *ton logion kuriou*, 'the word of the lord'. **[8]** MT *ûlᵉrāʿāh ûlᵉdāber*, 'and disaster and pestilence': G lacks what looks like an addition in MT (the phrase closes v. 8). G makes a fine contrast in vv. 8, 9 between 'prophesying war' and 'prophesying *šālōm*' which is lost in MT. Many mss read 'famine' (*rāʿāb*) for 'disaster' (*rāʿāh*); the triad fits the general redaction of the tradition, but is not one actually used in Jeremiah (cf. 27.8, 13). For 'many countries and great kingdoms' cf. 'many nations and great kings' (25.14; 27.7). **[9]** MT *ʾašer-šᵉlāḥō yhwh beʾᵉmet*, '(the prophet) whom Yahweh has sent in truth': i.e. truly sent, cf. *beʾᵉmet šᵉlāḥanī yhwh*, 'in truth Yahweh sent me' (26.15). Note the rather different principles behind the similar phrases: in 26.15 the self-asseveration must be taken at face value; in 28.9 a more empirical form of verification is formulated. The regulation in Deut. 18.22 may be modified here or even narrowed down (cf. Davidson 1964, 414). **[10]** MT *'et-hammōṭāh*, 'the yoke-bar': cf. NEB 'the yoke', JPSB 'the bar'; G plur., cf. RSV. The plur *mōṭōt* is used in v. 13; 27.2, but sing. in v. 12. MT *wayyišbᵉrēhû*, 'and he broke it': masc. suffix (referring to *ʿōl*, 'yoke', in v. 11, where the meaning of the action is stated?); BHS suggests changing it to fem. *-rehā* (*w* of MT a dittography from next word). **[11]** G lacks 'Nebuchadnezzar', 'within two years'. **[12]** RSV 'sometime' is not represented in the text but may be a fair interpretation of *wayᵉhî . . . 'aḥᵃrê*; Bright, 198: 'But then, sometime after . . .'. Cf. 42.7 for a definite period of waiting before the divine word was heard. **[13]** MT *wᵉʿaśîtā*, 'but you will make': G *kai poiēsō*, 'but I will make'; RSV follows G, NEB and JPSB follow MT. MT may be read as meaning Hananiah's action has only had the effect of making the servitude harder. **[14]** G lacks 'these', 'Nebuchadnezzar', 'and they shall serve him and also the beasts of the field I have given him'. The last part of v. 14 is probably an addition from 27.6b (cf. BHS). **[15]** Cf. 14.14–15; 23.21, 25–7, 32; 27.14–16. **[16]** MT *hinᵉnī mᵉšallēḥᵃkā*, 'look, I am sending you': i.e. dismissing you from the land of the living (to death). There is a word-play here with *lōʾ-šᵉlāḥᵃkā yhwh*, 'Yahweh did not send you', in v. 15 in which, although Yahweh *did not* send him, he *will* send him now (two senses of *šlḥ*). MT *kī-sārāh dibbarta ʾel-yhwh*, 'because you have spoken rebellion against Yahweh': G lacks the phrase. Cf. *kī dibber-sārāh ʿal-yhwh*, 'for he has spoken rebellion against Yahweh', Deut. 13.6 (EV 5). Deut. 18.20–21 uses a different criterion from this one (i.e. to speak a word Yahweh has not spoken is to speak presumptuously [*bᵉzādōn*]) which, though similar, is quite distinct from the charge in 28.16; Deut. 13.6 (EV 5). The absence of the charge in G suggests that MT has been expanded under Deuteronomistic influence (cf. Thiel 1981, 10) in the second edition; the same charge is made against Shemaiah in 29.32 (also lacking in G). Davidson 1964, 415, suggests that in the two places where the Deuteronomistic charge is made it may be the case that Jeremiah is accusing the representatives of Deuteronomic orthodoxy of being themselves in a state of rebellion against Yahweh. **[17]** G simply reads 'and he died in the seventh month', i.e. a couple of months after his original proclamation. Cf. Ezek. 11.13 for a death notice but with 'no element of direct encounter' (Zimmerli 1979, 260); Acts 5.1–6, for the death of another Ananias (Hananiah) due to a lie.

Lys 1979; Mottu 1975

The variant account of 27.16–22 provided by 28 introduces into the tradition a fascinating conflict between two named prophets in which Jeremiah behaves in a very distinctive fashion. He appears as a quite different character from the more dominant presentation of him in the major strands of the book. Part of that difference is due to the heterogeneous origins of the cycle 27–29 and part to the nature of the story told in 28. Yet in 27 Jeremiah is represented as denouncing *all* the prophets who proclaim the kind of message which is typified by Hananiah's declaration of the divine word. In reality the position adopted by Jeremiah in 27.12–15, 16–22 renders his response to Hananiah both unnecessary and incomprehensible. Why should Jeremiah listen to a particular instantiation of a message he already has dismissed as false? If what the prophets say is a lie (*šeqer*), then Hananiah, who says the same thing and in the same way (i.e. in the name of Yahweh, cf. v. 2; 27.14–15, 16), is a liar. Why should Jeremiah treat a liar with such sensitivity? Why should he respond in a dignified manner instead of heaping abuse on Hananiah's head? Why should he wish Hananiah to be right? Why should he accept the breaking of his own performative message and go his way? All these questions may be answered in terms of the structure of the story. It is an independent story and only owes to 27 certain features necessary for it to be a variant account (e.g. the conflict of prophets, the performance with the yoke-bars, the expectation of an imminent return of temple furnishings, king and people). To understand the story it needs to be heard (read) as quite independent of its present context and treated as an exchange between two prophets complete in their independence of what precedes and follows the story of their encounter. The holistic approach which insists on integrating each individual story with all the other traditions in the collection will only expose the contradictions between 28, its present context and the rest of the tradition.

In this analysis of 28 the encounter between Hananiah of Gibeon and Jeremiah is treated as a story rather than a historical account of a real event (in contrast to Koch 1969, 204 who regards it as the report of an eye witness who is completely reliable; formal analysis of story in Koch, 200–10). It is a story in which some of the details necessary for understanding it are provided by its present context but its main thrust is concerned with asserting yet again (i.e. in the context of Part III) the truth of the word proclaimed by Jeremiah *the prophet* (a subtle development in MT). This assertion is achieved in an indirect way by focusing on another prophet and allowing the *deity* to distinguish between them. If princes and people have validated Jeremiah's message in 26, now Yahweh himself puts the seal of approval on Jeremiah's preaching in relation to the king of Babylon motif. Hananiah serves this purpose (cf. Uriah in 26.20–3) and is of no other importance in the story. At the end of the account his dead body will invalidate his message and also vindicate Yahweh's word as spoken by Jeremiah (hence v. 14). In 26, 28 two dead prophets are introduced into the tradition, but both only serve to highlight the word of Yahweh as uttered by Jeremiah.

Hananiah ben Azzur from Gibeon is introduced in v. 1 as a prophet who encounters Jeremiah the prophet in the temple on a particular occasion (MT's overload of dating information is indicative of redactional problems of fitting the story into its present context). Nothing more is known about Hananiah (like Uriah ben Shemaiah he is only known because his story has been put into Jeremiah's story). He shares with Jeremiah a number of features: he is a Yahwistic prophet who speaks the word of Yahweh; he comes from outside Jerusalem (wherever Gibeon may be located); he addresses Jeremiah in the presence of the priests and people *in the temple* (cf. 7.2; 26.2). In some ways he is the mirror image of Jeremiah. The only discernible difference between the two men is the ideology of each. Hananiah is presented as a *šālōm* prophet (by implication of v. 9), Jeremiah is a prophet of war (cf. v. 8). The story is therefore a clash of ideologies (Mottu rightly discerns the ideological nature of the conflict but fails to scrutinize Jeremiah's ideology). It is difficult to delineate the ideological holdings of Hananiah because the story only provides two pieces of information about his work: his message in vv. 2–4 and his action in vv. 10–11. If these are sufficient for analysing his theory and his praxis (an unlikely possibility), it may be said of him that he represented the anti-Babylonian element in Judaean society. His position is close to that behind 24.4–7; 27.22; 29.10–14, except that he appears to have believed in a more imminent implementation of such a programme. In the context of 27–29 the only point separating him from the presentation of Jeremiah is a matter of timing.

Too much is said about Jeremiah in the tradition and too little about Hananiah for a satisfactory analysis of the differences between the two prophets. G's use of *pseudoprophetēs* to qualify Hananiah may be an idiosyncrasy of that edition, but it does expose the ideology of the redactors. Whatever Hananiah's status and belief system may be, they cannot be explicated from the story because he is essentially the foil for a presentation of Jeremiah as the 'true' prophet. This is a presentation much assisted by the story's opposing of two prophets in which one appears to be very self-assertive and the other a quiet listener and humble servant of Yahweh (cf. the analysis in Lys). One speaks and acts, the other listens, responds, goes away, listens to Yahweh and *then* speaks the divine word. A story of subtle relationships and movements which is remarkably different from all the other stories in the tradition where Jeremiah never listens to anybody but denounces and asserts all the time. In such stories the other prophets are silent or have words put in their mouths, but always they are denounced from the moment Jeremiah opens his mouth. Chapter 28 is so different from those accounts that it is necessary to draw attention to its eirenic presentation of the two prophets in order not to overemphasize the significance of the representation of

Jeremiah here (many exegetes use 28 as if it were a picture of the normal Jeremiah approach to other people – it is not). The peculiarities of 28 should warn the exegete against treating it as anything other than a disjunctive story in the tradition. It is in the unfolding of the story that the eirenic features appear but by its conclusion death and destruction have put an end to such pleasantries.

Hananiah's initial statement declares that Yahweh has broken (*šābartī*, 'I have broken', v. 2) the yoke of the king of Babylon. This announcement allows the story to be linked to the yoke-bars motif of 27 (it is further linked in v. 10). So Hananiah may be viewed as a representative of those in Judah who opposed the Babylonians and who believed that Yahweh would break their power. As evidence of his claim Hananiah says that in two years time the temple furnishings will return to the temple. This verification element links the story with the controversy in 27.16, 18–22 and associates Hananiah with the prophets who make such a claim (27.16). It is a mistake to accuse Hananiah of making the temple vessels into a fetish and belonging to a world where such commodities are viewed as prior to people (*contra* Mottu, 62–3). With the furnishings the king and people will return to Jerusalem. Temple and people belong together (cf. Haggai, Malachi), and not as commodities or fetishes, but as symbols of the creator Yahweh's rule of the world (cf. Levenson 1984b). Hananiah's concern with the furnishings is part of the contextualization of the discussion in the cycle, and not evidence of his involvement on the side of the subjective interests of the ruling class against the objective interests of the Judaean people (*contra* Mottu). The controversy in 27.16, 18–22; 28.2–4 is about the return of the furnishings as the symbol of Yahweh's breaking the imperial power of the empire which has enslaved the peoples of the region. Hananiah sides with those aspirations of the people, hence he addressses Jeremiah in the temple in the presence of priests *and people*. If Zedekiah is on the throne (v. 1) and Hananiah announces that Jeconiah *king of Judah* will return to Jerusalem, then he cannot be accused of serving the interests of the ruling class. He is in defiance of Zedekiah, the court and the Babylonians. Against the might of Babylon he risks his own personal safety by opposing the word of Yahweh to the present state of power politics in Jerusalem. Small wonder that he is dead by the end of the story!

Jeremiah the prophet responds to Hananiah in similar circumstances to the delivery of the original divine word: in the presence of the priests and the people in the temple. His reaction to the divine word is paradigmatic: 'May Yahweh do so' (*kēn ya'aśeh yhwh*). He listens quietly and then he speaks. He speaks to affirm Hananiah's words: 'May Yahweh indeed fulfil your words. Far be it from him that he should appear to oppose the return of the exiles to this place.' The formality of the speech probably represents the correct response to the utterance of the divine word (cf. 26.19). A similar soft answer appears in 26.12–14 and on both occasions Jeremiah adds a rider to his response – 'but, howbeit, only' (*'ak*). General agreement with a situation or belief is expressed, *but* a few dissenting points may yet be made (cf. *'ak* in 12.1). These points usually constitute the heart of the matter and have a tendency to reverse the agreement expressed with the sentiments just enunciated. Jeremiah's reservation is spoken to Hananiah and to all the people and represents a pertinent contrast between the long tradition of war prophets and the innovative word of the *šālōm* prophet (vv. 8–9). It is a strong riposte to Hananiah. It calls into question Hananiah's position by raising doubts about its backing warrants. In opposing Hananiah (if that is what Jeremiah is doing in vv. 8–9) Jeremiah sides with tradition against innovation; with the word of judgment against the word of salvation. Yet it could be said that in the terms of v. 8 Hananiah was in fact proclaiming war, i.e. Yahweh's war, against a great kingdom. Yahweh's breaking of Babylon would fit a tradition of his mighty acts against the nations on behalf of his own people (cf. Isaiah on Assyria in Isa. 10.12–19). Jeremiah's criterion for *šālōm* oracles in v. 9 is an interesting adaptation of Deut. 18.20–2, but it is not the Deuteronomistic criterion of fulfilment. It is not so much a narrowing down of Deut. 18.22 as a separation of war oracles from *šālōm* oracles. Oracles announcing war against the nations have the backing of a very long, and therefore honourable, tradition; oracles proclaiming *šālōm* lack any such warrant and must therefore justify themselves. The only backing warrant suggested for them is their fulfilment. When they happen they authenticate their speaker. Thus Jeremiah's response to Hananiah achieves a stalemate. The people must wait and see whether Hananiah is right or not; whether Yahweh has sent him or not.

As a blocking move it is a brilliant reply: full of subtle nuances and interesting possibilities. It appears to leave the issue open, but it has really closed it because the weight of tradition is now against

Hananiah. What can he do? He cannot just wait two years, for that would expose him to ridicule and an empty career. He could return to Gibeon and become yet another prophet from the Benjaminite territory who had gone to Jerusalem and been destroyed by the opposition there. But had not Yahweh of hosts spoken to him, and what could he do but obey (cf. Amos 3.8)? So he acted – the time for words being over, he backed his words with an appropriate action. He took the yoke-bars from Jeremiah's neck (here we need 27.2 because the necessary information is lacking in 28.1, cf. Rudolph, 172–3) and broke them. Accompanying his action are the words used on such occasions: 'Thus says Yahweh: even so (*kākāh*, cf. 13.9; 19.11; 51.64) will I break the yoke of the king of Babylon' (v. 11). If we assume an original setting of Jeremiah making and wearing the yoke as an act creating the servitude of Judah to Babylon (distorted in its present position in 27.2–4, 11) Hananiah now destroys that act with a divinely willed performance. Word and act match, and the prophet is the performer of both. Furthermore, the possibility of one prophetic performance cancelling out another prophet's act is raised here, but not developed (see on 36.23; cf. I Kings 13; 22.5–28). Jeremiah also acts. He goes his way (from the temple, but whither is not stated). The first encounter is over and the two prophets part. Silence develops between the two figures.

The extent to which the second part of the story (vv. 12–16) mirrors the first (Lys, 474–5) may be disputed. The direct intervention of Yahweh is absent in vv. 1–11 (contrast 26.1; 27.1, but cf. 29.1–29) but appears in v. 12. Both figures respond to each other in the first part whereas Hananiah is inert in vv. 12–16. The divine word comes to Jeremiah in v. 12 but is singularly absent in vv. 1–11 (except as reported by a prophet). In the first part Jeremiah is acted upon, but he acts in vv. 13, 15 ('go, tell Hananiah . . . and Jeremiah . . . said to . . . Hananiah'), whereby Hananiah is acted upon by the deity. Activity and passivity are elements in the two parts, but Jeremiah is never a completely inert figure in the way that Hananiah is in part two. Mirror-imaging is not the best description of the two parts of the story, except in so far as it is a broken mirror. This fracture inverts some of the elements, but part two picks up the disjunctive element introduced by *'ak* in v. 7 and develops that in a way not foreseen in vv. 1–11.

If Jeremiah has no real answer to Hananiah's claim (cf. von Rad 1965, 209–10) and has to go his way, v. 12 resolves his dilemma by introducing the divine word directly into the story. After the events of vv. 10–11 the word comes to Jeremiah in private (at least no public place is denoted in contrast to vv. 1, 5, 7). By himself Jeremiah cannot refute Hananiah, though he may make some canny observations; he must receive the divine word in order to do that. This feature of the story links it with the explanation of the vision in 24 and Jeremiah's role in the community in 42.1–7. No longer the one who initiates the action or speaks the word directly to a given situation, he requires a divine response to a situation before he may speak freely. Now the familiar form of the word comes to him: 'Go, tell Hananiah, "Thus says Yahweh . . ." '. At last the strains of an old sound are heard and Jeremiah may act and speak with confidence. The message for Hananiah (cf. the Pashhur incident in 20.1–6 following the act of 19.1–2, 10–11) reverses his act of vv. 10–11 but increases the severity of what the performance represents. Hananiah may have broken wooden bars, but iron ones will replace them (G, MT differ on who makes the new bars). The divine speech ends there, perhaps because it has affirmed Jeremiah's act of wearing the bars. The editors wish to press on in the matter of Hananiah versus Jeremiah, so v. 15 skips over a number of necessary moves and has Jeremiah confront his opponent. No longer does he speak in reasonable tones, though he does repeat his opening gambit 'listen now . . .' (vv. 7, 15 *šᵉmaʿ-nāʾ*). But the open question of v. 9 about whether a prophet of *šālōm* might have been sent (*šlḥ*) by Yahweh is a closed assertion in v. 15: 'Yahweh has not sent you (*lōʾ-šᵉlāḥᵃkā*)'. Instead of bringing *šālōm* to the people he has made them trust in falsehood (*šeqer*). He will, however, be sent (*šlḥ*) by Yahweh, but in the sense of *sent* from this life into death – 'you will die' (v. 16, *ʾattāh mēt*). In v. 11 Jeremiah had gone his own way after the first encounter with Hananiah; now after the second encounter Hananiah goes the way of all flesh. He dies because he is in rebellion against Yahweh (cf. Deut. 13.6; a similar charge is made against Shemaiah in 29.32). Between the true sending of Yahweh (v. 9) and Hananiah stands the lie (*šeqer*) spoken by him. The editors record his death in the seventh month of that year and thus round off the story in a neatly symmetrical way (cf. Pelatiah's fate in Ezek. 11.13).

The story ends there without comment on Hananiah's fate. There is none to mourn him or to bury him (contrast I Kings 13.29), but then the tale is not about Hananiah as much as it is about the confirmation of Yahweh's word as spoken by Jeremiah. In effect the story says: there will be no return of the temple furnishings or of Jeconiah and the exiles to Jerusalem. That is the point of the first edition of 27 (G) and 28 affirms it. The complication of the matter in 27.22 (MT) has no direct bearing on 28. The prophet from Gibeon who supported the belief that furnishings and exiles would return from Babylon has been executed by Yahweh of hosts (or the Babylonians?) and with his execution that party political scheme is at an end. Yahweh has spoken through his prophet Jeremiah and there is an end to the matter. The redactors pass on to a different subject.

Chapter 28 has been analysed without remainder and its interpretation appears to be unproblematical. Some of the things said by Hananiah will resurface elsewhere in the tradition and will be noted when they do (see on 29.10), but the story is straightforward by the standards of the book of Jeremiah. However, the chapter has attracted much special attention, especially in relation to questions about false prophecy and criteria for evaluating different prophets (cf. Hossfeld und Meyer 1973, 90–103; Kraus 1964; Lys, 477–82; Overholt 1970, 24–48; Wolff 1983, 67–73). The chapter offers no criteria for distinguishing between prophets because it is set in a tradition where Jeremiah is already established as the true prophet (e.g. 26.15–16) and in the confrontation between Jeremiah and Hananiah there are no differentiating marks which single out one of the prophets as true or false. The implication of II Kings 18.19–25 that when there are rival claimants to divine revelation one of them is probably lying would appear to be the point behind 28 (cf. De Vries 1978, 72). But identifying the liar is beyond the wit of man and, if even Jeremiah required a subsequent revelation to know that Hananiah was lying, therefore the story does not set out criteria for making such judgments. All the subtle exegesis of many commentators on 28 should not be allowed to conceal that lack of a criteriology. Distinguishing between prophets who proclaim radically different divine words may be an existential problem rather than an academic one (rightly Lys, 478), but sophisticated exegesis which reads into the story many elements from other ideologies will not provide what is already lacking in the text (*contra* Lys, Mottu). A careful exegesis of 28 will not produce evidence to back Jeremiah against Hananiah because there is no such evidence either in the text or in the world at large. Because Yahweh is not at hand but is the hidden god who is afar off (23.23), 'there could be no standard method of any sort by which he granted revelation' (von Rad 1965, 209). That factor may help to explain why Jeremiah is 'so much at sea' (von Rad's phrase) in his encounter with Hananiah. The irony of 23.28 should not be overlooked in the analysis of 28: 'let the prophet who has a dream tell the dream, but let him who has my word speak my word faithfully'. Hananiah speaks that divine word, yet it is declared a lie. So when the divine word may be a lie, prophecy itself becomes an activity in which true and false are indistinguishable. Without a redactional framework which can provide the necessary theological guidance for reading reality, prophecy is a mute witness.

Reading 28 as a clash between a central prophet (Hananiah) and a peripheral prophet (Jeremiah) in which the accusation of being a false prophet functions as the equivalent of witchcraft accusations in other cultures (cf. Wilson 1980, 247–51; 1984, 74–80) is an interesting approach to the material, but founders on being incoherent as a conceptual analysis of Jeremiah. Apart from his speaking in the temple, an activity much more frequently posited of Jeremiah, there is no evidence for Hananiah being a central prophet. Jeremiah has much better claims to that role, but the amassing of discrete traditions about Jeremiah make it impossible to determine his status in relation to central or peripheral prophecy (cf. the fluctuating analysis of Isaiah in Wilson 1980, 270–4). The concept of a peripheral prophet with support from members of the central establishment (Wilson 1980, 248) indicates the incoherence of such an analysis and the way the tradition represents Jeremiah as freely moving about the temple and the royal residence, with many powerful supporters, hardly supports the thesis of his peripheral status. The suggestion that Hananiah was Jeremiah's replacement after the death of Josiah (Johnstone 1967, 55) cannot be sustained by the text. If Hananiah had been a central prophet since Josiah's death he would most certainly have been deported by the Babylonians or so discredited by the collapse of the pro-Egyptian party that he would never have survived the changeover of power in 597. There is insufficient evidence in 28 to provide any account of Hananiah's social status, and therefore the encounter between the two prophets cannot be analysed using sociological factors or be assumed to be anything other than a paradigmatic story.

The Marxist analysis of 28 undertaken by Henri Mottu is an interesting approach to the text, but it collapses under the weight of its own ideological jargon. It has to posit of Hananiah so many things which are neither in the text nor necessarily held by Hananiah as to render the exposition almost worthless. Hananiah is set up as a straw man and then knocked down and buried under the Marxist terminology of Althusser, Gramsci, Sartre and others. None of this is justified by the text, which is quite capable of denigrating Hananiah but chooses not to attack his character, history or associations. Hananiah cannot even be identified from the text as a proponent of that Zion-orientated ideology which van der Woude identifies as the mark of the pseudo-prophet (van der Woude 1969). So when Mottu attacks Hananiah for being on the side of the powerful he is reading into the text what his theory tells him must be there. But consider the setting: in the temple of Zedekiah's day, i.e. with Babylonian overlords exercising the real power through their vassal, this prophet from Gibeon (not Jerusalem), this outsider or peripheral figure, proclaims the judgment of Yahweh on Babylon. How does that make Hananiah a participant in the power relationships of his time? If the authorities hear Hananiah, he will be executed (cf. 29.21–23). Hananiah risks all with his future-orientated faith that Yahweh will bring back furnishings, king and people. He may be wrong but not on the grounds that he lacks faith or praxis, is not open to the future, serves the powers that be or is trapped in the past. Jeremiah's response to him is far more anchored in the past than the future, yet many commentators praise him as being innovative in 28. This is a complete misreading of the text. Exegetes are generally so eager to praise Jeremiah and denigrate Hananiah that they read into the text much that is simply not there. To say that Yahweh will bring back the king, i.e. displace the present occupant of the throne, is an act of brave faith, however mistaken it may be. It is both radical and revolutionary in its political context and cannot be construed as support for the ruling classes. It is quite the opposite! Mottu accuses Hananiah of stealing Isa. 9.4 (the breaking of the yoke of the oppressor; but cf. 30.8!) and making a commodity of it (Mottu, 62; cf. 23.30 for the motif of stealing the divine words). Hananiah is also accused of 'parrotry of Isaiah' (Lys, 480) because in the sixth century he repeats what Isaiah said in the eighth (but what about the argument in v. 8 which uses the ancient tradition of the prophets of war? – is that not parrotry also?). Yet there is nothing in all these accusations which cannot be made of the Jeremiah represented in the tradition.

The point of representing these criticisms of Hananiah is simply to contrast the exegetical superstructure of so much modern analysis of 28 with what the text itself actually says about him. If so much extraneous material must be imported into the text in order to damn Hananiah, the resultant eisegesis is doing something other than explaining the text. Such misguided readings of 28 are based on the presupposition that it is history and that Hananiah's falseness is being demonstrated by the text. Neither is the case. 28 may be a cleverly constructed story (cf. Lys' structuralist analysis) but its point is very simple: the temple furnishings are not coming back (nor is the king). Babylon rules!

The cycle in which Hananiah's story is set has as its dominant motif the falseness (*šeqer*) of what *all* the prophets say (27.10, 14, 15, 16; 28.15; 29.9, 21, 23, 31), and in such a context Hananiah *the prophet* is inevitably a speaker of what is false. As the figure opposite Jeremiah his is the role characterized by the term *šeqer*. It is unnecessary, however, to construct a closely argued account of just why Hananiah of Gibeon is false. His falseness is part of the given in the story (demonstrated by Yahweh's only contribution in vv. 13–14) because in conjunction with Jeremiah he must be false. If he takes a different view from the bearer of the tradition he must be wrong. The redaction is committed to Jeremiah, *therefore Hananiah is false*. As Wilson rightly observes: 'the observer can decide which of the prophecies to believe only if he has already recognized the authority of one prophet or the other' (1980, 250). The process of authentication is prior to the encounter between the two prophets and is determined at the redactional level of the tradition. So it is futile to seek to demonstrate the falseness of Hananiah's position or to justify his condemnation as *šeqer*. Nor is it necessary for the modern exegete to join in the editorial excoriation of Hananiah with further denunciations of lying prophets who manipulate divine words for their own ends. The matter of prophecy is not so simple that the term *šeqer* may be bandied about with such certitude, and the remarks of Dodds on the Pythia's trance in relation to her priests' interpretation of her words hold good for this aspect of biblical prophecy:

> We cannot see into the minds of the Delphic priesthood, but to ascribe such manipulation in general to conscious and cynical fraud is, I suspect, to oversimplify the picture. Anyone familiar with the history of modern spiritualism will realise what an amazing amount of virtual cheating can be done in perfectly good faith by convinced believers (1973, 74).

29.1–23

29 1 These are the words of the letter which Jeremiah the prophet sent from
Jerusalem to the elders of the exiles, and to the priests, the prophets, and
all the people, whom Nebuchadnezzar had taken into exile from Jerusalem
to Babylon. 2 This was after King Jeconiah, and the queen mother, the
eunuchs, the princes of Judah and Jerusalem, the craftsmen, and the smiths
had departed from Jerusalem. 3 The letter was sent by the hand of Elasah
the son of Shaphan and Gemariah the son of Hilkiah, whom Zedekiah king
of Judah sent to Babylon to Nebuchadnezzar king of Babylon. It said: 4
'Thus says the LORD of hosts, the God of Israel, to all the exiles whom I
have sent into exile from Jerusalem to Babylon: 5 Build houses and live in
them; plant gardens and eat their produce. 6 Take wives and have sons and
daughters; take wives for your sons, and give your daughters in marriage,
that they may bear sons and daughters; multiply there, and do not decrease.
7 But seek the welfare of the city where I have sent you into exile, and pray
to the LORD on its behalf, for in its welfare you will find your welfare. 8 For
thus says the LORD of hosts, the God of Israel: Do not let your prophets and
your diviners who are among you deceive you, and do not listen to the
dreams which they dream, 9 for it is a lie which they are prophesying to you
in my name; I did not send them, says the LORD.

10 For thus says the LORD: When seventy years are completed for
Babylon, I will visit you, and I will fulfil to you my promise and bring you
back to this place. 11 For I know the plans I have for you, says the LORD,
plans for welfare and not for evil, to give you a future and a hope. 12 Then
you will call upon me and come and pray to me, and I will hear you. 13 You
will seek me and find me; when you seek me with all your heart, 14 I will
be found by you, says the LORD, and I will restore your fortunes and gather
you from all the nations and all the places where I have driven you, says the
LORD, and I will bring you back to the place from which I sent you into exile.

15 Because you have said, "The LORD has raised up prophets for us in
Babylon," – 16 Thus says the LORD concerning the king who sits on the
throne of David, and concerning all the people who dwell in this city, your
kinsmen who did not go out with you into exile: 17 "Thus says the LORD of
hosts, Behold, I am sending on them sword, famine, and pestilence, and I
will make them like vile figs which are so bad they cannot be eaten. 18 I
will pursue them with sword, famine, and pestilence, and will make them
a horror to all the kingdoms of the earth, to be a curse, a terror, a hissing,
and a reproach among all the nations where I have driven them, 19 because
they did not heed my words, says the LORD, which I persistently sent to you
by my servants the prophets, but you would not listen, says the LORD." –
20 Hear the word of the LORD, all you exiles whom I sent away from
Jerusalem to Babylon: 21 "Thus says the LORD of hosts, the God of Israel,

concerning Ahab the son of Kolaiah and Zedekiah the son of Maaseiah, who are prophesying a lie to you in my name: Behold, I will deliver them into the hand of Nebuchadrezzar king of Babylon, and he shall slay them before your eyes. 22 Because of them this curse shall be used by all the exiles from Judah in Babylon: 'The LORD make you like Zedekiah and Ahab, whom the king of Babylon roasted in the fire,' 23 because they have committed folly in Israel, they have committed adultery with their neighbours' wives, and they have spoken in my name lying words which I did not command them. I am the one who knows, and I am witness, says the LORD." '

[MT 29] = G 36. **[1]** MT *wᵉʾēlleh dibᵉrē hassēper*, 'and these are the words of the document': *wᵉ*, 'and', connects 29 with 28. Weiser, 249, translates the phrase as a title: 'This is the story of the letter.' 51.60 represents Jeremiah as writing a book and sending it to Babylon; for the idea of a prophet writing (a letter) to somebody cf. Elijah's writing (*miktāb*) to king Jehoram (II Chron. 21.12–15). The letter may not be authentic (cf. Williamson 1982, 306–7), but it reflects a period when 'Prophetic words are gaining canonical status' (Ackroyd 1973, 154), cf. Zech. 1.5–6. MT *yeter ziqᵉnē haggōlāh*, '(to) the rest of the elders of the exile': G lacks *yeter*, followed by RSV. MT may reflect the result of the trouble referred to in v. 22 or *yeter* may be out of place and belong with 'all the people' (cf. Nicholson, 44; for the second view cf. Volz, 266). Rudolph, 182, suggests the sense of 'preeminence' for *yeter* as in Gen. 49.3, meaning the most prominent elders. **[2]** A parenthetical insertion based on II Kings 24.14–16; cf. 24.1. For 'queen mother' see on 13.18. MT *wᵉhassārīsīm*, 'and the eunuchs': not necessarily castrates (unless in charge of the harems, cf. on 24.1), cf. Potiphar (Gen. 39.1), who was married (though his wife's behaviour with Joseph may suggest a certain lack in her husband!); cf. 38.7. MT *śārē yᵉhūdāh wirušālaim*, 'princes of Judah and Jerusalem': G *kai pantos eleutherou*, 'and every freeman'. **[3]** MT *bᵉyad*, 'by the hand of . . . ': v. 3 continues from v. 1 after the interruption of v. 2; the means of sending the letter is not clear. Perhaps by diplomatic bag (Thompson, 545), but cf. 51.60 (an ancient subversive practice?): Jeremiah is here a man of power with access to diplomatic dispatches. Elasah may have been a brother of Ahikam (26.24), and Gemariah (cf. 36.12?) may have been a son of Josiah's high priest (II Kings 22.4, 8). G lacks 'Nebuchadnezzar'. MT *lēʾmōr*, 'saying': RSV 'It said'. **[4]** MT *ʾᵃšer-higᵉlētī*, 'whom I have exiled': the shift from third person to first is awkward (cf. v. 7); BHS suggests emending with S to *hoglᵉtāh*, 'who have been exiled'. The contents of the letter appear in vv. 4–7. **[6]** MT *wᵉtēladᵉnāh bānīm ūbānōt*, 'and let them give birth to sons and daughters': lacking in G. MT *wᵉʾal-timʿāṭū*, 'and do not become few': cf. *pen-tamʿiṭēnī*, 'lest you make me few', 10.24. **[7]** MT *hāʿīr*, 'the city': G *tēs gēs*, 'the country' = *hāʾāreṣ*. Unless taken in a distributive sense MT is unlikely and exegetes prefer G (e.g. Weiser,

Rudolph, Bright). Loss of cult and deportation have not ruled out prayer to Yahweh in a foreign land; some exegetes read the text as evidence of the replacement of the temple cult by the synagogue (Volz, 270; Janssen 1956, 109–10). The notion of praying for a heathen land is unique in the Hebrew Bible, even if self-interest is the ground for such activity (*kī biš*ᵉ*lōmāh yihyeh lākem šālōm*, 'for in its well-being is your own well-being'). Yet if there is to be no return from Babylon (G 27.19–22; MT 28), it makes sense to pray for the well-being of the new (home) land. **[8–9]** Rudolph reads these verses after v. 15; they have no place in the letter but belong to the highly edited section which separates the letter from responses to it (vv. 24–29). These additions belong to the cycle's twin foci of Babylon and 'false' prophets. Bright, 208, regards vv. 8–9 as giving needed reinforcement to the preceding piece and leading into vv. 10–14. **[8]** MT *'el-ḥ*ᵃ*lōmōtēkem*, 'to your dreams': BHS reads 'their dreams' with G[26]. MT *'attem maḥl*ᵉ*mīm*, '(which) you cause to be dreamed': Rudolph treats as a textual error; G *ha humeis enupniazesthe*, 'which you dream', i.e. *hēm ḥōl*ᵉ*mīm*, 'they dream' (cf. v. 9). **[9]** MT *b*ᵉ*šeqer*, 'with a lie': Vrs *šeqer*, 'it is a lie, a falsehood'. **[10]** Cf. 25.11–12, where 'seventy years' is also mentioned. The secondary nature of vv. 10–14 should be obvious from the fact that both places refer to seventy years, yet each is dated quite differently (25 = 605; 29 = 597). Here the addition corrects the view that exile in Babylon is to be permanent, a view easily deduced from vv. 4–7 and corresponding to the subseuqent experience of millennia of Jewish life in Babylon! See on 25.11–12 for discussion of range of meaning of 'seventy years'. **[11]** MT *'ānōkī yāda'tī 'et-hammaḥ*ᵃ*šābōt '*ᵃ*šer 'ānōkī*, '*I* know the plans which I': lacking in G (probably due to homoioteleuton: *'ānōkī* . . . *'ānōkī* with the translator's eye moving from the first to the second *'ānōkī*). G lacks *n*ᵉ*'um yhwh*, 'says Yahweh'. MT *'aḥ*ᵃ*rīt w*ᵉ*tiqwāh*, 'a latter end and a hope': i.e. a hoped-for future (cf. Bright, 209 hendiadys); cf. 31.17 for these two terms. G *tauta* 'these things'. **[12]** MT *wah*ᵃ*laktem*, 'and you will go'; meaning? Perhaps spoken from the second temple and therefore an allusion to worship in a rebuilt shrine. Treated as secondary by many commentators; lacking in G. S lacks 'and I will hear you' (BHS). MT may include variants in vv. 12–13. **[13]** Cf. Deut. 4.29 of which this verse is virtually a citation (cf. Thiel 1981, 15). G[S] lacks 'and you will find when you seek me' (MT). **[14]** MT *w*ᵉ*nimṣē'tī lākem*, 'and I will be found by you': G *kai epiphanoumai humin*, 'and I will manifest myself to you'. G ends verse at this point (cf. BHS). What follows in MT has little to do with Babylon in particular but refers to widespread dispersion among many nations. MT *w*ᵉ*šabtī 'et-š*ᵉ*būt*ᵉ*kem* (Q) 'and I will restore your fortunes': K *š*ᵉ*bīt*ᵉ*kem*, 'your captivity'. The phrase *šūb š*ᵉ*būt*, 'restore the fortunes', occurs in 30.3, 18; 31.23; 32.44; 33.7, 11, 26; 48.47; 49.6, 39; Lam. 2.14; Deut. 30.3; for its meaning cf. Baumann 1929; Dietrich 1925; Holladay 1958, 110–15; Johnson 1962, 67 n. 4. **[15]** Cf. Deut. 18.15, 18. **[16–20]** G lacks these verses (except for G[L] which has the order 14, 16–20, 15, 21–23); they are another addition to the letter sequence and have no relevance to the Babylonian community (cf. 24.8–10 for similar sentiments but a different use of the figs metaphor). Note vv. 15, 20 both end with the word *bābelāh*, 'to Babylon', but vv. 16–20 are too long and different for G's lack to be due to homoioteleuton. **[17]** 'I will make them *like* disgusting figs (*katt*ᵉ*'ēnīm haššō'ārīm*)': cf. 24.2, 3. The vision of the two baskets of figs in 24 may have contributed the root metaphor here but in v. 17 it is Yahweh who *makes* the citizens uneatable figs, whereas 24 offers no explanation for the equation of the community with bad figs. If 24 is behind this usage then the writer has not grasped its meaning (cf. Rudolph, 186) and uses a masc. qualifier for a fem. noun (contrast 24.2, 3). **[18]** Cf. 15.2–4, where many of these terms are used, especially the triad sword, famine, pestilence (reversed order). Cf. note on 27.8 for listing of the triad references. K *lzw'h*; Q *l*ᵉ*za'*ᵃ*wāh*, 'a horror', as in 15.4. MT *w*ᵉ*lišrēqāh*, 'and for a whistling, hissing', cf. 18.16; 19.8; a few mss read *w*ᵉ*liq*ᵉ*lālāh*, 'and for a curse' (BHS). **[19]** MT *haškēm w*ᵉ*sālōaḥ*, 'rising early and sending': see on 7.13, 25. Some mss read *'*ᵃ*lēhem*, 'to them', as *'*ᵃ*lēkem*, 'to you', probably in view of *š*ᵉ*ma'tem*, 'you would (not) listen', which is the clichéd form of this motif throughout the tradition (Rudolph attributes it to a mechanical copying of the phrase cf. 25.3–4; 26.5). G^OL, S = *šāma'tū*, 'they would (not) listen'. **[21]** G lacks 'the son of Kolaiah', 'the son of Maaseiah', 'Nebuchadrezzar' (only example of normal spelling in 27–29), 'who are prophesying a lie to you in my name'. **[22]** MT *'*ᵃ*šer qālām*, 'whom he roasted': a possible word-play on *ben-qōlāyāh*, 'the son of Kolaiah' – but his name is as close to *qll*, 'curse', so the word-play might be with *q*ᵉ*lālāh*, 'curse' (cf. Carroll 1981, 191). *qlh*, 'roast'; *qll*, 'curse', *qōlāyāh*, 'Kolaiah' all share word-play elements, though MT lacks *qōlāyāh* in v. 22 (note defective spelling of *'eḥāb* for *'aḥ'āb*). **[23]** MT *ya'an* *'*ᵃ*šer 'āśū n*ᵉ*bālāh b*ᵉ*yiśrā'el*, 'because they have committed folly in Israel': 'to commit folly in Israel' is an idiomatic phrase for some outrageous act contrary to the good order of the community, hence its use even here to describe acts perpetrated in Babylon! Certain heinous activities are associated with the idiom: rape (Gen. 37.7); premarital loss of virginity discovered after marriage, indicative of an active sex life before marriage (Deut. 22.21); vicious rape (Judg. 20.6, 10); breach of the holy war rules applying to sacred property (Josh. 7.15); violation of a woman (cf. II Sam. 13.12–13). Apart from sacrilege, wanton sexual acts appear to be the meaning of 'folly in Israel'; cf. Gerleman 1974; Phillips 1975. Whether the wives referred to here were Babylonian cannot be inferred from the text, but Nebuchadrezzar's penchant for roasting people (Dan. 3) may have been sufficient reason for the fate of the two prophets. Bright, 209, attributes their execution to their seditious words but that also is only an inference from the context of the cycle. G lacks *šeqer*, 'falsehood, lie'. K *hwyd'*; Q *hayōdē'a*, 'the one who knows' (K *hū ' yōdē'a*, 'he who knows');

lacking in G. A dittography due to *wāʿēd*, 'and witness'; BHS reads *'ānōkī* . . . (*hā*) *ʿēd*, 'I am . . . (the) witness'. Adultery is a secret practice but Yahweh witnesses it, so its inherent falseness (*šeqer*) is exposed by the fate of the two prophets — This accusation makes the command in v. 6 'take wives' appear quite ironic!

The third chapter in the cycle is a much expanded account of an exchange of letters between Jerusalem and Babylon (vv. 3–7, 25–29, 31–32). The deportation of 597 has taken place and there appears to be a state of normal communication between the two communities (cf. v. 3). Jeremiah the prophet is presented as a figure of authority writing letters to the leaders of the deportees in Babylon, setting out the strategy for survival there. In this cycle he is clearly the leader of both communities, advising, condemning and encouraging the social leaders of the people in Jerusalem and Babylon. Even at so great a distance as that between the two territories he may command and send the divine word (cf. 51.59–64; Bright treats the book of oracles against Babylon as a magical act after 29.32). Like the legendary Elijah (II Chron. 21.12–15), Jeremiah can react at a distance to events by means of the written word. This role of the writing prophet is a major feature of Part III (e.g. 29.1; 30.2; 36.2; cf. 51.60) and reflects the later development of the prophet in the direction of becoming a canonical figure. In the story of this letter he is associated with important Jerusalem people (v. 3 Elasah and Gemariah) who are part of a royal delegation to Babylon (not to be confused with 51.59). His role, therefore, in the cycle is that of an authoritative figure moving about Jerusalem, advising foreign nations on foreign policy (27), confronting an anti-Babylonian prophet (28), and proclaiming a policy of co-operation with the Babylonians to the Judaeans now living in Babylon. The interests behind the cycle are clearly Babylonian, though whether on behalf of the communities in Babylon or those descendants of the original deportees who returned to Palestine after the fall of Babylon cannot be determined from the text (the redactional notes of vv. 1–2 would be unnecessary in earlier times).

In spite of the disjunctive additions which appear to be part of the contents of the letter, the letter itself is brief and straightforward. It advises the deportees to settle down to permanent exile. This is the clear message of its contents (vv. 5–7) and agrees with the view expressed in 28 that there would be no return from Babylon. The oracular format of the letter (v. 4) makes the policy expressed in it the word of Yahweh. It therefore provides divine sanction for the way of life of the Babylonian communities and is quite unique in the biblical traditions. The people who have moved to the new territory are counselled to settle down to a normal social life (cf. similar instructions relating to Palestinian territory in 32.15). Such an existence consists of building houses, planting gardens for the production of food, marrying and giving in marriage in order to reproduce the community's stock of people and increase its population. These are all long-term projects which produce a firmly established society with an open-ended future. It can go on developing as long as it does not diminish its stock (v. 6b). The well-being (*šālōm*) of this community is however bound up with the well-being (*šālōm*) of the city (MT) or country (G) of Babylon, hence the people must intercede (*hitpalᵉlū* in contrast to 7.16; 11.14; 14.11) with Yahweh on behalf of the well-being of their new home. This is civil religion at its very best, and virtually unique in the Bible: domesticity and devotion, hard work and prayer all contributing to *šālōm*. After the terrible events of invasion, deportation and life in an alien land, *šālōm* is to be found in a blend of normal existence and prayerful conformity to Babylonian life. Unique though the prescriptions may be in the Bible, they are a remarkably acute assessment of the situation and a blueprint for millennia to come.

The strategy for survival in a foreign land is completed in v. 7. The fate of the exiles is bound up with the fate of their new territory and the *šālōm* element in the strategy is a relational one between deportees and overlord culture. This makes the *šālōm* feature quite unique in the tradition in that it affects others (i.e. foreigners) and is not directed by Yahweh solely towards Judah (contrast v. 11). However, the letter is supplemented by a number of additions which have nothing to do with its contents but which reflect the present context of that letter. These are supplementary expositions designed to balance the letter and link it with the anti-prophetic theme of the cycle.

An oracular statement in vv. 8–9 denounces the prophets and diviners. These are not identified in the text, but the redaction's placing of the piece after vv. 5–7 permits, rather than necessitates, identifying them as deported prophets and diviners (cf. v. 1; G *pseudoprophētai*). Commentators interpret the attack on their activities as a further polemic against the prophetically inspired view that the exile would be a short one (cf. 27.16; 28.3). This is a possible interpretation based on inference but not on what the text says. It simply warns against being deceived by prophets and dreamers (i.e. those who divine by dreams). Such agents do not come from Yahweh and what they prophesy is false (*šeqer*). These are clichéd charges in the tradition and without further clarification in the text could mean anything. If the oracle is taken at face value it asserts what is stated so often in the polemic against the prophets: they deceive (cf. 4.10) by means of what they prophesy and dream (cf. 23.25–32). Nothing more is said about them, whether they are Judaean or foreign, in Judah or Babylon. What they do is false and Yahweh has not sent them (cf. 28.15). The reference to diviners (v. 8 *qōsᵉmīm*) only occurs elsewhere in 27.9 (but the prophets attacked in 14.14 produce worthless divination [*qesem*]), which raises the question whether 29.8 is a displacement of 27.9 or vice versa (27.9–11 is odd in its address to foreign prophets, but then 27–29 is an odd cycle). In 27–29 there appears to be a steady shift of a few elements to cover a wide diversity of situations and these movable phrases consequently lose their semantic force. The present position of vv. 8–9 taken in the context of 27–29 may imply prophetic and divinatory processes which claimed that there would be no exile or a short one. The letter explaining the permanence of the new life in an alien land is then a counterbalance to such behaviour. The point could have been made much more clearly in the text, if that is indeed what vv. 8–9 purport to be.

A further addition to the text occurs in vv. 10–14. It also appears to be a counterbalance to what precedes it (if Rudolph is followed in reading vv. 8–9 after v. 15 then the counterbalancing effect of vv. 10–14 to vv. 5–7 becomes quite apparent). For if vv. 5–7 assert the permanence of the exile, vv. 10–14 speak of a return to the homeland (v. 10 'this place' i.e. Jerusalem or the temple, cf. 27.22; 28.3). These two motifs do not necessarily contradict each other but vv. 10–14 look suspiciously like the message of the prophets in the cycle who are declared to be prophesying falsehood. It only differs from what they say in having a longer time sequence – seventy years instead of two years. The seventy years motif which appears also in 25.11–12 indicates the end of Babylonian rule (cf. 27.7 where three generations or a long time is given as the duration of that domination) and presumably identifies the unit as a post-exilic creation. As the return to the homeland never became a very popular movement the strategy for building a permanent life in Babylon proved to be very wise counsel.

The presence of the seventy years motif in v. 10 set in the cycle of 27–29 produces an unintended irony. In 28.9 a prophecy of *šālōm* requires fulfilment before it can be determined whether Yahweh sent the prophet or not. Although Hananiah is not condemned on the grounds of the failure of his prediction (28.9 does not function as a criterion in 28), his two years look very modest beside seventy years. A prediction of seventy years time would be absurd if either 28.9 or Deut. 18.22 was imposed as a test of authenticity. Nobody would be alive after another seventy years to be able to verify the speaker's genuineness and hence the criterion is not designed for long term predictions (if such were conceived of in biblical times). The speaker of vv. 10–14 need not be charged with being a false prophet because there are no grounds for considering the statement to be anything other than an after the event proclamation. Its function in 29 is to correct the impression rightly given by vv. 5–7 that exile would be permanent. There may be very few Jews in Iraq today, but the Jewish presence in Babylonia has been a permanent one. The restoration motif of v. 10 reflects that return to Palestine which a few descendants of the exiles made. This point needs to be underlined: those who went into exile in 597 were not those who returned in the century following the fall of Babylon in 539. Few, if any, of the original exiles lived so long that they could even contemplate returning to a land which they had left in their youth. The bulk of those who 'returned' had never known life in Palestine – it was a new and risky venture for them.

The restoration of the exiles in vv. 10–11 is given an oracular grounding and made the fulfilment of Yahweh's 'good word' (*dᵉbārī haṭṭōb*). For Yahweh has plans of well-being (*maḥšᵉbōt šālōm*, contrast 18.11) rather than disaster for the people. The future hope planned by Yahweh is developed in vv. 12–14 along pietistic lines and fused in v. 14 with the much more general return from the diaspora of all the scattered exiles. The influence of Deuteronomistic language here indicates redactional development of the piece in a direction quite distinct from vv. 10–11. There Yahweh restores the exiles from Babylon, after which they call upon him when they go (to the temple? MT v. 12) and pray to him. But in vv. 13–14 the restoration takes place after the scattered ones have sought Yahweh. The two different sequences of events probably reflect the two distinctive views of future restoration: an act of divine grace in which the deity initiates the movement (cf. 31.33–4) and a situation in which the people turn to Yahweh and he responds graciously (cf. 3.12; 4.1–2, 3–4; Deut. 30.1–10). In the first the return is Yahweh keeping his word (cf. NEB 'I will take up your cause and fulfil the promise of good things I made you'); in the second the deity restores the diaspora as a result of their response to him. As they both refer to rather different returns they should not be confused (cf. Emmerson 1984, 9–55, for analysis of the two distinctive strands as they affect the editing of the book of Hosea). The expansion of the unit in terms of the restoration of the diaspora has the effect of making v. 14 contradict the motif in v. 18. The post-exilic hope that the diaspora would return to Palestine conflicts with those elements in the tradition which write off any exilic community outside Babylon or any deportation other than that of 597.

The attack on the prophets is resumed in vv. 15, 21–23 but MT interrupts it with an onslaught on the Jerusalem community (lacking in G). This interpolation in vv. 16–19 would be better read after vv. 10–14 where it would afford a strong contrast between the different futures posited for the exiles of 597 (and all the diaspora) and those who remained behind in the land of Judah. The sequence vv. 15, 21–3 (G) identifies the prophets under attack as ones in the Babylonian community (if vv. 8–9 were to be incorporated into this section that would solve the problem of identification there). Apparently once the deportees settled down in various parts of Babylonia they developed normal social structures which included the emergence of prophets (v. 15 hardly refers to the prophets of the redactional heading in v. 1 as the community would not then have spoken of Yahweh raising up for them prophets). These prophets are recognized as coming from Yahweh, presumably in fulfilment of Deut. 18.15, 18 (the late addition to the Deuteronomistic law parallels the lateness of this material in 29). Because they are accepted as such by the people, an oracle is given against them (v. 20, lacking in G, is required in MT to provide an introduction to vv. 21–2 because of the disruption of vv. 16–19 which have isolated v. 15). In vv. 21–23 these prophets are identified as Ahab and Zedekiah (a peculiarity of the cycle is the naming of prophets against whom Jeremiah speaks). They also are accused of prophesying falsehood (*šeqer*) in the divine name. Nothing of what they say is given in the text, so again the redactional context may be to taken to imply that they are prophesying against Babylonian rule (like Second Isaiah?). Such an implication is in keeping with the charge against Hananiah (28) and the foreign prophets (27.9–10) but is *not* a necessary reading of the text. The redaction of 29 is particularly poor in the provision of adequate information which would allow each unit to be understood clearly.

The fate of the two prophets at the hands of Nebuchadrezzar is proof of their falseness and their adultery. In the attack on prophets of 23.14 adultery is one of the charges but there it is probably some involvement in illicit cults (see on 5.7–8); here the accusation of adultery concerns sexual activities with the wives of their neighbours. How could Jeremiah living in Jerusalem have known what was going on in secret (cf v. 23b) so many hundreds of miles away? To ask that question is to answer it. He could not have known such matters, unless they were common gossip in Babylon of the kind that would be mentioned in dispatches back to the homeland. This seems highly unlikely as it presupposes that vv. 21–23 belong to the letter and that adultery was tolerated at such a level. While it may be encouraging to discover that normal domestic concourse had been resumed to the point that adultery could be practised among the exilic communities, it might be wiser to assume that either a story is involved here or one further example of the denigration of the prophets so typical of the cycle is intended by the allusion. If the story is read as having any historical content then it must be treated as a product of the Babylonian exilic communities and not as the output of Jeremiah or the Jerusalem people.

The legends about Nebuchadrezzar collected and circulated in the Aramaic half of the book of Daniel include stories about his predilection for roasting people, so the tale about Ahab and Zedekiah may belong to the same provenance. They are a famous couple roasted by Nebuchadrezzar (the elements of word-play in v. 22 make the story a macabre example of gallows humour in the Bible), indeed so well-known is the tale that the exiles use it as a curse. Such a curse is used to explain their falseness. They are a famous example of sexual behaviour which is characterized as 'folly in Israel', i.e. 'deluded ignorance' (von Rad 1962, 267), a class of acts which bring appalling suffering in their wake because they disrupt the sexual harmony of the community. As prophets they would have had greater access to married women because of their special holy status as men of god (e.g. II Kings 4.11–17; cf. Isa. 8.3). Yet such adultery would require great secrecy, or else all the parties to it (note no women are mentioned as victims of the same fate) would have suffered whatever the consequences of the great sin were at that time and in that society. Falseness (*šeqer*) is the essence of adultery, hence the connection between prophesying falsehood and being adulterers. From the charge of prophesying falsehood it is but a step to accusing the 'false' prophet(s) of committing other kinds of false behaviour. The roasting of the prophets is *proof* of their falseness (whether due to sedition, *šālōm* preaching or just the story line) and whatever else may be charged against them. The reference to Yahweh as witness suggests a legal analogy: cf. Deut. 19.15, where two or three witnesses are required for a charge to be sustained; presumably the deity as witness would outrank this demand! But adultery in secret would only have the deity as witness, and his execution of the criminals by the hand of his vassal Nebuchadrezzar must be taken as proof of guilt (cf. the later rabbinic interpretation of disease and sickness as proof of sinfulness).

The question may be asked whether such a charge of adultery might not be a technique for controlling prophets. To be accused of the deed would certainly curtail a prophet's activities and either silence him or make him cautious. There is no evidence to confirm this analysis, though the biblical traditions use the charge as a metaphor of idolatry when they wish to denounce particular communities (cf. 2.20–25; 3.1; Hos. 3; Ezek. 23). However, the charge of not having been sent by Yahweh and of speaking falsehood in the divine name may have had a controlling function in the community, so the additional accusation of adultery may not have been necessary. It is the execution of Ahab and Zedekiah which allows the interpretation of their fate to be made in terms of having committed adultery. The story of their wretched fate at the hands of the cruel despot Nebuchadrezzar highlights a feature of the cycle: the death of prophets. Hananiah, Ahab and Zedekiah all die, and presumably because of opposition to Nebuchadrezzar (cf. Uriah in 26.23, who dies at the hands of Jehoiakim). Being a prophet in opposition to the Babylonians is a very risky calling, and those who embraced such a ministry must have been very brave, if perhaps foolish, Yahwists. Small wonder that Jeremiah the prophet was a supporter of Babylon and lived, according to the tradition, to be an old man. It is a wise prophet who knows which side to support and who does not allow nationalistic fervour to displace self-interest.

What is curious, however, is the number of commentators who praise Jeremiah endlessly for his bravery and equally condemn out of hand the other prophets for kowtowing to authority. According to the cycle of 27–29, all the risks being taken were by those prophets who preached against Babylon and encouraged resistance to Babylon at home. No risks were taken by those who praised the Babylonians and encouraged submission to their cruel yoke. Conformity to imperialist power was no doubt the wise thing to encourage, but such pusillanimity should not be praised by exegetes as risk-taking. As the oracles against Babylon (50–51) show, there is an alternative position to conformity.

The interpolated attack on the Jerusalem community in vv. 16–19 (not in G) allows a striking contrast to be made between the exiles in Babylon (vv. 5–7) and those who did not go into exile. The future for the exiles is one of settled domesticity and well-being (*šālōm*), whereas Jerusalem's king and people face a horrible future of destruction. Invasion, with its concomitant death by butchery, starvation and disease, will attend them and the deity will make them like rotten fruit. The figs metaphor may be derived from 24.1–3, but it is used in a quite different way from the vision of the two baskets of fruit (perhaps the influence is from 29.17 and 24.1–3 represent a further development). In the vision the figs represent the status of the two communities (exiled and domestic), here the deity turns the home community into something resembling (v. 17 '*like* disgusting figs') rotten figs (rotten in the sense of being too bad to eat – fruit gone off). The people will be driven from their homeland and wherever they are exiled the deity will pursue them with the triad of devastations. Thus wherever they go they will be an object of horror and the nations will hiss them, use them as a curse (v. 18, cf. v. 22), an occasion of appalment and a reproach (cf. 25.9, 18; 42.18; 44.8, 12, 22; also 49.13, 17; 51.37). This terrible pursuit by Yahweh is caused by the people's rejection of the prophetic word.

The horrific fate of Jerusalem and its people in contrast to the *šālōm* of the exiles (in spite of the fact that those exiled in 597 are accused of the same rejection of the divine word in 25.4; 26.5) is not only hyperbolic but also has a political function. It serves the interests of the Babylonian groups. It promotes those who can trace their ancestry to the exiles of 597 over those who remained in the land or who were deported at a later period. The deportation of 597 represents the *Mayflower* of the reconstructed Jerusalem community. All those who were not a part of that event are the special enemies of Yahweh and will be hunted down by him until completely annihilated. Yahweh's future plans (vv. 10–11) only concern the exiles in Babylon, and the myth of the extinction of all other occupants of Palestine (cf. II Chron. 36.20–1) facilitates this belief.

To read the various units in 29 in this way represents an attempt to explain why the tradition should contain strands (such as 24; 29.16–19; 44) where every community, except those in Babylon, is written off in relation to Yahweh's good pleasure for the future. Why is such undisguised hatred of the Jerusalem community so rampant in these strands? Is it simply hyperbole? Ought the exegete not to ask the question 'whose interests are served by such denunciations?'? According to Ezra and Nehemiah political elements came from the Persian court to reorganize Jerusalem, its economy and religion. Are, then, the strands in the Jeremiah tradition which display kindness towards the Babylonian groups and abuse the Jerusalem community in such vilifying terms not evidence of party bias reflecting a situation in which there was conflict between representatives of both communities? Such an explanation, however tentatively it may be advanced here, would help to account for a hostility towards everything non-Babylonian which cannot be explained in any other way.

29.24–32

24 To Shemaiah of Nehelam you shall say: 25 'Thus says the LORD of hosts,
the God of Israel: You have sent letters in your name to all the people who
are in Jerusalem, and to Zephaniah the son of Maaseiah the priest, and to
all the priests, saying, 26 "The LORD has made you priest instead of Jehoiada
the priest, to have charge over every madman who prophesies, to put him
in the stocks and collar. 27 Now why have you not rebuked Jeremiah of
Anathoth who is prophesying to you? 28 For he has sent to us in Babylon,
saying, 'Your exile will be long; build houses and live in them, and plant
gardens and eat their produce.' " '

29 Zephaniah the priest read this letter in the hearing of Jeremiah the
prophet. 30 Then the word of the LORD came to Jeremiah: 31 'Send to all
the exiles, saying, "Thus says the LORD concerning Shemaiah of Nehelam:
Because Shemaiah has prophesied to you when I did not send him, and has
made you trust in a lie, 32 therefore thus says the LORD: Behold, I will
punish Shemaiah of Nehelam and his descendants; he shall not have any
one living among this people to see the good that I will do to my people,
says the LORD, for he has talked rebellion against the LORD." '

[24] MT *wᵉ'el-šᵉmaʿyāhū hanneḥᵉlāmī tō'mar lē'mōr*, 'and to Shemaiah the Nehelamite you shall say saying': NEB deletes 'you shall say, saying', G lacks 'saying'; Rudolph, 186–7, treats as a title 'Concerning Shemaiah from Nechlam'. Nehelam is unknown as a place name in the Bible. The gentilic form may refer to a place name or a family; the uncertainty about the name suggests that its form here is part of the literary creation of the story and is opposed to Jeremiah the Anathothite (another gentilic form, v. 27). Yaure 1960, 306–9, understands the name to be Shemaiah the dreamer (cf. v. 8; 27.9; 23.17; 14.14), a prototype of Barjesus, i.e. Elymas the magician, in Acts 13.6–12. He is a prophet inspired by dreams; the Niphal form of *ḥlm*, 'dream', hardly supports this suggestion. **[25]** G lacks 'Thus says Yahweh of hosts, the god of Israel, saying'. MT 24, 25 overload the piece with forms of *'mr*, 'say'. G 'I did not send you in my name; and to Sophonias son of Maasaios the priest say' is a much shorter text than MT, which has developed the story to make it refer the prophetic statement to the priests and people as well. G lacks any reference to a letter at this point (cf. v. 29), whereas MT has *sᵉpārīm*, 'letters', here but *sēper*, 'letter', in v. 29. **[26]** MT *lihyōt pᵉqidīm*, 'to be overseers': G *genesthai epistatēn*, 'to be overseer'. MT *bēt yhwh*, 'house of Yahweh': many mss, Vrs *bᵉbēt*, 'in the house'. MT *lᵉkol-'īš mᵉšuggāʿ ūmitᵉnabbē'*, 'over every man who is mad and plays the prophet': i.e. crazy prophesying; 'madman', *mᵉšuggāʿ*, is a synonym for prophet (II Kings 9.11; Hos. 9.7). Cf. 20.2 for the overseer priest with the authority to beat unruly prophets. **[27]** MT *lō' gāʿartā*, 'you not rebuke': G *suneloidorēsate*, '(why do) you (plur.) rebuke'. G is quite different from MT in that the piece is directed against the two named characters rather than against Jeremiah. Hence they are challenged about rebuking Jeremiah (G), whereas MT demands of Zephaniah (the brother of Zedekiah in v. 21?) that he should have beaten Jeremiah of Anathoth. MT *hammitᵉnabbē'*, 'who is playing at being a prophet': cf. NEB 'who poses as a prophet'. **[28]** MT *kī ʿal-kēn šālaḥ*, 'for therefore he sent': G^V *dia tou mēnos toutou*, 'during the course of this month'. **[31]** A few mss, G* lack 'the exiles' (BHS); note *lākem* 'to you' here and in v. 27 where the two communities and their prophets are contrasted. Cf. 28.15 for the motif 'making the people trust to what is false'. **[32]** MT *wᵉlō'-yir'eh*, 'and he will not see': G *tou idein*, 'to see' = *lir'ōt*. G *humin*, 'to you' = *lākem*, for MT *lᵉʿammī*, 'to my people'. G lacks 'for he has uttered rebellion against Yahweh', cf. 28.16; Deut. 13.6 (EV5).

In a rather confused section dealing with exchanges of letters between Babylon and Jerusalem the theme of false prophets is continued. MT and G differ in their presentation of the story: in the Hebrew the priest Zephaniah ben Maaseiah (cf. 21.1; 37.3; 52.24) is challenged about his failure to control Jeremiah who is posing as a prophet (cf. NEB), whereas in the Greek the priest is berated for rebuking Jeremiah. In MT *letters* are sent from Babylon concerning the behaviour of the (pseudo-) prophet Jeremiah (cf. II Kings 10.1 for the motif of sending letters to stir up trouble), but in G the material is oracular rather than epistolary. The section appears to be an exchange of abuse between Shemaiah (cf. Uriah ben Shemaiah 26.20) the Nehelamite and Jeremiah the Anathothite (the only occurrence of this gentilic form in the tradition; for similar gentilic forms of Anathoth, cf. I Chron. 12.3; 27.12; II Sam. 23.27 = I Chron. 11.28). As such it is an argument between two prophets, each accusing the other of being wrong. In MT it would appear that this form of mutual abuse is carried on via letters and at a great distance. However, the exchange incorporates the temple priest in charge of madmen who play at being prophets (i.e. act the part of a prophet). In Shemaiah's letter the priest is upbraided for not keeping Jeremiah of Anathoth in check, thus implying the temple location of Jeremiah's activity. The view of Jeremiah as a crazy play-acting prophet is interesting in that it demonstrates the ease with which prophets may abuse each other. This type of abuse, i.e. accusations of posing as a prophet, telling lies, not being sent, making people trust in falsehood, is the stock-in-trade of prophetic conflict. There is no good reason for treating the language used as anything other than the fulminations against one another of members of the *same* profession. That the exchanges are so vituperative and defamatory is part of the process of denunciation common to all prophets. It is the rhetoric of prophecy.

The cause of Shemaiah's attack on Jeremiah is his view of the length of the exile (v. 28, *'ᵃrukkāh hī'*, 'it is long', refers to the exile, though the phrase lacks an object, because the rest of the verse is a citation of v. 5). Whereas Jeremiah's letter says nothing about the length of the exile because it does not admit of an end to it, Shemaiah's inference from it is not incorrect. From the standpoint of there being an end to the exile (i.e. Shemaiah's position) the logic of the letter from Jeremiah would entail a lengthy period before any such change in fortunes. Also from Shemaiah's viewpoint such discouraging information coming from Jerusalem must have militated against his own endeavours to maintain the deportees' courage and confidence that soon they would return to their own land. Hence his letter(s) to Zephaniah demanding to know why the overseer had not chastized Jeremiah for such irresponsible behaviour (cf. 20.1–2 for what Shemaiah would have considered the proper response to an irresponsible prophet).

Because Jeremiah is a temple prophet in this cycle (cf. 28.1, 5) it is natural in this story that he should be present for Zephaniah's reading of the letter. Perhaps the overseer summoned him so that he could listen to the complaint about his attitude and behaviour coming from Babylon. Zephaniah's role in the story is minimal: he receives the letter(s) and conveys its (cf. v. 29, 'this letter', in contrast to MT v. 25) contents to Jeremiah. He is part of the story because the priests are one of the main elements in the cycle (27.16; 28.1, 5; 29.1, 25) and much of what happens in the various stories takes place in the presence of the priests. Whether he disciplines Jeremiah or not is not mentioned in this story because its concern is with the exchange between the two prophesying figures. In vv. 30–31 Jeremiah's response is oracular. Yahweh replies to letters yet! The reply to Shemaiah is a public one addressed to all the exiles. Because he has misled the people by making them trust a lie (presumably *šeqer* refers to an implicit proclamation that the exile would be a short one, cf. 27.16; 28.2–4; though no statement of Shemaiah's to that effect appears in the unit) he will be punished by the deity. The reference to Yahweh's visitation (*pqd* v. 32, cf. v.10) ironically mirrors the divine visit of v. 10 and contrasts the fate of Shemaiah and his descendants with that of the descendants of the exiles. When the restoration does take place Shemaiah and his people will have no part in it (cf. 23.34 for the notion of the punishment of a man and his household). Shemaiah's fate is due to his having spoken rebellion against Yahweh (cf. Hananiah's fate 28.16 and the ruling in Deut. 13.5). Thus the Shemaiah story is a fragmentary variant of Hananiah's story and we must assume that the similarities imply that Shemaiah was a preacher of a short exile (a point not stated in the text though perhaps hinted at in v. 28).

What is most curious about the stories in this cycle is the fact that in spite of Hananiah and Shemaiah making the people trust in a lie (cf. the role of Ahab and Zedekiah among the exiles 28.21), only these prophets are punished and the people are not condemned for believing their falsehoods. In the context of the cycle this may not be particularly remarkable but within the tradition it is noteworthy. That Ahab and Zedekiah could commit adultery (29.23) without the community being condemned for adulterous behaviour is peculiar. It is odd in the light of the whole tradition and that oddity justifies the analysis of the material in the cycle as literary creations rather than historical events. The many peculiarities of 27–29 are best explained as being due to the independent origins of the cycle, which have produced a quite late and legendary image of Jeremiah the prophet whose status as the source of the divine word in the community makes him the dominant figure, whether in the Jerusalem temple or among the communities in Babylon. He now bestrides both countries like a prophetic colossus, and opposition to his viewpoint is evidence of being false. More than that, a prophet whose divine word differs from Jeremiah is guilty of 'having uttered rebellion against Yahweh' (Deuteronomistic influence on MT here, cf. Deut. 13.5). Thus to oppose Jeremiah is to be in rebellion against Yahweh. That is the main point of the cycle in its most fully developed form, though the attack on certain views about the duration of the exile is an important element in that presentation. Because certain ideological points dominate the cycle, there is no concern with denouncing the communities which have followed the false proclamations of the condemned prophets (29.16–19 is no exception to this point).

This interpretation of the letter(s) of 29 as fabrication(s) within the cycle of 27–29 differs considerably from that of many exegetes who regard the letter of Jeremiah as a genuine historical document (e.g. Dijkstra 1983). That a prophet might communicate the divine word by written form (tablet or letter) is known from the Mari archives and Akkadian sources (cf. Moran 1969; Pritchard 1969, 623–7), but the biblical traditions do not present the prophets as communicating by such means. The occasional writing of a message for the future is indicated in Isa. 8.1–2; 30.8, but only the Chronicler appears to attribute letter writing to a prophet (Elijah in II Chron. 21.12–15). As the Chronicler has a more developed role for prophets such as Elijah and Jeremiah (cf. II Chron. 35.25 where Jeremiah utters a lament for the dead Josiah, a lamentation conspicuously absent from the book of Jeremiah!), his work cannot be regarded as corroborative evidence of the *historicity* of the story in 29. Dijkstra's claim that 'we may have in Jer xxix 24–32 a complete copy of a real *document humaine*' (1983, 321) is a misreading of the tangled elements in 29.24–32 and fails to take into account the complex traditions forming the cycle of 27–29. In the context of 27–29 the dominant motif is Jeremiah's denunciation of the prophets 'who are prophesying lies' (cf. 27.10, 14, 15, 16; 28.15; 29.9, 21, 23, 31, where *šeqer* is the evaluation of what *all* the other prophets have to say) and, by means of the letter device, that polemic is extended to include the prophets in Babylon in 29. Such a fabrication serves the cycle's main thrust better as an interpretation of 29 than the vain search for evidence of a real letter submerged beneath the surface of the heavily edited narrative.

The book of the restoration of the fortunes: 30–31

A feature of the Jeremiah tradition is the presence of fragments of future hopes scattered throughout the book but lacking a coherent structure and presentation (e.g. 3.14–18; 12.14–17; 16.14–15; 17.24–26; 22.2–4; 23.5–6, 7–8; 24.4–7; 29.10–14; 42.7–12). This lack of a sustained hope is made good with an independent cycle in 30–31 which gathers together numerous poems about the restoration of the nation to its own land and the rebuilding of people, cities and economy. To these poems are added two narrative collections which develop the theme of the restoration of the fortunes (32–33). The central motif of these chapters is future salvation, though the occasional sour note can be detected (e.g. 30.5–7, 23–24; 31.22a, 29–30; 32.3–5, 23–24, 28–35). The hopes expressed by the restoration of the fortunes motif (30.3, 18; 31.23; 32.44; 33.11, 26; cf. 29.14) are modest ones and envisage a future of bucolic pleasures, political and economic security and the reversal of the bitter experiences of the past.

Following on, in the present redaction of the tradition, from Jeremiah's letter to Babylon, the cycle is represented as another of his writings. On four different occasions Jeremiah is said to have written things: 29.1; 30.2; 36.2 (this occasion is developed into the work of his amanuensis Baruch); 51.60. Two of these writings were sent to Babylon and two were addressed to the nation in Palestine – two were destroyed (51.63; 36.23–26, though this scroll was rewritten, 36.32) and two, presumably, were preserved. These different acts of writing should be interpreted as symbolic gestures – as adding something to the spoken word. In 36 and 51.59–64 the significance of the written form lies in its eventual destruction: Jehoiakim condemns himself by his act and Babylon is destroyed by the sinking of the book in the waters of the Euphrates. The letter of 29.4–7 clearly had to be written in order to be sent to Babylon. Only the writing of the book of the restoration of the fortunes remains unexplained. If, however, the writing of the word is part of the magical gesture (cf. Num. 5.23), then the collection of salvation poems in written form is itself one of Jeremiah's performative acts whereby the future is brought into existence. He who is so associated with the destruction of city and nation is here made the one who proclaims the reversal of the word of judgment and the dawn of a new age of restoration. The Book of Consolation affirms a good future for the people of Yahweh: a future not only spoken by Jeremiah but written in a book at the command of Yahweh.

If the cycle adds a dimension lacking in the tradition (cf. the building and planting motifs of 1.10), it also raises problems about its origins and connection with Jeremiah. Apart from the redactional 30.1–3 there is nothing in the cycle which would associate it with him, though there are a number of editorial elements which link it with the book of Jeremiah (e.g. 30.12–14, 23–24). Many commentators attribute it to the prophet Jeremiah, either after the collapse of Jerusalem or in the days of Josiah (e.g. Rudolph; cf. Raitt 1977, 106–27). Since he had proclaimed the complete destruction of city, land and people without residue it is difficult to see how Jeremiah could perform such a volte-face as is entailed in attributing 30–31 to him (see also on 31.1–6). As the cycle shows the marked influence of Hosea and Second Isaiah in places (e.g. 30.9, 10–11; 31.2–6, 7–9; 10–14, 18–20) and shares some common elements with the Ezekiel tradition (e.g. 31.29–30, 33, 38–40), it is preferable to attribute it to the anonymous circles during and after the exile which cherished expectations of restoration (the descendants of the prophets of *šālōm*?). The vagueness of this attribution is balanced by the lack of information available for determining the issue in a reliably historical manner and the contradictions inherent in crediting Jeremiah with the authorship of the cycle.

Deuteronomistic and post-Deuteronomistic influences on the cycle are minimal (cf. 31.31–34), though Böhmer, Herrmann and Thiel find numerous examples and traces of such activity in the text. If the Deuteronomistic outlook on the future may be summarized as the possibility of restoration on the grounds of the nation's turning (*šūb*), then there is little of such influence in the poems (cf. 31.21–22a). The alternative to such a view of future hope is the belief that a divine act of reversal and restoration will create the new age. This is the driving force of the poems in the cycle. Yahweh's love for his people will bring them back from afar and set them up in their own land, and never again shall they be disturbed (cf. Hos. 11.8–9). Apart from the fragments in the tradition already noted, this view of divine action is quite foreign to the spirit of Jeremiah as represented in the poetry and prose sections of the book. There Yahweh's hatred of his people, his fierce wrath and his overwhelming determination to destroy them for ever is the opposite of the love, compassion and tenderness which breathe through 30–31. Here the spirit is more akin to Hosea's and Second Isaiah's, and the cycle must be viewed as having its home in the circles which developed the Hosea-Second Isaiah outlook on the future in the Persian period. That such a cycle is incorporated into the Jeremiah tradition may be due to the redaction of the tradition at a time when such poems were in circulation, and their attachment to Jeremiah gave them a setting they would otherwise have lacked. It also gave them that authority which by now the figure of Jeremiah had acquired. To attribute them to the Jeremiah of the tradition was to underwrite their significance. Thus Jeremiah also became associated with the bucolic hopes for the future and even was made responsible for them. This process suggests a period when material required to be attached to more authoritative work in order to gain a hearing (cf. Ezek. 40–48; Zech. 9–11; 12–14; Malachi). Only the developed theological figure of the tradition could provide this status, and not the rejected 'historical' individual dimly discernible in the text (*contra* Raitt 1977, 126). The attribution of 30–31 to Jeremiah rounds off the development of the paradigmatic figure of the prophet: he now bestrides the culture like a colossus and determines both fate and future of Judah, whether in exile (29.1, 4–7) or its own land (30–31), of the deportees and remnant of 597 (24), of the refugees who flee to Egypt (44), and even of mighty Babylon (50–51). Not only is this achieved by word of mouth (note the almost liturgical quality of 'says Yahweh' in parts of 30–31), but it is also accomplished by the power of his pen.

30.1–4

30[1] The word that came to Jeremiah from the LORD: 2 'Thus says the LORD,
the God of Israel: Write in a book all the words that I have spoken to you.
3 For behold, days are coming, says the LORD, when I will restore the
fortunes of my people, Israel and Judah, says the LORD, and I will bring
them back to the land which I gave to their fathers, and they shall take

possession of it.' 4 These are the words which the LORD spoke concerning Israel and Judah:

[MT 30] = G 37. [3] MT $w^{e}\check{s}abt\bar{\imath}$ 'et-$\check{s}^{e}b\bar{u}t$ '$amm\bar{\imath}$ $yi\acute{s}r\bar{a}$'$\bar{e}l$ $w\bar{\imath}h\bar{u}d\bar{a}h$, 'and I will restore the fortunes of my people Israel and Judah': for the idiom $\check{s}\bar{u}b$ $\check{s}^{e}b\bar{u}t$, 'restore the fortunes', cf. 29.14 (Notes). BHS treats 'Judah' as an addition to the text here and in v. 4 (cf. Rudolph, 189). This is unnecessary unless 'Israel and Judah' are to be understood as an explanatory gloss on 'my people'; cf. 31.1, 'all the families of Israel'.

The cycle opens with a lengthy redactional introduction which represents the collected poems, sayings and prose pieces in 30–31 as the words of Yahweh spoken to Jeremiah and written by him in a book. The book constituted by this collection is often referred to by scholars as 'the Book of Consolation' because virtually all its contents refer to the salvation of the community. It is therefore in striking contrast to the bulk of the Jeremiah tradition.

The introductory sentence of v. 1 is the standard formulaic preface to the various blocks of material in the tradition (e.g. 7.1; 11.1; 18.1; 21.1; 32.1; 34.1, 8; 35.1; 40.1) and its use here integrates the independent cycle of 30–31 into the book of Jeremiah. Its secondary nature is also evidenced by the fact that what follows in vv. 2–4 contains an overload of further redactional material stressing the oracular nature of the cycle, to which v. 1 adds yet another assertion of the divine origin of Jeremiah's work. The representation of Jeremiah writing all the divine words in a book reflects a period when the spoken word has become the written word and there has been a significant shift in the role of the prophetic figure. By attributing all that follows to Jeremiah, the salvation oracles of a later period are given an authority which they would not have had by themselves. This book written by Jeremiah becomes a statement about the future (cf. 51.60; Isa. 30.8) which is summarized by v. 3. The fortunes of Yahweh's people will be restored (the idiom $\check{s}\bar{u}b$ $\check{s}^{e}b\bar{u}t$ may contain a word-play on $\check{s}\bar{u}b$) in the future when Yahweh brings back ($ha\check{s}ib\bar{o}t\bar{\imath}m$ an important use of $\check{s}\bar{u}b$ in the tradition) the people to the land given to their fathers. The least that is presupposed by this introduction is the exile of 587. To delete 'Judah' from vv. 3–4 in order to make the cycle refer to northern Israel and therefore represent the preaching of the young Jeremiah in the time of Josiah (cf. Rudolph, 188–9; Lohfink 1981) is quite unwarranted. The expansion of the term 'my people' as 'Israel and Judah' may reflect the recognition of the widespread dispersal of various tribal elements over a long period of time and the hope that in the future they would all be reunited in their own land (cf. 2.4; 31.1; Ezek. 37.15–23; contrast Zech. 11.7–14). This is more akin to the Chronicler's work with its programmatic appeal to all Israel, and it may be the case that the Book of Consolation is intended to be part of the argument for a unified and inclusive community in the future (cf. Williamson 1977b for such an analysis of Chronicles). Given Jeremiah's backing the collection of discrete materials is presented as the divine word in oracular form (hence the repeated 'says Yahweh', using different forms in v. 3 and the further introductory title in v. 4). All these hopes for the future are Yahweh's word to Jeremiah and, in a period when that figure had acquired either legendary status in the community or had become the focal point of the tradition, therefore authoritative.

When so many diverse elements are collected together and presented as the work of one person yet clearly contain the influences of other circles (e.g. Second Isaiah's), it becomes very difficult for the modern exegete to tease out the different strands and attribute them to specific sources with any degree of accuracy. The Book of Consolation poses this problem in its most extreme form (cf. the oracles against the nations in 46–51), and in the following analysis it will be argued that the collection is both anonymous and contains many disparate elements. Similarities between 30–31 and the poems in Second Isaiah cannot be demonstrated to be the influence of Jeremiah on the anonymous prophet of the exile (*contra* Paul 1969), without too many assumptions being made in one direction. Only in the final redaction is the cycle incorporated into the Jeremiah tradition and therefore attributed to him by means of the editorial vv. 1–4. Constructing complex accounts of how the one person could be prophet of judgment and *also at the same time* speaker of salvation (e.g. Raitt 1977 and many exegetes) involves too many major presuppositions to be a correct analysis and applies to the finished work of redaction rather than the supposed figure behind the tradition (cf. Kaiser 1975, 223, for similar strictures about treating Isaiah as a preacher of repentance).

The position of 30–31 as an independent cycle following on immediately from another independent cycle in 27–29 may be explained in terms of the associative links between the dominant motif of the good Yahweh will do to his people in 30–31 and the reference to that motif in 29.32. There Shemaiah of Nehelam is denied a share in that good, whereas in 30–31 the substantive elements in that good fortune are illustrated in a series of poems. From all these benefits Shemaiah and his descendants will be excluded. Furthermore, 30–31 focus on the restoration of the fortunes of Israel and Judah where 27–29 concentrate on the subjugation and dispersal of the community. What is taken away to and by Babylon is restored to the land of Israel in 30–31. Thus the two cycles work quite well together as a balanced account of judgment and destruction on the one hand and salvation and restoration on the other hand. Their origins and central motifs are very different, but together they form a dialectical element in the tradition which links past (judgment) and future (restoration) through the proclamation of the word of Yahweh by Jeremiah (the prophet).

30.5–7

5 'Thus says the LORD:
We have heard a cry of panic,
of terror, and no peace.
6 Ask now, and see,
can a man bear a child?
Why then do I see every man
with his hands on his loins like a woman in labour?
Why has every face turned pale?
7 Alas! that day is so great
there is none like it;
it is a time of distress for Jacob;
yet he shall be saved out of it.'

---

[5] MT *kī-kōh 'āmar yhwh*, 'for thus says Yahweh': a redactional addition which turns the report of the nation's distress into a divine oracle and typifies the overload of redactional indicators of oracularity in vv. 1–5a. MT *šāmā'nū*, 'we have heard': G *akousesthe*, 'you will hear'. Rudolph, 188, reads *šāma'tī*, 'I have heard', to balance *rā'ītī*, 'I have seen' in v. 6b; cf. Volz, 281, who reads 'I have heard' and accounts for MT as being due to the influence of 6.24. Böhmer 1976, 57, also reads *šāma'tī*. MT *paḥad*, 'terror': a term associated with the day of Yahweh motif (cf. Isa. 2.10–17; Amos 5.18–20; Zeph. 1.18; Böhmer, 57–8); this motif does not appear in the Jeremiah tradition (apart from in 46 and 47). **[6]** G has a double reading of the line 'why do I see every man with his hands upon his hips?' which represents in part an inner-Greek corruption (Janzen 1973, 29). MT *kayyōlēdāh*, 'as a woman giving birth': cf. 31.8; Micah. 5.2 (EV 3); lacking in G in spite of its double reading, hence a late gloss in MT (Rudolph, 190; Janzen, 49). MT *l^eyērāqōn*, '. . . to paleness': i.e. every face turns green (cf. *yereq*, 'green, grass'). G *eis ikteron egenēthē*, 'to become pale', reading *hwy* (v. 7) as *hyw* (*hāyū*); cf. BHS, which incorporates it into v. 6. G (Ziegler, 350; cf. Ziegler 1958, 97; Janzen, 29) represents inner-Greek corruption and a number of doublets here. **[7]** MT *hōy*, 'woe, alas': cf. G, BHS; Janzen, 73. MT *ūmimmennāh yiwwāšē'a*, 'and from it he shall be saved': before the addition of vv. 10–11 the original form of this phrase may have been 'and will he be saved from it?', cf. Bright, 297; Holladay 1962b, 53–4; Lundbom 1975, 33.

The first poem in the collection has very little to do with the introductory phrase in v. 5a or v. 4. The poem is a description of human response to the terrible day of Yahweh. Panic seizes the people, and even the men are terrified to the point where they are behaving like pregnant women giving birth (MT). The effect of the occasion on the men is to make them act pregnant: hands on hips and faces turning green! Such a transformation of men (see on 31.22b) into creatures caught in the agonies of childbirth indicates the aweful terror of that day. Trembling and horror without any wellbeing (*šālōm*) seize the community and the state of the men is graphic evidence of the disaster. The day is so great that there is none to match it. Such a nonpareil day is described as 'a time of distress for Jacob'. Nothing in this report of public reaction to the terrifying time of suffering suggests an oracular announcement, though the last phrase in v. 7 may represent a hint of (divine) salvation or a word of despair. It is this terrible scene which raises the curtain on the restoration of the fortunes cycle.

The image of destruction as comparable to a woman giving birth, i.e. the sudden onslaught of pains over which the person has no control, is to be found in 4.31; 13.21b; 49.24; 50.43, but here it is used in a different way. As a metaphor of the community suffering invasion the image is striking, but in the poem here it is used to convey something beyond that experience. The men of the community, i.e. members of the nation rather than a metaphor of it, are the ones seized by pains as if they were pregnant women. It is the transformation, even the transmogrification, of the normal patterns of life which characterizes this particular day (cf. 31.22 for a different transformation). Depicted in this manner the day cannot simply be 597 or 587 for, apart then from the inappropriateness of v. 7b, 'he shall be saved out of it' (but see Notes), there is something preternatural about it. Only the almost apocalyptic catastrophe of 4.23–26 comes close to the mood of this poem, and its significance must be sought in that direction. What the poem is about is the day of Yahweh. This is a motif to be found in many prophetic traditions (e.g. Isa. 2.10–17; 13.6–16; Obad. 15–21; Joel 2.1–11, 30–32 [MT 3.3–5]; Zeph. 1.14–18), though it is lacking in the Jeremiah tradition (apart from elements in the oracles against the nations e.g. 46.10; 47.4). Whatever the motif may have contributed to understanding various historical disasters (cf. Amos 5.18–20), its real function is to point forward to a time when all the nations which have opposed Israel for so long will be destroyed by the deity. In that destruction Zion and Jacob will escape (cf. Joel 2.32; Obad. 17, 18; Zeph. 3.11–20). As a preface to the collection of salvation oracles the poem creates the atmosphere for the development of that point.

30.8–9

8 'And it shall come to pass in that day, says the LORD of hosts, that I will break the yoke from off their neck, and I will burst their bonds, and strangers shall no more make servants of them. 9 But they shall serve the LORD their God and David their king, whom I will raise up for them.'

---

[8] MT *'ullō mē'al ṣawwā'rekā*, 'his yoke from your neck': = Isa. 10.27; who is 'you' here? G *autōn*, 'their', i.e. the people; Rudolph, 190, reads 'his' (BHS), i.e. Jacob's. MT *ûmōsrōtekā*, 'and your bonds': G 'their', cf. BHS, RSV. MT *wᵉlō'-ya'abᵉdû-bō*, 'and they shall not serve him': cf. *'bd b* in 22.13, 'they shall not use him as a servant' (24.14; 27.7). G 'they shall no longer serve foreigners'; *autoi*, 'them', for *bō*, 'him'. **[9]** Cf. Hos. 3.5, '. . . and they shall seek Yahweh their god and David their king': both texts use the same Hebrew phrases *'et(-)yhwh 'ᵉlōhêhem wᵉ'et dāwid malkām*. On the relationship between the two references cf. Emmerson 1984, 101–13, who allows for the possibility that Hos. 3.5 belongs to the primary stratum of Hosea.

A brief prose unit speaks of the future in terms of a divine liberation of the people from servitude to foreigners (contrast the divine imposition of such servitude in 27–28; for a different use of these images cf. 2.20; 5.5). This futuristic hope is also found in Isa. 10.27a (cf. Isa. 9.4). Its position here is as an explanation of the phrase 'but he shall be saved out of it'. Jacob, i.e. Judah-Israel, will be freed from foreign domination (cf. v. 3), and the only servitude it will know in the future is to Yahweh and its own king (cf. Amos 9.11 for the figure of the deity raising up [*'āqīm*, 'I will raise up'] the fallen booth of David). No longer will the nation serve foreign kings but their own Davidic king will be their ruler. This belief in the restoration of the deposed dynasty of David also appears in 23.5–6 where it is an appendix to the cycle on royal matters. It represents a hope which was kept alive in certain circles after 587 (cf. 33.14–16, 17, 21–22, 26; Ezek. 34.23–24; 37.24–25), a hope which *never* materialized. The belief that Yahweh would break the yoke of foreigners is also to be found elsewhere (e.g. Nahum 1.13, where Assyria's domination is brought to an end by Yahweh). But the combination of the two hopes in vv. 8–9 reflects some circle which identified the defeat of the foreigners as the occasion when expectations about the revival (*qūm*) of the royal house would be realized.

The distance between different parts of the tradition can be seen in a comparison of 30.8–9 with 2.25; 3.13 where 'strangers' have a rather different meaning. In the pious discourses of 2–3 'strangers' refer to alien cults among which the people pursue their own goals. In the cycles represented by 25.8–14; 27–29; 30–31, 'strangers' and 'servitude' belong to the experience of foreign domination. The resolution of such servitude will mean the service of their own god and king, a very different concept from that condemned in the discourses. The common elements of 30.9 and Hos. 3.5 point to the shared streams of tradition which the book of Jeremiah has in common with so many other biblical traditions. It is therefore unnecessary to maintain that the hope for David refers to Jeremiah's early preaching (*contra* Weiser, 269; cf. Böhmer 1976, 60), because the association of Jeremiah with the time of Josiah is a very late strand in the tradition which does not represent an actual preaching ministry before 609. The raising up of a king for the people (cf. the raising up of a prophet in 29.15; Deut. 18.15, 18) indicates the non-existence of a king of their own and therefore points to a period when the Davidic house was no longer a sovereign power in the land (cf. Amos 9.11). Domination by foreigners characterizes the post-587 period (especially after 539, when the Persians did not permit independent kings in the provincial areas of the empire). Although Hos. 3.5 may be an authentic element in the Hosea tradition (cf.

Emmerson), its use in 30.9 would not necessarily indicate the same hope as expressed by Hosea, though if applied to Judah it would presumably reflect the loss of monarchy (cf. Hos. 3.4). The presence of similar elements in different traditions raises difficult questions about interpretation. The most difficult of these concerns the precise relationship between original meaning and present setting. In the cycle of 30–31 the restoration of the fortunes of Israel and Judah is the controlling motif which determines the meaning of the various elements in the collection. The elements have their own specific meanings but those are subordinated to the central thrust of the cycle. Discrete strands contribute to that cycle but lose much of their original force by being associated with so many different elements. Thus the near apocalyptic sense of distress in 30.5–7 is developed by the addition of vv. 8–9 in the direction of a much more mundane outlook on the future as a time when foreign domination will disappear and the Davidic house will rule again.

30.10–11

10 'Then fear not, O Jacob my servant, says the LORD,
nor be dismayed, O Israel;
for lo, I will save you from afar,
and your offspring from the land of their captivity.
Jacob shall return and have quiet and ease,
and none shall make him afraid.
11 For I am with you to save you, says the LORD;
I will make a full end of all the nations
among whom I scattered you,
but of you I will not make a full end.
I will chasten you in just measure,
and I will by no means leave you unpunished.'

[10–11] = 46.27–28. G lacks them here because the oracles against the nations precede the cycle of 30–31 in G. G usually lacks such doublets, though whether by reason of omitting repeats or because such repeats are a feature of the second edition represented by MT divides scholars (the latter is the more likely case). **[10]** 46.27 lacks *nᵉ'um yhwh*, 'says Yahweh'. MT *'abdī ya'ᵃqōb*, 'my servant Jacob': cf. 'Jacob my servant', Isa. 44.1; 45.4; also 48.20. Throughout Second Isaiah the names Israel, Jacob, Judah, Jerusalem, Zion are used interchangeably to refer to the exiles or those living around and in Jerusalem (e.g. 40.1–2, 27; 41.8, 21, 27; 42.24; 43.14–15; esp. 48.1–2). **[11]** Cf. 46.28, where the first line repeats the first line of the previous verse and the phrase *kī-ʾitt^{e}kā ʾanī*, 'for I am with you' (v. 11; cf. 1.8) is at the end of the first line. MT *h^{a}piṣōtīkā*, 'I have scattered you': 46.28 *hiddaḥtīkā*, 'I have driven you'. MT *ʾak ʾōt^{e}kā*, 'only of you': 46.28 *w^{e}ʾōt^{e}kā*, 'but you'. For the motif 'discipline with justice' cf. 10.24. Cf. 4.27; 5.10, 18 for the motif 'not make a full end'.

This brief poem expresses hope for the people's return from captivity in terms derived from the circles which produced Second Isaiah and added elements to the Jeremiah tradition. It combines the motif of the return with the belief in the destruction of the nations. If Yahweh has not spared his own people, then the nations will suffer even more than Israel (cf. 25.29). Again the context of the piece is Israel's exile and the nations' domination over the people, and its content concerns the reversal of these factors. The tendency of the poems to refer to the people as Israel or Jacob rather than Judah (apart from redactional and additional strands, e.g. 30.3, 4; 31.23–24, 27, 31) is not a reflection of the northern origins of the poems but indicates the use of a wide variety of terms for Judah in the exilic and later periods (hence Zion in 30.17; 31.6, 12, 38–40). This kind of language is at home in the Second Isaiah tradition and reflects the development of the patriarchal stories in the sixth century as a means of bypassing the problems of history in favour of theological constructs (cf. Van Seters 1975). In a context of salvation the patriarchal image of Jacob is more congenial than the historical images of the nation. Thus it is that the community may be called 'Jacob my servant' in a cycle far removed from the other use of 'servant' in the tradition (e.g. 2.14). The god who is far off (cf. 23.23) will save the nation which is afar in captivity and return it to its homeland, where it will enjoy peace and quiet (without the panic referred to in v. 5). The saviour god will annihilate the enemies of Jacob (*kālāh*, cf. Nahum 1.9) among whom the exiles have been scattered.

In a period of such divine annihilation (cf. v. 7) it is important to be able to make a distinction between the nations and Israel. That differentiation is made in terms of a partial destruction of Israel in contrast to the complete wiping out of the other nations. This division between the divine punishment of Israel and destruction of the nations makes vv. 10–11 fit the cycle of 30–31 better than the cycle of 46–51 (cf. 46.26). The view of Israel's sufferings in the period described by v. 11 is that of just (*mišpāṭ*) discipline. Such an understanding of the nation's appalling experience is the same as that expressed in the communal prayer of 10.24–25. There the community prays for Yahweh's just measure (*mišpāṭ*) of correction lest he make them too few to survive (cf. 29.6; 30.19), but also appeals to him to pour out his anger on those nations who not only do not know him but also have laid *Jacob* waste. Part of the function of the coming great apocalyptic destruction of the nations will be Yahweh's just annihilation of all those who have destroyed Israel. In that terrible period Israel will again suffer, but will survive, and in returning to the homeland will face a secure future because there will be none left to induce any further panic (v. 10).

The priestly oracle of salvation (an important form in the construction of the oracles of Second Isaiah, cf. Isa. 41.10, 13, 14; 43.1, 5; 44.2; 54.4; Westermann 1969, 68–9, 71–3) provides the initial motif of the poem 'fear not'. Often it announces the assuring word of confidence after a lament has stated the individual or communal complaint about present circumstances. As such vv. 10–11 would make a fitting response to vv. 5–7, where the terrible day of Jacob's distress may be regarded as equivalent to a formal lament (vv. 8–9 interrupt the connection and must be regarded as secondary additions to the cycle). The great liturgical songs of confidence which characterize much of Second Isaiah provide a fitting note of comfort for the community enduring Jacob's distress. 'Fear not my servant Jacob, you will be saved and will return from distant lands to enjoy peace and quiet in your own land without hindrance from others.' This reassurance of salvation, i.e. return to the homeland, necessarily contains a reference to the destruction of the other nations because from 597 onwards the foreign powers have plagued Jacob's existence. Although suffering greatly at the hands of these nations, Jacob has not undergone complete annihilation. In the coming destruction of the nations Jacob will survive still to enjoy a good future. Hints of this belief can be found in Part I of the tradition (cf. 4.27b; 5.10, 18) and, although ambiguous, give rise to certain tensions within the text there. The different streams which feed the tradition provide the formal elements of these contradictions, but the communities which developed the traditions were no doubt able to resolve the difficulties to their own satisfaction.

30.12–17

12 ‘For thus says the LORD:
Your hurt is incurable,
and your wound is grievous.
13 There is none to uphold your cause,
no medicine for your wound,
no healing for you.
14 All your lovers have forgotten you;
they care nothing for you;
for I have dealt you the blow of an enemy,
the punishment of a merciless foe,
because your guilt is great,
because your sins are flagrant.
15 Why do you cry out over your hurt?
Your pain is incurable.
Because your guilt is great,
because your sins are flagrant,
I have done these things to you.
16 Therefore all who devour you shall be devoured,
and all your foes, every one of them, shall go into captivity;
those who despoil you shall become a spoil,
and all who prey on you I will make a prey.
17 For I will restore health to you,
and your wounds I will heal,
says the LORD,
because they have called you an outcast:
“It is Zion, for whom no one cares!” ’

---

[12] MT *’ānūš l^{e}šibrēk*, ‘incurable is your fracture’: G *anestēsa suntrimma*, ‘I have brought destruction’; *l^e* may be emphatic here (Nötscher 1953, 380) cf. 9.2 (EV 3), but Rudolph, 190, reads it as *lāk šibrēk* (cf. BHS). For *’ānūš*, ‘incurable’, cf. v. 15a; 15.18; 17.9, 16. **[13]** MT *’ēn-dān dīnēk l^{e}māzōr*, ‘there is none who pleads your cause, concerning injury’: for *māzōr*, ‘injury’, cf. Hos. 5.13; ‘oozing infection’ (Andersen and Freedman 1980, 413) from *zūr*, ‘squeeze pus’, cf. Isa. 1.6. MT is either a failure to understand the metaphor or a variant (cf. Bright, 271); Rudolph reads *rikkukīm*, ‘soothings, alleviation’ (cf. *rukk^{e}kāh baššāmen*, ‘soothing with oil’, Isa. 1.6). NEB ‘there can be no remedy for your sore, the new skin cannot grow’; RSV ‘no medicine for your wound, no healing for you’. MT *r^{e}pu’ōt*, ‘healings’; Rudolph treats as a gloss, though it correctly interprets *t^e‘alāh*, ‘comes up’, i.e. ‘new skin coming on the wounded flesh’ (NEB); cf. 46.11. **[14]** MT *mūsar ’akzārī*, ‘the discipline of a cruel one’: cf. 6.23; 50.42; if the absolute form *mūsār* is read, then the phrase means 'cruel discipline'. The lines 'because your guilt is great, because your sins are flagrant' are probably a repetition from v. 15b (G lacks v. 15, which may be due to the repeated lines in 14–15). **[15]** MT *tiz'aq*, 'you cry out': masc. form, but the whole poem uses fem. forms because it refers to the city Zion. MT *'āśītī 'ēlleh lāk*, 'I have done these things to you': cf. 4.18 *'āśō 'ēlleh lāk* 'he has done these things to you' (see BHS). **[16]** MT *lākēn kol*, 'therefore all': but there is no logical connection between vv. 15, 16 which would justify *lākēn*; Rudolph, 192, treats as a dittography and reads *wᵉkol*, 'and all' (BHS). MT *kullām baššᵉbī yēlēkū*, 'all of them will go into captivity': G *kreas autōn pan edontai*, 'all eat their own flesh' = *kullōh bᵉśārām yō'kēlū*. MT probably represents variants: 'all your foes, all of them'. K *s'syk*; Q mss *šōsaik* = *šōssaik* (BHS), 'your plunderers' (*šāsas* a form of *šāšāh* cf. BDB, 1042): K an Aramaized form. Some G recensions produce v. 15b in the middle of v. 16. **[17]** Rudolph reverses the first two clauses as being more appropriate and transfers *nᵉ'um yhwh*, 'says Yahweh', to the end of the verse. G has 'from the grievous wound' for MT 'from your wound'. MT *ṣiyyōn*, 'Zion': G *thēreuma hēmon*, 'our prey' = *ṣēdēnū*.

This longer poem describes the condition of the nation or city (the personification is feminine) in metaphors drawn from illness and injury. Some of the metaphors appear in poems in Part I (cf. 8.18–22; 10.19; 14.17). If the poem appears to be out of place in a collection of salvation oracles its inclusion in the cycle may be justified by the concluding vv. 16–17 (added for that purpose?). The community has suffered greatly because of its own shortcomings (cf. Isa. 1.5–6) and has been abandoned by its lovers (cf. 2.25, 33; 3.1–2). It is a wretched sight – battered and broken, bleeding and oozing pus, untreated and without medical attention. Different meanings may be given to these metaphors, but within the cycle the dominant significance of the poem is probably as a lament for the terrible damage done to the nation by invasion and deportation. The savage attacks on it by the Babylonians have destroyed the body politic and the desperately wounded woman lies there bleeding to death. The images and their significance are suddenly reversed in vv. 16–17 and the broken flesh becomes whole again. The deity provides the healing which is lacking in the community. He turns the tables on the enemy and they go into captivity because they have despised the outcast Zion.

The poem summarizes the community's recent history in terms which identify the causes of its terrible condition as the number and strength of its sins (vv. 14b, 15b) and yet permit the transformation of its state. There is in the poem a fluctuating explanation which makes Yahweh the enemy because of the community's sinfulness and yet blames the external enemies for what has happened. If the terrible wounds are really self-inflicted (vv. 12–15), the possibility of healing comes about because the deity acts against the adversaries of the city. The two different kinds of explanation belong to separate sections of the poem (vv. 12–15, 16–17) and are only loosely connected (*lākēn*, 'therefore', in v. 16 lacks logical force). But without a reversal of the community's state the poem would have no place in this cycle. The identification of the victim as Zion in v. 17 (different in G) accounts for the feminine forms used throughout the poem and confirms the view that the cycle is about Judah and Jerusalem, whatever names are used in the different sections. The enemy is not identified in specific terms, though elsewhere the destruction of the Babylonians is justified on the grounds of their treatment of Judah, Israel and Zion (50.28, 33–34; 51.6, 10, 24, 35, 49; cf. the reversal of fates in Isa. 49.25–26; 51.22–23).

30.18–22

18 'Thus says the LORD:
Behold, I will restore the fortunes of the tents of Jacob,
and have compassion on his dwellings;
the city shall be rebuilt upon its mound,
and the palace shall stand where it used to be.
19 Out of them shall come songs of thanksgiving,
and the voices of those who make merry.
I will multiply them, and they shall not be few;
I will make them honoured, and they shall not be small.
20 Their children shall be as they were of old,
and their congregation shall be established before me;
and I will punish all who oppress them.
21 Their prince shall be one of themselves,
their ruler shall come forth from their midst;
I will make him draw near, and he shall approach me,
for who would dare of himself to approach me?
says the LORD.
22 And you shall be my people,
and I will be your God.'

---

[18] MT *hinᵉnī-šāb šᵉbūt*, 'look, I will restore the fortunes': cf. 29.14; 30.3;

31.23; 32.44; 33.7, 11, 26; 48.47; 49.6, 39 for this concept. G lacks 'of the tents': a pastoral image balancing 'dwellings' in the Hebrew poetry. For *rahēm*, 'have compassion', in a positive sense in the Jeremiah tradition, only here and 31.20; 33.26; cf. 12.15; Isa. 49.10, 13, 15; 54.8, 10; 55.7; 60.10. G *kai aichmalōsian autou*, 'and his prisoners', for MT *ūmiškᵉnōtāyw*, 'and his dwellings' = *ūšᵉbītō* (BHS). MT *'īr 'al-tillāh*, 'the city upon its tell', i.e. the mound of the ruins of a city; the sing. may refer to Jerusalem or be a collective referring to the rebuilding of the towns of Judah. MT *wᵉ'armōn 'al-mišpāṭō*, 'and the citadel upon its accustomed place': *mišpāṭ* here may mean 'plan' (cf. BDB, 1049), 'proper place' (JPSB), 'familiar household' (NEB), 'accustomed place' (Rudolph), 'rightful place' (Weiser), 'where it used to be' (RSV). **[19]** G lacks *wᵉhikbadtīm wᵉlō' yiṣ'ārū*, 'and I will make them honoured and they will not be insignificant': cf. Job 14.21 for the contrast between being honoured and being despised. Cf. 10.24; 29.6 for the motifs of population and depopulation. **[20]** MT *wᵉhāyū bānāyw kᵉqedem*, 'and their sons shall be as of old': G *kai eiseleusontai hoi huioi autōn hōs to proteron*, 'and their sons shall go in (= *ūbā'ū*?) as before'; cf. 46.26b; Lam. 5.21. MT *wa'ᵃdātō*, 'and its assembly': i.e. its sacred congregation (cf. 26.9, 17, where *qhl* is used). The sacral protected status of the community is demonstrated by the divine punishment (*pqd*) of its oppressors. **[21]** MT *wᵉhāyāh 'addīrō mimmennū*, 'and its leader shall be from it': Rudolph reads this as *wᵉhāyāh 'addīr mēhem*, 'and their leader shall be from them', i.e. one of their own rather than their oppressors, cf. vv. 8–9. Cf. 14.3; 25.34–36 for *'addīr*, 'leader, chieftain, noble'; for *mōšēl*, 'ruler' cf. 22.30; 33.26; Micah 5.2 (MT 1). Deut. 17.15 stipulates that the king should come 'from the midst of your brethren'; here the leader is a cultic figure rather than a king, as 21b makes clear. G *kai sunaxō autous, kai apostrepsousin pros me*, 'and I will gather them, and they shall return to me', for *wᵉhiqrabtīw wᵉniggaš 'ēlāy*, 'and I shall bring him near and he shall approach me'. MT *'ārab 'et-libbō*, lit. 'he gives his mind in pledge': i.e. who would dare risk giving his mind as security to be so bold as to approach me? Cf. NEB 'no one ventures of himself'. **[22]** G lacks this verse; it may be a pious addition here summing up the force of vv. 18–21 or reflecting 31.1. The shift in person indicates its secondary nature.

The devastations caused by invasion and defeat reduced the Judaean territory to a landscape of ruins and greatly depopulated areas. Any restoration of the fortunes of the people (vv. 3, 18) would have to focus on programmes of rebuilding and repopulation. These are therefore the concern of this poem. The reconstruction of the community, in particular the towns, strongholds, population and organization of the sacred assembly, is the core of the restoration of the people's fortunes. The key to this concept is *šûb*, the 'turning' or 'reversal' of what the long years of destructive neglect have entailed for Judaean society. The divine anger and hatred are turned to compassion (*rḥm*), the mounds of ruins are transformed into cities as used to be the case (*mišpāṭ*), the funerary laments and bitter weeping (cf. 9.17–22; 14.17; Lamentations) are changed to songs and sounds of merrymaking, and the pathetically few people become many and weighty with honour. Things will become the way they used to be (v. 20 'as they were of old'). The sacred congregation will once again be constituted before the divine presence and will have a protected status (cf. 2.3). And instead of being dominated by foreigners (cf. v. 8; 27.12–15), their leader will be one of their own people. Furthermore, access to the divine presence will be permitted to the leader (G different) so that the assembly will be a properly constituted and represented cultic community. The absence of a king here (contrast v. 9; 23.5; 33.17, 21) indicates a programme of rebuilding the community as a theocratic assembly in which the royal status of the leaders is not an important element (cf. Ezek. 40–48). Yet the main features of the poem are to be found in a number of sources elsewhere: e.g. rebuilding of the cities of Judah (Isa. 44.26–28; 49.17; Ezek. 36.10, 33–36), repopulation of the nation (3.16; Isa. 49.20–21; 54.1–3; Ezek. 36.8–15), and the setting of the divine sanctuary in the midst of the people (Ezek. 37.26–28). All these shared elements are indicative of the restoration programme of the Persian period.

The glossator's addition of v. 22 makes an admirable summary of the poem by spelling out the implications of the great restoration of the nation's fortunes. The people will become Yahweh's people and he their god (cf. 31.1, 33; 32.38). They will become a theocracy in which the ruler will be one of their own people (cf. Micah 5.2) and foreign oppression will disappear under divine protection. All the defective institutions of the past will be put right and a harmonious community will enjoy in the future a mythical past (cf. v. 20). Elements of this hope betray the influence of Deuteronomistic ideas in which the historical plan of Yahweh is designed to produce the result specified in v. 22 (cf. Deut. 7. 6; Herrmann 1965, 221–2). The great upheavals of the sixth century have created the conditions in which, with the restoration of Israel's fortunes, the plan may be realized. The destruction of the old institutions has cleared the ground for rebuilding a new community which will combine the old and the new in the proportions believed to be desirable. Then the reciprocal relationship of v. 22 will be achieved.

30.23–24

23 Behold the storm of the Lord!
Wrath has gone forth,
a whirling tempest;
it will burst upon the head of the wicked.
24 The fierce anger of the Lord will not turn back
until he has executed and accomplished
the intents of his mind.
In the latter days you will understand this.

[23–24] = 23.19–20 (see Notes there).

The occurrence of these verses in two rather different contexts raises questions about the appropriateness of the unit in either place. It would be difficult to demonstrate that one context is better than the other (polemic against the prophets cycle in 23 or Book of Consolation cycle in 30), though some commentators (e.g. Bright, 152) think that the verses make a splendid fit in 23.19–20. Here the image of the divine storm breaking on the heads of the wicked may seem inappropriate contextually, but if the oppressors of Jacob are understood as the wicked a case may be made for reading vv. 23–24 as a reminder of the divine wrath about to fall upon the foreign nations (cf. vv. 8, 11, 16, 20b). It is not a strong case, but neither placement of these verses is contextually felicitous. 31.1 picks up the final line of the unit and identifies the turning back of the divine anger (*šūb*) with the restoration of the people to their own land. This use of *šūb*, 'turn', provides a closure for vv. 18–22 (cf. *šāb š^e^būt*, 'turn the fortunes') and also with v. 3, so that a case could be argued for greater integration of the unit in 30 than 23. Only in the future, i.e. the latter days, will the people understand that Yahweh's destruction of the wicked is the prelude to the nation's restoration of fortunes in the homeland. The terrible day of Jacob's distress (v. 7) is also the time when Yahweh will turn the people's fate. In the cycle in 23 the wicked are identified with the prophets; here they are the oppressors of Israel. G has the repeat also, so the placing of the unit here (as well as in 23.19–20) reflects the double use of it in the first edition. Such floating units, of which the Jeremiah tradition has a considerable number, demonstrate the flexibility of the redactional construction of the book without contributing to the exegete's task of understanding why doublets should be used.

31.1–6

31[1] 'At that time, says the LORD, I will be the God of all the families
of Israel, and they shall be my people.'
2 Thus says the LORD:
'The people who survived the sword
found grace in the wilderness;
when Israel sought for rest,
3 the LORD appeared to him from afar.
I have loved you with an everlasting love;
therefore I have continued my faithfulness to you.
4 Again I will build you, and you shall be built,
O virgin Israel!
Again you shall adorn yourself with timbrels,
and shall go forth in the dance of the merrymakers.
5 Again you shall plant vineyards
upon the mountains of Samaria;
the planters shall plant,
and shall enjoy the fruit.
6 For there shall be a day when watchmen will call
in the hill country of Ephraim:
"Arise, and let us go up to Zion,
to the LORD our God." '

[MT 31] = G 38. **[1]** MT *lᵉkōl mišpᵉḥōt*, 'to all the families of': G *tō genei*, 'to the family'. The plur. may represent the development of the second edition in terms of the widespread diaspora; cf. 'all the families of the house of Israel', 2.4; 'all the families of the kingdom of the north', 1.15; 'all the families of the north', 25.9 (see Notes on 1.15; 25.9). This verse functions as a heading to the collection in 31 (cf. 30.3, 4); 30.22 is a simpler form of v. 1. **[2]** MT *māṣā' ḥēn bammidbār 'am śᵉrīdē ḥāreb*, lit. 'he found grace in the wilderness the people survivors of the sword': G *euron thermon en eremō meta olōlotōn*, 'I found him warm in the desert with them that were slain by the sword'; cf. Ex. 32.12–17 for the motif 'find grace, favour'. Rudolph, 192, reads *kammidbār*, 'as in the wilderness', i.e. not in the wilderness as such but *like* finding in the desert a survivor from a battle. The oracular introduction *kōh 'āmar yhwh*, 'thus says Yahweh', is formal here, as the divine speech does not begin until v. 3b (cf. Bright, 280; Rudolph). MT *hālōk lᵉhargī'ō yiśrā'ēl*, lit. 'going to find him rest Israel': BHS reads *hōlēk lᵉmargō'ō* (with A, Symm; cf. 6.16) 'going for his rest'; cf. *lō' targī'a*, 'you will not find rest', Deut. 28.64. **[3]** MT *mērāḥōq yhwh nir'āh lī*, 'from afar Yahweh appeared to *me*': G *autō*, 'to him', and lacking *wᵉ*, 'and', of next word suggests *lō*, 'to him', is what MT should be. MT *'ᵃhabtīk*, 'I have loved *you*'; fem. object here refers to 'virgin Israel' of v. 4 rather than the 'he' of v. 2. MT *mᵉšaktīk ḥāsed*, lit. 'I drew you (with) loving devotion': cf. the similar metaphor in Hos. 11.4 *māšak ḥesed*, 'draw (with) loving devotion' (this is a reconstructed reading of MT there, cf. Andersen and Freedman 1980, 580–1; BHS); the parallel use of *'hb*, *ḥsd* allows 'love' to translate either or both words (cf. Ps. 36.11 [EV 10] for *māšak ḥesed* metaphor). G *eis*, '(I drew you) in (compassion)'. In v. 3 the sense of *māšak*, 'drew', is strengthened by the reference to 'from afar' at the beginning of the verse (cf. 30.10 'I will save you from afar'): the magnetic pull of love, even from far away. **[4]** MT *bᵉtūlat yiśrā'ēl*, 'O virgin Israel': for the epithet cf. v. 21; 18.13; Amos 5.2. MT *bimḥōl mᵉśaḥᵃqīm*, 'in the dance of the merrymakers': G *meta sunagōgēs paizontōn*, 'with the company of those who play', i.e. dance; cf. v. 13; 30.19 (different terms are used in 33.11 for merrymaking). The motif of building (29.5; 30.18; 31.4, 38) used in Part III contributes to its listing in 1.10 (cf. the planting motif also in 29.5; 31.5, 12). Note the triple *'ōd* . . . *'ōd* . . . *'ōd*, 'again . . . again . . . again' (vv. 4–5). **[5]** MT *nāṭ'ū nōṭ'īm wᵉḥillēlū*, 'the planters planted and they will profane': *ḥillēl*, 'profane', here means to treat something as common by using it (cf. Deut. 20.6; 28.30 for profaning by use; Lev. 19.23–25 for rules about the uncircumcised fruit of trees [i.e. fruit with foreskins] becoming available for food in the fifth year). Rudolph, 194, follows Cornill, 333, and reads *nōṭ'ē nᵉṭā'īm yᵉḥallēlū*, 'the planters of plants will profane', i.e. those who do the planting will enjoy the fruit themselves rather than others (cf. Isa. 65.21–22; contrast Amos 5.11). Rudolph treats the phrase as an additional gloss from Deut. 28.30 (cf. BHS); it differs in person and number from *tiṭṭᵉ'ī*, 'you (fem.) will plant'. G *phuteusate kai ainesate*, 'plant and praise' (i.e. *hll* for *ḥll*). The phrase 'the mountains of Samaria' only occurs here and Amos 3.9 (cf. 'the mountain of Samaria', I Kings 16.24; Amos 4.1; 6.1). **[6]** MT *qār'ū nōṣrīm*, 'the watchman cried out': G *klēseōs apologoumenōn*, 'those who plead in defence cry out'.

A collection of poems in 31.2–22 is given a unifying theme by the addition of the titular v. 1. The introductory phrase 'at that time' connects with 30.24b. In the future (i.e. the time of understanding according to 30.24b) Yahweh will become the god of all the families of Israel and they shall become his people. Such a reference to 'all the families' (MT not G) reflects the diaspora with its many scattered communities of Israelites and Judaeans throughout the Persian and Greek empires. The restoration of fortunes in the future will include the reunification of all the clans, and these together will constitute the people of Yahweh. As a preface to the bucolic poems in the collection v. 1 indicates how the poems were understood by the editors.

The poems in 31.2–22 differ from those in 30.5–7, 10–21 in a number of ways, though both collections share the same theme of restoration. One minor difference is the use of the term 'Ephraim' (31.6, 9, 18, 20) to describe the territory of the people. Except for 4.15 and 7.15, the word is not used in the Jeremiah tradition, so its repeated employment in these poems has persuaded some commentators that the poetry represents the early preaching of the young Jeremiah to northern Israel in the period when king Josiah was extending his territory to include what had been the kingdom of Israel (e.g. Volz, Rudolph). This viewpoint has influenced some exegetes (cf. Bright, 285), but is unlikely to be correct. The eroticism of some of the language used (e.g. v. 3), the deeply emotional and idyllic images of pastoral life (worthy of a Breughel), and the strong links between the poetic expressons and the traditions of Hosea and Second Isaiah all point in directions other than the author of the bitter denunciations of Judaean life which dominate the tradition. To imagine that Jeremiah bottled up these feelings until some forty years later and then gave expression to them after 587 (e.g. Lindars 1979) is as unnatural as it is unlikely. The poems breathe an air of delight, are bucolic idylls which rejoice in life lived in a rural setting punctuated by occasional visits up to Jerusalem (cf. Zech. 3.10; 8.3–8); they are hardly the utterances of a man depicted throughout the tradition as sour and alienated from all communal activities and as incapable of speaking kindly without adding even more words of judgment (e.g. 28.7–9, 15–16; 42.9–12, 13–22). These representations of Jeremiah may only be creations of different strands put together by the redactors, but they do not assist in producing an image of Jeremiah which would make him the most likely speaker of the poems in 31. The fictional Jeremiah created by the tradition is temperamentally incapable of uttering such images of love and merrymaking – the last representations of him in the tradition are of his haranguing the communities in Egypt (44) and cursing the Babylonians (51.59–64). Those are characteristic poses of the man

Jeremiah and it is against a backdrop of such images that the sudden shift to love poetry and songs supportive of the people is so unlikely. These are poems which delight in how communities live; they bless and praise rather than damn and curse. They are at home in the world of Second Isaiah and later (e.g. Isa. 60.1–62.12; 65.17–25; 66.7–14, 22–3), though they may imitate some elements in Hosea (cf. Lindars 1979, 51).

The foregoing argument is an attempt to account for the radically different atmosphere and world of the poems in 30–31 (cf. the prose appendices in 31.23–34, 38–40; 32; 33). The only grounds for attributing the poems to Jeremiah are the redactional introduction in 30.1, which has no necessary connection with the contents of the book, and the late reference to building and planting in 1.10. All exegetes recognize the artificiality of these editorial features, and the denial of the poems to Jeremiah does not detract from their meaning, power or importance. The inclusion of these idylls of salvation in the tradition represents one aspect of Judaean society in the Persian period: its hopes for the future. By being attributed to a book written by Jeremiah their incorporation into the tradition is facilitated and they are given the kind of authority associated with Jeremiah by the makers of the book of Jeremiah.

The first poem in 31 is presented as an oracular statement, though the deity does not speak until v. 3b. Israel is represented as somebody (MT a people) who has escaped the sword, like a man finding nourishment in the desert. The images suggest a miraculous escape from destruction, though without defining what the catastrophe may have been (the exile? the terrible storm of Yahweh? the time of Jacob's distress?). From afar (cf. 30.10; 23.23) Yahweh appears to him (G) and speaks words of great love to the nation. Here the image changes to that of a woman much beloved of the speaker, and he reassures her of his love which is such that it draws her to him. What this declaration of love means is set out in vv. 4–6. She, the virgin Israel, will be built again and, adorned with tambourines, she will join the dance of the merrymakers celebrating victory (cf. Ex. 15.20; Judg. 11.34; I Sam. 18.6). The vineyards will be replanted and those who planted them will enjoy their produce. The old ways will come back ('again . . . again . . . again') and there will even be days when in the hill country of Ephraim the guardians will summon the people to go on pilgrimages to Yahweh in Zion.

It is a wonderful idyll of restoration which spells out what it is to be a woman loved by Yahweh. Its links with Hosea and the late elements in Isaiah point to a continuing poetic tradition which depicts the restoration of the fortunes of Yahweh's people (*šûb šᵉbût*) in terms drawn from simple rural life in which the divine blessing produces fertility, prosperity, security and merrymaking. This future is danced (cf. v. 13) and sung, and what the villagers produce they enjoy. No longer does the shadow of the invader frustrate all their work or rapacious troops curtail travelling to the shrine in Jerusalem. The rebuilt community is one in which work and worship are integrated; past and future have become as one (cf. 2.2–3). The pilgrimage to Jerusalem is part of the restoration (cf. Ps. 120–34, esp. 122, 126, 127, 133), and suggests a unified land which no longer knows north and south as rival kingdoms. This is more than an idyllic reconstruction of the past, for no such past ever really existed (the so-called split after Solomon's time demonstrates the non-unity of the clans). The use of Ephraim in these poems takes up the old name of Israel but applies it to a territory of which Zion is the cult centre and outside Jerusalem is the rural area of Israel. The nation living in its own land as an agricultural economy with Zion as its centre is an idyll which has no past, though it may well have a future (cf. 41.5 for a very different pilgrimage to Jerusalem).

31.7–9

7 For thus says the LORD;
'Sing aloud with gladness for Jacob,
and raise shouts for the chief of the nations;
proclaim, give praise, and say,
"The LORD has saved his people,
the remnant of Israel."
8 Behold, I will bring them from the north country,
and gather them from the farthest parts of the earth,
among them the blind and the lame,
the woman with child and her who is in travail, together;
a great company, they shall return here.
9 With weeping they shall come,
and with consolations I will lead them back,
I will make them walk by brooks of water,
in a straight path in which they shall not stumble;

for I am a father to Israel,
  and Ephraim is my first-born.'

---

[7] G lacks *śimḥāh*, 'gladness'. MT *b^e rō'š haggōyīm*, 'at, for the head of the nations': cf. *rē'šīt haggōyīm*, 'the first of the nations', Amos 6.1. The raucous public commotion (*rnn, ṣhl*, cf. Isa. 24.14) may be an expression of chauvinistic pride or may represent an imaginary procession of the nations, at the head of which is Jacob; for the shrill neighing (*ṣah^a lū*) of public performances cf. 5.8. BHS suggests *hārīm*, 'mountains', for 'nations'. MT *hōša' yhwh 'et-'ammekā*, 'save O Yahweh your people': G *esōsen kurios ton laon autou*, 'the lord *has* sav*ed his* people'; i.e. *hōšī'a . . . 'ammō*. The final phrase *'et š^e erīt yiśrā'ēl*, 'the remnant of Israel', may be an additional gloss (Rudolph, 195), cf. 23.3; it is in G. **[8]** MT *bām 'iwwēr ūpisseaḥ*, 'among them the blind and the lame': G *en heortē phasek*, 'in the feast of passover' = *b^e mō'ēd pēsaḥ*; for the blind and lame cf. II Sam. 5.6, 8; Isa. 35.5–6. MT *hēnnāh*, 'hither, here': Rudolph reads *hinnēh*, 'look, behold', and takes it with v. 9 (BHS). The imagery of vv. 8–9 is shared with Isa. 35; 40.3–5; 41.17–19; 42.16; 43.5–6; 44.3–4; 48.20; 49.9–13. **[9]** MT *yābō'ū*, 'they shall come': G *exēlthon*, 'they went forth' = *yāṣ'ū*. MT *ūb^e taḥ^a nūnīm* 'and with supplication for favour': cf. 3.21; Dan. 9.18. G *kai en paraklēsei*, 'and with consolation', suggests *ūb^e tanḥūmīm*; cf. EVV. This makes a better contrast with 'weeping' than MT: they went out weeping but will be led (back) with 'consolations'.

In this poem great joy and much noise is caused by the return of the diaspora from the north (cf. Isa. 43.6) and everywhere else (cf. 6.22). This great return mimics the terrible invasion route of the cruel enemy which had brought about the original scattering of the people (e.g. *miyyark^e tē-'āreṣ*, v. 8; 6.22, 'from the farthest parts of the earth'). It reverses the fate of the nation in the past. But it does so in subtly different ways: the mighty army which came down from the north and destroyed Judah-Jerusalem was an appallingly fierce and vicious force (4.13; 5.15–17; 6.22–26), whereas the army of people which now returns to its own land includes the blind and the lame, as well as the pregnant and those who have given birth recently. One is a very human procession of the weak and those who carry the promise of new life for the nation; the other an almost superhuman force of mighty warriors whose weaponry was like an open grave (5.16). The first brought death with it and left behind it a dead kingdom. The second brings with it life and the remaking of the land into a place full of joy and prosperity (cf. vv. 12–14). The feminine images in these poems are characteristic of the restoration theme: a land filled with overflowing life. In the poems about the destruction of city and nation the feminine is an image of the raped and violated nation – the victim. Now the great reversal (*šûb šᵉbût*) transforms the feminine back into its active state of that which gives life and sustains it. From the passivitiy of destruction to the activity of giving birth and drawing love from the other (v. 3), the feminine imagery in the tradition demonstrates the polarities of the life of the community.

The return from other lands is heralded in v. 7 as a procession for the chief of the nations and explained in v. 9 on the grounds that Yahweh is the father of the nation, Ephraim is his first-born (Volz takes v. 9 with v. 6, and other exegetes suggest reading vv. 7, 9c with v. 6 as the conclusion to vv. 2–6). The old pride in the nation has been reawakened with the return of the exiles from so many different lands (this is not the return from Babylon but a later diaspora's regathering to the land). This is the head of the nations, this is Yahweh's first-born son (cf. Ex. 4.22). That the old name Ephraim is used in this fashion suggests an allusion to the story of how Ephraim, who was not the first-born son, *became* the first-born in reality (cf. Gen. 48.8–20; it is a moot point whether Jeremiah reflects Genesis or vice versa, cf. Brodie 1981, 46–51). Thus the nation which suffered the humiliation and devastation of defeat and scattering to the ends of the earth is brought back in triumph as Yahweh's heir to the land. The nation's fecundity and good fortune are due to Yahweh being its father. The shift in the gender of the metaphors used of the relationship between Yahweh and Israel is characteristic of the biblical writers' use of images drawn from family and communal life for describing the shared life of deity and people. Israel is both Yahweh's mistress (wife) and son – the one loved by him. The multiplicity of metaphors used, masculine and feminine, positive and negative, should warn the modern exegete to exercise caution when reading the text from a contemporary ideological viewpoint (see on 4.30–31).

The great assembly (*qāhāl gādōl*) which comes in triumph from so many parts of the world and which travels with such ease along well-watered, straight paths is an image shared by the poem and the poetry of Second Isaiah. This common poetic tradition may also account for the positive feminine images which abound throughout the cycle (on Second Isaiah cf. 49.8–23; 51.17–20; Gruber 1983). With the fall of Babylon great hope developed among some of the exiles, and in the subsequent centuries the many scattered communities focused on Zion as their centre and made pilgrimages there (in reality and in fantasy). The poems in the cycle represent some of these hopes as well as the reconstruction of urban and rural areas in the Persian period.

31.10–14

10 'Hear the word of the LORD, O nations,
and declare it in the coastlands afar off;
say, "He who scattered Israel will gather him,
and will keep him as a shepherd keeps his flock."
11 For the LORD has ransomed Jacob,
and has redeemed him from hands too strong for him.
12 They shall come and sing aloud on the height of Zion,
and they shall be radiant over the goodness of the LORD,
over the grain, the wine, and the oil,
and over the young of the flock and the herd;
their life shall be like a watered garden,
and they shall languish no more.
13 Then shall the maidens rejoice in the dance,
and the young men and the old shall be merry.
I will turn their mourning into joy,
I will comfort them, and give them gladness for sorrow.
14 I will feast the soul of the priests with abundance,
and my people shall be satisfied with my goodness,
says the LORD.'

---

[10] MT *bā'iyyīm*, 'in the coastlands, among the islands': cf. 2.10; Isa. 41.1, 5; 42.4, 10, 12; 49.1; 51.5; 59.18; 60.9; 66.19; Ps. 97.1; Zeph. 2.11. MT *wᵉ'imrū*, 'and say': an unnecessary gloss? (cf. BHS); but cf. v. 7. MT *ūšᵉmārō kᵉrō'eh 'edrō*, 'and will keep him as a shepherd his flock': cf. Isa. 40.11 *kᵉrō'eh 'edrō yir'eh*, 'as a shepherd his flock he will feed'. **[11]** MT *kī-pādāh . . . ūgᵉ'ālō* 'for he has ransomed . . . and redeemed him': these are terms which appear frequently in Isa. 40–55 but, apart from 31.11; 15.21; 50.34, not at all in the Jeremiah tradition. **[12]** MT *bimrōm-ṣiyyōn*, 'on the height of Zion': Rudolph treats this as a Judaean correction (as he does for 30.17b) of *behārīm*, 'on the mountains', deleting *ṣiyyōn*. MT *wᵉnāhᵃrū*, 'and they shall shine, be radiant': cf. 51.44b; Isa. 60.5; Ps. 34.6 (EV 5), the only other occurrences of the verb. MT *'al-dāgān wᵉ'al-tīrōš wᵉ'al yiṣhār*, 'over the new grain, the new wine, and the oil': this list of the triple products of the fertile land of Canaan occurs frequently in Deuteronomy (e.g. 7.13; 11.14; 12.17;

14.23; 18.4; 28.51); also Hos. 2.10 (EV 8); Joel 1.10; 2.19; Hag. 1.11. The terms refer to the products 'in an unmanufactured state' (Driver 1896, 193), and relate Yahweh's goodness (*ṭūb yhwh*) to the new growth of the land. G *epi gēn sitou* . . . , 'to a land of corn . . .'. MT *k^{e}gan rāweh*, 'as a watered garden': cf. Isa. 58.11 (Ezek. 36.35 likens the new land to the garden of Eden). G *hōsper xulon egkarpon*, 'like a fruitful wood'. **[13]** MT *b^{e}māḥōl ūbaḥurīm*, '. . . in the dance, and young men . . .': G *en sunagōgē neaniskōn*, 'in the assembly of youth', cf. v. 4. MT *yaḥdāw*, adv., 'together': G *charēsontai*, 'shall rejoice' = *yaḥdū* (*ḥādāh*, 'rejoice'). The scene represented by G is that of virgins (*b^{e}tūlōt, parthenoi*; MT collective?) enjoying the dance of youth and old men rejoicing. MT *w^{e}hāpaktī*, 'and I will overturn', i.e. 'transform'. G lacks *w^{e}niḥamtīm*, 'and I will comfort them'. MT *migōnām*, 'from sorrow': G *megalunō*, 'I will make great', taken with next verse where it appears as a doublet of *w^{e}riwētī*, 'I will make great (i.e. *ribbītī*, cf. BHS) and cheer with wine (*methusō*) . . .' **[14]** MT *w^{e}riwwētī nepeš hakkōh^{a}nīm dāšen*, lit. 'I will saturate the appetite of the priests with fatness', i.e. satiate the priests with food and drink: G 'sons of Levi' in place of *dāšen*, 'fatness'.

The poem in vv. 10–14 is linked to vv. 7–9 by the use of similar terms in vv. 7, 10 (cf. the triple verbs 'proclaim, give praise, and say', v. 7; 'hear, declare, say' v. 10; the use of 'nations' in both poems). Subject matter is also shared, as both pieces celebrate the return of the scattered people to their own land. Where they differ is in the more strongly pastoral imagery of vv. 10–14 and the focus on the fertility of the land to which the dispersed return (cf. vv. 4–5). Fewer metaphors are used and the dominant image is of Yahweh the shepherd gathering his scattered flock (a dispersal caused by Yahweh himself, v. 10) and tending it as a responsible shepherd. The basis of both poems is the declaration that Yahweh has saved, ransomed and redeemed his people (vv. 7b, 11). In vv. 12–14 the exiles return to Zion and become radiant over the goodness of Yahweh: this goodness is the agricultural products of the land. The new grain, grape and olive proclaim the goodness of Yahweh in the abundance of food, wine and oil and in the harvest celebrations of such productivity great joy is experienced by the community. With this fertility of land and animals the life of the people (i.e. its spirit, *nepeš*) is like a watered garden, knowing no further dearth of anything. The young virgins join in the dance of youth (G) and the old men make merry (cf. v. 4), and Yahweh transforms mourning and sorrow into joy and happiness (cf. 33.11). As in v. 6, prosperity and cultic life belong together, so that the priests are sated with food and drink.

All the scarcities of the past have disappeared in the great transformation of restoration to the homeland (cf. Second Isaiah's imagery and message). Thus the evil intended and executed by Yahweh in the past is overturned (*hpk*) by his shepherding of the people back to a fecund land of prosperity.

31.15–20

15 Thus says the LORD:
'A voice is heard in Ramah,
lamentation and bitter weeping.
Rachel is weeping for her children;
she refuses to be comforted for her children,
because they are not.'
16 Thus says the LORD:
'Keep your voice from weeping,
and your eyes from tears;
for your work shall be rewarded,
says the LORD.
and they shall come back from the land of the enemy.
17 There is hope for your future,
says the LORD,
and your children shall come back to their own country.
18 I have heard Ephraim bemoaning,
"Thou hast chastened me, and I was chastened,
like an untrained calf;
bring me back that I may be restored,
for thou art the LORD my God.
19 For after I had turned away I repented;
and after I was instructed, I smote upon my thigh;
I was ashamed, and I was confounded,
because I bore the disgrace of my youth."
20 Is Ephraim my dear son?
Is he my darling child?
For as often as I speak against him,
I do remember him still.
Therefore my heart yearns for him;
I will surely have mercy on him,'
says the LORD.

---

[15] The formulaic introduction 'thus says Yahweh' does not introduce a divine saying (v. 16 begins the divine speech), but (cf. v. 3) indicates a redactional unit, vv. 15–20, which is to be treated as the divine word by the receiving community (hence the additional *nᵉ'um yhwh*, 'says Yahweh', in vv. 16, 17). MT *bᵉrāmāh*, 'in Ramah, in the upland, on the height': BHS reads *bārāmāh* because Ramah always has the article. MT *bᵉkī tamrūrīm*, 'bitter weeping': cf. 6.26; Hos. 12.15. The use of Rachel as a figure of the community weeping for its dead children may be an allusion to the story of Rachel's death in childbirth (Gen. 35.16–20). It is possble that *rāḥēl*, 'ewe-lamb', is the sense here rather than Rachel, one of the wives of Jacob (cf. Gaster 1969, 605–6). According to I Sam. 10.2 Rachel's tomb is at Zelzah in Benjaminite territory, not far from Ramah (I Sam. 8.4); Gen. 35.19 places it near Bethlehem, on the way from Bethel. Whether these different accounts agree is a matter of debate. The image of the mother weeping for the dead children may be an echo of the folk belief that women who die in childbirth haunt the earth in search of their babies (cf. Gaster 1969, 605). **[16]** G lacks *nᵉ'um yhwh*, 'says Yahweh'. **[17]** G *monimon tois sois teknois*, 'a lasting (place) for your children': a shorter text than MT which stresses the children's (future) stability. MT emphasizes the return of the children (*bānīm*, 'children', rather than EVV '*your* children'): *wᵉšābū . . . wᵉšābū*, 'and they shall return . . . and they shall return' (vv. 16, 17). Delete *nᵉ'um yhwh*, 'says Yahweh'. **[18]** MT *šāmō'a šāma'tī . . . yissartanī wā'iwwāsēr*, 'I have really heard . . . you have disciplined me and I was disciplined': cf. the repeats in 17.14. MT *hᵃšībēnī wᵉ'ašūbāh*, 'bring me back that I may come back': word-play on *šūb*; *šūb* is used in vv. 16, 17, 18, 19. The image of Ephraim as an untrained calf (*kᵉ'ēgel lō' lummād*) reverses the figure of Ephraim as a trained heifer (*'eglāh mᵉlummādāh*) in Hos. 10.11 (note the gender variations with reference to Ephraim). **[19]** MT *kī-'aḥᵃrē šūbī niḥamtī*, 'for after my turning I repented': exegetes think a word has fallen out of this sentence; Rudolph reads *šabtī*, 'I turned', after *šūbī* (lost by haplography) and translates 'after my going astray I turned back' (cf. BHS; Bright). G *aichmalōsias mou* 'my captivity' = *šibyī*; Driver 1937–8, 119–20, follows G and Rudolph to read 'for after my captivity (I turned) (and) repented'. He treats *hiwwād'ī* ('I was instructed') as from *yd'*, 'was humbled', rather than *yd'*, 'know'. G *estenaxa eph' hēmeras aischunēs*, 'I groaned for the days of shame' = *'ānaqtī 'al-yᵉmē bōšet* rather than 'I smote upon my thigh; I was ashamed'. **[20]** MT *hᵃbēn yaqqīr* 'is a precious son . . . ?': G lacks the interrogative *hᵃ-* and the linking *'im*, 'is (he a darling child)?'. MT *kī-middē dabbᵉrī bō*, 'for as often as I speak about him'. RSV translates *bō* as 'against him', but cf. Bright, 282; Driver, 120, understands *dbr b* as 'to turn the back on' or 'reject' (followed by NEB; cf. JPSB's 'turned against him'). Rudolph reads *dabbᵉrī* as *hinnākᵉrī*, 'I estrange myself against him' (cf. Ecclus. 11.34; BHS). MT *hāmū mē'ay lō*, 'my inward parts (i.e. emotions or intestines) thrill for him': cf. BDB, 242; EVV 'heart' may be a fair translation here if the physical and emotional senses of 'innards' are understood. The visceral feelings referred to describe the physically powerful urges a mother feels for her son or lovers for each other. Bright, 275, translates as 'I am filled with yearning for him'. The parallel phrase *raḥēm ʾaraḥamennū* may also have an equally physical sense beyond the standard translation of 'I will surely have compassion'; cf. Trible 1978, 45, 'motherly-compassion'.

Anderson 1978; Lindars 1979; Trible 1976; 1978, 40–50

The poem in vv. 15–20 is made up of a number of distinctive elements, vv. 15–17, 18–19, 20 (cf. Weiser, 279–82), bound together by the redactional markers 'thus says Yahweh', 'says Yahweh' (vv. 15, 20). These elements are independent of each other but have been forged into a poem by the incorporation of v. 15 as an oracular statement, though it clearly is not one, into what looks like a series of dialogue poems. Ephraim and Yahweh are the main speakers in vv. 18–20, though the figure of Ephraim can hardly be posited of the speaker of v. 15 or the female addressed in vv. 16–17. The terrible mourning of v. 15 is responded to by Yahweh in vv. 16–17, and the bemoaning oneself (*mitnōdēd*) of vv. 18–19 is replied to by the deity in v. 20. In vv. 15–17 the mother is the speaker and addressee; in vv. 18–20 the son is speaker and addressee. The connection between the two is redactional because each element is about something quite distinctive. The lamenting Rachel of v. 15 is a distraught mother who mourns the disappearance of her children – 'for they are not' (*kī ʾēnennū*). The divine response in vv. 16–17 is shaped by v. 15 (whether by association or in terms of cannot be determined) to the extent that images of weeping are common to both pieces, but it deals with the return of the exiled children, whereas v. 15 is about the death of the mother's children. Her children no longer exist, and that is why she refuses to be comforted. It is not a case of her children having gone away but of their annihilation. The fragment constituted by v. 15 does not fit this context, and would be better treated by exegetes as an independent poem. However, the context of the cycle allows the response to transform the utter despair of the mother into a word of hope for the future. The juxtapositioning of the two pieces modifies the meaning of v. 15. In vv. 18–19 the nation speaks as a man complaining about his youth and the deity responds in very strongly maternal and visceral terms in v. 20. The tone and images of vv. 18–20 are very different from those of vv. 15–17. Many exegetes also include vv. 21–22 in the poem (e.g. Anderson, Bright, Condamin, Duhm, Hyatt, Thompson), but speaker and addressee are quite distinctive in these verses, and the deity's position is also sufficiently different for the unit to be treated in isolation from what precedes it (following Weiser, Rudolph).

The redactional unit formed by associating different poems together produces a number of striking images in which the bitter feelings of the community as mother are balanced by the erotic-maternal urgings of the deity as mother. Between these two sets of images the community as son struggles to come to terms with a regretted past by appealing to the deity to turn him back. Some of the metaphors used in vv. 18–20 reflect similar images used in the Hosea tradition (e.g. Hos. 4.16; 10.11; 11.8–9), and both the cycle and Hosea share the representation of Yahweh's very emotional involvement with the community. It is that overwhelming love (cf. 31.3; Hos. 11.8) which warrants the hope that Ephraim will not be destroyed (Hosea) or will find mercy and turning (31.18, 20). As a woman the community is shattered by the loss of its people (wiped out in the cruel invasions, sieges, killings and executions), as a man the community bemoans its disgraceful youthful past, and as a mother the deity's innards heave with maternal feelings whenever she considers her son. In the strength of such feelings and emotions the future of the community lies and the idyllic elements of the cycle are of a piece with such representations of the relationship between Yahweh and the people.

Rachel weeping for her children in Ramah is a strange metaphor in the independent v. 15. Its precise meaning is not clear, especially as the word *rāḥēl* may be understood as 'ewe-lamb'. Rachel, the wife of Jacob, is hardly ever mentioned outside the stories of Jacob (apart from the grave notice in I Sam. 10.2 and as part of a simile in Ruth 4.11), though there are some associations between the cycle 30–31 and the Genesis stories which would make the allusion to her appropriate here (cf. Brodie 1981). The term Ramah may combine a reference to Rachel's burial mound and the transit camp of 40.1 where the Judaean captives were herded on their way to exile in Babylon. Again, it is quite possible that *rāmāh* means 'height' here, and the image is one of a mother sheep lamenting on the highlands the loss of her lambs. Whichever figure is understood by the metaphor, the meaning remains the same: the mother of the community bitterly laments the loss of her children. The verse is a lament in response to the complete destruction of the community and represents a word of judgment in the cycle. Only in combination with vv. 16–17 is the judgment aspect transformed.

Yahweh's answer to the lament is given by the redaction which appends vv. 16–17 to v. 15. It commands the woman not to weep because her children will return (*šābû*) from the land of the enemy. There is a reward for all her labours on behalf of her children. The content of this response is repeated in v. 17. If a core is to be sought for the cycle, it might be found in the sentence *w*[e]*yēš-tiqwāh l*[e]*'aḥ*[a]*rîtēk*, 'and there is hope for your future' ('and' links the hope with *yēš śākār*, 'there is reward', of v. 16; G has a shorter v. 17). The reward for the woman's work is the hope for the future. Finding the right nuance for *'aḥ*[a]*rîtēk* is difficult: it may refer to the future (RSV) or what happens *afterwards*, i.e. after the mother's death. In this latter sense it is an allusion to the woman's posterity (cf. NEB margin; also 29.11 NEB); she will leave descendants after her (NEB). This may make a better connection between v. 17 and the reference to Rachel in v. 15 because Rachel died in childbirth, and to a woman dying in childbirth the only comfort that may be given is that of reassurance about the welfare of the child. However, the metaphorical representation of the community as a mother weeping for her children in vv. 16–17 should not be taken to the point where it is the community which is dying but its children are surviving. The weeping of v. 16 refers to the exile of some of the people and the reassurance of vv. 16–17 applies to the return of those exiles. The mother's children will return to her, and thus the despair of v. 15 is reversed. In reality of course the children died, but later generations were able to return to the old homeland. The metaphors of vv. 15, 16–17 refer to different things; hence their redactional combination tends to obscure what is being said about each situation. However, the hope for the future is the return, which is a dominant motif in 31 (e.g. vv. 8–9, 10–12, 16–17, 21).

The subject matter of vv. 18–19 is really quite different from vv. 16–17. There is no talk about a return of the children but a penitential confession by Ephraim (cf. 3.21–23 for this kind of liturgical statement). Ephraim moves to and fro in lamentation about his condition and confesses to having been disciplined like an untrained calf. The image is that of a domesticated animal which has not yet been trained properly, so it has wandered away and has to be flogged in order to make it return. Ephraim, i.e. the community, appeals to Yahweh to turn him back effectively. He acknowledges having gone astray and confesses to having repented (*nḥm*). After instruction he admits his shame and humiliation caused by his youthfulness (or in his youth? contrast 2.2–3). The reference to repentance is unusual in the cycle as all the images of salvation are of the divine initiative irrespective of human response, so this extract from a confessional lament is quite out of place in the cycle. Set within this poem it may be read as a transformed element in the dialogic exchanges between Yahweh and community, but it reflects a very different notion of potential salvation from the rest of the cycle. In 30–31 repentance is not a prerequisite of salvation (cf. Hos. 11.8–9).

The divine response to this confession is an expression of the deity's powerful feelings for her son. Mother Yahweh speaks affirmatively (G but interrogatively in MT) of Ephraim as her son who is very precious (*yaqqīr*) and an absolute delight (*šaʿašuʿīm*, cf. Isa. 5.7; Prov. 8.30–1) to her. Every time she speaks of him she remembers just what he means to her and her insides moan for him (cf. Trible 1978, 45, 'my womb trembles for him'). So she most surely will have mercy on him. The images of overwhelming feminine love for her son characterize the deity's view of the community and bespeak a glowing future for it. What that future may be is not spelled out in the divine answer to the lament, but within the context of the whole poem and the cycle may be deduced to be either the return to the homeland or the prosperous building up of the community in the fertile land of their ancestors. Yahweh's love for Ephraim is so strong, so visceral, that the child will encounter mercy in spite of his foolish youthfulness. The Hosea tradition and the Book of Consolation belong together at this point, and in order to express the intensity of Yahweh's feelings for the people feminine metaphors are employed. The community as mother (cf. vv. 15, 16) becomes the people as son and Yahweh as mother (vv. 18–19, 20), and the bitter weeping of the bereaved mother is transformed by Yahweh's uterine love. The different units contribute various images to the development of this metaphoric statement about the community's future as the child of the powerful and possessive mother deity, and that compulsive love will guarantee the future. The rhetoric of the poem is 'replete with female semantics' (Trible 1978, 50) and should be noted as such (see on 4.30–31). It should not, however, be over-elaborated in theological terms because the words used are but metaphors and the tradition contains a wide range of variable figures of speech which may contribute to the construction of a sensibly balanced theology of divine-human interaction using both masculine and feminine terminology.

31.21–22

21 'Set up waymarks for yourself,
make yourself guideposts;
consider well the highway,
the road by which you went.
Return, O virgin Israel,
return to these your cities.
22 How long will you waver,
O faithless daughter?
For the LORD has created a new thing on the earth:
a woman protects a man.'

---

[21] MT *ṣiyyunīm*, 'sign-posts, markers': G *Siōn*, 'Zion'. MT *tamrūrīm*, cf. v. 15, where the same word means 'bitter' (from *mrr*), but here must be derived from *tmr*, 'palm-tree, post', cf. 10.5, i.e. 'sign-posts' (NEB). Giesebrecht, 169, reads it as *timōrīm*, 'posts', i.e. artificial palms; cf. BHS *tīmōrīm*, 'palm-like columns'. G *timōrian*, a transliteration of the Hebrew. MT *lam*[e]*sillāh*, 'the highway': a motif used in Isa. 40.3; 49.11 to describe the return from exile (cf. Isa. 62.10); G *eis tous ōmous*: 'to the path' (reading *oimous*). MT *'ēlleh*, 'these': cf. v. 8 *hēnnāh*, 'here'; G *penthousa*, 'mourning' = *'*[a]*bēlāh* (BHS). **[22]** MT *habbat haššōbēbāh*, 'faithless daughter': cf. 3.14, 22, 'faithless sons'; *šūb* has the sense of waywardness here (cf. NEB) and balances *titḥammāqīn*, 'twisting and turning'. MT *n*[e]*qēbāh t*[e]*sōbēb gāber*, 'a female . . . a man': perhaps the most difficult half-line in the book of Jeremiah. G *en sōtēria perieleusontai anthrōpoi*, 'in safety men shall go about'. For the motif of Yahweh doing something new (*'ōśeh ḥ*[a]*dāšāh* rather than *bārā' ḥ*[a]*dāšāh*), cf. Isa. 43.19. The crux of the matter is the translation of *t*[e]*sōbēb* (assonant word-play with *šōbēbāh*?): 'protects' (RSV), 'turned into' (NEB), 'courts' (JPSB), 'shall compass' (AV). Duhm, 251 emends it to *tissōb*, 'turned into', cf. Zech. 14.10 (cf. NEB), and suggests that the phrase is probably a proverb which can be used in a number of different ways. Here its function may be that of a mocking gloss which points out that Israel appears first as a son, then as a woman (a post-exilic gloss). Volz, 278, 283, treats v. 22b as an addition which is quite incomprehensible, reads *b*[e]*'ereṣ t*[e]*šūbāh*, 'in the land of return', and treats *n*[e]*qēbāh*, *gāber* as glosses to v. 27b, which he reads as part of v. 22. Giesebrecht, 170, relates *t*[e]*sōbēb* to *sbb* in

Deut. 32.10 with the meaning 'protect', i.e. the woman protects the man; cf. Ehrlich 1912, 322. Cornill, 342, follows Duhm's emendation and reads v. 26 immediately after v. 22. Condamin, 225, 227–8, reads . . . *tāšūb lᵉgeber*, '(the woman) returns to her husband', i.e. Israel returns to Yahweh, making the new thing reflect 3.1. Hyatt, 1034, appears to agree with Condamin. Weiser, 282, understands the phrase as 'the woman surrounds the man' and sees in it a hint of the renewal (i.e. the new thing created by Yahweh in the land) of the creation blessing of fruitfulness in Gen. 1.28; cf. Jer. 31.27. Both Weiser and Rudolph, 198, admit that the phrase is completely mysterious as to its meaning, though each offers some clarification of it. Rudolph, 199, suggests *nᵉqabbāh tᵉsōbab gᵉbirā(h)*, 'the cursed one changes to queen', cf. 30.20–21. Bright, 282, provides a literal translation: 'a female shall compass a man', but comments, 'the meaning is wholly obscure, and it might have been wiser to leave the colon blank . . . Quite possibly we have here a proverbial saying indicating something that is surprising and difficult to believe, the force of which escapes us.' Anderson 1978, 477, 'encompass, enfold', i.e. will be the agent of new life in the new age. Holladay offers a rather different account of v. 22, treating it in relation to 30.6, where the men behave like women; now the sex roles will be reversed again and the female will have priority, initiative, dominance over the male. 'Your warriors have become female? Look: the female will surmount the warrior! Take heart; come home' (1966b, 239). Lundbom 1975, 33–4, treats the line as ironic, expressing shock and surprise at the defeat of Israel's soldiers: 'My, a new thing on earth! The woman must protect the soldier.' This forms an *inclusio* for the core of the cycle with 30.6, which Lundbom regards as saying the same thing as 31.22b (cf. Holladay 1962b, 53–4, for the view that 30.7, 'yet he shall be saved out of it', is an ironic question with an implicit negative answer). The wide range of opinions on v. 22b is indicative of the difficulties of interpreting the phrase; it is both lapidary and over-rich in possible meanings (e.g. *sbb* means 'surround', 'encompass', 'enclose', 'encircle', 'march around', 'turn around'). Sexual connotations may well be present in view of v. 20, and the proverbial nature of the saying (a view taken by many exegetes; cf. Carroll 1981, 327 n. 25) may allude to this aspect of community life by means of an oblique reference to future fertility: 'the woman encircles, i.e. wraps herself around, the man' (perhaps 'the vagina envelops the penis'). This reference to vigorous sexual intercourse is shorthand for the renewal of the community (cf. v. 8). As a bawdy proverb it may not suit the metaphorical role it has to play in vv. 21–22 (hence the problems of understanding it), but it provides a fine closure of the cycle with 30.6, where the mimicry of pregnancy by men in a time of trouble will be replaced by the real thing when Yahweh creates something new in the land. Not role reversal (cf. Isa. 4.1) is the point of the saying, but an affirmation that when Yahweh acts creatively women will be women and men will be men – and ever the twain shall meet and become one flesh! Hence the repopulation of the community.

The cycle of poems is concluded with a short poem which provides a closure with 30.5–7 but transforms the terrible gloom of the prefatory poem. Speaker and figure change from vv. 15–20, though the community is still addressed. The masculine image of Ephraim in vv. 18–20 becomes the feminine figure of the virgin daughter, but the deity probably retains a parental role in the poem without specification of gender. The scattered exiles are commanded to make preparations for returning home by marking out their route. Milestones and signposts will assist them to return by the highway along which they went into exile. The woman here addressed is not the mother figure of vv. 15–17 but the people in exile. They are described in v. 22a as wavering, i.e. turning to and fro without making any real progress, and faithless (a use of *šûb* which links the poem to the circle which produced 3.12, 14, 21–23; cf. Hos. 14.1 [MT 2]). In tone the poem is quite different from the more idyllic pieces of vv. 2–6, 7–9, 10–14 and suggests a reluctance on the part of the exiles to return to the cities. This failure to return to the homeland is what earns Israel the epithet 'faithless' (*šôbēbāh*) and hints at some of the problems in the Persian period, when returning to the land of Israel must have represented a quite unpleasant prospect for many families living outside that land. Yet nothing should prevent their return, because Yahweh has created something new in the land (MT *bā'āreṣ* is better translated 'in the land' than 'in the earth' with EVV). What that new thing may be is far from clear, but in its present context it is presented as an argument for returning home.

Much has been written already on the meaning of v. 22b, and little of it will bear repeating. The mystification expressed by various exegetes as to its meaning is quite understandable and the terseness of the three-word half-line allows great scope for speculative interpretations. Two points are worth making: as the closure of the cycle the verse may be more influenced by 30.5–7 than by v. 21 and the use of a punning word-play (*šôbēbāh – t^esôbēb*) reduces the semantic content of the statement because paronomasia inevitably narrows down meaning in favour of sound or *double entendre*. Both these points should warn against over-confidence in seeking a definitive meaning for the phrase 'a female encompasses the virile'. If the saying is also proverbial (e.g. Duhm and others), then its significance may be lost to us because such aphorisms are often confined to particular cultures and without further explication may be meaningless to outsiders. The bawdy interpretation of the words (cf. the mocking style of 30.6) underlines a further obscurity because, in spite of its universal character, obscene and ribald language is highly particularized in individual cultures (this is even true of euphemisms: e.g. feet, knees, hand are terms for genitals in Hebrew but not in English).

Many of the explanations offered entail emending the text or involve exegesis which only succeeds in terms of what is known as using the form *obscurum per obscurius* (i.e. explaining what is obscure by something which is more obscure). The temptation to use this form is strong when such a difficult half-line presents itself in a context where explanations must be provided. It is tempting to pick up words and phrases in the immediate context and to build them into an exegesis which is coherent and interesting. Thus the stress may be put on Yahweh's new creation, and role(?) reversal may be emphasized so as to explain v. 22b in terms of the Genesis creation stories (connections between the cycle and the stories of Genesis have been noted and the two sets of stories may have come into existence together or have been recited in the same liturgical circles). In the first Genesis account Yahweh creates male and female (Gen. 1.27) and in the second story he creates the man, puts him to sleep, takes a rib from his body and builds it into a woman (Gen. 2.7, 21–23; note the sleep motif in Jer. 31.26). Now, where once the rib encircled the man and woman was made from it, things will be reversed and the woman will encircle the man. The brief saying may reflect such a meditation on the story of how men and women came to be the way they are, especially in terms of their sexual passions for each other. This explanation would fit the tenor of the context about the rebuilding of the community by means of repopulation and would harvest the various nuances of gender in the poems. It is, however, purely a speculative reconstruction of a possible setting for a proverbial half-line.

The wiser course for the exegete is to admit ignorance and acknowledge that ancient texts occasionally do baffle the modern hermeneut. 31.22b is one such baffling text. It may have been a witty gloss or addition to the poem when it was first produced but the humour eludes the modern mind. Perhaps the amount of exegetical activity aroused by the text is equivalent to those lengthy explanations of jokes indulged in by the humourless – and with as much point! In the final analysis I must admit that I do not know what v. 22b means.

31.23–26

23 Thus says the LORD of hosts, the God of Israel: 'Once more they shall use these words in the land of Judah and in its cities, when I restore their fortunes:

"The LORD bless you, O habitation of righteousness,
O holy hill!"

24 And Judah and all its cities shall dwell there together, and the farmers and those who wander with their flocks. 25 For I will satisfy the weary soul, and every languishing soul I will replenish.'

26 Thereupon I awoke and looked, and my sleep was pleasant to me.

---

[23] G *eulogēmenos kurios epi dikaion oros to hagion autou*, 'blessed be the lord on his righteous holy mountain'. Bright, 282, treats the terms *ṣedeq*, 'righteous', and *qōdeš*, 'holy', as titles of Yahweh rather than epithets of the temple mount. **[24]** MT *wᵉnāsʿū*, 'and they shall wander (with the flock)': BHS follows Vrs and reads *wᵉnōsʿē*, 'and those who wander . . .', i.e. shepherds. NEB deletes 'Judah and all his cities' as an addition. MT *bāh*, 'in her': RSV 'there'; probably a reference to *ʾereṣ*, 'land', in v. 23, rather than the temple region. **[25]** MT *wᵉkol-nepeš dāʾᵃbāh*, 'and every soul languishes': i.e. every one who is hungry, cf. v. 12; either the relative *ʾᵃšer* should be understood or the adjectival form *dᵉʾēbāh* should be read. **[26]** MT *wāʾerʾeh*, 'and I saw': BHS suggests *wᵉʾerweh*, 'and I was refreshed' (cf. Rudolph, 200); cf. v. 14. The line is enigmatic and may be a marginal comment on the utopian nature of the collection (i.e. the hopes are merely a dream). Some exegetes (e.g. Weiser, 283–4; Rudolph) treat *ʿal-zōʾt*, 'for this reason', as indicative of a citation and translate what follows as a quotation of a well-known song. It may represent an editorial note indicating a prediction of future pastoral well-being using incubatory techniques or revelation through dreams (cf. John Bunyan's sojourn in Bedford gaol which produced *The Pilgrim's Progress*). JPSB treats 'sleep' as 'the vision in the preceding verses'. Bright, 283, confesses to being baffled by the verse.

To the collection of poems in the cycle 30–31 have been added five units which expand the theme of restoration by a series of reversal motifs (vv. 23–26, 27–30, 31–34, 35–37, 38–40). These deal with specific sayings (cf. vv. 23, 26, 29, 34) and motifs and have the effect of defining more clearly the future awaiting the nation in its own land. As they are discrete units, it is difficult to locate them in any particular period or social setting. They concern the restoration of Judah and Israel in terms of repopulation around the cult centre, the reversal of the divine maleficence towards the nation, the making of a new covenant to replace the old broken agreement, a divine guarantee of the permanence of the people analogous to the fixity of the heavenly bodies, and the rebuilding of the city as a reversal of its profanation referred to in 7.30 – 8.3. Each of these motifs may represent a specific social issue in the Persian period.

The first of the five additions hints at the restoration of the temple mount when Yahweh restores the people's fortunes. When the great instauration happens, then the nation will once more be able to use the old blessing, 'blessed be Yahweh on the true (*ṣedeq*, i.e. legitimate) habitation (*nāwēh*, cf. Ex. 15.13; but see 50.7), the holy mountain' (cf. G). It will be a time of solidarity between farmers and shepherds when both will live together in the land. At the same time those who are weary with thirst and languish from hunger will be refreshed and fed. It will be a time of plenty which will reverse the harsh experiences of the present era. The dream of peace and prosperity in the land with Yahweh's presence on the sacred temple mount is recognized in v. 26 as the product of sleep. Waking up from sleep the speaker acknowledges the pleasantness (*'ārbāh*, contrast 6.20) of what he has seen. The enigmatic quality of v. 26 makes it difficult to determine the precise meaning of the text (as the exegetical opinions in the commentaries indicate). As a marginal gloss it may represent the editor's response to the idyll, without necessarily implying a scepticism about the difference between the harsh reality of his own world and the dream-like qualities of the future hope. If the vision of such a benign state is the product of dream techniques used by seers (apocalyptic?) to foresee the future, it is ironic to find it included in the Jeremiah tradition which includes material so hostile to the use of dreams (cf. 23.25, 27–28, 32; 27.9; 29.8). However, the irony need only be noted as a possible reflection on the text and the indeterminate meaning of the statement renders all particular interpretations subject to dispute. The hope expressed in the images of vv. 23–25 is closely related to the bucolic joys of the poems in 30–31, with the additional element of the temple mount from whence the blessing of Yahweh (cf. the development of this motif in MT) will characterize the life of the restored communities throughout the land of Judah. If there is to be a resurgence of an old saying indicative of Yahweh's presence in the (rebuilt is implied though not stated) temple it should be contrasted with 3.16–17, where a different saying (relating to the ark of the covenant) will no longer be used. Both motifs have the same meaning: there will come a time when the presence of Yahweh in the land (Jerusalem in 3.17) will be so palpable that territory and people will thrive in the most wonderful of ways. Small wonder that the hope of vv. 23–25 should be viewed as the product of a most pleasant sleep.

31.27–30

27 'Behold, the days are coming, says the LORD, when I will sow the house of Israel and the house of Judah with the seed of man and the seed of beast.
28 And it shall come to pass that as I have watched over them to pluck up and break down, to overthrow, destroy, and bring evil, so I will watch over them to build and to plant, says the LORD. 29 In those days they shall no longer say:

"The fathers have eaten sour grapes,
and the children's teeth are set on edge."

30 But every one shall die for his own sin; each man who eats sour grapes, his teeth shall be set on edge.'

---

[27] MT *wᵉzāraʿtī*, 'and I will sow': for *zrʿ* as a figure of repopulating the land cf. Hos. 2.25 (EV 23); as a metaphor of scattering the people from their land cf. Zech. 10.9. The term is used in Num. 5.28 for the insemination of a woman which is analogous to sowing a field; so Yahweh will inseminate the communities with people and animals. **[28]** MT *šāqadtī*, 'I have watched': a positive use of *šqd*, cf 44.27 for its negative application (see on 1.12 for a neutral use of the term). G *kathairein kai kakoun*, 'to pull down and to maltreat', lacking two of the four terms in MT used to describe Yahweh's evil actions against the nation. The six metaphors of divine action only occur here and in 1.10, though various selections of them appear in 12.14–17; 18.7, 9; 24.6; 31.40; 42.10; 45.4 (for meanings see on 1.10; cf. Bach 1961). **[29]** MT *lōʾ-yōʾmᵉrū ʿōd*, 'they shall no longer say': = 3.16; 23.7; cf. 16.14. The phrase is the opposite of *ʿōd yōʾmᵉrū* 'once more they shall say' in v. 23, but both statements refer to the reversal of the nation's contemporary misfortunes. The use of *bayyāmīm hāhēm*, 'in those days', links an independent citation to the future hope of v. 27. MT *bōser*, 'unripe, sour grapes': cf. Isa. 18.5; Ezek. 18.2; Job 15.33. The proverb cited here and rebutted in v. 30 also appears in Ezek. 18.2, where it is debated at much greater length (18.1–32; cf. Zimmerli 1979, 378–87, for discussion). Lam. 5.7 touches on the same point without using the gnomic saying. **[30]** Cf. Deut. 24.16 for the same sentiment and reversal of the dogma of inherited retribution set out in the Decalogue (Ex. 20.5; Deut. 5.9); cf. II Kings 14.6. Mayes 1979, 326, relates the Deuteronomic law to the human administration of justice and argues that it is therefore not directly comparable with the divine justice of the Decalogue. The discussion of the matter in Ezek. 18.25, 29 suggests that divine rulings may be behind the debate (e.g. 'the way of Yahweh is not just'), but here vv. 29–30 hardly afford sufficient information to determine whether divine or only human justice is involved.

The first of the three future hopes ('look, the days are coming', vv. 27, 31, 38) for reversals of the past concerns the repopulation of the land by the two communities, Israel and Judah. Yahweh is represented as the virile progenitor who will sow the two houses with people and animals. This striking figure (cf. Hos. 2.23 [MT 25]) reflects the relationship between deity and land in the nature cults, where the maintenance of fertility is sustained by the cult in terms of the divine insemination of the earth and of humans. The terrible losses of human and animal life in the invasions of the land and the destruction of the cities (cf. 7.20) will be reversed in the future. This divine sowing of the communities will be a direct reversal of his previous policy of watching over them for evil purposes (cf. 18.11; 21.10). That policy was characterized by the disruption of all civilized life and the deity's negative attitude towards his people (summarized by the use of the four redactional motifs used throughout the tradition: 'pluck up', 'break down', 'overthrow', 'destroy'). These four negative terms are reversed by the two positive redactional figures 'build', 'plant'. The arid and deserted landscapes produced by Yahweh in his anger will now be cultivated again and human civilization will flourish in the future. The scrutiny (*šqd*) of evil with which Yahweh destroyed the nation will become a scrutiny of building and planting which will result in the great reversal of the nation's fate.

To this oracular proclamation of Yahweh's future transformation of man and beast in Israel and Judah has been added a further citation (cf. vv. 23, 26) which may also be found in Ezek. 18.2. Apparently as a result of the preaching of certain parties about the causes of the invasion, destruction and exile of the community being due to the long history of idolatry and rebellion (typical of the sermons in 7; 11; 25.1–7; 26. 2–6; Ezek. 16; 20; 23), there had grown up in the land a proverb to the effect that the fathers had eaten ssour grapes but the children's teeth have been set on edge (cf. 2.5,9). The proverb summarizes in the most succinct way the belief in inherited guilt and punishment – it is later generations who must pay for the sins of the fathers (cf. Job 21.19). The Ezekiel tradition attempts to combat this claim with assertions of the opposite belief. Here the addition to vv. 27–28 regards the future as a time when such a saying will have no validity. In that future each individual (cf. Ezek. 18.25–29; 33.17–20) will die for his own guilty actions. As part of a much debated controversy (cf. Lam. 5.7; Deut. 24.16) after the fall of Jerusalem such a fragment as vv. 29–30 has a rightful place in the Jeremiah tradition, though perhaps not here in a cycle of poems and prose additions about future salvation. For it introduces into the images of a great and prosperous future a chill note about the human condition (cf. Isa. 65.20b). Although in the future nobody will suffer for any misdeeds other than their own, there will be those who misbehave to the point of being executed! Everybody will bear the responsibility of their own actions. As a note of realism among the golden dreams of the utopian future it is quite out of place. In view of the next addition with its equally utopian image of a time when nobody will need to teach his neighbour divine knowledge because everybody will automatically possess that knowledge, it is even more inappropriate (see on v. 34). However, in this reversal of a popular saying of the time an old criticism is being transformed and the further implications of v. 30 should perhaps not be scrutinized too closely.

31.31–34

31 'Behold, the days are coming, says the LORD, when I will make a new
covenant with the house of Israel and the house of Judah, 32 not like the
covenant which I made with their fathers when I took them by the hand to
bring them out of the land of Egypt, my covenant which they broke, though
I was their husband, says the LORD. 33 But this is the covenant which I will
make with the house of Israel after those days, says the LORD: I will put my
law within them, and I will write it upon their hearts; and I will be their
God, and they shall be my people. 34 And no longer shall each man teach
his neighbour and each his brother, saying, "Know the LORD," for they
shall all know me, from the least of them to the greatest, says the LORD; for
I will forgive their iniquity, and I will remember their sin no more.'

[31] Rudolph, 201, deletes 'and the house of Judah' because it is lacking in v. 33; he understands 'house of Israel' to refer to the northern kingdom and not the whole people north and south. The reference to Judah may be an expansion (cf. v. 27; Bright, 283), but in that case 'Israel' should be understood as the whole nation and not the northern kingdom. **[32]** MT *hēpērū 'et-bᵉrītī*, 'they broke my covenant': cf. 11.10; 14.21; 33.20; Thiel 1970. MT *wᵉ'ānōkī bā'altī bām*, 'but I was their husband': *bā'al* may also be translated 'lord, baal', cf. 3.14. G *egō ēmelēsa autōn*, 'I loathed them' = *gā'altī* (cf. Heb. 8.9), which makes a better divine response to the broken covenant. **[33]** MT *bēt yiśrā'ēl*, 'house of Israel': a few mss *bᵉnē*, 'children . . .'. MT *'aḥᵃrē hayyāmīm hāhēm*, 'after those days': a curious phrase in the light of the formal 'days are coming' of v. 31; cf. v. 29; Martin-Achard 1974, 156 n. 49. Bright, 277, 'when that time comes', makes the two phrases equivalent (cf. Rudolph, 202–3). Perhaps the writer has synthesized two motifs: the coming days of restoration *after which bᵉrīt ḥᵃdāšāh*, 'a new covenant' (or divine obligation) will be enacted; it being a further event in the programme of restoration'; cf. Perlitt 1969, 180 who refers it to the 'dark present'. Weiser, 288, refers the strange phrase to the extension of the historical horizon into the eschatological. Many mss read *wᵉnātattī*, '*and* I will put (my *tōrāh* in their midst)'. The formulaic 'I will be their god and they shall be my people' appears in various forms in 7.23; 11.4; 13.11; 24.7; 30.22; 31.1; 32.38. The inscribing of the *tōrāh* on the mind (*lēb*, EVV 'heart') is a metaphorical transformation of an external practice whereby what the law stands for is interiorized; cf. the similar transformation of the figure of circumcision in 4.4 (enjoined upon the people as something they must do for themselves); Deut. 30.6 (a divine enactment). 9.25–26 represent a rather different strand of tradition. **[34]** MT *kī 'eslaḥ la'ᵃwōnām*, 'for I will forgive their iniquity': for the motif of forgiveness in the Jeremiah tradition see 5.1, 7; 33.8; 36.3; 50.20 (cf. Amos 7.2; Isa. 55.7). In Num. 14.18–20 Yahweh's forgiveness (*nś', slḥ*) of the people's iniquity (*'āwōn*) is seen as a history of continual forgiveness (*nś'*), from the exodus to the time when the prayer of Moses was written ('even until now'); cf. Solomon's prayer for forgiveness in I Kings 8.30–50.

Anderson 1964; Bright 1966a; Buis 1968; Herrmann 1965, 179–85, 195–204; Martin-Achard 1974; Weippert 1979

The third addition to the cycle envisages the making of a *new bᵉrīt* (the only occurrence in the Hebrew Bible where *bᵉrīt*, 'covenant' [?] 'obligation' [?], is qualified by *ḥᵃdāšāh*, 'new') in the future indicated by the formulaic 'look, days are coming' (cf. vv. 27, 38). A reversal motif is incorporated in the piece in that the new *bᵉrīt* will replace the old one broken by the community's fathers in the past. That broken *b^erît* had reversed the relationship of Yahweh with the people by making him disgusted with the nation (v. 32 G), but when the new *b^erît* is instituted the house of Israel will become Yahweh's people and he their god (once more?). If the motif *b^erît* is a common one in Dueteronomistically influenced traditions, the concept of newness associated with it here is less clear. This particular instantiation of *b^erît* interiorizes the divine *tôrāh* in the minds of the people, and such interiorization may constitute the *new* element in *b^erît* (cf. Swetnam 1974 for the interpretation of the new feature as the making available in the synagogues [or wherever Israelites are to be found] of copies of the Mosaic Law). As a consequence of such internalization there will be 'the cessation of tradition' (Westermann 1964, 219); i.e. the human teaching of the knowledge of Yahweh will cease because each person will know Yahweh (already). Every class of persons in the nation ('from the least of them to the greatest') will know the deity, and this state of knowledge will reverse the accusations made in 5.1–5; 8.7. A further consequence of the new *b^erît* will be the divine forgiveness of the nation's iniquity (contrast 5.1, 7a). So in the future to which this oracular statement looks forward the dire straits into which the fathers of the community had brought the nation in 587 will be reversed by the making of an *unbreakable* new *b^erît* (as in the discourses of 2–3, only two generations are described: the past and the future, though a third one [i.e. the one receiving this declaration] may be discerned, cf. 2.9).

The *b^erît* motif is not a dominant element in the Jeremiah tradition, though it appears in that strand often identified as Deuteronomistic (cf. Herrmann; Thiel 1981, 23–28). A number of different *b^erît* feature peripherally in the traditions: e.g. the ark of the covenant (3.16), the covenant preached by Jeremiah (11.2, 3, 6, 8), the *new* covenant appended to the cycle of 30–31 (31.32, 33), Yahweh's covenant with day and night which affords an analogue of the future covenant between Yahweh and the dynasy of David (33.20–2, 25), a covenant made between king Zedekiah and the people of Jerusalem (34.8, 10, 13, 15, 18), the covenant of the exodus period (34.13; cf. 31.32) and the covenant of the future whereby the people will join themselves to Yahweh permanently (50.5; cf. 32.40). These mainly refer to future hopes about the organization of the community, though a few are allusions to the past. In envisaging a new *b^erît* the author of this oracle ignores the problems of the past and foresees a form of relationship between Yahweh and nation which will avoid the defects of the old system of *b^erît* by virtue of internalizing the divine instructions (*tôrāh*). It is a pious hope rather than a programme of social organization and it may be described quite fairly as utopian. Such utopianism is a feature of the futuristic elements in the prophetic anthologies (cf. Blenkinsopp 1983, 105) and represents a fundamental weakness of biblical prophecy. The individuals within the nation will not need to teach one another the knowledge of Yahweh (is this awareness and experience of the deity [cf. 5.4–5; 9.24] or the practice of justice [cf. 22.15–16] or something quite undefined?) because each one will know it already and the nation's iniquity will be forgiven. Bright rightly asks important questions of this utopian outlook: 'And what of the still further future? Will the people thereafter sin no more?' (1966a, 195). His answer to these queries is correct without being penetrating: 'That is a question that lies beyond Jeremiah's field of vision. The new covenant is God's final, gracious provision for his people; the question of its continuing endurance does not enter his mind.' That is the very nature of utopian thought – it predicts a splendid future but is unable to show how such a state may first be achieved and then maintained permanently without disintegration into the chaos which preceded it. The old covenant may have been broken, but it is assumed that the new one will not be (on the analogy of the tables of the law only being broken once?). If the people will really know Yahweh in such an interior manner then the future will be sinless – a veritable utopia and the triumph of hope over experience. Such coming days have yet to come, and it is worth pondering again some words of Immanuel Kant on the difficulty of producing a just society: 'from so crooked wood as man is made out of, nothing completely straight can be built' (Kant 1963, 18).

Whatever the problems of utopian visions of the future, the exegesis of vv. 31–34 is straightforward and the interpretation of the piece would be simple were it not for the fact that many commentators insist on reading 31.31–34 as 'one of the profoundest and most moving passages in the entire Bible' (e.g. Bright, 287; cf. Thompson, 579–80). This Christian appreciation of a minor and prosaic hope for the future, often identified with the new covenant of the New Testament (cf. Heb. 8.8–13; 10.15–17), while irrelevant for the meaning of the text, complicates the treatment of the section because there is a large literature devoted to its interpretation from the viewpoint of Christian theology. In this reading of the new *b^erît* passage the future hope for the house of Israel becomes a prediction of the Christian gospel:

> So we must go beyond Jeremiah's word, and beyond B.C. We must follow Jeremiah's word ahead to the gospel, for it is to the gospel that it points us and drives us; and until it has driven us there it has not discharged its function. We hear Jeremiah's word, '. . . I will make a new covenant . . .' – and that is promise. We also hear the gospel word, 'This cup is the new covenant in my blood' – and that is fulfillment (Bright 1966a, 204).

Part of this perspective on the text is a striving to demonstrate that it comes from Jeremiah (e.g. Bright, 287; 1966a, 192–3; discussion in Martin-Achard, 149–52), though the question of authorship can hardly affect the meaning of the statement. If Bright clamours for Jeremiah's responsibility for its sentiments, others regard it in varying degrees as coming from the prophet of Anathoth (probably the majority of exegetes: e.g. Martin-Achard, 151, attributes its paternity to Jeremiah; Rudolph, 201, assigns it to his early preaching to the northern kingdom). The Deuteronomistic shaping of the language and thought allows some scholars to associate it with that redaction of the tradition rather than with Jeremiah (e.g. Böhmer, Herrmann, Nicholson, Thiel). Others attribute it to a disciple of Jeremiah (e.g. Coppens 1963; Mowinckel 1942, 93–6) or a post-exilic scribe (Duhm, 255). Among those exegetes who assign it to Jeremiah himself, some regard it as including his response to Deuteronomistic views (Martin-Achard, 163) or his reaction to the failure of the reform of 621 (Anderson, 229). Deuteronomistic influence must be acknowledged in the passage, but in view of the fact that the Deuteronomists do not themselves at any point in their writings propose a new covenant, not even in the late piece on the restoration of Israel in Deut. 30.1–10, it must be questioned whether they are responsible for this addition to the cycle. The attribution of authorship in the Jeremiah tradition is a moot point, especially in relation to 30–31, and, though I favour a post-exilic dating for 31.31–34, a dogmatic position is to be avoided. However, I would regard the relation between 31.31–34 and the Deuteronomistic strand in the tradition to be one of critical dialogue (cf. Wisser 1983, 223–4). The Deuteronomists believed that the covenant had been broken and therefore had become inoperable. Late additions to their work allow for the possibility of Yahweh's restoration of the nation and the divine circumcision of its mind after it has turned back to him (Deut. 30.1–10). But of a new covenant the Deuteronomists know nothing (cf. Buis, 13 for the possible connections between 31.31–34 and Deut. 30.1–10). The author of 31.31–34 transcends that limitation by asserting the divine initiative beyond human turning and the making of a new *b^e^rīt*. It is a post-Deuteronomistic hope but one which has learned its theology from Deuteronomism and made the leap of hope into the utopian future. In that future the broken *b^e^rīt* would be transformed in the creation of a new *b^e^rīt* which would transpose *tōrāh* from the stones of the Mosaic legend or the documents of scribes to the mind of the community. This movement from literal to symbolical indicates the metaphorical status of *b^e^rīt* in 31.31–34 (cf. the new mind and spirit of Ezek. 36.26). The *b^e^rīt* motif, asserts this future hope, did not come to an end with 587 as the logic of Deuteronomism demands, but has a future when Yahweh will act to transform the nation.

The use of *b^e^rīt* as a metaphor to describe a state where the community will automatically keep the divine *tōrāh* must be considered a postscript to Deuteronomistic uses of *b^e^rīt* because it transforms those uses in a very radical way. This future *b^e^rīt* is not an obligation between two parties with national and moral regulations which may be kept or broken, but a metaphor of an arrangement with an imaginary community (what Bultmann 1955 calls an 'eschatological concept') which rescues a resonant word (*b^e^rīt*) from oblivion. The utopian society characterized by this metaphor of *b^e^rīt* does not and cannot exist, yet like all the additions to the cycle vv. 31–34 utilize motifs and sayings from the past to construct an idyll of the future. Transformations of such an idyll may produce fertile soil for new movements to develop in ways unimaginable by the author (e.g. the rise of Christian communities), but in terms of the Jeremiah tradition the images and language of the piece reflect upon and transform motifs of a disintegrating and fragmented society to be found in chapters 4–21. In the restoration of the nation the deity will act to create the kind of society which previous generations failed so miserably to achieve.

31.35–37

35 Thus says the LORD,
who gives the sun for light by day
and the fixed order of the moon and the stars for light by night,
who stirs up the sea so that its waves roar –
the LORD of hosts is his name:
36 'If this fixed order departs
from before me, says the LORD,
then shall the descendants of Israel cease
from being a nation before me for ever.'
37 Thus says the LORD:
'If the heavens above can be measured,
and the foundations of the earth below can be explored,
then I will cast off all the descendants of Israel
for all that they have done,
says the LORD.'

---

[35] NEB treats this verse as a prose introduction to the oracular poem in v. 36 and v. 37 as a prose conclusion to it. G has v. 37 before vv. 35, 36. MT *ḥuqqōt*, 'fixed orders': cf. *ḥuqqīm*, v. 36; *ḥuqqōt*, 33.25; *ḥoq-'ōlām*, 'permanent limit', 5.22; these are what von Rad (1972, 107 n. 7) calls ' "orders" in creation . . . orders of heaven and earth'. In 33.20, 25 the orders of night and day are described as Yahweh's *bᵉrīt* with day and night. Volz, 283, reads *ḥōqēq*, 'fixed' (moon), followed by Rudolph, 204 (cf. BHS). MT *rōga' hayyām wayyehᵉmū gallāyw yhwh ṣᵉbā'ōt šᵉmō*, 'he disturbs the sea so that its waves roar – Yahweh of hosts is his name' = Isa. 51.15b; G *kai kraugēn en thalassē*, 'and a roaring in the sea . . .'. **[36]** MT *'im-yāmušū haḥuqqīm hā'ēlleh*, 'if these fixed orders depart': i.e. are removed or fail. As the fixed orders of creation exist before Yahweh's presence, so does the seed (*zera'*, i.e. descendants) of Israel; both are permanent. **[37]** G lacks 'thus says Yahweh', and has *hupsōthē*, 'be raised' (= *yārumū*) for MT *yimmaddū*, 'be measured'. MT *wᵉyēḥāqrū*, 'and (they) be searched out, explored': G *kai ean tapeinōthē*, 'and if (they) be sunk'. G lacks 'all' (*kol*) before 'seed of Israel'.

The fourth addition is a hymnic poem which affirms the permanence of the seed (i.e. race NEB; offspring JPSB; descendants RSV) of Israel and Yahweh's maintenance of it for ever. Yahweh of hosts (cf. Isa. 51.15) is the one who has provided the sun to give light during the day and the moon and stars to light up the night (cf. Gen. 1.14–18), and these permanent orders of creation are analogues of Israel's permanence as a nation before Yahweh. This late hymn is the only element in vv. 23–40 which does not directly reverse a saying or past event and it may once have been a hymnic conclusion to the cycle before vv. 23–34, 38–40 were added (cf. Bright, 286–7). It summarizes the word of restoration which dominates 30–31 using cosmic figures as metaphors of Israel's guaranteed future and reflects the late glossing of prophetic texts with allusions to the power of *Yahweh of hosts* (cf. Amos 4.13; 9.5–6; Crenshaw 1975). The hymn presents Israel's descendants as having a permanent existence before the divine presence (contrast the more negative use of created orders in 5.20–25) and contrasts quite strikingly with much of the Jeremiah tradition which emphasizes the doom-laden future of the nation because of its past sins or its current state. In the oracles about the prosperous future the possibility of sin and destruction is almost entirely absent (see on 31.30). The optimism of the dogma of permanent favoured status before Yahweh gives the book of Jeremiah a tension between present misery and future prosperity which reverses the usual dialectic of absolute judgment and contingent hope analysed by the theological scrutineers of the tradition. After 587 the word of absolute destruction began to give way to words of hope (though see on 44, where destruction remains decreed of the communities in Egypt) and these are to be found concentrated in 30–33. The permanence of Israel through its descendants on the basis of created orders of the universe (i.e. Israel's existence is equivalent to such a fixed order of nature; cf. Second Isaiah's equivalences between the creation of the world and the creation of Israel through the exodus and the return from exile) is a parallel motif to the new *b^e^rīt* of 31.31–34 which implies, without specific articulation, a permanent future without sin in which the whole nation will know Yahweh. These additions to the cycle (vv. 23–40) point to the development of beliefs (in the Persian period?) in the absoluteness of Israel's restoration and prosperity in the future. No such disaster as 587 would ever again destroy the nation, for its future existence is of the order of one of Yahweh's decrees of creation, i.e. permanent (cf. 32.40; 33.17–26; 50.4–5, 20). And this Yahweh himself says – oracular indicators are used four times in MT to stress the intensity and importance of this hymnic affirmation.

31.38–40

38 'Behold, the days are coming, says the LORD, when the city shall be rebuilt for the LORD from the tower of Hananel to the Corner Gate. 39 And the measuring line shall go out farther, straight to the hill Gareb, and shall then turn to Goah. 40 The whole valley of the dead bodies and the ashes, and all the fields as far as the brook Kidron, to the corner of the Horse Gate toward the east, shall be sacred to the LORD. It shall not be uprooted or overthrown any more for ever.'

---

[38] MT *hinnēh yāmīm*, 'look, days . . .', lacks *bā'īm* (supplied masoretically by Q reading in text): lack of representation in K may be due to haplography of *n'm*, 'says' (cf. BHS); Vrs read 'are coming' (*bā'īm*). MT *hā'ir lyhwh*, 'the city for Yahweh': or 'the city of Yahweh', cf. NEB 'in the Lord's honour' (analogous to *lᵉdāwid*, 'for David', in the titles in the book of Psalms). Rudolph, 206, suggests 'by' Yahweh, cf. 31.4. For the two locations 'tower of Hananel' (Neh. 3.1; 12.39) and 'corner gate' (II Kings 14.13; II Chron. 26.9) cf. Zech. 14.10; '(from) . . . *to*' may be represented in MT by *hpnh* with *he locale* (so Driver, 1937–38, 120) or *l* 'to' lacking due to haplography (cf. BHS). **[39]** K *qwh*; Q *qāw*, 'line' (K construct form *qᵉwēh*, cf. BDB, 876). MT *negdō*, 'in front of *it*': G *autōn* ' . . . *them*'; *wᵉnāsab gō'ātāh*, 'and shall turn to Goath': G *kai perikuklōthēsetai kuklō ex eklektōn lithōn*, 'and it shall be encompassed with a circle of choice stones'. The locations 'hill of Gareb', 'Goath/Goah' are unknown; Bright, 283, relates them to the west on the grounds that v. 38 refers to the north and v. 40 to the south and east. **[40]** G lacks 'and the whole valley of the dead bodies and the ashes': the 'valley' (*'ēmeq*) may be an allusion to the fire-cult practised in the valley (*gay'*, 7.31–32) but need not be so understood. It may simply refer to an area where terrible slaughter once took place. K *hšrmwt*; Q *haššᵉdēmōt*, 'fields' (K incomprehensible): a possible reference to *šᵉdēh māwet*, 'field of death', i.e. cemetery (cf. V *regionem mortis*; Ug. *šd mt*, 'field of Mot'; Lehmann 1953), though here it may just mean 'fields' for cultivation (cf. Croatto und Soggin 1962); G = K. MT *'ad . . . 'ad* 'as far as (the brook Kidron), as far as (the corner)': Rudolph, Bright follow Volz, 283, and read *'al*, 'above', for the first *'ad* (MT due to scribal miscopying). MT *lō'-yinnātēš wᵉlō' yehārēs 'ōd lᵉ'ōlām*, 'it shall not be uprooted or overthrown again for ever': *ntš*, *hrs* belong to the thematic list of 1.10.

The final addition to the cycle is the third of the 'days are coming' series which reverses old sayings, practices and occurrences. In this piece the rebuilding of Yahweh's city, i.e. Jerusalem, is described in terms of the area which will be reconstructed so as to represent the sacred territory that will remain inviolable for ever. The plucking up *(ntš)* and overthrowing *(hrs)* of the city in the past (587 and subsequently?) will be reversed in the future building of the area, and its special relation to Yahweh *(qdš)* will make it the holy city (this motif appears in Isa. 48.2; 52.1). Such sacred status will afford the city permanent protection. The images of the city in 7.30 – 8.3 are here reversed, and the rebuilding of the city is given an oracular justification which may have been intended to provide backing for a particular building project (cf. Zech. 14.10–11; Ezek. 40–48). So the coda to the cycle ends with the rebuilt Jerusalem, Yahweh's city, facing a prosperous future under permanent divine protection (cf. Isa. 4.5–6), with its terrible past completely reversed.

32.1–15

32[1] The word that came to Jeremiah from the LORD in the tenth year of
Zedekiah king of Judah, which was the eighteenth year of Nebuchadrezzar.
2 At that time the army of the king of Babylon was besieging Jerusalem,
and Jeremiah the prophet was shut up in the court of the guard which was
in the palace of the king of Judah. 3 For Zedekiah king of Judah had
imprisoned him, saying, 'Why do you prophesy and say, "Thus says the
LORD: Behold, I am giving this city into the hand of the king of Babylon,
and he shall take it; 4 Zedekiah king of Judah shall not escape out of the
hand of the Chaldeans, but shall surely be given into the hand of the king
of Babylon, and shall speak with him face to face and see him eye to eye; 5
and he shall take Zedekiah to Babylon, and there he shall remain until I
visit him, says the LORD; though you fight against the Chaldeans, you shall
not succeed"?'

6 Jeremiah said, 'The word of the LORD came to me: 7 Behold, Hanamel
the son of Shallum your uncle will come to you and say, "Buy my field
which is at Anathoth, for the right of redemption by purchase is yours." 8
Then Hanamel my cousin came to me in the court of the guard, in
accordance with the word of the LORD, and said to me, "Buy my field which
is at Anathoth in the land of Benjamin, for the right of possession and
redemption is yours; buy it for yourself." Then I knew that this was the
word of the LORD.

9 And I bought the field at Anathoth from Hanamel my cousin, and
weighed out the money to him, seventeen shekels of silver. 10 I signed the
deed, sealed it, got witnesses, and weighed the money on scales. 11 Then I
took the sealed deed of purchase, containing the terms and conditions, and
the open copy; 12 and I gave the deed of purchase to Baruch the son of

Neriah son of Mahseiah, in the presence of Hanamel my cousin, in the presence of all the Jews who were sitting in the court of the guard. 13 I charged Baruch in their presence, saying, 14 "Thus says the LORD of hosts, the God of Israel: Take these deeds, both this sealed deed of purchase and this open deed, and put them in an earthenware vessel, that they may last for a long time. 15 For thus says the LORD of hosts, the God of Israel: Houses and fields and vineyards shall again be bought in this land." '

[MT 32] = G 39. **[1]** K *bšnt*; Q *baššānāh*, 'in the (tenth) year': cf. 28.1 for this K–Q variation. The introductory formula for the reception of the divine word is the same as that in 21.1; 34.1, 8; 35.1; 40.1; and similar to 7.1; 11.1; 18.1, which have *lē'mōr*, 'saying', instead of a temporal clause indicating the occasion on which the word was received. For the eighteenth year of Nebuchadrezzar, cf. 52.29, which places the deportation of 587 then (counting his first year as 604/3), but 25.1; 52.12; II Kings 25.8 (counting from 605) refer the deportation to his nineteenth year; cf. Soggin 1984, 251, on the discrepancy, which can hardly be attributed to two different chronological systems in Jer. 52 (*contra* Malamat 1968, 150). **[2]** Verses 2–5 are a redactional parenthesis setting out the reason for Jeremiah's imprisonment (cf. 37.11–14 for a different account; 34.2–3 for a summary of the charge here). MT *hannābī'*, 'the prophet': lacking in G. **[3]** Cf. 37.21 for the imprisonment motif and 34.2 for the message of v. 3. **[4]** Cf. 34.3; K *'ynw*; Q *'ēnāw*, 'his eyes': MT lit. 'and his mouth will speak with his mouth and his eyes will see his eyes', cf. NEB 'he will speak with him face to face and see him with his own eyes'. **[5]** MT *'ad-poqᵉdī 'ōtō*, 'until I visit him': cf. 15.15; 27.22; 29.10 where *pqd* means 'to visit graciously' (cf. Ruth 1.6; Ps. 65.10 [EV 9]) and that would appear to be the meaning here (hence the motif of peaceful death in 34.4–5). G lacks second half of verse from after 'and remain there' (*kai ekei kathieitai*); G^A *apothaneitai*, 'and die' (cf. 22.12, 26). Zedekiah died in prison (52.11); some exegetes think that the editor has here confused Zedekiah with Jehoiachin (cf. 52.31–34; Duhm, 261; Volz, 299; Hyatt, 1043–4). **[6]** MT *wayyō'mer yirmᵉyāhū hāyāh*, 'and Jeremiah said . . . came . . .': G *egenēthē* = *wayᵉhī*; MT *'ēlay*, 'to me': G *pros Ieremian*, 'to Jeremiah' (cf. 'to me', v. 8). This is not Jeremiah's response to Zedekiah but the beginning of the symbolical-magical act of vv. 6–15, of which vv. 1–5 are the editorial setting of the transaction. The text does not indicate to whom Jeremiah spoke (MT), hence G is better as an introduction to the divine word. **[7]** Hanamel ben Shallum: cf. Hananel in 31.38. MT *mišpaṭ haggᵉ'ullāh*, 'the right, duty, custom of redemption': cf. Lev. 25.25–28 for some of the rules about kin obligations to purchase land in the family. For the divine word as anticipating the future behaviour of people cf. 13.12–13. **[8]** MT *ben-dōdī*, lit. 'the son of my uncle', i.e. 'cousin'. G lacks *kidᵉbar yhwh*, 'according to the word of Yahweh'. BHS treats 'which is in the land of

Benjamin' as additional (a superfluous gloss Rudolph, 208); G has the phrase before 'which is in Anathoth'. MT *ūlᵉkā haggᵉʾullāh qᵉnēh-lāk*, 'and to you belongs (the right of *mišpaṭ*?) the redemption, buy for yourself': G *kai su presbuteros*, 'and you are the oldest', i.e. the closest of kin (?). MT *mišpaṭ hayᵉruššah*, 'the right of possession', varies the form of v. 7. MT *wāʾēdaʿ kī dᵉbar-yhwh hūʾ*, 'then I knew that this was the word of Yahweh': a most unusual example of confirmation of the divine word in the tradition. **[9]** Apparently the land was bought unseen by Jeremiah! Cf. 37.12, where he takes the opportunity to visit it during a lull in the siege (see on 37.11–15). G lacks 'which was in Anathoth' and '(weighed out to him) the silver'. It is not possible to determine the value of this transaction since we do not know the size of the field or the exchange rate of the silver shekel. As it stands the story presents a Jeremiah who has both money and property. **[11]** MT *hammiṣwāh wᵉhaḥuqqīm*, 'the order and the statutes': lacking in G, NEB; JPSB, 'according to rule and law'; 'the contract and the prescriptions', Bright, 237. The legal terminology may indicate the rules governing contracts: the sealed copy was for a permanent record and the open copy was for consultation (cf. Hyatt, 1045; Bright, 237–8; the Elephantine Letters [Porten 1968]). **[12]** Baruch ben Neriah ben Mahseiah: cf. 36.4–32; 43.3–7; 45. MT *ḥᵃnamʾēl dōdī*, 'Hanamel my uncle': some mss, Vrs read 'son of my uncle', i.e. 'cousin', as in vv. 8, 9. MT *ūlᵉʿēnē hāʿēdīm hakkōtᵉbīm*, 'and in the sight of the witnesses who wrote . . .': G 'and in the sight of those standing and writing . . .'. **[14]** Rudolph treats the opening phrase as a mechanical gloss after 'saying' (cf. BHS). G lacks 'these deeds', 'the sealed'. The storing of the deeds in a ceramic jar may be for their protection over a long period, which hardly suggests that the open copy was for consultation.

The story of Jeremiah's purchase of a field in Anathoth belonging to his kin appears in a heavily edited chapter which develops a number of themes at great length (vv. 1–5, 16–25, 26–35, 36–41, 42–45). It is complicated by being placed after an introductory account of Zedekiah's arrest and imprisonment of Jeremiah during the siege of Jerusalem in 588–7. This particular theme is presented a number of times in the tradition, though on each occasion there are significant variations in the story of the encounter between Jeremiah and Zedekiah (or his delegation) which make a complex pattern of motifs (cf. 21.1–7; 32.1–5; 34.1–7; 37.1–15, 16–21; 38.1–6, 14–28). These constitute a major theme in the narratives of the book of Jeremiah. However, it is not happily presented as an introduction to the buying of the family plot in Anathoth as it represents an occasion when access to the city from the north was freely available to Jeremiah's relative in spite of Jerusalem being *under siege* at the time! Jeremiah's visit to Benjaminite territory is explained in 37.12 as occurring during a tactical withdrawal by the Babylonians but no such explanation is offered in 32.1–5. Rather Jeremiah is depicted as being shut up in the courtyard at a time when the Babylonians had shut up the city so as to prevent exit or access. If the story of the land purchase is read apart from its present redactional position sense may be made of it (to a certain degree), yet its placing here must be taken into account on two counts. The story is a positive statement about the future (cf. v. 15), hence belongs with the additions to the cycle of 30–31. It is a statement of Jeremiah's actions, rather than words, for the future which, because of their magical nature, create that future. The second count concerns the contrast set up between Jeremiah's constricted circumstances in vv. 1–5 and the great freedom with which he manipulates the future so as to secure it for the nation. His actions while under open arrest preserve for the Jews a future of conventional buying and selling.

There are other problems with the story of Jeremiah's purchase of family land which undermine treating it as a historical event and demonstrate it to be a paradigmatic account of how the future was secured by Jeremiah *the prophet* (MT). In 11.21–23 the men of Anathoth are represented as seeking Jeremiah's life (the interpretation taken by most conventional exegetes), yet in 32.7–8 a relative from Anathoth offers him land. Had the quarrel, in spite of its lethal potentialities, been settled between the two parties? If it had not been amicably solved, what likelihood was there that Jeremiah could ever make use of his piece of land among people who wished to kill him? The purchase of land during a harsh siege by the Babylonians may be presented as hope for the future in the text, but in real-life terms such an action would be the most foolhardy of treasonous acts. Consider the matter. In a time of invasion and siege why buy land that might never be occupied? Might it not be the case that a man who was prepared to make such a purchase was in fact a traitor, a collaborator with the enemy who stood to gain after the nation's defeat? It is not a fanciful argument – it is similar to the accusation made against Jeremiah in 37.13. A man who proclaimed that the Babylonians would capture the city and the king, yet who at the same time bought up land, must have come under suspicion immediately. The tradition knows no such accusation but does emphasize that the seizure of Jeremiah was due to his opposition to Judah in favour of the enemy *in a time of war* (the most absolute form of high treason). For this treachery he was arrested (cf. 32.3; 37.13–15; 38.1–6). It therefore seems most unlikely that the story of the purchase of family land should be understood as a literal act of Jeremiah's; it should be read as one more presentation of *Jeremiah the prophet* behaving in a paradigmatic manner with reference to the community's future. *The* prophet here *creates* the positive future spoken of in his oracles in 30–31 by means of a piece of family business in which he secures property against the distant future ('many days', v. 14) when once more (*'ōd*, cf. 31.23, 29) houses, fields and vineyards will be bought and sold in the land.

The encounter between Jeremiah and Zedekiah reflects the one constant in that theme – the Babylonians will prevail against city and king. If in 21.6–8 nobody escapes the savage butchery of the Babylonians, here Zedekiah is reassured that he will be taken to Babylon after confronting Nebuchadrezzar and there he must remain until Yahweh visits him (cf. 27.22). In 34.5 Zedekiah is apprised of his own death in Babylon, a death which will be 'in *šālōm*' (Yahweh's gracious visit of 32.5?), with the proper funeral arrangements following. Here the precise details of the divine visitation are left unstated because the redactors' concern is with a rather different future. In Babylon there is no future (but horror and death), whereas in the land of Palestine there is a future. That future is now secured by Jeremiah's actions. What is spoken and written in 30–31 is here made good by the first act of the future.

For reasons unstated in the text, Jeremiah's cousin Hanamel offers him family land as his to purchase by right. The divine word does not command Jeremiah to go and buy land but simply informs him that land will be offered for sale to him. When Hanamel appears, Jeremiah knows that what he had heard was indeed Yahweh's word (an unusual point of confirmation in the tradition, cf. I Sam. 10.1–7). Here we have *the prophet* (MT) whose every anticipation and action is governed by the divine word and whose knowledge of what is happening in the world is mediated to him by that word (cf. 11.21–23; 13.12–13). So Hanamel's offer of land is accepted by Jeremiah, and for seventeen shekels of silver (seven ounces) he buys family territory in the land of Benjamin. It would be pointless to speculate on Jeremiah the man of means and property because the tradition provides no hints as to how someone so universally spoken against could also be so well appointed as to buy land with silver on the spur of the moment. The paradigmatic prophet is always adequately equipped and furnished, no matter what the emergency (cf. the stories of Elijah and Elisha). The transaction of buying and selling land is scrupulously observed: written deeds, sealed and open, witnesses in particular and in general (the Jews in the court reveal how open Jeremiah's arrest is, though their presence is fundamentally important because what they are observing is *their* title-deed to land in the future). Baruch ben Neriah, appearing in the tradition for the first time, becomes the custodian of the deeds which are placed in a ceramic jar for preservation. In the presence of this assembled host Jeremiah proclaims the meaning of his action: 'houses and fields and vineyards shall again be bought in this land'. This is Yahweh's word, and the prophet's action will one day, a long time from now, create Judah's future because it is the first purchase of land in and for that future.

The family land bought by Jeremiah is like the field of Ephron which Abraham bought in order to bury his dead (Gen. 23), an earnest of the future and a land claim legitimately acquired. The small plot of land in Anathoth will become a symbol of the whole land and the prophet is the first man to own property in the new age when Yahweh restores the fortunes of Israel. Ironically Jeremiah will be dead by then, and as a childless man (the conventional interpretation of 16.1–2) his piece of property will have passed on to others. However, the niceties of legal requirements have been observed and the act is more important than the fact that Jeremiah will never see that land. Its purchase by *the* prophet is what matters because it stakes a claim to the future *in the land* for the people. The future is not in Babylon (*contra* 24.4–7; 29.4–7) but here in Judah – which is why the story is set in the period of Jeremiah's arrest during the siege by Babylon. The terrifying present is reversed by his act in buying Palestinian land. Zedekiah may go to Babylon (with his courtiers, supporters and other citizens), but Yahweh has a future for the land of Judah (cf. 42.7–12). The jar containing the title deeds to that field in Anathoth, wherever it may be hidden (did it survive the fall of Jerusalem? foolish question because it is not that kind of story), contains Judah's future and the divine word acting through *the prophet* has already created that future. The Babylonians may lay siege to the city, take it and raze it to the ground, but the future has been secured.

32.16–25

16 'After I had given the deed of purchase to Baruch the son of Neriah, I
prayed to the LORD, saying: 17 "Ah Lord GOD! It is thou who hast made
the heavens and the earth by thy great power and by thy outstretched arm!
Nothing is too hard for thee, 18 who showest steadfast love to thousands,
but dost requite the guilt of fathers to their children after them, O great and
mighty God whose name is the LORD of hosts, 19 great in counsel and
mighty in deed; whose eyes are open to all the ways of men, rewarding every
man according to his ways and according to the fruit of his doings; 20 Who
hast shown signs and wonders in the land of Egypt, and to this day in Israel
and among all mankind, and hast made thee a name, as at this day. 21
Thou didst bring thy people Israel out of the land of Egypt with signs and
wonders, with a strong hand and outstretched arm, and with great terror;
22 and thou gavest them this land, which thou didst swear to their fathers
to give them, a land flowing with milk and honey; 23 and they entered and
took possession of it. But they did not obey thy voice or walk in thy law;
they did nothing of all thou didst command them to do. Therefore thou hast
made all this evil come upon them. 24 Behold, the siege mounds have come
up to the city to take it, and because of sword and famine and pestilence
the city is given into the hands of the Chaldeans who are fighting against
it. What thou didst speak has come to pass, and behold, thou seest it. 25
Yet thou, O Lord GOD, hast said to me, 'Buy the field for money and get
witnesses' – though the city is given into the hands of the Chaldeans." '

---

[16] MT *wā'etpallēl 'el-yhwh*, 'and I prayed to Yahweh': contrast the presentation of Jeremiah in 7.16; 11.14; 14.11. **[17]** MT *lō'-yippālē' mimmᵉkā kol-dābār*, 'nothing is too difficult for you': this half-line links the prayer to the oracular sermon in vv. 26–35 by virtue of the similar half-line in v. 27b; cf. the question in Gen. 18.14a, *hᵃyippālē mēyhwh dābār*, 'is anything too difficult for Yahweh?'. G *apokrubē*, 'hidden', for *pl'*, 'wonderful, difficult, extraordinary'. The occurrence of *hinnēh*, 'look', may be linked to *hinnēh* in v. 24, where the prayer may be said to continue after the extolment of Yahweh in vv. 18–23 (cf. Bright, 294). Deuteronomistic elements are to be found in the prayer (cf. Thiel 1981, 31–4). **[18]** G lacks 'of hosts is his name', and links *yhwh* with 'great' in v. 19, where the occurrence of *pantokratōr* indicates a displaced *ṣᵉbā'ōt*, 'hosts', i.e. 'all-powerful'. The recital of Yahweh's favour and vengeance (cf. Ex. 20.5–6; Deut. 5.9–10) contrasts with 31.29–30 but indicates the rhetorical nature of such liturgical recitations. **[19]** This verse appears to contradict the principle of extended guilt in v. 18, but prayers such as this one (cf. Neh. 9.6–37; Dan. 9.3–19) are made up of many clichés and conventional lines, so should not be scrutinized for precision of principle or thought. G lacks 'and according to the fruit of his doings'. **[20]** MT *'ad-hayyōm hazzeh*, 'to this day': i.e. the present time, whenever the speech may be given (cf. Childs 1963 on this formulaic phrase); cf. v. 31; 3.25. JPSB understands the phrase to mean 'with lasting effect', whereas RSV, NEB provide 'and' (added to MT by BHS) before it as the logic of the statement demands. MT *kayyōm hazzeh*, 'as at this day': i.e. 'like today' or 'this very day', cf. 11.5; 25.18; 44.6, 23; DeVries 1975, 52 n. 78. **[21]** Cf. Deut. 4.34; 26.8–9. **[23]** K *wbtrwtk*; Q *ūbᵉtōrātᵉkā*, 'and in your law'; cf. 30.3 where the taking possession of the land is also posited of the future. The sense of v. 23 is to be found in 9.13; 11.8; 44.10, 23. **[24]** MT *hassōllōt bā'u hā'īr*, 'the siege ramps have come to the city': G *ochlos*, 'a mob, crowd', for 'mound, siege rampart' (33.4; cf. 6.6); it presupposes the success of the siege. G lacks *wᵉhinnᵉkā rō'eh*, 'and look, you see': i.e. the deity may observe his handiwork of the destroyed city. **[25]** MT *wᵉhā'ēd 'ēdīm*, 'and make witnesses': i.e. get witnesses. G follows v. 10 instead here: 'and I wrote the deed (*biblion*, 'book') and sealed it and got witnesses'. The command 'buy the field for silver' is not part of vv. 7–8, but reflects the ultimate lesson drawn from the story in v. 44, 'fields shall be bought for silver'.

The twin motifs of vv. 1–15, the siege and Jeremiah's purchase of the field for silver, are developed in various ways in the additional material appended in 32. In vv. 16–25 Jeremiah is represented as making a great prayer of praise to Yahweh and recital of the nation's disobedient past in order to point up the absurdity of buying land during a siege. The juxtaposition of the two motifs allows for a meditation on the theme that nothing is too marvellous (i.e. impossible) for the deity, and hence out of the most unlikely circumstances he will create the possibility of a good future (developed in the other sections). The language of the prayer is very conventional, Deuteronomistic and reflects the great litanies of the Persian period and later (e.g. Neh. 9.6–37; Dan. 9.3–19). It is more akin to the prayers used by groups in worship than by individuals (cf. Volz, 300) and is only loosely integrated with the theme of buying the field (thus Bright, 289–91, reads vv. 16–17a, 24–25, as Jeremiah's prayer and vv. 17b–23 as an insertion). As the leader of the prayer Jeremiah is presented as a major liturgical figure and the addition indicates a significant development in the treatment of the prophetic stories in the tradition.

32.26–35

26 The word of the Lord came to Jeremiah: 27 'Behold, I am the Lord, the
God of all flesh; is anything too hard for me? 28 Therefore, thus says the
Lord: Behold, I am giving this city into the hands of the Chaldeans and
into the hand of Nebuchadrezzar king of Babylon, and he shall take it. 29
The Chaldeans who are fighting against this city shall come and set this
city on fire, and burn it, with the houses on whose roofs incense has been
offered to Baal and drink offerings have been poured out to other gods, to
provoke me to anger. 30 For the sons of Israel and the sons of Judah have
done nothing but evil in my sight from their youth; the sons of Israel have
done nothing but provoke me to anger by the work of their hands, says the
Lord. 31 This city has aroused my anger and wrath, from the day it was
built to this day, so that I will remove it from my sight 32 because of all the
evil of the sons of Israel and the sons of Judah which they did to provoke
me to anger – their kings and their princes, their priests and their prophets,
the men of Judah and the inhabitants of Jerusalem. 33 They have turned
to me their back and not their face; and though I have taught them
persistently they have not listened to receive instruction. 34 They set up
their abominations in the house which is called by my name, to defile it. 35
They built the high places of Baal in the valley of the son of Hinnom, to
offer up their sons and daughters to Molech, though I did not command
them, nor did it enter into my mind, that they should do this abomination,
to cause Judah to sin.'

---

[26] G 'to me' for MT 'to Jeremiah', cf. v. 16, where Jeremiah is the speaker. What follows in vv. 28–35 is an entirely different oracular attack on the nation, which is quite inappropriate in this context of appendices to 30–31. This formula is found in 33.19, 23; cf. 31.1; 35.12; 37.6. **[27]** Cf. v. 17; the spelling out of this claim does not appear until vv. 37–41. MT *yhwh ᵓᵉlōhē kol-bāšār*, 'Yahweh, the god of all flesh': cf. *ᵓēl ᵓᵉlōhē hārūḥōt lᵉkol-bāśār*, 'El, the god of the spirits of all flesh', Num. 16.22; said of Yahweh in Num. 27.16. G *krubēsetai*, 'be hidden', for MT *yippālēᵓ*, 'difficult, wonderful' cf. v. 17. **[28]** Cf. v. 36. MT *hinᵉnī nōtēn ᵓet-hāʿīr hazzōᵓt*, 'I am giving this city': G *dotheisa paradothēsetai*, 'shall certainly be given' = *hinnātōn tinnātēn* (cf. BHS); cf. 34.2. G lacks 'the Chaldaeans and into the hands of Nebuchadrezzar'; cf. the shorter MT of v. 3. **[29]** Cf. 37.10 for the motif of the Chaldaeans burning the city (not in 32.3–5); cf. 34.2; 39.8 for the burning of the city or parts of it. Cf. 19.13 for the motif of offerings to other gods on the roofs. **[30]** A summary of Israel's and Judah's idolatrous history is provided in vv. 30–35; for v. 30 cf. 7.30. The two nations contrast with the essential orientation of 32.44 on Judaean and southern territory, but this is part of the Deuteronomistic glossing of the tradition (cf. Thiel 1981, 33–4). The phrase 'work of their hands' refers to idols, cf. 1.16; cf. 7.18–19 for the provocation of Yahweh to anger by involvement in other cults. G lacks the second half of v. 30. **[31]** MT *wᵉʿad hayyōm hazzeh*, 'and to this day': cf. v. 20. The hyperbolic nature of this harangue should be apparent from the reference to the day Jerusalem was built – a period long before Judah took possession of the city. However, 'from that day to this day' makes a fine rhetorical point. Cf. 7.25–26 for a similar piece of rhetoric about the exodus. The syntax of v. 31 is most awkward and quite similar to 52.3 (cf. Bright, 296). **[32]** Cf. the gloss in 2.26b. **[33]** MT *wᵉlammēd*, 'and taught': if read as an infinitive absolute it may have the force of *wāʾalammēd* 'and I taught', so Rudolph, 210 (cf. BHS). The idiom *haškēm wᵉlammēd*, 'rising early and teaching', is a variation of a form which appears frequently in the sermons of the tradition (e.g. 7.13, 25; 11.7; 25.4; 26.5; 29.19; 35.14, 15; 44.4). Many of these idioms refer to the prophets, but the teaching process is not identified here, though in view of the cultic matters criticized it might refer to the priestly role of teaching (*tōrāh* is normally used to describe that function of the priests, cf. Deut. 33.10). For the turning of the back on the deity, though here it is a metaphor of the rejection of the divine teaching, cf. the cult act described in Ezek. 8.16 (the language is quite different from 32.33). **[34]** Cf. 7.30. **[35]** Cf. 7.31; 19.5; see on 7.30–34 for interpretation of the fire-cult (*contra* Bright, 296). MT *lᵉhaʿabīr*, 'to pass': i.e. to dedicate to Molech rather than 'to offer up' (RSV); Bright, 296 translates correctly 'in order to cause to pass [through the fire]', i.e. 'to devote', but spoils his treatment by insisting 'But sacrifice of sons and daughters is meant'. The phrase 'to cause Judah to sin' is an additional point here to those made in 7.31; 19.5. S adds 'in Tophet' after 'Baal' (BHS); G has *Moloch basilei*, 'king Moloch'. K *hḥṭy*; Q *haḥᵃṭī*, 'to cause to sin'.

The prayer of Jeremiah gives way to a lengthy oracular harangue of the city and then of Judah and Israel. In spite of the repetition of the claim that nothing is impossible for Yahweh, the point of this affirmation of divine omnipotence is postponed yet again by editors who wish to make further comments on the Babylonian siege of Jerusalem and to recite extracts from a monothematic history of the two communities. In this outburst the burning of the city after the siege is accounted for in terms of the long history of idolatry in Israel and Judah. Not because Zedekiah failed to surrender was the city burned (cf. 38.17–18) nor because of the evil done by Zedekiah and Jehoiakim (52.2–3), but as a result of a continous history of barbarous and idolatrous practices. Also the city had aroused divine anger since its very foundation! Thus the fall of Jerusalem is more than accounted for in this oracular sermon. In spite of being quite out of place in the development of the field buying motif, the sour note of vv. 28–35 (some exegetes would limit the harangue to vv. 29b–35) betrays the influence of the circles which edited the Jeremiah tradition by means of attacks on pagan practices (e.g. 1.16; 7.16–20, 30–34; 9.12–16; 11.1–13; 19.3–9, 11b–13). These attacks represent a dismissal of the religious practices favoured by other groups in the city and the land in favour of a more Yahwistic type of religion which concentrated solely on Yahweh as the cult and national god. Hence the pejorative descriptions of cultic life and the association of such worship with the destruction of Jerusalem. Yahweh gave the city into the hands of the Babylonians, thereby demonstrating his anger against such cults. Curiously his wrath is said to have been aroused since the city was first built, long before the Judaeans had taken possession of it, though such a view may simply be the hyperbole of outrage against groups with different cultic outlooks. Sermons of denunciation should not be regarded as models of accurate description or fair comment: the producers of these harangues may have believed that Jerusalem had always been part of their history and that some profound explanation was required to account for its destruction (the syntax of v. 31 is awkward, see on 52.3). The events of 588–7 were too good an opportunity for the Yahweh-alone party not to use them in its ideological battles with other parties favouring different cultic arrangements.

32.36–41

36 'Now therefore thus says the LORD, the God of Israel, concerning this city of which you say, "It is given into the hand of the king of Babylon by sword, by famine, and by pestilence". 37 Behold, I will gather them from all the countries to which I drove them in my anger and my wrath and in great indignation; I will bring them back to this place, and I will make them dwell in safety. 38 And they shall be my people, and I will be their God. 39 I will give them one heart and one way, that they may fear me for ever, for their own good and the good of their children after them. 40 I will make with them an everlasting covenant, that I will not turn away from doing good to them; and I will put the fear of me in their hearts, that they may not turn from me. 41 I will rejoice in doing them good, and I will plant them in this land in faithfulness, with all my heart and all my soul.'

---

[36] G lacks 'therefore'. MT *'attem 'ōmᵉrīm*, 'you say': G sing. *su legeis*; a transformation of vv. 3, 28, whereby Yahweh's claim to be giving the city to the Babylonians is made out to be a claim by the people (MT) or the prophet (G). G *kai en apostolē*, 'and by banishment', for MT *ûbaddāber* 'and by pestilence'; the triad 'sword, famine, pestilence' appears throughout the later prose sections of the tradition (e.g. v. 24; 14.12; 21.7; 24.10; 27.8, 13; 29.18; 42.17, 22; 44.13). **[37]** MT *mikkol-hā'ᵃrāṣōt*, 'from all the lands': G *ek pasēs tēs gēs*, 'out of all the land'; MT refers to the diaspora rather than the exile to Babylon. MT *'el-hammāqōm hazzeh*, 'to this place': possibly the temple, though the city or the land may be intended, if the speaker was in the cult place. **[38]** Cf. 7.23; 11.4; 24.7; 30.22; 31.1, 33. **[39]** MT *lēb 'eḥād wᵉderek 'eḥād*, 'one mind and one way': Bright, 290, 'singleness of mind and of purpose'; G *hodon heteran kai kardian heteran*, 'another way and another heart', i.e. reading *'eḥād* as *'aḥēr*; S *ḥdt'* = *ḥādāš*, 'new', cf. Ezek. 11.19; 36.26. MT *kol-hayyāmīm*, 'all the days', i.e. permanently; for the sentiments here cf. Deut. 4.10; 5.29; 6.24; 14.24; 31.13; Thiel 1981, 35. **[40]** MT *bᵉrīt 'ōlām*, 'a permanent covenant': Ezek. 16.60; 37.26; cf. the new covenant of 31.31; Weippert 1981b, 95–102, for a treatment of 32.36–41; 31.31–34 as variations on a theme. MT *lō'-'āšūb mē'aḥᵃrēhem lᵉhēṭībī 'ōtām*, 'I will not turn from following them to do them good': NEB 'to follow them unfailingly with my bounty'; G lacks 'to do them good'. **[41]** MT *wᵉśaśtī 'ᵃlēhem*, 'and I will rejoice over them': G *kai episkepsomai*, 'and I will visit (to do good to them)'; cf. Deut. 30.9 for the motif of Yahweh's joy (*lāśūś*) over his people. The planting (*nṭ'*) motif is a further occurrence of the set of motifs used in 1.10 to summarize the message of the tradition. The Deuteronomistic phrase 'with all my heart and all my soul' is uniquely applied to Yahweh here.

The excoriation of the community finally gives way to a more positive oracular statement whereby the deity reverses the terrible destruction wrought by the Babylonians (it is the people who claim that the city has been given over to the king of Babylon) and promises to gather all the dispersed exiles from all the countries to which he has driven them in his fierce anger (described in a triad of 'anger, wrath and indignation'). The editors have almost got around to developing the buying of the field motif! The great reversal of the diaspora will involve the return of the exiles to a safe homeland where the deity will genuinely (*be'ᵉmet*, 'in truth', cf. 26.15) plant them (cf. 21.7; 31.28; 42.10; Amos 9.15). Part of this restoration process will be the making of a permanent *bᵉrīt* with the people which will guarantee them perpetual protection by the deity. The binding of Yahweh in a permanent obligation to do good to his people will make good the most obvious defects in previous *bᵉrīt* arrangements which regularly broke down in outbursts of divine anger. The future permanent agreement between Yahweh and people is characterized by a tenderness, joy and concern implemented by the deity with 'all his mind and being' which contrasts significantly with his bouts of brutal anger in the past (cf. Deut. 28.16–68). The dream of the Deuteronomists that the people should fear Yahweh all the days of their life will also be realized in the future because Yahweh will put that fear within them (cf. the interiorization of *tōrāh* in 31.33) so that they do not turn away from him. Permanent loyalty will exist between both parties, and the deity will not desist from doing good to his people. The motif of the permanent *b^erīt* is a feature of the future expectations of various traditions (e.g. Ezek. 16.60; 37. 26; Isa. 55.3; 61.8; cf. Raitt 1977, 200–6), and is indicative of a profound desire for perpetual security, based on divine protection, without having to have recourse to the kind of human behaviour which would placate the deity (except in so far as the deity makes such behaviour automatic). It is a utopian dream of a time when the flawed character of human communities will disappear for ever, a time when deity and community will delight in each other without the prospect of disintegrating forces producing tears in paradise.

32.42–44

42 'For thus says the LORD: Just as I have brought all this great evil upon this people, so I will bring upon them all the good that I promise them. 43 Fields shall be bought in this land of which you are saying, It is a desolation, without man or beast; it is given into the hands of the Chaldeans. 44 Fields shall be bought for money, and deeds shall be signed and sealed and witnessed, in the land of Benjamin, in the places about Jerusalem, and in the cities of Judah, in the cities of the hill country, in the cities of the Shephelah, and in the cities of the Negeb; for I will restore their fortunes, says the LORD.'

---

[42] Cf. 19.15; 35.17, where the evil is spoken of; the good promised (*dōbbēr*, '[I] speak') to the people is that to which vv. 37–41 allude. Cf. the similar reversal in 31.28. **[43]** Cf. v. 36. MT plur., G sing. 'say': for the land without man or beast cf. 9.10. In v. 36 the popular saying refers to the city (cf. v. 28); here it refers to the land which is more appropriate for the field buying motif. MT *haśśādeh*, 'the field': sing. as collective for land, fields. **[44]** MT *hāhār . . . hašš^epēlāh*, 'the hill country . . . the lowland': cf. Deut. 1.7; Josh. 9.1 for these technical terms describing areas of the territory according to the compass points. This listing appears in 17.26; 33.13. These two terms refer to the mountains and the lowland, i.e. to wherever there are cities in the land of Judah and Benjamin. The restoration of the fortunes (of the cities) motif is an important feature of the cycle 30–31 with its prose appendices (cf. 30.3, 18; 31.23; 33.26; also 29.14).

The heavily expanded chapter finally reflects on the significance of the story of Jeremiah's buying family land (adequately stated in v. 15). The emphasis on there being nothing that is impossible for Yahweh (vv. 17b, 27) is presumably intended to anticipate objections to the assertion that Yahweh will restore the land and the fortunes of the cities of Judah. From the standpoint of the land during the Babylonian period such a restoration must have seemed very unlikely, hence affirmations of Yahweh's power are very necessary (though they are not directly linked to the restoration motif). The oracular statement of vv. 42–44 reverses the evil brought upon the people by Yahweh and their forlorn observation of a land from which man and beast have been banished. How can there be hope in such a time? Will normal life ever return to Judah? To these questions the editors proffer the answer 'yes'. Yes: because Yahweh's great No to land and people has been reversed and he now speaks 'yes' to their hopes. But the guarantee of such positive expectations is not simply the oracles of promise but the transactions carried out by the prophet Jeremiah in the very days when the Babylonians were besieging Jerusalem. The Babylonians will not dominate the land for ever, but there will come a time when the buying and selling of land for silver will again be part of life in the land. Jeremiah's act of familial loyalty creates the future. All the things he did – signed and sealed deeds, acquired witnesses, bought land for silver – will take place when Yahweh restores the fortunes of the cities of Judah. These cities are listed in geographical regions: around Jerusalem, throughout Judah, in the highlands and the lowlands, and in the south and north (land of Benjamin). So the restoration of the fortunes of the people (cf. 30.3) includes the resumption of property deals throughout the cities of Judah (cf. 31.23), in all its territories (cf. 17.26; 33.13). These property transactions, of which Jeremiah's act is the great sign and portent, are indicative of the restoration of normal living conditions no longer subjected to foreign overlords, invasions or sieges. The frightful experiences of the cities during the sixth century will be reversed in the future. Thus Jeremiah's divinely inspired (vv. 6–8) response to his cousin's invitation to buy family land resonates beyond his own time, beyond the era of ruined cities and deserted landscapes into a future when all Judah will once again be able to move freely about their own land buying and selling property. Such images are not utopian but betoken the very stuff of community life.

33.1–13

331 The word of the LORD came to Jeremiah a second time, while he was
still shut up in the court of the guard: 2 'Thus says the LORD who made the
earth, the LORD who formed it to establish it – the LORD is his name: 3 Call
to me and I will answer you, and will tell you great and hidden things which
you have not known. 4 For thus says the LORD, the God of Israel, concerning
the houses of this city and the houses of the kings of Judah which were torn
down to make a defence against the siege mounds and before the sword: 5
The Chaldeans are coming in to fight and to fill them with the dead bodies
of men whom I shall smite in my anger and my wrath, for I have hidden
my face from this city because of all their wickedness. 6 Behold, I will bring
to it health and healing, and I will heal them and reveal to them abundance
of prosperity and security. 7 I will restore the fortunes of Judah and the
fortunes of Israel, and rebuild them as they were at first. 8 I will cleanse
them from all the guilt of their sin against me, and I will forgive all the guilt
of their sin and rebellion against me. 9 And this city shall be to me a name
of joy, a praise and a glory before all the nations of the earth who shall hear
of all the good that I do for them; they shall fear and tremble because of all
the good and all the prosperity I provide for it.

10 Thus says the LORD: In this place of which you say, "It is a waste
without man or beast," in the cities of Judah and the streets of Jerusalem
that are desolate, without man or inhabitant or beast, there shall be heard
again 11 the voice of mirth and the voice of gladness, the voice of the
bridegroom and the voice of the bride, the voices of those who sing, as they
bring thank offerings to the house of the LORD:

"Give thanks to the LORD of hosts,
for the LORD is good,
for his steadfast love endures for ever!"

For I will restore the fortunes of the land as at first, says the LORD.

12 Thus says the LORD of hosts: In this place which is waste, without
man or beast, and in all of its cities, there shall again be habitations of
shepherds resting their flocks. 13 In the cities of the hill country, in the cities
of the Shephelah, and in the cities of the Negeb, in the land of Benjamin,

the places about Jerusalem, and in the cities of Judah, flocks shall again pass under the hands of the one who counts them, says the LORD.'

[MT 33] = G 40. **[1]** MT *šēnīt*, 'a second time': i.e. subsequent to the word of 32.6–8 or 32.26, thus making 33.1–13 (a series of such divine words) a supplement to 32 (cf. Thiel 1981, 37); cf. 1.13 for *šēnīt*. 32.2b; 33.1b are redactional notes providing the same setting in the life of Jeremiah for 32–33, but much of the material presupposes a devastated Judah and Jerusalem (e.g. 32.43; 33.10, 12), hence the siege context is thematic rather than historical (cf. Rudolph, 215). **[2]** MT *ʿōśāh yhwh yōṣēr ʾōtah* 'who made it, Yahweh who formed it': G *poiōn gēn kai plassōn autēn*, 'who made the earth and formed it'. Rudolph, 214 reads *ʿōśeh wᵉhāyāh*, 'who made and it is there', and *ʾōtiyyāh*, 'what is to come' (cf. Isa. 41.23; 44.7): 'what has happened', i.e. the past, and 'what is to come', i.e. the future. 'Yahweh is his name': cf. 32.18b. **[3]** MT *ūbᵉṣurōt*, 'and inaccessible (things)': *bṣr* is often used of cities to describe their fortified impregnability (cf. 15.20, where it refers to a wall); a few mss read *nṣr*, 'guarded, secret', cf. Isa. 48.6 *ūnᵉṣurōt wᵉlōʾ yᵉdaʿtām*, 'and hidden things which you have not known', virtually the same phrase as here. **[4f.]** MT *malkē*, 'kings of': G *basileōs*, 'king of', cf. 22.18, 21. MT seems to suggest that there were many royal palaces in the city. The text of vv. 4b, 5a is hopelessly corrupt in MT (cf. Bright, 296; Rudolph, 214): lit. 'which were torn down to the siege ramparts and to the sword 5 coming to fight the Chaldaeans and to fill them (with) the corpses . . .'. G lacks 'coming' and reads 'bulwarks, ramparts' for 'sword', but otherwise is the same as MT. Some description of fortifying the city against the siege may be behind the present text (cf. Isa. 22.10), but without rewriting the whole piece coherence must remain lost. **[5]** MT *mēhāʿîr hazzōʾt*, 'from this city': G *ap' autōn*, 'from them' = *mēhem*. The hiding of the divine face is a metaphor of anger and destruction, of Yahweh's withdrawal of his protection and favour cf. Isa. 8.17; 54.8; 64.6. **[6]** MT *ʾᵃrukāh*, 'healing': lit. 'lengthening', i.e. the new flesh which replaces the wound; cf. 8.22; 30.17; Isa. 58.8; used of repairing the temple (II Chron. 24.13) and rebuilding the walls of Jerusalem (Neh. 4.1 [EV 2]). Some Vrs read *lāhem*, 'to them', i.e. the houses for *lāh*, 'to her', i.e. the city. MT *ʿᵃteret*, 'abundance': this form only appears here (from *ʿtr*, 'be abundant'); G *kai poiēsō*, 'and I will make', suggests *wᵉʿābadtī* (an Aramaism cf. 7.29 G). Duhm, 272, reads *ʿᵃtidōt*, 'treasures' (cf. Isa. 10.13); Rudolph, 214, suggests *ʿēt rewaḥ*, 'a time of refreshment' (cf. BHS); cf. *ʿᵃṭeret* 'crown of (peace and truth)'. MT *šālōm weʾᵉmet*, 'peace and truth': if treated as a hendiadys, 'true peace', 'genuine well-being'. **[7]** Some G mss have 'Jerusalem' for 'Israel', which fits the context of 32–33 better (cf. Rudolph). **[8]** K *lkwl*; Q *lᵉkol*, 'all': K a scribal error. **[9]** MT *wᵉhāyᵉtāh*, 'and it will be': i.e. she, the city, will be . . . cf. v. 6. MT *lī lᵉšēm śāśōn*, 'to me a name of joy': G *eis euphrosunēn*, 'for joy'; NEB 'This city will win me a name', deleting 'joy' as an addition. Volz, 308, reads the consonants *lylšm* as an abbreviation for Jerusalem, followed by Rudolph (cf. Bright, 292): 'Jerusalem shall be a source of joy.' MT *'ōtām*, 'them': i.e. the citizens of Jerusalem rather than the nations; BHS deletes or would read *'ōtāh*, 'her', cf. *lāh*, 'to her', at the end of the verse. **[10]** MT *bammāqōm-hazzeh*, 'in this place': i.e. Jerusalem. Cf. 32.36, 43. **[11]** Cf. 7.34; 16.9; 25.10. MT *tōdāh*, 'praise': G *dōra*, 'gifts'; cf. 17.26 for the bringing of thank-offerings (*tōdāh*) to the (rebuilt) temple. The liturgical chant of v. 11b is formulaic (cf. Ps. 106.1; 107.1; 118.1; 136). Cf. Job 42.10 for the motif of 'restoring the fortunes', though there Job is given twice as much as he had before; here inevitably the land can only be restored 'as at first' – nothing has been lost by its terrible destruction! **[13]** Cf. 17.26; 32.44; the formal listing of territorial areas has a different purpose in each reference (e.g. temple offerings, the buying of land, the pasturing of flocks) and a different order of areas. MT *'al-yᵉdēmōneh*, 'under the hands of him who counts': i.e. the tally-keeper (Bright, 296) who counted the sheep returning to the fold at night; whatever its precise meaning the phrase indicates a period when sheep would safely graze and always be accounted for by the shepherds.

If the expansion of 32 shows much Deuteronomistic editorial influence, the supplement to it in 33 is a post-Deuteronomistic postscript to the cycle of salvation expectations in 30–31 (cf. Thiel 1981, 37). This supplement is made up of two collections of oracular pieces, one dealing with the reconstruction of Jerusalem and the land (vv. 2–9, 10–11, 12–13) and the other devoted to the revival of the Davidic dynasty (vv. 14–16, 17–18, 19–22, 23–26).

33 is linked to 32 by means of a redactional note which places Jeremiah's reception of the divine word in the same situation as that of his buying Hanamel's field (v. 1; 32.2, 8). However unsuitable such a context may be for this material, it indicates the editorial concern to pack all the positive elements into the siege period, so that even before the city had fallen its future rise should be announced. The restoration of commercial deals in the land (32) and the rebuilding of Jerusalem and the cities of Judah (33) are underwritten by allusions to Yahweh as creator (e.g. 32.17; 33.2). Thus creation and redemption are bound together (cf. the fusing of these two motifs in Second Isaiah). In both supplements the figure of Jeremiah is developed in ways different from other strands in the tradition, e.g. he makes lengthy prayers typical of the post-exilic period (32.17–23) and he is invited to call upon the deity for the revelation of great mysteries (33.3; cf. the figure of Daniel to whom Yahweh reveals

such matters as are hidden from others concerning the future). In 33.4–9 the inaccessible things concern the rebuilding of a Jerusalem partially knocked down to fight off the Chaldaeans (assuming vv. 4b–5a refer to the siege defences project) and destroyed by the enemy. The future holds healing, i.e. rebuilding, for the city: a metaphor used in the poems to describe precisely the one thing lacking in the community (cf. 8.22). In the restoration of the fortunes of Judah and Jerusalem (Israel in present texts) the rebuilding of the nation will reproduce the conditions prevailing at the beginning of its history (contrast 32.31). And in this restoration sin and guilt will be cleansed and forgiven (cf. 31.34).

The modern reader may feel that the destruction of city and land, the death of so many people and the deportation of various citizens would constitute both punishment and cleansing-forgiveness, especially as the guilty generations all would have been dead when this reconstruction began. However, these sermons and meditations on restoration should not be read as realistic descriptions of social history, but as theological reflections on abstract notions which have to do with cultic matters in the period of the second temple. Only with the forgiveness of the past and the cleansing of guilt and rebellion could the renewed city and temple become again a place which would yield joy, praise and glory to Yahweh. The various generations between the events of 597–87 and the speaker's period (cf. 'this very day', 32.20, 31) are invariably absent in the tradition's handling of destruction and restoration (cf. 2.9; 7.25–26; 32.21–23). So the generation of the reconstruction period requires forgiveness and cleansing for the crimes of their distant ancestors (cf. 31.32–34). When the past is completely reversed then the renewed community will become a repository of Yahweh's goodness. The bounty enjoyed in this period will shake and terrify the nations, and thus will the new age reverse that period when the Chaldaeans were breaking down the walls of Jerusalem and butchering its inhabitants. Yahweh's restoration of the fortunes of Judah and Jerusalem in the future will be everything the present is not – hence the setting of the material in the period of the siege.

Two further oracular statements embellish this reconstruction expectation: vv. 10–11 are a variation on 32.36, 43 or, perhaps, one of three treatments of a popular saying about the desolation of city (32.36) and land (32.43); vv. 12–13 also deal with the same view of the city or land as a wasteland, but envisage a return of shepherds and flocks. These future expectations are based on reversals of the past (and contemporary?) experiences of the community. Where once no human or animal sounds were heard (cf. 9.10), now shall be heard all the normal sounds of human activity, typified by weddings (cf. the merrymaking of the maidens and young men in 31.4, 13) and liturgical processions to the temple. The resurgence of these noisy human encounters reverses the note of their cessation in 7.34; 16.9; 25.10. In a few lines denoting sexual activity and worship v. 11 reconstructs the communal life of the nation without expansive details of rebuilding the temple (contrast Ezek. 40–48). The sounds of animals throughout the land are implied (without articulation) in vv. 12–13, when the culture will become once again a thriving pastoral civilization. Once all the cities are rebuilt and reinhabited in the listed districts (cf. 17.26; 32.44), pastoral life will thrive again. These are all simple images of the restoration of a way of life disrupted and destroyed by the Babylonian incursions into Palestine. They are neither profound nor utopian, but represent the return to normal urban and rural life after the disappearance of the Babylonians in the Persian age. The loss of stability and security after the emergence of Babylon in 605 is apparent from these hopes about the future, and most of the elements in 30–33 provide a very simple but clear meaning for the dominant motif of 'the restoration of the fortunes of Judah' (i.e. Israel).

33.14–26

14 'Behold, the days are coming, says the LORD, when I will fulfil the
promise I made to the house of Israel and the house of Judah. 15 In those
days and at that time I will cause a righteous Branch to spring forth for
David; and he shall execute justice and righteousness in the land. 16 In
those days Judah will be saved and Jerusalem will dwell securely. And this
is the name by which it will be called: "The LORD is our righteousness."

17 For thus says the LORD: David shall never lack a man to sit on the
throne of the house of Israel, 18 and the Levitical priests shall never lack a
man in my presence to offer burnt offerings, to burn cereal offerings, and to
make sacrifices for ever.'

19 The word of the LORD came to Jeremiah: 20 'Thus says the LORD: If
you can break my covenant with the day and my covenant with the night,
so that day and night will not come at their appointed time, 21 then also
my covenant with David my servant may be broken, so that he shall not

have a son to reign on his throne, and my covenant with the Levitical priests my ministers. 22 As the host of heaven cannot be numbered and the sands of the sea cannot be measured, so I will multiply the descendants of David my servant, and the Levitical priests who minister to me.

23 The word of the LORD came to Jeremiah: 24 'Have you not observed what these people are saying, "The LORD has rejected the two families which he chose"? Thus they have despised my people so that they are no longer a nation in their sight. 25 Thus says the LORD: If I have not established my covenant with day and night and the ordinances of heaven and earth, 26 then I will reject the descendants of Jacob and David my servant and will not choose one of his descendants to rule over the seed of Abraham, Isaac, and Jacob. For I will restore their fortunes, and will have mercy upon them.'

G lacks vv. 14–26. They should be regarded as an addition to the second edition of Jeremiah (MT). Cf. 23.5–6, of which vv. 14–16 are a development. **[14]** MT *'et-haddābār haṭṭōb*, 'the good word': i.e. the promise cf. 29.10; this may refer to 23.5–6, though curiously Israel appears in 23.6 but not here in vv. 15–16 (see on 23.5–6). **[15]** Cf. 23.5, where the language of v. 14, is used, hence the terms here are different: *'aṣmīaḥ . . . ṣemaḥ ṣᵉdāqāh*, 'I will cause to sprout . . . a true shoot'; word-play on *ṣmḥ* lacking in 23.5 ('and he shall reign as king and deal wisely' does not appear in 33.14–16; though many mss add it). **[16]** MT *bayyāmīm hāhēm*, 'in those days': 23.6 'in his days'. MT *wirūšālaim tiškōn*, 'and Jerusalem will dwell': 23.6 *wᵉyiśrā'ēl yiškōn*, 'and Israel will dwell'; in spite of Israel in v. 14 the use of Jerusalem here reflects the modification of 23.6. In 23.6 the branch is named using a pun on Zedekiah's name (appendix to royal cycle), in 33.16 the context of the rebuilding of Jerusalem (vv. 6–13) may have infleunced the text's development into a statement about the name of the city. A few mss, S read *šᵉmō*, 'his name' (cf. 23.6); Rudolph, 216, inserts *haššēm*, 'the name', following G^O,L^, Theod, V (cf. BHS). Cf. Ezek. 48.35 for a different name of the city (*yhwh šāmmāh*, 'Yahweh is there'). The significance of the phrase 'this (is the name) which one will call her "Yahweh is our vindication" ' probably refers to the reconstruction of land and city, as much as the reemergence of the Davidic dynasty. MT may represent the transition of the name from the branch to the city. **[17]** MT *lō'-yikkārēt lᵉdāwid*, 'there shall not be cut off for David': i.e. there shall never be lacking for David an occupant of the throne; note 'house of Israel', where Israel stands for Judah and Israel (v. 14). **[18]** MT *wᵉlakkōhᵃnīm halᵉwiyyim*, 'and for the priests, the levites': i.e. the levitical priests, a typically Deuteronomistic phrase (Deut. 17.9, 18; 18.1; 24.8; 27.9; Josh. 3.3; 8.33; cf. Ezek. 43.19; 44.15). The same idiom (*lō'-yikkārēt*) is used of the appointment of priests as for the occupant of the throne. **[19]** Cf. v. 23; 32.26; 35.12; 43.8 for this shortened form of the reception of the divine word formula (slight expansion in 43.8). **[20]** MT *'im-tāpērū 'et-bᵉrītī hayyōm*, 'if you could break my *bᵉrīt* of the day': for this unusual grammatical form of an absolute with suffix in a construct chain cf. MT Lev. 26.42; Num. 25.12; v. 21 uses the normal form *bᵉrītī . . . 'et-dāwid*, 'my *bᵉrīt* . . . with David'. The creation of the day and night by Yahweh (cf. Gen. 1.5; 8.22) is here described by the term *bᵉrīt*, indicating its meaning as a fixed obligation rather than an agreement between two parties (cf. the fixed orders of 31.35–36). **[21]** MT *wᵉ'et-halᵉwiyyim hakkōhᵃnīm*, 'and with the levites, the priests': a transposition of the normal order (cf. vv. 18, 22; either of which should be read here, cf. BHS). **[22]** Cf. Gen. 22.17 for similar images of the stars and sand as figures of the multitudinous descendants of Abraham; here they apply to the royal and priestly houses. MT *mᵉšārᵉtē 'ōtī*, 'who minister to me': governs only the priests; Rudolph, 218, reads *mᵉšārᵉtay 'ittō*, 'my ministers with him' (BHS). **[24]** The two families here presumably refer to Israel and Judah (v. 14), though it is possible that David and Levi (vv. 17–22) are intended, or even Jacob and David (v. 26). MT *lipnēhem*, 'before them'; who are 'them'? The same question may be asked of *hā'ām hazzeh*, 'this people', i.e. those who acknowledge that Yahweh has rejected the two families. Perhaps they are Jews who agree with the critique offered by Jer. 2–20 and who are attacked here by supporters of a different ideology. **[25]** Cf. v. 20. MT *bᵉrītī yōmām*, 'my *bᵉrīt* by day': perhaps *yōm*, 'day' (BHS on vv. 20, 25); Rudolph follows Duhm, 277, in reading *bārā'tī*, 'did I not create day?'. MT *ḥuqqōt*, 'the ordinance of': cf. 31.35, 36. **[26]** MT *mōšᵉlīm*, 'ruling': plur. i.e. rulers; G^O.L^, Theod, S read sing. K *'šwb*; Q *'āšīb*, 'I will restore': cf. 32.46 for conclusion of supplement (see also 33.11; 49.39). The phrase *dāwid 'abdī*, 'David my servant' (vv. 21.26) should be compared to 'Nebuchadrezzar my servant' (25.9; 27.6).

Notably absent from the future expectations listed in the cycle of 30–31 and its supplements is any detailed account of the restoration of the royal house of David (touched on in 30.9, 21). When the fortunes of Judah are restored by Yahweh, peace and prosperity will descend upon the land and its cities, but what about the royal and priestly houses? The expectations hint at the rebuilt temple and the services which will take place there (cf. 30.20–21; 31.23, 40; 33.11), and assert the divine forgiveness and cleansing (31.34; 33.8). But no clear statement appears about the revival of the royal house (apart from 30.9) or the organization of the cult. It is hardly surprising, then, that these lacunae should be made good in a supplement to the cycle and its supplements in the second edition of the tradition (MT).

The additional supplement provides four oracular statements

which assert the revival of the house of David in conjunction with the levitical priesthood as *permanent* elements of social organization in the future. Never again will David's dynasty lack an occupant on the throne (or, presumably, suffer the humiliation of deposed kings and puppet client kings as happened during the Babylonian period). Never again will the temple be destroyed (implicit in v. 18) nor will the levitical priests be excluded from sacral duties there (cf. Ezek. 44.15–27). The future envisaged here is one ruled over by a Davidic figure on the throne (the word 'king' is not used, but *mōlēk*, 'reign', is in v. 21; cf. 23.5) and a levitical priest officiating in the temple. Permanent royal leadership and perpetual levitical sacrifice will characterize this future. The order of that permanency is given in terms of the created orders of day and night (cf. 31.35–36) and guaranteed by means of the fertility of the royal and priestly houses – they will multiply the way the legends of the patriarchal stories envisage the nation increasing. These hopes (vv. 14–22; 23.5–6; 30.9) represent a minority report in the Jeremiah tradition and reflect sources in the Persian period which still hoped for a revival of the Davidic house. They were unsuccessful, though the expectations about a levitical organization of the temple cult reflect the reality of the Chronicler's time (perhaps he also entertained hopes of a restoration of the Davidic monarchy, cf. Williamson 1977a).

The devastations of the sixth century persuaded some people that Yahweh had rejected the two families (cf. Amos 3.2), but the saying to this effect (v. 24) would be reversed when Yahweh restored the fortunes of the nation. The final word in the cycle and its supplements is *wᵉriḥamtīm*, 'and I will have mercy upon them'. That divine mercy will reverse all the devastations of the past and revive the destroyed institutions in a new age when the seed of Abraham, Isaac, and Jacob will enjoy all the expectations ever entertained for the nation. Only in Yahweh's mercy could that happen.

34.1–7

34[1] The word which came to Jeremiah from the LORD, when Nebuchadrezzar king of Babylon and all his army and all the kingdoms of the earth under his dominion and all the peoples were fighting against Jerusalem and all of its cities: 2 'Thus says the LORD, the God of Israel: Go and speak to Zedekiah king of Judah and say to him, "Thus says the LORD: Behold, I am giving this city into the hand of the king of Babylon, and he shall burn it with fire. 3 You shall not escape from his hand, but shall surely be captured and delivered into his hand; you shall see the king of Babylon eye to eye and speak with him face to face; and you shall go to Babylon." 4 Yet hear the word of the LORD, O Zedekiah king of Judah! Thus says the LORD concerning you: "You shall not die by the sword. 5 You shall die in peace. And as spices were burned for your fathers, the former kings who were before you, so men shall burn spices for you and lament for you, saying, 'Alas, lord!' " For I have spoken the word, says the LORD.'

6 Then Jeremiah the prophet spoke all these words to Zedekiah king of Judah, in Jerusalem, 7 when the army of the king of Babylon was fighting against Jerusalem and against all the cities of Judah that were left, Lachish and Azekah; for these were the only fortified cities of Judah that remained.

[MT 34] = G 41. **[1]** The formulaic reception of the divine word introductory note here is of the expanded kind which includes the occasion of its reception, cf. 21.1; 32.1; 34.8; 35.1; 40.1 (simple form, i.e. lacking occasion, 7.1; 11.1; 18.1; 30.1). Cf. 21.1–2; 32.2; 37.3–5 for the siege and variations on this encounter between Jeremiah and Zedekiah; v. 7 gives further details of the occasion. G *kai pasa hē gē archēs autou*, 'and all the country of his dominion': MT expanded by 'and all the peoples', 'kingdoms'. These represent the military contingents from the subjugated states of the empire. MT *wᵉʿal-kol-ʿārehā*, 'and against all her cities': i.e. the towns of Judah associated with Jerusalem, cf. 19.15; G *kai epi pasas tas poleis Iouda*, 'and against all the cities of Judah'. **[2]** 'Go and speak to Zedekiah': the only version of the Jeremiah encounter with Zedekiah series of stories which has Jeremiah initiating the contact (by divine command). MT *hinᵉnī nōtēn ʾet*, 'look, I am giving': G *paradosei paradothēsetai*, 'shall certainly be delivered', cf. 32.28. G has *kai sullēmpsetai autēn*, 'and he shall take it' (= *ūlᵉkādāh*) after 'the king of Babylon', cf. 32.3. Rudolph, 218 treats 'and he shall burn it with fire' as a *vaticinium ex eventu* added to the text. **[3]** Cf. 32.4; 39.5–7; Ezek. 17.11–21. Zedekiah's rebellion against his overlord is the reason for this personal confrontation with the king of Babylon. Rudolph regards 'and you shall go to Babylon' as a later *vaticinium ex eventu* which conflicts with the death notice of v 5. G* lacks 'and his mouth shall speak with your mouth' (BHS). **[4]** G lacks 'you shall not die by the sword'. Bright, 216, reads this verse as a conditional offer that if Zedekiah heeds Yahweh's word and surrenders, then Nebuchadrezzar will spare his life (cf. 38.17–18); cf. Rudolph, 220. **[5]** MT *bᵉšālōm tāmūt*, 'you will die in peace': hardly captures the essence of Zedekiah's experiences at Riblah, where he witnesses the execution of his sons, is blinded and taken to Babylon (39.5–7). Rudolph transposes 'in Jerusalem' from the end of v. 6 (where it is superfluous) to here and reads *bᵉšālōm* as *bīrūšālāim*. The promise to Zedekiah then becomes one of death in his own city rather than Babylon. For the mourning rites specified here cf. 22.18; II Chron. 16.14; 21.19. The burial honours afforded the king confirm the view that interment in Jerusalem is intended. MT *ūkᵉmiśrᵉpōt ʾᵃbōtekā*, 'and as the burnings of your fathers': i.e. the kindling of fires for your ancestors (cf. NEB); spices are not necessarily implied by the term used (cf. RSV, JPSB, Bright, 214). G *eklausan . . . klausontai*, 'they wept . . . they shall weep': a free translation of mourning rites (cf. BHS). **[6]** 'Jeremiah *the prophet*': cf. 32.2; 'the prophet' is lacking in G. Bright, 214, deletes 'the prophet', 'of Judah' (with G) as redundant. **[7]** G lacks 'which were left': G^A = MT. If only Lachish and Azekah were left, the campaign must have been nearing its climax; cf. Lachish Letters IV on the fate of Azekah (Pritchard 1969, 321–2). On the relation of the Lachish ostraca and 34.7 cf. Migsch 1981, 246–53 (with analysis of vv. 1–7 on 99–111).

The theme of Jeremiah and Zedekiah during the Babylonian campaign against city and land appears in a variety of different forms in the tradition: a delegation sent by Zedekiah to Jeremiah (21.1–7; 37.3–10), a summons of Jeremiah to an interview with the king (37.16–21; 38.14–27), and a divine sending of Jeremiah *to* Zedekiah (34.1–7). The Babylonian presence is a constant of the stories, though in 37.5 it has withdrawn temporarily, but the situation of Jeremiah varies considerably. He may be at large somewhere in the city (probably the temple if he can be found with such ease), in prison for the offence of speaking in such terms to the king (32.3–5), secretly summoned from the cells (37.16–17), or summoned from constraint to the temple (38.13–14). The response to the delegation is always a word of unmitigated destruction (21.6; 37.8–10), but in his encounters with the king Jeremiah allows for the possibility that Zedekiah may save his own life, and that of his house, by surrendering to the Babylonians (38.17–23; cf. 34.4–5; but not in 37.17).

These variations on a theme indicate how a few motifs may be used in the tradition in a number of different ways to put across certain theological perspectives. The absolute word of judgment against the city and the contingent possibility of survival are combined in these stories in accordance with the pattern of absolute-contingent elements used in the prose sections of the tradition (e.g. 7.1–15; 21.3–7, 8–10; 25.3–7, 9–11; 26.2–6; 36). Hence the various accounts of Jeremiah's encounter with Zedekiah, or his delegation, shift between a declaration of Zedekiah's inevitable fate (along with that of the city and citizens) at the hands of the Babylonians and an affirmation of the possibility of king and city avoiding that fate.

Intransigence in the face of the enemy will lead to the destruction of everybody (21.6–7), whereas surrender to the princes of the king of Babylon will entail survival for city, king and his house (38.17). The peculiarity of 34.2–5, apart from its distinctive element of the prophet being sent by Yahweh to the king rather than receiving a delegation from the king or a summons to speak to him, is its combination of an announcement of the fate of city and king with an oracle of deliverance addressed to Zedekiah (vv. 2–3, 4–5). An editor has fused together two halves of quite discrete pieces to produce a strange amalgam of material which, as it stands, requires substantial rewriting in order to become coherent.

The two elements of vv. 2–3, 4–5 formally contradict each other. In the first piece the burning of the city is announced and Zedekiah's deportation to Babylon after confrontation with the Babylonian king is asserted. In the second oracular statement a personal word of reassurance is addressed to Zedekiah (v. 4) in which the king is assured of a proper and conventional royal burial in his own land. He will not be killed in battle but will die in peace (*bᵉšālōm*, i.e. well-being) and his body will be accorded the full honours of a royal funeral (cf. II Chron. 16.14; contrast 22.18–19). Such a funeral ceremony could only take place in his own land (contrast the fate of Shallum 22.11–12) and hardly at the termination of a siege. If 38.17 were to be read here it could be argued that vv. 4–5 imply a call to surrender with a promise of a quiet life leading eventually to a traditional burial. The present text of 34.4–5 does not make that connection but in order to make sense of what are contradictory accounts some such background explanation is required.

The prediction of the death of kings and their subsequent obsequies would appear to be a problematical feature of certain biblical traditions. The contrast between 34.4–5 and 39.5–7 is considerable because by no stretch of the imagination can Zedekiah's fate be described as 'dying in peace'. The term *šālōm* cannot be said to cover the experiences of witnessing the execution of one's sons, the blinding of oneself, deportation in fetters to a foreign land, and one's eventual death there (52.10–11). It is also highly unlikely that such a wretched prisoner should then be accorded the full state funeral honours of a foreign country after his death in prison. Thus the oracle of 34. 4–5 must be regarded as an utterance with reference to peaceful demise in Jerusalem and read *as if* it contained an *implicit* conditional force (cf. Bright, 216) which would contrast it to vv. 2–3. This is not a necessary reading of the text, because the two oracles may be understood as contradictory on the grounds that predictions about the fate of kings are problematic in the Hebrew Bible. Thus the prophetess Huldah predicts a gathering to his grave in peace (*bešālōm*) for king Josiah (II Kings 22.20), whereas he was slain by Pharaoh Neco at Megiddo (II Kings 23.29). Problems of interpreting the prediction of Jehoiakim's lack of proper burial in 22.18–19 have been noted already, so allowance must be made for a considerable gap between conventional oracles of the death and burial of kings and the actual fate of those kings. The combination of two discrete oracles in 34.2–5 without adequate editing to relate them to each other (along the lines of 38.17–18) provides the exegete with a range of possible explanations, but only the pattern of stories about Jeremiah in relation to Zedekiah may justify an exegetical approach.

The oracular material is enveloped in contextualizing notes about the siege of Jerusalem under the king of Babylon (vv. 1, 6–7). Nebuchadrezzar's campaign in the land of Judah had reached the point where only two other towns, Lachish and Azekah, remained uncaptured. Thus the fate of Jerusalem was virtually sealed. Once those towns were taken the Babylonians could devote their whole attention to breaching Jerusalem and then confront king Zedekiah with the consequences of his breach of vassalage to Nebuchadrezzar (see on 39.5). Hence the urgency of Jeremiah's commission to speak to Zedekiah. Time was short and the king's fate hung in the balance.

34.8–22

8 The word which came to Jeremiah from the LORD, after King Zedekiah
had made a covenant with all the people in Jerusalem to make a proclamation
of liberty to them, 9 that every one should set free his Hebrew slaves, male
and female, so that no one should enslave a Jew, his brother. 10 And they
obeyed, all the princes and all the people who had entered into the covenant
that every one should set free his slave, male or female, so that they would
not be enslaved again; they obeyed and set them free. 11 But afterward they
turned around and took back the male and female slaves they had set free,
and brought them into subjection as slaves. 12 The word of the LORD came
to Jeremiah from the LORD: 13 'Thus says the LORD, the God of Israel: I
made a covenant with your fathers when I brought them out of the land of
Egypt, out of the house of bondage, saying, 14 "At the end of six years each
of you must set free the fellow Hebrew who has been sold to you and has

served you six years; you must set him free from your service." But your fathers did not listen to me or incline their ears to me. 15 You recently repented and did what was right in my eyes by proclaiming liberty, each to his neighbour, and you made a covenant before me in the house which is called by my name; 16 but then you turned around and profaned my name when each of you took back his male and female slaves, whom you had set free according to their desire, and you brought them into subjection to be your slaves. 17 Therefore, thus says the LORD: You have not obeyed me by proclaiming liberty, every one to his brother and to his neighbour; behold, I proclaim to you liberty to the sword, to pestilence, and to famine, says the LORD. I will make you a horror to all the kingdoms of the earth. 18 And the men who transgressed my covenant and did not keep the terms of the covenant which they made before me, I will make like the calf which they cut in two and passed between its parts – 19 the princes of Judah, the princes of Jerusalem, the eunuchs, the priests, and all the people of the land who passed between the parts of the calf; 20 and I will give them into the hand of their enemies and into the hand of those who seek their lives. Their dead bodies shall be food for the birds of the air and the beasts of the earth. 21 And Zedekiah king of Judah, and his princes I will give into the hand of their enemies and into the hand of those who seek their lives, into the hand of the army of the king of Babylon which has withdrawn from you. 22 Behold, I will command, says the LORD, and will bring them back to this city; and they will fight against it, and take it, and burn it with fire. I will make the cities of Judah a desolation without inhabitant.'

---

[8] Cf. v. 1 for introductory formula. G lacks 'all', 'which are in Jerusalem', 'to them'. MT *liqrō' lāhem dᵉrōr*, 'to proclaim to them liberty': cf. vv. 15, 17; Isa. 61.1; Ezek. 46.17; Lev. 25.10. In Ezek. 46.17; Lev. 25.10 the use of *dᵉrōr* refers to the year of jubilee, but no such connection applies here, though Sarna 1973, 148–9, makes 588–7 a sabbatical year (cf. BDB, 204). Heb. *dᵉrōr*, 'freedom, emancipation, liberty', cf. Akk. *andurāru* (Weinfeld 1972a, 153). **[9]** MT *ḥopšīm lᵉbiltī ʿᵃbād-bām bīhūdī 'āḥīhū 'īš*, '. . . free, so that none should serve among them, of a Jew, his brother, anyone': Heb. awkward (part of this line is repeated in v. 10); cf. 22.13; 25.14 for *ʿbd b*, 'to make serve'. **[10]** MT *wayyišmᵉʿū*, 'and they obeyed': G *kai epestraphēsan*, 'and they turned' = *wayyāšūbū* (cf. v. 11). G lacks *ḥopšīm . . . wayᵉšallēḥū*, 'free, so that they would not be enslaved again; they obeyed and released'. **[11]** G lacks most of v. 11; its shorter text reads *kai eōsan autous eis paidas kai paidiskas*, 'and gave them over to be men-servants and maid-servants'. K *wykbyšwm*; Q *wayyikbᵉšūm*, 'and they subdued them': i.e. 'brought them into bondage (again)'; K represents Hiphil use, Q the more normal Qal. The uses of *šūb*, 'turn, change, repent' (vv. 11, 15, 16) should be noted. Bright, 221, relates the change of policy to the lifting of the siege (cf. vv. 21–2; 37.5); this may be implied by v. 21, but the editor has not presented the story in such terms. **[12]** Two introductory formulae are used here to indicate the reception of the divine word: 'and the word of Yahweh came to Jeremiah' + '(the word which came to Jeremiah) from Yahweh'; cf. vv. 1, 8; 33.1; 32.26; G lacks 'from Yahweh'. **[13]** Cf. 7. 22; 'out of the house of bondage', cf. Ex. 20.2; Deut. 5.6. **[14]** MT *miqqēṣ šeba' šānīm*, 'at the end of seven years': following Deut. 15.1, 12; G *hex etē*, 'six years', followed by RSV. It is *in* the seventh year (Ex. 21.2; Deut. 15.12), rather than at the end of it (Deut. 15.1), that the debt bondage comes to an end. MT *'ašer-yimmākēr lᵉkā*, 'who has been sold (or has sold himself) to you': indicates the servitude was due to debt bondage. The Deuteronomistic concluding sentence (cf. Thiel 1981, 42) about the fathers refusing to obey Yahweh (cf. 7.24, 26; 11.8), apart from being stereotypical, may indicate a tendency for the law on manumission to be ignored (cf. Mendelsohn 1949, 85–91); cf. Neh. 5.1–13. **[15]** MT *wattāšubū 'attem hayyōm watta'ᵃśū*, 'but you turned, you, today, and you did . . .': G lacks *'attem* and reads the verbs as third person plur. The use of *hayyōm*, 'today', is curious but it may be a contrast between the right action of the people *now* and the failure of the fathers *bᵉyōm*, 'on the day', when Yahweh commanded them to keep his covenant (cf. DeVries 1975, 241–3). The technical language for making a covenant *krt bᵉrīt* (cf. McCarthy 1978, 91–5) appears in vv. 8, 13, 15, 18; cf. II Kings 23.3, where king Josiah also makes a covenant. In a Deuteronomistically influenced text it is hardly surprising to find a king 'cutting' a *bᵉrīt*. Cf. 7.10, 11, 14 for 'in the house which is called by my name.' **[16]** MT *'ašer-šillaḥtem ḥopšīm lᵉnapšām*, 'whom you had set free to their desire': cf. Deut. 21.14, *wᵉšillaḥtah lᵉnapšah*, 'and you will release her to her desire'. RSV 'you shall let her go where she will'; *npš* here may mean 'to do what one wishes' or 'to go where one wishes'. Though where the released slaves could have gone after Zedekiah had freed them during a siege is a moot point (to their own land after Nebuchadrezzar's withdrawal? Cf. v. 21; 37.11–12). They must have remained in, or close to, the city for them to have been taken back into debt bondage! G* lacks 'and you brought them into subjection to be'. **[17]** A word-play on *dᵉrōr*: you did not proclaim *dᵉrōr*, 'freedom', to your brother (G only has one variant here); look, I am proclaiming *dᵉrōr* to sword, pestilence and famine (a dominant triad in the prose sections of the tradition). K *lzw'h*; Q *lᵉza'ᵃwāh*, 'for a horror': cf. 15.4; 24.9; 29.18 where the same phrase appears. **[18]** MT *wᵉnātattī 'et-hā'ᵃnāšīm . . . hā'ēgel 'ašer kārᵉtū lišᵉnayim wayya'bᵉrū bēn bᵉtārāyw*, 'and I will make the men . . . the calf which they cut in two and passed between its parts': EVV, Ehrlich 1912, 331, read *kā'ēgel*, 'like the calf'; this strange statement may mean that the deity will treat the people like the animal they cut up, i.e. kill them. Driver 1937–38, 121–2, alters *lᵉpānāy* to *lipnē*, 'like', i.e. 'like the calf'. Here the ritual is an acted-out curse where the animal is a substitute for the parties to the *bᵉrīt*, and those who breach it suffer the same fate (cf. Rudolph, 225; McCarthy 1978, 94; Weinfeld 1972a, 102–4). It reflects a ceremony of self-cursing (Rudolph); cf. Gen. 15.7–18 for a similar ritual of cutting up an animal and passing between the pieces in the making of a *b^erît*. Bright, 220, transposes 'the young bull' after 'they cut' and makes v. 20 the continuation of the main verb (*ntn*). G quite different here: *epoiēsan ergazesthai autō*, '(which) they made to serve it', i.e. (presumably) to sacrifice the calf, a rather vague rendering of MT *krtw . . . btryw*. Whether G did not understand the ritual alluded to in MT, confused the two occurrences of *krtw*, found the ceremony offensive or had a Hebrew text which lacked any reference to the calf practice is a moot point. G (= *'ašer 'āb^edû lišrātô*) may point to a reading of the phrase as an allusion to the golden calf incident, but this is unlikely (cf. Giesebrecht, 192). **[19]** G has a shorter text than MT: 'the princes of Judah, and the powerful men, and the priests, and the people'. MT *hassārisîm*, 'officials': not necessarily 'eunuchs', cf. JPSB, 'the officials'; 29.2; 38.7; 52.25. MT *w^ekōl 'am hā'āreṣ*, 'and all the people of the land': hardly the rabble or peasants but the landed gentry who might have possessed debt slaves; cf. 1.18 where 'its princes, its priests and the people of the land' may refer to the leading classes of society. **[20]** MT *w^enātattî 'ôtām*, 'and I will give them': refers back to the beginning of v. 18, with 'them' identified in vv. 18a, 19. G lacks 'and into the hand of those who seek their lives': for the phrase cf. 21.7. Cf. 7.33; 16.4; 19.7b for v. 20b; also Deut. 28.26. **[21]** G lacks 'and into the hand of those who seek their lives'. MT *hā'ōlîm mē'alêkem*, 'who are going up from you': i.e. 'withdrawing', cf. 21.2. Only vv. 21–22 provide a setting for the *b^erît* ceremony (cf. vv. 6–7, which are hardly suitable for what follows). **[22]** A combination of 37.8 and 9.11b.

David 1948; Lemche 1976; Sarna 1973

The word of salvation to Zedekiah (34.4–5) is followed by a Deuteronomistically edited attack on him in relation to a specific ritual act which the king, and his officials, has failed to carry through to its proper and permanent conclusion. Thus the word of assurance to the king – fulfilled in the going up of the Babylonians from the city (v. 21) – is arrested and changed to the command of destruction. Such may be the purport of this strange tale of the royal edict which the leading classes failed to sustain by subsequent public actions.

The king's proclamation of freedom to the slaves is a story unique in biblical traditions (cf. Neh. 5.1–13, where Nehemiah the governor persuades the nobles and officials to return to the people the mortgaged properties, goods and interest charges they have exacted from them). It betrays the Deuteronomists' interest in the making and breaking of *bᵉrīt*, and relates the destruction of the city of Jerusalem to the abrogation of this particular *bᵉrīt* (cf. 17.19–27, where the burning of Jerusalem is a punishment for breaking sabbath regulations). In a tradition where so many poems denounce the community for incorrigible corruption and prose sermons harangue the people about the nation's long history of idolatry and rebellion against Yahweh, these specific examples of what caused Jerusalem's destruction are redundant as well as difficult to explain. They appear to be midrash-type explanations added to the tradition which reflect the exegetical activity of communities in the Persian period rather than accounts of historical events prior to the fall of Jerusalem. As such they use the catastrophe of a previous age to underline the importance of keeping sabbath or ceremonial agreements between people.

The grounds for this interpretative approach to vv. 8–22 are manifold. In the midst of a terrible siege, with most of the outlying towns devastated (cf. vv. 6–7), why should the king and his nobles suddenly decide to liberate their slaves? Many different explanations have been offered by various exegetes: for military reasons (e.g. David, Rudolph); out of self-interest so as not to have to feed them (cf. Volz, 318; Duhm, 280); as an act of repentance (cf. v. 15; Weiser, 312); because it was the sabbatical year and, besides, an Egyptian force had relieved the siege temporarily (cf. v. 21; 37.5; Sarna). This appearance of a relief force from Egypt may have occasioned the Babylonian withdrawal, thereby allowing the leading classes to rescind their agreement (Sarna, 144). Many such rationalizing explanations may be provided to make good the absence of an editorial account of *why* Zedekiah should behave so out of character (in terms of the Jeremiah tradition cf. 38.19, 24–27) in the middle of the Babylonian onslaught. But they fail to carry conviction because they read the story as historical rather than as midrashic (Duhm treats vv. 12–22 as midrash and the product of the later supplementer of the tradition). If the community's fathers had not practised the manumission rules (v. 14), why should Zedekiah's generation suddenly institute them during a time of war? Where would the slaves have gone once they were released? What if they had refused to go, on the grounds that they preferred to stay with their masters (cf. Ex. 21.5–6; Deut. 15.16–17)? What space of time had elapsed between the making of the *bᵉrīt* and the turning (*šūb*) of the leading citizens to renege on it? What were the freed people doing during that period? The lull in the siege caused by the withdrawal of the Babylonians is represented as the occasion for Jeremiah to leave the city and head for home (37.11–13); would the newly released slaves have done the same? Did the ruling citizens lavish on their erstwhile slaves the bounty the law demanded of them (Deut. 15.13–14) and, if they did (what kind of *b^erît* based on Deut. 15.12–18 could have avoided providing such compensation?), where did they acquire such provisions during a siege?

Many questions, no answers! The text offers no explanations nor the kind of information which would permit the careful exegete to recreate the events behind the story. Yet the questions must be asked in order to justify a different reading of the account and to explain why the exegete must view sceptically the temptation to read the story as if it were to be taken literally. As the story appears in its edited form in vv. 8–22 it is an amalgam of various strands and motifs. It uses the ruling of Deut. 15.12 but read in terms of Deut. 15.1, so that a specific regulation about individual debt slaves becomes a general proclamation of liberty to *all* slaves *at the same time*. Behind this confusion of regulations there may be some notion of a sabbatical year or even the year of jubilee (cf. Lev. 25.10, 25–28; Ezek. 46.17; Lemche), but not in any coherent form. The freeing of the slaves may be explained by modern exegetes in terms of *Realpolitik*, which would account for the act of general liberation, but the editor attributes it to the law on the release of slaves whose debt has been paid off by six years of servitude. These are two very different things. No connection with sabbatical or jubilee years is made by the redaction of the text, though vague notions of these (theoretical?) institutions may not be far from that process (depending upon the social setting of the editors of these midrashic elements in the Jeremiah tradition). The *b^erît* ceremony is represented as a temple ritual (v. 15), though the regulations for releasing slaves have no specifications for a cultic setting of the rite (except for those slaves who do not wish to go free! Ex. 21.6). Here a parallel with Josiah's *b^erît*-making in the temple should be noted (II Kings 23.1–3) and an explanation found for the general nature of the act. Like king Josiah, king Zedekiah also made a *b^erît*. He, too, made it with *all* the people (v. 8 MT; II Kings 23.3). The similarities end there, but if 34.8–22 is midrashic at all, it is so because so much of the story is made up of allusions to and citations of other writings on the subject of slaves and their release and from the Deuteronomistic corpus. In v. 9 the motivation of the proclamation of liberty to the slaves is given as 'that no one should enslave a Jew, his *brother*'. Now this is *not* the law on the release of slaves as set out in Ex. 21.1–11; Deut. 15.12–18 because that does not contemplate the ending of bondage but the regulation of the practice. It is closer to the spirit of Lev. 25.39, which also aspires to preventing the enslavement of 'your *brother*' (cf. Deut. 15.1b). Thus the story in vv. 8–11 should be read as a midrash on slave rulings set into the Jeremiah tradition and reflecting the teaching programme of later communities (cf. 7.5–7; 17.19–27). The reversal of the *bᵉrīt* in v. 11 allows for a Deuteronomistically shaped sermon (cf. Nicholson 1970, 64–5) to teach its lessons by making connections between the abrogated *bᵉrīt* and the destruction of Jerusalem and the cities of Judah.

The story in vv. 8–11 is but the background to the divine word which comes to Jeremiah as a response to the turning of the princes and the people (vv. 8, 12). What follows in vv. 13–22 is Yahweh's word to Jeremiah without any instructions for its delivery to the king and his nobles or the people (nor any report of his so delivering it – though that is also absent for vv. 2–5). In the sermon the *bᵉrīt* between Yahweh and the people who came out of Egypt is stated in terms of the ruling about the release of slaves in the seventh (MT) year. Although this follows Deut. 15.12 inflected by v. 1, as befits the Deuteronomistic influence on the redaction, Ex. 21.1–6 would fit the point better as it is the first of the ordinances (*mišpāṭīm*) prefacing the making of that *bᵉrīt* (cf. Ex. 24.3–8). In keeping with the view expressed in the prose sermons in the tradition (e.g. 7.22–26; 11.7–8; 17.21–23), it is asserted that the exodus generation did not keep that *bᵉrīt* (v. 14b; cf. 31.32). The people of Zedekiah's time are represented as having been different from that generation because they had turned (v. 15, *šūb*) and behaved rightly in the divine eyes (contrast 7.25–26; 16.11–12). This right behaviour consisted of making a *bᵉrīt* in the temple – a different matter, perhaps, from the original *bᵉrīt* between Yahweh and people in that it was between the people and their slaves or, more likely, between the king and the slave-owning people (cf. vv. 8, 15, 16). However, the making of such *bᵉrīt* counts as virtue. It constitutes turning (in spite of all the assertions in Part I about the incapacity of the people to turn!) and is therefore to be praised. Unfortunately, however, the turning did not last and soon (how soon?) the people had profaned the name (v. 16) by subjugating the freed slaves again (profaned because the proclamation of liberty was carried out as a sacral act in the temple).

This turning back from the *b^e^rīt* to which they had turned occasions a divine word-play (v. 17): the people failed to proclaim liberty to their neighbours (the slaves or more general?), so Yahweh proclaims liberty to 'sword, pestilence, famine' against them. Those who transgressed the *b^e^rīt* will bear the curse implicit in the ritual making of that *b^e^rīt* – the hacked animal becomes an analogue of their fate (cf. Judg. 19.29; I Sam. 11.5–11). All those involved in the ceremony will be given over to the enemy and their corpses will provide food for the birds and beasts. At this point the story alludes to the withdrawal of the Babylonians, but not by way of explaining the occasion of the *b^e^rīt*. The retiral of the siege army is a necessary condition of Yahweh commanding them to come back and destroy the city with fire after capturing it. Thus the fate of Jerusalem is directly related to the abrogated *b^e^rīt*, and Zedekiah's fate is bound up with that treachery (a very different account from vv. 2–5; 38.17–23). To the question 'why did Jerusalem fall?' this particular story answers: 'because Zedekiah and his companions (listed in v. 19) turned from the *b^e^rīt* and profaned the divine name'. Could a better story be told to teach the community the importance of making *and keeping b^e^rīt*? I doubt it. If great Jerusalem fell because Zedekiah and his lords broke faith with the common people and discarded solemn agreements, then the community must pay careful attention to these matters because even *one* of the *mišpāṭīm*, if broken, could lead to terrible destruction (cf. Neh. 5.13).

35.1–19

35[1] The word which came to Jeremiah from the LORD in the days of Jehoiakim the son of Josiah, king of Judah: 2 'Go to the house of the Rechabites, and speak with them, and bring them to the house of the LORD, into one of the chambers; then offer them wine to drink.' 3 So I took Jaazaniah the son of Jeremiah, son of Habazziniah, and his brothers, and all his sons, and the whole house of the Rechabites. 4 I brought them to the house of the LORD into the chamber of the sons of Hanan the son of Igdaliah, the man of God, which was near the chamber of the princes, above the chamber of Maaseiah the son of Shallum, keeper of the threshold. 5 Then I set before the Rechabites pitchers full of wine, and cups; and I said to them, 'Drink wine.' 6 But they answered, 'We will drink no wine, for

Jonadab the son of Rechab, our father, commanded us, "You shall not drink wine, neither you nor your sons for ever; 7 you shall not build a house; you shall not sow seed; you shall not plant or have a vineyard; but you shall live in tents all your days, that you may live many days in the land where you sojourn." 8 We have obeyed the voice of Jonadab the son of Rechab, our father, in all that he commanded us, to drink no wine all our days, ourselves, our wives, our sons, or our daughters, 9 and not to build houses to dwell in. We have no vineyard or field or seed; 10 but we have lived in tents, and have obeyed and done all that Jonadab our father commanded us. 11 But when Nebuchadrezzar king of Babylon came up against the land, we said, "Come, and let us go to Jerusalem for fear of the army of the Chaldeans and the army of the Syrians." So we are living in Jerusalem.'

12 Then the word of the LORD came to Jeremiah: 13 'Thus says the LORD of hosts, the God of Israel: Go and say to the men of Judah and the inhabitants of Jerusalem, Will you not receive instruction and listen to my words? says the LORD. 14 The command which Jonadab the son of Rechab gave to his sons, to drink no wine, has been kept; and they drink none to this day, for they have obeyed their father's command. I have spoken to you persistently, but you have not listened to me. 15 I have sent to you all my servants the prophets, sending them persistently, saying, "Turn now every one of you from his evil ways, and amend your doings, and do not go after other gods to serve them, and then you shall dwell in the land which I gave to you and your fathers." But you did not incline your ear or listen to me. 16 The sons of Jonadab the son of Rechab have kept the command which their father gave them, but this people has not obeyed me. 17 Therefore, thus says the LORD, the God of hosts, the God of Israel: Behold, I am bringing on Judah and all the inhabitants of Jerusalem all the evil that I have pronounced against them; because I have spoken to them and they have not listened, I have called to them and they have not answered.'

18 But to the house of the Rechabites Jeremiah said, 'Thus says the LORD of hosts, the God of Israel: Because you have obeyed the command of Jonadab your father, and kept all his precepts, and done all that he commanded you, 19 therefore thus says the LORD of hosts, the God of Israel: Jonadab the son of Rechab shall never lack a man to stand before me.'

[MT 35] = G 42. **[1]** Cf. 21.1; 32.1; 34.8; 40.1 for the introductory formula with note of the occasion of Jeremiah's reception of the divine word, though in this instance 'the days of Jehoiakim' is a very general notice (cf. 26.1; 36.1 for other narratives purportedly set in the period of Jehoiakim). **[2]** MT *'el-bēt*, 'to the house': *bēt* can mean 'household' or 'community, members of a clan', cf. vv. 3b, 5a, *bēt hārēkābîm*, 'the Rechabite community'. However, here it probably refers to the house in the city to which they moved when the Babylonians invaded the land (v. 11) rather than the community (*contra*

Rudolph, 224; Bright, 189). Had they been living in tents in the city, the text would have stated it to demonstrate their fidelity to the ancestral command, but then the contrast between vv. 10–11 would have been lost. Here Jeremiah goes (*hālōk*; hardly Bright's 'Seek out') to the *house* where they stay in order to take them to Yahweh's *house* (*bēt yhwh*). Neither the irony of the Rechabites living in the city (in a house at that!) nor their visiting a house where the deity lives is apparent to the writer. **[3]** MT *ben-yirmᵉyāhū*, 'the son of Jeremiah': one of the *three* Jeremiahs mentioned in the tradition, cf. 1.1; 52.1; G *Ieremin*, 'Jeremin'. **[4]** MT *bᵉnē ḥānān ben-yigdalyāhū ʾîš hāʾᵉlōhîm*, 'the sons of Hanan ben Yigdaliah, the man of god': i.e. the prophetic guild of Hanan . . . the prophet. This is the only occurrence of the term 'man of god' to describe a mantic figure in the Jeremiah tradition; the phrase is used of Samuel, Elijah, Elisha and various anonymous figures (e.g. I Sam. 2.27–36; I Kings 13.1–10). Jeremiah's relationship with this guild is not known. On Hanan's name cf. Hananiah 28.1, 5, 10, 12, 13, 15, 17; a few minor Vrs read *bᵉnē*, 'guild', as *ben*, 'son of (Hanan)'. G *Godoliou* = *gᵉdalyāh* (cf. 40.7) for Yigdaliah. 'Maaseiah ben Shallum, keeper of the threshold': cf. 52.24, where such a post appears to be an important one; this may be the same Maaseiah father of Zephaniah the priest in 29.25; 52.24. **[5]** G has 'a jar of wine' for MT's 'jars, pitchers or bowls of wine'. **[6]** Jonadab ben Rechab, the founder of the community, appears in II Kings 10.15–17, 23; the group is related to the Kenites in I Chron. 2.55. Only the story in Jer. 35 tells of their anti-cultivation (viticulture, agriculture and house-building) outlook which rejects the values of urban and farming cultures (in favour of a pastoralist economy?). It cannot therefore be determined whether 35 is a fabrication of the writer or reflects an actual separatist group in Judaean life; the point of the story is not affected, whichever may be the case. **[7]** G *kai ampelōn ouk estai humin*, 'and a vineyard you shall not have': for MT *lōʾ-tiṭṭāʿū wᵉlōʾ yihyeh lākem*, '(a vineyard) you shall not plant nor shall you have'. MT *ʾattem gārîm šām*, 'you shall wander as aliens there': i.e. having no fixed abode and therefore behaving like aliens (*gērîm*) in Judaean society. **[9]** MT *wᵉśādeh wāzeraʿ*, 'or field or seed': perhaps this should be read with Ehrlich 1912, 332, as *ûśᵉdēh-zeraʿ*, 'and fertile soil', as in Ezek. 17.5 (cf. Rudolph, 226; BHS). **[11]** MT *ḥēl ʾᵃrām*, 'the army of the Syrians': G *dunameōs tōn Assuriōn*, 'the might of the Assyrian'; S 'Edom'. MT *wannēšeb bîrûšālāim*, 'and (so) we live in Jerusalem': some explanation is required for their infidelity to the communal rule about not living in houses and therefore a fortiori not in cities. Cf. I Macc. 2.29–41 for a similar breach of faith due to military pressure. The story-teller does not appear to be aware of the irony of the situation or the contradiction between Rechabite principle and practice in v. 11. **[12]** G has 'to me' for MT 'to Jeremiah': cf. 1.4, 11, 13; 2.1; 34.12 for this short introductory formula for the reception of the divine word. **[14]** MT *hūgam ʾet-dibrē yᵉhōnādāb*, 'the words of Jonadab have been upheld': i.e. observed, obeyed. G lacks 'to this day, for they have obeyed their father's command'. MT *haškēm wᵉdabbēr*, 'rising early and speaking': i.e. urgently speaking (7.13; 25.3; cf. urgently sending 7.25; 25.4; 26.5; 29.19; 35.15; 44.4; II Chron. 36.16; urgently witnessing 11.7; urgently teaching 32.33); RSV 'persistently . . .'. **[15]** MT *haškēm wᵉšālōaḥ*, 'rising early and sending': i.e. urgently sending (7.25; 25.4; 26.5; 29.19; 44.4; II Chron. 36.15). The stereotypical phrase 'all my servants the prophets' (7.25; 26.5; 29.19; 44.4; cf. 'his servants . . .' 25.4) has no specific meaning other than as a blanket approval of prophets. It lacks identification of what prophets are considered to be Yahweh's and only identifies their message in terms of general warnings against evil ways and idolatry (cf. the negative generality of 28.8). **[17]** G lacks 'because . . . not answered' explanation in MT. **[18]** G has a shorter introduction than MT: 'therefore thus says the lord' and a slightly different description of the Rechabite behaviour. **[19]** G lacks MT introductory phrases and ends the chapter with the phrase *pasas tas hēmeras tēs gēs*, 'all the days of the earth' (cf. *kol-yᵉmē hā'āreṣ*, Gen. 8.22). MT *lō'-yikkārēt*, 'shall not be cut off': i.e. lacking, cf. 33.17–18, where the house of David and the levitical priesthood are assured of a similar future to the Rechabites. The propinquity of these two sections in the tradition, though quite independent in origins, underlines the irony of a belief in the one case (Rechabites) that continuity and permanence are the reward for fidelity to principles and in the other (David and Levi) the confidence that such a reward may be gifted by Yahweh in spite of infidelity in the past.

Part III closes with two stories set in the reign of king Jehoiakim, thus forming a closure with 26. The strange tale of the Rechabites in 35 provides a positive contrast to the infidelity of the nation and Zedekiah's community in 34.8–22. If the abrogated *bᵉrīt* of that story accounts for the Babylonian destruction of Jerusalem and the cities of Judah, the narrative of the Rechabite fidelity to its cultural past points up the way communities could survive.

The story is set about ten years before the *bᵉrīt* ceremony of 34.8–11, presumably in the last year of king Jehoiakim, when the Babylonians invaded the land and eventually deported Jehoiachin. This invasion forced the Rechabite community to move into the city of Jerusalem, thus making them betray their cultural heritage of having nothing to do with settled modes of life. To this end they had shunned cultivating vineyards, working arable land or building houses. The definition of their way of life in negative terms emphasizing their rejection of urban civilization and the values of sedentary culture is attributed to their loyalty to their clan ancestor Jonadab (a figure associated with one of Jehu's political and religious bloodbaths, II Kings 10.15–27). In obedience to his command they had maintained a community which rejected urban and agrarian ways in favour of what may only be surmised to be pastoralist quasi-nomadic ways (reflecting the values of the desert culture?). Apart from this story, we know nothing about this group and it would be idle to speculate on how they lived or what their relation to the urban areas (e.g. Jerusalem) may have been. Their living in tents and refusing to drink wine appear in 35.6–10 to symbolize their rejection of viticulture and the building of permanent houses. But did they also not eat anything which might be produced by agriculture? Were they purely a meat-eating group or were leguminous plants permitted? The story only focuses on the matter of their not drinking wine and the explanation for it. Whether there were internal contradictions in their way of life is not the concern of the editor of this account.

Jeremiah is brought into contact with the Rechabites by means of an oracular instruction to perform a symbolic action (of all the dramatic actions presented in the tradition this one is the most symbolical and the least performative). He is sent (*hālōk*, 'go', cf. 13.1; 19.1) to the house in the city where the Rechabites are staying (whether he is sent from the temple is not made clear) in order to take them and bring them to Yahweh's house. Again it would be futile to speculate on what the Rechabites might have thought of a deity who dwelled in a magnificently built house but, presumably, they would have rejected such a religion. However their thoughts on the matter are not part of the story. There in the temple he is to offer the Rechabite clan wine to drink. Jeremiah carries out these instructions and takes the Rechabites to a chamber of a prophetic guild in the temple (MT). His access to such a place may imply friendliness between him and the *b^e^nē* Hanan or a shared working area. The story shows Jeremiah as one having access to the temple (contrast 36.5), influence there and the kind of authority which can command groups of people such as the Rechabites (cf. 19.1; 32.12). These may be features only of the story and should not be used to construct images of the historical Jeremiah. In the temple room he sets out pitchers of wine and cups and commands the Rechabites to drink. They refuse to drink wine and explain why they behave in such a peculiar manner. They are being faithful to their ancestor's command. They must, however, excuse their residency in Jerusalem as the Babylonian invasion has forced them to break faith in the matter of where and how they live.

The divine word explaining the significance of this act now follows (vv. 12–17). The key to understanding what has taken place is the refusal of the Rechabites to drink wine (whether they now live in a house or simply in Jerusalem is not the focus of the story). That refusal demonstrates their fidelity to the ancestral command and such obedience to commands is one of the demands of the prose sermons in the book of Jeremiah (for Deuteronomistic influence in 35 cf. Thiel 1981, 44–8). Jeremiah is now to go (*hālōk*, v. 13) to the men of Judah and the citizens of Jerusalem (cf. 4.4; 11.2, 9; 17.25; 18.11; 32.32) and declare to them the significant contrast between the loyalty of the Rechabites to their cultural values and the disloyalty to Yahweh of their own behaviour. The evidence for that infidelity is the rejection of the prophetic mission sent by Yahweh to the people (v. 15; 7.25; 25.4; 26.5; 29.19; 44.4; cf. II Kings 9.7; 17.13, 23; 21.10; 24.2; Ezra 9.11; Dan. 9.10; Amos 3.7; Zech. 1.6). In this explanation it is assumed that the people have been witnesses of the incident with the Rechabites or have had the matter explained to them at some point in Jeremiah's speech. The text offers no evidence of this, and it must be assumed that vv. 12–17 belong to the editorial explanation of the Rechabite refusal to drink wine in the temple. The Rechabite culture is presented as the outcome of obedience to an ancient command and thus affords a contrasting image of Judaean society which is represented as the opposite. That refusal to obey the prophetic warnings to turn and amend their way of life (cf. 7.5–7; 25.3–6; 26.3–5; 36.3, 7) will bring upon the communities great evil (cf. 6.19; 11.11, 23; 19.3, 15; 32.42; 36.31; 42.17; 44.2; 45.5).

In contrast to the word condemning Judah and Jerusalem is the word given to the Rechabites (vv. 18–19): their fidelity to the past is rewarded with the guarantee of their continual survival in the future. The phrase used to assert this, 'Jonadab . . . shall never lack a man . . .', is a post-Deuteronomistic one (cf. 33.17–18) in that the normal form of the Deuteronomistic statement is a conditional assertion (cf. I Kings 2.4; 8.25; 9.5; II Chron. 6.16; 17.8). That the second edition of Jeremiah contains 33.17–18 is ironic in view of 35.19 being a reward for faithful duty done in the past (not the Deuteronomistic motif which speaks of future fidelity). Yet David and the levitical priests are also rewarded in the same way as the Rechabites in spite of past infidelities. The editing of 35 has produced a number of ironies by setting the story in the days of Nebuchadrezzar's invasion against Jehoiakim. Thus the residency of the Rechabites in a city has to be ignored in the claim that they have been faithful to their ancestor's rules and only their refusal to drink wine is made the test of their loyalty (would eating bread have been an equally good test?). The Rechabites do not figure in any of the stories of the fall of Jerusalem, so perhaps 35 should be treated as a fabricated story rather than a historical account.

The curious tale of the Rechabites appears here after the story of Zedekiah's abrogated *b^erît* and, to some degree, makes an effective contrast. Disloyalty to the past brings destruction (34.15–16), and its opposite (35.8–10) guarantees a permanent future. The parallels between the Rechabite culture and the nation's history are far from exact but the traditionists use a simple parallel to offer yet again a theologized account of why city and country were destroyed by the Babylonians. Hints as to how the future might have been secured are contained in both stories.

36.1–32

36[1] In the fourth year of Jehoiakim the son of Josiah, king of Judah, this
word came to Jeremiah from the LORD: 2 'Take a scroll and write on it all
the words that I have spoken to you against Israel and Judah and all the
nations, from the day I spoke to you, from the days of Josiah until today. 3
It may be that the house of Judah will hear all the evil which I intend to do
to them, so that every one may turn from his evil way, and that I may
forgive their iniquity and their sin.'

4 Then Jeremiah called Baruch the son of Neriah, and Baruch wrote
upon a scroll at the dictation of Jeremiah all the words of the LORD which
he had spoken to him. 5 And Jeremiah ordered Baruch, saying, 'I am
debarred from going to the house of the LORD; 6 so you are to go, and on a
fast day in the hearing of all the people in the LORD's house you shall read
the words of the LORD from the scroll which you have written at my dictation. You shall read them also in the hearing of all the men of Judah who
come out of their cities. 7 It may be that their supplication will come before
the LORD, and that every one will turn from his evil way, for great is the
anger and wrath that the LORD has pronounced against this people.' 8 And
Baruch the son of Neriah did all that Jeremiah the prophet ordered him
about reading from the scroll the words of the LORD in the LORD's house.

9 In the fifth year of Jehoiakim the son of Josiah, king of Judah, in the
ninth month, all the people in Jerusalem and all the people who came from
the cities of Judah to Jerusalem proclaimed a fast before the LORD. 10 Then,

in the hearing of all the people, Baruch read the words of Jeremiah from the scroll, in the house of the LORD, in the chamber of Gemariah the son of Shaphan the secretary, which was in the upper court, at the entry of the New Gate of the LORD's house.

11 When Micaiah the son of Gemariah, son of Shaphan, heard all the words of the LORD from the scroll, 12 he went down to the king's house, into the secretary's chamber; and all the princes were sitting there: Elishama the secretary, Delaiah the son of Shemaiah, Elnathan the son of Achbor, Gemariah the son of Shaphan, Zedekiah the son of Hananiah, and all the princes. 13 And Micaiah told them all the words that he had heard, when Baruch read the scroll in the hearing of the people. 14 Then all the princes sent Jehudi the son of Nethaniah, son of Shelemiah, son of Cushi, to say to Baruch, 'Take in your hand the scroll that you read in the hearing of the people, and come.' So Baruch the son of Neriah took the scroll in his hand and came to them. 15 And they said to him, 'Sit down and read it.' So Baruch read it to them. 16 When they heard all the words, they turned one to another in fear; and they said to Baruch, 'We must report all these words to the king.' 17 Then they asked Baruch, 'Tell us, how did you write all these words? Was it at his dictation?' 18 Baruch answered them, 'He dictated all these words to me, while I wrote them with ink on the scroll.' 19 Then the princes said to Baruch, 'Go and hide, you and Jeremiah, and let no one know where you are.'

20 So they went into the court to the king, having put the scroll in the chamber of Elishama the secretary; and they reported all the words to the king. 21 Then the king sent Jehudi to get the scroll, and he took it from the chamber of Elishama the secretary; and Jehudi read it to the king and all the princes who stood beside the king. 22 It was the ninth month, and the king was sitting in the winter house and there was a fire burning in the brazier before him. 23 As Jehudi read three or four columns, the king would cut them off with a penknife and throw them into the fire in the brazier, until the entire scroll was consumed in the fire that was in the brazier. 24 Yet neither the king, nor any of his servants who heard all these words, was afraid, nor did they rend their garments. 25 Even when Elnathan and Delaiah and Gemariah urged the king not to burn the scroll, he would not listen to them. 26 And the king commanded Jerahmeel the king's son and Seraiah the son of Azriel and Shelemiah the son of Abdeel to seize Baruch the secretary and Jeremiah the prophet, but the LORD hid them.

27 Now, after the king had burned the scroll with the words which Baruch wrote at Jeremiah's dictation, the word of the LORD came to Jeremiah: 28 'Take another scroll and write on it all the former words that were in the first scroll, which Jehoiakim the king of Judah has burned. 29 And concerning Jehoiakim king of Judah you shall say, "Thus says the LORD, You have burned this scroll, saying, 'Why have you written in it that the

king of Babylon will certainly come and destroy this land, and will cut off
from it man and beast?' 30 Therefore thus says the LORD concerning
Jehoiakim king of Judah, He shall have none to sit upon the throne of David,
and his dead body shall be cast out to the heat by day and the frost by night.
31 And I will punish him and his offspring and his servants for their iniquity;
I will bring upon them, and upon the inhabitants of Jerusalem, and upon
the men of Judah, all the evil that I have pronounced against them, but
they would not hear." '

32 Then Jeremiah took another scroll and gave it to Baruch the scribe,
the son of Neriah, who wrote on it at the dictation of Jeremiah all the words
of the scroll which Jehoiakim king of Judah had burned in the fire; and
many similar words were added to them.

[MT 36] = G 43. **[1]** G has *pros mē*, 'to me', for 'to Jeremiah', cf. 32.26; 35.12. The fourth year of Jehoiakim was 605, the year of the battle of Carchemish, though the drama about to unfold is set in 604 (v. 9). The standard reception of the divine word introductory formula is used in v. 1b with the occasion specified first, cf. 16.1; 27.1. **[2]** MT *'al-yiśrā'ēl*, 'against Israel': G^BS have 'Jerusalem', G^A 'Israel'. MT represents the later edition which knows Israel, Judah, nations as the tripartite objects of Jeremiah's preaching, but the content of the scroll suggests that 'Jerusalem and Judah' are the target of what follows (cf. vv. 9, 31). The aim of the scroll is to turn the house of Judah (v. 3), though the normal order is 'Judah and Jerusalem' in the other prose sermons; cf. Wanke 1971, 61. Duhm, 289, regards 'and against all the nations' as a superstitious (i.e. 'touch wood') rounding off of the introduction. MT *m^egillat-sēper*, 'a book-scroll': only here, v. 4 and Ps. 40.8 (EV 7); Ezek. 2.9; on its constitution cf. Hicks 1983. The force of *'al*, 'against' or 'concerning', is debatable in v. 2: the summary of 36 in v. 29 favours 'against' (cf. Rietzschel 1966, 130; Rudolph, 228); other exegetes prefer 'concerning' (e.g. Weiser, 320, 323; Bright, 176, 179). **[3]** MT *'ûlay*, 'perhaps, it may be': cf. v. 7; 26.3; Amos 5.15. Thiel 1981, 49–51, regards vv. 3, 7, 31 as the Deuteronomistic redaction of the story; v. 31 shows that the possibility mooted in vv. 3, 7 is lost by the king's attitude, though the scroll is directed to the people. In this strand forgiveness (*slḥ*) is determined by turning (*šûb*), rather than a divine gift (contrast 31.31–34; 33.8). The scroll is addressed to 'the house of Judah' (*bêt y^ehûdāh*), but the syntax of v. 3 is plural rather than collective. **[4]** MT *wayyiqrā' . . . 'et*, 'and he summoned . . .'; cf. v. 18, where MT has *'el*; a few mss here have *'el*. 'Baruch ben Neriah': cf. 32.12, 13; of all the references to Jeremiah writing something (29.1; 30.2; 51.60), this is the only case of his using an amanuensis. It must reflect a strand in the tradition which elevates Baruch's importance (cf. 43.3; 45). MT *'ašer-dibbēr 'ēlāyw*, 'which he spoke to him': ambiguous phrase meaning either 'which he (Yahweh) spoke to him (Jeremiah)' or 'which he

(Jeremiah) spoke to him (Baruch)'. **[5]** MT *'ᵃnî 'āṣûr 'ûkal lābô' bêt yhwh*, 'I am restrained, I am unable to enter the house of Yahweh': why? Cf. *'āṣûr*, 33.1; but hardly this kind of constraint if he may go into hiding (vv. 19, 26). See Comm. **[6]** G lacks *ûbā'tā 'attāh*, 'you go, you yourself', and reads *en tō chartiō toutō*, 'in *this* scroll', for MT 'in the scroll which you have written at my command the words of Yahweh'. MT *bᵉyôm ṣôm*, 'on a fast day': presumably the next time a fast is observed in the temple, unless a specific future event is in mind – according to v. 9 it was virtually another year before a fast was proclaimed. **[7]** MT *tippōl tᵉḥinnānām*, 'their supplication will fall': cf. 37.20; 38.26; 42.2, 9 for this idiom (also Dan. 9.18, 20). **[8]** MT *yirmᵉyāhû hannābî'*, 'Jeremiah *the prophet*': G lacks 'the prophet'. Cf. v. 10, where a similar statement indicates Baruch's carrying-out of Jeremiah's command. As a summary v. 8 completes the first telling of the story; are vv. 9.26 a variant account of vv. 4–8? (cf. vv. 9–10, 11–19, 20–26, where the scroll is read on three separate occasions). **[9]** MT *baššānāh haḥᵃmišît*, 'in the fifth year': G^{BS} *en tō etei tō ogdoō*, 'in the eighth year'; G^{A} = MT. G 'all the people in Jerusalem and the house of Judah' for MT 'and all the people who came from the cities of Judah to Jerusalem'. The people can hardly be the subject of 'they proclaimed a fast before Yahweh'; presumably the cultic authorities called the fast (cf. Rudolph, 230). **[10]** Cf. 35.4 where the chamber of the *bᵉnê* Hanan is used by Jeremiah. The chamber here was either extremely large or an open area for 'all the people' to have heard the reading. The combination of motifs drawn from large-scale temple gatherings for public speeches (cf. 7.2; 26.2) and the more intimate meetings in rooms (cf. 35.4; 36.10, 12, 20) has made the story confusing at this point. Gemariah ben Shaphan: cf. 26.24; II Kings 22.3 for Shaphan the secretary; as v. 12 makes clear, Gemariah was not the secretary (*hassōpēr*, lit. 'the scribe'). Cf. 26.10 for reference to the New Gate; I Kings 7.12 for the various courts of the temple. **[12]** MT *wayyēred bêt-hammelek*, 'and he went *down* to the house of the king': cf. 22.1; 26.10. The named individuals here are the council or, what Bright, 180, calls, 'the cabinet ministers'. Whether Hananiah (*ḥᵃnanyāhû*) the father of Zedekiah here is the prophet Hananiah (*ḥᵃnanyāh*) cannot be determined from the text. G has variations of some of the names in v. 12 (cf. BHS). **[14]** Yehudi *ben* Nethaniah *ben* Shelemiah *ben* Cushi: the listing of three generations suggests a very important figure, but as Yehudi is an unknown person otherwise, it is possible that *wᵉ'et*, 'and . . .', has dropped out before the name of Shelemiah (even Baruch does not warrant such an ancestry, cf. 32.12); cf. Rudolph, Bright, Wanke, etc. MT *wayyābō*, 'and he came . . .': G *katebē*, 'went down', an accurate understanding of Baruch's movement. **[15]** MT *šēb*, 'sit down': G *palin*, 'again' = *šûb*, i.e. 'read it again'. Bright treats MT as evidence of the courtesy with which the princes treated Baruch and further proof of their friendliness towards him. **[16]** MT *pāḥᵃdû 'îš 'el-rē'ēhû wayyō'mᵉrû 'el-bārûk*, 'they were afraid to one another and they said to Baruch': syntax awkward; G lacks 'to Baruch' which eases the text. If 'and they said' were transposed to before 'to one another' (cf. Volz, Rudolph, Bright), good sense would follow. The fear expressed by the princes may be dictated by Josiah's response to a similar reading of a book (II Kings 22.11; Volz, 328), but they may be afraid simply on behalf of Baruch (and Jeremiah once they establish his hand in the matter vv. 17–19); cf. McKane 1965b, 118–21. Why they should express surprise or fear if what they had just heard had been Jeremiah's preaching for the previous twenty years (v. 2) is difficult to imagine. Their reaction would make more sense if this were the first occasion on which they had heard such dire warnings of imminent destruction (hence the reaction in 26.7–9). **[17]** MT *'ēk*, 'how': G* *pothen*, 'whence' (*mē'ayin*); G^{B} *pou*, 'where' (*'ayyēh*). MT *mippīw*, 'from his mouth': lacking in G; it anticipates v. 18 and belongs to Baruch's knowledge rather than what the princes know. RSV 'Was it at his dictation?' assumes something like *h^{a}mippīw*, 'was it from his mouth?', and suggests an awareness of Jeremiah's presence 'in absence' among the princes. **[18]** G has 'Jeremiah' after 'to me': this makes better sense as it identifies the source and authority for Baruch's scroll without the over-subtle allusions of MT. G lacks *badd^{e}yō*, 'with ink': Giesebrecht, 199; Ehrlich 1912, 334, treat the original as 'by my hand' (*b^{e}yādī*, 'by my hand', or *b^{e}yād*, 'by hand'). **[20]** MT *ḥaṣērāh*, 'to the court(yard)': hardly in winter when it would have been too cold for such sessions! Giesebrecht, 200, suggests *ḥadrāh*, 'inner chamber' or 'his cabinet'. Many mss, G, Vrs have 'these' after 'all the words'. Presumably the scroll was left behind to facilitate giving the king a modest summary of its contents suitably toned down or perhaps to heighten the tension of the story by delaying the moment when king and scroll would encounter each other. **[22]** G lacks 'in the ninth month'. MT *bēt haḥōrep*, 'autumn-house': cf. Amos 3.15; NEB 'winter apartments'. MT *w^{e}'et-hā'āḥ l^{e}pānāyw m^{e}bō'āret*, 'and the brazier before him was burning': Vrs read *w^{e}'ēš*, 'a fire'; G lacks 'burning'. **[23]** MT *šālōš d^{e}lātōt w^{e}'arba'āh*, 'three or four columns': on the nature and substance of these cf. Hicks 1983, 49–57; *delet*, 'door', only occurs here in the Hebrew Bible in the sense of 'column' or 'writing board'. MT *yiqrā'ehā b^{e}ta'ar hassōpēr*, 'he would cut it with a penknife': the 'he' is ambiguous, but presumably refers to the king (cf. v. 25). **[24]** MT *w^{e}lō' pāḥ^{a}dū w^{e}lō' qār^{e}'ū 'et big^{e}dēhem*, 'but they did not fear nor did they rend their garments': cf. v. 16; a word-play contrast appears here using *qr'*, 'cut, rend', to describe the king's response to the scroll and his failure to respond properly (cf. Josiah's rending, *qr'*, of his garments when he heard the words of the book found in the temple, II Kings 22.11). This verse condemns the king and his courtiers (G *hoi paides autou*, 'his servants', possibly 'his youths', i.e. his children) and it is unlikely that a distinction is being made, by using *kol-'^{a}bādāyw*, between them and the princes (*śārīm*) of vv. 12–16. Neither servants nor princes rend their garments. **[25]** 'Delaiah': G *Godolias*; G^BS lack the negative element *mē*, hence make the named individuals persuade the king to burn the scroll! G lacks the final clause 'but he would not listen to them'. Cf. 26.22 for Elnathan ben Achbor. The mildly sympathetic picture presented of some of the princes in this story may reflect the motif of the support of Jeremiah by the princes in 26.16. However, the point of v. 25 may be to stress Jehoiakim's obduracy rather than the opposition of the princes. **[26]** G lacks 'and Shelemiah ben Abdeel': perhaps due to homoioteleuton (BHS). MT *wayyastirēm yhwh*, 'but Yahweh hid them': G *kai katekrubēsan*, 'but they were hidden' (= *wayyissāterū*, 'but they had hidden themselves'?). MT is probably a false dittography due to *way^ehī* in v. 27 (Rudolph, 232) and represents a miraculous development of the text which is quite unique in the book of Jeremiah. **[27]** MT *w^e'et-hadd^ebārīm*, '*and* the words': G *pantas tous logous*, '*all* the words', i.e. (the scroll), all the words. For the introductory reception formula cf. 33.1; 35.12 (lacking occasion); 43.8. **[28]** G lacks 'former' and 'first' as qualifications of the scroll. **[29]** G lacks 'and concerning Jehoiakim the king of Judah': possibly due to homoioteleuton (cf. end of v. 28; BHS). MT is emphatic *'attāh śāraptā*, 'you, you have burned . . .'. The king's summary of the scroll reflects the destruction of 587! Cf. 9.10–11; 32.43 for the devastation of 'man and beast'. **[30]** Cf. 22.18–19 for the casting out of the corpse of Jehoiakim. The fate of the king's body may reflect ironically the image of him sitting in his winter quarters heating himself beside the brazier (v. 22). In 22.30 similar language describes Jehoiachin's lack of a successor 'to sit upon the throne of David'; ironically Jehoiachin himself, for the few months he was king, falsifies this threat of Jehoiakim lacking a successor on the throne! For the problem of 'the predicted fate of kings' see on 22.18–19; 34.4–5. **[31]** G lacks MT *'et-^{ca}wōnām*, 'their guilt, iniquity': the use of *pqd* is sufficient to indicate punishment (cf. 29.32). The introduction of 'the inhabitants of Jerusalem and . . . the men of Judah' (cf. vv. 3, 9) by the editor here (Thiel's Deuteronomists) is the only hint given of the people's reaction to the reading of the scroll. It is out of place in a denunciation of the royal house. Cf. 19.15; 35.17 for the judgment against the nation. **[32]** MT *w^eyirm^eyāhū*, 'and Jeremiah': G *kai* . . . *Barouch*, 'and . . . Baruch'; MT has Jeremiah carry out the instruction of v. 28 (cf. vv. 2, 4), whereas G assumes Baruch made the arrangements (the divine word shows no awareness whatever of Baruch's existence). It is idle to speculate on what additional material the second scroll may have contained (for such speculations cf. Holladay 1976a, 169–74; 1983, 149), but the supposed difference between the two scrolls implies a passage of time between the event of vv. 20–26 and the response of v. 32.

Kessler 1966; Nicholson 1970, 39–45; Wanke 1971, 69–69

Part III ends as it begins with a confrontation between Jeremiah and the community in the time of Jehoiakim. But there are subtle differences between 36 and 26. In 26 Jeremiah is present all the time but king Jehoiakim never appears. His absence is palpable, however, because of the redactors' dating of the story and their supplement (26.20–3) about the killing of the prophet Uriah ben Shemaiah. In 36 Jeremiah is only present for the preparation of the scroll (vv. 4–7) and in the aftermath of its burning (vv. 27–32). For the three readings of the scroll he is absent. The third reading takes place in the king's chamber (v. 20), and his presence is sensed in the second reading (v. 16). Throughout the readings of the scroll Jeremiah is present in his absence, i.e. awareness of him shapes the responses to the scroll (e.g. vv. 17–19, 26). The going into hiding of Jeremiah and Baruch (vv. 19, 26; cf. I Kings 17.3; 18.13) reflects the motif of a king who is prepared to kill prophets. In the editing of the two stories the purpose of the public declaration or reading of Jeremiah's words is the same: the attempt to persuade the community to turn (*šūb*, 26.3; 36.3, 7). The roles of the various strata of society differ in the two stories: in 26 the priests and prophets are ranged against Jeremiah, the princes and elders appear to support him, and the people fluctuate in their loyalty. In 36 no response is given for the people (v. 10, cf. v. 31b), the princes are sympathetic towards Baruch, the king is completely hostile towards the two creators of the scroll, and there is no mention of the priests and prophets. How Jeremiah avoids trouble is unclear in both stories, but survive he does, no matter what the king intends.

The most important differences between 26 and 36 concern Baruch and the fate of the king. If 26 represents the vindication of Jeremiah without clarifying precisely what happens to him, in 36 his presence is no longer necessary for the divine word to be heard in society. Between the two stories the motif of the divine word itself has come to the fore, and that is symbolized by Baruch's role as a scribe writing down what Jeremiah says and then reading it out in various chambers of the temple and palace. The written word has *replaced* Jeremiah. The scroll may be burned in the story (v. 23), but it can be rewritten (v. 32) in a way that an executed Jeremiah could not be repeated. If 26 ends in some confusion about what happened to Jeremiah, 36 is very clear on what happened to the divine words. *They were burned.* They were rejected by the king and, implicitly according to v. 31, by all the people. It is not necessary for the story to emphasize the rejection of the word by the people and the princes. The readings of the scroll in the presence of the worshippers in the temple and before the princes in the palace are the means whereby the scroll arrives in the chamber of the king for its third and fateful reading. The failure of all the groups to respond properly (i.e. by repentance and rendering of garments, v. 24) condemns them outright. Thus the writing of the words and the delegation of their reading to Baruch the scribe are symbolic actions whereby the community is exposed to the divine words and the various responses seal the fates of king, princes and people. By the end of Part III the fate of Jerusalem and Judah is determined by the ashes of that scroll lying under the king's brazier.

The dating of the story in 605–4 (vv. 1, 9, or 601, cf. G) may be a purely redactional matter, but it makes a close connection between Jehoiakim's action in burning the scroll and the emergence of Babylon as the dominant power in international politics (hence the summary of the scroll's contents in v. 29). As the scroll is read out to the people thronging the temple at the fast, and as it moves through the various echelons of Judaean society on its way to the king, the nation's destiny is determined. When the king dismisses its claims by burning it, he seals the fate of himself and his people. The threats and curses in the scroll are not destroyed by the king's apotropaic act but released by it. All that follows in Part IV is but the working out of that fate (cf. 52.2–3). Symbolic of that fact is the way the story ends with a brief account of the process of rewriting the scroll and developing its venomous message with further additions (v. 32). The king may burn the scroll, but he cannot prevent its contents becoming operative (cf. the broken flask of 19.1–2, 10–11; the drowned book of 51.59–64). In this story of a prophetic act the irony lies in the fact that it is the king himself who releases the fatal word rather than the prophet. Jeremiah delegates his authority to Baruch, but the king brings down upon himself and his people the destruction of the nation at the hands of the king of Babylon. The king may have been opposing the power of the spoken word with his own undoubted power in the community, but the point of the story is that such royal power is inferior to the prophetic word. Against Yahweh's word there is no effective power, not even that of a prophet-killing king.

Apart from forming a closure with 26, 36 should be read in conjunction with II Kings 22 (cf. Isbell 1978). The story of king Josiah's response to the finding of the book of the law in the temple is the counterpart to the tale of Jehoiakim's burning of the scroll.

Both stories belong together and, Deuteronomistic editing apart, provide paradigms of how to respond to the hearing of the divine word (or not as the case may be). Josiah's reaction to the reading of the book by Shaphan the scribe (hence Baruch in Jer. 36) is to rend his garments (II Kings 22.10–11; which explains why Jehoiakim and his courtiers are condemned in such terms as 36.24). His next response is to send his servants to inquire of Yahweh on behalf of himself, the people and all Judah because the nation is in dire trouble over their failure to obey the words of the book. This inquiry takes the form of a consultation with the prophet Huldah who assures the delegation that the words mean what they say and that the nation is doomed (II Kings 22.14–17). She also conveys an individual message for king Josiah which promises him a peaceful death because of his reaction to the curses of the book (II Kings 22.18–20). Josiah's weeping and torn garments, his concern for the nation and his consultation with a prophet represent the correct way to respond to the divine word in its written form. That story cannot be ignored in reading the account of the scroll of Jeremiah's words delivered by Baruch to the people, the princes and, finally, to the king. In spite of the apparent concern of the princes for the safety of Baruch and Jeremiah (vv. 16–19), they do not respond to the actual words read out to them. Throughout 36 there is no response to the scroll's contents: people, princes, king and courtiers *all* are represented as ignoring the contents of the scroll. Thus 36 reverses the paradigmatic response of Josiah to the words of the book.

The parallels between 36 and II Kings 22 contribute to accounting for Jeremiah's absence in vv. 9–26 and Baruch's presence in the story. In the Josiah story the source of the book is veiled, but its contents are validated by a prophetic source at some distance from the palace. It is read to the king by Shaphan the secretary. Chapter 36 also presents a story of a king being read to by a secretary from a scroll which has been validated by a prophetic authority outside the palace. As Josiah's book comes from the temple, we would expect Jeremiah to have lodged the scroll of his sayings in the sacred house from which he did so much of his work. However, if this had been the case, the pattern of II Kings 22 would have been broken and the king would have heard the words from Jeremiah himself rather than from a scribal figure. Furthermore, the editing of the book of Jeremiah invariably presents the prophet and king Jehoiakim as two figures who never encounter one another (hence the king's inexplicable absence from 26). By absenting Jeremiah from the temple, a role is created for Baruch the scribe and the parallel maintained to II Kings 22. Such structural symmetry is impressive, though v. 5 attempts to explain why Jeremiah could not go to the temple. Exegetes have offered various explanations for his debarment from the cult centre: e.g. he is banned on the grounds of levitical impurity (Duhm, 290), or because the temple priesthood opposed him for his behaviour on previous visits to the temple (e.g. 20.1–6; 26.2–15; cf. Volz, 328; Weiser, 325; Bright, 179). The view of Jeremiah as a trouble-maker simply does not explain how he moves so freely about the temple (e.g. 22.1; 29.24–29; 35.2–11). If he had been barred after 20.1–6 or 26.2–15 (assuming either story to be historical), then surely he would have been excluded even more categorically after Baruch's performance in 36. Yet a few years later (?) in 35.2–11 we find him introducing a group of Rechabites into the temple! The text offers no reason for the temple being inaccessible to him, but the story requires him to be debarred, otherwise there will be no role for Baruch the scribe. So Jeremiah is excluded from going to the temple to speak his words and therefore has to write them and delegate Baruch to deliver them at the next large public gathering.

The introduction of Baruch as a companion and amanuensis of Jeremiah has persuaded many scholars that 36 affords clues as to how the book of Jeremiah came to be written, and Baruch has been credited with the production of 'memoirs' which are to be found in many of the prose sections of Jeremiah (e.g. Duhm; Mowinckel 1914; Muilenburg 1970; cf. Rietzschel 1966; Wanke). There is little warrant for this reading of 36, and it should be noted that only in 36 is the writing of Jeremiah's work attributed to Baruch. Elsewhere Jeremiah writes his own material or, at least, nobody is credited with writing it for him (29.1; 30.2; 32.10; 51.60). These references may not reflect historical events, but they do not attribute Jeremiah's scribal activities to Baruch. Furthermore, the parallel account of 36.1–3 which appears in 25.1–7 does not present Jeremiah's summary of his twenty-three years of preaching in written form (hinted at in 25.13?), but as a further proclamation. The turning of the spoken word into writing occurs in 36 as part of a symbolic act and Jeremiah's use of Baruch is not a necessary element of the divine command (i.e. Yahweh does *not* order Jeremiah to acquire for himself a scribe to whom he may delegate the writing of the divine words). Baruch's role may be accounted for by the pattern of II Kings 22, but the thesis that 36 represents the taking over of the tradition by the Deuteronomistic scribal school (as II Kings 22 provides a possible legitimation of the book of Deuteronomy) cannot be ruled out altogether (cf. Carroll 1981, 15–16). There is a Baruch strand in the tradition (e.g. 32.12–13, 16; 36; 43.3, 6–7; 45) which, although brief and obscure, may reflect the beginning of an independent figure within the book which develops significantly in post-Jeremiah literature. Here, as the writer of the sayings of Jeremiah (36.4, 32), Baruch lays claim to authority by association and delegation, but too much should not be made of this claim because it is registered only in 36 and not elsewhere in the blocks of material in the book (though the other references to him confirm the degree of his association with Jeremiah). To focus on Baruch in 36 is to miss the point of the story:

> . . . it may be concluded that the central concern of this narrative is not with a description of how the book of Jeremiah had its beginnings, much less with a mere recording of an incident, albeit an important one, in the prophet's life, but rather with the manner in which Yahweh's Word as proclaimed by the prophet was rejected by Israel as personified in the king and actualized in his deeds (Nicholson 1970, 45).

The story of the fate of the scroll in 36 is one of the finest pieces of writing in the book. It is an example of Judaean storytelling at its best and, especially in vv. 11–19, 20–26, creates a number of striking dramatic moments which brilliantly illuminate scenes of potential conflict and disaster. (An alternative and undramatic account of the story may be implied by v. 8!) Suspense is built up and maintained by a sequence of three very different readings of the scroll. These are encapsulated by two introductory pieces (vv. 1–3, 4–8) and two concluding sections (vv. 27–31, 32). At the end of the story the fate of the nation is sealed, and yet Jeremiah and Baruch have only just written the scroll (again). The introductory material sets the scene for Baruch's visit to the temple whenever a suitable occasion presents itself. Thereafter Jeremiah disappears from sight and is replaced by the scroll. At a great public fast the temple is crowded with people seeking to appease Yahweh because of the Babylonians or a terrible drought (the reason for the fast is not given, but exegetes relate it to the military threat of Babylon or the terrible drought of 14.2–6; cf. Holladay 1981, 71–2, for the linking of both motifs). At this gathering Baruch gives his first public reading of the scroll. Nothing is recorded of its reception, but Micaiah ben Gemariah hears it and goes down to the palace where the princes are gathered. Thus the word is about to penetrate further into the corridors of power

Baruch is summoned to the palace, and there he gives a second reading of the scroll. What the princes hear (cf. v. 29, the force of which is lost by the redactional introduction of vv. 1–3) makes them afraid, and they recognize the fact that the king must hear these words. Once they have elicited from Baruch the source of the scroll, they counsel him to hide and they go to the council chamber where the king is. So the scene is set for the third reading, and this time only the scroll is present. Neither the presence of Baruch nor that of Jeremiah can distract from that document. The king is warming himself by a fire because it is winter. Jehudi reads the scroll to him. As the sections are read the king cuts them off with a knife and casts them into the fire. Thus king and court condemn themselves. Even though urged by some of the princes not to burn the scroll, the king refuses to listen. Instead he issues orders for the seizure of Jeremiah and Baruch, but they have hidden themselves (G). So at the end of the *third* reading of the *short* scroll, it is in ashes, the authors of it are in hiding and the king remains in his chamber unopposed.

Why did the king burn the scroll? To show his contempt for it? To counteract its terrible power? To frustrate the onslaught of the Babylonians of which it spoke? To show where the real power in the kingdom lay? The text offers no answers to these questions. The presentation of Jehoiakim in Jeremiah and the Deuteronomistic history is such that the burning of scrolls and the execution of prophets are to be expected of him. However, as the leader of the country, what else could he do to turn back the power of Babylon? Clearly neither he nor his councillors believed that the prophetic word provided any defence against the Babylonians (cf. McKane 1965b, 118–30). However much some of the princes may have felt that the scroll should not have been burned, none of them acted correctly according to the story-teller (v. 24). If v. 29 is a fair summary of the scroll's contents, then it offered no means of resisting the invaders. The redactional setting of the story within a pattern of proclamation and turning (vv. 3, 7, 31) obscures the absoluteness of the word of judgment (whether the scroll is imagined to have contained the oracles in 4–6 or not). Against the power of the written-spoken word (cf. 51.59–64) Jehoiakim exercised his royal authority to destroy it by burning the scroll.

Is that the end of the prophetic word? Does a king outrank a prophet? Is royal power the effective word in the kingdom? What of

Yahweh's word? Is that also hidden with those who cannot face the king's wrath? What now? The divine word strikes again (v. 27) and Jeremiah is ordered to repeat the process as before. This time there will be a special word for Jehoiakim (vv. 29–31): the image of the king sitting there by the fire burning the scroll is picked up in the cursing of the king. He will die without a successor on the throne and his body will be flung out (cf. the fate of Hananiah 28.16) to face heat by day and cold by night (cf. 22.19). The redactor uses this opportunity to include the nation in the word of judgment (v. 31b). Finally, the instructions of v. 28 are carried out (v. 32, cf. v. 8) and once more the scroll of words exists in Jerusalem. The written words of Yahweh are not easily destroyed, not even by a king!

With the disintegration of the nation brought about by the fall of king, city, and land and the development of the prophetic word in a written form, it becomes possible to discern the emergence of the idea of the word over against society. Committed to writing, the word has a permanence beyond the exigencies of human existence and can survive even the absence of its original bearer. The written word begins to transcend time and place and, in 36, we may catch a glimpse of an important transformation of theological thought in the exilic and later periods. George Steiner makes a similar point:

> The locus of truth is always extraterritorial; its diffusion is made clandestine by the barbed wire and watch-towers of national dogma . . . The mortal clash between politics and verity, between an imminent homeland and the space of the transcendent, is spelt out in *Jeremiah* 36–39. King Jehoiakim seizes the scroll dictated by God's clerk and bookkeeper. He cuts out the offending columns and casts the entire text into the consuming flame (governments, political censors, patriotic vigilantes burn books). God instructs the prophet: 'Take thee again another scroll and write on it all the words that were written on the first.' The truth will out. Somewhere there is a pencil-stub, a mimeograph machine, a hand-press which the king's men have overlooked. 'So Jeremiah abode in the court of the prison till the day that Jerusalem was taken; and he was *there* when Jerusalem was taken.' The formulaic specification is magnificent in meaning. The royal city, the nation are laid waste; the text and its transmitter endure, *there* and *now*. The Temple may be destroyed; the texts which it housed sing in the winds that scatter them (1985, 21).

PART FOUR

The Fall of Jerusalem and Aftermath

37–45

The rejection of the divine word in 36 determines the fate of Jerusalem and the people. Part IV spells out the consequences of that act and presents an image of Jeremiah as a passive figure undergoing maltreatment at the hands of various social groups. Jeremiah's passivity is intimated in 36 by his delegation of Baruch to write and read out the scroll of his words to the people. It is further developed throughout 37–45 (with the exception of 39.15–18; 43.8–13), though the delegated status of Baruch is limited to 36. Neither figure is the central focus of the tradition, and it is therefore not possible to develop a reading of Part IV as the passion narrative of Jeremiah (*contra* Kremers 1953; Zimmerli 1981; cf. Welten 1977). This is not possible because, as in 36, the figure of Jeremiah fades from view at certain points of the narrative (e.g. 40.7 – 41.18; 45.3–5). Only the word counts, and the bearer of that may be Jeremiah, Baruch (36) or, even, Seraiah (51.59). Jeremiah's sufferings are incidental in Part IV and provide opportunities for further proclamations of that divine word (hence the repetitions in 37–38). When the word is not present Jeremiah is absent (as in 40.7 – 41.18). 37.2b summarizes the first half of Part IV: king, officials and people 'did not listen . . . to the words of Yahweh which he spoke *by means of* Jeremiah the prophet'. Jeremiah is simply the instrument of the divine word or its expression (cf. Ackroyd 1968b, 52). Even in Egypt (43.8–13; 44) his only function is the declaration of the word.

Part IV consists entirely of prose narratives (with the exception of the poetic couplet in 38.22b) dealing with Jeremiah's imprisonment in the dungeons (37) or cistern (38), the fall of Jerusalem (39.3–10), the rescue of Jeremiah from prison by the Babylonians (39.11–14) or from among the deported Judaeans at Ramah (40.1–6), the community under Gedaliah's governorship, including the governor's assassination and the rebellion of Ishmael ben Nethaniah (40.7 – 41.18), the leadership of Johanan ben Kareah and Jeremiah's consultative role among the remnant of Judah (42.1 – 43.3), the flight to Egypt of that remnant (43.4–7), Jeremiah's performative magic against Egypt (43.8–13), a lengthy and highly edited sermon with responses directed against the Jewish communities in Egypt (44), and a brief lament with reply relating to Baruch (45). Nothing unifies these stories except the unfolding of the divine word as it shapes the fate of the community. The element of hope to be found in Part III (e.g. 29.4–7, 10–14; 30–31; 32.6–15, 36–44; 33) is almost entirely absent in Part IV. It can be detected in a few places: e.g. 39.15–18; 40.7–12; 42.9–12; 45.5. But these are all very modest expressions of potential well-being set into contexts of overwhelming destruction. The militancy with which the Egyptian connection is denounced (42–44) contrasts with the pro-Babylonian tendency of 27–29 (counteracted by 30–31) and hints at ideological conflict between the different Jewish communities in Palestine, Babylon and Egypt from the sixth century onwards. Apart from a consistent attitude to Egypt, the figure of Jeremiah supports the Palestinian community in Part IV and both Palestinian and Babylonian in Part III.

37.1–2

37[1] Zedekiah the son of Josiah, whom Nebuchadrezzar king of Babylon made king in the land of Judah, reigned instead of Coniah the son of Jehoiakim. 2 But neither he nor his servants nor the people of the land listened to the words of the LORD which he spoke through Jeremiah the prophet.

[MT 37] = G 44. **[1]** MT *wayyimᵉlāk-melek ṣidqiyyāhū*, 'and Zedekiah reigned as king': G lacks *malek* – a dittography in MT unless read as *hammelek*, '(Zedekiah) the king'; cf. 23.5 for MT idiom. G lacks 'Coniah ben Jehoiakim', thereby making v. 1 the fulfilment of 36.30; i.e. Zedekiah becomes king instead (*antitaḥat*) of Jehoiakim. **[2]** MT *wᵉlō'šāma'*, 'but he did not listen': this is the central point of 37–39, but it is expanded in the title here to emphasize the collective responsibility of the leadership: '*he* and his servants and the people of the land'. This third group appears in 1.18;

34.19, where they refer to the landed gentry, though some exegetes regard them as the people in general (e.g. Rudolph, 236). If they are the common people, then 37.2 follows 36 by indicting the three strata of king, princes and people (36.10, 24, 31). MT *dibber bᵉyad yirmᵉyāhū hannābî*, 'he spoke by means of Jeremiah the prophet': G lacks 'the prophet'; *bᵉyad*, lit. 'by the hand of', frequently means 'by the agency of', 'instrumentality of', cf. II Kings 9.36; 17.13, 23 (often of prophets).

Part IV is introduced by a titular statement to the effect that Zedekiah took over from Jehoiakim (G), but he *too* did not listen to Yahweh's words delivered by Jeremiah. This title summarizes the content of 37–39 and anticipates by way of explanation the fall of Jerusalem. It opens the final part of the book (G order) with a clear statement to the effect that even a change of king did not avert the nation's fate (sealed in 36). Zedekiah continues his predecessor's policy of ignoring the words of Jeremiah. All that follows will unfold the consequences of that attitude, and again the words of Jeremiah (i.e. Yahweh's word) will dominate the narratives. In the second edition (MT) Jeremiah's prophetic status is emphasized (cf. 34.6). In spite of the stories which appear in Part IV and elsewhere in the tradition (e.g. 21.1–7; 34.8–22), nothing needs to be known about Zedekiah's reign beyond the dismissive preface to the block in 37.2. As the fall of Jerusalem comes into focus, it is sufficient to know that the Babylonian replacement on the throne proved to be no more receptive to the divine word mediated through the agency of Jeremiah than all the other kings. The destruction of Jerusalem may be heard through the filter of the motif of a leadership which failed to grasp the significance of the prophetic ministry of Jeremiah. That summary judgment is unique among the parts which make up the book in that it anticipates what is to happen by offering an account of the reason why before allowing the story to unfold in its own way.

37.3–10

3 King Zedekiah sent Jehucal the son of Shelemiah, and Zephaniah the priest, the son of Maaseiah, to Jeremiah the prophet, saying, 'Pray for us to the LORD our God.' 4 Now Jeremiah was still going in and out among the people, for he had not yet been put in prison. 5 The army of Pharaoh had come out of Egypt; and when the Chaldeans who were besieging Jerusalem heard news of them, they withdrew from Jerusalem.

6 Then the word of the LORD came to Jeremiah the prophet: 7 'Thus says the LORD, God of Israel: Thus shall you say to the king of Judah who sent you to me to inquire of me, "Behold, Pharaoh's army which came to help you is about to return to Egypt, to its own land. 8 And the Chaldeans shall come back and fight against this city; they shall take it and burn it with fire. 9 Thus says the LORD, Do not deceive yourselves, saying, 'The Chaldeans will surely stay away from us,' for they will not stay away. 10 For even if you should defeat the whole army of Chaldeans who are fighting against you, and there remained of them only wounded men, every man in his tent, they would rise up and burn this city with fire." '

---

[3] MT *wayyišlaḥ hammelek ṣidqiyyāhū*, 'and Zedekiah the king sent . . .': = v. 17; 38.14; cf. 21.1. Jehucal is Jucal in 38.1. Zephaniah ben Maaseiah appears in 21.1; 29.25. The delegation here (Jehucal, Zephaniah) differs from that given in 21.1 (Pashhur [cf. 38.1], Zephaniah). G lacks 'the prophet' as a qualifier of Jeremiah. MT *hitpallel-nā' ba'ᵃdēnū*, 'pray on our behalf': cf. *dᵉrāš-nā' ba'ᵃdēnū*, 'inquire on our behalf', 21.2. **[4]** MT *bā' wᵉyōṣē' bᵉtōk hā'ām*, 'coming in and going out among the people': G *ēlthen kai diēlthen dia mesou tēs poleōs*, 'came and went through the midst of the city'. K *hkly'*; Q *hakkᵉlū'*, cf. 52.31 for K–Q: *hakkele'*, 'prison, confinement', vv. 15, 18. This verse anticipates vv. 13–15; cf. 32.2–5. **[5]** G lacks 'who were besieging Jerusalem'. Cf. 34.21–22 for the Babylonian withdrawal. **[6]** G lacks 'the prophet'. **[7]** MT *kōh tō'mᵉrū*, 'thus will *you* (plur.) say': i.e. the delegates; G sing. which, with *pros se*, 'to you', for MT *'etkem 'ēlay*, 'you to me', refers to Jeremiah. **[8]** MT *ūśᵉrāpuhā bā'ēš*, 'and burn it with fire': cf. 34.2; 38.3. It is regarded as an additional gloss (Rudolph, 238; cf. BHS); see v. 10 also. **[10]** MT *'īš bᵉ'ohᵒlō*, 'each in his tent': G *hekastos en tō topō autou*, 'each in his place'. BHS treats 'burn . . . with fire' as a possible gloss. Cf. II Chron. 24.23–24 for the motif of the defeat of the Judaeans by a *few* enemies; II Sam. 5.6–8 for the element of contempt in this verse.

The first block of material in Part IV is 37.3 – 38.28 (analysis in Migsch 1981, 125–80; Pohlmann 1978, 49–93; Wanke 1971, 95–102). It consists of a series of variations on encounters between Jeremiah and Zedekiah. These encounters take two very different forms: in one set Zedekiah sends a delegation to the prophet (21.1–2; 37.3), in the other set he summons Jeremiah for an interview (37.17; 38.14). One group of stories relates to a prophet who has his freedom to move about the city (37.4 G), the other focuses on an imprisoned Jeremiah (37.15; 38.13; cf. 32.2–3). All the stories must be regarded as variations on a theme rather than as historical accounts of independent events in the intertwined lives of Zedekiah and Jeremiah (cf. Bright, 233; Skinner 1922, 258 n. 1 on 37–38 as two accounts of the *same* story). Apart from 38.17, every encounter between the king and the prophet, whether by delegation or summons, has the same result. The message remains the same throughout: the king of Babylon or the Chaldaeans will take the city (34.4–5 may be regarded as a modification of the harsh forecast). The severity with which the enemy will treat the occupants of the city varies in the telling (cf. the gradations of 21.5–6, 7, 8–10), but only 38.17 affords any escape for king and city. The theme, with all its variations and its outworking in 39.1–10, is the only point of contact between Jeremiah and Zedekiah (just as 36 is the only story where Jeremiah and Jehoiakim almost encounter each other). This underlines the dominant motif of parts III and IV – the movement of the divine word in Jerusalem. The tradition has little interest in the story of Jeremiah or the activities of the kings; only the encounter with the word is the concern of the redactors who have put together these stories.

The variation on the delegation motif in 37.3–10 (see on 21.1–7) sets the event in the lull caused by the Babylonian withdrawal from the siege of Jerusalem to meet the Egyptian force (v. 5; 34.8–22 is set in this period too). 21.2 has the delegation approach Jeremiah so that his intercession with the deity may lead to a Babylonian withdrawal. 38.3 does not make it clear why Jeremiah should intercede with the deity, but the motif reflects the theme of Jeremiah *the prophet* (MT). An explanation is required here because Jeremiah ought to have been under arrest during the siege (cf. 32.2–5). The king had had him arrested for his treasonous proclamation about the triumph of the Chaldaeans, but in anticipation of vv. 12–15 in this telling of the story he is at liberty. In 34.21–22 the withdrawal of the Babylonians is made to coincide with the *b*ᵉ*rīt* releasing the debt slaves, and their return is viewed as the punishment for the profanation of that obligation. Here the raising of the siege is accounted for in terms of an Egyptian military expedition against the Babylonians. The possibility of hope facilitates the sending of the delegation to the intermediary. However, the message remains what it has always been. The Chaldaeans will return and take the city. The Egyptian intervention will peter out and no confidence is to be placed in it. Furthermore, even if the Babylonian army were to be defeated by the Judaeans (never mind the Egyptians), it would not help the city. Here the prophet uses irony to make his point: a defeated army would still conquer Jerusalem because even its wounded soldiers would rise from their beds to capture the city (cf. the irony in II Sam. 5.6–8 with reference to the taking of Jerusalem). If 21.1–7 in its treatment of the delegation theme asserts the inevitability of the city's defeat and the death of everybody in it, 37.7–10 reasserts that lesson but reinforces it by relating it to the false hopes raised by the appearance of the Egyptians on the horizon. Even under such circumstances there is no hope for Jerusalem.

37.11–16

11 Now when the Chaldean army had withdrawn from Jerusalem at the approach of Pharaoh's army, 12 Jeremiah set out from Jerusalem to go the land of Benjamin to receive his portion there among the people. 13 When he was at the Benjamin Gate, a sentry there named Irijah the son of Shelemiah, son of Hananiah, seized Jeremiah the prophet, saying, 'You are deserting to the Chaldeans.' 14 And Jeremiah said, 'It is false; I am not deserting to the Chaldeans.' But Irijah would not listen to him, and seized Jeremiah and brought him to the princes. 15 And the princes were enraged at Jeremiah, and they beat him and imprisoned him in the house of Jonathan the secretary, for it had been made a prison. 16 When Jeremiah had come to the dungeon cells, and remained there many days.

---

[12] MT *laḥaliq miššām bᵉtōk hā'ām*, lit. 'to divide from there among the people': the last phrase appears in v. 4, where it is used as a reference to this incident, but in order to place vv. 6–10 before what transpires in vv. 13–15; cf. II Kings 4.13, where the phrase *bᵉtōk 'ammī*, 'among my own people', indicates one's kinsfolk (hardly its meaning in v. 4). The expression 'to divide' (Piel *ḥillēq*) can refer to apportioning land (cf. Josh. 19.51; Micah 2.4; Joel 4.2 [EV 3.2]; Dan. 11.39), but Jeremiah hardly was a distributor of land. G *tou agorasai*, 'to buy': an attempt to understand *ḥlq*. The word may refer to his inheritance (cf. Rudolph) as described in 32.6,15 (so Bright, 229), but that transaction took place when Jeremiah was under arrest and the tradition knows nothing of his release until 39.14! **[13]** MT *ba'al pᵉqidut ūšᵉmū yir'īyyāyh*, lit. 'master of the guard and his name (was) Irijah': G *kai ekei anthrōpos, par' hō kateluen, Sarouias*, 'and there a man with whom he lodged, Saruia'; a rather different account of the matter. Cf. 20.2 for the Benjamin Gate. G lacks 'the prophet' as in vv. 2, 3, 6. **[14]** G Saruia for Irijah (S Neriyah as in v. 13). The Heb. word for 'desert' in vv. 13–14 is *nōpēl*, i.e. 'fall away, go over to'; cf. 21.9. **[15]** G lacks MT *bēt hā'ēsūr*, 'prison' (cf. JPSB; other EVV 'imprisoned'). MT's two 'houses' (prison, Jonathan's) represent variants, as *bēt hā'ēsūr* is unnecessary in view of the final clause.

[16] MT *kī bā'*, 'when he went . . .': G *kai ēlthen*, 'and he came' = *wayyābō'*. RSV is a poor translation here (other EVV superior) and necessitates reading v. 16 as the beginning of the next piece rather than the end of this section. MT *'el-bēt habbōr w^e'el-haḥ^anuyōt*, lit. 'to the house of the pit (i.e. dungeon, cistern), and to the cells': hendiadys 'dungeon cells'; cf. the variant story in 38.6 where Jeremiah is put in a pit or cistern (*bōr*). G *chereth* for *haḥ^anuyōt*. 'And he remained there many days': end of this particular story; cf. v. 21; 38.13, 28.

A rather different story is now set in the period of the Babylonian withdrawal from the siege. In 32.2–5 Jeremiah had been put under house arrest in the guard court for his proclamation of the Chaldaean destruction of Jerusalem. In this version of that motif he is stopped as he attempts to leave the city and thrown into the dungeons. Thus there are two different traditions in the book about Jeremiah's fate during the siege. In one he is restricted severely in his movements but may receive visitors and transact business (32.6–15; very much like Socrates waiting for hemlock). In the other he is at liberty to move about the city (37.4) and preach sedition to the people (38.1). The variants of this tradition give different reasons for his incarceration in the dungeons and for his eventual escape from them. All the variations of the two traditions allow the redactors to drive home the primary message of the Babylonian destruction of everything, though even here variants appear in the fate of Zedekiah (34.4–5; 38.17) and the city (38.17).

Jeremiah in his freedom chooses to leave the city to go to his homeland in Benjaminite territory. The text (v. 12) is not clear about his reason for doing this, but relates it to the division of land. This may refer to Jeremiah's purchase of land in 32.6–15, though no such connection is made directly by the editors. It is much more likely that the story is told in order to explain why Jeremiah was thrown into the cells. He chose to leave the city when the opportunity presented itself and suffered the consequences of his actions. Such an explanation requires Jeremiah to have had his freedom at the time and also necessitates the withdrawal of the Babylonians. The editions differ about the precise details of the story: G presents his experience as the result of a citizen's arrest by the man with whom he lodged, whereas MT has him arrested by an officer of the guard. He is charged with deserting to the enemy. This charge he denies as being false (*šeqer*, 'it is false', v. 14). In 21.8–10; 38.2 he advocates desertion to the citizens so it is hardly surprising that he should now suffer arrest for appearing to be following his own advice. Enraged by his disloyalty the princes beat him (different princes from 26.16; 36.19?) and imprison him in the dungeons (variants obscure v. 15). There he remains a long time.

37.17–21

17 King Zedekiah sent for him, and received him. The king questioned him secretly in his house, and said, 'Is there any word from the LORD?' Jeremiah said, 'There is.' Then he said, 'You shall be delivered into the hand of the king of Babylon.' 18 Jeremiah also said to King Zedekiah, "What wrong have I done to you or your servants or this people, that you have put me in prison? 19 Where are your prophets who prophesied to you, saying, "The king of Babylon will not come against you and against this land"? 20 Now hear, I pray you, O my lord the king: let my humble plea come before you, and do not send me back to the house of Jonathan the secretary, lest I die there.' 21 So King Zedekiah gave orders, and they committed Jeremiah to the court of the guard; and a loaf of bread was given him daily from the bakers' street, until all the bread of the city was gone. So Jeremiah remained in the court of the guard.

---

[17] MT *wayyiqqāḥēhū*, 'and he received him': G *kai ekalesen auton*, 'and he called him'. Contrast the secret meeting here in the palace with the meeting in the temple of 38.14. **[18]** MT *wayyō'mer*, 'and he said': cf. NEB 'Then . . . said'; better than RSV 'also'. Jeremiah's question is naive in the extreme (contrast 26.14–15) in the context of deserting in a time of war, but the interview strand should be read independently of its present context. G sing. '*you* put me in prison', i.e. the king is responsible for his imprisonment (cf. 32.3). **[19]** K *w'yw*; Q *wᵉ'ayyēh*, 'but where . . .?': Thiel 1981, 53–4 treats v. 19 as a redactional verse from the Deuteronomistic editing; cf. 27.9, 16; 29.8. **[20]** Cf. 36.7 for the supplication motif (*tᵉḥinnāh*). **[21]** Cf. 32.2 for the court of the guard. In 52.6–7 the breaching of the city wall coincides with the exhaustion of the food supply. MT *wayyēšeb yirmᵉyāhū baḥᵃṣar hammaṭṭārāh*, 'and Jeremiah remained in the court of the guard': = 38.13, 28; cf. 37.16b. Volz, 332; Rudolph, 243, transpose 38.24–28 to follow 37.21 (cf. BHS).

Jeremiah's incarceration in the dungeons is terminated in this version of the story by a summons from the king (v. 17; cf. 38.14, but contrast 38.7–13; 34.2). No details are given about how the king knew that Jeremiah had been thrown into the cells, nor are the stages of his release noted in the text. The text passes in silence over the movements required to transfer Jeremiah from his erstwhile prison to the king's palace, though it notes that the interview was 'in secret' (v. 17, *bassēter*). Curiously the king blithely inquires about a divine oracle, as if vv. 7–10 were unknown or all that had passed between king and prophet on other occasions had been forgotten. This minor point confirms the view that there is only a set of motifs which is used repeatedly in different ways to construct variations on a theme rather than a historical event behind the variant accounts. In this particular version of the interview motif Jeremiah reasserts his message of the king's deliverance into the hand of the Babylonian king and adds a plaintive question about his own imprisonment (v. 18). The question may be naive in the light of Jeremiah's constant preaching of sedition, but here it reflects the independent interview motif rather than the integrated strands of 37–38.

The main feature of the interview motif (37.17–21; 38.14–28; cf. 34.2–5) is the eirenic exchange between king and prophet. Death is much spoken of (37.20; 38.15–16, 19–20, 24–26) and there is between the two men a sympathy which is strikingly absent from much of the tradition. Zedekiah is presented as a person quite prepared to ease Jeremiah's position, but also as a man somewhat afraid of his official advisors. As a man afraid he appears to be quite human (38.19, 24–27) and rather different from the redactional material which blames him for the fall of Jerusalem (37.1–2; 52.1–3; cf. May 1956, 103–5 on Zedekiah). He is susceptible to Jeremiah's pleas and capable of overriding the wishes of his princes. Thus he accedes to Jeremiah's entreaty and releases him from the dungeon in which he would inevitably have died. He can save the prophet's life by freeing him and by assigning him a daily food allowance; an allowance facilitated by confining him to the court of the guard. There Jeremiah would have lived out the siege and have been in a better position than the citizens, not confined, but exposed to the hazards of finding food in a time of war. Yet no credit is granted to the king in the tradition (cf. Obadiah's role in I Kings 18.13). The story of how Jeremiah survived the terrible siege of Jerusalem is told a number of times in 37.17–21; 38.7–13, 24–28. But his survival is hardly a concern of the tradition; rather, it is more interested in recording how the purveyor of the divine word came to be alive after the catastrophe and to be still the bearer of that word. The irony of vv. 18–19 raises an interesting point (attributed to Deuteronomistic influence according to some exegetes), but the text does not develop it.

38.1–6

38[1] Now Shephatiah the son of Mattan, Gedaliah the son of Pashhur, Jucal the son of Shelemiah, and Pashhur the son of Malchiah heard the words that Jeremiah was saying to all the people, 2 'Thus says the LORD, He who stays in this city shall die by the sword, by famine, and by pestilence; but he who goes out to the Chaldeans shall live; he shall have his life as a prize of war, and live. 3 Thus says the LORD, This city shall surely be given into the hand of the army of the king of Babylon and be taken.' 4 Then the princes said to the king, 'Let this man be put to death, for he is weakening the hands of the soldiers who are left in this city, and the hands of all the people, by speaking such words to them. For this man is not seeking the welfare of this people, but their harm.' 5 King Zedekiah said, 'Behold, he is in your hands; for the king can do nothing against you.' 6 So they took Jeremiah and cast him into the cistern of Malchiah, the king's son, which was in the court of the guard, letting Jeremiah down by ropes. And there was no water in the cistern, but only mire, and Jeremiah sank in the mire.

[MT 38] = G 45. **[1]** G lacks 'and Pashhur the son of Malchiah': cf. 21.1 for Pashhur ben Malchiah; 37.3 for Jehucal ben Shelemiah. Is Gedaliah the son of the Pashhur of 20.1? **[2]** = 21.9. Rudolph, 240, treats the verse as a marginal gloss (cf. BHS); Bright, 230, thinks of it as a genuine citation by the princes. K *yḥyh*; Q *w^{e}ḥāyāh*: 'and shall live': an addition forming a doublet with *wāḥāy*; 21.9 lacks *wāḥāy*, 'and live'. **[3]** Cf. 21.7; 32.28; 34.2. **[4]** G 'and they said' for MT 'and the princes said': Rudolph suggests *hā'ēlleh*, 'these', has dropped out after 'princes' due to haplography (cf. BHS). For the idiom 'weakening the hands' cf. Lachish Letter VI for the same phrase; the opposite idiom appears in 23.14. Cf. 29.25–28 for other complaints about Jeremiah's defeatist attitude. **[5]** MT *hinnēh-hū' b^{e}yed^{e}kem*, 'look, he is in your hands': cf. *wa'^{a}nī hin^{e}nī b^{e}yed^{e}kem*, 'but as for me, look, I am in your hands', 26.14. MT *kī-'ēn hammelek yūkal 'et^{e}kem dābār*, 'for the king can do nothing against you': G *hoti ouk ēdunato ho basileus pros autous*, 'for the king was not able to withstand them'. MT stresses the king's weakness, G the power of the princes. **[6]** G lacks 'and they took Jeremiah', 'Jeremiah by ropes', and reads 'and he was in the mire' for MT 'and Jeremiah sank in the mire'.

The second account of Jeremiah's adventures during the events leading up to the sacking of Jerusalem follows the pattern of the first story in 37. He is arrested by the princes, thrown into a cistern, rescued from there, granted an interview with the king and has his conditions of restraint ameliorated. The pattern may be similar, but the details are quite different: the circumstances of his arrest are no longer the attempt to leave the city to visit Benjaminite territory but one of the occasions when Jeremiah was trying to persuade the citizens to desert to the Babylonians. This time when arrested, Jeremiah is thrown into a cistern in the court of the guard (contrast 37.15) by permission of the king. He is rescued from there by an Ethiopian official with the king's permission, whereas in 37.17 a royal summons appears to have gained him his release from the dungeons. The royal interview now takes place in the temple rather than the palace, and the exchanges between Zedekiah and Jeremiah are much longer than in 37.17–20. As variations on a theme there are inevitably divergent elements in the accounts which cannot be harmonized (*contra* Bright, 234). Such disharmonious features point to the development (independently?) of doublets in the tradition about the fate of Jeremiah during the siege (cf. the two stories of his release by the Babylonians in 39.11–14; 40.1–6). These doublets allow for considerable interplay between different motifs in the tradition: e.g. the occasion of Jeremiah's arrest in 37.12–14 is linked to property in the land of Benjamin (cf. 32.6–15), whereas in 38.1 it is related to his public preaching which permits an editorial citation in 38.2. In the first account of the interview with the king an ironic point is made about the other prophets (37.18–19); in the second interview a symmetrical connection is made between Jeremiah's experience in the cistern and the fate of the king's harem at the hands of the Babylonians (38.6b, 22).

The charge of desertion in the first story becomes one of seditious preaching in the second account (37.13; 38.4). 21.9 is cited in 38.2 (cf. 45.4 for the idiom 'having one's life as a prize of war'), and Jeremiah is charged with weakening the war effort against the Babylonians (in 21.8–10 the desertion motif is a redactional development of an original statement about complete destruction, hence the appearance of 21.9 in 38.2 points to editorial activity). It is Jeremiah's preaching *to all the people* (v. 1) which attracts the attention of certain princes rather than his arrest by Irijah (37.14b). In a time of war such seditious preaching must be regarded as a capital offence, and Jeremiah is to be considered fortunate that he was not executed summarily (cf. 26.20–23). Once more the prophet appears in a situation which could lead to his death (cf. 26.8, 11, 15, 16, 24; 36.19, 26), but as usual he leads a charmed existence. He may have to hide or be smuggled out of danger, but he always survives. He may even, as on this occasion, be flung into a dungeon or cistern where death is inevitable and only a matter of time. Yet out of these depths also he is rescued. A charmed existence is how his life appears in the different stories in the tradition. But the charge of treason should be noted not only as an element in this version of 37–38 but especially by exegetes who insist on reading the tradition as the representation of an *imitatio jeremiae* (e.g. Polk 1984). At no point is this type of reading more problematical than on the issue of Jeremiah as a traitor (cf. Schoneveld 1976, 194–205; Carroll 1981, 276). The clash of ideologies behind 38.2–4 is not articulated in the story, but the modern exegete would be well advised not to side with one or the other ideology too easily. Jeremiah's stance in this story is acutely criticized by the princes, and his contribution to the defeat of Jerusalem, though unquantifiable, quite notable. Such treachery is well defined by the princes in the charge 'this man is not seeking the welfare (*šālōm*) of this people, but their harm (*rā'āh*)' (v. 4b).

In the exchange between the princes and the king Zedekiah is exposed as a ruler who cannot control his officials. This may be a correct reading of the story, but Zedekiah could hardly have defended Jeremiah against such a charge of treason without revealing himself to be a traitor as well. In the set of stories he clearly has sufficient power to modify the actions of the princes (37.17; 38.10, 14), but even the king cannot release a traitor like Jeremiah and permit him to undermine further the attempt to repulse the Babylonians. The variation in the pattern whereby it is Zedekiah who imprisons Jeremiah for his treasonous talk should be noted (32.3). However, the presentation of some of the princes in 36; 37–38 is quite unsympathetic, and the king appears in the stories as a foil to them. If they are hostile and cruel towards Jeremiah then the king will be represented as kind and sympathetic towards him. These are but the structures of the story-telling techniques and reflect motifs within the tradition. They should not be extrapolated into a psychological profile of either king or princes.

The princes succeed in their attempt to silence Jeremiah by persuading the king that the man is too dangerous for the community's well-being (*šālōm*). He concedes to their wishes and Jeremiah is thrown into an *empty* (cf. 2.13b?) cistern (in a full one he would have drowned!). The princes are more interested in preventing him from damaging the war effort than in killing him (MT v. 6, 'letting Jeremiah down *by ropes*'!). However, the possibility of his death may be mooted by his confinement to an empty cistern (cf. v. 9; 37.20); though such a place also facilitates his being rescued. By confining him there the princes make Jeremiah available for any interviews the king may wish to grant his obdurate prophet. To have killed him outright would have been the ruination of a good story!

38.7–13

7 When Ebed-melech the Ethiopian, a eunuch, who was in the king's house, heard that they had put Jeremiah into the cistern – the king was sitting in the Benjamin Gate – 8 Ebed-melech went from the king's house and said to the king, 9 'My lord the king, these men have done evil in all that they did to Jeremiah the prophet by casting him into the cistern; and he will die there of hunger, for there is no bread left in the city.' 10 Then the king commanded Ebed-melech, the Ethiopian, 'Take three men with you from here, and lift Jeremiah the prophet out of the cistern before he dies.' 11 So Ebed-melech took the men with him and went to the house of the king, to a wardrobe of the storehouse, and took from there old rags and worn-out clothes, which he let down to Jeremiah in the cistern by ropes. 12 Then Ebed-melech the Ethiopian said to Jeremiah, 'Put the rags and clothes between your armpits and the ropes.' Jeremiah did so. 13 Then they drew Jeremiah up with ropes and lifted him out of the cistern. And Jeremiah remained in the court of the guard.

---

[7] G lacks *'îš sārîs*, 'a eunuch': cf. 29.2, where *sārîsîm* may refer to officials rather than eunuchs (cf. Rab*saris* in 39.3, 13). In 39.16 Ebed-melech is not qualified in this manner, though he may have been a eunuch (cf. Bright, 231) because he appears to be part of the king's household. MT *'ebed-melek*, 'Ebed-melech', i.e. 'servant of the king': cf. Obadiah 'servant of Yahweh' (I Kings 18.3–16), a man in charge of the king's household and also given to rescuing prophets in trouble. The king is placed at the Benjamin Gate, cf. 37.13 (an echo of the other story?). **[9]** G lacks introductory 'my lord the king' and has a different reading from MT: G 'you have done evil in what you have done to kill this man with hunger'. MT accuses the princes as if vv. 4–5 were not part of the story; it also has variants *'ēt kol-'ašer 'āśû*, 'all that they did', and *'ēt 'ašer-hišlikû 'el-bōr*, 'their casting into the cistern', which are both the object of *hērē'û*, 'they did evil'. G inevitably lacks 'Jeremiah the prophet'. MT *wayyāmāt*, 'and he has died': a trace of Jeremiah's death notice? Revocalize to *wᵉyāmut*, 'that he may die' (BHS). MT *mippᵉnē hārāʿāb kī ʾēn hallehem ʿōd bāʿīr*, 'because of starvation, for there is no more bread in the city': a curious explanation when Jeremiah's plight is more one of suffocation or exposure than lack of food. If the bread supplies in the city had been exhausted, hauling him from the cistern would not have made him any the less hungry! Exegetes regard this clause as a mistaken gloss (Bright, 227n.) or an addition from 37.21 (BHS; Volz). According to 52.6–7 the siege ended with the exhaustion of the food supply; 38.9 reflects a different viewpoint. **[10]** MT *šᵉlōšīm ʾᵃnāšīm*, 'thirty men': generally regarded as a mistake by commentators (G *triakonta*, 'thirty') and corrected to *šᵉlōšāh*, 'three', following one ms (cf. Hitzig, 301; II Sam. 23.13). G lacks 'Jeremiah the prophet', reading only *auton*, 'him'; also 'the Ethiopian'. **[11]** MT *bᵉyādō*, 'with him': lacking in G. MT *ʾel-taḥat hāʾōṣār*, 'to under the storehouse': G *tēn hupogeion*, 'the underground'; read with Ehrlich 1912, 304, *meltaḥat*, 'wardrobe', cf. II Kings 10.22 (followed by most commentators). K *hsḥbwt*; Q *sᵉḥābōt*, 'rags, clouts': K definite article from v. 12. G lacks *baḥᵃbālīm*, 'by ropes': MT influenced by v. 6 (it is unnecessary for the rags to be lowered by rope; they can be thrown down the cistern!). **[12]** G has a shorter text: 'and he said, Put these under the ropes. And Jeremiah did so.' **[13]** G *auton*, 'him', for MT 'Jeremiah'. MT *wayyēšeb yirmᵉyāhū baḥᵃṣar hammaṭṭārāh*, 'and Jeremiah remained in the court of the guard' = v. 28; 37.21.

The one novel section in the second version of Jeremiah's imprisonment and interview with the king is 38.7–13. The story of Ebed-melech's rescue of the prophet is the only element in the two variant accounts which explains *how* Jeremiah was extricated from the cistern down which the princes had put him. 37.17 passes over the logistics of the matter, but the development of the cistern element (*bēt habbōr*, 'the house of the cistern', 37.16) in 38.6 requires some account of the transition of Jeremiah from that parlous position to his encounter with the king. A new character is introduced into the story: Ebed-melech an Ethiopian (conceivably a eunuch), who served in the king's household (cf. Obadiah's role as overseer of Ahab's household, I Kings 18.3). His intervention with the king on behalf of Jeremiah indicates that the story is quite independent of its present context in that the king's participation in Jeremiah's plight (vv. 4–5) is incompatible with his orders to rescue the prophet (v. 10). The king has consented to Jeremiah's death ('let this man be put to death . . . he is in your hands', vv. 4–5) and can hardly be expected to change his mind now (G v. 9 is more aware of vv. 4–5 than MT). In 37.12–14 Jeremiah is arrested at the Benjamin Gate; here in v. 7b

Ebed-melech finds the king there. As the story unfolds, Ebed-melech is represented as making a number of journeys: from the king's house to the Benjamin Gate, back to the king's house and then to the cistern in the court of the guard. He is a busy but conscientious official who clearly has access to the king and can sway his actions and decisions. His representations on behalf of Jeremiah are successful, and in some detail the story explains how he rescued the incarcerated prophet (vv. 11–13; briefer in G).

No explanation is offered in the text of the reasons for Ebed-melech's actions towards Jeremiah, though 39.15–18, which also refers to him, may allude to one possible reason – his trust in Yahweh. The two pieces are not connected (39.18 may echo 38.2; cf. 45.5, though the editors have not chosen to place the motifs together). Perhaps Ebed-melech represents that strand of sympathy between Jeremiah and the princes which occurs at various points in the tradition (e.g. 26.16; 36.17–19). On occasions an official figure is presented in the text as assisting the prophet during a crisis in his career (cf. 26.24; 38.7–13; even Baruch in 36.5). The introduction of Ebed-melech into 37–38, with the intimation of his fate in 39.15–18, may point in the direction of the development of the tradition. Variant stories allow for development and embellishment, and the figures of Baruch and Ebed-melech represent examples of this creative aspect of the growth of the book (much developed in post biblical literature). The story of Ebed-melech introduces a new character into a set of stories and permits mediation between certain features of the basic story. Balancing the hostility of the princes is the concern of the Ethiopian official and the three men who assist him (v. 10). The king's decision to supply Jeremiah with his daily bread (37.21) becomes Ebed-melech's pointing out to the king the prophet's lack of food. The same motifs are manipulated in different ways, and the historical fantasy (cf. Pohlmann 1978, 79–80) of the Ethiopian official becomes a third account of how Jeremiah came to be under arrest in the court of the guard during the final days of the siege. Such scope for variation belongs to the art of story-telling and that art is a dominant feature of Part IV (especially in 37–41).

38.14–23

14 King Zedekiah sent for Jeremiah the prophet and received him at the third entrance of the temple of the LORD. The king said to Jeremiah, 'I will ask you a question; hide nothing from me.' 15 Jeremiah said to Zedekiah, 'If I tell you, will you not be sure to put me to death? And if I give you counsel, you will not listen to me.' 16 Then King Zedekiah swore secretly to Jeremiah, 'As the LORD lives, who made our souls, I will not put you to death or deliver you into the hand of these men who seek your life.'

17 Then Jeremiah said to Zedekiah, 'Thus says the LORD, the God of hosts, the God of Israel, If you will surrender to the princes of the king of Babylon, then your life shall be spared, and this city shall not be burned with fire, and you and your house shall live. 18 But if you do not surrender to the princes of the king of Babylon, then this city shall be given into the hand of the Chaldeans, and they shall burn it with fire, and you shall not escape from their hand.' 19 King Zedekiah said to Jeremiah, 'I am afraid of the Jews who have deserted to the Chaldeans, lest I be handed over to them and they abuse me.' 20 Jeremiah said, 'You shall not be given to them. Obey now the voice of the LORD in what I say to you, and it shall be well with you, and your life shall be spared. 21 But if you refuse to surrender, this is the vision which the LORD has shown to me: 22 Behold, all the women left in the house of the king of Judah were being led out to the princes of the king of Babylon and were saying.

"Your trusted friends have deceived you
  and prevailed against you;
now that your feet are sunk in the mire,
  they turn away from you."

23 All your wives and your sons shall be led out to the Chaldeans, and you yourself shall not escape from their hand, but shall be seized by the king of Babylon; and this city shall be burned with fire.'

---

[14] MT *wayyiqqaḥ 'et-yirmᵉyāhū hannābī' 'ēlāyw*, 'and Jeremiah the prophet was brought to him': G *kai ekalesen auton pros heauton*, 'and called him to himself'. The third entrance (G 'the house of Aselisi', cf. G^{AS}) of the temple is unknown; but yet again the text associates Jeremiah with the temple. Duhm, 305, follows Giesebrecht, 208, and reads *mābō' haššālīšīm* (MT *haššᵉlīšī*, 'third'), 'the entrance of the officers', cf. II Kings 11.4–8. MT *šō'ēl 'ᵃnī 'ōtᵉkā dābār*, 'I will ask you something': cf. NEB, JPSB; better than RSV 'question'. The force of *dābār* here may be 'oracle', i.e. 'prophetic word' (cf. Bright, 231); this would parallel 37.17, where a divine oracle is sought. The phrase 'hide nothing from me' (cf. v. 25; I Sam. 3.17; II Sam. 14.18) may reflect the motif of the reluctant speaker withholding the divine word (e.g. 26.2; 42.4b; cf. Janzen 1981, 97–105). The word sought by the king is given in vv. 17–18. **[15]** The exchange here is similar to the rational conversation between the two parties in 37.18–20. The storyteller's art focuses on a realistic aspect of the encounter, rather than the more frequent stereotypical clichés which characterize the tradition. **[16]** MT *bassēter*, 'in secret': cf. 37.17; lacking in G here. It may well be asked 'what is swearing in secret'?, but the motif belongs to the pattern of the stories in 37–38 and occurs here for that reason. 16b contradicts v. 5. MT *ḥay-yhwh 't ᵃšer 'āśāh-lānū 'et-hannepeš hazzō't*, lit. 'as Yahweh lives who has made for us this life': Q omits K *'t* (a scribal error). Cf. v. 9 for 'these men' (note 'this man', v. 4; 'these men', vv. 9, 16). G lacks 'who are seeking your life': the phrase reflects the option motif of 21.7; cf. 34.20, 21. **[17]** G lacks 'the god of hosts, the god of Israel'. MT *'im-yāṣō' tēṣē'*, 'if you will really go out', i.e. surrender. Whether the Babylonians would have spared king and city after a lengthy siege is a matter of speculation, but the king's surrender hardly would have made good his breach of trust against Nebuchadrezzar in the first place. The options of vv. 17–18 reflect the motif in v. 2; 21.8–9, but with the added element of the king's surrender sparing the city. **[18]** Cairo geniza fragments lack 'the princes of'; G lacks 'from their hands'. **[19]** Jeremiah's campaign to persuade people to desert is represented by v. 19 as a successful one. Zedekiah's pliability has limits, and this reason may be an excuse for not following Jeremiah. Whichever course of action Zedekiah follows he faces a nasty future – whether from the Babylonians (39.5–7) or from those who feel betrayed by him. **[20]** Cf. the *šālōm* oracle of 34.4–5 for a similar word of well-being (*wᵉyīṭab lᵉkā*, 'it shall be well with you'). MT *lō' yittēnū*, 'they will not give': i.e. it will not happen, they will not hand you over to the Jews who have deserted. **[21]** MT *zeh haddābār ᵃšer hir'anī yhwh*, 'this is the thing which Yahweh has showed me': not a vision as such (cf. 24.1), though it may be an imaginative conjuring up of a scene typical of invaded cities and the fate of the harems of defeated kings. **[22]** Cf. Obad. 7 for the poem. MT *'anšē šᵉlōmekā*, 'your trusted friends': cf. 20.10 for a similar motif of treachery among familiar friends. The sinking of the foot (MT, but many mss 'feet') into the mire parallels Jeremiah's sinking into the mire in v. 6b. **[23]** G lacks 'all', 'from their hand', 'with fire'; MT *tiśrōp*, 'burn': a few mss *tiśśārēp*, 'shall be burned'; cf. G *katakauthēsetai*.

The extended interview between Zedekiah and Jeremiah in the ch. 38 version of their encounter has a number of distinctive points. It is conducted in the temple complex rather than in the royal palace. A secret oath is sworn by the king to protect Jeremiah, and the prophet (MT) offers Zedekiah the possibility of escaping his fate by surrendering to the Babylonians. The king explains his reluctance to surrender because of the threat posed by the citizens who have surrendered already. Jeremiah repeats and expands his message about the fate of king and city in terms of what will happen to the royal harem. A brief piece of poetry is used to portray the king's plight. These additional features make for a more interesting exchange of opinions between king and prophet and indicate some of the story-teller's skills. The dialogue between Zedekiah and Jeremiah (also in vv. 24–26) presents the king as pusillanimous in his relations with other people, though only up to a point in that he refuses to kow-tow to Jeremiah's threats about the future. This characterization of him also appears in vv. 4–5, where he allows the princes to act against Jeremiah. The Zedekiah of the interviews strand is a man trapped between the Babylonians and his own princes: he cannot resolve his problems because whichever way he turns he faces disaster. Even though v. 17 may hint at a resolution of his difficulty, it can hardly be taken seriously. The Babylonians are besieging the city (the withdrawal of 37.11 is not represented in 38); the princes are determined to defend Jerusalem, and Zedekiah cannot oppose them. Whether he surrenders or fights, he faces the anger of the Babylonians as their vassal, and if he surrenders he must bear the wrath of the betrayed people and princes as well as that of those who are outside the city already. Jeremiah's advocacy of such betrayal can hardly be palatable to him. It does, however, represent the motif of choice epitomized by v. 2 and it is used in vv. 17–18 to offer Zedekiah the option available to the citizens. Yet what Zedekiah appears to want from Jeremiah is a divine oracle (37.17; 38.14): a word which will transform his situation (cf. 21.2b; 37.3). That transformation would entail the withdrawal of the Babylonians, not his surrender to them. Surrendering to the king of Babylon could only bring about his destruction because he would have to face charges of disloyalty (hence 39.5b). Jeremiah fails to persuade Zedekiah to surrender because it is not a proper option open to him. The unrealistic assurances of the prophet cannot convince him. Elements of his dilemma are well presented by the developed dialogue of vv. 14–23.

The novelty of the surrender offer in v. 17 illustrates the freedom with which the writers develop the theme of the interview and the motifs of that theme. It is part of the logic of the siege-surrender material but extended to the king it breaks down. The king cannot surrender in the way an ordinary citizen might, because he is the one responsible for the siege in the first place. Since he is Nebuchadrezzar's vassal, the termination of the siege will bring about his own downfall. Sympathy towards Jeremiah permits the interview, control of the princes allows him to promise protection; but his pliability has limits, and he compromises with both prophet and princes by pleasing neither. Jeremiah's final word to him is an oracular one (v. 21 is not necessarily a vision, though the force of 'Yahweh has shown me' will allow for a visionary element) depicting the outcome of his failure to surrender. This word depicts the fate of the royal women and children. The harem will go to the victorious army, as is the inevitable fate of women in war: rape, concubinage, abuse and exploitation. Their treatment symbolizes the defeat of the kingdom, as does the leading out of the royal sons to their captors (it is not specified in v. 23, but execution would be their most probable end, cf. 39.6). Pathos is added to this picture of the fall of Jerusalem by the placing of the brief poem of v. 22b in the mouths of the women as they are led out to endure the lot of women wherever men gain complete power over them. They mock Zedekiah with a conventional poetic outcry, castigating him for his deception by his companions and sneering at his plight. The snatch of poetry also makes connections between Jeremiah's erstwhile internment in the cistern (v. 6b) and Zedekiah's figurative position. The *seizing* of Jeremiah by the princes (37.14) is reprised now by the *seizing* (*tpś*) of Zedekiah by the king of Babylon (v. 23b). This terrible picture of what lies in store for the king constitutes Jeremiah's last word in the interview strand (what follows in vv. 24–28 represents no exchange between king and prophet) and reiterates the harshness of 21.7 (cf. 37.17b for much greater brevity of sentiment). In refusing the possibility of surrender Zedekiah has not only sealed his own fate but also guaranteed the destruction of the city (v. 18). Thus the extended interview of 38 allows the king's responsibility for the fate of Jerusalem to be fully demonstrated, and the interview strand may be regarded as serving just this precise purpose in the tradition (cf. 37.2).

38.24–28

24 Then Zedekiah said to Jeremiah, 'Let no one know of these words and you shall not die. 25 If the princes hear that I have spoken with you and come to you and say to you, "Tell us what you said to the king and what the king said to you; hide nothing from us and we will not put you to death," 26 then you shall say to them, "I made a humble plea to the king that he

would not send me back to the house of Jonathan to die there." ' 27 Then all the princes came to Jeremiah and asked him, and he answered them as the king had instructed him. So they left off speaking with him, for the conversation had not been overheard. 28 And Jeremiah remained in the court of the guard until the day that Jerusalem was taken.

---

[24] Cf. v. 16; this section would fit better after 37.20, especially in view of the reference to 'the house of Jonathan' in v. 26 (cf. 37.15). It would then not appear to be a modification of Zedekiah's promise in v. 16. The section vv. 24–28 may well be a variant of 37.20–21 added at the end of the interview section and inverting the speakers. **[25]** MT *mah-dibbartā 'el-hammelek . . . ūmah-dibber 'ēlekā hammelek*, 'what you said to the king . . . and what the king said to you': G *ti elalēsen soi ho basileus . . . kai ti elalēsen pros se ho basileus*, 'what the king said to you . . . what the king said to you'! BHS transposes 'and what the king said to you' to immediately after 'what you said to the king', cf. Volz, 332–3; Rudolph, 242. RSV, NEB assume this rearrangement of the MT (JPSB follows its order). The story variants have placed together conflicting offers to spare Jeremiah's life, thus rendering neither of the parties guilty of planning his death. **[26]** Cf. 37.20. **[27]** MT *ṣiwwāh hammelek*, 'the king commanded': some mss, Vrs *ṣiwwahū*,' (the king) commanded *him*'. MT *wayyaḥ^a^rišū mimmennū kī lō'-nišma' haddābār*, lit. 'and they were silent for him because the thing (word) had not been heard': G *kai apesiōpēsan, hoti ouk ēkousthē logos kuriou*, 'and they were silent because the word of the lord was not heard'. **[28]** = 37.21; 38.13b + 'until the day that Jerusalem was taken': this addition links with the next section which in MT begins in v. 28b with a repeat of 'that Jerusalem was taken' (see Notes on 39.1). Bright, 229, reads 39.15–18 immediately after 38.28a. This transposition makes sense as the completion of Jeremiah's activities in the court of the guard, but the MT order has the advantage of associating Ebed-melech's deliverance with Jeremiah's release when the Babylonians freed him.

The final element in the collection of pieces constituting the Jeremiah-Zedekiah interview motif explains how Jeremiah is confined to the court of the guard rather than returned to the cistern. In 37.20 the transference from the dungeons to the court is effected by Jeremiah's own request, whereas 38.24–28a do not explain precisely how the change came about but emphasizes the way Jeremiah escaped from death at the hands of king *and* princes. According to v. 26 the request of 37.20 is employed, but it is put in the king's mouth rather than Jeremiah's. This change of speaker reflects the inversion of activity between 37.20–21 and 38.24–26. In the first account of Jeremiah's escape from the dungeons and interview with the king, Jeremiah does the speaking (from v. 18) and the king acts in accordance with what he says (v. 21). In the second account the king and Ebed-melech speak, with Ebed-melech and Jeremiah acting (38.9–13). But in the third account the king does all the speaking; Jeremiah says nothing yet acts according to the king's commands. The effect of 38.24–28 on the whole story is ironic in that the section reverses the role of the princes and presents the king as seeking Jeremiah's protection. In v. 27 the princes, who had sought his death in v. 4, are now happy to accept from his lips the explanation provided by the king. Gone is all hostility against Jeremiah, and the one who throughout the story faces death in various forms without the protection of the authorities protects the king from his princes! Only 38.7–13 provides a mediating position between these two versions with the presentation of Ebed-melech as a supportive third party. His role in the story saves Jeremiah from the embarrassing situation of having to prevaricate about his conversation with the king into which he is put by vv. 24–27.

Irony abounds in the final exchange between Zedekiah and Jeremiah: in order not to die Jeremiah must not speak a truth which the tradition represents him as constantly speaking. He must equivocate with the princes and use an explanation concocted by the king which happens to be Jeremiah's own words in the first version of the story (37.20)! The irony of 38.25 may be modified by viewing the statement as the king's imaginative projection on to the princes, but in v. 27 they appear to be satisfied by the request for a transfer to a more congenial place of confinement. Jeremiah is protected by the king by protecting the king from the princes. Conscious irony on the writer's part may be discernible here. At the same time it would be inadvisable to take Jeremiah's 'white' lie in vv. 24–27 too seriously, though recent writers on prophetic conflict have noted it carefully (e.g. Crenshaw 1971, 59). If moral issues are to be imported into the scrutiny of prophecy then it may be of some importance, but in the context of a story variation it is only an element used by a storytelling technique to explain how Jeremiah overcame the hostility of king and princes. The image of the ranting prophet reduced to 'lying' to protect the king or himself from the hostility of the princes is ironic within the context of the whole tradition, but hardly so from the viewpoint of the exchanges between king and prophet in 37.17–20 or 38.14–23. It is hardly the intention of the writers to present

Jeremiah as a liar by their development of the theme of his interview with the king.

The varied material in 37.3 – 38.28a represents the growth of a section of the tradition in terms of reworking a limited number of motifs in a number of different ways. The creation of stories about the fate of Jeremiah during the siege and the way he survived the twin rigours of starvation and royal opposition subtly illustrates the storyteller's art in the book of Jeremiah and leads up to the final collapse of Jerusalem. Apart from securing a food supply for Jeremiah nothing is changed by the stories, though the introduction of Ebed-melech provides a concrete example of the truth of Jeremiah's preaching about the possibility of survival (38.2; 39.15–18). The word spoken and read out in the time of Jehoiakim (36) remains as the background to 37–38 (in spite of a slight modification in 38.17), and the network of variations on Jeremiah in the dungeons and in encounters with the king allows a certain suspense to be maintained before the fate of king and city is unfolded.

39.1–14

39[1] In the ninth year of Zedekiah king of Judah, in the tenth month,
Nebuchadrezzar king of Babylon and all his army came against Jerusalem
and besieged it; 2 in the eleventh year of Zedekiah, in the fourth month, on
the ninth day of the month, a breach was made in the city. 3 When Jerusalem
was taken, all the princes of the king of Babylon came and sat in the middle
gate: Nergal-sharezer, Samgar-nebo, Sarsechim the Rabsaris, Nergal-
sharezer the Rabmag, with all the rest of the officers of the king of Babylon.
4 When Zedekiah king of Judah and all the soldiers saw them, they fled,
going out of the city at night by way of the king's garden through the gate
between the two walls; and they went toward the Arabah. 5 But the army
of the Chaldeans pursued them, and overtook Zedekiah in the plains
of Jericho; and when they had taken him, they brought him up to
Nebuchadrezzar king of Babylon, at Riblah, in the land of Hamath; and he
passed sentence upon him. 6 The king of Babylon slew the sons of Zedekiah
at Riblah before his eyes; and the king of Babylon slew all the nobles of
Judah. 7 He put out the eyes of Zedekiah, and bound him in fetters to take
him to Babylon. 8 The Chaldeans burned the king's house and the house
of the people, and broke down the walls of Jerusalem. 9 Then Nebuzaradan,
the captain of the guard, carried into exile to Babylon the rest of the people
who were left in the city, those who had deserted to him, and the people
who remained. 10 Nebuzaradan, the captain of the guard, left in the land

of Judah some of the poor people who owned nothing, and gave them vineyards and fields at the same time.

11 Nebuchadrezzar king of Babylon gave command concerning Jeremiah through Nebuzaradan, the captain of the guard, saying, 12 'Take him, look after him well and do to him no harm, but deal with him as he tells you.' 13 So Nebuzaradan the captain of the guard, Nebushazban the Rabsaris, Nergal-sharezer the Rabmag, and all the chief officers of the king of Babylon 14 sent and took Jeremiah from the court of the guard. They entrusted him to Gedaliah the son of Ahikam, son of Shaphan, that he should take him home. So he dwelt among the people.

[MT 39] = G 46. G lacks vv. 4–13, possibly due to homoioteleuton (vv. 3, 13 have virtually the same list of Babylonian officers' names). MT 39.1–10, cf. 52.4–16; II Kings 25.1–12 for essentially the same material. 39.1–2 interrupt the connection between 38.28b ('when Jerusalem was taken' transposed by RSV to 39.3a; cf. JPSB n. i) and 39.3 (Rudolph, 243, treats them was a parenthetical summary from 52.4–7aα). **[1]** Cf. 52.4; G^BS 'ninth *month*' for MT 'ninth year'. According to most of the texts the siege of Jerusalem started in January 588 and finished in July 587 (see on 52.12). The MT phrase *wᵉhāyāh ka'ᵃšer nilkᵉdāh yᵉrūšālāim*, 'now when Jerusalem was taken', in 38.28b should be followed by 39.3 'and all the princes came . . .', but the editors provide vv. 1–2 as a background to the events of 39 (everything in 37.3–38.28a is set in this period). G^BS lack 'in the tenth month'. **[2]** Cf. 52.5–7a. MT 'fourth': a few mss, S 'fifth'. MT *hobqᵉ'āh hā'īr*, 'the city was breached': i.e. the city wall was penetrated, cf. 52.7a; II Kings 25.4a. As a redactional title to 39, vv. 1–2 constitute a summary of the siege, but the other accounts of the matter are ambiguous because they associate the breaching of the city (*wattibbāqa' hā'īr*) with the breaking out of the besieged rather than the penetration of the city by the Babylonians. RSV circumvents any misunderstanding by prefixing 38.28b to v. 3, whereas in MT v. 3 looks like the next stage of the siege after the breaching of the wall. **[3]** MT *bᵉša'ar hattāwek*, 'in the middle gate':unknown location. Bright, 241, reads 38.28b; 39.3, 14 together after 39.1–2, 4–10 and before 39.11–13. The list of Babylonian officers is confused in MT, cf. v. 13; Rudolph, 245; Bright, 243. Nergal sar-ezer occurs twice in MT: the four names of v. 3 become three in v. 13 and in the emended list of many modern exegetes appear as Nergalsarezer, the prince of Sin-magir (a district), the Rabmag (a high official), Nebushazban the Rabsaris (a diplomatic or military rank rather than chief eunuch, cf. 29.2; 34.19; [38.7?]), cf. Rudolph, 245. MT *wᵉkol-šᵉ'rīt śārē*, 'and all the rest of the princes of': 'rest' may be a gloss due to dittography (cf. BHS); it is lacking in v. 13. Cf. Ehrlich 1912, 342: *yeter*, 'rest', would be more suitable, cf. v. 9. **[4]** MT *wayᵉhī ka'ᵃšer rā'ām ṣidqiyyāhū*, 'and when Zedekiah saw them': Volz, 342–3, reads *rā'āh*, 'saw it', i.e. the breach of

v. 2; MT represents an adjustment of the text to v. 3. MT *wayyēṣē derek hā'ᵃrābāh*, 'and *he* went out in the direction of the Arabah': i.e. towards the Jordan valley (cf. v. 5). Only Zedekiah acts according to MT, but v. 5; 52.7 indicate the action was taken by him and his warriors; various mss, Vrs read plur., cf. BHS *wayyēlᵉkū*, 'and they went', as in 52.7. **[5]** S, a few mss read 'and all his army was scattered from him' after 'in the plains of Jericho' as in 52.8; II Kings 25.5. 'Riblah, in the land of Hamath': cf. II Kings 23.33; on the river Orontes it was the Syrian headquarters of Nebuchadrezzar from which he conducted his campaign against Judah. MT *wayᵉdabbēr 'ittō mišpāṭīm*, lit. 'and he spoke with him judgments': i.e. pass sentence upon, cf. 1.16. NEB understands Zedekiah to be the subject of the verb 'and he pleaded his case before him'; JPSB 'and he put him on trial' conveys the sense of the idiom entirely adequately. **[8]** MT *bēt hā'ām*, 'the house of the people': cf. 52.13, where temple, palace and all the houses of Jerusalem are burned; S *bāttē*, 'houses of . . .'. Cf. II Kings 25.9. Rudolph inserts 'of Yahweh and the houses of', cf. BHS. No 'house of the people' is known for Jerusalem nor is there any evidence in the Hebrew Bible that the temple was ever called by such a demotic title. Bab. Talmud *Megillah* 27a understands the phrase to refer to the synagogue; cf. Landsberger 1949 for the temple as the meaning of *bēt hā'ām*. **[9]** MT repeats *wᵉ'ēt yeter hā'āmōn*, 'and the rest of the artificers' (see on 52.15), cf. Prov. 8.30; followed by Rudolph, Bright. MT *nᵉbūzar-'ᵃdān rab-ṭabbāḥīm bābel*, 'Nebuzaradan, the chief of the butchers of Babylon': an archaic title but meaning marshal or captain. Nebuzaradan, '(the god) Nabu has given seed', is regarded as having become a proselyte in later years (tractate *Sanhedrin* 95a–96b): small wonder in view of 40.2–5! The irony of v. 9 should be noted: both those who deserted and those who remained in the city were deported, whereas the options proclaimed by Jeremiah offered survival only to those who deserted and death to those who remained in the city (cf. 21.8–9; 38.2). **[10]** MT *wīgēbīm*? cf. 52.16; II Kings 25.12: of uncertain meaning; ST 'fields', V 'cisterns' (*gēbīm*); perhaps '(vineyards) and cisterns' but other texts *ūlᵉyōgᵉbīm*, 'and ploughmen, field labourers'. MT *bayyōm hāhū'*, 'on that day': i.e. the same day; it may represent an editorial link between v. 10 and v. 11 (Bright, 243, takes it with v. 11). **[11]** Rudolph suggests transposing vv. 11–12 to before 40.2a, 1b, 2b (cf. BHS). MT *bᵉyad*, 'by means of (Nebuzaradan)': cf. 37.2. Two stories are told about the release of Jeremiah (39.11–14; 40.1–6): in this one the emperor himself plays a role; in both Nebuzaradan is the main actor. **[12]** MT *wᵉ'ēnekā śīm 'ālāyw*, lit. 'and put your eyes on him': i.e. look after him. **[13]** Cf. 40.2; an attempt to harmonize vv. 11–12 with vv. 3, 14; cf. Rudolph, 246, where his rearrangement of the text eases some of the problems. **[14]** Rudolph, 245, regards 'to Gedaliah ben Ahikam ben Shaphan' as an addition from 40.6 (cf. Weiser, 345); it is an attempt to harmonize rather different accounts of Jeremiah's release from prison or rescue from deportation. MT *wayyēšeb bᵉtōk hā'ām*, 'and he remained among the people': cf. 37.4; 40.6. G lacks 'to the house'; RSV 'home', NEB 'the Residence'.

Textual confusions abound in 39.1–14 and most commentators rearrange the text to make better sense of it (e.g. Rudolph reads 38.28b; 39.3, 11–12, 14 with 39.1–2, 4–10, 13 bracketed as redactional and secondary). The details of the fall of Jerusalem are to be found in 52.4–16 and II Kings 25.1–12 so they are unnecessary here except as background to the account of what happened to Jeremiah when the city fell. Appended to the various accounts of how Jeremiah fared during the siege and his residence in the court of the guard are two stories of how the Babylonians liberated him (39.3, 11–12, 14; 40.1–6). These stories are the equivalent of the variations on the interview motif and indicate the variety of story-telling used to portray Jeremiah in 37–40.6; 42–45. The stories cannot be harmonized, but they share central themes: Nebuzaradan the commander freed Jeremiah, and once freed Jeremiah elected to stay in Judah rather than go to Babylon. The details and circumstances of each story are different. The image of Jeremiah in Part IV is that of a man who belongs 'among the people' (37.4, 12; 39.14c; 40.6) and, the imprisonment stories and 40.7–41.10 apart, he is so represented in all the stories (typified by 42.1–2).

The fall of Jerusalem results in the devastation of the city and its great buildings (v. 8; cf. 32.29), the capture and execution of all the nobles and the deportation of the citizens (see on 52.4–16). According to v. 10 all that is left in the land are a few poor people who are allowed to take over the vineyards and fields. However, this assertion is in conflict with v. 14, where some important people remain behind to govern the land. It also conflicts with the information given about Gedaliah's community in 40.7–41.18 (see on 41.10). The contradictions between the different accounts in 39–41 are more obvious because the redactors have placed 39.4–10 in this context. Discrete traditions contribute to making the picture of Judaean life in the aftermath of the fall of Jerusalem rather confused; though the confusion is no greater than exists for any block of biblical literature measured against its historical background (e.g. the exodus and Ex. 1–24; settlement of the land in Joshua and Judges: the origins of the monarchy and I Samuel). The deportation of all the people, deserters from the city and survivors of the siege, to Babylon undermines the claim attributed to Jeremiah that remaining in the city would lead to death whereas deserting would secure life. Again the discrepancy is brought to our attention by the editing which places in close proximity the two different traditions. The contradiction is hardly an important one, but it does underline the nature of the material in the book as a collection of diverse stories associated with Jeremiah but lacking a coherent and harmonious unity.

In the first account of Jeremiah's release from the court of the guard he is made the special object of concern of *Nebuchadrezzar* (whether v. 11 imagines the emperor to be present in Jerusalem or at Riblah is a moot point because v. 6 is not part of the rescue operation). Thus the one who had advocated the Babylonian cause for so long is rewarded by his sponsors (?) with special consideration after a harrowing siege. This is in keeping with the view of Jeremiah as the friend of Babylon (cf. 27–29; but contrast 50–51) and belongs to the logic of that strand of tradition. It is hardly necessary to speculate on whether the story is realistic or otherwise (cf. the idyll of 40.1–6), but the element of choice offered in 40.4–5 is absent here. Jeremiah is to be looked after in general terms, and Nebuzaradan is to implement whatever the friend of Babylon wishes to be done in particular. After release from confinement Jeremiah is given into the keeping of Gedaliah ben Ahikam (cf. 26.24) ben Shaphan and so remains among the people. This story of his residing in the land does not belong to a deportation tradition (which is why the editorial placement of 39.4–10 is so confusing), but reflects a rather different account of the organization of life in the land after the fall of Jerusalem. Those who supported Babylon in the period before the destruction of Jerusalem and the people are allowed to live in the land (40.4–5 offers an account of Jeremiah's release in relation to the deportation). Jeremiah now becomes part of Gedaliah's group (cf. 40.6). The tradition knows nothing more about Jeremiah in relation to Gedaliah and therefore can only assert that he was a member of it. As a last word on the matter it is noted that 'he remained among the people' (cf. 37.4, 12; 40.6). This point is hardly compatible with v. 10, but presupposes a quite different tradition of life after the loss of Jerusalem as the centre of life in the land. Jeremiah 'among the people' is one of the dominant images of the stories in Part IV and is a rather distinctive element in the book.

39.15–18

15 The word of the LORD came to Jeremiah while he was shut up in the court of the guard: 16 'Go, and say to Ebed-melech the Ethiopian, "Thus says the LORD of hosts, the God of Israel: Behold, I will fulfil my words against this city for evil and not for good, and they shall be accomplished before you on that day. 17 But I will deliver you on that day, says the LORD, and you shall not be given into the hand of the men of whom you are afraid. 18 For I will surely save you, and you shall not fall by the sword; but you shall have your life as a prize of war, because you have put your trust in me, says the LORD." '

---

[15] The introductory formula word-order is peculiar in MT: 'and to Jeremiah came the word of Yahweh'. G lacks 'while he was shut up': this makes better sense than emphasizing the constraints upon him in relation to the command of v. 16 'Go'! **[16]** MT *hālōk*, 'go': cf. 13.1; 19.1; 35.1. If the redactional note in v. 15 is taken at face value then the command of v. 16 is absurd (cf. Duhm, 312; but Bright, 232, feels it should not be taken literally: 'Either he sent the message, or Ebed-melek came to visit him'). Rationalizations apart, vv. 15–16 represent stereotypical language-usage by the editors without thought for content. Jeremiah is a prophet who comes and goes (cf. BHS b–b on 39.14) by divine command and so the word here is given such an introduction even though it is unsuitable for the circumstances indicated by MT. K *mby*; Q *mēbī*, 'bringing', i.e. fulfilling: cf. 19.15; 21.10 for the motifs used here. G lacks *w^ehāyū l^epāneḵā hayyōm hahū'* lit. 'and they shall be before you on that day': i.e. the words will be performed in your presence the same day; cf. v. 10 for *bayyōm hahū'*; dittography from v. 17? (cf. BHS; Cornill, 410–11). **[17]** MT *w^elō' tinnātēn b^eyad hā'^anāšīm '^ašer-'attāh yāgōr mipp^enēhem*, 'and you shall not be given into the hand of the men of whom you are afraid': this assurance would fit the Zedekiah of 38.19–20 better than the Ebed-melech of 38.7–13. The men who are feared cannot be the princes (*contra* Bright, 232) because 'on that day' they either would be killed or would have to flee for their lives. If Ebed-melech had anything to fear from them it would have been before the Babylonian penetration of the city. Cf. 22.25 for the affirmative form of this sentence (i.e. the giving of Coniah into the power of those whom he fears). **[18]** Cf. 21.9; 38.2; 45.5b for the metaphor 'your life as a prize of war', but here it does not refer to deserting from the city (see on 45.5). MT *kī mallēṭ '^amallet^ekā*, 'for I will surely deliver you': lit. let you escape.

Inserted between the two accounts of Jeremiah's release from confinement by Nebuzaradan is an oracular statement given to

Ebed-melech before the siege was terminated. Like so much else in 37–39 it is out of place in the logical scheme of things, but the editors may have wished to link together the fate of both men. The imprisoned Jeremiah and the Ethiopian official both would survive the siege and its aftermath. Although the oracle given to Ebed-melech would be more appropriate after 38.7–13, its present position (like an afterthought) emphasizes the fulfilment of the divine word and the relation between deliverance and trust in Yahweh.

39.15–18 is virtually a midrash built out of phrases and motifs from the whole tradition (cf. Duhm, 312–13). The way these are put together suggests a late source developing the tradition by means of concrete examples which demonstrate the truth of Jeremiah's preaching (Ebed-melech here and Baruch in 45 are prime instances of this technique). As evidence of this reading of the text the awkwardness of vv. 15–18 may be adduced. Jeremiah is confined to the court of the guard (a form of house arrest), yet is *sent* (*hālōk*, 'go') to the king's house where Ebed-melech works (where else would he be sent?). This is a perfectly good idiom from the tradition (cf. 13.1; 19.1; 35.1) and reflects the presentation of Jeremiah as an actor who responds to cues from Yahweh (e.g. 'go', 'go down', 'stand'). But it does not fit Jeremiah's situation during the siege. Ebed-melech is then made a witness of the fulfilment of the divine word (*'before you* on that day', v. 16) and incorporated into the message (vv. 17–18; cf. Baruch in 45.4–5). The motif of being given into the power of the enemy is one used to describe the Babylonians (cf. 21.7; 22.25) but can hardly have that meaning here. Why should the Chaldaeans wish to harm Ebed-melech in particular? Fear of other Jews is introduced in 38.19, but different language is used so v. 17 is not citing that motif. As an official of the king Ebed-melech may have had the same enemies as Zedekiah, and his escape after the breaching of the city wall may be the point of vv. 17–18. The view that he feared the princes who were Jeremiah's enemies because he had assisted the prophet to escape from the cistern and had accused the princes of doing evil (38.9; Bright) is an unlikely meaning of v. 17. The princes could have killed him at any stage in the siege until the Babylonians breached the wall, and then they would have had to devote their energies to escaping rather than to the settling of old scores. Furthermore, to interpret v. 17 in this fashion is to assume a historicity to 38.7–13 and to ignore the lack of hostility between the princes and Jeremiah in 38.27. All the elements in 37–39 should be read as stories rather than history and their lack of compatibility with each other should be noted as evidence for that reading of them.

Jeremiah and Ebed-melech are two figures who did not desert to the Babylonians during the siege, yet survived the ordeal of those days. 39.11–14; 40.1–6 deal with Jeremiah's fate as a 'friend of Babylon'. 39.15–18 present a rather different account of how survival was possible: as the result of a divine oracle. The extent to which this oracle is to be linked to Ebed-melech's action in rescuing Jeremiah in one of the stories about the siege is difficult to determine. According to v. 18 Ebed-melech's deliverance is due to his putting his trust in Yahweh (cf. 17.7–8, where such trust rules out fear). No direct connection is made between the rescue of Jeremiah and Ebed-melech's own escape from danger (that lack of connection is much facilitated by the separation of 39.15–18 from 38.7–13). Not his attitude towards Jeremiah but his trust in Yahweh underwrites Ebed-melech's fate. In the fall of Jerusalem the Ethiopian will survive (i.e. have his life as a spoil of war) because of his trust. Thus is the man who trusts in Yahweh blessed (17.7), and Ebed-melech becomes an example of the pious whose survival in whatever circumstances depends only upon their trust in Yahweh. Gone is the option of 38.2, and now only trust in Yahweh is required. This is the lesson drawn by a pious editor from the stories of Jeremiah in the siege of Jerusalem.

40.1–6

40[1] The word that came to Jeremiah from the LORD after Nebuzaradan the
captain of the guard had let him go from Ramah, when he took him bound
in chains along with all the captives of Jerusalem and Judah who were being
exiled to Babylon. 2 The captain of the guard took Jeremiah and said to
him, 'The LORD your God pronounced this evil against this place; 3 the
LORD has brought it about, and has done as he said. Because you sinned
against the LORD, and did not obey his voice, this thing has come upon you.
4 Now, behold, I release you today from the chains on your hands. If it
seems good to you to come with me to Babylon, come, and I will look after
you well; but if it seems wrong to you to come with me to Babylon, do not
come. See, the whole land is before you; go wherever you think it good and
right to go. 5 If you remain, then return to Gedaliah the son of Ahikam, son
of Shaphan, whom the king of Babylon appointed governor of the cities of
Judah, and dwell with him among the people; or go wherever you think it
right to go.' So the captain of the guard gave him an allowance of food and

a present, and let him go. 6 Then Jeremiah went to Gedaliah the son of Ahikam, at Mizpah, and dwelt with him among the people who were left in the land.

[MT 40] = G 47. **[1]** The text is in disorder here. The formulaic introduction of a divine oracle appears without the oracle itself following (unless vv. 2–3 are it). Cf. 32.1; 34.1, 8; 35.1 for the formula. Rudolph, 247, rearranges the text: 39.11f.; 40.2a,1b, 2b–6a, 1aβ, 6b, deleting 1aα (cf. BHS); Bright, 244 regards v. 2 as resuming 39.11–13aα, with 40.1b as a parenthesis explaining the circumstances under which Jeremiah was found. Ramah: cf. 31.15; the assembly point for the deportation of the citizens (the modern *er-Rām* five miles north of Jerusalem?). MT *wᵉhū'-āsūr*, 'and he was bound': lacking in G. Q *bā'ziqqīm*, 'in manacles': K *ba'ᵃziqqīm* (? cf. BHS; Judg. 9.41 MT). The image of Jeremiah 'among the people' (37.4, 12; 39.14; 40.5, 6) is here matched by 'Jeremiah among all the exiles' (*bᵉtōk kol-gālūt*). **[2]** MT *wayyiqqaḥ rab-ṭabbāḥīm lᵉyirmᵉyāhū*, 'and the captain of the guard *took* Jeremiah': *lᵉ* an Aramaism; NEB 'set him free', JPSB 'took charge of'; Bright, 241 'had . . . brought'. Cf. 39.14, where Jeremiah is taken (*lqḥ*) from the court of the guard rather than from among the deportees at Ramah. The speech made by Nebuzaradan in vv. 2b–3 is in impeccable Deuteronomistic language (cf. Thiel 1981, 58–61). This is typical of speeches put into the mouth of foreigners (cf. 22.8–9; Rahab the whore in Josh. 2.8–14 makes such a theologically correct speech). **[3]** G has a shorter text: 'the lord has done it because you sinned against him and did not listen to his voice.' In v. 2 'you' is sing., but plur. in v. 3 (a characteristically Deuteronomistic number shift). K *dbr*; Q *haddābār*, '*the* word': cf. Lam. 2.17 for the motif of the fulfilled word. **[4]** MT *min-hā'ziqqīm 'ᵃšer 'al-yādekā*, 'from the manacles (cf. v. 1) which are on your hand': many mss, Vrs read 'your hands'; *ydk* may be dual form (cf. Wanke 1971, 105), cf. 38.22. G lacks v. 4b (from 'but if it seems wrong'): MT is due to dittography (cf. Volz, 346); cf. BHS for adjustments with v. 5. **[5]** MT *wᵉ'ōdennū lō'-yāšūb wᵉšubāh*: unintelligible. G *ei de mē, apotreke kai anastrepson*, 'but if not, go away and return' (translating MT yields lit. 'but he was still not turning, and turning'): Rudolph, 246, follows Volz, 346, *'im ṭōb bᵉ'ēnekā lāšebet šubāh*, 'if it be pleasing in your eyes to return, return' (cf. BHS). Rudolph refers this to 39.14 and understands it as a reference to freedom of movement rather than returning (cf. BHS b–b on 39.14). MT *'ᵃšer hipqīd melek-bābel bᵉ'ārē yᵉhūdāh*, 'whom the king of Babylon appointed over the *cities* of Judah': surely the Judaean cities had been destroyed by the Babylonians! Cf. 34.22b. G has *en gē Iouda*, 'in the land of Judah' (= *bᵉ'ereṣ* for *bᵉ'ārē*), which makes sense of the material in the context of its setting (i.e. the aftermath of the fall of Jerusalem). MT *'ᵃruḥāh ūmaś'ēt*, 'an allowance and a position': G *dōra*, 'a gift'; *maś'ēt* can refer to a present from a superior person (cf. Gen. 43.34; II Sam. 11.8) or largesse in general.

Cf. 52.34 for the continual *'ᵃruḥāh* given to Jehoiachin by Evil-merodach; here the 'allowance' may refer to 'a meal for the journey' (*'rḥ*, 'travel, journey'). Nebuzaradan's actions may represent simple courtesy in terms of hospitality or the lavish treatment of a special person. **[6]** Mizpah: the location of Mizpah is uncertain. A number of exegetes favour *tell en-naṣbe* (e.g. Bright, 244; Thompson, 653) about eight miles north of Jerusalem (41.4–6, 12–16), though *nebī samwīl* (five miles to the north of Jerusalem) and *tell el-bīre* also have advocates (cf. Rudolph, 246). 41.17–18; 42.1–2 suggest that Jeremiah was in Bethlehem! MT *wayyēšeb 'ittō bᵉtōk hā'ām hanniš'ārīm bā'āreṣ*, 'and he remained with him among the people who were left in the land': cf. 37.21; 38.13, 28; 39.14 for the motif of Jeremiah remaining in a particular place and 37.4, 2; 39.14; 40.5, 6 for the image of Jeremiah 'in the midst of the people'.

The second account of Jeremiah's rescue by the Babylonians is very different from the story which has him released from the court of the guard (39.14). In this version Jeremiah is taken into exile among the other deportees (*gālūt yᵉrūšālaim*, 'the exile of Jerusalem' v. 1) and is in chains. At Ramah where the prisoners are stockaded before the long journey to Babylon he is discovered by Nebuzaradan and released. This is a very different story from the instructions to the guard to look after him by releasing him from the courtyard where he has spent the siege (39.11–12, 14). It is unnecessary to harmonize these two stories as if they could be merged together to produce a sequential account of two releases, one in Jerusalem and the other in Ramah after having been picked up wandering about the streets of Jerusalem (cf. 'while not exactly harmonious . . . not necessarily contradictory', Bright, 245–6). In the present state of the text MT presents an absurd picture of the preacher going into exile and being made the recipient of a sermon preached to him by the pagan military commander Nebuzaradan. At some point in the redaction an oracular statement by Jeremiah about the fall of the city given in Deuteronomistic language has been turned into a pious outburst by the Babylonian soldier. Once again the biblical writers present the heathen as first-class Deuteronomists, and only the Judaeans appear to be theologically illiterate (cf. 22.8–9). If the two strands are untangled, a story of Jeremiah's deportation with the exiles is found to be mixed up with a proclamation about the city's fall. In spite of a shorter text G contains the confusion.

The two stories of how Jeremiah escaped death in the burning city are based on similar motifs: release by the Babylonians, his remaining in the land of Judah instead of going to Babylon (what price 24 now?), and his association with Gedaliah ben Ahikam ben Shaphan. 40.1–6 develops these motifs more fully than the story in 39.11–12, 14. Nebuzaradan gives Jeremiah the option to go to Babylon or remain in the land of Judah (G). He accepts Jeremiah's decision to stay in Judah and sends him to Gedaliah. The parting gift (v. 5b) need not be understood as Babylonian homage to the great man, but may only be a courteous provision of food for the journey to Mizpah from Ramah. That the Babylonians took pains to look after Jeremiah may be interpreted as the storyteller's art, but it could reflect the belief that Jeremiah had been a Babylonian agent and therefore deserved to be rewarded now that his activity had been successful in demoralizing the citizens of Jerusalem (38.4; cf. Winckler 1903, 170, for the now unfashionable view that the prophets were agents of or friendly towards foreign powers). In both stories the Babylonians are represented as knowing about Jeremiah and as being concerned for his welfare.

Both accounts of Jeremiah's association with Gedaliah run counter to the motif of the destruction of the land with only the poor remaining (39.10; 52.16; II Kings 25.12; II Chron. 36.17–21; cf. Ezra 1.3–4). On the contrary, a thriving community developed around Gedaliah, who was himself an important official figure in Jerusalem society (cf. 40.9–12; 41.10). It is therefore from this group that the association with Jeremiah must be derived, and the stories are to be read as reflecting the discrete motif of 'survival *in the land of Judah*'. This strand is technically in conflict with other strands in the tradition which denounce the Palastinians (e.g. 24) or regard only the community in Babylon as the recipients of divine care (e.g. 29.4–7). The presentation of Jeremiah as actively *choosing* to stay in Judah and associate himself with Gedaliah underwrites the legitimation of the community with its centre at Mizpah. Thus the stories provide an ironic reflection on many of the elements in the book of Jeremiah.

Gedaliah's community 40.7 – 41.18

The traditions in 40–44 about the aftermath of the fall of Jerusalem have a unique section in 40.7 – 41.18 where Gedaliah's governorship of the settlements which survived the Babylonian onslaught is depicted (cf. II Kings 25.22–26). Its uniqueness lies in the fact that Jeremiah is completely absent from the story until 42.1–2. In the series of crises faced by the community during and after the assassination of the Babylonian appointed governor Gedaliah *Jeremiah plays no part*! He is entrusted to Gedaliah in 39.14, and in 40.6 goes to Gedaliah from Ramah, but in the material on Gedaliah's community he disappears until the crises are over. His absence is inexplicable except on the grounds that II Kings 25.22–26 has no place for him either. In the story of Gedaliah Jeremiah has no role and therefore must disappear from the picture until the hostages move to Bethlehem. He then becomes instrumental in guiding the community and goes to Egypt with them (42–43). However, his disappearance in a time of crisis is noteworthy, especially in the book which purports to tell his story. Part IV stresses the image of Jeremiah 'among the people', but in the disintegration of Gedaliah's community he is nowhere to be found (an extension of his imprisonment theme?). When Jerusalem fell and when Gedaliah was assassinated Jeremiah is out of harm's way or absent (cf. David when Saul fell on Mount Gilboa). The tradition makes no observations about these factors and may even be unaware of the significance of the fact that Jeremiah is absent in 40.7–41.18.

The story of Gedaliah's assassination and the break-up of his community is told without reference to Jeremiah because the editors had it in this form. They know nothing of Jeremiah's involvement with the community until it is ready to flee to Egypt. Thus the tradition links Jeremiah with the beginning and end of the community, but cannot find a place for him during the crises of that community. This is all the more remarkable in that the tradition presents Jeremiah as 'the prophet for all seasons'. Yet as the hopes for reconstructing communal life in Judah blossom and fade *Jeremiah is conspicuously absent*. How can this be? If the book of Jeremiah were a historical work, there would be insuperable problems here, but in a collection of stories constructed around the bearer of the word the absence of that bearer in 40.7 – 41.18 is less problematic. Apart from inheriting stories which lacked Jeremiah in them, his absence in the critical period of the rise and collapse of Gedaliah's community facilitates the subsequent disintegration of the survivors. When Jeremiah does reappear it is too late for him to prevent the headless rush to Egypt (42–44). Hence his absence which strikes the modern reader as inexplicable may not have been such an enigma for the ancient editors. The historical-critical approach which scrutinizes the text very closely may note anomalies of which the writers of that text may have been unaware. These may make for poor history, but they can contribute to the storyteller's art. In telling the story of Gedaliah's community are the editors blithely unaware that they have left out Jeremiah?

In Jeremiah's absence other figures come to the fore. Gedaliah as governor of the community is central until his tragic assassination. In his place Ishmael ben Nethaniah emerges briefly as the focus of the story and his banditry threatens to remove the people from Judah. But he is quickly displaced by Johanan ben Kareah, who behaves like the community's natural leader by rescuing the hostages and making decisions about the future of the people. Only after the crisis is over does Jeremiah reappear in order to perform his prophetic role and give guidance to the people. The general pattern of Part IV is resumed in 42–43 where Jeremiah is presented as warning the community against going to Egypt and having his warning rejected. His passivity, so characteristic of Part IV and typified by his absence from the story of Gedaliah's community, is reinforced as a motif in the tradition by the account of his being taken to Egypt (presumably against his own wishes). Briefly in 42.10–12 Jeremiah announces the possibility of divine mercy to the community on condition they remain in the land of Judah (cf. Ackroyd 1968b, 37–54). This moment of possibility is rejected and the work begun by Ishmael is continued by Johanan. The people go into exile in Egypt and thus reverse the legendary history of the nation as the movement of people from Egypt to the land of Canaan. At the same time the story of Jeremiah in part IV which began with him in the empty cistern (cf.

37.16; 38.6) ends with him in Egypt, just like part of the story of Joseph whose brothers put him in an empty cistern (*bōr*, Gen. 37.22–24) and then sold him to Midianites (or Ishmaelites!) who took him to Egypt (Gen. 37.25, 28, 36).

40.7–12

7 When all the captains of the forces in the open country and their men
heard that the king of Babylon had appointed Gedaliah the son of Ahikam
governor in the land, and had committed to him men, women, and children,
those of the poorest of the land who had not been taken into exile to Babylon,
8 they went to Gedaliah at Mizpah – Ishmael the son of Nethaniah, Johanan
the son of Kareah, Seraiah the son of Tanhumeth, the sons of Ephai the
Netophathite, Jezaniah the son of the Maacathite, they and their men. 9
Gedaliah the son of Ahikam, son of Shaphan, swore to them and their men,
saying, 'Do not be afraid to serve the Chaldeans. Dwell in the land and
serve the king of Babylon, and it shall be well with you. 10 As for me, I will
dwell at Mizpah, to stand for you before the Chaldeans who will come to
us; but as for you, gather wine and summer fruits and oil, and store them
in your vessels, and dwell in your cities that you have taken.' 11 Likewise,
when all the Jews who were in Moab and among the Ammonites and in
Edom and in other lands heard that the king of Babylon had left a remnant
in Judah and had appointed Gedaliah the son of Ahikam, son of Shaphan,
as governor over them, 12 then all the Jews returned from all the places to
which they had been driven and came to the land of Judah, to Gedaliah at
Mizpah; and they gathered wine and summer fruits in great abundance.

[40.7–9] Cf. II Kings 25.22–24. **[7]** MT *kol-śārē haḥ^a^yālīm ^'a^šer baśśādeh*, 'all the princes of the armies which were in the field': i.e. the forces in the open country which had not been destroyed by the Babylonians. G^BAS^ *kai parekatethento autō andras kai gunaikas autōn*, 'and they committed to him the men and their wives', for MT *hipqīd 'ittō ^'a^nāšīm w^e^nāšīm wāṭāp ūmiddallat hā'āreṣ*, 'and had committed to him men, women, and children, those of the poorest of the land'. MT influenced by 39.10; 52.16; it represents a harmonization of two discrete views of the aftermath of the fall of Jerusalem. **[8]** G lacks 'and Jonathan' due to haplography of Johanan: lacking in a few mss, Vrs, II Kings 25.23; also RSV but see other EVV. It therefore follows that many Vrs read *ben qārēaḥ*, 'son of Kareah', for MT *b^e^nē-qārēaḥ*, 'sons of Kareah'. K *'wpy*; Q *'ēpay*, 'Ephai' (K Opay): G, V follow K. MT *wīzanyāhū*: a few mss, II Kings 25.23, *w^e^ya^'a^zanyāhū*; Jezaniah – Jaazaniah. **[9]** MT *mē'^a^bōd*, 'of serving': II Kings 25.24, *mē'ab^e^dē*, 'of the servants of', i.e. the

Chaldaean officials; G *apo prosōpou tōn paidōn tōn*, 'before the children of'. Cf. Lam. 5.8. **[10]** MT *yōšēb*, 'dwell': G *kathēmai enantion humōn*, 'dwell in your presence'. Cf. 15.1 for the motif of standing before. With Gedaliah as mediator between people and Babylonians there is no role for Jeremiah in the community! MT *beʿārēkem*, 'in your cities': G *en tais polesin*, 'in the cities' = *beʿārīm*; cf. v. 5. The seizure (*tpś*) of towns may represent the successes of the military in the field (v. 7). **[11]** MT *bekol-hāʾarāṣōt*, 'in all the lands': EVV, 'other countries'; G *en pasē tē gē*, 'in all the land'. **[12]** G lacks 'then all the Jews came from all the places to which they had been driven'.

The images presented of Gedaliah's community in vv. 7–12 depict a society beginning to re-establish itself after the disasters of 588–7. No dating is provided in the text so it is not possible to determine whether the events of 40–41 took place immediately after the fall of Jerusalem or some years later (see on 52.30). Once Gedaliah is established as the Babylonian appointed leader of the community and governor of Judah the various factions in the land rally to him. Military leaders, their forces with them, join him, among whom are notable individuals (named in v. 8). Jews who had fled during the invasion and siege now return to their homeland. They are all prepared to associate with Gedaliah ben Ahikam as their legitimate leader. Thus Gedaliah finds himself in charge of many people, including military forces, with Mizpah as his centre. In v. 10 he is represented as the community's mediator with the Babylonians. One ostensible reason put forward by the text for the gathering together of the people to Gedaliah and their resettlement in the land is the need for the ingathering of the harvest. A good summer had produced abundant fruit, grapes and oil and there was a pressing need for them all to be harvested. Gedaliah could deal with political matters but he needed workers for the fields and vineyards (cf. 32.15). So the community begins to emerge in relation to the tasks facing it, and stability is created in response to nature's prodigality (cf. 31.5, 12).

The story of Gedaliah's community represents a different account of the aftermath of the fall of Jerusalem from the view that all the people were deported and only some of the poorest left to look after the land (39.9–10; 52.15–16; II Kings 25.11–12). Many people, including those important enough to have their names registered in terms of their families, remained in the land and these were joined by others who recognized Gedaliah's authority. The fertility of the land hardly suggests a recent invasion and siege. Such foreign intrusions into a country usually devastate all food resources and leave behind them the consequences of a scorched earth policy. However, the products listed, vines ('wine' presupposes vineyards and the due processes of wine-making), summer fruits and oil, represent crops which may not have required the constant supervision which the invasion and siege will have destroyed. Furthermore, the time-gap between the ending of the siege and the period depicted in 40.7–12 may have been sufficiently long for the vineyards to have been tended. But images of a devastated land occupied by the huddled masses of the poor are completely absent from the depiction of the circumstances prevailing under Gedaliah's governorship. For him and the people under his command a new age is beginning – one of stability and plenty. As presented in 40.7–12 there is an idyllic quality about the new community. The exiles driven away from home in recent years come flocking back to their homeland (vv. 11–12) and participate in the great harvesting: 'and they gathered wine and summer fruits in great abundance' (v. 12b).

40.7–12 reads like the fulfilment of the future hopes expressed in the poems of 30–31 or the idylls of Second Isaiah (cf. Baltzer 1961, 33–7). It certainly suggests a very different view of life in the land of Judah after 587 from other strands in the book of Jeremiah which denounce the Judaeans in favour of the deportees in Babylon (e.g. 24.4–7; 29.16–19). With the emergence of Gedaliah's community, hope returns to the land and the future of the many people who associate themselves with him begins to look bright.

40.13 – 41.3

13 Now Johanan the son of Kareah and all the leaders of the forces in the open country came to Gedaliah at Mizpah 14 and said to him, 'Do you know that Baalis the king of the Ammonites has sent Ishmael the son of Nethaniah to take your life?' But Gedaliah the son of Ahikam would not believe them. 15 Then Johanan the son of Kareah spoke secretly to Gedaliah at Mizpah, 'Let me go and slay Ishmael the son of Nethaniah, and no one will know it. Why should he take your life, so that all the Jews who are gathered about you would be scattered, and the remnant of Judah would perish?' 16 But Gedaliah the son of Ahikam said to Johanan the son of Kareah, 'You shall not do this thing, for you are speaking falsely of Ishmael.'

41[1] In the seventh month, Ishmael the son of Nethaniah, son of Elishama, of the royal family, one the chief officers of the king, came with ten men to

Gedaliah the son of Ahikam, at Mizpah. As they ate bread together there at Mizpah, 2 Ishmael the son of Nethaniah and the ten men with him rose up and struck down Gedaliah the son of Ahikam, son of Shaphan, with the sword, and killed him, whom the king of Babylon had appointed governor in the land. 3 Ishmael also slew all the Jews who were with Gedaliah at Mizpah, and the Chaldean soldiers who happened to be there.

---

[13] Johanan ben Kareah: cf. v. 8. 40.13–43.5 refer to him in this fashion, hence MT *bᵉnē qārēaḥ* (v. 8) may be incorrect. **[14]** Baalis, king of the *bᵉnē Ammon*: cf. 27.3; Ezek. 21.18–32 [MT 23–37] for Ammonite opposition to Babylon. The plot against Gedaliah may be part of this campaign against the Babylonians. MT *lᵉhakkōtᵉkā nepeš*, 'to strike you mortally': cf. v. 15; NEB 'to assassinate you'. G lacks 'ben Nethaniah' and 'ben Ahikam'. **[15]** MT *bassēter*, 'in secret': as in 37.17; 38.16. This would appear to be a literary device in 37–40 used to convey a dramatic sense of the conspiratorial nature of the meetings and interviews delineated. MT *šᵉ'ērīt yᵉhūdāh*, 'the remnant of Judah': cf. v. 11. **[16]** K *t'š*; Q *ta'ᵃśeh*, 'you shall (not) do'. MT *kī-šeqer 'attāh dōbēr 'el*, 'for you are speaking falsely of': cf. 43.2 *šeqer 'attāh mᵉdabbēr*, 'you are telling a lie'. **[MT 41]** = G 48. **[1]** Cf. II Kings 25.25; 'in the seventh month': the year is not identified, but the sequence in II Kings 25 implies that it was the same year as the fall of Jerusalem (cf. 'in the fourth month', 39.2). Zech. 7.5; 8.19 refer to a fast in the seventh month which may be associated with the assassination of Gedaliah (or is the assassination dated to this month because of the fast?). G *Elasa* for Elishama. G lacks 'and the chiefs of the king', MT *wᵉrabbē hammelek*, i.e. one of the king's chief officers: also lacking in II Kings 25.25, NEB; a dittography in MT (cf. Rudolph, 250; BHS). **[2]** G lacks 'the son of Ahikam, son of Shaphan, with the sword and killed him'. MT *wāyyamet 'ōtō*, 'and he killed him': Vrs 'they killed him'. **[3]** MT *'et-gᵉdalyāhū bammiṣpāh*, 'with Gedaliah at Mizpah': G lacks 'with Gedaliah'; a gloss identifying the Jews who were killed. As all the Jews at Mizpah were not killed (v. 10), the word *bammiṣpāh* is problematic (G has it). Duhm, 317, considers it a gloss to *šām*, 'there'; Rudolph, 250, reads *bammišteh*, 'at the feast' (cf. BHS). MT consists of a series of direct object indicators *wᵉ'ēt . . . 'et . . . wᵉ'et . . . 'ēt* governed by the final two words of v. 3, *hikkāh yišmā'ē'l*, 'Ishmael smote'.

A second account of the gathering of the military leaders with their forces to meet with Gedaliah at Mizpah is given in 40.13–16 (this is lacking in the II Kings 25 version). In this story there is no influx of refugees from foreign lands or great gathering of fruits and the vintage, but the commanders gather to inform Gedaliah of a conspiracy against his life. This conspiracy is organized by the

Ammonites and centres on Ishmael ben Nethaniah (cf. 36.14). Johanan ben Kareah also informs the governor of the plot in a secret session with Gedaliah. In this private interview (modelled on the Zedekiah-Jeremiah interviews?) Johanan volunteers to assassinate Ishmael and thereby save the community of the remnant of Judah. As a would-be champion of the governor Johanan emerges as the military leader of the new community (cf. 41.11). However, Gedaliah refuses to believe that there is a conspiracy against him and declines permission for an assassination attempt. Thus he appears to be a good, eirenic leader who is not prepared to allow Judaeans to slaughter each other on the strength of rumours.

41.1–3 (cf. II Kings 25.25) provides a brief account of Ishmael's successful assassination of Gedaliah, his companions and the Babylonian soldiers stationed at Mizpah. Apparently this slaughter takes place in the 'seventh month', some three months after the fall of Jerusalem. This may seem too brief a period to cover the return of the foreign exiles and the great harvest ingathering, but the account in II Kings 25 knows nothing of these developments which appear exclusively in the Jeremiah tradition. Yet Ishmael must have been well-known to Gedaliah to have shared a meal with him, especially after the warning issued by Johanan. As a member of the royal family Ishmael would have had some standing in the land, though not necessarily in Gedaliah's community. Perhaps behind his animosity towards Gedaliah (why would Gedaliah not realize this?) lay loyalty to the family of Zedekiah which had been outrageously butchered by the Babylonians (cf. 39.6–7; 52.10–11). Gedaliah by his association with Babylon and his acceptability to Nebuchadrezzar as a governor would have been a traitor to the people of Judah in Ishmael's eyes. In killing him and all those in league with him Ishmael may have struck a blow against the Babylonian domination of Judah. This explanation would make the assassination one further act in the long conflict between pro-Babylonian and anti-Babylonian forces in Judaean politics since the Babylonians first penetrated the land in 597. Other possibilities may be mooted also: Ishmael may represent anarchic guerilla forces operating against the Babylonian settlements in Judah or, as 40.14 suggests, he may have been part of other conspiracies against the Babylonians (cf. 41.10b). The simple story of Gedaliah's assassination may be read in many different ways for political motives, but the text affords little serious information to account for it. As the story appears in II Kings 25 it could hardly be simpler or briefer. Developed at some length in 40.7 – 41.18 the story becomes no clearer in spite of added details. With ten men Ishmael is able to kill governor, companions and the Babylonian soldiers! The eleven men are then able to take captive all the other people in Mizpah and transport them towards Ammonite territory (41.10). The lack of realism in the story becomes more obvious in 41.11–18 when Johanan's forces reappear (from where?), chase Ishmael, and retrieve the captives. It is difficult to read the stories making up the account of Gedaliah's community as realistic descriptions of history or as serious accounts of what happened. At best they may be regarded as tales told about the assassination of the Babylonian appointed governor Gedaliah. They expand the much briefer account in II Kings 25.22–26 and prepare the way for further stories about Jeremiah among the people (cf. 42.1–6).

With the assassination of 41.2 the story of Gedaliah comes to an end. The fate of his community (cf. II Kings 25.26) remains in suspense for some further time (cf. 41.4 – 43.7). The future which dawned so brightly with Gedaliah, the return of the exiles and the ingathering of the harvest is snuffed out by a malcontent of the royal house. The innocent and good Gedaliah, the mediator and spokesman of the community in its relations with Babylon, becomes one more murdered victim of a brutal age (cf. Baltzer 1961, 35, who sees a striking similarity between the stylization of Gedaliah and the figure who suffers so starkly in Isa. 53). With his death the stability of the community is wrecked and hopes of a good future in Judah are shaken. Ishmael's act of defiance against a hated enemy (i.e. the Babylonians and one of their collaborationists) now threatens the security of the renascent country and it remains to be seen whether those who survive the attack can control Ishmael and persuade their Babylonian overlords of their own lack of complicity in the conspiracy.

41.4–10

4 On the day after the murder of Gedaliah, before any one knew of it, 5
eighty men arrived from Shechem and Shiloh and Samaria, with their beards shaved and their clothes torn, and their bodies gashed, bringing cereal offerings and incense to present at the temple of the LORD. 6 And
Ishmael the son of Nethaniah came out from Mizpah to meet them, weeping

as he came. As he met them, he said to them, 'Come in to Gedaliah the son of Ahikam.' 7 When they came into the city, Ishmael the son of Nethaniah and the men with him slew them, and cast them into a cistern. 8 But there were ten men among them who said to Ishmael, 'Do not kill us, for we have stores of wheat, barley, oil, and honey hidden in the fields.' So he refrained and did not kill them with their companions.

9 Now the cistern into which Ishmael cast all the bodies of the men whom he had slain was the large cistern which King Asa had made for defence against Baasha king of Israel; Ishmael the son of Nethaniah filled it with the slain. 10 Then Ishmael took captive all the rest of the people who were in Mizpah, the king's daughters and all the people who were left at Mizpah, whom Nebuzaradan, the captain of the guard, had committed to Gedaliah the son of Ahikam. Ishmael the son of Nethaniah took them captive and set out to cross over to the Ammonites.

---

[4] MT *way^ehī bayyōm haššēnī l^ehāmīt 'et-g^edalyāhū*, lit, and it came to pass on the second day with reference to the killing of Gedaliah'. **[5]** Shiloh: G Salem; cf. 7.14; 26.6. The three towns Shechem, Shiloh, Samaria appear in MT in alphabetical rather than geographical order. MT *ūmitgōd^edīm*, 'and gashed', i.e. their bodies cut: cf. 5.7; 16.6; 47.5; 48.37; I Kings 18.28; the funeral rites described here are forbidden by Deut. 14.1. Such a late (cf. Mayes 1979, 238) prohibition may reflect a rejection of the self-laceration custom of mourning associated with pagan religion. MT *ūl^ebōnāh*, 'and frankincense'. It is generally assumed that *bēt yhwh* refers to the temple in Jerusalem because to posit a temple in Mizpah would be an over-subtle reading of the text (cf. Giesebrecht, 216); cf. Ackroyd 1968a, 25–8; Jones 1963, 14–16, on the relation of v. 5 to the question about cultic practices in Jerusalem during the exile. **[6]** MT *hōlēk hālōk ūbōkeh*, idiomatic for 'weeping as he went': G *autoi eporeuonto kai eklaion*, 'they were going along weeping'. MT makes Ishmael dissemble by weeping, whereas G follows the logic of the story and has the pilgrims weep. Why Ishmael should weep *and* invite the pilgrims to meet Gedaliah is less than clear. G lacks MT's *way^ehī kip^egōš 'ōtām*, 'and when he encountered them'. **[7]** MT *'el-tōk habbōr*, 'to the midst of the cistern': G lacks *tōk*; a dittography of (*'el-*)*tōk* (*hā'īr*), '(to) *the midst of* (the city)'. The lack of a verb is supplied by S (= *wayyašlīkēm*, 'and he cast them') before 'to the midst of the cistern'. The cistern (*habbōr*) motif of 37–38 appears here and reflects storytelling techniques used in Part IV. G lacks 'he and the men with him'. **[8]** MT *bām*, 'among them': G *ekei*, 'there' = *šām*. The story told by the ten men is presumably a lie to buy off Ishmael, for what would mourning pilgrims be doing with supplies buried in the fields! However, realism should not be expected in such stories as make up the account of Gedaliah's community. **[9]** G lacks 'the bodies of the men'. MT *b^eyad-g^edalyāhū*, 'by the hand of Gedaliah': G *phrear mega touto estin*, 'this is the great cistern' = *bōr gādōl hū'*. Cf. I Kings 15.22 for king Asa's association with Mizpah. **[10]** MT *wayyišb*^{e}, 'and he took captive': G *kai apestrepsen*, 'and he brought back' = *wayyāšeb*. G lacks 'all the people who were left in Mizpah', 'Nebuzaradan', 'and Ishmael ben Nethaniah took them captive'. A few mss, G^{OL} read *wayyaškēm*, 'and he rose early', for *wayyišbēm*, 'and he took them captive' (cf. BHS).

The supplements attached to the story of Gedaliah's assassination are so tantalizingly brief and disconnected that it is difficult to determine what is happening or why. On the second day, i.e. the day after, of the murder eighty pilgrims arrive from a variety of famous cultic cities on their way to the Jerusalem temple. Their long pilgrimage is endured in a state of mourning – beards removed, clothes torn, bodies gashed – and it must be presumed that they are responding to the fall of the city and the destruction of the temple. As 41.1 sets the stories in the seventh month, the pilgrimage may be associated with the great pilgrimages of that season (cf. Lev. 16.29 for the setting of the Day of Atonement ritual in the seventh month). Whether as response to 587 or as an annual pilgrimage to Jerusalem in the seventh month, it is a curious affair and not referred to elsewhere in the Hebrew Bible. Ishmael persuades the pilgrims to meet Gedaliah in Mizpah, and there he kills seventy of them. How realistic an account the story may be is hard to imagine, because the eleven killers massacred seventy pilgrims while the rest of the people (v. 10) stood and watched. Yet they spared ten pilgrims on the grounds that they had hidden stores of wheat, barley, oil and honey in the fields. Then, having dumped the corpses in a large cistern, killers and captives all left to go to the Ammonites. Put together like this the elements in vv. 4–8, 9–10 hardly make any sense, but part of the incoherence may be due to the combination of discrete strands in the chapter (e.g. 1–3, 10; 4–9 are quite independent of one another, cf. Pohlmann 1978, 115–8). With v. 8 the ten pilgrims spared disappear from the story, and in v. 10 the people who were not present at Gedaliah's meal (v. 1) are taken captive. Not much coherence is gained by separating the strands, because in each story the community appears to be passive in the extreme as Ishmael and his ten men terrorize governor, town, garrison and people. It is a most remarkable story and, considering that Gedaliah represented Babylonian authority in a recently subjugated land and therefore must have had ample troop support, quite unreal.

Even as a fiction Ishmael ben Nethaniah is a difficult character to understand. His killing of Gedaliah and the Babylonian soldiers is the act of a patriot, but his slaughter of the pilgrims is an outrage and suggests a psychotic bandit. Put together, the stories are unconvincing because they mix two very different types of activity. The bandit story might well fit the period in which it is set, but in that case the pilgrims would have had an armed escort or would not have been wandering about in a land only beginning to recover from the depredations of invasion and the consequences of so many plundered cities. That the stories may reflect aspects of the period need not be denied, but they should not be read as historical accounts of the aftermath of Jerusalem's destruction. They are better understood as stories used to fill in the interstices of the account given in II Kings 25.22–26 and built around the characters of Ishmael ben Nethaniah (villain) and Johanan ben Kareah (hero).

41.11–15

11 But when Johanan the son of Kareah and all the leaders of the forces with him heard of all the evil which Ishmael the son of Nethaniah had done, 12 they took all their men and went to fight against Ishmael the son of Nethaniah. They came upon him at the great pool which is in Gibeon. 13 And when all the people who were with Ishmael saw Johanan the son of Kareah and all the leaders of the force with him, they rejoiced. 15 So all the people whom Ishmael had carried away captive from Mizpah turned about and came back, and went to Johanan the son of Kareah. 15 But Ishmael the son of Nethaniah escaped from Johanan with eight men, and went to the Ammonites.

---

[12] MT *'et-kol-hā'ªnāšīm*, 'all the men': *to stratopedon autōn*, 'their army'. MT *'el-mayim rabbīm 'ªšer bᵉgib'ōn*, 'at the great waters which are in Gibeon': cf. II Sam. 2.13; for Gibeon cf. 28.1. Rudolph, 252, favours reading *bᵉgeba'*, 'in Geba'. In view of Ishmael's flight to the Ammonites these details favour identifying Gibeon with *nebī samwīl* rather than *tell en-naṣbe* (cf. Blenkinsopp 1972, 100). Bright, 255, allows for the possibility that Ishmael may have followed a circuitous route, so that *tell en-naṣbe* may still be indicated; see on 40.6. **[13]** G lacks 'and they rejoiced' (*wayyiśmāḥū*). Bright, 249, reads vv. 13a, 14aβ, 13b, 14aαb, transposing the MT for the sake of clarity. **[14]** G is much shorter than MT, reading only *kai anestrepsan pros Iōanan*, 'and they returned to Johanan'.

The reappearance of Johanan ben Kareah, the military leaders and their forces in vv. 11–12 prompts the question 'where were they during the assassination of Gedaliah?'. Their absence during the crisis is most curious and remarkable. Such a military force would have protected Gedaliah, especially as 40.14 indicates that Johanan knew about the plot. Yet he seems to disappear, taking his men with him, until it is too late to sustain the community's existence. Then after the kidnapping of the remnant of the community in v. 10 (note the presence of the king's daughters among Gedaliah's charges in spite of 38.22–23; 39.9), Johanan and his forces return in order to rescue them. Like Jeremiah's absence throughout the crisis, the temporary disappearance of Johanan and his troops is another mystery of 40.7 – 41.18.

The mere appearance of Johanan and troops is sufficient to rescue the kidnapped people. Once they are informed (by whom?) about Ishmael's activities, the military commanders and their troops pursue the bandits and overtake them by the great pool of Gibeon (another story motif like the great cistern made by king Asa). Ishmael loses control of the hostages once military opposition appears, and the kidnapped people easily elude their captors and turn to Johanan. In the ensuing confusion Ishmael and *eight* of his men escape (v. 15; does this imply that two of his men were killed? cf. v. 2). They join the Ammonites and disappear from the story. Ishmael's contribution to 40.7 – 41.18 is to have struck the death-blow of Gedaliah's community.

41.16–18

16 Then Johanan the son of Kareah and all the leaders of the forces with him took all the rest of the people whom Ishmael the son of Nethaniah had carried away captive from Mizpah after he had slain Gedaliah the son of Ahikam – soldiers, women, children, and eunuchs, whom Johanan brought back from Gibeon. 17 And they went and stayed at Geruth Chimham near Bethlehem, intending to go to Egypt 18 because of the Chaldeans; for they were afraid of them, because Ishmael the son of Nethaniah had slain Gedaliah the son of Ahikam, whom the king of Babylon had made governor over the land.

---

[16] MT *'ᵃšer hēšīb mē'ēt yišmā'ē'l*, 'which he recovered from Ishmael': cf.

NEB, JPSB. RSV follows an emended text reading *šābāh 'ōlām*, 'he took them captive' (cf. Hitzig, 320; Rudolph; BHS). Johanan did not rescue the people 'from Mizpah'. G lacks 'the son of Kareah from Mizpah after he had slain Gedaliah the son of Ahikam'. MT *g^ebārīm 'anšē hammilḥāmōh* 'men' i.e. 'soldiers': G *dunatous andras en polemō*, 'men mighty in battle'; understanding *gbrym* as *gibbōrīm* 'warriors' (a few mss read this form); cf. 43.6. It is unlikely that Ishmael took captive soldiers along with all the other people listed in vv. 10, 16b. MT *w^esārisīm*, 'and eunuchs': cf. 38.7; it is possible that these were eunuchs in the service of the princesses (cf. Rudolph, 252) rather than high-ranking officials. MT *w^eṭap*, 'and children': lit. 'toddlers'; G *kai ta loipa*, 'and the residue'. Cf. 43.6. **[17]** MT *b^egērūt kimhām*, 'at Gerut-kimham': K *kmwhm*; Q *kimhām*; Vrs have different forms of a place name. Cf. II Sam. 19.37–38 for the proper name Chimham. The hapax legomenon *gērūt* may refer to a lodging-place, inn or khan (cf. BDB, 158).

The final element in this stage of the story of the disintegration of Gedaliah's community represents Johanan's return with the captives. He does not, however, return to Mizpah but settles at some lodging area near Bethlehem. There the remnant of the community regroup in order to emigrate to Egypt. Sound reasoning is behind this decision: once the Babylonian authorities discover what has happened to the garrison at Mizpah and to Gedaliah their representative they will act harshly against the occupants of the area. In spite of the propaganda about the generous nature of the Babylonians in 39.11–14; 40.1–5, their reactions to Ishmael's activities would have been a good deal less kind. Those who had failed to fight off Ishmael and his *ten* men and thereby protect Gedaliah or even their own interests could hardly have expected much support from a retaliatory Babylonian expedition (such a campaign may account for the deportation of 583, cf. 52.30). One minor absurdity may be noted in v. 16b, where reference is made to 'men, men of war' as being among the captives taken by Ishmael. How a handful of bandits captured such soldiers (cf. v. 3) is beyond imagination, though in keeping with the style of storytelling in 41. If it is a mistaken interpretation of 'men', it is a mistake maintained by both editions (G, MT).

With the disappearance of Ishmael Johanan ben Kareah emerges as the dominant figure in the community. But having failed to prevent the assassination of Gedaliah and not having captured Ishmael he is not able to hold the people together in the land of Judah. Ishmael has effectively killed off any positive future in the homeland.

42.1–6

42[1] Then all the commanders of the forces, and Johanan the son of Kareah and Azariah the son of Hoshaiah, and all the people from the least to the greatest, came near 2 and said to Jeremiah the prophet, 'Let our supplication come before you, and pray to the LORD your God for us, for all this remnant (for we are left but a few of many, as your eyes see us), 3 that the LORD your God may show us the way we should go, and the thing that we should do.' 4 Jeremiah the prophet said to them, 'I have heard you; behold, I will pray to the LORD your God according to your request, and whatever the LORD answers you I will tell you; I will keep nothing back from you.' 5 Then they said to Jeremiah, 'May the LORD be a true and faithful witness against us if we do not act according to all the word with which the LORD your God sends you to us. 6 Whether it is good or evil, we will obey the voice of the LORD our God to whom we are sending you, that it may be well with us when we obey the voice of the LORD our God.'

[MT 42] = G 49. **[1]** MT *wizanyāh*, 'Jezaniah': cf. 40.8; G *Azarias*, 'Azariah', cf. 43.2; here and in 43.2 (G 50.2) G makes Azariah the son of *Maasaeas* rather than of Hoshaiah. **[2]** 'Jeremiah the prophet': one of the very few occurrences in G of the epithet 'the prophet'. Cf. Gen. 20.7 for the association of prophet and intercession. The supplication (*tᵉḥinnāh*) motif appears in 36.7; 37.20; 38.26. G lacks *baʿᵃdēnū*, 'for us'; S lacks 'for all this remnant'; MT has both variants. MT *miqqāṭōn wᵉʿad-gādōl*, 'from the smallest to the greatest': cf. variations in 6.13; 8.10; 16.6; 31.34; 42.8. **[3]** MT *ʾᵉlōhekā*, 'your god': a few mss, S '*our* god', cf. 37.3. **[4]** G lacks 'the prophet' and reads 'our god' for MT 'your god'. MT *ʾᵃšer-yaʿᵃneh yhwh ʾetkem*, 'which Yahweh shall answer you': Volz, 354, reads *ʾᵉlōhēkem*, 'your god', for *ʾetkem*, 'you', on the grounds that Yahweh answers the prophet, not the people (followed by Rudolph, cf. BHS); G lacks 'you'. Cf. 26.2; 38.15 for the motif of withholding the divine word. **[5]** MT *ʾᵃšer yišlāḥᵃkā yhwh*, 'with which Yahweh sends you': cf. v. 21; 43.1 for this sending (*šlḥ*) motif. **[6]** K *ʾnw*; Q *ʾᵃnaḥnū*, 'we' (K *ʾᵃnū*, 'we', is common in post-biblical Hebrew but only appears in the Hebrew Bible here). Thiel 1981, 64, regards v. 6 as a pious repetition of v. 5 explaining it in Deuteronomistic terms; cf. Pohlmann 1978, 126–7.

The last stage in the story of the fate of Gedaliah's community unfolds in 42.1 – 43.7 (analysis in Pohlmann 1978, 123–59; Wanke 1971, 116–33). Jeremiah returns to the centre of the stage but displays an utter unawareness of recent events and alludes not at all to the assassination of Gedeliah. The crises of the community are not referred to him until the disappearance of Ishmael and the retreat of the refugees to near Bethlehem (if 42.1 is read as linked to 41.16–18 by virtue of 'then', it may be assumed that the meeting of 42.1–2 takes place near Bethlehem). Then he emerges as the prophetic figure in the community to whom all may seek for guidance. The figure of 37–38 who makes humble supplication to the king becomes the one who may intercede with the deity for all the people. This is not only a case of role reversal but also a contrast with the figure of Part I (cf. 7.16; 11.14; 14.11) who is forbidden to intercede on behalf of the people. This presentation of Jeremiah as the prophet of the community no longer forbidden to pray for it reveals a significant change in the status of that community before Yahweh. Jeremiah can behave like an authoritative prophetic figure because the community is acceptable to Yahweh. With the fall of Jerusalem the hostility of the deity against the people of Judah (cf. 40.2–3) has been dissipated, and the community constituted by the remnant now enjoys his favour to the extent that Yahweh is prepared to listen to the prophet. In the strands of the tradition where intercession is prohibited Jeremiah is not represented as a prophet, but here he is *Jeremiah the prophet* (v. 2 both editions; 4 MT). Thus 42 reflects a quite distinctive element in the book of Jeremiah and one which differs significantly from that strand which identifies the divine pleasure exclusively with the exiles in Babylon (cf. 24.4–7; 29.4–7, 10–14). Not in Babylon but in Judah lies the real hope for the future (cf. Ackroyd 1968a, 57; 1968b, 37–54). Whether that hope can be sustained is the question under discussion in this chapter, and the assassination of Gedaliah appears to be irrelevant to the answer.

The whole community, its military leadership and all its ranks, gathers to Jeremiah to seek help from the deity. Jeremiah's prowess as a prophet is tacitly recognized by the formal request for his mediation with the deity. He agrees to intercede with the deity on their behalf and to convey to them everything said to him by Yahweh. They in turn agree to act in conformity with whatever the divine answer may be. An editorial note (v. 6) reinforces that affirmation.

42.7–17

7 At the end of ten days the word of the LORD came to Jeremiah. 8 Then he summoned Johanan the son of Kareah and all the commanders of the forces

who were with him, and all the people from the least to the greatest, 9 and said to them, 'Thus says the LORD, the God of Israel, to whom you sent me to present your supplication before him: 10 If you will remain in this land, then I will build you up and not pull you down; I will plant you, and not pluck you up; for I repent of the evil which I did to you. 11 Do not fear the king of Babylon, of whom you are afraid; do not fear him, says the LORD, for I am with you, to save you and to deliver you from his hand. 12 I will grant you mercy, that he may have mercy on you and let you remain in your own land. 13 But if you say, "We will not remain in this land," disobeying the voice of the LORD your God 14 and saying, "No, we will go to the land of Egypt, where we shall not see war, or hear the sound of the trumpet, or be hungry for bread, and we will dwell there," 15 then hear the word of the LORD, O remnant of Judah. Thus says the LORD of hosts, the God of Israel: If you set your faces to enter Egypt and go to live there, 16 then the sword which you fear shall overtake you there in the land of Egypt; and the famine of which you are afraid shall follow hard after you to Egypt; and there you shall die. 17 All the men who set their faces to go to Egypt to live there shall die by the sword, by famine, and by pestilence; they shall have no remnant or survivor from the evil which I will bring upon them.'

---

[7] MT *wayᵉhî . . . wayᵉhî*, 'and it happened . . . that (the word) came': an unusual variation on the formulaic reception of the divine word introduction. Apart from the double *wayᵉhî* caused by the temporal phrase preceding the formal statement, the passage of time indicator is unique in the book of Jeremiah (cf. 28.12, where the precise amount of time is *not* indicated). Cf. 33.1; 35.12; 43.8 for the formulaic phrase and 1.4, 11, 13; 2.1; 16.1 for its variant form. **[8]** Cf. v. 2; 6.13; 8.10; 16.6; 31.34 for variations of the phrase 'from the smallest to the greatest'. **[9]** G much shorter: *kai eipen autois outōs eipe kurios*, 'and he said to them Thus says the lord'. **[10]** MT *'im-šôb tēšᵉbû*, 'if you will surely stay': correcting MT scribal error *šôb* to *yāšôb*, cf. Vrs. The verbs 'build' (*bnh*), 'pull down' (*hrs*), 'plant' (*nṭ'*), 'pluck up' (*ntš*) are those of 1.10; cf. 18.7–9, where they are also employed in conjunction with divine repentance (*nḥm*). **[11]** Cf. 40.9 for the motifs of fearing the Chaldaeans and serving the king of Babylon. The motif of the divine presence in deliverance appears in 1.8, 19b. **[12]** MT *wᵉriḥam 'etkem*, 'and he will have mercy on you': G *kai eleēsō humas*, 'and I will have mercy on you'. MT *wᵉhēšîb 'etkem 'el-'admatkem*, 'and he will restore you to your land': G *kai epistrepsō* . . . 'and *I* will restore . . .'; this may reflect an exilic perspective (cf. Bright, 256) but could also be a statement about the displacement of the people at Bethlehem (cf. 41.17–18; Rudolph, 254). **[14]** G lacks MT *lē'mōr lō'*, 'saying No'. **[16]** Cf. 39.5 (*wayyaśśigû*) for the image of the sword *overtaking* (*taśśîg*) those who flee away. MT *wᵉhārā'āb . . . šām yidbaq 'aḥᵃrêkem*, 'and the hunger . . . there shall cleave after you': i.e. cling to you wherever you go. BHS reads *wᵉhāyāh* for *wᵉhayᵉtāh* and suggests *bᵉmiṣraim*, '*in* Egypt', for MT *miṣraim* '(to?) Egypt'. **[17]** MT *wᵉyihyū*, 'and they (died)': better as BHS *wᵉhāyāh*, 'and it shall be', i.e. come to pass (cf. v. 16). G also has 'and all the strangers' after 'all the men' = *wᵉkol-hazzārīm* (cf. *hazzēdīm*, 'the insolent', 43.2). Cf. Thiel 1981, 63, on v. 17 as a Deuteronomistic element; for the triad sword, famine, pestilence, cf. 14.12; 21.7, 9; 24.10; 27.8, 13; 29.17–18; 32.24, 36; 34.17; 38.2; 42.22; 44.13.

The passivity of Jeremiah is a dominant element in Part IV (broken only in 39.16, where the command is anomalous), and nowhere is it more obvious than in 42.7, where Jeremiah waits ten days for the divine word to come to him. The figure who moves about so much in Part I becomes quite passive in Part III and almost inert in Part IV. Things happen to him more frequently and he is more the victim of circumstances than an activist. This representation of him reflects his status as bearer of the divine word: a word whose bearer is rendered otiose, once it has been rejected (cf. 36.23–26; 37.1–2). Even in this story of the community's consultation with him, he must wait for the word to come to him instead of being the one who possesses it and delivers it without delay (cf. 28.12, where his passivity is also an element in the story). No details are given about his techniques for receiving the word (contrast Num. 22.38–23.5; 24.1–3; II Kings 3.14–16); only the length of time it took for the communication to occur (cf. the passage of time in the visions of Daniel: Dan. 8.15–17, 27; 9.1–2, 20–3; 10.1–21). Speculations about the time factor in v. 7 would be too eisegetical for sound interpretation, but the movement away from the presentation of Jeremiah as the one to whom the word comes before he acts towards the figure of the one who seeks the word in order to speak to a particular situation should be noted. It is not a movement developed in the tradition in an articulated way, but here it is consonant with the passivity of Jeremiah as a major feature of Part IV.

On reception of the divine word Jeremiah summons the community along with its leaders and addresses a sermon to all of them. The sending (*šlḥ*) motif which plays a large part in the tradition is used in v. 9 in a rather different manner: it is the community which *sends* Jeremiah to Yahweh with its supplication (cf. v. 21, where Yahweh *sends* Jeremiah with the answer; 43.1). The answer to that inquiry is set out in vv. 10–17 in terms of possible alternatives. Yahweh's intention towards the community is positive – he will create the conditions for normal life in the land (using the motifs of 1.10, 'building', 'planting', to convey this message). This change of attitude towards the community is due to divine repentance (*nḥm*), which reveals a change of mind by Yahweh. Recent devastations of the community ('pulling down', 'plucking up', cf. 1.10) belong to the past of which the deity repents. Such a figure as repentance used of Yahweh simply asserts a change of attitude and policy (cf. 18.8, 10) and represents the standard anthropomorphic language used of the deity by biblical writers. It is unwise to single out the repentance motif for a criticism of such language and it is unnecessary for exegetes to be peculiarly sensitive to this particular metaphor (I Sam. 15.11, 29, 35 suggest that such sensitivity is an ancient problem). All language about god is metaphorical and problematic, but no biblical exegesis would be possible if certain metaphors were singled out for criticism. Repentance is a human activity also posited of the deity, and one means of expressing the view that the past need not be overdeterminative of the future. It is the language of possibility and renewal, and when used of the deity indicates such changes in his attitude towards the community that its future becomes an open one. A good future is now possible for the people.

The conditionality of this future is an important element in the sermon. *If* is the opening word of v. 10. *If* the people are prepared to remain (*šūb*) in their own land, then a positive future is a possibility. The factors operating against that future are dismissed as inconsequential: divine hostility is gone (cf. 29.11); fear of the emperor is to be displaced by divine protection and mercy (v. 12: G and MT differ about *who* shows mercy and *who* permits residence in the land). If the people can overcome their legitimate fears about the consequences of the Babylonian reaction to the assassination of Gedaliah (whether this is the point of v. 11 is difficult to determine, but may be understood implicitly to be so because of the present editing of 41–42), then a secure residence in Judah is possible. If, on the other hand, the people are determined to flee to Egypt, then their future will be disastrous, even though there are very good reasons for leaving Judah: safety, food and security. There in Egypt they will encounter all the evils they had left Judah to avoid (v. 16). The familiar triad – sword, famine, pestilence – will destroy them in Egypt. Thus the sermon is typical of the sermons in the tradition (e.g. 7.3–7; 11.3–5; 18.7–10; 22.3–5) which present the future in terms of either-or: *either* the people must behave in a particular fashion *or* they face destruction. In this form of the sermon the alternatives are: *either* stay in Judah and live *or* go to Egypt and perish (a reversal of the options offered in 21.8–10!). The positive future lies in the land of Judah or nowhere. Yahweh's repentance only holds good for life in Judah – elsewhere his intention is evil (v. 17).

42.18–22

18 'For thus says the LORD of hosts, the God of Israel: As my anger and my
wrath were poured out on the inhabitants of Jerusalem, so my wrath will
be poured out on you when you go to Egypt. You shall become an execration,
a horror, a curse, and a taunt. You shall see this place no more. 19 The
LORD has said to you, O remnant of Judah, "Do not go to Egypt." Know
for a certainty that I have warned you this day 20 that you have gone astray
at the cost of your lives. For you sent me to the LORD your God, saying,
"Pray for us to the LORD our God, and whatever the LORD our God says
declare to us and we will do it." 21 And I have this day declared it to you,
but you have not obeyed the voice of the LORD your God in anything that
he sent me to tell you. 22 Now therefore know for a certainty that you shall
die by the sword, by famine, and by pestilence in the place where you desire
to go to live.'

---

[18] G lacks 'of hosts'. Cf. 44.12 for the same four epithets 'execration', 'horror', 'curse', 'taunt'; three of the four appear in 29.18; and two in 24.9; 25.18 (all these references use four epithets). The outpouring of the divine anger motif occurs in 7.20; 44.6; cf. 32.31; 33.5; 36.7. For the curses of Egypt cf. Deut. 28.15–68. **[19]** Because Rudolph, 256, and Bright, 252, read 43.1–3 between 42.18 and 19, they insert the phrase 'and Jeremiah said' at the beginning of v. 19 (cf. BHS). G has *kai nun*, 'and now', before 'know for a certainty', i.e. surely know (*yādoʿa tēd^{e}ʿū*). G lacks 'that I have warned you this day'. **[20]** K *htʿtym*; Q *hitʿētemy* 'you have erred' (K a scribal error); MT *hitʿētem b^{e}napšōtēkem*, lit. 'you have erred at the cost of your lives'. G *eponēreusasthe en psuchais humōn*, 'you have done wickedness in your souls' = *h^{a}rēʿōtem* for *hitʿētem*. G lacks 'to the lord your god', 'our god', and 'our god so declare to us'. The sending (*šlḥ*) motif dominates the chapter, cf. vv. 5, 6, 9, 20, 21; cf. 43.1, 2. **[21]** G lacks 'and I have declared to you this day', 'your god', and *ul^{e}kol*, 'and concerning everything'. **[22]** G lacks 'know for a certainty that'. See Notes on v. 17, for the triad sword, famine, pestilence.

Some commentators favour transposing 43.1–3 between 42.18 and 19 in order to sharpen the force of the dialogue (e.g. Bright, 258), but the expansion of the prose of 42 is such that it is hardly necessary to rearrange the chapter to improve its logic. 42.18–22 appears to anticipate the people's refusal to listen to Jeremiah and their determination to go to Egypt. These points are not made until 43.1–3, but the editors have already introduced the going to Egypt motif in 41.17 and have expanded it in 42.13–17. The attention of the hearers of the tradition is therefore well prepared for the people's response in 43.2–3. In devising and expanding the sermon of 42.9–22 the editing has focused on the choice between staying in the land of Judah and going to the land of Egypt. 42.18–22 is a further statement about the journey to Egypt which describes Egypt in terms drawn from the tradition about the fate of Jerusalem. 43.4–7 will deal with the actual flight to Egypt, but 42.18–22 hammers out the consequences of that possibility. Thus 42.9–22 is made up of three verses about the benefits of remaining in the land of Judah and ten verses about the horrors of going to Egypt (cf. the proportion of blessings to curses in Deut. 28).

In vv. 18–22 Jeremiah is presented as a faithful warner of the community. He addresses the people: 'O remnant of Judah – Do not go to Egypt' and this warning is reinforced by reassurances that such a journey will most certainly (vv. 19, 22) result in the forfeiture of the people's lives. The horror expressed about going to Egypt reflects the anti-Egyptian outlook behind Deut. 28 (cf. Mayes 1979, 348–51, for discussion of the post-Deuteronomistic aspects of this chapter) and the antipathy towards all things Egyptian held by certain circles in Judah. In going to Egypt the people would appear to be reversing the original divine act of redemption which brought the people out of Egypt. In Deuteronomistic circles such an apostate act was unthinkable, and contrary to divine command (cf. Deut. 17.16b; 28.68a). Hence to go to Egypt was to enter into the realm of the curse and to become an execration oneself (vv. 18b; 44.12). Merely by fleeing to Egypt the people would bring down upon their own heads the wrath of Yahweh; that very wrath which had destroyed Jerusalem so recently.

The emphasis by the people on their willingness to obey (vv. 5–6) can now be seen to be a literary device of the editors whereby the enormity of the people's disobedience is underlined (vv. 13, 21). In going to Egypt they will never see the land of Judah again (v. 18), but they will die (vv. 16, 17, 20, 22) without any survivors (v. 17b). Thus the remnant of Gedaliah's community is presented as tottering on the brink of annihilation. Will they be so foolhardy as to go to Egypt?

43.1–7

431 When Jeremiah finished speaking to all the people all these words of
the LORD their God, with which the LORD their God had sent him to them,
2 Azariah the son of Hoshaiah and Johanan the son of Kareah and all the
insolent men said to Jeremiah, 'You are telling a lie. The LORD our God did
not send you to say, "Do not go to Egypt to live there"; 3 but Baruch the
son of Neriah has set you against us, to deliver us into the hand of the
Chaldeans, that they may kill us or take us into exile in Babylon.' 4 So
Johanan the son of Kareah and all the commanders of the forces and all the
people did not obey the voice of the LORD, to remain in the land of Judah.
5 But Johanan the son of Kareah and all the commanders of the forces took
all the remnant of Judah who had returned to live in the land of Judah from
all the nations to which they had been driven – 6 the men, the women, the
children, the princesses, and every person whom Nebuzaradan the captain
of the guard had left with Gedaliah the son of Ahikam, son of Shaphan; also
Jeremiah the prophet and Baruch the son of Neriah. 7 And they came into
the land of Egypt, for they did not obey the voice of the LORD. And they
arrived at Tahpanhes.

[MT 43] = G 50. **[1]** G lacks both occurrences of 'their god'. Cf. 42.5 for the motif of Yahweh sending (*šlḥ*) Jeremiah to the people. **[2]** Cf. 42.1 for these two figures (G Azariah the son of *Maasaeas*). MT *wᵉkol-hā'ᵃnāšīm hazzēdīm*, 'and all the insolent men': G lacks 'insolent'; MT anticipates the community's answer to Jeremiah. MT *'ōmᵉrīm*, '(they) say': G *hoi eipantes*, 'who say' = *hā'ōmᵉrīm* (MT lit. 'and Azariah . . . said . . . and all the men . . . say'); Giesebrecht, 220, reads as *wᵉhammōrīm* '(insolent) and rebellious' cf BHS. G has *legontes*, 'saying', after 'to Jeremiah'. MT *šeqer 'attāh mᵉdabbēr*, 'falsehood you are speaking': G lacks 'you are speaking'; cf. 40.16 for a similar accusation. MT *'ᵉlōhēhū*, 'our god': G *pros hēmas*, 'to us' = *'ēlēhū*. **[3]** MT *massīt 'ōtᵉkā bānū*, 'has incited you against us': *sūt* instigated or seduced, cf. 38.22; Deut. 13.7 (EV 6); Job 2.3. NEB better than RSV. **[5]** G lacks 'from all the nations to which they had been driven there' and reads *en tē gē*, 'in the land', for MT *bᵉ'ereṣ yᵉhūdāh*, 'in the land of Judah'; cf. 40.12. **[6]** MT *'et-haggᵉbārīm* 'the men': G *tous dunatous andras*, 'the mighty men', cf. 41.16b. MT *wᵉ'et-bᵉnōt hammelek*, 'and the daughters of the king': as in 41.10, i.e. the princesses. Both MT and G read 'Jeremiah *the prophet*'. **[7]** Tahpanhes (*taḥpanḥēs*): cf. 2.16; 44.1; Daphne, modern tell Defneh, in north-east Egypt.

The response of the community to Jeremiah's presentation of the options available to them contains a fine irony. They accuse him of telling a lie (*šeqer*). This accusation against Jeremiah is highly ironic in a book which represents him as constantly accusing other people of speaking lies (*šeqer*, e.g. 8.8; 9.4 [EV 5]; 14.14; 23.25, 26, 32; 28.15; 29.21). It also demonstrates how easily the accusation may be made against any speaker and how prejudiced a judgment it may be. Further irony may be glimpsed in the explanation offered in v. 3 that behind Jeremiah's false speaking is the figure of Baruch ben Neriah. This accusation that Baruch has incited (*sūt*) Jeremiah to lie is ironic in that throughout the book of Jeremiah the prophet is always presented as a man quite capable of acting on his own initiative (i.e. at Yahweh's command). Yet the irony is in keeping with the depiction of Jeremiah as a passive figure in Part IV. Only at the instigation of some other person may he be regarded as becoming active in these stories. A conspiracy is detected behind his advocacy of staying in Judah rather than fleeing to Egypt. That conspiracy is attributed to Baruch, and the accusation itself may represent the suspicion that Jeremiah and Baruch have plans for self-aggrandisement in advocating such a policy. They certainly could be expected to benefit from the Babylonian reaction to the assassination of Gedaliah because they were not implicated in it (hence their complete absence from that part of the story?). Johanan and Azariah would most likely face the wrath of the Babylonians and could expect to die for their failure to protect the Babylonians' appointee. The other people would have to face deportation to Babylon (cf. v. 3). These legitimate fears account for the rejection of Jeremiah's warnings against going to Egypt, though they do not explain why Baruch is accused of inciting Jeremiah to adopt such a standpoint.

The sudden appearance of Baruch in this story is inexplicable. Up to this stage of Part IV he is completely absent from the story of Jeremiah, but now he is introduced into the story in order to explain why the prophet is so hostile towards the plan to go to Egypt. Jeremiah's claim to be speaking Yahweh's words is rejected as falsehood (*šeqer*), and the hand of Baruch is detected behind his words. Why should that be? Where was Baruch during the fall of Jerusalem? Where has he been during the period when Gedaliah was organizing the community and after the assassination? Where was he when the people consulted Jeremiah? Chapter 45 attempts to answer the question about Baruch's survival of the destruction of

Jerusalem, but all the other questions (like so many questions raised by a serious reading of the tradition) cannot be answered *from the text.* Baruch appears very infrequently in the book of Jeremiah and his appearance in 43.3 (cf. v. 6) may be regarded as part of that process whereby the tradition created and developed a subsidiary figure to accompany Jeremiah at certain points of the story (e.g. 32.12–13, 16; 36; 45). What Baruch represents in the story-telling pattern of the tradition is a debatable matter (cf. Wanke 1971, 154–6; Pohlmann 1978, 198–204), but, rejecting the theory that he is the author of much of the book, whatever view is taken of him he remains a very *minor* figure in the story of Jeremiah. His surfacing in that story at 43.3, 6 reflects the creation of a secondary character whose role is far from being well defined and who therefore remains an aleatory figure in the book.

The outcome of the rejection of Jeremiah's stand against going to Egypt is the journeying of everybody, including Jeremiah and Baruch, to the land of the curses. Although v. 5 represents the whole community, i.e. all the remnant of Judah, as going to Egypt, this should be read as an ideological rather than a literal statement. It can hardly be maintained that the land of Judah was completely denuded of people and that everybody went to Egypt. The groups of people associated with Johanan ben Kareah may have fled to Egypt, but all the other groups of people left throughout the land of Judah must have remained (cf. Lam. 5). This analysis would appear to be confirmed by the deportation of seven hundred and forty-five people to Babylon in 582 (52.30); a deportation which may have been the result of the assassination of Gedaliah. The impression is given in 40.7 – 43.7 that everybody in the land associated themselves with Gedaliah and that therefore the whole remnant of Judah went into exile to Egypt. If such an impression is intentional, then it must reflect the ideology of the editors, who wish to write off all the people left in Judah (cf. 39.9–10; 52.15–16). Such an ideological presentation is in keeping with the sermon of 42.9–22, which offers divine protection to the remnant of Judah and then in 43.1–3 indicts the remnant for rejecting that offer. The actual people (among whom it may be supposed were those who would be deported in 582) who went on living in the land of Judah are of no interest to the editors. Jeremiah and Baruch go to Egypt or, more precisely, are taken to Egypt, and the editorial attention focuses on that area. What remains behind in Judah ceases to have any significance for the tradition and may be deemed not to exist. But this non-existence should not be confused with social reality; it is but an ideological blank space in the tradition.

With the descent of the people to Egypt the story of Gedaliah's community comes to an end. What follows in 43.8–13 and 44 is a number of statements against Egypt and the Jewish com*munities* in Egypt, but the groups which constituted Gedaliah's community are no longer the subject of the tradition. The great hopes associated with Gedaliah are dead, and the possibility of a renewed people in the land of Judah is now in the past. As if to emphasize the passivity of Jeremiah, he is not only accused of being Baruch's puppet (or ventriloquist's dummy) but is taken to Egypt (presumably cf. 42.13–22) against his wishes. Thus he becomes a pathetic victim of other people's fears and plans and is branded a liar into the bargain. Those who go to Egypt, including Jeremiah and Baruch, now enter the area of the curses and cannot hope for anything other than a miserable life under Yahweh's curses – 'and you shall become an execration, a horror, a curse, and a taunt' (42.18b). This, then, is the fate of Jeremiah – the victim of other men's incompetence and plans. But the tradition is not concerned with his fate – this is not a biography of Jeremiah – so the account of the people's flight to Egypt only mentions the taking of Jeremiah and Baruch there in passing (e.g. v. 6c). All those who go to Egypt are enclosed in the editorial condemnation 'they did not obey the voice of Yahweh' (v. 7). Thus under disobedience and the aweful power of the curses uttered by Jeremiah against going to Egypt Gedaliah's community face a future without hope after the shattering of their hopes for life in the land of Judah.

43.8–13

8 Then the word of the LORD came to Jeremiah in Tahpanhes: 9 'Take in
your hands large stones, and hide them in the mortar in the pavement which
is at the entrance to Pharaoh's palace in Tahpanhes, in the sight of the men
of Judah, 10 and say to them, "Thus says the LORD of hosts, the God of
Israel: Behold, I will send and take Nebuchadrezzar the king of Babylon,
my servant, and he will set his throne above these stones which I have hid,
and he will spread his royal canopy over them. 11 He shall come and smite
the land of Egypt, giving to the pestilence those who are doomed to the
pestilence, to captivity those who are doomed to captivity, and to the sword

those who are doomed to the sword. 12 He shall kindle a fire in the temples of the gods of Egypt; and he shall burn them and carry them away captive; and he shall clean the land of Egypt, as a shepherd cleans his cloak of vermin; and he shall go away from there in peace. 13 He shall break the obelisks of Heliopolis which is in the land of Egypt; and the temples of the gods of Egypt he shall burn with fire." '

---

[8] Cf. 33.1; 35.12; 42.7 for this form of the reception of the divine word formulaic introduction. Jeremiah's reception of the word in Egypt maintains his prophetic status there and is a form of the OAN strand in the tradition (cf. 46; 51.59–64). **[9]** MT *qaḥ*, 'take': cf. 25.15; 36.2; negative command (*lō'-tiqqaḥ*, 'do not take') in 16.2. MT *bammeleṭ bammalbēn 'ašer*, 'in the cement, in the brick-mould which': lacking in G; meaning of Hebrew uncertain, cf. NEB 'in cement in the pavement'; JPSB 'in mortar in the brick structure'. The word *meleṭ* only occurs here and may mean 'mortar, cement', cf. Bright, 259, 'in the clay flooring [?]'; *malbēn* appears in II Sam. 12.31, where it may refer to 'brick-making', and Nahum 3.14 'brick-mould', where it may mean 'terrace of bricks' (cf. KB, 527; KB³ II, 555f.; Driver 1937–38, 122; 'quadrangle', BDB 527); The two words are variants in MT; G *en prothurois*, 'in the vestibule'. A, Theod. *en tō kruphiō*, 'in secret'. Rudolph, 258, regards *malbēn* as a dittography of *meleṭ*, 'clay soil' (cf. BHS). MT *le'ēnē 'anāšīm yehūdīm*, 'in the sight of the men of Judah': lit. 'to the eyes of the men, the Jews'; cf. 28.1, 5, 11, where words and actions are performed *in the sight of* various social strata. **[10]** G lacks 'of hosts, the god of Israel'. G lacks 'my servant' in the phrase 'Nebuchadrezzar the king of Babylon', cf. 25.9; 27.6, where the fullest form of the phrase appears in MT but the whole phrase is lacking in G 25.9. G 34.6 lacks 'my servant', but has *douleuein autō*, 'to serve him', which may reflect MT (cf. Tov 1979, 83–4) which, in turn, probably influenced 43.10 (se Notes on 27.6). MT *weśamtī*, 'and *I* will place': G *kai thēsei*, 'and *he* will place' = *weśām*. MT *ṭāmāntī*, '*I* have hid': G *katekrupsas*, '*you* have hid'. K *šprwrw*; Q *šaprīrō*: the word only occurs here and is of doubtful meaning; possible meanings are 'canopy, pavilion, carpet' (cf. BDB, 1051). **[11]** K *wb'h*; Q *ūbā'*, 'and he will come'. Cf. 15.2 for the incantatory words *'ašer lammāwet lammāwet wa'ašer laššebī laššebī wa'ašer laḥereb leḥāreb*, 'those who are for death to death, those who are for captivity to captivity, and those who are for the sword to the sword'. Rudolph suggests the last motif (sword) may be an addition (cf. BHS), as there is no essential difference between death and the sword. RSV, JPSB translate *māwet* respectively as 'pestilence', 'plague', which distinguishes it from 'sword' = death. The terms in the list are stereotypes, cf. 15.2 (death, sword, hunger, captivity) and reflect the magical performance of Jeremiah. **[12]** MT *wehiṣṣattī*, 'and *I* will kindle': Vrs 'and *he* will kindle' = *wehiṣṣīt*; cf. other verbs '*he* will burn them' or '*he* will carry them captive'. Here 'them' must refer to the gods (i.e. the idols) rather than the temples in which the fires are kindled. MT *w*e*'āṭāh*, 'and he will wrap himself up': i.e. as a shepherd wraps himself up in his garment, so king Nebuchadrezzar will wrap himself up in the land of Egypt. This is a graphic image of Babylon's complete domination of Egypt, cf. JPSB. G *phtheiriei*, 'search for lice': i.e. as a shepherd searches his garment for lice, cf. RSV, NEB; this suggests *'āṭāh*, 'grasp, pick' (cf. Isa. 22.17), rather than *'āṭāh*, 'wrap oneself'. Rudolph favours 'delouse', cf. BHS. The image of Nebuchadrezzar departing in peace (*b*e*šālōm*) may favour G imagery. **[13]** MT *'et-maṣṣ*e*bōt bēt šemeš*, 'the standing stones of Beth-shemesh': i.e. the sacred pillars of the house of the sun; G *tous stulous Hēlioupoleōs*, the pillars of Heliopolis. MT *'*a*šer b*e*'ereṣ miṣrāyim*, 'which is in Egypt': written from a Palestinian perspective. G *tous en Ōn*, 'which are in On': a double rendering Heliopolis – On. Giesebrecht, 221, treats MT as a late gloss to distinguish the *bēt šemeš* which is in Egypt from the Palestinian one. MT *w*e*'et-bātē '*e*lōhē-miṣrayim*, 'and the houses of the gods of Egypt': i.e. the temples, but G *kai tas oikias autōn*, 'and their houses' (= *bātēhem*), may be a more general reference to the houses of the town, as the burning of the temples is referred to in v. 12 (cf. Giesebrecht).

In Egypt the divine word comes to Jeremiah and he becomes active once more in the performance of a magical act. He is commanded to take large stones and hide them somewhere in the area of the door of the Pharaoh's house (i.e. his official residence when visiting that part of Egypt) in Tahpanhes. This strange performance is to be carried out in the sight of the Jews who fled with Jeremiah to that town. The words accompanying this magic act are given in vv. 10–13 so that the witnesses understand what is happening. The dramatic actions of carrying large stones and burying (?) them in the brick terracing outside the royal residence must have bewildered the onlookers. Whether the performance should be regarded as a literal one (how would the Egyptian guards have responded to a foreigner digging up their premises?) or an enactment elsewhere with theatrical overtones is a moot point. But the spoken words explaining the meaning of the action clarify whatever obscurities cloak the action depicted in v. 9. Jeremiah's transportation of stones to the royal residence in Tahpanhes signifies Yahweh's sending (*šlḥ*) and taking of Nebuchadrezzar (Yahweh's servant in MT) to Egypt where he will set up his throne on the very spot where Jeremiah hid the stones. Thus Jeremiah brings Nebuchadrezzar to Egypt by his performative magic. To this explanation of the drama vv. 11–13 add a number of details: the Babylonian invasion of Egypt will devastate the land and its people will be consigned to death or deportation (cf. 15.2). This incantation chanted over the land of Egypt effectively brings about the destruction of the people (cf. 51.59–64, where Babylon is similarly spoken against). The temples of the gods of Egypt will be fired and Nebuchadrezzar will have complete control over Egyptian territory (cf. G and MT images in v. 12). The obelisks of Heliopolis will be shattered also and the houses burned. These details are only given in the spoken part of the ritual action – they are the meaning of the incantatory aspects of Jeremiah's performance.

Thus the first act of Jeremiah in Egypt is to bring about its destruction. Such ritual magic (cf. 46) is characteristic of the presentation of Jeremiah in certain strands of the tradition (e.g. 13.1–11; 19.1–2, 10–11; 25.15–17; 51.59–64). He creates and presides over the annihilation of the enemy (e.g. Judah, Jerusalem, Egypt, Babylon) by his performance of certain acts accompanied by incantation, curses and magical utterances. Each of the victims of his actions in due course undergoes the fate conjured up for it. The extent to which Egypt suffered a devastating invasion by the Babylonians is debatable because the evidence for the Babylonian incursion into Egypt suggests a military campaign to curb Egyptian interference in Babylonian matters rather than a punitive campaign of destruction (e.g. Pharaoh Amasis appears to have retained his throne and to have established friendly relations with Babylon; cf Pritchard 1969, 308). However, the important thing in the tradition is not the historicity of these acts but the power of the word manipulated by Jeremiah and linked to his performative magic. The condemnation of Egypt epitomized by the act of v. 9 is part of the strong anti-Egyptian strand in the book at this point (42.13–22; 43.8–13; 44; 46). By presenting this strand in conjunction with one of Jeremiah's formidable magic acts accompanied by incantation (v. 11), the editors increase the force of the rejection of the community which fled to Egypt. No sooner have they fled from the potential threat of Babylon in the land of Judah (42.11–12) than they must face Yahweh's sending for Nebuchadrezzar to invade the very land to which they fled in order to avoid him! Their disobedience against the warnings of Jeremiah has trapped them in a place where Yahweh's wrath is about to descend.

44.1–14

44[1] The word that came to Jeremiah concerning all the Jews that dwelt in the land of Egypt, at Migdol, at Tahpanhes, at Memphis, and in the land of Pathros, 2 'Thus says the LORD of hosts, the God of Israel: You have seen all the evil that I brought upon Jerusalem and upon all the cities of Judah. Behold, this day they are a desolation, and no one dwells in them, 3 because of the wickedness which they committed, provoking me to anger, in that they went to burn incense and serve other gods that they knew not, neither they, nor you, nor your fathers. 4 Yet I persistently sent to you all my servants the prophets, saying, "Oh, do not do this abominable thing that I hate!" 5 But they did not listen or incline their ear, to turn from their wickedness and burn no incense to other gods. 6 Therefore my wrath and my anger were poured forth and kindled in the cities of Judah and the streets of Jerusalem; and they became a waste and a desolation, as at this day. 7 And now thus says the LORD God of hosts, the God of Israel: Why do you commit this great evil against yourselves, to cut off from you man and woman, infant and child, from the midst of Judah, leaving you no remnant? 8 Why do you provoke me to anger with the works of your hands, burning incense to other gods in the land of Egypt where you have come to live, that you may be cut off and become a curse and a taunt among all the nations of the earth? 9 Have you forgotten the wickedness of your fathers, the wickedness of the kings of Judah, the wickedness of their wives, your own wickedness, and the wickedness of your wives, which they committed in the land of Judah and in the streets of Jerusalem? 10 They have not humbled themselves even to this day, nor have they feared, nor walked in my law and my statutes which I set before you and before your fathers.

11 Therefore thus says the Lord of hosts, the God of Israel: Behold, I will set my face against you for evil, to cut off all Judah. 12 I will take the remnant of Judah who have set their faces to come to the land of Egypt to live, and they shall all be consumed; in the land of Egypt they shall fall; by the sword and by famine they shall be consumed; from the least to the greatest, they shall die by the sword and by famine; and they shall become an execration, a horror, a curse and a taunt. 13 I will punish those who dwell in the land of Egypt, as I punished Jerusalem, with the sword, with famine, and with pestilence, 14 so that none of the remnant of Judah who have come to live in the land of Egypt shall escape or survive or return to the land of Judah, to which they desire to return to dwell there; for they shall not return, except some fugitives.'

[MT 44] = G 51. 1–30. **[1]** Cf. 25.1 for the reception of the divine word formula. The site of Migdol is uncertain, but it may be near Tahpanhes (to the east of it, cf. Rudolph, 258; Ex. 14.2). MT *ūb*^{e}*nōp*, 'and in Memphis': cf.

2.16; lacking in G. Memphis was the capital of Lower Egypt. Pathros was in Upper Egypt. These towns and areas represent Jewish communities which had settled in Egypt over a long period and 44.1 should not be read as a continuation of 43.8–13. **[2]** G lacks 'this day' and 'of hosts'. The representation of the cities of Judah as a waste or ruin (*ḥorbāh*) reflects the belief that during the exile there were no people living in the land of Judah (cf. II Chron. 36.21; but cf. Lam. 5). This belief favoured the exiles in Babylon (24.4–7) because it left the land vacant for their return. Cf. 25.11; 34.22; 35.17; 36.31; 40.2–3 for the motifs of evil and desolation in operation against Jerusalem and Judah. **[3]** G lacks 'to serve': MT *l^eqaṭṭēr la^{ʿa}bōd*, 'to burn to serve', is overloaded. It is better to understand *qṭr*, 'burn', as in 'offer sacrifice', cf. NEB, JPSB, rather than 'burn incense', cf. 1.16; 7.9. MT *^{ʾa}šer lōʾ y^edāʿūm*, 'which they did not know them': G *hois ouk egnōte*, 'which you did not know'. MT adds *hēmmāh ʾattem wa^{ʾa}bōtēkem*, 'they, you, and your fathers': cf. 2.5–9, where different generations are accused of such behaviour. It is an absurd feature of these sermons that the nation is accused of persistent idolatry throughout their existence yet always in terms of gods which they have not known! Either they worshipped them constantly or they did not know them, but hardly both. Cf. 7.9; 19.4 for the unknown gods motif. **[4]** Cf. 7.25; 26.5; 29.19; 35.15 for the motif of sending Yahweh's servants the prophets (*haškēm w^ešālōaḥ*, 'rising early and sending'). Here the function of the prophets is reduced to warnings against 'this matter of abomination' (*ʾet d^ebar-hattōʿēbāh hazzōʾt*), i.e. idolatry; cf. 7.10; 32.35; 44.22 for the motif 'doing this (these) abomination(s)'. **[5]** Cf. 7.13b, 26; 11.8; 25.4, 7; 29.19; 34.14; 35.14, 15 for the motif of not listening. The point made about *qṭr* in v. 3 applies throughout 44 (e.g. vv. 5, 8, 15, 17, 18, 19, 21, 24). **[6]** Cf. v. 2. MT *l^eḥorbāh lišmāmāh*, 'a ruin a waste': possibly variants, but some mss, Vrs read 'a ruin *and* a waste'. Cf. 42.18 for the pouring out of the divine wrath on Jerusalem; also 7.20 where the burning motif is associated with the outpouring of anger. Cf. 7.17, 34; 11.6; 33.10; 44.6, 9, 17, 21 for the phrase 'in the cities of Judah and in the streets of Jerusalem'. MT *kayyōm hazzeh*, 'as at this day': cf. vv. 22–23; 11.5; 25.18; 32.20. **[7]** MT *yhwh ^{ʾe}lōhē ṣ^ebāʾōt ^{ʾe}lōhē yiśrāʾēl*, 'Yahweh god of hosts, god of Israel': G *kurios pantokratōr*, 'lord almighty', i.e. Yahweh of hosts. The evil (*rāʿāh*) committed here is different from that of v. 2 (Yahweh's evil); it refers to the moral injury that is self-inflicted through idolatry rather than the destruction caused by Yahweh (cf. Thiel 1981, 72). Cf. 27.13, 17 for the why question motif. MT *l^ebiltī hōtīr lākem š^eʾērīt*, 'in order not to leave for yourselves a remnant': the motif of complete annihilation runs through this chapter (cf. vv. 12, 14, 27). **[8]** MT *l^emaʿan hakrīt lākem ū*, 'in order to cut off yourselves and': an addition from v. 7? (cf. Rudolph, 260; BHS). Cf. 25.18; 42.18 for the motifs 'curse', 'taunt'; 7.18b–19 for the notion of provoking the deity to anger; 26.6, 'a curse for all the nations of the earth'; 25.6; 32.30 for provoking Yahweh to anger by the work of your/their hands (cf. Deut. 31.29; I Kings 16.7; II Kings 22.17 = II Chron. 34.25). The theme of settling in Egypt appears in vv. 8, 12, 14, 28; 42.15, 22. **[9]** MT *w*ᵉ*'ēt rā'ōt nāšāyw*, 'and the evil of his wives': *n*ᵉ*šēhem*, 'their wives', is assumed by EVV; cf. BHS. I Kings 11.4; 15.13 indicate a plurality of wives; G *kai tōn kakōn tōn archontōn humōn*, 'and the evil of your princes', cf. vv. 17, 21. G lacks 'and your own evil'; S lacks 'and the evil of your wives'. For the rhetorical question of v. 9 cf. 3.6; 7.17. **[10]** MT *lō' dukk*ᵉ*ū*, 'they were not crushed': cf. *m*ᵉ*dukkā'īm*, 'crushed', Isa. 19.10; meaning crushed by remorse, cf. NEB. G *kai ouk epausanto*, 'and have not ceased': = *nikl*ᵉ*'ū*? Vrs have different readings which suggest MT is uncertain; Rudolph, 260, *nik'ū* (*k'h*, Niph., 'be disheartened, cowed'), cf. Dan. 11.30; Ps. 109.16. G lacks 'nor have they feared'. MT *b*ᵉ*tōrātī ūb*ᵉ*ḥuqqōtay*, 'in my law and in my statutes': G *ton prostagmatōn mou*, 'my ordinances' = *b*ᵉ*ḥuqqōtay*. G lacks 'before them' and reads '*their* fathers' for MT '*your* fathers'. Cf. 9.13; 26.4; 32.23, for the motif of not walking in Yahweh's *tōrāh*. **[11]** G is briefer than MT: 'therefore thus says the lord behold I set my face'. Cf. 21.10 for the motif of setting the face against (city/people) for evil. **[12]** MT *baḥereb bārā'āb*, 'by sword, by famine': many mss, Vrs 'by sword *and* by famine', so RSV but cf. NEB, JPSB. Cf. vv. 18, 27 for the consumption (*tmm*) motif; 42.17, 18 for many of the elements in v. 12; also 21.9; 27.13; 38.2; 42.16, 22. In v. 11 Yahweh sets his face, in v. 12 the people set their faces (*śīm pānīm*, 'to set faces', idiom for determination); the same behaviour of deity and remnant leads to confrontation and only one party can win, cf. v. 28b 'whose word shall stand' (G, cf. MT, which spells out the point further). Cf. 42.18b for the fourfold designation of the remnant 'execration, horror, curse, taunt'. G has three terms rather than four. **[13]** Cf. 42.18a; the triad sword, famine, pestilence are to be found throughout the tradition, cf. Notes on 42.17. This verse forms a conclusion to Jeremiah's sermon by making an equation between the sins of the remnant in Egypt and those of the people of Jerusalem (cf. Thiel 1981, 73). G^{BS} lack 'pestilence'. **[14]** Cf. 42.17; a citation and paraphrase of 42.17b. G lacks *šām*, 'there' (to live in the land of Egypt) and 'to live', *lāšebet*. MT *kī lō'-yāšūbū kī 'im-p*ᵉ*lēṭīm*, 'for they shall not return except fugitives': the last phrase contradicts 14a, 'there shall be no fugitive (*pālīṭ*) or survivor (*śārīd*) belonging to the remnant of Judah'. It is regarded as a gloss by many commentators (e.g. Duhm, Volz, Rudolph, Bright); an addition to v. 14 in view of v. 28a, which asserts that a few will escape from Egypt and return to Judah. Cf. 22.27 for the phrase *'ᵃšer-hēmmāh m*ᵉ*naśś*ᵉ*'īm 'et-napšām lāšūb . . . lō'-yāšūbū*, 'to which they desire (lit. they lift up their souls) to return . . . they shall not return'.

A prolix sermon in 44 concludes Part IV in such a manner that it forms a closure with the equally long diatribe against idolatrous practices which opens Part I (i.e. chapter 2; 1 and 45 are parallel additions to the blocks forming the tradition). The long-winded discourse against involvement with other gods is addressed to the fugitive communities of Jews in the land of Egypt (both upper and lower parts of that land). Thus v. 1 is not a continuation of 42.13–22 but a more general attack on communal religion similar to the discourses of 2–3 which are addressed to 'all the families of the house of Israel' (2.4b). That so many communities should be scattered throughout the land of Egypt reflects a period when the Jews were well settled in Egypt and not the immediate aftermath of the fall of Jerusalem. Ideologically 44 sets out to deny divine favour to such communities and the sermon must be read as reflecting the interests of other groups. Whether those interests belong to the Jerusalem community (second temple period?) or the exiles in Babylon (cf. 24.4–7) cannot be determined from the text. The hostility towards Egypt is a feature of 42–44 which is shared by Deuteronomistic circles, and many elements in 44 point to a Deuteronomistic influence on the construction of the sermon (analysis in Thiel 1981, 69–81; cf. Pohlmann 1978, 166–82). The sermon is a mosaic of phrases and motifs drawn from many of the prose discourses in the book of Jeremiah, and there is little in 44 which represents an independent tradition (with the possible exception of v. 1).

Despite the prolix nature of the sermon it may be divided into a number of sections. In vv. 2–14 Jeremiah makes a lengthy statement, though hardly to all the different communities of Jews living throughout the land of Egypt (contrast v. 15b). This statement may be divided into three parts: vv. 2–6, 7–10, 11–14 (cf. Pohlmann 1978, 168–72). These parts consist of a review of the idolatrous past of Judah and Jerusalem which brought about the disaster of 587, an indictment of the people to whom the sermon is addressed, and a statement of Yahweh's punishment of the remnant of Judah now living in the land of Egypt. Each part is filled out by citations and paraphrases of pieces from elsewhere in the tradition. The key motifs in the sermon include the burning (*qiṭṭēr*) of sacrifices to other gods (vv. 3, 5, 8, 15, 17–19, 21, 23, 25), the fate of the remnant of Judah in Egypt (vv. 12, 14, 28), the lack of any survivors of the coming judgment (vv. 7, 11, 14, 27, 28), and the attack on the familial cults of the people (vv. 7, 9, 14, 20–21, 24–25). All these motifs may be found in the prose collections of 7.1–8.3; 11.1–13; 19.1–13; 25.1–7; 26.2–6; 32.23–35; 42.13–22, and only the setting of the sermon in

Egypt allows for nuances of variation in the handling of so many clichés.

There is no reason to assume that 44 represents an authentic sermon of Jeremiah preached to the many communities scattered throughout Egypt (*contra* Bright, 265). Such an assumption fails to recognize the redactional nature of v. 1 (cf. 7.1; 11.1; 18.1; 21.1; 30.1; 32.1; 34.1, 8; 35.1; 40.1) which renders what follows impossible as a literal performance. It also refuses to acknowledge the clichéd nature of the material constituting the sermon as an ideological rejection of 'unreal' situations, in the sense that the communities criticized are constructs of the tradition itself. There is nothing in 44 which permits a glimpse of the historical Jewish communities in Egypt, communities which were to be so important in the following centuries for the development of the Jewish religion. The fact that everything said about these communities in Egypt is also said at length about the people of Judah and Jerusalem is indicative of the ideological nature of 44. Ideology reduces all distinctions to the same level of unreal similarity in order to condemn discrete entities in blanket terms. Such an ideology can be detected in the writings of the Deuteronomistic school and other writings influenced by them (cf. Thiel 1981, 93–115). The central feature of Deuteronomistic ideology is the claim that the states of Israel and Judah were destroyed because of cultic and idolatrous practices. This claim is dominant in 44 and the prose sermons of the tradition, and it is difficult to deny a Deuteronomistic influence at some level in the construction of the book of Jeremiah. Even if the influence belongs to a post-Deuteronomistic level of tradition construction, the ideological handling of cultic malpractices and idolatrous beliefs owes much to the influence of the Deuteronomists.

To underline the importance of cultic purity and the avoidance of rituals tainted with paganism the sermon in 44 extends the critique of Judah and Jerusalem to the communities living in Egypt. The catastrophe of 587 is not viewed as the end of Yahweh's wrath (contrast 42.10–12) but a major instantiation of it. That wrath continues to burn against similar cultic practices, and no matter where they are cultivated the devotees of such cults are exposed to summary judgment. Two strands run through the sermon in its present form; v. 1 applies the sermon to all the communities in Egypt and vv. 11–14 refer it to the remnant (cf. 40.11 – 43.7) which fled to Egypt. To these two strands is added a midrashic section in vv. 15–29, 20–23, 25 which develops 7.17–19 as a particular example of idolatry leading to destruction. Throughout the sermon the state of the land of Judah is represented as a place where nobody lives any more (e.g. vv. 2, 6, 22). Such desolation is the result of idolatry, and it will befall the Jews who now live in Egypt. Thus the disasters of the past are used by the editors to present a case for their own ideological outlook. The association of the past with idolatry and disaster makes connections between ideology and history which must be viewed as part of a complex of arguments about the nature of cultic worship in the Persian period when the second temple became the focus of rival claims about power and control (cf. Haggai, Zechariah, Chronicles, Ezra-Nehemiah and Isa. 56–66).

The three parts of the sermon outline the history of the past (vv. 2–6) in terms of offering sacrifices to other gods, the persistent sending of the prophets, and the rejection of such messengers and the destruction of Jerusalem 'as at this day' (v. 6). The present is represented by vv. 7–10, which accuse those addressed of having forgotten such matters because they behave in the same way as their fathers and therefore endanger their own lives to the point of being cut off (*krt*) without any remainder (*šᵉ'ērît*, v. 7). The future (vv. 11–14) uses a word-play on the divine setting of the face against those who set their face to go to Egypt (vv. 11–12). That fate which befell Jerusalem will befall them (v. 13), and none will escape (v. 14). An additional phrase allows for a few fugitives to survive.

44.15–19

15 Then all the men who knew that their wives had offered incense to other gods, and all the women who stood by, a great assembly, all the people who dwelt in Pathros in the land of Egypt, answered Jeremiah: 16 'As for the word which you have spoken to us in the name of the LORD, we will not listen to you. 17 But we will do everything that we have vowed, burn incense to the queen of heaven and pour out libations to her, as we did, both we and our fathers, our kings and our princes, in the cities of Judah and in the streets of Jerusalem; for then we had plenty of food, and prospered, and saw no evil. 18 But since we left off burning incense to the queen of heaven and pouring out libations to her, we have lacked everything and have been consumed by the sword and by famine.' 19 And the women said, 'When we burned incense to the queen of heaven and poured out libations to her, was it without our husbands' approval that we made cakes for her bearing her image and poured out libations to her?'

[15] MT *qāhāl gādōl*, 'a great assembly': cf. 31.8 (26.17, *qᵉhal hāʿām*, 'assembly of people'); a great crowd or, more likely, the sacred congregation of worshippers. BHS suggests *qōl*, 'voice', for *qāhāl*. The clause 'and all the people who dwelt in the land of Egypt, in Pathros' is regarded as an addition (e.g. Rudolph, Bright, BHS) because it is most unlikely that all the people throughout Egypt attended Jeremiah's sermon. Rudolph, 260, regards it as a gloss to 'a great assembly'. S '*and* in Pathros': i.e. in (Lower) Egypt and Pathros (Upper Egypt), cf. Rudolph. **[16]** Cf. 43.1–2, where all the people also refuse to listen to Jeremiah. **[17]** MT *'et-kol-haddābār 'ᵃšer-yāṣā' mippīnū*, lit. 'everything which comes out of our mouth': idiomatic for vowing, cf. Num. 30.3, 13; 32.24; Judg. 11.36. Cf. v. 25, where *ndr*, 'vow', is used. MT *limᵉleket haššāmayim*, 'to the hosts of the heavens': many mss *lml'kt*; G *tē basilissē tou ouranou*, 'to the queen of heaven' = *lᵉmalkat* . . . cf. 7.18. The queen of heaven probably refers to some form of the Ishtar cult or Isis as she would be known in Egypt. **[18]** Cf. v. 17 for vocalization of 'queen of heaven'. G lacks 'and poured out libations to her'. MT *tāmᵉnū*, 'have consumed us': cf. vv. 12, 27 for this motif (*tmm*). **[19]** MT *wᵉkī-'ᵃnaḥnū*, 'and when we': G^L *kai hai gunaikes eipon hote kai*, 'and the women said and when', cf. S; = *wᵉhannāšīm 'āmᵉrū wᵉkī*. Cf. RSV, NEB but JPSB = MT. Vocalization of 'queen of heaven' as in vv. 17, 18. MT *lᵉhaʿᵃṣibāh*, lit. 'to fashion': *h* lacks a mappiq, which would make the word mean 'to fashion *her*', i.e. shaping her image on the cakes or making the cakes in the shape representative of her.

The response to Jeremiah's sermon comes from a great assembly of people from *all over Egypt* (cf. S). MT identifies the location of the people as Pathros, i.e. Upper Egypt, but it is unlikely that people travelled from so far afield to hear a recent immigrant preach. This aspect of the response is part of the editorial story which represents Jeremiah as preaching a sermon on proper techniques of worship and the people as responding to him. In typical fashion (cf. 43.1–2) they refuse to listen to what he says (v. 16) and thereby condemn themselves as obdurate as well as apostate. The sermon requires no response as such, so the reply of the people in vv. 15–19 should be regarded as a development of the sermon along different lines. It singles out the motif of burning (*qṭr*) sacrifice to other gods (cf. vv. 3, 5, 8, 21, 23, 25) and has the men of the assembly defend the cultic practices of their wives (v. 15; cf. v. 9, where the behaviour of wives is also part of the indictment of history). However, vv. 17–18 represent the cult of the queen of heaven as a communal matter whereas vv. 15,19 (cf. S) present it as a feminine cult performed by the women with their men's approval (cf. v. 25). The discrepancy between these two viewpoints may be due to the rhetoric of the edition, especially in v. 17, where stereotypical language predominates.

At first sight vv. 15–19 look like a midrash on 7.17–18, but a scrutiny of both pieces will reveal significant differences. In 7.17–18 a familial cult involving all the members of the family is condemned, but in 44.15, 19 a feminine cult of devotion to the queen of heaven is singled out as an example of sacrificing to other gods. The two pieces have in common the queen of heaven motif and the pouring out of libations to her accompanied by cakes (*kawwānīm*) bearing her image (only in 44.19). They are clearly about the same cult, but the treatment of that cult is different in both places. The midrashic quality of the treatment is such that a common core may be presupposed for the story, but disparate contexts determine some of the differences. In 7.1 – 8.3 a collection of responses to cultic abuses prefaces an independent sub-block of material; in 44 a highly edited attack on idolatrous worship throughout history focuses in particular on the cult of the queen of heaven (e.g. vv. 17–19, 25). Like so many parallel accounts in the tradition (e.g. 7.1–15; 26 or 37–38) a common feature may be discerned in the stories, but on each occasion the form of the story is significantly different from other treatments of the material. In 7.17–18 the family cult devoted to the goddess is an example of the outrageous behaviour of the people in 'the cities of Judah and the streets of Jerusalem' and it provokes the deity to great anger (v. 20; in spite of the subtle argument of v. 19 about the self-injury of idolatry). In 44.17 the same cult is spoken of, but from the viewpoint of its participants. It refers to the past, to the time when the people practised such things 'in the cities of Judah and the streets of Jerusalem'. But in v. 18 there is a confession that the cult has not been active since those days. Thus the cult of vv. 17–18 has nothing to do with the charge in v. 8 of offering sacrifices to other gods in the land of Egypt! The tie-in between the two may be v. 15, but v. 19 is ambiguous in that it may refer to current activity or past behaviour (the participial form *mᵉqaṭṭᵉrīm* allows either, cf. 33.18). Reference to the men's knowledge of their wives' behaviour (v. 15. *hᵃmibbalʿᵃdē*, 'was it apart from?', in v. 19 is more oblique, but it implies that the men knew about the practice) makes the cult an exclusive female one, but implicates the men in the guilt attached to involvement with such other gods. It is, however, quite a different presentation from

7.17–18, where men and children are as involved in the cult of the queen of heaven as the women. Inconsistent editing is a major feature of the Jeremiah tradition (cf. McKane 1981), and evidence of that inconsistency may be detected in a comparison of 7. 17–18 and 44. 15, 19, 17–18.

In v. 17 the men (cf. v. 15 where MT is clearer than RSV 'then all the men answered Jeremiah') affirm that they will go on doing what they did when they lived in Judah. The break with the past of v. 18 is a temporary one, interrupted by the destruction of Jerusalem and the flight to Egypt no doubt, but the people are determined (v. 16 have vowed) to return to the old cultic ways which had worked so well in the past. A very interesting argument is put forward in vv. 17–18. In the past when the cult of the queen of heaven was in operation the community enjoyed prosperity (*ṭōbīm*), i.e. they had food and never saw disaster. But having desisted from the practice of that cult they have lacked everything (*kōl*), i.e. they have been consumed by sword and famine. The argument is essentially a *post hoc ergo propter hoc* one, but implicit in its presentation is the view that the cult of the queen of heaven guaranteed prosperity. Proof of that claim is to be found in the recent terrible disasters which befell the community when they abandoned the goddess. No account is given of that change, so it is not possible to determine whether a new cult policy had been adopted or the old practice allowed to fall into desuetude. Some exegetes (e.g. Weiser, 372; cf. Thiel 1981, 75) relate the period of prosperity to the long reign of Manasseh (695–641) when pagan cults were tolerated, and the change of fortunes to the time of Josiah when such cults were annihilated in the savage massacres of the reform instituted by that king (cf. II Kings 23.4–20). The sudden death of Josiah (II Kings 23.29) was the beginning of Judah's decline into disaster and exile. This reading of 44.17–18 identifies the reforming zeal of Josiah with the cause of Judah's run of disasters and Manasseh's toleration of many cults as the basis of Judah's prosperity. It is an interesting reading of the text, but by no means a necessary interpretation of it (e.g. Volz, 365, relates the cessation of the cult to the time of Zedekiah and not to Josiah's reform). To read 44.17–18 against a background provided by II Kings 22–23 is to assume a historicity for the Josiah story which is by no means warranted by the Deuteronomistic stories (cf. Hoffmann 1980). Yet if the hand of the Deuteronomists is to be detected in 44 (cf. Thiel 1981, 74), then it may well be the case that vv. 17–18 are intended to be a reflection on that Deuteronomistically constructed reform. However, there are no direct connections between vv. 17–18 and the story of Josiah's reform of the cult (of either a linguistic or a theological nature). The generality of the contrast in vv. 17–18 is such that the argument may be read simply as a statement of justification for resuming an old cultic practice without representing a confirmation of the Deuteronomistic history. It is an *ad hoc* argument put in the mouths of the people by the editors in order to demonstrate the incorrigibility of the people no matter what they have suffered. As v. 22 indicates, a different interpretation of the 'facts' may be offered, so v. 17 underlines the obduracy of the community.

An interesting feature of the argument of vv. 17–18, whatever its origins or editorial nature may be, is the similarity it bears to the thesis offered by David Hume in his *The Natural History of Religion*. In this work Hume argues that the original religion of mankind is polytheism, out of which arises monotheism. But because of 'a kind of flux and reflux in the human mind' nations move from polytheism to theism and then back again (Hume 1976, 51–57; cf. Mackie 1982, 188–90). 44.17–18 illustrates Hume's 'flux and reflux' thesis to some extent, though v. 18 may not warrant the inference that the people shifted from polytheistic to monotheistic practices. The Deuteronomistic history's presentation of the nation's long history of shifting loyalties from Yahweh to the gods and back to Yahweh (or from the gods to Yahweh to the gods) is a fine example of what Hume had in mind. A further interesting point about the argument of vv. 17–18 is its *post hoc* nature. It appears to argue from experience in order to make connections between events and beliefs (though the reverse form of the argument is offered in vv. 21–22). It is therefore a very good example of the unsatisfactory nature of such arguments. The interpretation of experience depends upon prior (or even *a priori*) beliefs which are then confirmed by experience. But the same set of experiences will confirm different beliefs because of the primacy of belief over experience. Thus the editors use one set of experiences (disaster) to ground two different sets of beliefs. Neither set of beliefs is warranted by the evidence offered for it because such beliefs are originally independent of experience. Belief in Yahweh or the queen of heaven is prior to the prosperity or disaster associated with such commitment. In 44 logic is on the side of neither the community nor the editors, though the sermon illustrates this principle very well. Perhaps the Deuteronomists (or the editors of 44 and other sermons in Jeremiah) really did think that logic and experience were on their side because so much in the book of Jeremiah uses the fall of Jerusalem to argue for certain beliefs and practices, but as the author of Job knew only too well, the logic of belief can be a very poor interpreter of experience.

44.20–23

20 Then Jeremiah said to all the people, men and women, all the people who had given him this answer: 21 'As for the incense that you burned in the cities of Judah and in the streets of Jerusalem, you and your fathers, your kings and your princes, and the people of the land, did not the LORD remember it? Did it not come into his mind? 22 The LORD could no longer bear your evil doings and the abominations which you committed; therefore your land has become a desolation and a waste and a curse, without inhabitant, as it is this day. 23 It is because you burned incense, and because you sinned against the LORD and did not obey the voice of the LORD or walk in his law and in his statutes and in his testimonies, that this evil has befallen you, as at this day.'

---

[20] MT *hā'ōnīm 'ōtō dābār*, lit. 'who answer him a word': i.e. who made the response of vv. 16–19. **[21]** MT *h*ᵃ*lō' 'et-haqqiṭṭēr '*ᵃ*šer qiṭṭartem*, 'is it not the burning which you burned?': i.e. the sacrifices made in the cities of Judah and the streets of Jerusalem; cf. *qṭr* in vv. 3, 5, 8, 15, 17–19, 23, 25. Burning incense (RSV) is too narrow an application of *qṭr*. MT *w*ᵉ*'am hā'āreṣ*, 'and the people of the land': cf. 1.18; 34.19; 37.2. Whether it refers to the landed gentry or the common people here is difficult to determine. In Jeremiah it often refers to the wealthy (e.g. 34.19) but most of these were supposed to have been deported to Babylon, so Jeremiah could hardly have been addressing them in Egypt. However, 44 is built up out of phrases from the tradition and does not represent a historical reflection of life in Egypt. The people in general may be meant in v. 21; cf. 37.2. MT *'ōtām zākar yhwh*, '*them* Yahweh remembered': G lacks 'them'; some exegetes read *'ōtāh*, 'it' (e.g. Rudolph, 262; cf. BHS), in agreement with following verb. MT *watta'*ᵃ*leh 'al-libbō*, 'and it came into his mind': for the idiom (all in the negative) cf. 7.31; 19.5; 32.35; the negative form may be understood here by virtue of the introductory *h*ᵃ*lō'*, 'did not . . .?'. **[22]** G lacks *mē'ēn yōšēb*, 'without inhabitant': cf. v. 2 *w*ᵉ*'ēn bāhem yōšēb*, 'and there is no inhabitant in them' (i.e. in the cities). MT *k*ᵉ*hayyōm hazzeh*, 'as is the case this day': cf. vv. 6, 23. For the evil doings as a motive for divine destruction cf. 4.4b; 21.12b; 26.3; Deut. 28.20; vv. 22–23 have an apologetic character in the sermon and constitute an explanation for Yahweh's judgment (cf. Thiel 1981, 75). **[23]** G lacks *kayyōm hazzeh*, 'as is the case this day': cf. vv. 6, 22. Cf. 16.10; 40.3 for the motif of sinning against Yahweh; the motif of not walking in his testimonies only appears here. Cf. v.10 for the motif of not walking in Yahweh's *tōrāh* or his statutes. The image of evil befalling (*qr'*) the nation occurs in 32.23; Deut. 31.29.

Two responses to the people's response to Jeremiah are attributed to Jeremiah (vv. 20–23, 24–28). Thus the sermon is turned into a debate, with both sides responding to each other in an antiphonal manner (cf. the two strands of response in vv. 15, 19, 17–18), by its present editing. In his first answer (v. 20, cf. v. 15 for the men and women to whom he replies) Jeremiah responds to the point about the people having offered sacrifice in the land of Judah in the past, but makes no acknowledgment of the queen of heaven cult (that occurs in his second answer in v. 25). He offers an entirely different explanation of the fate of the people. It was because Yahweh remembered such sacrifices and was unable to go on bearing them any more that he destroyed the land. So the popular explanation of the connection between worship and fate is inverted by Jeremiah to account for the present desolate state of the land of Judah. Both parties to the dispute accept the same principle: fate of land is bound up with worship of the god. The people claim that their abandoning of their god (i.e. the queen of heaven) caused the terrible experiences of the past. Jeremiah in principle agrees with that explanation but offers it on behalf of a different god. In strongly anthropomorphic language he represents Yahweh as remembering the past behaviour of the community and the various social strata and becoming unable to put up with the burden of evil deeds any longer. For these reasons the land became 'a desolation and a waste and a curse' (cf. v. 12) and not for the reasons offered by the people.

The different claims made by the people and Jeremiah using the same data underline the hopelessness of using experiences and 'facts' to explain ideological positions. Jeremiah's response in vv. 21–23 embodies a distinctive conception of history and an alternative account of the destruction of Judah to that of the people (cf. Thiel 1981, 75–6, who describes this account as Deuteronomistic). Without such a prevenient theology the 'facts' of 587 would remain uninterpreted and both people and Jeremiah would share the same experiences without disagreeing about the meaning of what had happened to them. The Deuteronomistically influenced theology of 44 provides an alternative explanation to that of the people, but the case for both positions is determined by the ideologies of the parties to the dispute and cannot be decided independently of one ideology or the other.

44.24–30

24 Jeremiah said to all the people and all the women, 'Hear the word of the
Lord, all you of Judah who are in the land of Egypt, 25 Thus says the Lord
of hosts, the God of Israel: You and your wives have declared with your
mouths, and have fulfilled it with your hands, saying, "We will surely
perform our vows that we have made, to burn incense to the queen of heaven
and to pour out libations to her." Then confirm your vows and perform
your vows! 26 Therefore hear the word of the Lord, all you of Judah who
dwell in the land of Egypt: Behold, I have sworn by my great name, says
the Lord, that my name shall no more be invoked by the mouth of any man
of Judah in all the land of Egypt, saying, "As the Lord God lives." 27
Behold, I am watching over them for evil and not for good; all the men of
Judah who are in the land of Egypt shall be consumed by the sword and by
famine, until there is an end of them. 28 And those who escape the sword
shall return from the land of Egypt to the land of Judah, few in number;
and all the remnant of Judah, who came to the land of Egypt to live, shall
know whose word will stand, mine or theirs. 29 This shall be the sign to
you, says the Lord, that I will punish you in this place, in order that you
may know that my words will surely stand against you for evil: 30 Thus
says the Lord, Behold I will give Pharaoh Hophra king of Egypt into the
hand of those who seek his life, as I gave Zedekiah king of Judah into the
hand of Nebuchadrezzar king of Babylon, who was his enemy and sought
his life.'

---

[24] G lacks 'all Judah who are in the land of Egypt'. Some exegetes delete 'to all the people and' because in v. 25 only the women are addressed (*watt^edabbērnāh*, 'and you [fem.] said'), cf. Rudolph 262; Pohlmann 1978, 176–7; BHS; Bright, 262. **[25]** G lacks 'of hosts'. MT *'attem ūnᵉšēkem*, 'you and your wives': G *humeis gunaikes*, 'you women' = *'attēnāh hannāšīm*; MT represents v. 20 and the editing of the chapter as Jeremiah's responses to *all* (vv. 1, 15, 20, 24) the people. MT *'et-nᵉdārēnū*, 'our vows': cf. v. 17 where an idiom is used instead of *ndr* for vowing. The homologation (cf. G *has hōmologēsamen*, 'which we have agreed to') of vows in v. 25 reads v. 19 as a declaration of intent rather than a statement of past historical actions. MT *lᵉqaṭṭēr limᵉleket haššāmayim*, 'to burn to the works of the heavens': see on v. 17

for the queen of heaven cult (G) and on v. 3 for *qṭr* as 'burn', meaning to sacrifice. MT *tāqīmnāh*, 'confirm': regarded as an abnormal form (cf. GK 72k), perhaps *tāqēmnāh* or *teqīmenāh* (cf. BHS). MT *we'āśōh ta'aśenāh 'et-nidrēkem*, 'and really perform your vows': a few mss read *niskēkem*, 'your libations'; this reading fits better in that vows *and* libations are part of the affirmation. G lacks the word; Bright, 262, reads 'By all means perform them'; NEB 'and make your words good' (cf. BHS). **[26]** Cf. vv. 1, 15 for the address to all (Judah) who live in Egypt; cf. 22.5 for the divine swearing by himself. Duhm, 333, treats this verse as ironic. Cf. 4.2; 5.2; 12.16; 16.14, 15; 23.7, 8; 38.16 for the oath *ḥay-yhwh* 'as Yahweh lives'; here *ḥay-'adōnāy yhwh*, 'as the lord Yahweh lives' (G *zē kurios kurios*, G^B *zē kurios*). **[27]** MT *hinenī šōqēd 'alēhem*, 'look, I am watching over them': the watching (*šqd*) motif appears in 1.12; 31.28 (cf. 5.6); for evil here but for good in 31.28. Cf. 21.9; 39.16 for the phrase 'for evil and not for good'; cf. v. 12 for consummation by sword and famine. **[28]** G lacks *mimmennī ūmēhem*, 'mine or theirs'. BHS treats 'who came to the land of Egypt to live there' as a 'false addition' (Rudolph, 262). It hardly fits the annihilation of the community in Egypt referred to at the end of v. 27 or the few fugitives who escape to Palestine. Cf. 42.15, 19; 44.12, 14 for the attack on the remnant; the association of the remnant with knowing (*yd'*) appears in 42.19, 22. Cf. Deut. 18.21 for knowing (*yd'*) the word which Yahweh has *not* spoken; here the survivors *know* that Yahweh has spoken (i.e. his word stands) because the community has been annihilated. Hence some survivors are needed in order to act as witnesses to the confirmation (*qūm*) of Yahweh's word. Cf. v. 14b where a few fugitives survive from the destruction of the remnant (cf. discussion in Thiel 1981, 77–81; Ehrlich 1912, 351). **[29]** MT *wezō't-lākem hā'ōt*, 'this is the sign for you': this is the only occurrence of sign in this sense in the book of Jeremiah (cf. 10.2; 32.20, 21). G has a shorter reading: 'and this (is) the sign to you that I will visit you for evil'; BHS explains the lack of 'in this place in order that you may know that my words shall surely stand against you' in terms of homoioteleuton (*'alēkem . . . 'alēkem*). Perhaps this is correct, but the briefer G text introduces v. 30 more succinctly than MT's repetition of the idea in v. 28b (with the addition of *ne'um-yhwh*, 'says Yahweh'). Cf. vv. 11, 27 for the motif *lerā'āh* 'for evil'. **[30]** G lacks 'Pharaoh': due to haplography? MT *'et-par'ōh ḥopra'*, 'Pharaoh Hophra': this king ruled Egypt 589–570 and was killed in a rebellion. He was succeeded by Amasis (570–526). Hophra's troubles are here made the sign of the destruction of the remnant or so understood by the editors. The parallel between Hophra and Zedekiah is made in stereotypical language, cf. 19.7; 21.7; 22.25; 34.20, 21; thus the remnant will suffer a fate similar to the end of Jerusalem when Zedekiah was given into the hand of his enemy – Nebuchadrezzar.

The second response of Jeremiah to *all* the people (cf. v. 20) is a development of a reply to the women involved in the cult of the queen of heaven (cf. v. 19). In the editing of the sermon the women's cult is combined with the address to all the people of the Jewish communities in Egypt so that a particular cultic practice is generalized as the behaviour of all the communities. This permits the editorial ideology to condemn all the exogenous groups outside Palestine (i.e. Egypt, though presumably not Babylon) by means of a sermon and a debate in which Jeremiah acts as the divine mouthpiece for dismissing as idolatrous Yahwistic practices in the land of Egypt (cf. v. 26). The mixing together of discrete elements in 44 constitutes an ideological dismissal of thriving communities elsewhere.

Jeremiah responds to the women's cult of the queen of heaven with biting irony (e.g. v. 25b). This is achieved by turning the statement of practice in v. 19 into a declaration of intent on the women's part in v. 25. The implication of the men in the women's cult (cf. vv. 15–19, 20, 24) allows the condemnation of a special ritual (cf. Ezek. 8.14) to become a wholesale rejection of 'all Judah who dwell in the land of Egypt'. It also facilitates the divine forswearing of even the practice of Yahwism in Egypt (v. 26). The swearing by the name of Yahweh is a mark of the genuine worship of Yahweh (cf. 4.2), but here it is ruled out as a permissible way of life in Egypt (cf. 5.2 for the practice as a mask for false behaviour). Such a blanket condemnation of the cult of Yahweh in Egypt must represent an ideological conflict between Palestine (?) and Egypt over cultic matters at some period after the fall of Jerusalem (e.g. in the second temple era? Cf. the tensions between the two areas in matters cultic as evinced by the Elephantine documents, Porten 1968, 105–50, 278–98). The complete writing off of the Jewish communities in Egypt betrays xenophobic prejudices against rival groups practising Yahwism outside the 'holy land' of Palestine, and Jeremiah is used to give these prejudices respectability. Their fate is to be the same as befell Jerusalem in 587 and is expressed in terms of the divine watching (*šqd*) for evil rather than good (e.g. v. 27a; 31.28; cf. 1.12). Whether the voice of the pro-Babylonian exiles (cf. 24.4–7; 29.10–14) strand in the tradition should be detected in 44 is a moot point.

The annihilation of the remnant of Judah in the land of Egypt is a dominant motif in 42.13–22 and 44. This motif is expressed most clearly in 44.27b, where the whole community ('all the men of Judah who are in the land of Egypt') is to be wiped out by sword (i.e.

invasion) and famine. A lack of survivors is one of the features of this motif (cf. 42.17, 22; 44.14). It is therefore strange to read in v. 28a that there will be survivors who will escape the slaughter and return to the land of Judah (cf. v. 14 'except some fugitives'). Having put an end (*'ad-kᵉlōtām*, 'until there is an end of them') to the remnant in v. 28b it is odd to find survivors making their way *back to Judah*! This returning motif (*šûb*) is such a feature of the tradition that its occurrence here is in keeping with the book of Jeremiah as a whole, though out of place in 44.27–28. It may be regarded as an editorial addition to the attack on the Egyptian communities (cf. the addition to v. 14). Whether it represents an addition in the light of historical experience (i.e. Jews from Egypt returned to Palestine over the years) or a literary motif added to the story in order to highlight the complete destruction of the communities in Egypt in terms of surviving witnesses to it is a debatable matter. Without survivors there could be no meaning to the claim 'in order that you may know that my words will surely stand against you for evil' (v. 29b: lacking in G; cf. Ezek. 6.8–10 for a similar argument).

The concluding point of the sermon is the establishment (*qûm*) of the divine word. In the destruction of the Jewish communities in Egypt that word (v. 28; words in MT, v. 29) will stand as confirmed by events (the competition between 'mine or theirs' in v. 28 belongs only to MT). As a sign of the fulfilment of the divine word v. 30 refers to the defeat of Pharaoh Hophra (though the reference is presented as a prediction). This suggests a date after 570 for the editing of the sermon (or the addition of v. 30 to it). In the events surrounding the fall of Hophra the editors detect the establishment of the divine word against the Jewish communities throughout Egypt. Thus his fall is described in stereotypical language from the tradition and compared with the defeat of Zedekiah by Nebuchadrezzar. So the divine word against the remnant in Egypt is of the same order as the word against Jerusalem (cf. 42.18). Strictly speaking a holistic reading of the book of Jeremiah would arrive at the conclusion that all the Jewish communities, apart from the one in Babylon, are written off as the objects of Yahweh's implacable wrath. That may well be the point of 44. However, the voice behind 44 may be that of the cultic community in Jerusalem, among whom may be exiles returned from Babylon (hence v. 28). In Jeremiah's attitude to the people in Egypt there may be detected a strong anti-Moses parallel (cf. Alonso Schökel 1981).

45.1–5

45[1] The word that Jeremiah the prophet spoke to Baruch the son of Neriah,
when he wrote these words in a book at the dictation of Jeremiah, in the
fourth year of Jehoiakim the son of Josiah, king of Judah: 2 'Thus says the
LORD, the God of Israel, to you, O Baruch: 3 You said, "Woe is me! for the
LORD has added sorrow to my pain; I am weary with my groaning, and I
find no rest." 4 Thus shall you say to him, Thus says the LORD: Behold,
what I have built I am breaking down, and what I have planted I am
plucking up – that is, the whole land. 5 And do you seek great things for
yourself? Seek them not; for, behold, I am bringing evil upon all flesh, says
the LORD; but I will give you your life as a prize of war in all the places to
which you may go.'

[MT 45] = G 51.31–35. **[1]** Cf. 36.1–4. The introductory phrase *haddābār ʾᵃšer dibber yirmᵉyāhū hannābīʾ ʾel-bārūk ben-nēriyyāh*, 'the word which Jeremiah the prophet spoke to Baruch ben Neriah', is quite different from the formulaic reception of the word introductions used throughout the book (cf. 51.59). MT *bᵉkātᵉbō ʾet-haddᵉbārīm hāʾēlleh*, 'when he wrote *these words*': what words? In its present position 45.1 gives the impression that 44 is the content of Baruch's writing. This makes no sense, as the dating of 45.1 to 605 (Jehoiakim's fourth year) places the writing at least twenty years before the supposed event of 44. Although 45 should follow 36, where 'these words' would have a logical force (cf. Bright, 184), its placing after 44 removes any reference to 36 and makes it a more general reference to 'the well-known words' (Rudolph, 262) of Jeremiah. The dating in 1b confuses that point (cf. Skinner 1922, 346). **[2]** G lacks 'the god of Israel'. **[3]** G begins the verse with *hoti*, 'because' = *kī*; lacking in MT due to haplography (*bārūk* in v. 2). G repeats *oimmoi oimmoi*, 'woe, woe'. **[4]** MT *kōh tōʾmar ʾēlāyw*, 'thus you will say to him': a change of person from v. 3 (him – you) which suggests the phrase is a later addition (cf. Wanke 1971, 133). Cf. 1.10 for the motifs used in v. 4. MT *wᵉʾet-kol-hāʾāreṣ hīʾ*, 'that is, the whole earth': *hīʾ* makes the meaning of this phrase uncertain (cf. JPSB); G lacks the clause. Rudolph, 264, reads *ʾakkeh*, 'I will smite'; Driver 1937–38, 122–3, reads *ʾᵃnī makkeh*, 'I am smiting'. MT is a gloss (cf. Giesebrecht, 226) relating the divine action to the land rather than the people (as in v. 5). **[5]** MT *kol-bāśār*, 'all flesh': i.e. mankind, cf. 12.12; 25.31; 32.27; not the land but all mankind will undergo the destruction brought about by Yahweh – why then should Baruch complain or seek great things for himself? Cf. 39.16, where Yahweh is bringing evil upon the city. MT *wᵉnātattī lᵉkā ʾet-napšᵉkā lᵉšālāl*, 'and I will give you your life for booty': i.e. 'but you shall save your life and nothing more' (NEB). Cf. the idiom *hāyᵉtāh . . . nepeš . . . lᵉšālāl*, 'to have (one's) life for booty', 21.9. 38.2; 39.18. This is an ironic figure of speech which assures the recipient of survival but nothing else, using an image drawn from the aftermath of battle when the victors divide the booty (*šālāl*). In 21.9 = 38.2 it is linked to survival (*ḥāyāh*), in 39.18 it is associated with escape (*mallēṭ*), and here it is related to survival wherever Baruch goes (*tēlek*). 21.9; 38.2 are general offers to the community; 39.18; 44.5 are directed to named individuals (Ebed-melek, Baruch). After the onslaught the only booty such people will possess will be their own lives! Thiel 1981, 86, regards 44.5 as basic and 21.9; 38.2; 39.18 as imitations used by the Deuteronomists (cf. Duhm, 336).

Part IV ends surprisingly with a short piece about Baruch's lament which is dated to the year 605. Coming immediately after the lengthy section on the aftermath of the fall of Jerusalem (39.11 – 43.7) and the denunciations of the Jewish communities in Egypt (44), it appears to make connections with 36 which are out of place after 44. The editorial arrangement of it here may be parallel to the concluding of Part III with 35–36, which do not follow chronologically from 32–34. Chronological sequence is seldom followed by the editors of the book of Jeremiah and it is arguable that 45 makes an appropriate ending to Part IV by alluding to 36 and 26, where the material is set also in Jehoiakim's reign (cf. discussion in Thiel 1981, 82–90). As the closing story it concludes the block of material rather than continues the theme of 42, 44. Furthermore, the redactional presentation in vv. 1–2 reflects the standard treatment of the stories in the tradition by giving them settings which have no original connection with the material in the first place. The unit of 45 is the lament with response in vv. 3–5 (cf. Wanke 1971, 135), and the editorial introduction is precisely what raises the problem of appropriateness. An original lament with response is quite appropriate as a closure of Part IV because the denunciations of the communities in Egypt have introduced the question of survival (cf. 44.7, 14, 27, 28). The oracular response to this question appears in 45.4–5 and asserts the divine gift of survival. Survival and nothing else is the point of the metaphor in v. 5b. The editing which transforms the generality of this oracular declaration into a personal oracle to Baruch ben Neriah breaks the connection between 45.3–5 and 44 but links it to 36. That transformation uses a concrete example to make the point about the futility of seeking self-aggrandizement (v. 5 *g^e^dōlōt*, 'great things') in the period characterized by 44 (vv. 3–5) or 'these words' (i.e. 605 if v. 1b is read in terms of the final form of the text or 587 if this phrase is understood as a general reference to Jeremiah's preaching). A different interpretation of *g^edōlōt* is offered by de Boer (1973, 33–5), who treats it as a reference to divine, superhuman acts (cf. 33.3), and the complaint as an attempt by Baruch to persuade Yahweh to change his mind about destroying his people.

The presence of 45 at the end of Part IV may be compared to the addition of 1 as a prologue to Part I. In the first edition of Jeremiah (G) the four parts are enclosed by lengthy discourses against idolatry (2, 44). To this collection have been added a prologue (1) and an epilogue (52 = II Kings 24.18–25.30). It is possible that 45 represents a parallel development to 1. In 1 the individual figure of Jeremiah is introduced as the speaker of the tradition which follows and the prologue ends with a divine promise of protection (1.19b). 36 introduces the figure of Baruch as the amanuensis of Jeremiah and credits him with the writing of Jeremiah's words. Now in 45 as a parallel to I Baruch is addressed and given a promise of survival. The connecting link between the two chapters is signalled by 1.10 and 45.4 which share similar motifs. If 45 is a good deal less substantial than 1 that reflects the minor role played by Baruch in the book of Jeremiah. The effect of 45 as a conclusion to the book (before the addition of the epilogue in 52) is to make Baruch the last figure in the tradition (a role played by Jehoiachin in 52) rather than Jeremiah (cf. Bogaert 1981a, 172–3). This irony is achieved by the development of a brief strand in the tradition which provides Jeremiah with Baruch as a companion or assistant. Those exegetes who maintain the theory that Baruch is the *author* or *writer* of the book of Jeremiah (or parts of it) may regard 45 as a kind of author's colophon by means of which the writer puts himself into his work. A more likely explanation is to read 45.1–2 as the editorial development of the figure of Baruch in the tradition by associating him with a saying of (or attributed to) Jeremiah (cf. Wanke 1971, 133–6).

The introductory formula in v. 1a is a very distinctive one in the book of Jeremiah, though 51.59 is virtually the same and shares the structure of 45.1 (cf. 46.13; 50.1, where a similar formulaic introduction is used but with Yahweh as the speaker). Jeremiah *the prophet* (epithet also in G) makes an oracular proclamation in response to his companion Baruch's lament. These two elements, Jeremiah *as* prophet and Baruch, reflect late developments of the tradition and the association of the oracle with 605 allows the editors to respond to 36. Without that editorial point (v. 1b) the piece could be read as a response to the plight of Baruch in 43.3, 6 (cf. Wanke 1971, 141) and as forming a closure with 43.1–7. The reason for Baruch's lamentation can only be speculated about (cf. Bright, 185–6) because there is nothing in the tradition to suggest that Baruch was anything other than an inert figure who did Jeremiah's bidding. 43.3 may hint at activity on his part, but that may be attributable to the paranoia of the community's leaders. The lament of 45.3 would fit the laments in Part I and it may therefore reflect a further development of the character of Baruch by attributing to him sentiments which Part I at times appears to associate with Jeremiah, though the language of v. 3 is quite different from that of the laments in 11–20 (cf. Wanke 1971, 134 n. 6).

In a time characterized by the breaking down of what the deity had built and his plucking up of what he had planted (cf. the reversal of these motifs in 31.28), the individual may not hope for the realization of his ambitions. Each use of the motifs listed in 1.10 is distinctive in the tradition (cf. 12.14–17; 18.7, 9; 24.6; 31.40; 42.10) and here Yahweh, who is always the actor implementing these terms (with the exception of 1.10 where Jeremiah takes that role), is represented as reversing his former policy. The terms of 45.4 which view the past as a period of divine building and planting (!) and the present as a change in the deity's attitudes therefore constitute a different view of life from that represented by 42.10 (the dating in v. 1b may preserve the deity from the charge of being peculiarly fickle in his dealings with the community). Rapid changes in the fortunes of the people are assimilated into the theological outlook of the editors by the use of the metaphors set out in 1.10. These cover the positive and negative aspects of the period and enable a wide range of assessments of events and social trends to be incorporated into a coherent theological perspective. Behind everything which happens is the deity establishing the conditions of normal life or destroying the bases of communal living. Prosperity and disintegration are his doing, and the proper response of communities (or even individuals as 45.4–5 suggest) to his activity is to align themselves with whatever is the current mode of that action (e.g. 12.16–17; 42.10). If seeking great things for oneself in a time of great destruction for all flesh (v. 5; cf. 12.12; 25.31) is a futile aspiration, the response to the lament is not entirely negative. It allows the speaker the reassurance of survival. Using a metaphor which is also used in 21.9; 38.2; 39.18 Baruch is promised survival wherever he goes. As the figure of speech is ironic this may be cold comfort but it is a better alternative to being dead! The metaphor describes the gift of survival in terms drawn from the practice of war. After the fighting the victorious troops plunder the corpses, towns and whatever they can lay their hands on in order to take away with them the spoils of war. In the terrible evil coming upon everybody Baruch also will receive war booty – his own life. Devastation will be so great that just surviving may be described as acquiring the plunder of war. The sweep of the destruction, i.e. 'evil upon *all flesh*', is so complete that we may detect in 45.5 an allusion to the suprahistorical war against all the nations (cf. 12.12; 25.31; 30.5–7) associated in prophetic forecasts with the end of time. In such a time surviving is the most that can be hoped for (cf. 30.7b), and Baruch is reassured of such survival. Thus the ironic metaphor corrects his grandiose expectations by drawing his attention to the period in which he lives and warning him to adjust his aspirations to a more realistic perspective.

The parallel between Baruch's prospects for the future and the reassurance of deliverance given to Ebed-melech (39.15–19) is strengthened by the use of the same ironic metaphor. Ebed-melech is assured that he will not be slain in the siege or destruction of Jerusalem but will be rescued (*mlṭ*) by the deity. The figurative statement 'you shall have your life as booty' (39.18) is more positive in his case because it is related to his trust in Yahweh and to a situation less overwhelming than the evil befalling all flesh in 45.5. Apart from the fact that they share the same metaphor the relative positions of the two pieces in the tradition should be noted. Both are technically out of place and ought to be attached to other points of the book. However, the editors have placed both of them immediately after stories of great destruction. In 39.3–10 a version of the destruction of Jerusalem is given and followed by two accounts of Jeremiah's escape from imprisonment in the fallen city. Sandwiched between these accounts is the promise of deliverance to Ebed-melech. All three stories contribute to toning down the story of Jerusalem's destruction by focusing on those who survive it. So in 45 the word of survival addressed to Baruch is placed immediately after the prolix sermon of destruction directed against the communities of Jews in Egypt. The complete annihilation of those communities is emphasized in 44, but the placing of 45 serves to modify the note of doom to some extent by announcing the possibility of survival to Baruch who in 43.6 is taken down to Egypt. So a moment of hope (strictly delimited) is allowed to penetrate the utter gloom. Communal devastation cannot be avoided, but in all the great slaughter named individuals survive as the booty of war. That hope is not articulated any further (except in the book of 30–31), but the beginnings of a pattern may be detected in the editing of Part IV (cf. the juxtaposing of doom and salvation elements in the arrangement of Isa. 1–12). In 45 Baruch symbolizes such hope, though whether as an earnest of the future or as a survivor whose very survival emphasizes the dimensions of the destruction is more difficult to determine. Governed by anxiety, caution and modesty, the Jeremiah tradition makes few sweeping gestures in the direction of a positive future (even 30–31 are modest in comparison with other traditions). Thus the figure of Baruch is quite unrealized in the book of Jeremiah.

The concluding of Jeremiah's work with this brief glimpse of Baruch (G but not MT) draws attention to the son of Neriah and reminds the reader of the half-glimpsed association between Jeremiah and Baruch. In 32.12–13 Baruch is party to Jeremiah's purchase of land, but the significance of that involvement is neither stated nor developed. He is Jeremiah's companion in the flight to Egypt (43.6) and is even held responsible for Jeremiah's advocacy of living in the land of Judah (43.2–3). 36 presents him as the prophet's amanuensis and delegated authority in the matter of writing and reading out the scroll of Jeremiah's life's work. The glimpses of him are too enigmatic and inchoate for a theory of them to be established or even a pattern detected. In two pieces he is associated with the future: mere (?) survival in 45.5 and the reconstruction of the land in 32.12–15. The other two glimpses of him *hint* at his replacement of Jeremiah *as if* in the development of the tradition's redaction he represents the next generation (of the community?). In later literature the relationship between Jeremiah and Baruch is that of father and son (metaphorically speaking).

He is the means whereby Jeremiah's words are passed on to the future. The structure of 45.1 is essentially the same as 51.59 (cf. 46.13; 50.2) and both introduce sons of Neriah. Baruch and Seraiah are probably brothers, and both are used in similar ways by Jeremiah. Baruch is used to convey the written word of doom to the people and king Jehoiakim; Seraiah is commissioned as a delegate of Jeremiah's written word of doom to deliver it to Babylon in the fourth year (cf. 45.1b) of Zedekiah's reign. If the structural particularity of 45.1

and 51.59 is significant, even if only to the extent of allowing both stories to be read together, then the pieces may be read as statements about the future in which the tentativeness of 45 becomes the definite affirmation of 51.59–64 (cf. Wanke 1971, 140–3). Seraiah enacts and thereby creates the destruction of Babylon and therefore the deliverance of Israel (cf. 50.17–20). His brother is less creative in this respect but his survival in 45.5 may be an oblique allusion to a future beyond Yahweh's bringing of evil upon all flesh.

This reading of the few references to Baruch in the book of Jeremiah is necessarily a tentative one. It cannot be regarded as *the* meaning of the texts or even perhaps as the most likely reading of them. The most precise interpretation of the data on Baruch would be a restatement of what each text says about him, but that would fail to elicit the significance of Baruch in the tradition. More grandiose theories about him as the author of the book of Jeremiah go beyond the evidence by reading 36 as a paradigm of the tradition and as a historical account without allowing for the literary creativeness of the editors. Baruch remains an enigma in the tradition, and that is a fitting role for the figure whose survival became his spoils of war!

PART TWO

46.1 – 51.64

The oracles against the nations 46–51

> The prophets who preceded you and me from ancient times prophesied war, famine, and pestilence *against many countries and great kingdoms* (28.8).

Formal oracles against the nations (OAN) are to be found in the major prophetic anthologies (Isa. 13–23; Ezek. 25–32) and the smaller collections associated with prophetic figures (Amos 1.3–2.3; Nahum; Obadiah; cf. Joel 3; Zeph. 2–3). The book of Jeremiah is no exception to this pattern, though the two editions vary in their placing of the collection and the order of the nations denounced.

The conventional nature of these oracles is established by their widespread occurrence in so many different prophetic traditions, but the origins of the OAN form are unknown. Comparative material from Mari demonstrates the existence of the practice of prophesying against foreign nations in a culture other than those represented by the Bible (cf. Malamat 1966; Moran 1969). This evidence only indicates the popularity of the practice in the ancient Near East, it affords no information about the origins or development of the form. However, it may lend weight to the view that the OAN are the oldest form of prophetic oracle (cf. Hayes 1968, 86–7), a point echoed in the statement attributed to Jeremiah in 28.8. If the origins of the form are beyond our knowledge, there is no lack of scholarly speculation about the setting in life out of which it may have arisen (e.g. Christensen 1975; Clements 1975, 58–72; Hayes 1968; Reventlow 1962, 56–75).

The story of the prophet Balaam being summoned by Balak, king of Moab, to curse Israel (Num. 22–24) suggests a ritual of cursing (and blessing) which could be operated against foreign enemies in a period of potential conflict. No such ritual appears elsewhere in the Bible, but the OAN may reflect cultic activity directed against the nation's enemies as a means of encouraging the people and defeating the foe (cf. Isa. 7.7–9; 8.9–10). A ritual of blessing and cursing in which the king is assured of his triumph over the national enemy (cf. Ps. 2; 110) might well include the cursing of the adversary in the form of an oracle delivered by the cult prophet. Such oracles accompanied by the magical rituals of the cult may have determined foreign policy by encouraging the kings to make war or to desist from ill-advised campaigns (cf. I Kings 22; II Kings 13; Fohrer 1967, 257–61; Christensen 1975). The context of this activity is seen by some scholars as the covenant festival (e.g. Reventlow 1962, 65), though the complete lack of information in the text should render such specificity open to serious questioning. Mowinckel associates the OAN with the enthronement of Yahweh festival but not as part of the festal ritual proper:

> . . . they mark extempore inspirations and improvisations of the cult prophet, only loosely connected with the festival, and taking place before the crowd, which was eating and drinking and playing in the temple courts (1962, I, 154).

The incorporation of collections of OAN into the traditions of Amos, Isaiah, Jeremiah, and Ezekiel raises a number of problems. If the form represents threats against the enemy or veiled assurances for Judah, it does not sit well with the denunciatory oracles directed against Israel and Judah in these traditions. This combination of disparate forms may require modifying the account of OAN as oracles supporting the nation to include the notion that they may occasionally serve to disabuse the people of false notions of security (cf. Clements 1975, 64). Amos 1–2, in their present redaction, illustrate this function by combining attacks on the nations with a thoroughgoing vilification of Israel. However, it cannot be shown that the same speaker uttered both OAN *and* diatribes against Israel of Judah. The association of the two is a feature of the redaction of the traditions, and it may represent the marriage of incompatible partners rather than a modification of the OAN. Different forms of activity may have been incorporated into the same tradition without requiring a rationalization of the role of the eponymous figure associated with it. Yet if the OAN cannot be related to a specific setting in the life of the community, their significance becomes much more difficult to determine. Clements is undoubtedly right in his assessment:

> That any one sphere of Israel's life, the royal court, the cultus or the military organization of the state with its inheritance of holy war ideology, formed the exclusive setting of the category of the oracles against foreign powers cannot be regarded as established. Rather we must regard these prophecies as a distinctive genre of their own which drew from many aspects of Israel's life (1975, 72).

As a distinctive genre the OAN are independent of the contexts in which they now appear, and this inevitably causes problems of interpretation in relation to the larger traditions into which they have been integrated by the editorial processes which created those traditions.

A comprehensive account of the OAN cannot be given in a commentary, but the central problem of the OAN for the interpretation of the book of Jeremiah is the relation between them and the Jeremiah of the other strands in the book. How can the preacher of the destruction of Jerusalem and Judah also be the speaker of the OAN in 46–51? The simplest answer to that question is – he cannot be the speaker of all the different levels of tradition in the book. That would appear to be the correct response to such a question. However, many exegetes attribute 46–51 to Jeremiah (in varying proportions), and so the obvious becomes a matter of dispute. Leaving aside convoluted theological arguments (cf. Raitt 1977) which argue for a shift in the prophet's outlook after 587, the crux of the matter focuses on the role of Babylon in 27–29 and the attitude expressed towards Babylon in 50–51. It is difficult to reconcile the proclamation of submission to Babylon in 27–29 and the announcement of its destruction as the work of the same speaker when both sets of material are dated to the same period (cf. 27.1; 28.1; 51.59). The representation of Babylon (Nebuchadrezzar) as Yahweh's servant (27.6) *and* as the dragon (51.34) indicates the incompatibility of the imagery as well as authorship. Neither tradition may be attributable to Jeremiah; both cannot be so attributed. The separation of the OAN into two distinct collections, 46–49 and 50–51, may ease the problem of attribution because the nations denounced in 46–49 represent opposition to Babylon as well as opponents of Judah and a nationalistic prophet might well speak out against them (cf. Bardtke 1935; 1936). However, all attempts to attribute the OAN of 46–51 to Jeremiah depend upon the prior theory that the book represents the utterances of the historical Jeremiah rather than the construction of the editorial framework. Only in that framework does such an attribution appear (e.g.; 46.1, 13; 47.1; 49.34; 50.1) and nothing in the poems necessitates identifying the speaker as Jeremiah (see on 50.1). If Jeremiah's connection with the OAN is the creation of the editing processes, then the whole debate about how the authorship of 27–29 and 50–51 is to be reconciled is beside the point. The editorial presentation of Jeremiah is as a prophet to the nations (1.5, 10) and 46–51 provide the OAN which warrant such a description.

46–51 contain some of the finest, as well as the most difficult, poetry in the book of Jeremiah (e.g. 46.3–12, 14–24; 48.1–10; 50.35–38a; 51.20–23). Similarities between the poems of 46–51 and those in 4–6, 8–10 raise the question of whether the two collections of poetry have a common source or one is modelled on the other. If the latter is the case, then an argument may be mounted for viewing 4–6, 8–10 as imitated OAN describing the (Babylonian) destruction of Jerusalem. This would support the view of Jeremiah as a nationalistic prophet speaking against the nations (Bardtke): a dominant element in the tradition which has been extended in Part I to make him a speaker against Jerusalem. This is simply one interpretation among many of the implications of the shared poetic elements of 46–51 and 4–6, 8–10. 46–51 also share common features with the OAN of Isaiah, Amos and Obadiah and poetry elsewhere in the Bible (e.g. cf. 48.45–46 with Num. 21.28–29; see Notes on 46–51 for parallels) and such shared aspects point to the stereotyping of OAN in the different collections throughout the Bible. They also weaken the arguments for a specific authorship of any single tradition. The genre OAN must be regarded as independent of the traditions into which they have been incorporated and as *one more level* of tradition within those books. Hence the editorial links which connect the poems of 46–51 with Jeremiah (46.1, 13; 47.1; 49.34; 50.1) are necessary in order to relate this specific collection to the redactional framework governing the book of Jeremiah.

The division of 46–51 into two parts, 46–49 and 50–51, permits certain differences between the collections to come into focus. The nations denounced in 46–49 (excluding 49.28–39) represent Judah's neighbours and belong to the socio-political history of the nation over a number of centuries. These poems may therefore reflect encounters between Judah and its neighbours during the eighth to the sixth century (cf. Rudolph 1963; Ogden 1982) rather than the onslaught of the Babylonians against Judah's traditional opponents from 605 onwards. But the defeat of Egypt by Babylon at Carchemish in 605 (cf. 46. 2, 6) must be regarded as an important element in the poems and it is possible to read the collection in the light of Babylonian dominance in the sixth century. Bardtke's interpretation of the poems as Jeremiah's preaching against the enemies of Josiah's expansionist plans in the years 617–615 (1935, 236–9; 1936, 242) cannot be ruled out *a priori*, but is too precise an identification of the background of stereotypical poems and too dependent on the redactional presentation of Jeremiah as a prophet in the time of Josiah (1.2; 25.1, 3). It does, however, illustrate one approach to 46–49 as war oracles determining foreign policy (cf. Christensen 1975, 208–49). Christensen's analysis of 46–49 divides them into genuine OAN of Jeremiah (46.2–12, 13–24; 47.1–7; 49.28–33, 34–39) and archaic OAN (48.1–47; 49. 1–6, 7–22, 23–27). This division allows the stereotypical and distinctive elements in the OAN of 46–49 to be related to the Jeremiah tradition without furnishing arguments for attributing them to Jeremiah. In 50–51 a different spirit may be detected (termed 'eschatological orientation' by Christensen 1975, 208) as well as a different enemy, namely Babylon. The length of the oracular collection against Babylon in conjunction with a number of distinctive features in it justifies the separate treatment of 50–51 (cf. Christensen 1975, 249–80; Wiklander 1978, 43–5). Apart from the lengthy material against Moab in 48 with its depiction of a hubristic enemy of Yahweh, the foe attacked in 50–51 is at times less the historical Babylon than a mythical creature (cf. the dragon of 51.34) symbolizing opposition to Yahweh (cf. the representation of Babylon in Isa. 13–14 and Tyre in Ezek. 28). Such a presentation of the destroyer of Jerusalem slips history and moves in the direction of apocalyptic (Christensen). Babylon becomes a symbol of the oppressor of Yahweh's people and the fully redacted 50–51 ceases to be solely the product of the sixth century. Zion as victim is an important feature of this cycle which distinguishes it from 46–49 (with the exception of 48.27): e.g. 50.6–7, 17–20, 28, 29, 33–34; 51.10, 11, 24, 34–37, 49–51. Whether this motif is an integral part of the cycle or a later glossing of 50–51 (cf. Fohrer 1981, 50–2) is a moot point and does not affect the interpretation of the work as it now stands. With the destruction of Babylon (whether as

Nebuchadrezzar's kingdom or as a cipher of whatever imperial power dominates the people of Israel) the vindication of Zion and Israel is guaranteed and the cycle reflects the worshipping community's liturgy of triumph. Such a reflection is quite lacking in 46–49, especially in view of the grace notes scattered throughout these OAN (e.g. 46.26b; 48.47; 49.6, 39).

The hubris of the enemy (Moab in 48, Babylon in 50–51) which attracts the wrath of Yahweh (48.26, 29–30, 35, 42; 50.24–27, 31–32; 51.6, 11, 25–26, 56) is a motif to be found in other OAN (e.g. Isa. 13–14 against Babylon; Ezek. 28 against Tyre) and suggests that some OAN transcended their origins in xenophobic curses against other nations to become statements of a theological nature against hubris of any form (cf. Isa. 2.12–17). Yahweh's vengeance reflects Yahweh's imperium which may be the background to the developed use of the OAN (on *nāqām*, *neqāmāh*, 'vengeance, vindication' in the Bible and especially the book of Jeremiah cf. Mendenhall 1973, 69–104). Against the imperial dominance of the empire (in particular Babylon) the OAN pose Yahweh's power on behalf of his people. This opposition makes 46–51, 50–51 especially so, very different from the other levels of tradition in the book of Jeremiah which are so scathing against Yahweh's people and more akin to the cycle of salvation oracles in 30–31. The two cycles 30–31, 50–51 may be read together because, though having different origins and interests, they share the motif of the restoration of Israel. In 30–31 that restoration is focused on without much emphasis on external enemies (apart from 30.12–16), whereas in 50–51 the enemy is the main focus with minor allusions to the vindication of Zion and the return of the exiles. The differences between the cycles are more significant than the shared motif of restoration, but both traditions contribute to the more positive aspects of the book of Jeremiah.

A full treatment of the themes of 46–51 can only arise out of the exegesis of the poems, but two further features of the OAN may be noted here. Many exegetes detect the influence of holy war concepts in the poems (e.g. Bach 1962; Christensen 1975, 184–93) as well as elsewhere in the Jeremiah tradition (cf. 4.5–8; 6.1–5; 15.7–9). Such concepts are not a distinctive feature of Israelite religion but represent the general beliefs of ancient Near Eastern societies that their gods intervened on their behalf against their enemies (cf. M. Weippert 1972). In the OAN Yahweh fights against Israel's enemies, especially against Egypt (46.10, 15, 25), Philistia (47.4, 7), Moab (48.26, 35,

44), Ammon (49.5), Edom (49.10, 13, 15–16), Damascus (49.27), Elam (49.35–38), and Babylon (50.13–15, 24–25, 31–32, 34, 45; 51.1–2, 11, 12, 24, 25–26, 29, 36–37, 40, 44, 52–53, 55–57). This motif is reversed in Part I (4–6), where the enemy comes against Jerusalem at Yahweh's bidding (e.g. 5.15–17; 6.6). Such a reversal of a traditional form suggests that the fall of Jerusalem was justified in the development of the tradition by the use of the OAN genre in a transformed mode, and this may warrant the view that the relevant poems in Part I reflect a later stage of the development of the book. The other notable feature of the OAN is the allusion to magical practices in 51.59–64 with reference to Babylon and the use of ciphers in 50–51 (e.g. 51.1, 41). Incantation and prestidigitation with a background in magical activity are important elements in the book of Jeremiah (e.g. 13.1–7; 19.1–2, 10–11; 25.15–17; 43.9–13) and may be presupposed for the OAN. The ciphers used (cf. 25.26) can hardly be intended to conceal the identity of the victim (clearly stated throughout 50–51), so must be accounted for in terms of magical tricks designed to bring about the downfall of specific opponents through the creation of ill omens against them. Prophecy and magic are particularly associated in the OAN (cf. Fohrer 1967, 257–61) and the manipulation of oracles (as in 51.59–64) makes a fitting conclusion to the cycle in MT. Gesture, word, incantation and ritual activity combine in the OAN to bring about the downfall of the imperial enemy and the termination of the words of Jeremiah at this point (only in MT 51.64b) concludes the story impressively with the doom of Babylon.

This analysis of 46–51 inevitably brings to the fore the considerable differences between the two editions of Jeremiah (G and MT). In the MT positioning of 50–51 it is difficult to avoid the impression that the editors have deliberately concluded their work with the ritual dismissal of Babylon as the last word of Jeremiah. G, with its very different order, represents a less impressive editorial arrangement and conclusion. MT ends on a dramatic note; G is much more modest in concluding with the story of Baruch's worries about his future. Whether the defeat of Babylon (in the past?) accounts for the difference cannot now be determined, but the different editions point to divergent editorial presentations of the OAN. In G they are where they would be expected to be – as Part II of the tradition (cf. Isaiah, Ezekiel) and integrated with the cup of the wine of wrath story (G 32.15–29 = MT 25.12–29). MT separates them from that story and turns 25.15–38 into a closure of Part I rather than the beginning of Part II. The motif of the cup (*kōs*) is common to 25.15–17, 27–29 and some of the OAN (49.12; 51.7), but is used quite differently in each instance. In 25.15–17, 27–29 *all* the nations drink it (including Jerusalem and Judah according to the addition in v. 18) because Yahweh's work of evil begins at Jerusalem but will not finish there. Thus all the nations (Babylon as well) share in the wrath of Yahweh which the events of 587 presage. In the development of the OAN against Edom the victim must drink the cup because those who did not deserve to drink it have had to partake of it. Who are these? Most likely 49.12 refers to Judah and this allusion is very different from 25.29. 51.7 represents Babylon as the golden cup in Yahweh's hand which has made the whole earth drunk. The metaphor is the same as in 25.15–17, but here it is Babylon rather than Jeremiah who administers the deadly vinous potion to the nations. However, the cup metaphor is only a passing reference to Babylon because the point of the poem in 51.6–10 is the sudden transformation in the fortunes of Babylon; from being Yahweh's golden cup one moment to being broken herself the next moment (how are the mighty fallen!). So the cup metaphor holds together a cluster of different motifs.

The difference between G and MT is compounded by a different order of nations attacked in the respective presentations of the OAN:

G	MT (EVV)
Elam	Egypt
Egypt	Philistia
Babylon	Moab
Philistia	Ammon
Edom	Edom
Ammon	Damascus
Kedar	Kedar
Damascus	Elam
Moab	Babylon

G places the material in MT 25.15–38 at the end of the OAN whereas in MT this section is separated from the OAN by Parts III and IV. The order of MT approximates more closely to the list of nations in 25.19–26 (it is *not* the same order) than does G (i.e. G 32.5–12), but little may be deduced from that approximation except that there may have been an *attempt* in the second edition to make the order conform (cf. Janzen 1973, 116). Some exegetes have discerned a geographical (e.g. Pfeiffer 1941, 487) or chronological (e.g. Hyatt, 1104) order in MT, but no discernible order can be detected in G. The position of the OAN in G, with its list of nations in no particular order, must be regarded as original and the arrangement of them in MT as a secondary development of the tradition.

46.1

46[1] The word of the LORD which came to Jeremiah the prophet concerning the nations.

[MT 46] = G 26. **[1]** MT *'ᵃšer hāyāh dᵉbar-yhwh 'el-yirmᵉyāhū hannābī' 'al*, lit. 'what came (as) the word of Yahweh to Jeremiah the prophet concerning': this curious form of a stereotypical introduction also appears in 14.1; 47.1; 49.34 (14.1 lacks *hannābī'*, 'the prophet'); cf. 1.2. G lacks v. 1 because it integrates the OAN with 25.15–38 in G 25.14–32.24 and therefore has no need of a separate title like MT. MT *'al-haggōyim*, 'concerning the nations': many mss 'against *all* the nations'; cf. 25.13b, *'ᵃšer-nibbā' yirmᵉyāhū 'al-kol-haggōyim*, 'which Jeremiah prophesied against all the nations'. Rudolph, 264, 268, adds 'in the fourth year of Jehoiakim the son of Josiah, king of Judah' from v. 2b because he regards 46.1 – 49.33 as oracles belonging to the fourth year of Jehoiakim (49.34 is dated to the beginning of Zedakiah's reign). Cf. 45.1b.

A formulaic reception of the divine word notice functions as a title to the collection of OAN. As an editorial note it uses the form which occurs in 14.1; 47.1; 49.34 and, to some extent, in 1.2. It has three elements: the divine word, Jeremiah *the prophet*, and the nations. These explain the general description of Jeremiah in 1.5c as 'a prophet to the nations' (*nābī' laggōyim*). In denouncing the enemy nations Jeremiah functions as a nationalistic prophet.

46.2

2 About Egypt. Concerning the army of Pharaoh Neco, king of Egypt, which was by the river Euphrates at Carchemish and which Nebuchadrezzar king

of Babylon defeated in the fourth year of Jehoiakim the son of Josiah, king of Judah:

---

[2] MT *l^e^miṣrayim*, 'concerning Egypt': section title, cf. 23.9; 48.1; 49.1, 7, 23; the longer title here is also to be found in 47.1; 49.28; cf. 49.34; 50.1. The section title may be separated from the occasion notice which follows: as a general title to 46 and because the detailed specifications of the rest of v.2 apply only to vv.3–12 (cf. v. 13). The occasion is 605 when Babylon defeated Egypt at Carchemish. Cf. 25.1; 36.1; 45.1 for this date. Whether Rudolph, 268, is justified in shifting the date notice to v. 1 in order to make 46.1 – 49.33 a block of material parallel to 25.1ff. and 36.1ff. is a moot point, but MT does not present it in this fashion. The dating owes something to 25.1 in that 25.19 identifies the Egyptians as the first of the recipients of the cup of Yahweh's wrath.

Egypt

The first nation addressed is Egypt (cf. 25.19, but G puts Elam first in 25.14–20; cf. Isa. 19; Ezek. 29–32). As all the OAN are declarations of defeat and destruction (though allowance is made for subsequent recovery in certain cases, cf. 46.26b; 48.47; 49.6, 39), the editorial dating of v. 2 may reflect an attempt to relate some poems to specific historical events. 605 was a fateful year for Egypt because its defeat by the Babylonians at Carchemish established Babylon's power throughout Palestine and curtailed effectively Egyptian control of Palestine. The denunciation of Egypt in 46 may be read in conjunction with 25.1–11, but in view of 50–51 is better read in the light of 25.15–17, 19–26. Were it not for 45, which has links with 46.2, the condemnation of Egypt in 46 would follow in MT immediately after the denunciations of Egypt in 43.8–13 and the Jewish communities there in 44. The enormous hostility felt towards Egypt and evidenced by 42.13 – 44.30 as much as 46 reflects political as well as ideological factors in the tradition. Between 609 and 587 pro-Egyptian elements in Judaean politics contributed significantly to national policy and, to some extent, were behind the revolts against Babylonian imperial power which brought Jerusalem to ruins. Deuteronomistic ideology viewed Egypt with extreme hostility and regarded any form of involvement with it, be it political, religious or residential, as apostasy against Yahwism and betrayal of the nation's history. After 605 the emergence of pro-Babylonian forces in Judaean political life created factions within the body politic. The extent to which the oracles against Egypt in 46 represent the output of such factions or the standard responses to the misfortunes of foreign nations is difficult to determine. Various strands in the book of Jeremiah reflect the partisan politics of both parties (cf. 26.20–23; 37.7–10 for traces of pro-Egyptian sentiments; 27–29, 39–40 for pro-Babylonian attitudes) but the oracles of 46–51 run counter to both outlooks in that they treat all foreign nations as the intended victims of Yahweh's wrath.

46.3–12

3 'Prepare buckler and shield,
and advance for battle!
4 Harness the horses;
mount, O horsemen!
Take your stations with your helmets,
polish your spears,
put on your coats of mail!
5 Why have I seen it?
They are dismayed
and have turned backward.
Their warriors are beaten down,
and have fled in haste;
they look not back –
terror on every side!
says the LORD.
6 The swift cannot flee away,
nor the warrior escape;
in the north by the river Euphrates
they have stumbled and fallen.
7 Who is this, rising like the Nile,
like rivers whose waters surge?
8 Egypt rises like the Nile,
like rivers whose waters surge.
He said, I will rise, I will cover the earth,
I will destroy cities and their inhabitants.
9 Advance, O horses,
and rage, O chariots!
Let the warriors go forth:
men of Ethiopia and Put who handle the shield,
men of Lud, skilled in handling the bow.

10 That day is the day of the Lord GOD of hosts,
a day of vengeance,
to avenge himself on his foes.
The sword shall devour and be sated,
and drink its fill of their blood.
For the Lord GOD of hosts holds a sacrifice
in the north country by the river Euphrates.
11 Go up to Gilead, and take balm,
O virgin daughter of Egypt!
In vain you have used many medicines;
there is no healing for you.
12 The nations have heard of your shame,
and the earth is full of your cry;
for warrior has stumbled against warrior;
they have both fallen together.'

---

[4] MT *wa'ᵃlū happārāšīm*, 'and mount the stallions: cf. Watson 1984, 380; *pārāš* means 'horse, steed' as well as 'horseman' (4.29) or 'charioteers'. G lacks 'and', and this lack gives the commands of the Egyptian officers a more realistic staccato manner, cf. EVV. MT *mirqū hārᵉmāpḥīm*, 'polish the lances': G *probalete ta dorata*, 'advance the spears', i.e. raise the spears; Rudolph, 266, follows Ehrlich 1912, 352, in reading it as *hērīqū*, 'empty', i.e. draw, unsheath (cf. Ps. 35.3) the lances (BHS *hāriqū*). **[5]** MT *madoū'a rā'ītī*, 'why do I see?': i.e. what is it that I see?; lacking in G due to 'simple scribal lapse' (Janzen 1973, 109). MT *ūmānōs nāsū*, lit. 'and the fleeing they flee': the noun *mānōs*, 'flight', may reflect an enclitic *m* (so Watson 1984, 380), so the phrase is to be understood as if it were an infinitive absolute with finite verb (i.e. *nōs nāsū*), 'really fleeing' or 'fleeing to and fro', cf. Rudolph, 266; Bright, 301, 'they flee pell-mell'. MT *māgōr missābīb*, 'terror on every side': cf. 6.25; 20.3, 4, 10; 49.29; Lam. 2.22; Ps. 31.13 (MT 14); Bach 1962, 51 n. 3, translates it as 'ambush' (cf. Watson). **[6]** MT *'al-yānūs*, 'do not flee': the jussive force here expresses the view that the swift *cannot* flee cf. GK 107p. G lacks 'river'; BHS deletes it. **[7]** MT *kannᵉhārōt yitgā'ᵃšu mēmāyw*, 'like rivers whose waters surge': plurals of amplification (Watson 1984, 381); cf. v. 8a. **[8]** The answer to the question in v. 7; deleted by Rudolph as unnecessary (cf. BHS). G lacks part of the line (8a); it also lacks 'city and' in v. 8b. **[9]** MT *wᵉyēṣᵉ'ūsᵉ'u haggibbōrīm*, 'and let the warriors go forth': G *exelthate . . .* 'go forth . . .' = *ṣᵉ'ū*, cf. NEB; Bright, 302; BHS. 'Put': G *Libues*, 'Libyans'; but Put is hardly Libya (cf. Nahum 3.9). It is more likely to be Punt on the Somali coast (cf. Rudolph, 268). MT *wᵉlūdīm*, 'and Ludim': not the Lydians of Asia Minor but an African people under the control of Egypt (cf. Gen. 10.13). Cf. Nahum 3.9 *pūṭwᵉlūbīm*, 'Put and the Libyans'; see comments in Thompson, 689. MT *tōpᵉśē dōrᵉkē qāšet*, lit. 'handlers of, benders of the bow': variants or, more likely, an erroneous repetition of *tōpᵉśe* from previous clause *tōpᵉśē māgēn*, 'handlers of the shield'; most exegetes delete it (cf. BHS). **[10]** G lacks *ṣᵉbā'ōt*, 'of hosts'. MT *ḥereb*, 'the sword': but perhaps *ḥarbō*, 'his sword', should be read due to haplography (cf. BHS); G *hē machaira kuriou*, 'the sword of the lord'. There may be a hint or element of word-play in the word *miṣṣārāyw*, 'on his foes', in an oracle about *miṣrāyim*, 'Egypt', though Egypt does not occur in v. 10; cf. v. 11; Watson. **[11]** K *hrbyty*; Q *hirbêt*, 'you have multiplied': K represents the old feminine ending, cf. 2.33; 3.4. Watson 1984, 382–3, detects rootplay and pun in *ᶜᵃlī gilᵉᶜād*, 'go up (to) Gilead', and *ṣōrī*, 'balsam, balm, storax', and *miṣrāyim*, 'Egypt'; word-play may be detected in *ᶜᵃlī*, 'go up', and *tᵉᶜālāh*, 'healing' (lit. the new flesh which *comes up* in the healing of a wound). Cf. 8.22 for the association of Gilead with healing. For the epithet 'virgin daughter' personifying a nation cf. 18.13; 31.4,21; Amos 5.2 ('virgin Israel'); Jer. 14.17 ('virgin daughter my people'); Isa. 47.1 ('virgin daughter Babylon'); Isa. 23.12 ('virgin daughter Sidon'). **[12]** MT *qᵉlōnēk*, 'your cry': cf. G. *phōnen sou*, 'your voice' (= *qōlēk*). NEB. RSV, JPSB, 'your shame', is a poor match for *ṣiwḥātēk*, 'your outcry'. In late Heb. *qōlan* means 'shouter, crier': unattested in biblical Hebrew but possible here or *qōl*, 'voice' with afformative – (*ā*)*n* (cf. Watson 1984, 382 n. 62); cf. Bright, 302 n.

A brilliant poem in vv. 3–12 fits the redactional introduction in v.2. It is one of the finest poems in the book of Jeremiah, and skilfully uses word-play, assonance, simile, metaphor, personification and certain structural patterns (cf. analysis in Watson 1984, 379–83). Dominant motifs include uses of *ᶜālāh*, 'go up, rise' (vv. 4, 7, 8, 9, 11), *gibbōr*, 'warrior' (vv. 5, 6, 9, 12), and *'ereṣ*, 'earth' (vv. 8, 10, 12). The poem moves from a graphic depiction of the call to war to the complete rout of the Egyptian army as its warriors flee from the enemy – an enemy never directly identified because in the background of the disastrous encounter 'in the north (country) by the river Euphrates' (vv. 6, 10) lurks the figure of Yahweh (v. 10a). The real enemy is Yahweh, hence the Babylonians do not appear in the poem. Egypt's defeat is the focus, and from the Judaean perspective of the poet the lord Yahweh is the host at the slaughter of the ancient enemy (cf. v. 10). Behind the ideology of the poem may be detected elements of the holy war motif (cf. Bach 1962) used to construct this oracle of doom.

Whether the oracle was uttered before, during or after the defeat of the Egyptian army at Carchemish cannot be determined from the text because the conventional nature of such oracles allows them to be interpreted as curses against the enemy by way of debilitating their campaign or as celebrations of their defeat. The battle between Egypt and Babylon at Carchemish was not one involving Judah, so the poem can hardly be read as a determinative of Judaean policy. It does, however, cleverly represent the *real* enemy of Egypt as being Yahweh and therefore the Babylonian defeat of the Egyptian army as the triumph of Yahweh's vengeance over *his* adversaries. Thus an event of international significance is drawn into the realm of Judaean ideology and made to conform to the domestic theology of a minor state on the edges of the two empires engaged in the struggle for dominance. Describing the encounter at Carchemish in the *north* (cf. 1.13–14; 4.5; 6.1, 22; 25.9 for the reverberations of this motif in the tradition) as Yahweh's day, i.e. a day of vengeance (*yōm nᵉqāmāh*) belonging to him, and as the time of the lord Yahweh's sacrifice (*zebaḥ la'dōnāy yhwh*), the poem domesticates international affairs in terms of Judaean religious matters (cf. Isa. 34.5–8; Ezek.39. 17–20; Zeph. 1.7 for similar motifs.)

In vv. 3–4 the Egyptian officers are heard barking commands at their troops to mount up in preparation for battle, but in vv. 5–6 the warriors are beaten back and flee, only to fall by the river (MT v.5a has the poet witness the rout of the Egyptians). Having summarized the battle in vv. 3–6 the poet describes it further in 7–9 and explains it in vv. 10–12. The mighty power and, even, hubris of Egypt is depicted in vv. 7–8 as the rising of the waters of the Nile – an image which captures admirably the essence of Egypt. Behind the repetitions of vv. 7–8a (MT) may be an allusion to the cosmic mythology of the waters of chaos shared by many nations in the ancient Near East (cf. Gen. 1.2; Bright, 306; Christensen 1975, 218; May 1955, 16). The surging of the Nile becomes a figure of the Egyptian army's pursuit of conquest and power and at the same time alludes to the destructive forces released by the waters of chaos which threaten to engulf the civilized world. Egypt is chaos and its war aims are a hubristic endeavour to cover the earth and destroy (cf. Isa. 10.5–16 for a description of Assyria as a destructive form of hubris). So the Egyptian warriors and their auxiliary troops go forth to do battle in the north (v. 9). But the day of battle belongs to Yahweh as his day of vengeance (cf. Isa. 2.12–17 for Yahweh's day against all hubristic attitudes and enterprises). The confident march of the Egyptians is but to the place of Yahweh's sacrifice, and his sword (cf. G) will devour the Egyptians. So the military expedition becomes a scene of ritual slaughter and there is no hope for the Egyptians. Against Yahweh's slaughter there can be no healing, in spite of all the efforts made by Egypt to find a cure for disaster (v. 11; cf. 8.21–22).

46.13

13 The word which the LORD spoke to Jeremiah the prophet about the coming of Nebuchadrezzar king of Babylon to smite the land of Egypt:

---

[13] Cf. 37.2; 50.1 for similar elements of the formulaic reception of the divine word introduction. G *en cheiri*, 'by the hand of': MT *'el*, 'to' (Jeremiah) = *b*^e^*yad*, 'by means of', as in 37.2; 50.1. G lacks *hannābî'*, 'the prophet'.

The redactional introduction to the poem in vv. 14–24 identifies the occasion of that utterance as Nebuchadrezzar's invasion of Egypt. In view of the poem's reference to 'a gadfly from the north' (v. 20) and 'a people from the north' (v. 24), that identification would appear to be a reasonable one. However, Nebuchadrezzar did not invade Egypt until 568–7, some forty years after the defeat of Egypt at Carchemish, so the appropriateness of the attribution of the poem to Jeremiah is questionable. The association of the two poems together is justifiable on the grounds that they represent two periods of Egyptian defeat by the Babylonians and define Egypt's fate in terms of Babylonian domination. Commentators who wish to attribute vv. 14–24 to Jeremiah do so on the grounds that he may have uttered it in 604 when the invasion of Egypt by Babylon appeared likely to happen (cf. Bright, 308; Thompson, 691; Rudolph, 271). A date *c.* 587 may be indicated by 37.6–10 which would make the poem an attack on the pro-Egyptian party in Jerusalem by denouncing their hopes of Egyptian support with an oracle of doom against Egypt. The most likely period for the poem is the two decades after the fall of Jerusalem (cf. Cornill, 450–1). This would make vv. 14–24 similar to the denunciation of Egypt in 43.8–13 (cf. Hyatt, 1107; Ezek. 29–32). Apart from the images of invasion in the poem, the word-play on the Pharaoh's name in v. 17 reflects the fact that Hophra (Apries) was in power then (Cornill, 451). The force of the word-play should not be exaggerated: it is over-subtle and may be more imaginary than real (G specifically identifies Necho as the Pharaoh and therefore relates it to 605 rather than after 589).

Such difficulties in dating a poem are characteristic of all biblical interpretations because the highly metaphorical and allusive language of biblical poetry permits a wide range of meaning. The problem of meaning is compounded in the book of Jeremiah by the editorial framework, which may have no necessary connection with the poetry and prose attached to it. Part of the difficulty with 46.13 is the conventional dating of Jeremiah's ministry to the 620s, so that by 566–7 he would have been very old indeed (i.e. in his eighties cf Duhm, 239). Exegetes who do not place Jeremiah's work as early as 1.2 indicates are relieved of this minor problem and may envisage Jeremiah prophesying twenty years after his arrival in Egypt. However, only the editorial note attributes vv. 14–24 to Jeremiah, and that may be regarded as more schematic or formal than accurate (cf. Volz, 395). A dating of the poem to 605–4 is necessary only if v. 13 reflects v. 2 and is judged to be a continuation of the defeat of Egypt depicted in vv. 3–12. The most natural reading of v. 13 is to relate the poem which follows to the invasion of Egypt by Nebuchadrezzar and therefore to the period of 568–7. No editorial dating is given, so v. 13 should be read as the redactors' introduction by way of commentary on vv. 14–24. As the *prophet* (lacking in G) of the tradition Jeremiah is credited with the oracle against Egypt, so that the poem describing the collapse of Egypt against the onslaught from the north becomes an oracular utterance. The occasion of the oracle is given in the most general terms in v. 13 but without sufficient detail (stereotyped or otherwise, cf. v. 2) to permit the modern reader to determine the precise intention of the editors. Such editorial glossing of the text is part of the development of the tradition, but has the effect of historicizing what may have been originally a quite different type of utterance (i.e. the curse against the enemy). The poem may *now* be read as a commentary on Nebuchadrezzar's campaign against the Egyptians rather than the calling down on the Egyptians of bad luck and misfortune in the future.

46.14–24

14 'Declare in Egypt, and proclaim in Migdol;
proclaim in Memphis and Tahpanhes;
Say, "Stand ready and be prepared,
for the sword shall devour round about you."
15 Why has Apis fled?
Why did not your bull stand?
Because the LORD thrust him down.
16 Your multitude stumbled and fell,
and they said one to another,
"Arise, and let us go back to our own people
and to the land of our birth,
because of the sword of the oppressor."
17 Call the name of Pharaoh, king of Egypt,
"Noisy one who lets the hour go by."
18 As I live, says the King,
whose name is the LORD of hosts,
like Tabor among the mountains,
and like Carmel by the sea, shall one come.
19 Prepare yourselves baggage for exile,
O inhabitants of Egypt!
For Memphis shall become a waste,
a ruin, without inhabitant.
20 A beautiful heifer is Egypt,
but a gadfly from the north has come upon her.
21 Even her hired soldiers in her midst
are like fatted calves;
yea, they have turned and fled together,
they did not stand;
for the day of their calamity has come upon them,
the time of their punishment.
22 She makes a sound like a serpent gliding away;
for her enemies march in force,
and come against her with axes,
like those who fell trees.
23 They shall cut down her forest,
says the LORD,
though it is impenetrable,
because they are more numerous than locusts;
they are without number.
24 The daughter of Egypt shall be put to shame,
she shall be delivered into the hand of a people from the north.'

[14] G lacks 'in Egypt and proclaim', 'and in Tahpanhes': MT, cf. 44.1; Isa. 11.11. Cf. 4.5 for the three verbs 'declare' (*higīd*), 'proclaim' (*hašmi'a*), 'say' (*'āmar*). MT *s^ebībekā*, 'round about you': G *tēn smilaka sou* 'your yew tree' = *subb^ekēk* cf. 21.14; MT changes gender here (cf. *lāk*, 'yourself'), BHS corrects it and in v. 15 (cf. Rudolph, 270). **[15]** MT *maddū'a nisḥap 'abbīrekā*, lit. 'why are your bulls prostrated?': i.e. why are your mighty ones (warriors?) prostrate? G *dia ti ephugen ho Apis*, 'wherefore has Apis fled?' (G[B] *apo sou*, 'from you'). G represents *nisḥap* read as two words, *nās ḥap*, 'Hapfled', where Hap is Apis the sacred bull reverenced as the incarnation of the Egyptian god Ptah. Giesebrecht, 231, reads *nās ḥap 'abbīr^ekā lō' 'āmad*, '(why) has Apis fled . . . your bull not stood?' (cf. Cornill, 452); Rudolph, 270, prefers MT (cf. BHS) with suffix gender of 'mighty ones' adjusted. **[16]** MT *hirbāh kōšēl*, lit. 'he increased one stumbling': G *kai to plēthos sou ēsthenēsen*, 'and your multitude has fainted' = *wah^amōn^ekā kāšal*, 'and your crowd has stumbled'; Rudolph suggests *rahab hārab kāšal*, 'the mighty Rahab has stumbled' (cf. BHS), i.e. Egypt has stumbled (cf. Isa. 30.7 for Rahab [the mythical sea monster] as an epithet of Egypt). Giesebrecht, 231, reads *'erb^ekā*, 'your mixed multitude', i.e. the foreign troops among them (cf. 50.37; Ezek. 30.5; see also 25.20). Christensen 1975, 218–19, offers the conjectural emendation *rābb^e(kā)*, 'your champion', based on *rīb* as an epithet applied to the deity (cf. 50.34; 51.36). MT *wayyō'm^erū*, 'and they said': transpose to beginning of clause (cf. G *hekastos . . . elalei*, 'each . . . said'). MT *mipp^enē ḥereb hayyōnāh*, 'because of the sword of the oppressor': cf. 25.38; G *apo prosōpou machairas Hellēnikēs*, 'from the Greek sword' = . . . *hayy^ewāniyyāh*. **[17]** MT *qār^e'ū šām par'ōh*, 'they called there, "Pharaoh . . ." ': G *kalesate to onoma Pharaō Nechaō* . . . 'call the name of Pharaoh Necho . . .' = *qir^e'ū šēm* . . .; BHS treats 'king of Egypt' as an addition to the text. MT *šā'ōn he'^ebīr hammō'ēd*, lit. 'battle noise who lets pass the appointed time': meaning uncertain, but possibly a reference to mistimed battle strategy (cf. 25.31; 48.45, where *šā'ōn* represents the noise of war). The Pharaoh is the *din* of war no doubt, but to little effect. Bright, 306, conjectures a pun on his personal name or royal titles; NEB 'King Bombast, the man who missed his moment'; JPSB 'Braggart who let the hour go by'; Christensen 1975, 218, 'Big Noise, who missed his chance!' The use of *he'^abīr* may be a pun on Pharaoh Hophra's name Apries, i.e. *w'ḥ-ib-r'* (cf. Thompson, 692), G transliterates *Saōnesbiemōēd*. **[18]** MT *hammelek yhwh ṣ^ebā'ōt š^emō*, 'the king Yahweh of hosts is his name': G *kurios ho theos*, 'the lord god'. MT '*the* king' (cf. 48.15b) contrasts with v. 17 'king of Egypt', thus emphasizing Yahweh as the real, i.e. effective, king, so unlike the windbag who cannot seize the right moment for action. Rudolph, 270, inserts *gibbōr*, 'warrior', after *kī* in v. 18b and adds *'ōyēb*, 'foe', to the end of it (cf. BHS): *'ōyēb* is lacking due to haplography and *gibbōr* because of homoioteleuton. **[19]** MT *yōšebet bat-miṣrāyim*, lit. 'inhabitress, daughter Egypt': cf. 'virgin daughter Egypt', v. 11; and the more frequent 'daughter my people' (e.g. 8.19, 21, 23 [EV 9.1]). It represents a personification of the people of Egypt as a woman. Cf. 2.15; 9.10 (EV 11) for similar motifs of the Judaean cities and Jerusalem becoming ruins without inhabitants. **[20]** MT *yᵉpēh-piyyāh*, 'pretty': better with many mss, *yᵉpēpiyyāh*. MT *qereṣ miṣṣāpōn bā' bā'*, lit. 'a fly from the north has come, has come': *qereṣ* (a hapax leg.) is of uncertain meaning, 'fly, gadfly' (stem *qrṣ*, 'nip, pinch', cf. Prov. 6.13; 10.10; 16.30; Job 33.6); G *apospasma*, 'shred, something torn off'. Cf. Isa. 7.18 for a direct entomological allusion as a figure of invasion and defeat. Many mss, GS read *bā' bāh*, 'has come upon her'; some exegetes delete the second *bā'* as a dittography. **[21]** MT *kᵉ'eglē marbēq*, 'like calves of the stall': i.e. stall-fed, fat calves as a simile of well-fed, fat warriors (cf. Isa. 10.16 for fatness as a figure of soldiers); the hired ones in her midst are mercenaries. The phrase *'ēt pᵉquddāh* (suffix variable), 'time of . . . punishment', appears in 6.15; 8.12; 10.15; 49.8; 50.27, 31; 51.18 (cf. 'year of . . .' 11.23; 23.12; 48.44). **[22]** MT *qōlāh kannāḥāš yēlēk*, 'her voice like the snake it goes': G *phōnē hōs opheōs surizontos*, 'their voice is like a hissing snake'; Bright, 304 reads 'Hear her hiss like a snake', following G (*šōrēq*). Rudolph, 270, reads *kᵉnaham yōlᵉdāh*, 'like the groaning of one giving birth' (cf. BHS); Christensen 1975, 219–20, suggests *qalāh kᵉnāḥāš zāḥal*, 'quickly like a snake she glides away' (cf. Micah 7.17, where *nāḥāš* and *zāḥal* occur in parallel). MT *bᵉḥayil*, 'in force': G *en ammō*, 'in the sand' = *bᵉḥōl*. MT *lāh*, 'against her': many mss *lāk*, 'against you'. **[23]** MT *kārᵉtū*, 'they have cut down': G *ekkopsousin*, 'they will cut down'. MT *kī lō' yēḥāqēr*, 'for it cannot be searched': i.e. it is impenetrable; Rudolph favours reading plur here, '*they* cannot be searched' (cf. BHS). Cf. 21.14; 22.7 for the forest (trees) image in terms of destruction (Isa. 10.33–34 have similar figures); some exegetes see in the figure of woodmen chopping down an impenetrable forest the continuation of the snake imagery of v. 22 (i.e. they cut down the forest in order to attack the snake, e.g. Bright, 306). This is unlikely, as the image changes in v. 22b and v. 23 stresses the *numerical* force of the invaders by virtue of which they can cut down even impenetrable forests. MT *kī rabbū mē'arbeh*, 'for they are more numerous than locusts': a hint of word-play on *rābāh* 'to be many', and *'arbeh*, 'locust-swarm', cf. Nahum 3.15 (a different image is used in relation to locusts). **[24]** MT *hōbīšāh bat-miṣrāyim*, 'daughter-Egypt is put to shame': Egypt personified as a young woman is raped by her invaders from the north. Christensen 1975, 220, treats the two occurrences of *bat*, 'daughter' (vv. 19, 24), as *bᵉtūlat*, 'virgin', cf. v. 11. Cf. 13.22, 26 for sexual violence as an image of the shaming of a people.

The second poem on Egypt's defeat focuses on the Egyptian experience of and response to invasion from the north (like the poems in 4.5 – 6.26 the foe from the north is not identified, except for the editorial 46.13). In the Egyptian towns the people are warned (cf.

v. 14; 4.5) to prepare for destruction. Behind the invasion is Yahweh's defeat of Egypt (MT) or his rout of the Egyptian god Apis (G). As expressions of that triumph are the incompetence of the Pharaoh (v. 17) and the failure of the Egyptian mercenaries to withstand the invading forces (v. 21). Thus the poem depicts the invasive defeat of Egypt in terms of Yahweh's activity and thus reflects the holy war motif also apparent in vv. 3–12. Contrasts are made between Yahweh, the Egyptian god Apis (G) and the king of Egypt. Yahweh is the effective power behind the political events of the period, whereas the bull-god of Egypt cannot stand against him nor can the Egyptian king act effectually. In vv. 17, 18 the king of Egypt is represented as a noise (windbag?) who cannot seize the opportune moment (a reflection on 37.7–10?), but the king, identified as Yahweh of hosts (cf. 48.15b; 51.57; also 8.19; 10.7, 10), who acts with power, is the very one who will bring the invader against Egypt. Behind Babylon's defeat of Egypt is Yahweh, and therefore the kudos accruing from that triumph belongs to the Judaean god. In Egypt's destruction is the vindication of Judaean ideology, and the fate of the people of Egypt is the same as that of Judah and Jerusalem (v. 19; a compensation for the fall of Jerusalem or just shared misery?).

In vv. 20–24 a series of theriomorphic metaphors describes Egypt's plight. Egypt is a beautiful heifer savaged by a nipper (the literal meaning of *qereṣ*) from the north. This graphic image of a cow plagued by a vicious species of insect is very appropriate to Egypt because of its theriomorphic cult of the gods. The inroads made by the Babylonians destroy Egypt's beauty. Even her mercenaries (cf. v. 9), like well-fed cattle, have fled in the face of the enemy. The imagery changes in v. 22 to depict Egypt's response to the invasion by means of a simile: she is like a snake hissing at (NEB) or gliding away (RSV) from attack. The snake image again reflects the Egyptian use of serpents as symbols of the gods and insignia of royalty. But Egypt as a snake is a figure of impotent reaction to threatened existence. The invading forces are powerful and numerous (vv. 22–23), and come against her with axes (cf. Ps. 74.5). Again the images change (though some exegetes relate the felling of the trees to the snake metaphor), and like a forest Egypt is chopped down by the axe-men. No matter how impenetrable that forest may be, the invading army is too numerous to be deterred from complete destruction of Egypt. An entomological image, locusts, is used to indicate the sheer numbers of soldiers penetrating the Egyptian territory. That image may appropriately reflect Egyptian uses of insects in religion, but the connection should not be exaggerated, as the point of v. 23 concerns vast numbers rather than locusts as such. The final image of Egypt's defeat is that of a young woman (daughter) violated by the invading troops. Behind the metaphor of national defeat is the all too real practice of occupying armies raping the women of conquered territories. Given over to the northern invader Egypt is a woman (cf. virgin, v. 11) violently ravished.

The Judaean perspective of this poem may be detected in v. 18, where the invader is described in terms reflecting geophysical features of the land of Israel. Two mountains, Tabor and Carmel, regarded as magnificent and impressive sights, are used to depict the enemy who 'shall come' (*yābō'*). These form part of a divine oath that Egypt will be invaded most surely and are rather strange and fantastic images of such an event (cf. Duhm, 340). To the poet's satisfaction Egypt will be exiled and Memphis become a waste (in contrast to Carmel's fertile aspect).

46.25–26

25 The LORD of hosts, the God of Israel, said: 'Behold, I am bringing punishment upon Amon of Thebes, and Pharaoh, and Egypt and her gods and her kings, upon Pharaoh and those who trust in him. 26 I will deliver them into the hand of those who seek their life, into the hand of Nebuchadrezzar king of Babylon and his officers. Afterward Egypt shall be inhabited as in the days of old, says the LORD.'

---

[25] G has a shorter text: 'Behold, I will avenge Amon her son on Pharaoh, and upon them that trust in him.' MT introductory formula is unusual in that it lacks *kōh*, 'thus' (cf. 48.1, 40; 50.18; 51.33). MT *'āmōn minnō'*, 'Amon of Thebes': cf. *minnō' 'āmōn*, Nahum 3.8; Amon was the chief god of Thebes, the capital of Upper Egypt (cf. Ezek. 30.14–16). Rudolph, 272, detects a type of word-play in the two words and suggests that *wᵉ'al-par'ōh*, 'and against Pharaoh', might be *wᵉ'al-pārōh*, 'and against his bull' (but cf. BHS); he also treats the absence of 'and Egypt . . . upon Pharaoh' from G as due to homoioteleuton (BHS; Bright, 305, rightly regards the phrase as an expansion in MT). NEB prints vv. 25–26 as poetry (followed by Thompson, 694), whereas most translations and exegetes treat them as prose. **[26]** G lacks v. 26; cf. 21.7; 44.30 for the motifs in v 26a. MT *wᵉ'aḥᵃrē-kēn tiškōn kimē-qedem*, 'afterwards it will dwell as in the days of old': i.e. Egypt will be inhabited as of old. Cf. 48.47; 49.6, 39 for a similar note of recovery in the oracles against the nations.

A brief prose statement (contrast NEB) summarizes the preceding poem as Yahweh's punishment of Egypt, her gods and institutions. Those Egyptians who trust in these things will be delivered into the power of Nebuchadrezzar and his troops. Thus the poem in vv. 14–24 is enclosed in two editorial comments identifying the enemy of Egypt as Nebuchadrezzar and the power behind him as Yahweh. The final sentence in v. 26 reverses the judgment of Egypt by hinting at a restoration of its inhabitation in the future just like the old days (cf. the more stereotypical restoration of the fortunes of Moab, the Ammonites, and Elam in 48.47; 49.6, 39). Whether this is a realistic note caused by Egypt's survival of the Babylonian invasion of 568 or a modification of the word of judgment because of the Jewish communities living there cannot be determined due to the brevity of the statement. It probably reflects a more positive view of Egypt than is to be found elsewhere in the book of Jeremiah (cf. the prose additions to the oracle denouncing Egypt in Isa. 19.18–25).

The oracles against Egypt conclude with the prosaic summary of vv. 25–26. These brilliant poetic denunciations of Egypt reveal how the oracles against the nations appropriate the political victories of Babylon in order to make statements about Yahweh's activities. Defeated themselves by Babylon, the Jewish communities can only claim the Babylonian achievements as triumphs of their own god. Yet the military might of Babylon (itself to be challenged in 50–51) occasions some very fine poems in the tradition. These assimilate events from international politics to internal ideology and use a combination of oracles of doom and holy war motifs to forge a statement about the *reality* of what is happening in the world at large.

46.27–28

27 'But fear not, O Jacob my servant,
   nor be dismayed, O Israel;
for lo, I will save you from afar,
   and your offspring from the land of their captivity.
Jacob shall return and have quiet and ease,
   and none shall make him afraid.

28 Fear not, O Jacob my servant,
says the LORD,
for I am with you.
I will make a full end of all the nations
to which I have driven you,
but of you I will not make a full end.
I will chasten you in just measure,
and I will by no means leave you unpunished.'

[46.27–28] = 30.10–11 with minor variations: 30.10 has *n^e'um yhwh*, 'says Yahweh', which appears in 46.28 where v. 27a is repeated (lacking in 30.11). 46.28a is necessarily different from 30.11a, which ends with an additional *l^ehôšî'ekā*, 'to save you'. For the motif 'I will not make a full end' cf. 4.27; 5.10, 18. Cf. Notes on 30.10–11.

The appearance of this poem here and in 30.10–11 raises questions about its original location (G only has it here) and its function in the oracles against the nations (see on 30.10–11). In MT the verses are between the oracles against Egypt and Moab, whereas in G they follow Egypt but *precede* the material against Babylon (G 27–28). Israel's return from captivity is a motif used in the oracles against Babylon (e.g. 50.4–5, 17–20; cf. vv. 33–34), so 46.27–28 may originally have been a marginal gloss on 50.2–5 which became displaced by editorial activity (cf. Hitzig, 348; Janzen 1973, 93–4). G represents the verses as a preface to the Babylon collection (cf. Isa. 14.1–3 for a similar prefatory approach to anti-Babylon material), whereas the changed order of MT vitiates that function of the piece. If the verses are read as a postscript to the oracles against Egypt they may be understood as making a contrast between the fate of Egypt and the future of Israel. However this is an inappropriate reading in the light of the final sentence of 46.26 where Egypt's restoration is alluded to because v. 28 refers to the complete annihilation (*kālāh*) of the nations. Such a reference suits 50–51 better than 46.25–26, though it is arguable that these verses are a late addition to the poems in 46. What 46.26b and 27–28 share is the motif of restoration and that link may be sufficient for the present position of vv. 27–28.

The editorial differences between G and MT entail distinctive interpretations of the material in terms of the discrete development of the tradition in its two editions. In 30.10–11 the oracle of salvation contributes to modifying the word about 'a time of distress for Jacob' (lacking in G) by using a poem belonging to the circle from which the poems of Second Isaiah emanated (cf. 30.4–7). Such a function is less clear for 46.27–28 (MT) and the superiority of G here must be acknowledged.

47.1

47[1] The word of the LORD that came to Jeremiah the prophet concerning the Philistines, before Pharaoh smote Gaza.

[MT 47] = G 29. **[1]** G lacks all this verse except for the titular phrase *epi tous allophulous*, 'against the Philistines' = MT *'el-pᵉlištîm*; this looks like the original title (cf. 46.2; 48.1; 49.1, 7, 23, 28; Rudolph, 272–5), perhaps a variation of *lipᵉlištîm*, 'concerning the Philistines'. Katzenstein 1983, 250, regards MT as authentic in spite of G lacking the expansion (cf. Bright, 311, who allows for the possibility that the addition is 'factually correct and furnishes us with the actual occasion of the prophecy'; Janzen 1973, 114, regards G as original). Cf. 14.1; 46.1; 49.34, for this form of the reception of the divine word notice.

Philistia

A short poem against the Philistines (cf. Amos 1.6–8; Isa. 14.29–32; Ezek. 25.15–17; Zeph. 2.4–7; Zech. 9.5–7 for other oracles against Philistia) is prefaced by an editorial introduction which identifies it as an oracular utterance of Jeremiah *the prophet* and its occasion as the period before the Egyptians attacked the Philistine city of Gaza (all this information belongs to the second edition of Jeremiah). The phrase 'before Pharaoh smote Gaza' raises a problem because the poem speaks of the threat to the Philistines as coming from the north (v. 2; cf. Isa. 14.31) rather than the south, whence an Egyptian campaign would come. It is arguable that the secondary introduction is not a statement about an Egyptian attack but an indication that the poem refers to a defeat inflicted on the Philistines *before* the more recent Egyptian onslaught on Gaza. Apart from the general principle that prose introductions have no necessary connection with the poems to which they are attached, the poems themselves are of such a general nature that it is difficult to discern in them precise information about specific historical events. The editors represent Jeremiah as uttering an oracle against the Philistines and provide further background detail by means of a reference to an Egyptian invasion of Philistine territory. Exegetes disagree about the occasion of this attack on Gaza: it may refer to Pharaoh Necho's defeat of the city Kadytis (probably Gaza) in 609 (cf. Herodotus II, 159; Oded 1977, 468), to Babylonian conquests in Palestine after the defeat of Egypt in 605 (cf. Wiseman 1956, 68–73), to the period of Necho's defeat of Nebuchadrezzar in 601 (cf. Katzenstein 1983, 250). The first edition of the text lacks this editorial material and therefore leaves the occasion of the poem to be deduced from the poetry itself. Such a deduction is hardly facilitated by the allusive phrases in the poem, some of which have been interpreted in relation to a rebellion of Ashkelon against Esarhaddon the Assyrian emperor (cf. Tadmor 1966, 100). The wisest course here may be to admit to ignorance and uncertainty (cf. Bright, 312, 'we cannot be sure') rather than to date the occasion of Jeremiah's oracle to the fourth year of Jehoiakim and 47.1 to *c.* 600 (*contra* Katzenstein's confidence).

47.2–7

2 'Thus says the LORD:
Behold, waters are rising out of the north,
and shall become an overflowing torrent;
they shall overflow the land and all that fills it,
the city and those who dwell in it.
Men shall cry out,
and every inhabitant of the land shall wail.
3 At the noise of the stamping of the hoofs of his stallions,
at the rushing of his chariots, at the rumbling of their wheels,
the fathers look not back to their children,
so feeble are their hands,
4 because of the day that is coming to destroy
all the Philistines,
to cut off from Tyre and Sidon
every helper that remains.
For the LORD is destroying the Philistines,
the remnant of the coastland of Caphtor.
5 Baldness has come upon Gaza,
Ashkelon has perished.
O remnant of the Anakim,
how long will you gash yourselves?

6 Ah, sword of the LORD!
  How long till you are quiet?
Put yourself into your scabbard,
  rest and be still!
7 How can it be quiet,
  when the LORD has given it a charge?
Against Ashkelon and against the seashore
  he has appointed it.'

---

[2] Cf. 46.7–8 for the rising waters motif; it is combined with the overflowing (*šṭp*) motif in Isa. 8.7–8. MT *'ereṣ ūmᵉlō'āh 'īr wᵉyōšᵉbē bāh*, 'the land and its fullness, the city and those who dwell in it': = 8.16b. MT *kōl yōšēb hā'āreṣ*, 'every inhabitant of the land': many mss, Vrs read *yōšᵉbē*, '(all the) inhabitants of . . .'. **[3]** MT *mērip'yōn yādāyim*, lit. 'because of sinking of hands': i.e. terror-induced feebleness, cf. 6.24. Rudolph, 272, relates 3a to v. 2 and 3b to v. 4 (cf. BHS); cf. Christensen 1975, 212, who reads *'al-hayyōm*, 'in that day' at the end of v. 3. **[4]** MT *lᵉṣōr ūlᵉṣīdōn kōl śārīd 'ōzēr*, 'Tyre and Sidon every remaining helper': i.e. (cutting off) every last defender of Tyre and Sidon. G (*kai aphaniō*) *tēn Turon kai tēn Sidōna kai pantas tous kataloipous tēs boētheias autōn*, '(and I will destroy) Tyre and Sidon and all the rest of their allies': a prophecy against the Phoenician cities is strange in a poem about the Philistines, but the line may represent an expansion of the original poem (Christensen deletes *ūlᵉṣīdōn kōl* as an expansionary gloss). Cf. 27.3 for Tyre and Sidon in relation to Palestinian struggles against Babylon. G lacks 'the Philistines' in 4c. MT *'ī kaptōr*, 'the isle of Caphtor': G *tōn nēsōn*, 'the islands' = *hā'iyyīm*; for the belief that the Philistines came from Caphtor (i.e. Crete and adjacent islands) cf. Amos 9.7. Cf. 11.23; II Sam. 14.7 for the notion of wiping out a group so that not even a remnant (*šᵉ'ērīt*) is left. **[5]** Cf. 16.6; 41.5 for baldness or beards shaved off as signs of mourning. MT *nidmetāh*, 'destroyed' (EVV *dmh*) or 'silenced' (*dmm*): 'silenced' suits the context of mourning better than 'destroyed' (cf. Rudolph, Bright). G *aperriphē*, 'cast away'. MT *šᵉ'ērīt 'imqām*, 'the remnant of their valley': hardly intelligible; G *kai hoi kataloipoi Enakim*, 'and the remnant of the Anakim', cf. Josh. 11.22; RSV. The Anakim are a legendary race of giants believed to have inhabited Canaan before Israel moved there, remnants of which were associated with Gaza, Gath and Ashdod. Condamin, 309; Rudolph, 272, add 'Ashdod' to the text: 'Ashdod, the remnant of Anakim'. Cf. Zeph. 2.4 for the three place-names (Gaza, Ashkelon, Ashdod). Bright, 310, explains *'imqām* as 'strength' on the basis of Ugaritic *'mq* (cf. 49.4); followed by Christensen 1975, 212–13: i.e. 'the remnant of their strength'. MT *titgōdādī*, 'will you gash yourselves?': cf. 5.7; 16.6; 41.5 for the practice of self-laceration; Christensen emends the text to *titgōrārī* with 2QJer fragment 'will you whirl about' because it 'renders better sense here than the root *gdd*, "cut", of MT' (1975, 213). The funerary ritual of MT makes perfectly good sense in this context. **[6]** G lacks *hôy*, 'woe, ah'; cf. 51.35–37 for the sword image. **[7]** MT *'ēk tišqōṭī*, 'how can *you* rest?': Vrs 'How can *it* rest?' i.e. the sword. MT continues the address of v. 6a, but in v. 7 the sword is spoken of in the third person.

The poem against the Philistines has two parts: an oracle of doom in vv. 1–5 and a song of Yahweh's sword in vv. 6–7 (cf. the analysis in Christensen 1975, 213–15). Waters rise in the north (Babylon?) against the inhabitants of Philistia and this symbol of invasion (cf. Isa. 8.7–8) denotes such a devastating onslaught that the Philistines and their towns are swept away completely. It is such a frightening day of destruction that even the fathers will be too terrified (or weak) to turn to assist their children. The reference to Tyre and Sidon in v. 4 (if not an expansion of the text) may allude to an alliance between the Philistine and Phoenician cities, though no evidence survives of such a treaty. When the Babylonians swept into Palestine they would have attacked the Phoenician cities as well as the Philistine territory, so this allusion may be a trace of such a campaign (cf. Ezek. 26.28; 29.18–20 for the devastation of Tyre; the oracles against the nations in the Jeremiah tradition lack a section on Tyre). The responses of the Philistine citizens to the destruction are the inevitable funeral rites of baldness, silence and self-laceration (v. 5). In the hymn to Yahweh's sword (vv. 6–7) the identity of the warrior who fights against Philistia is given as Yahweh, and his sword is represented as being insatiable (cf. the hymn in 51.35–37).

The short poem against the Philistines is similar to much else in the poems of the OAN. Terrible slaughter befalls a people and, whatever the invading force may be in reality, behind it is inevitably the figure of Yahweh. Babylon is *not* identified as the invading enemy, but the holy warrior Yahweh is the one who wields the bloodthirsty sword against the designated victim. It is Yahweh who marches from the north to cut off the Philistines and the actual army (i.e. the stallions and chariots of v. 3a) is but the means he uses to vent his spleen against the foreign nations. Against the Philistine towns and the seacoast he has commanded and appointed his sword.

48.1–10

481 Concerning Moab.
Thus says the LORD of hosts, the God of Israel:
'Woe to Nebo, for it is laid waste!
Kiriathaim is put to shame, it is taken;
the fortress is put to shame and broken down;
2 the renown of Moab is no more.
In Heshbon they planned evil against her:
"Come, let us cut her off from being a nation!"
You also, O Madmen, shall be bought to silence;
the sword shall pursue you.
3 Hark! A cry from Horonaim,
"Desolation and great destruction!"
4 Moab is destroyed;
a cry is heard as far as Zoar.
5 For at the ascent of Luhith
they go up weeping;
for at the descent of Horonaim
they have heard the cry of destruction.
6 Flee! Save yourselves!
Be like a wild ass in the desert!
7 For, because you trusted in your strongholds and your treasures,
you also shall be taken;
and Chemosh shall go forth into exile,
with his priests and his princes.
8 The destroyer shall come upon every city,
and no city shall escape;
the valley shall perish,
and the plain shall be destroyed,
as the LORD has spoken.
9 Give wings to Moab,
for she would fly away;
her cities shall become a desolation,
with no inhabitant in them.
10 Cursed is he who does the work of the LORD with slackness; and
cursed is he who keeps back his sword from bloodshed.'

[MT 48] = G 31 (lacking vv. 45–47). **[1]** G lacks 'of hosts, the god of Israel' and the first occurrence of *hōbîšāh*, 'shamed' (a repetition in MT from next line). MT *hōbîšāh hammiśgāb wāḥāttāh*, 'shamed is the fortress and broken down': the feminine forms of the verbs suggest that *miśgāb* was understood as a place name (Rudolph, 274, corrects them, cf. BHS); cf. vv. 20, 38, 39, where this general confusion persists. In 46.24 *hōbīšāh* is used correctly because Egypt is personified as a young woman. **[2]** MT *tᵉhillat mō'āb*, 'the renown of Moab': cf. 49.25; 51.41; G *iatreia Mōab*, 'healing for Moab' = *tᵉ'ālat*. MT *bᵉḥešbōn ḥāšᵉbū*, 'in Hesbon they plot': word-play on *ḥšb*; G *agauriama en Esebōn*, 'glorying in Esebon' = *tᵉhillāh*. G lacks *lᵉkū*, 'come'. MT *gam-madmēn tiddōmmī*, 'also Madmen you shall be silent': Madmen is unknown but Dibon may be meant (Rudolph), cf. Isa. 15.9 where Dimon may be a word-play on Dibon (cf. BHS; Kaiser 1974, 69). In Isa. 25.10 *madmēnāh*, 'dung-pit' (cf. *dōmen*, 'dung', Jer. 8.2; 9.21; 16.4; 25.33) is used in a simile about Moab. Word-play on *dmm*, 'be silent', may be detected in the phrase, cf. G *kai pausin pausetai*, 'and she shall be completely silent', reading *mdmn* as *dāmōm* (infin. absol.). Kuschke 1961, 185; Dahood 1962b, 70 translate *gam* as 'with a loud voice (Madmen shall *wail*)', followed by Christensen 1975, 238. Silent (*dmm*) wailing with a loud voice introduces an oxymoron into the text! **[3]** MT *mēḥōrōnāyim*, 'from Horonaim': cf. v. 5; Isa. 15.5; Cornill, 463, reads *mē'ᵃbarīm*, 'from Abarim', cf. 22.20 (*ṣ'q*, 'cry', is used in both places), influencing Rudolph to read *mēhar 'ᵃbārīm*, 'from mount Abarim' (cf. BHS). MT *šōd wāšeber gādōl*, 'desolation and great destruction': cf. Isa. 59.7; 60.18, for the two terms together (without *gādōl*); 'great destruction' occurs in 4.6; 6.1. **[4]** MT *hišᵉmī'ū zᵉ'āqāh ṣᵉ'īrehā*, 'her little ones make a cry': cf. 49.20; 50.45 for *ṣᵉ'īrīm*, 'little ones', i.e. the insignificant or helpless ones (children). K *ṣ'wryh*; Q *ṣᵉ'īrehā*, cf. 14.3. G *anaggeilate eis Zogora*, 'proclaim to Zogora': lacking 'cry', cf. Isa. 15.5, *'ad-ṣō'ar*, 'to Zoar'; followed by RSV, NEB, BHS and many exegetes. **[5]** K *hlḥwt*; Q *halluḥīt*, 'Luhith', cf. Isa. 15.5 (K 'tablets, planks' makes no sense). MT *bibᵉkī ya'ᵃleh-bekī*, 'with weeping one goes up weeping': cf. Isa. 15.5 *bibᵉkī ya'ᵃleh-bō*, 'with weeping one goes up *on it*' (i.e. the ascent); BHS, Bright and others follow Isa. 15.5. MT *ṣārē ṣa'aqat-šeber*, 'the distresses of the cry of destruction': G lacks *ṣārē*, cf. RSV, NEB, BHS, Isa. 15.5. Driver 1937–38, 123, translates *ṣārē* as 'shrill cry', and deletes *ṣa'ᵃqat* as an explanatory gloss on it. **[6]** MT *wᵉtihyeynāh ka'ᵃrō'ēr bammidbār*, 'and be like Aroer in the desert': the meaning of this phrase is unintelligible. The fem. plur. (*hyh*) is odd but may be explained as second masc. plur. (cf. Bright, 314n.); *'ᵃrō'ēr* may be a corruption of *yᵉ'ō'ērū*, 'raise, rouse', in Isa. 15.5 (a variant in place of *šāmē'ū*, 'they have heard', in v. 6, but misplaced here?). G *hōsper onos agrios*, 'like a wild ass': i.e. *'ārōd*, 'wild ass' (Job 39.5), cf. *pere'* 2.24(MT); Rudolph deletes the word (cf. BHS); also Christensen. Duhm, 346, reads *ūtᵉḥayyunhā kᵉ'ar'ār bammidbār*, 'and eke out an existence as a juniper tree in the desert', cf. 17.6. Rudolph reads *wthynh* as *wᵉtaḥᵃnū*, 'and encamp (in the desert)', cf. BHS. **[7]** MT *bᵉma'ᵃśayik ūbᵉ'ōṣᵉrōtayik*, 'in your works and in your treasures': G *en ochurōmasin sou*, 'in your stronghold' = *bᵉmā'uzzayik* or *bimᵉṣudōtayik* or some such word; MT *ma'ᵃśayik* may represent a general term 'works' covering any defence work (cf. Janzen 1973, 19–20), but the doublet overloads the line. As variants MT may be an attempt to decipher an unreadable word (Volz, 405; cf. Weiser, 392); Christensen 1975, 238, deletes the second word. Note that Moab is personified as a woman here. K *kmyš*; Q *kᵉmôš*, 'Chemosh': K is a scribal error. K *yḥd*; Q *yaḥdāyw*, 'together': Q is a variation on the more usual *yaḥdāw*; cf. 46.12, 21; 49.3; K 'together' lacks *w* due to haplography (cf. v. 8). Many mss represent Q forms. **[8]** G lacks the second occurrence of *'îr*, 'city'. MT *hā'ēmeq . . . hammîšōr*, 'the valley . . . the plain': perhaps not collectives for 'valleys' and 'plains' but specific Moabite areas. Rudolph, 285, identifies the valley as the territory east of the Jordan and north of the Dead Sea (cf. Josh. 13.27) and the plain as the plateau north from the Arnon to the area of Heshbon (cf. Weiser, 392; Schottroff 1966). MT *'ᵃšer 'āmar yhwh*, 'which Yahweh has said': as if v. 8 were a citation of 33.22; Rudolph deletes as a dittography (cf. BHS). **[9]** MT *tᵉnū-ṣîṣ lᵉmō'āb*, 'give ? to Moab': meaning of *ṣîṣ* is dubious: G *sēmeia*, 'signs, marks', suggests *nēs*, 'standard' (4.6) or *ṣiyyūn*, 'road-mark' (31.21; cf. 'grave-mark,' II Kings 23.17; Giesebrecht, 236; BHS). RSV highly unlikely; NEB 'Let a warning flash to Moab': following G 'Set up a monument for Moab', i.e. her grave marker will indicate her complete destruction. A different approach is advocated by Moran 1958, 69–71, who argues for *ṣîṣ*, 'salt', on the basis of Ugaritic glosses in Akkadian texts: 'give salt for Moab' means 'salt her cities', a figure symbolizing the utter annihilation of a city by sowing its ruins with salt (cf. Judg. 9.45; Ecclus. 43.19). Hence NEB margin, 'Doom Moab to become saltings'. Cf. Gevirtz 1963 for the practice of sowing cities with salt. MT *nāṣō' tēṣē'*, Hebrew obscure: word-play or confusion may explain MT. Two verbs, *nṣh*, 'collapse in ruins', and *yṣ'*, 'go out', are combined when two forms of the one verb may be intended, cf. G *haphē anaphthēsetai*, 'kindling she shall be kindled' (*yṣt*, cf. 2.15; 9.9, 11 [EVV 10, 12]; 46.19). Rudolph, 275, reads *nāṣōh tiṣṣeh*, 'she shall surely fall in ruins' (cf. BHS; 4.7). MT may conceal an alternative reading *yāṣō tēṣē'*, 'she shall surely surrender' (cf. I Sam. 11.3; Isa. 36.16 for *yṣ'*, 'surrender'). **[10]** G lacks the repeat of *'ārūr*, 'cursed be . . .': v. 10 is regarded by many exegetes as a prose comment on the preceding poem (e.g. Duhm, Volz, Rudolph, Bright, Christensen); cf. 50.25; Judg. 5.23 for the motifs of Yahweh's work and human involvement in it.

Moab

A series of poems with prose comments constitutes the oracle against Moab (cf. Isa. 15–16; Amos 2.1–3; Zeph. 2.8–11; Ezek. 25.8–11 for similar oracles directed against Moab). Apart from the poems about Babylon in 50–51, there is nothing in the collection of 46–51 to match the length of the material on Moab (48 is longer than all the oracles against Moab in the other prophetic collections put together!). Small wonder that Cornill (462) should refer to its length as 'monstrous'. None of the other small nations (Philistines, Ammonites, Edom, Syria, Kedar or Elam) has so much attention devoted to it. Even Egypt is given less space in the collection. Why Moab should so dominate 46–49 cannot be explained and, as so little is known about Moab and its history (cf. van Zyl 1960), it is but speculation to suppose a special relationship existed between Judah and Moab which might have yielded so much material. No doubt 48 contains much older material which has been adapted and developed for the period after the fall of Jerusalem, but why Moab should be singled out for such expansion of resources is unknown. A further remarkable feature of 48 is the number of place names which appear in it which make it almost an atlas of Moabite territory (listed alphabetically and described in Rudolph, 284–8; cf. Schottroff 1966).

Moab shared with Judah and all the other minor states the devastations caused by the Babylonian invasions of Palestine during the period 605–582. Whatever Moabite activities against Judah may have involved (cf. II Kings 24.2), or whatever the extent of the revolt against Babylonian domination (cf. 27.3), Moab suffered the same fate as Judah and the other nations and had to submit to the imperial power of Babylon. This submission along with subsequent invasion of Arab tribes (cf. Bright, 323) helped to destroy Moab. The poems of 48 reflect much of the history of Moab without being specific to the point of describing actual events. Thus they are similar to all the poems in 46–51 which use metaphors and similes of destruction combined with allusions to Yahweh's warlike campaigns against the nations to provide a commentary on the sixth century. In the Moab collection place names take the place of specific details and give the impression of the deity roaming about the land of Moab slaughtering everything he encounters (echoes of Num. 21.13–14, 27–30 may be detected in 48).

As with so much of the poetry in the book of Jeremiah the division of 48 into individual poems or separate units is not really determined; nor do all exegetes agree on how many divisions should be made in the chapter (e.g. Bardtke 1936 has three: 1–13, 14–27, 28–47; Bright has five: 1–10, 11–17, 18–28, 29–39, 40–47; Rudolph has six: 1–10, 11–17, 18–28, 29–39, 40–42, 43–46). Prose elements in the poem also complicate the matter by breaking up the flow of the poetry (e.g. vv. 10, 12–13, 21–24, 26–27, 34–39). The complete poem is a mixture of distinctive forms: the summons to flee, announcements of judgment, laments and the summons to mourn, and oracles of doom (see analysis in Christensen 1975, 234–45). In dividing the poem into the sections suggested by Bright convenience rather than conviction has determined the division, and the fuzzy edges of each section should be kept in mind when scrutinizing the text.

The poem is introduced by the summarizing title 'concerning Moab' and there can be little doubt that title and contents agree. A further introductory statement makes the poem an oracular pronouncement and therefore Moab's experience of destruction a divine activity. Allowance must be made for textual difficulties in vv. 1–9 (see Notes), but otherwise the general meaning of the section is clear. Various towns in Moab are laid waste and the inhabitants of other towns are invited to flee from the onslaught of the destroyer. The famous defences of Moab are breached, and there is no hope of escape. Yahweh has spoken, and the people of Moab, along with their god Chemosh, must go into exile. In v. 10 a prose commentary (with poetic traces?) encourages (whom?) persistence in the slaughter by cursing those (the Babylonians? Arab tribes?) who would desist from killing. This is Yahweh's work (cf. 50.25), and all must participate in it with enthusiasm (cf. the curse in Judg. 5.23 against the inhabitants of Meroz for not assisting Yahweh against the enemy). If v. 10 reflects a trace of holy war terminology (cf. Bach 1962, 88), the curse may be directed against Judaeans who fail to pursue the defeated Moabites to the point of annihilation. Implied in this reading of v. 10 is an interpretation of the poem against Moab in terms of a Judaean campaign againt the Moabites. Such a campaign has been identified with Josiah's expansionist policies when that king tried to extend Judaean territory in the period of Assyrian decline (e.g. Bardtke 1936, 242; cf. Christensen 243–4). There may be an element of this in the poem, but too many features in 48 are shared with the other poems in 46–51 for such an interpretation to have a high level of probability. For it is unlikely that Judah instigated and pursued holy wars against all the nations listed in the oracles, especially against Egypt and Babylon. A glossing of the poems with holy war motifs or a transference of holy war language to describe the conquests of Babylon would provide a better reading of the material. The cursing of Meroz may bear on the interpretation of v. 10, but, Judg. 5 apart, the holy war motif knows nothing of unwilling or half-hearted participation. 48.10 and Judg. 5.23 have only the terms 'cursed' (*'ārūr*) and 'Yahweh' in common, and the list of curses (*'ārūr*) in Deut. 27.15–26 sets out apodictic rulings for the nation but does not envisage non-participation in the slaughter of foreigners as grounds for cursing. While one should not rule out Bardtke's interpretation altogether it is more likely that 48.10 represents a pious glossator's response to the destruction of the Moabites. It expresses the hope that the destroyer will not hold back from doing Yahweh's work until Moab is annihilated. It is a word of encouragement stated in negative terms.

48.11–17

11 'Moab has been at ease from his youth
  and has settled on his lees;
 he has not been emptied from vessel to vessel,
  nor has he gone into exile;
 so his taste remains in him,
  and the scent is not changed.'
12 'Therefore, behold, the days are coming, says the LORD, when I shall
send to him tilters who will tilt him, and empty his vessels, and break his
jars in pieces. 13 Then Moab shall be ashamed of Chemosh, as the house
of Israel was ashamed of Bethel, their confidence.'
14 'How do you say, "We are heroes
  and mighty men of war"?
15 The destroyer of Moab and his cities has come up,
  and the choicest of his young men have gone down to slaughter,
  says the King, whose name is the LORD of hosts.
16 The calamity of Moab is near at hand
  and his affliction hastens apace.
17 Bemoan him, all you who are round about him,
  and all who know his name;
 say, "How the mighty sceptre is broken,
  the glorious staff." '

---

[11] MT *Š^emārāyw*, 'his lees': i.e. the dregs of unfiltered wine; cf. vv. 32–33; Isa. 16.8–10 for further figures drawn from Moabite viticulture. **[12]** MT *ṣō'īm w^eṣē'uhū*, lit. 'benders and they will bend him': a word-play on *ṣ'h*, 'stoop, bend, incline' (cf. 2.20 where it is used in an obscene sense); Bright, 315, 320 tries to catch the word-play element with 'men to cant and decant him'. The figure is of Moab as a vessel being tipped over by tippers (RSV, 'tilters who will tilt him'). MT *yārīqū*, 'they shall empty': G *leptunousi*, 'they shall smash' = *yādēqqū*. G '*his* jars', for MT '*their* jars'. Rudolph, 276, treats 'therefore . . . says Yahweh' as an addition because in reality Jeremiah expected Moab's catastrophe to be in the near future and not in 'days are coming' (cf. Cornill, 466). Excluding the phrase assists reading v. 12 as poetry (cf. NEB, many exegetes). **[13]** 'Bethel': for Bethel as a deity or divine epithet cf. Porten 1968, 164–73; this prose addition to the poem need not be regarded as a pre-exilic element (*contra* Christensen 1975, 244–5), for an analogy between the gods of Moab (Chemosh) and Israel (Bethel) could be a glossator's comment in any period before or after 587. The fall of Jerusalem would not necessarily prevent 'so spiteful and self-righteous an attitude towards the northern kingdom' (Eissfeldt 1965, 363) being maintained among Judaeans. The particularity of the allusion may reflect a recognition of the similarity of Chemosh and Bethel as well as being a stray element from the Bethel redaction of Amos (cf. Coote 1981, 46–109). **[15]** MT *šuddad mō'āb wᵉʿāreyhā ʿālāh*, lit. 'Moab is destroyed, and her cities he has come up': cf. v. 18b, where *kī-šōdēd mō'āb ʿālāh bāk*, 'for the destroyer of Moab has come up against you' may be the way to read v. 15a (cf. BHS) or allow it to be changed to 'the destroyer of Moab has come up against her towns' (cf. Bright, 315). G 'Moab is ruined, his city' = *šuddad mō'āb ʿīrō*. G lacks v. 15c: a redactional gloss from 46.18. Christensen 1975, 238, follows Shafer 1971, 393–4, in understanding *mibḥar*, 'choicest', as 'fortress' (cf. G). **[16]** MT *'ēd*, 'ruin, calamity': G *hēmera*, 'day' = *yōm*. The imminence of Moab's destruction is conveyed by the term *qārōb*, 'near' (cf. Joel 1.15; 2.1; 4.14 [EVV 3.14]), and the phrase *mihᵃrāh mᵉ'ōd*; 'it hastens quickly'.

Two different elements constitute this section of the poem. In vv. 11–12 images drawn from wine-making are used to describe Moab's state and in vv. 14–17 the hubris of Moab meets its nemesis in the destruction of its warriors, fortresses and great reputation. Viticulture provides metaphors of undisturbed tranquility in v. 11, where Moab's state is described as one of unmolested security in the past (an idyllic and unreal description in view of the troubled history of all the small nations during the Assyrian period). Like the sediment in undisturbed wine Moab has been at ease from its youth (cf. the equally idyllic images of Israel's youth in 2.2–3); no one has poured him from vessel to vessel. Thus the taste and bouquet of the wine are unchanged and therefore unspoiled. The reputation of Moab's wine (cf. vv. 32–33; Isa. 16.8–10) is used to depict an untroubled nation (ancient viticulture should not be confused with modern techniques of wine blending or chateau bottling methods which produce sophisticated vintages) which has had no experience of exile (in contrast to Israel in 721 or Judah in 597 or 587?). This idyllic existence is about to be disrupted in a most violent manner: the deity will send against Moab those who will violently disturb the wines by tipping them over (the word-play is difficult to capture in English), emptying the drinking vessels, and smashing the jars (cf. 13.12–14) containing the wines. Such a brawl in the taverns (if this more modern image may be used of v. 12) will destroy Moab. A pious editor has added v. 13 in order to draw the religious lesson from the images of vv. 11–12. The destruction of Moab will cause disillusionment with the national god Chemosh. Such dissatisfaction with the god is likened to Israel's loss of faith in Bethel. It is hardly necessary to see in this simile a pre-exilic note, though such a dating cannot be ruled out. A Judaean editor could hardly have referred to the fall of Jerusalem as occasioning disillusionment with Yahweh (cf. 44.17–19), hence an allusion to the northern kingdom's syncretistic ways is appropriate here. Yahweh no less than Chemosh or Bethel failed to protect his nation but such a sensitive issue has other explanations in the tradition. As a passing comment on Moab's rude awakening from a tranquil past the point of v. 13 makes connections with Israel's past, but the shadow of 587 may be detected throughout the oracles against the nations whatever the precise dating of any individual poem or verse.

The images change completely in vv. 14–17 and return to the theme of vv. 2–9. Moab's destroyer (unidentified as is characteristic of all the poems in the OAN) has come up against its cities and fortresses and has destroyed its mighty warriors. The destroyer *comes up* and the young men (i.e. the troops) *go down* to slaughter (v. 15). In v. 16 the ruin of Moab is envisaged as being about to happen ('near at hand', 'hastens quickly') rather than as having happened already. This change of perspective depicts the slaughter as a process moving swiftly to its completion and is but a change of pace in the poetry. As the Moabites collapse against the enemy those, who are familiar with Moab's great reputation (cf. vv. 29–30) are invited to shake their heads in mourning (v. 17 *nudū*, cf. 15.5; 16.5; 18.16; 22.10; 31.18) at its loss and the attendant reversal of its powerful status.

48.18–28

18 'Come down from your glory,
and sit on the parched ground,
O inhabitant of Dibon!
For the destroyer of Moab has come up against you;
he has destroyed your strongholds.
19 Stand by the way and watch,
O inhabitant of Aroer!
Ask him who flees and her who escapes;
say, "What has happened?"
20 Moab is put to shame, for it is broken;
wail and cry!
Tell it by the Arnon,
that Moab is laid waste.
21 Judgment has come upon the tableland, upon Holon, and Jahzah, and
Mepha-ath, 22 and Dibon, and Nebo, and Beth-diblathaim, 23 and
Kiriathaim, and Beth-gamul, and Bethmeon, 24 and Keri-oth, and Bozrah,
and all the cities of the land of Moab, far and near. 25 The horn of Moab
is cut off, and his arm is broken, says the LORD.
26 Make him drunk, because he magnified himself against the LORD; so
that Moab shall wallow in his vomit, and he too shall be held in derision.
27 Was not Israel a derision to you? Was he found among thieves, that
whenever you spoke of him you wagged your head?
28 Leave the cities, and dwell in the rock,
O inhabitant of Moab!
Be like the dove that nests
in the sides of the mouth of a gorge.'

---

[18] K *yšby*; Q *ūš^{e}bī*, 'and sit': K is a scribal error. MT *r^{e}dī . . . ūš^{e}bī*, 'come down . . . and sit': cf. Isa. 47.1, where the dethroned daughter Babylon is spoken to in the same way. Rudolph, 276, favours reading *baṣṣō'āh*, 'in the filth' (vomit or excrement), for *baṣṣāmā'*, 'dry ground', in order to make a sharp contrast between her former glory and her present state (cf. the image of vomit in v. 26); cf. Bright, 315. G *en hugrasia*, 'in a damp place' (cf. S). MT *yōšebet bat-dībōn*, lit. 'inhabitress, daughter Dibon': cf. 46.19; G lacks 'daughter' (omitted by Christensen 1975, 238 with G). Cf. the suggestion in BHS that *bat* is a dittography of *(ywš)bt*. Dibon is the city north of the river Arnon where the Moabite Stone (Mesha's inscription) was found. Cf. v. 15a for v. 18bα. **[19]** Cf. 6.16 for a similar instruction. The subtle gender shift of MT (*nās*, 'him who flees' – *nim^{e}lāṭāh*, 'her who escapes') is lost in the Vrs, which read both words as masc. MT may be an expression of the totality of the fleeing population. Cf. 21.13; 22.23 for the epithet *yōšebet*, 'inhabitress', describing a town or location. **[20]** Cf. v. 1; 46.24. MT *kî-ḥattāh*, 'for *she* is broken': read *ḥat*, '*he* is broken', i.e. *it* (Moab); MT due to dittography. K *hylyly wz'qy* (cf. G); Q *hêlîlû ûzᵉ'āqû*, 'wail and cry': K sing., Q plur. Either is possible, as *yōšebet* is a collective. **[21]** K *mwp't*; Q *mēpā'at*, 'Mephaath': Vrs follow Q but G has K (*Mōphath*). 21–24 are a prose expansion which interrupts the poem. **[25]** G lacks *nᵉ'um yhwh*, 'says Yahweh'. The words 'horn' (*qeren*) and 'arm' (*zᵉrō'a*) are metaphors of strength (cf. Lam. 2.3 for *qeren* with reference to Israel). This may be the answer of the refugees to the question asked in v. 19b (cf. Rudolph, 278). **[26]** MT *wᵉsāpaq mō'ab bᵉqî'ō*, lit. 'and Moab shall *slap* in his vomit': *spq* means 'slap' (cf. Job 34.26) or 'clap' hands in anger or mockery (cf. Num. 24.10; Lam. 2.15; Job 27.23); also 'slap' the thigh in remorse and sorrow (cf. 31.19; Ezek. 21.17). Its occurrence here is difficult: RSV 'shall *wallow* in his vomit', NEB 'until he *overflows* with his vomit', JPSB 'shall vomit till he is drained'; G *kai epikroussei Mōab en cheiri autou*, 'and Moab shall *clap* his hands'. The figure may be one of splashing about in vomit or falling with a splash into vomit (cf. BDB, 796); though some connect *spq* with slapping the thigh out of rage and disgust with vomiting (*bᵉ* 'on account of', KB, 665; *spq* II, 'to vomit, be sick', KB³ III, 722, following Rudolph, 278). Syr. *spq*, 'throw up', i.e. 'spew forth his vomit' (cf. NEB; Driver 1950, 62): delete *bᵉ* as dittography (cf. BHS). The images of drunkenness reflect a standard metaphor of the divine anger (cf. 25.15–29; Isa. 49.26; 51.21–23; 63.6; also the imagery of 13.12–14). **[27]** K *nmṣ'h*; Q *nimᵉṣā'*, '*he* was found' (K fem.). G lacks *middê dᵉbāreykā*, 'as often as your words': Rudolph and others revocalize with Symm. *middê dabberᵉkā*, 'as often as you speak' (cf. BHS). MT *titnōdād*, 'you shook' (your head in derision); cf. 18.16; 31.18: a mocking or bewildered gesture. 26–27 are another prose expansion breaking up the flow of the poem and developing very different images from vv. 18–20. **[28]** Cf. 13.4; Isa. 2.21 for the image of hiding in the rocks. MT *bᵉ'ebᵉrê pî-pāḥat*, lit. 'on the sides of the mouth of the pit': cf. v. 43; i.e. make your refuge in the precarious places where birds make their nests – on the edges of chasms or gorges (contrast the nesting image of 22.23 as a figure of security).

A brief poetic section on the transmogrification of Moab (v. 18a) is expanded by two prose insertions (vv. 21–24, 26–27). In the poem the descent of Moab (from the throne, cf. Isa. 47.1) to sit on the dry ground (or in the excrement cf v. 26; Rudolph) is attested by questioning those who flee (vv. 19–20). Moab's power is broken (v. 20) and its inhabitants are advised to leave the cities in order to find protection in the steep sides of the gorges where birds make their nests (v. 28). The poem graphically conveys the sense of Moab's collapse by focusing on the fleeing inhabitants and the telling of the sad tale by the river Arnon (v. 20).

The flow of the poem is interrupted at two points: vv. 21–24 list the cities upon which judgment (*mišpāṭ*) has come (the names do not appear to be in any particular order, cf. Rudolph, 281), and vv. 26–27 describe Moab's plight in images more akin to vv. 11–12 than their present position. Both these pieces are in prose (though NEB, JPSB and some exegetes treat vv. 26–27 as poetry) and make observations about Moab which are tangential to the poem in vv. 18–20, 25, 28. The imagery of v. 26 shares with vv. 11–12 a setting in the world of brewing and wine-making, but the metaphors are used differently. Moab is to be made drunk (cf. 25.15–17; 51.6, 39) because it has opposed (*higdīl*, i.e. vaunted himself against) Yahweh (the how is not explained, but cf. v. 27). In such drunkenness Moab will be humiliated: wallowing about in vomit (cf. 25.27) is a figure of military destruction drawn from the experiences of being drunk and incapable. As in all human communities such degrading behaviour makes the victim an object of hilarity (*śᵉḥōq*, 'derision') to those who observe the floundering about and eventual collapse in the vomit and excrement produced by such drunkenness. Thus Moab is to be humiliated for its opposition to Yahweh by its attitude to Israel (v. 27). This is a rather different explanation of Moab's fate from the hubris and overweening self-confidence of vv. 7, 11, 14, 29–30 (cf. v. 42, where Moab's opposition [*higdīl*] to Yahweh is not linked to its attitude towards Israel). It reflects antagonism between Israel and Moab but does not identify the occasion (if occasion it be) of the hostility between the two nations. As neighbouring states Israel and Moab (and all the other small states) must have watched each other jealously over the centuries, and the fall of one would have been an occasion of great joy for the other (the OAN reflect the nationalistic envy in a most thorough-going fashion). Moabite taunts against Israel are viewed as grounds for the destruction of Moab (cf. Zeph. 2.8–11), and such taunts may have been a particular feature of Israelite-Moabite relations during the period when Babylon devastated Judah in 597 and 587. Nothing definite may be deduced from v. 27, but Moab's constant mocking of Israel (quite unjustified from an Israelite viewpoint) is turned around in v. 26 so that Moab also (*gam-hū'*, '*he* also') becomes an object of mockery. Israel's innocence is protested in the question 'was he found among thieves?'. Was this why every time Moab mentioned him there was a shaking of the head at him? How different this protestation of innocence or assertion of *amour-propre* is from the denunciations of the nation throughout the Jeremiah tradition! The shaking of the head (cf. 18.16) is quite justified in the poems and sermons making up the bulk of the book, but here in the OAN such criticism is out of place. Nationalistic pride turns the enmity of the nations into opposition against Yahweh and therefore into grounds for the divine judgment to fall on the mockers of Israel *and* Yahweh (cf. 50.29; 51.5, 11, 24, 35, 49–51).

48.29–39

29 'We have heard of the pride of Moab –
he is very proud –
of his loftiness, his pride, and his arrogance,
and the haughtiness of his heart.
30 I know his insolence, says the LORD;
his boasts are false,
his deeds are false.
31 Therefore I wail for Moab;
I cry out for all Moab;
for the men of Kir-heres I mourn.
32 More than for Jazer I weep for you,
O vine of Sibmah!
Your branches passed over the sea,
reached as far as Jazer;
upon your summer fruits and your vintage
the destroyer has fallen.
33 Gladness and joy have been taken away
from the fruitful land of Moab;
I have made the wine cease from the wine presses;
no one treads them with shouts of joy;
the shouting is not the shout of joy.

34 Heshbon and Elealeh cry out; as far as Jahaz they utter their voice, from Zoar to Horonaim and Eglath-shelishiyah. For the waters of Nimrim also have become desolate. 35 And I will bring to an end in Moab, says the LORD, him who offers sacrifice in the high place and burns incense to his god. 36 Therefore my heart moans for Moab like a flute, and my heart moans like a flute for the men of Kir-heres; therefore the riches they gained have perished.

37 For every head is shaved and every beard cut off; upon all the hands

are gashes, and on the loins is sackcloth. 38 On all the housetops of Moab and in the squares there is nothing but lamentation; for I have broken Moab like a vessel for which no one cares, says the LORD. 39 How it is broken! How they wail! How Moab has turned his back in shame! So Moab has become a derision and a horror to all that are round about him.'

---

[29] MT *šāmaʿnū*, '*we* have heard': G *ēkousa*, 'I have heard'; this is the only we-style form in 48 (v. 14 is reported speech), cf. Bardtke 1936, 245, for analysis. Cf. vv. 29–33 and Isa. 16.6–10; v. 36a and Isa. 16.11; v. 35 and Isa. 16.12; v. 34 and Isa. 15.4a, 5a, 6a. On Isa. 15–16 see Rudolph, 281–2; 1963, 130–43; Clements 1980, 150–6; Kaiser 1974, 57–75; v. 29 = Isa. 16.6 with variations (MT *gābᵉhō ū*, 'his loftiness and', is lacking in G; Isa. 16.6; *wᵉrum libbō*, 'and the haughtiness of his mind', is not in Isa. 16.6, which has *lō'-kēn baddāyw*, 'his boasts are false' cf. v. 30). **[30]** MT *ʿebᵉrātō wᵉlō'-kēn*, 'his arrogance and (is) not right': MT should be repunctuated (i.e. *atnah* shifted back a phrase) in order to read *wᵉlō'-kēn* with next word (cf. Isa. 16.6; BHS as in Rudolph, 280); G *erga*, 'works', for MT 'arrogance'. G lacks *nᵉ'um yhwh*, 'says Yahweh'. MT *baddāyw*, 'his idle talk': i.e. empty boastings, cf. 50.36; Job 11.3; G *ouchi to hikanon autou*, 'is it not his sufficiency?', i.e. 'is it not enough for him?' = *dayyō*. MT *lō'-kēn ʿāśū*, lit. 'not right *they* do'. **[31]** Cf. Isa. 16.7. MT *'el-'anšē qīr-ḥereś yehgeh*, 'for the men of Kir-heres *he* moans': Isa. 16.7 *la'ᵃšīšē*, 'for the raisin-cakes of (Kir-heres)', i.e. delicacies (cf. S. of Sol. 2.5; Hos. 3.1; II Sam. 6.19) associated with Kir-heres; *yehgeh* is the indefinite 'one' (a mistake for *'ehgeh*, 'I moan', cf. Bardtke 1936, 245; Q^{Or}). G lacks *ūlᵉmō'āb*, 'and for Moab', and duplicates '(Kir-)*ḥereś*' as *auchmou*, 'drought', i.e. dry place (?). **[32]** Cf. Isa. 16.8–9; v. 32 is shorter and uses only some of the lines from Isa. 16. MT *mibbᵉkī*, lit. 'from weeping': idiomatic for greater weeping *than* . . . but Isa. 16.9 *bibᵉkī yaʿzēr*, '*with* the weeping of Jazer (I weep)'; G *hōs klauthmon Iazēr*, '*as* the weeping of Jazer' = *kibᵉkī*. Rudolph, 282, suggests *mabbᵉkē*, 'springs' (*nbk*), cf. Job 38.16; i.e. springs of Jazer. Landes 1956, 31, connects *bky* with Ug. *npk*, 'fountain, well, source' (cf. Christensen 1975, 239); there may be an element of word-play here (Bright, 321). MT *haggepen śibmāh*, 'the vine Sibmah': G, Isa. 16.9 lack article; cf. 2.21; 6.9 for *gepen* as a figure of Israel. Christensen deletes the phrase for metrical reasons as a secondary conflation from Isa. 16.8 (though the citation is from 16.9!). MT *ʿad yām yaʿzēr*, 'as far as *the sea of* Jazer': *yām* repeated from previous clause (lacking in Isa. 16.8; G). MT *wᵉʿal-bᵉṣīrēk*, 'and upon your vintage': a few mss, Isa. 16.9, *wᵉʿal-qᵉṣīrēk*, 'and upon your harvest'. MT *šōdēd nāpāl*, 'the destroyer has fallen': Isa. 16.9, *hēdād nāpāl*, 'the shout has fallen', cf. v. 33; 25.30; 51.14. **[33]** Cf. Isa. 16.10. MT *mikkarmel ūmē'ereṣ mō'āb*, 'from Carmel *and from* the land of Moab': RSV, NEB combine these terms, though G lacks the first and Isa. 16.10 the second. They are clearly variants combined here in 48.33. MT *wᵉyayin* *mīqābīm hišbattī*, 'and the wine from the presses I have made to cease': Isa. 16.10, *lō' yayin bay^eqābīm*, 'there is no wine in the presses'; G lacks negative force because it reads *prōi* 'early' (= *haškēm*?) for *hišbattī*, cf. G Isa. 16.10. MT *lō'-yid^erōk hēdād*, 'the shout does not tread'! Isa. 16.10 *lō'-yid^erōk haddōrēk*, 'the treader does not tread': i.e. the grapes are not trodden into wine. MT *hēdād lō' hēdād* lit. 'a shout not a shout': a too subtle word-play, a mistake, or a gloss; Isa. 16.10, *hēdād hišbattī*, 'I have caused to cease shout'; i.e. the shouting associated with grape-treading is gone. Cf. 25.30, where *hēdād* alludes to the battle shout as well as the jubilant noise of workers producing the new season's wine. In Isa. 16.9 the shout (*hēdād*) which falls is that of battle (v. 32 *šōdēd*, 'destroyer'); thus the pun here may reflect 'the shouting (is of battle) not the shouting (of drunken grape-treaders)' in a context where images of grapes, wine, and drunkenness can mean disaster (vv. 12, 26, 33; 25.15–17, 27; 51.39). The same images may denote great joy (31.5, 12), but v. 33a clearly indicates that the context is not one of gladness and joy. Cf. 51.14 for the battle shout (*hēdād*). G *oude deilēs, ouk epoiēsan aidad*, 'nor in the evening, they did not make shouting': not helpful, but an attempt at translating an awkward text. Rudolph favours reading a verbal form of the second *hēdād*, i.e. *y^ehōdād* or *y^ehuddād*, 'burst into (song)', cf. BHS; Bardtke 1936, 246n. deletes the phrase as a gloss. Christensen 1975, 239, attaches the *m* of the next word (v. 34) to *hēdād* (i.e. *hyddm*) as an enclitic and reads 'The shout of harvest is no longer voiced'. **[34]** Cf. Isa. 15.4–6. RSV corrects to 'Heshbon and Elealeh cry out' from Isa. 15.4a: MT 'from the cry of Heshbon *to* Elealeh *to* Jahaz . . .'. 34–39 are prose, though v. 37 may be regarded as poetry (cf. Bright, 318), with vv. 34–36 as a conglomerate formed from Isa. 15.2–6; 16.11–12 (cf. Schottroff 1966, 184–7; Bardtke 1936, 246–7). **[35]** MT *ma^{ʿa}leh bāmāh*, lit. 'the one who raises a high place': something is missing here; G *anabainonta epi bōmon*, 'going up *on* high place', may be considered an improvement. Rudolph inserts *ʿōlāh* (cf. T) *ʿal* (with G) *hab*(*bāmāh*), i.e. '(one who offers up) a sacrifice upon the (high place)'; a double loss of *ʿlh*, but cf. Driver 1937–38, 124. Cf. Notes on 44.3, 5, 8, 15, 17–19, 21, 23, 25 for *qṭr* as 'burn' sacrifice in general rather than RSV's more limited 'burn incense'. Cf. Isa. 16.12 for reference to a different Moabite practice in the cult; the offering of sacrifice to the god(s) here is more in keeping with the Jeremiah tradition. **[36]** Cf. Isa. 16.11; 15.7. MT *yitrat ʿāśāh 'ābādū*, lit. 'the abundance he has gotten they are destroyed': i.e. the accumulated riches have gone; the similar phrase (*yitrāh ʿāśāh*) in Isa. 15.7 is developed in a different way. Christensen 1975, 239, transposes 'for the waters of Nimrim have become desolate' (v. 34; cf. Isa. 15.6) to the end of v. 36. **[37]** Cf. Isa. 15.2b–3. G *en panti topō*, '(every head) *in every place* (shall be shaved)'. Many mss, Vrs read 'all' before *māt^enayim*, 'loins', i.e. on *every* waist is sackcloth. Cf. 16.6; 41.5; 47.5 for the ritual marks of mourning. **[38]** Cf. Isa. 15.3. G lacks *kullōh mispēd*, 'all of it (is) mourning': i.e. nothing but mourning. MT *kikᵉlî 'ên-ḥēpeṣ bô*, 'as a vessel for which no one cares': cf. 22.28, where the same phrase (*'im* instead of *kᵉ*) is used of the discarded Coniah. NEB treats 'says Yahweh' as addition. **[39]** MT *'êk ḥattāh hêlîlû* 'how it is broken, they wail': cf. v. 20, where *ḥat* also should be read (BHS); A, Symm lack *hêlîlû* ('they howl' or 'howl'). Rudolph, 282, treats as an addition from v. 20 (cf BHS). Cf. v. 26 for *wᵉhāyāh . . . liśḥōq*, 'and (Moab) shall become a derision'; 17.17 for *mᵉḥittāh*, 'terror', i.e. object of terror.

The second part of 48 (dividing the chapter into vv. 1–28, 29–47 is an alternative way of reading the poem to its division into various parts) consists of poems and prose statements which continue the denunciation of Moab intertwined with laments for its fall. Much of vv. 29–38 is based on Isa. 15.2–7 and 16.6–11, and part two of the poem may be regarded as secondary development of vv. 1–28 (cf. Christensen 1975, 244). A comparison of vv. 29–38 and Isa. 15–16 will reveal a wide diversity of influence, usage and placement of the phrases and motifs of Isa. 15–16 in 48 and the question of originality of source, if raised at all, is perhaps not as easily answered as many exegetes think it is. An early dating of Isa. 15–16 (cf. Rudolph 1963, 142) would settle the matter in favour of the Isaiah tradition, but the problems of determining origin, date and reference of Isa. 15–16 must counsel the wise exegete to exercise a cautious agnosticism about the relation between the two different uses of the material on Moab (cf. Kaiser 1974, 60–65).

The hubris of Moab is stressed in v. 29 (cf. Isa. 16.6; G *hubrin Mōab*), and in v. 30 that arrogance is denounced by the deity (only in MT) as false. As in Isa. 16.6–7, the response to such hubristic arrogance is lamentation and mourning, though in 48.31 it is the speaker who wails for Moab rather than Moab who is invited to wail over its own plight. The focus of the mourning is the destruction of the land, in particular the cessation of the great wine-making production of Sibmah (hence the epithet '*vine* Sibmah'). The late summer harvesting reaches its climax in the vintage when a good season's hard work is crowned with the pleasures of the grape. Now mourning must descent upon Moab because the joy and pleasure of that occasion are gone, and the noise of drunken celebration (*hêdād*) is in reality the din of battle (*hêdād*, cf. 25.30–31). The mourning spreads throughout Moab (v. 34): everybody is shaved, gashed and dressed in sackcloth, everywhere there is lamentation, and even the speaker's heart wails like a flute for the Moabites. Yahweh has broken Moab like a discarded ceramic pot and, in fulfilment of v. 26, it has become an object of derision and terror to its neighbours. The section may well be secondary (cf. Rudolph, 280–2), but its images graphically lament the destruction of a proud people.

48.40–47

40 For thus says the LORD:
'Behold, one shall fly swiftly like an eagle,
and spread his wings against Moab;
41 the cities shall be taken
and the strongholds seized.
The heart of the warriors of Moab shall be in that day
like the heart of a woman in her pangs;
42 Moab shall be destroyed and be no longer a people,
because he magnified himself against the LORD.
43 Terror, pit, and snare
are before you, O inhabitant of Moab!
says the LORD.
44 He who flees from the terror
shall fall into the pit,
and he who climbs out of the pit
shall be caught in the snare.
For I will bring these things upon Moab
in the year of their punishment,
says the LORD.
45 In the shadow of Heshbon
fugitives stop without strength;
for a fire has gone forth from Heshbon,
a flame from the house of Sihon;
it has destroyed the forehead of Moab,
the crown of the sons of tumult.
46 Woe to you, O Moab!
The people of Chemosh is undone;
for your sons have been taken captive,
and your daughters into captivity.
47 Yet I will restore the fortunes of Moab
in the latter days, says the LORD.'
Thus far is the judgment on Moab.

---

[40] G lacks all of v. 40 except 'for thus says the lord'. Cf. 49.22 for elements of vv. 40–41. Many exegetes follow G and delete the rest of v. 40 as secondary from 49.22 (e.g. Rudolph, 283; contrary view in Weiser, 401 n. 3, based on the theory that G omits doublets, but against this position cf. Janzen 1973, 94–5). Cf. Ezek. 17.3 for the eagle image; Isa. 8.8b for the wings motif as a figure of invasion (or is it protection?). **[41]** MT *nitpāśāh*, 'is seized': Q^{Or} plur., but for plur. nouns with sing. verbs cf. Rudolph, 284. G lacks v. 41b: cf. 49.22 where the line occurs with Edom in place of Moab; some exegetes delete it here as an addition from 49.22 (cf. BHS). Cf. 4.31 for the birth-pangs seizing a woman and 30.6 for the transformation of men (*geber*, warriors?) into women in a time of awesome trouble. **[42]** Cf. v. 26 for *kī 'al-yhwh higdīl*, 'because he magnified himself against Yahweh'. Bardtke 1936, 249, concludes the poem with v. 42 (omitting vv. 37–41, 43–47) and uses this line as the theological grounding of the trilogy of poems in 48 (explained in the light of the Deuteronomistic reform, cf. Bardtke, 247–8). **[43]** Cf. Isa. 24.17 (*hā'āreṣ*, 'of the earth', instead of 'of Moab'; lacking *nᵉ'um yhwh*, 'says Yahweh'). G lacks 'says Yahweh'. MT *paḥad wāpaḥat wāpāḥ*, 'terror and pit and trap': fine example of assonance in Heb. **[44]** Cf. Isa. 24.18. K *hnys*; Q *hannās*, 'he who flees' (as Isa. 24.18, but lacking *wᵉhāyāh*, 'and it shall be . . .'), K = ? (refugee perhaps). If Isa. 24 belongs to the post-exilic period (cf. Kaiser 1974, 173–9; Miller 1976, 108), then this section of 48 must be from an equally late era (i.e. post-catastrophe of 587). The argument of v. 44a,b is essentially that of Amos 5.19. Minor variations between v. 44 and Isa. 24.18 include *mippᵉnē*, 'from' – *miqqōl*, 'from the sound of', and *min*, 'from' – *mittōk*, 'from the midst of'; the third line is quite different in both places. MT *kī-'ābī' 'ēleyhā*, 'for I will bring *upon her*': G *hoti epaxō tauta*, 'for I will bring *these things*' = *'ēlleh*; MT *'ēleyhā* and *'el-mō'āb*, 'against Moab', are probably variants. **[45]** Cf. Num. 21.28; 24.17b. S lacks v. 45a. MT *'ēš yāṣā'*, 'a fire has gone forth': many mss, Num. 21.28 read *yāṣᵉ'āh* (correct gender matching). MT *wᵉlehābāh mibbēn sīḥōn*, lit. 'and a flame from between Sihon': a few mss read *mibbēt*, 'from the house of' (i.e. the capital city, cf. Bright, 319; NEB 'the palace of Sihon'); Num. 21.28 *miqqiryat*, 'from the town of'. MT *pᵉ'at mō'āb*, 'the temples of Moab': i.e. the hair (lit. 'corner') on the side of the head (cf. 9.25 [EV 26]; 25.23; 49.32 where the phrase describes tribes who practise cutting their side locks); a personification of Moab as a man whose head has been destroyed by fire. Cf. Num. 24.17b. **[46]** Cf. Num. 21.19. MT *'ābad 'am-kᵉmōš*, 'the people of Chemosh is destroyed': or 'he has destroyed'; some Vrs, Num. 21.29 *'ābadtā*, 'you have destroyed'. **[47]** Cf. 30–31 for the 'restoration of the fortunes' motif (see Notes on 29.14); applied here to Moab and elsewhere to the Ammonites (49.6) and Elam (49.39). A hint of mercy towards Moab may be detected in Isa. 16.1–5 (contrast Zeph. 2.8–11). The phrase 'in the latter days' refers to the future (i.e. when all the destruction is over) without eschatological overtones (cf. Rudolph, 284), cf. 23.20; 30.24; Num. 24.1. It is equivalent to 'afterward' (*'aḥ^a rē-kēn*) in 46.26; 49.6. MT *'ad-hēnnāh mišpāṭ mō'āb*, 'thus far the judgment of Moab': cf. 51.64. The sheer length of the oracle against Moab has constrained an editor to add a note indicating its termination.

A further section comprising vv. 40–42, 43–44, 45–46, 47 concludes the lengthy poem against Moab and is presented as an oracular utterance (G is considerably shorter). The poem effectively ends at v. 42 (cf. Bardtke 1936, 249; Rudolph, 284, treats vv. 40b, 41b, 43–47 as secondary) with a theological explanation for Moab's destruction: *against Yahweh he magnified himself* (cf. v. 26). This assertion is neither explained nor spelled out, but it equates the fate of Moab with its hubris (cf. v. 29), and hubris is always regarded as a fatal defect in human communities (cf. Isa. 2.12–17; 10.5–15). Whether Moabite arrogance against Judah during the Babylonian slaughter of the Judaeans and the destruction of Jerusalem or long-standing antagonism between the neighbouring states is behind this accusation cannot be determined, but the OAN genre is clear testimony to the hostility felt by Judaeans towards their neighbours. Any defeat of or setback to the surrounding states would be a cause for Judaean celebration and yet fully in line with the fundamental religious outlook shared by Judah *and* Moab. The Moabite Stone (cf. Pritchard 1969, 320–1) provides evidence of the close affinity between Israelite and Moabite beliefs, and indeed the inscription 'reads almost like a chapter from the Bible' (Gibson 1971, 71). This shared religious outlook permits the defeat of the one to be the work of the other's god, hence the destruction of Moab becomes the triumph of Yahweh (just as Jerusalem's destruction in 587 may have been regarded as Chemosh's defeat of an old enemy) and Moab's offence self-aggrandizement against Yahweh (i.e. against Yahweh's people, cf. vv. 26–27; Zeph. 2.8, 10).

The concluding poems in vv. 43–46 contain elements to be found in Isa. 24.17–18b and Num. 21.19, 28; 24.17b. They therefore can hardly be considered original to 48, but reflect the many strands of anti-Moabite material in the Bible. Added to the poem of 48 they extend the denunciations of Moab (though vv. 43–44 must be regarded as a free-floating piece because in Isa. 24.17–18b it has no connections with Moab). These codas depict the ruination of Moab but add nothing of a serious nature to the argument of the poem. The shorter G edition lacking vv. 45–47 ends the poem on the note of terror for all the inhabitants of Moab in the year of divine judgment for them (MT adds oracular indicators).

The apparent reversal of the poem in v. 47 (cf. 49.6, 39) may surprise the modern reader but, in the light of 30–31, should not. After the destruction of Moab there will come a time when Yahweh (Judaean perspective) will restore the fortunes (*šûb šᵉbût*) of the devastated nation. This penultimate postscript simply asserts a future recovery of Moab. Nothing miraculous or wonderful is posited of this revival of Moab's fortunes – only a recognition of that nation's survival after the devastations depicted in the poem. A similar explanation may be offered for 30–31 (developed at greater length because the book is the product of Judaean communities which survived the destructions of the sixth century) and the use of the restoration of the fortunes motif throughout the book of Jeremiah. The motif is a statement about survival. Here it refers to Moab which, in spite of the depredations described repeatedly in the poem, survived at least to the period when 48 was edited in its final form (MT). The fact that similar motifs are used of different nations (e.g. Judah, Moab, Ammon, Elam, even Egypt) indicates a fair degree of stereotyping in the language of the tradition and demands a conventionalist interpretation of such motifs. Disaster is brought about by Yahweh (whatever the means may appear to be in the sphere of social reality) and the subsequent survival of such catastrophes represents his restoration of the fortunes of the nation so devastated. This restoration consists of the rebuilding of the community and the renewal of traditional modes of living (cf. 1.10; spelled out in 30–31). A further example of the conventionalist nature of many of the motifs in the tradition may be seen in the mourning language used of Moab in vv. 31–32, 36 (cf Isa. 16.7–10). The speaker (the 'I' of the poem) mourns for the destruction of Moab, just as the speaker of 4.19–21, 8.18–9.1; 10.19–20 bewails the disasters which have overtaken city and people. Whether these are the utterances of the nation or city personified or of the poet on behalf of either, they are conventional expressions of lamentation. It is therefore unnecessary to develop, in the case of the poems lamenting Jerusalem's fall, a theory of the prophet Jeremiah's self-identification with his people because such a theory then would be required for his self-identification with Moab! This would be an absurd theory. It is better exegesis to recognize how conventional these mourning songs are and to understand *all* of the poems as expressions of grief traditionally uttered over the fallen.

A wise editor has noted the excessive length of the poem about Moab and has brought it to a final conclusion (cf. G) with a note to the effect that 'here ends the sentence on Moab' (NEB). A similar editorial point is provided for the even longer attack on Babylon (cf. 51.64), but there it has a different effect. The meaning of the line 'thus far . . .' (*'ad-hēnnāh*) is not entirely clear: it is understood here to be a closing notice terminating the poem (just as 51.64 indicates the end of Jeremiah's words), but there are other interpretations of it. It has been seen as a temporal note indicating that until this point (i.e. the editor's notation) judgment (*mišpāṭ*) has been Moab's experience (e.g. Rothstein, 796). Thus things may be about to change for Moab. Until the new age of restoration dawns Moab must face destruction, but 'in the latter days' the nation will be rebuilt by Yahweh. A different explanation allows for the possibility that the phrase is a marginal note originally intended to mark off one oracle from another in older manuscripts, perhaps before the titular information was added to the poems (cf. Duhm, 352). Such marginal glosses may get displaced in the transmission of manuscripts and allowance must be made for this note being out of place (perhaps originally after v. 42 or v. 44).

49.1–6

1 Concerning the Ammonites.
Thus says the Lord:
'Has Israel no sons?
Has he no heir?
Why then has Milcom dispossessed Gad,
and his people settled in its cities?
2 Therefore, behold, the days are coming,
says the Lord,
when I will cause the battle cry to be heard
against Rabbah of the Ammonites;
it shall become a desolate mound,
and its villages shall be burned with fire;
then Israel shall dispossess those who dispossessed him,
says the Lord.'
3 'Wail, O Heshbon, for Ai is laid waste!
Cry, O daughters of Rabbah!
Gird yourselves with sackcloth,
lament, and run to and fro among the hedges!

For Milcom shall go into exile,
with his priests and his princes.
4 Why do you boast of your valleys,
O faithless daughter,
who trusted in her treasures, saying,
"Who will come against me?"
5 Behold, I will bring terror upon you,
says the Lord GOD of hosts,
from all who are round about you,
and you shall be driven out, every man straight before him,
with none to gather the fugitives.
6 But afterward I will restore the fortunes of the Ammonites, says
the LORD.'

[MT 49.1–6] = G 30.1–5 (Rahlfs 1935, 30. 17–21). **[1]** MT *malkām*, 'their king': Vrs Milkom, i.e. Molech, patron deity of Ammon, depicted here as acquiring Israelite territory by conquest. A good example of the religious ideas and language common to Israel, Moab and Ammon and typical of 48; 49.1–6. G 'Gilead' for 'Gad': cf. Num. 32.29 for Gad's possession of Gilead. **[2]** Rudolph, 286, regards v. 2a as an addition (cf. BHS) to be deleted as in 48.12; the line is in G. G lacks *b^enē-'ammōn*, 'of the Ammonites': Rabbah (cf. v. 3) is the capital of the territory (cf. modern-day Amman, capital of Jordan). Cf. 4.19 for 'the battle cry'; 30.18 for mound (*tēl*). MT *ūb^enōteyhā* lit. 'and her daughters': i.e. the outlying villages dependent upon Rabbah; G *kai bomoi autēs*, 'and her high places' = *ūbāmōteyhā* (but cf. v. 3). Rudolph, 289 treats v. 2d as an addition based perhaps on Zeph. 2.9b; cf. Cornill, 474, but Weiser, 404 n. 2, discerns a different logic in Zeph. 2.9b from Jer. 49.2b. MT *w^eyāraš yiśrā'ēl 'et-yōr^ešayw*, 'then Israel shall dispossess *those who dispossessed him*': G *kai paralalēmpsetai Israēl tēn archēn autou*, 'and Israel shall take possession of *his dominion*'. G lacks *'āmar yhwh*, 'said Yahweh': cf. 48.8, where *'^ašer 'āmar yhwh* suggests a citation; perhaps MT alludes here to the belief expressed by Zeph. 2.9b. **[3]** MT *hēlīlū ḥešbōn kī šudd^edāh-'ay*, 'Howl, Heshbon, for Ai is laid waste': Heshbon, though near the border, is a Moabite town (cf. 48.2, 34, 45) and no Ammonite Ai is known; Volz, 411, reads *šōdēd 'ālāh*, 'the destroyer has come up' (cf. 48.18), followed by Rudolph (cf. BHS); Duhm, 353, and Cornill, 475, favour reading *hā'īr*, 'the city (i.e. the capital) is destroyed'. MT *w^ehitšōṭaṭ^enāh bagg^edērōt*, 'and rush to and fro among the walls (i.e. hedges or sheep-folds)': lacking in G. NEB 'and score your bodies with gashes': *šūṭ*, 'rove about', but *šōṭ*, 'scourge, whip', as verb would support NEB translation (cf. Driver 1937–38, 124–5). Giesebrecht, 241, and other exegetes (e.g. Duhm, Rudolph) favour reading *gdd* for *gdr* (cf. *d-r* shift in 48.37), i.e. *mitgōd^edīm* (41.5) 'gashing yourselves' or *big^edudōt* (BHS) 'with gashes', cf. the funeral rites of 16.6; 41.5; 48.37.

MT is incomprehensible. MT *malkām*, 'their king': cf. v. 1 (G *Melchol*); cf. 48.7 for 'his priests and his princes together (shall go into exile)'; also Amos 1.15. **[4]** MT *bāʿᵉmāqīm zāb ʿimᵉqēk*, lit. 'in the valleys flowing your valley': G *en tois pediois*, 'in the plains'. Duhm, 353, explains *zb* as *z* (= *zeh*) *bᵉ* 'that is, in your valley' (explaining 'valleys'); followed by Rudolph (deleting 'valleys' cf. BHS) and others (cf. Driver 1937–38, 125). A different explanation is offered by Dahood 1959, 166–7, who understands *ʿmq* to mean 'strength' as in Ugaritic and reads MT as 'Why boast of your strength (enclitic *m*), your ebbing strength?'; followed by Bright, 324–5, and Christensen 1975, 225. Cf. 47.5. MT *habbat haššōbēbāh*, 'O faithless daughter': epithet used of virgin Israel in 31.22; G *thugatēr atimias*, 'dishonoured daughter' = *bat habbūšāh*. Duhm prefers *habbat hašša'ᵃnannāh*, 'O complacent daughter', cf. 48.11 (*ša'ᵃnan mō'āb*), followed by Rudolph (cf. BHS). Cf. 48.7 for the same image of trusting in treasures (i.e. strongholds?). A few mss, Vrs have 'who says' before 'Who will come against me?' (cf. Lam. 4.12 for the conviction of impregnability). **[5]** MT *paḥad . . . mikkol-sᵉbībāyik*, 'terror . . . from every side': i.e. from all around; cf. *māgor missābīb*, 'terror on every side' (6.25; 20.3, 10; 46.5; 49.29; cf. Christensen 1973). G *eipe kurios*, 'says the lord': lacking *'ᵃdōnāy . . . ṣᵉbā'ōt*, 'lord . . . hosts'. Rudolph deletes the whole phrase as an addition. G lacks *lannōdēd*, 'the wanderers', i.e. the stragglers (cf. NEB). **[6]** Lacking in G. Cf. 46.26 for the 'afterward' motif and 48.47; 49.39 for the 'restoration of the fortunes' idea. A prose addition to the poem against the Ammonites representing the subsequent revival of Ammonite fortunes (contrast Zeph. 2.9, which envisages a permanent wasteland for Moab and the Ammonites).

Ammon

The lengthy collection of material on Moab is followed by a series of much shorter pieces against neighbouring and more distant nations. In the first poem the Ammonites are the target of divine punishment (cf. Amos 1.13–15; Zeph. 2.8–11; Ezek. 21.20, 28–32; 25.1–7 for other anti-Ammonite statements). Rabbah, the chief town of the territory, is the focus of the oracular announcement and, as in all the OAN, its fate represents great destruction with concomitant mourning, exile and the reversal of national hubris. Nemesis pursues Ammon in this poem because of Ammonite domination of Gileadite territory. The Ammonite god Milcom having dispossessed Israel will in turn be dispossessed by Israel when the Ammonite towns are burned and Rabbah reduced to a mound (*tēl*). Echoes of the poems against Moab can be detected in vv. 1–5 (e.g. the reference to Heshbon in v. 3), especially the hubristic attitude of the nation (v. 4, cf. 48.7, 29). The brevity of the piece allows for no development of theme, variations or speaker's responses: great mourning comes upon the people (v. 3), but the poet does not join in the lamentation (contrast 48.31–35). An additional note in v. 6 recognizes the revival of Ammonite fortunes in a period after the devastations celebrated in the poem.

Some exegetes date the poem to *c.* 617 in the time of Josiah (e.g. Bardtke 1936, 251; Christensen 1975, 227), when Judaean nationalistic policy was one of territorial expansion. There is little in the poem to confirm or deny such an interpretation, and its stereotypical elements divorce it, to a great extent, from a specific situation, though v. 1 may point to some Ammonite infiltration of Judaean land. Ammon's defeat is inevitably the work of Yahweh, just as Gilead's loss is expressed in terms of Milcom's possession of land and cities. Theomachy, i.e. the battle of the gods, is an important element behind many of the poems in the collection of oracles against the nations because the defeat of a nation is the defeat of its god. Thus the fluctuating fortunes of Judah and its neighbours represent the flux of divine power and loss, though Judaean theology hardly permits the entertaining of the notion that Yahweh's defeat is entailed in Judaean disasters. Each nation presumably exempts its god from defeat but allows credit to be taken for the defeat of other nations (cf. Moabite Stone, the oracles of Second Isaiah). The brevity of vv. 1–5 does not allow for the development of themes and motifs found in the longer poems, so it is difficult to determine the extent to which the speaker is hostile towards Ammon or 'seems almost to express sympathy for the Ammonites' (Hyatt, 1117). That hint of sympathy may be the contribution of the editor who appended v. 6 to the poem and allowed for Yahweh's revival of the fortunes of Ammon, but in view of 46.26b; 48.47; 49.39 sympathy may be too strong a word for such stereotypical notes.

49.7–11

7 Concerning Edom.
Thus says the LORD of hosts:
'Is wisdom no more in Teman?
Has counsel perished from the prudent?
Has their wisdom vanished?

8 Flee, turn back, dwell in the depths,
O inhabitants of Dedan!
For I will bring the calamity of Esau upon him,
the time when I punish him.
9 If grape-gatherers came to you,
would they not leave gleanings?
If thieves came by night,
would they not destroy only enough for themselves?
10 But I have stripped Esau here,
I have uncovered his hiding places,
and he is not able to conceal himself.
His children are destroyed, and his brothers,
and his neighbours; and he is no more.
11 Leave your fatherless children, I will keep them alive;
and let your widows trust in me.'

[MT 49.7–11] = G 29.8–12. **[7]** G lacks 'of hosts'. The interrogative of MT (*ha'ēn 'ōd*, 'is there no longer . . . ?) is a simple assertion in G (*ouk estin eti*, 'there is no longer . . .'). MT *nisr^eḥāh ḥokmātām*, '(has) their wisdom been let loose': *srḥ*, 'go free, be unrestrained'; Rudolph, 288, 'rancid', cf. modern Heb. *srḥ*, 'stink'. NEB 'decayed'; Bright, 328, 'gone stale'. Cf. 7.28 for a similar structure to 'counsel has perished . . .'. **[8]** MT *hop^enū*, 'be turned back': Hophal imperative; Ehrlich 1912, 360, reads *hiṣṣāp^enū*, 'hide yourselves'. MT *'ēd 'ēśāw*, 'the calamity of Esau': G *duskola epoiēsen*, 'he has done (i.e. *'āśāh*) peevishly'; i.e. behaved badly. **[9]** Cf. Obad. 5. The image of gleaning appears in 6.9. MT *hišḥītū dayyām*, 'they would destroy their sufficiency': i.e. they would destroy no more than they needed for themselves; G *epithēsousi cheira autōn*, 'they shall lay their hands on' = *yāšītū yādām*. **[10]** Cf. Obad. 6. MT *ḥāśaptī*, 'I have stripped bare': cf. 13.26; Obad. 6, *neḥp^eśū*, 'is searched out', i.e. exposed. MT *w^eneḥbāh*, lit. 'and is hidden': GV and modern exegetes (e.g. Ehrlich, Rudolph and others) read infin. absol. *w^enaḥbōh*, 'to hide (themselves)'. MT *šuddad zar'ō w^e'eḥāyw*, 'his seed is destroyed and his brothers': Rudolph regards 'and his brothers' as incomprehensible, deletes it and transposes *w^e'ēnennū*, 'and he is no more', to follow 'his seed is destroyed' (cf. Bardtke 1936, 253). Christensen 1975, 230 understands *zr'* as *z^erō'a*, 'arm' (cf. G *epicheira adelphou autou*, '*forearm* of his brother') in the sense of 'strength', cf. 17.5, and reads the line as 'The strength of his allies is shattered'. MT *w^e'ēnennū*, 'and he is no more': cf. Symm, G^L, *ouk estin hos erei*, 'there is none who speaks', followed by Rudolph (also Bardtke) as *w^e'ēn 'ōmēr* (cf. BHS). Driver 1937–38, 125, transfers *'āz^ebāh* from v. 11 and reads *w^e'ēnām 'ōz^ebō*, 'and there was none to help him'. **[11]** MT *tib^eṭāḥū*, 'let them trust': masc. ending for fem. = *tib^eṭāḥnāh* (BHS).

Edom

Moab, Ammon, and now Edom (cf. different order in 25.21 and G) are grouped together in MT (the piece on Damascus interrupts G 29–31). The Edom piece is more like the Moab poem than the Ammon one in that it has been extended by prose material and shares common elements with OAN in other traditions (e.g. Obadiah and Isa. 34.5–15). Hostility towards Edom is to be found in many biblical sources and especially in relation to the Babylonian destruction of Judah (cf. Lam. 4.21–22; Ps. 137.1; Isa. 11.14b; 21.11–12; 63.1–6; Amos 1.11–12; Ezek. 25.12–14; 32.29; 35; Ps. 60.9–10 [MT 10–11]; Mal. 1.2–5; Ogden 1982). However, the degree of such antagonism is not reflected in the length of the poem which, though long, is by no means as developed as the material against Egypt, *Moab* and Babylon. The expansion of 49.7–11 owes much to other sources and therefore the length of the anti-Edomite piece is more a redactional matter, drawing together discrete strands of comparable material, than an indication of particular hostility towards Edom.

The poem itself is typical of the collection and, apart from the individual details of names and places which identify the antagonist, calls upon Edom (using the names of its towns Teman and Dedan) to flee from the enemy. Like the Ammonite poem it opens with questions, but these are about the state of wisdom in Edom. If the people of Edom still possess understanding and insight they will flee from the calamity of Esau. In the genealogical legends of Israel the nation's eponymous forebear has a brother called Esau: he lived in Edomite territory and indeed was known as Edom (Gen. 25.31; 32.3; 36.8–9, 43). Thus Israelites and Edomites were believed to be closely related kin groups. Common origins and common territorial interests would explain much of the mutual hostility between the two nations (cf. Gen. 19.30–38 for similar connections between Israel, Moab, and the Ammonites). The ferocity of Esau's (i.e. Edom's) destruction is explained in vv. 9–10 using figures which appear also in Obad. 5–6. Unlike the gleaning of the vineyards (cf. 6.9; 8.13) or the consideration of thieves, neither of which actions completely removes everything, the punishment of Esau has been a stripping of him naked. Nothing is left (the deity being less kind and more thorough than humans). No hiding places, no people nor neighbours: nothing remains to protect Edom or to afford the nation help. Such terrible devastations may reflect Babylonian incursions into Edomite territory, but any particular destruction of Edom may be included in such a brief poem.

The ending of the poem in v. 11 is strange: the nation is summoned to abandon its orphans and widows to Yahweh. He, the Judaean god, will protect the Edomite victims of his wrath. Such concern for the oppressed suggests a lack of serious hostility against Edom in the poem (cf. vv. 6, 39 for other eirenic attitudes towards foreign nations) and a possible allusion to the belief in Yahweh's protection of widows and orphans (cf. Deut. 10.18 and the epithets of Ps. 68.5, 'father of the fatherless and protector of widows'). Those among the Edomite widows who are prepared to trust Yahweh will find protection from him (cf. 17.7–8; 39.18 for the trust motif). It is a strange statement because Yahweh's role as a caring and protective figure is seldom applied to members of foreign nations. Whether such a note of concern for foreigners reflects a pre- or post-587 setting is a moot point.

49.12–22

12 For thus says the LORD: 'If those who did not deserve to drink the cup
must drink it, will you go unpunished? You shall not go unpunished, but
you must drink. 13 For I have sworn by myself, says the LORD, that Bozrah
shall become a horror, a taunt, a waste, and a curse; and all her cities shall
be perpetual wastes.'

14 I have heard tidings from the LORD, and a messenger has been
    sent among the nations:
  'Gather yourselves together and come against her,
    and rise up for battle!'
15 For behold, I will make you small among the nations,
    despised among men.
16 The horror you inspire has deceived you,
    and the pride of your heart,
  you who live in the clefts of the rock,
    who hold the height of the hill.
  Though you make your nest as high as the eagle's,
    I will bring you down from there,
                says the LORD.

17 'Edom shall become a horror; every one who passes by it will be horrified
and will hiss because of all its disasters. 18 As when Sodom and Gomorrah
and their neighbour cities were overthrown, says the LORD, no man shall
dwell there, no man shall sojourn in her. 19 Behold, like a lion coming up

from the jungle of the Jordan against a strong sheepfold, I will suddenly make them run away from her; and I will appoint over her whomever I choose. For who is like me? Who will summon me? What shepherd can stand before me? 20 Therefore hear the plan which the LORD has made against Edom and the purposes which he has formed against the inhabitants of Teman: Even the little ones of the flock shall be dragged away; surely their fold shall be appalled at their fate. 21 At the sound of their fall the earth shall tremble; the sound of their cry shall be heard at the Red Sea. 22 Behold, one shall mount up and fly swiftly like an eagle, and spread his wings against Bozrah, and the heart of the warriors of Edom shall be in that day like the heart of a woman in her pangs.'

---

[12] G is shorter here: 'for thus says the lord They who were not appointed to drink the cup, have drunk; and you shall by no means be cleared'. MT *'ēn mišpāṭām*, lit. 'there was no obligation on them': cf. 25.28–29; this deviates from the sense of 25.15–27, where Jerusalem and Judah are obligated to drink the cup, though v. 18 should be deleted as an addition to 25.15–29. In this context the forcing of the cup is made to apply to Edom. **[13]** Cf. 22.5; 44.26; 51.14 for the divine swearing by himself. MT *l*^{e}*ḥōreb*, 'a waste': lacking in G; possibly a dittography of *l*^{e}*ḥor*^{e}*bōt*, 'waste places'. Cf. 42.18b; 44.12 for similar fourfold execrations. 'Bozrah': cf. v. 22; the chief city of Edom (modern el-Busreiah). G *en mesō autēs*, 'in the midst of her' = *b*^{e}*tōkāh*. Bozrah is probably a figure for the whole land (cf. Isa. 34.6b) as Teman is in v. 7. **[14]** Cf. Obad. 1. **[15]** Cf. Obad. 2. **[16]** Cf. Obad. 3–4. MT *tip*^{e}*laṣt*^{e}*kā*: hapax legomenon, meaning uncertain; *plṣ*, 'shudder' (BDB, 814); *tplṣt*, 'shuddering, horror' (cf. KB, 1037, 'the horror caused by thee?'). NEB 'Your overbearing arrogance', cf. *mip*^{e}*leṣet*, 'horrid thing', used of some idolatrous object (I Kings 15.13); Bright, 331, thinks the two words may have the same sense (i.e. 'your horrible idol') and that *tplṣt* may be a contemptuous epithet for the Edomite god. Christensen 1975, 228, translates it as 'Your reputation for ferocity'; Driver 1937–38, 125, 'shuddering', i.e. 'Edom has mistaken men's shuddering horror of her misdeeds for fear of her prowess.' MT *hiššī' 'ōtāk*, 'has deceived you': many exegetes read *hiššī'at*^{e}*ka* (cf. Ehrlich 1912, 361; Rudolph, 288). G lacks *n*^{e}*'um yhwh*, 'says Yahweh'. Cf. 22.23 for the image of nesting as a figure of security. **[17]** Cf. 19.8. Much of vv. 17–22 is a patchwork of elements to be found throughout the book of Jeremiah. **[18]** = 50.40 with minor variations. G has *kurios pantokratōr* for MT *yhwh*, i.e. 'lord almighty'. Cf. Zeph. 2.9, where Moab and Ammon become like Sodom and Gomorrah (20.16 is more allusive). Christensen treats vv. 17–18 as secondary prose elements (also vv. 13a, 22b), but the rest as poetry. Cf v. 33b for v. 18b. **[19]** 49.19–21 = 50.44–46 (*mutatis mutandis*). MT *migg*^{e}*'ōn hayyardēn*, 'from the jungle of the Jordan': see Notes on 12.5b; G *ek mesou tou Iordanou*, '*from the midst of* the

Jordan' = Aram. *miggō'* (BHS). MT *'el-n^{e}wēh 'ētān*, 'to the perennial pastures': cf. NEB; i.e. permanent pasturage, here suddenly depopulated by the enemy (under the figure of a lion). Rudolph refers the phrase to the oases of the Jordan desert territory. MT *kī*, 'for': BHS *kēn*, 'so', follows Duhm, 336. MT *'argī'āh '^{a}riṣennū mē'āleyhā*, 'I will in a moment chase *him* from her': 50.44; Vrs 'them' (RSV margin); Rudolph, 288 reads *'erg^e'āh 'et-ṣō(')n mar'ītō*, 'I will startle the sheep of his flock' (BHS). MT *ūmī bāḥūr 'ēleyhā 'epqōd*, lit. 'and who is chosen? Over her I will appoint': Cornill, 482, and followed by many (e.g. Rudolph, Bright) *ūmibḥar 'ēleyhā 'epqōd*, 'and the choicest of her rams I will single out'. **[20]** MT *'īm-lō . . . 'īm-lō'*, 'surely . . . surely': the asseverative force reflects the formal oath style. MT *yisḥābūm*, 'they shall drag them': Rudolph, 290, reads *yissāḥ^{a}bū gam*, 'they will be dragged also' (BHS); Kselman 1970, 580, treats it similarly but reads the *m* as enclitic (followed by Christensen 1975, 230). MT *yaššīm '^{a}lēhem n^{e}wēhem*, lit. 'he shall devastate their fold on account of them': Rudolph reads *yiššōm* (cf. v. 17) 'shall be devastated' (BHS); MT Hiphil may have the force of the Qal. Kselman treats *'lyhm* as *'ullēhem*, 'nurslings' (cf. Gen. 33.13). **[21]** MT *ṣ^e'āqāh b^{e}yam-sūp nišma' qōlāh*, lit. 'cry is heard by the sea of reeds her voice': many mss read '*their* voice'; G, 50.46 lack *qwlh*. Rudolph reads *ṣā'^{a}qāh*, 'the cry from it'; Driver 1937–38, 126, interprets the line as 'the crying thereof (i.e. of the earth) is heard in the Red Sea: hark to it!'. The sea of reeds (*yam-sūp*) refers to the Egyptian border territory associated with the legend of the exodus (Ex. 14) and not the Red Sea (as in EVV but not JPSB). **[22]** Cf. 48.40–41. G 48.40 lacks 'shall mount up and'. MT *'al-boṣrāh*, 'against Bozrah': G *ep' ochurōmata autēs*, 'over her strongholds' = *'al-mib^{e}ṣāreha*. Rudolph, 290, deletes 'in that day' for metrical reasons.

The oracle against Edom (original form consists of vv. 7–8, 22a, 10–11 [Bardtke] or vv. 7–8, 10–11, 22 [Rudolph]) is expanded considerably by secondary material in vv. 12–21. These expansions reflect Obad. 1–4 and the anti-Babylonian collection in 50.44–46, but also use 19.8 and elements from 25.15–29. The fate which befell Judah in 587 (cf. 25.18) now becomes the destiny of Bozrah (v. 13). To some extent the development of the poem in vv. 7–11 may be due to post-587 considerations and the use of so many different strands from other contexts suggests common material against the nations available for such constructions. Apart from the occasional place name in a poem or the redactional introduction which provides a key to the interpretation, many of the poems have a generality of reference which permits them to be used interchangeably of different nations (e.g. vv. 14–16 could refer to any state, and its present application to Edom is determined by the context of vv. 7–22 and influenced by the title in Obad. 1a). This feature of the OAN may be detected also in the poems directed against Jerusalem in Part I.

The cup metaphor in v. 12 refers to the cup of the wine of the wrath of Yahweh sequence in 25.15–29, where all the nations are forced to drink the wine in order to be destroyed. Jerusalem and the cities of Judah are included in that list (perhaps not originally) and two points are developed from that inclusion (25.29; 49.12). The first reflection makes the punishment of Jerusalem the grounds for the destruction of the nations. In the second the fate of Jerusalem is recognized as being unwarranted (i.e. lacking justification, *'ēn mišpāṭ*), but, since it has happened, the punishment of Edom is *a fortiori* inevitable. 587 becomes the warrant for the annihilation of the nations and the OAN show a remarkable shift from the arguments of Parts I, III–IV, which elucidate good reasons for the destruction of Jerusalem. Hence the same language is used of Jerusalem and Edom (v. 13; cf. v. 17; 19.8; 42.18b; 44.12). The bitter lessons taught by 597 and 587 (cf. Lam. 4.12) have become the inspiration for denouncing the nations and exposing their hubristic outlook (v. 16; cf. 48.29–30; 49.4, 31; 50.31–32). Whether the enemy addressed in v. 14 is Babylon or some other foe cannot be determined from vv. 14–16, but the more developed vision of Obadiah suggests that Babylon is the force summoned to destroy Edom (cf. Obad. 10–14). Edom's fate comes from Yahweh and will involve a reversal of its standing among the nations; instead of being much feared it will become small and inferior to the other states (vv. 15–16). The first line of v. 16 is ambiguous in that the opening word is an obscure one which may refer to Edom's attitude or its effect on others (cf. EVV). But Edomite arrogance (*zᵉdōn lēb*) allied to this other feature of its existence has deceived the nation (cf. 4.10 for Jerusalem's deception), and its secure position in the rocks cannot protect it (cf. 21.13; 22.23) from Yahweh.

Further images are used to describe Edom's fall in vv. 17–22. Like Jerusalem, those who pass through it will be shaken by what they see. Unlike Jerusalem (cf. Isa. 1.9), Edom will become like Sodom and Gomorrah, the legendary cities of the plain overthrown by the deity (Gen. 19.24). The invading army is described as a lion coming up from the lush growth of the Jordan area and savaging the sheepfolds (v. 19). These images are continued in v. 20 as an explanation of Yahweh's plan against Edom. The young sheep are dragged away by the lion and the slaughter is such that the community (sheepfold) are appalled by the massacre, the report of which reaches as far as the border of Egypt. In v. 22 (cf. 48.40–41) the enemy is like an eagle attacking Bozrah, and the Edomite warriors become like women (cf. 51.30), unable to fight back.

49.23–27

23 Concerning Damascus.
'Hamath and Arpad are confounded,
for they have heard evil tidings;
they melt in fear, they are troubled like the sea
which cannot be quiet.
24 Damascus has become feeble, she turned to flee,
and panic seized her;
anguish and sorrows have taken hold of her,
as of a woman in travail.
25 How the famous city is forsaken,
the joyful city!
26 Therefore her young men shall fall in her squares,
and all her soldiers shall be destroyed in that day,
says the Lord of hosts.
27 And I will kindle a fire in the wall of Damascus,
and it shall devour the strongholds of Ben-hadad.'

[MT 49.23–27] = G 30.12–16. **[23]** 'Hamath and Arpad': petty states in central and northern Syria respectively (cf. Isa. 10.9; 36.19; 37.13). MT *nāmōgū bayyām dᵉ'āgāh*, lit. 'they melt in the sea (is) anxiety': Volz, 415, reads *nāmōg libbām middᵉ'āgāh*, 'their hearts melt from anxiety', and is followed by many exegetes (e.g. Rudolph, Bright). Christensen 1975, 245–6, uses a conjectural emendation *nmg (k)ym d'g(w)* and translates 'they melt away (in terror) like Yamm, they quiver in fear'. G represents the line with two verbs: *exestēsan*, *ethumōthēsan* 'they are amazed, they are angry'. Cf. 6.24 for the hearing of a report motif. **[24]** MT *wᵉreṭeṭ heḥᵉzīqāh*, 'and *she* has seized panic': read with Giesebrecht, 244, and others *-āh*, i.e. 'and panic has seized *her*'; *ṛṭṭ* is a hapax legomenon in MT, cf. Aram. *rᵉṭēṭ*, 'tremble'. G lacks v. 24b and it is deleted by many exegetes (e.g. Bardtke, Rudolph, Christensen); cf. 6.24b; 50.43b where a similar phrase occurs expressing a state of collapse in terms of a pregnant woman's seizure with birth pangs. **[25]** MT *'ēk lō' 'uzzᵉbāh 'īr tᵉhillāh*, lit. 'how *not* deserted (is) she, the city of praise': i.e. the city of renown is *not* deserted but the context demands an assertion of forsakenness rather than its denial; only V lacks *lō'*, 'not'. Some exegetes delete 'not' (cf. BHS), others explain *lō'* as a mistake for the emphatic *lamed* (*l*[e], cf. Nötscher 1953, 374; Christensen 1975, 246); Driver 1937–38, 126, treats *'zb* as 'helped'. Rudolph, 292, regards it as a marginal note of a reader who would award such a title only to Jerusalem. Q *t*[e]*hillāt* = *t*[e]*hillātī*, '*my* praise', parallel to *qiryat m*[e]*śōśī*, 'city of *my* joy', i.e. my joyful city (Jerusalem); most Vrs lack suffix. **[26]** = 50.30 with the addition of *ṣ*[e]*bā'ōt*, 'of hosts' (lacking in G). **[27]** Cf. Amos 1.14; v. 27b = Amos 1.4b. Ben-hadad represents the name of the Syrian dynasty in the ninth-eighth centuries (BCE) and also the names of individual kings (cf. I Kings 20).

———

Damascus (Syria)

The shortest oracle in the collection is the one against Damascus (the town stands for Syria) and in MT it belongs to a group of three pieces which deal with territories further afield than Judah's neighbouring states. The title 'concerning Damascus' (*l*[e]*dammeśeq*) reflects the identification of Syrian territory with its main city (cf. Amos 1.3–5; Isa. 17.1–3; Zech. 9.1), though the oracle also alludes to the cities of nearby states Hamath (cf. Zech. 9.2a) on the Orontes and Arpad near Aleppo. Reference to areas so far away from Judah (incorporated into the Assyrian empire in the late eighth century) is strange in oracles attributed to Jeremiah and has been explained as a reflection of the Assyrian conquests of a previous age using an archaizing tendency characteristic of epigonic literature of the fifth century (cf. Pfeiffer 1941, 508). It is less likely that the piece represents an anonymous eighth-century poem reapplied to Damascus in relation to a campaign of Nebuchadrezzar's against that area (though allowance must be made for this possibility, cf. Bright, 337). A reference to Syrian troops in II Kings 24.2 associates them with the curbing of Jehoiakim's activities *c.* 597, but the oracle against Damascus hardly belongs to such an anti-Judaean strand in the Deuteronomistic history.

The poem is very brief and consists of vv. 23, 24a, 25 (Bardtke 1936, 255), with v. 26 an addition from 50.30 and v. 27 a concluding appendix from Amos 1.4, 14 (cf. Rudolph, 292; Christensen 1975, 245–6, excludes much less). It depicts Damascus panic-stricken and routed – a famous city abandoned. The report of this catastrophe makes Hamath and Arpad extremely anxious. No account is given of the cause of the panic and no specific historical situation can be discerned at all in the poem (though Christensen, 248, relates it to the period of Josiah's political expansion). Rather it is Yahweh who destroys Damascus, hence the extract from Amos 1. Stereotypical phrases identify Yahweh as the opponent of the foreign nations, and it is possible to detect here a hint of apocalyptic orientation (cf. Pfeiffer).

49.28–33

28 Concerning Kedar and the kingdoms of Hazor which Nebuchadrezzar king of Babylon smote.
Thus says the LORD:
'Rise up, advance against Kedar!
  Destroy the people of the east!
29 Their tents and their flocks shall be taken,
  their curtains and all their goods;
their camels shall be borne away from them,
  and men shall cry to them: "Terror on every side!"
30 Flee, wander far away, dwell in the depths,
  O inhabitants of Hazor!
                says the LORD.
For Nebuchadrezzar king of Babylon
  has made a plan against you,
  and formed a purpose against you.
31 Rise up, advance against a nation at ease,
  that dwells securely,
                says the LORD,
that has no gates or bars,
  that dwells alone.
32 Their camels shall become booty,
  their herds of cattle a spoil.
I will scatter to every wind
  those who cut the corners of their hair,
and I will bring their calamity
  from every side of them,
                says the LORD.
33 Hazor shall become a haunt of jackals,
  an everlasting waste;
no man shall dwell there,
  no man shall sojourn in her.'

[MT 49.28–33] = G 30.6–11. **[28]** MT *ūlᵉmamlᵉkōt ḥāṣōr*, 'and the kingdoms of Hazor': G *tē basilissē tēs aulēs*, 'the queen of the courtyard' =

l^e^malkat ḥāṣēr. MT hardly makes sense with a reference to Hazor in an oracle about the bedouins of the eastern desert (vv. 30, 33 make it a place name), and most modern exegetes translate 'the kingdom of Hazor' quite differently. Cf. Isa. 42.11, *ḥ^a^ṣērîm tēšēb qēdār*, 'the villages Kedar inhabits'. Thus Bardtke, Rudolph, Christensen among others treat *ḥṣr* as 'encampments'; *maml^e^kōt* may mean 'chieftains' (cf. 1.15) and the phrase can be translated as 'village chieftains' (cf. Bright, 336). Cf. 2.10 for Kedar as a designation of the eastern desert region. K *nbwkdr'ṣwr*; Q *n^e^bûkadre'ṣṣar*, 'Nebuchadrezzar': K a scribal error perhaps under the influence of Hazor (*ḥṣwr*). Bardtke 1936, 255, and Christensen 1975, 209, delete 'which Nebuchadrezzar king of Babylon smote' as unoriginal (an expansionary gloss). MT *w^e^šād^e^dû*, 'and destroy': G *kai plēxate*, 'and fill', i.e. destroy? (cf. *apolesai* in 29.4 [MT 47.4]; BHS). **[29]** Cf. 4.20; 10.20 where the destruction of bedouin encampments provides images of the disaster befalling the speaker's people. MT *māgôr missābîb*, 'terror on every side': cf. 6.25; 20.3, 4, 10; 46.5 (see on 19.14 – 20.6). **[30]** Cf v. 8a for v. 30a. MT *nudû m^e^'ōd*, 'wander greatly': G lacks *nudû*. Rudolph, 292, treats 'dwell in the depths' as an addition from v. 8 (cf. Rothstein). MT *yōš^e^bē ḥāṣōr*, 'inhabitants of Hazor': G *kathēmenoi en tē aulē*, 'those who live in the courtyard', cf. v. 28. G lacks *n^e^'um yhwh*, 'says Yahweh'. Rudolph regards 'king of Babylon' as an addition because it disrupts the metre; it may be an expansionary gloss (Christensen); G lacks 'Nebuchadrezzar'. Cf. v. 20a for plan (*'ēṣāh*) and purpose (*maḥ^a^šābāh*) with Yahweh as subject. K *'lyhm*, 'against them'; Q *'^a^lēkem*, 'against you' (lacking in G^BS^). **[31]** Cf. Ezek. 38.10–11. G lacks *n^e^'um yhwh*, 'says Yahweh': deleted by Rudolph (cf. BHS) because Nebuchadrezzar is the speaker. **[32]** MT *q^e^ṣûṣē pē'āh*, 'those who cut the corner (of their hair)': cf. 9.25 (EV 26); 25.23; i.e. the Arabs of the desert who clip the hair of their temples. MT *ûmikkol-'^a^bārāyw* 'and from every side of *him*': Vrs have plur. suffix '. . . of them'; Rudolph reads the unsuffixed *'^a^bārîm*, i.e. '(from every) side'. **[33]** MT *ḥāṣōr*, 'Hazor': G *hē aulē*, 'the courtyard', as in vv. 28, 30. 33 appears to consist of phrases from the book of Jeremiah: cf. 9.10 (EV 11); 10.22; 51.37 for 'haunt of jackals', 'desolation' (33a); 33b = v. 18b. It is an editorial conclusion to the poem.

Kedar

The redactional introduction to the poem associates the oracle with Nebuchadrezzar's campaign against the Arabian tribes of Kedar and the kingdoms of Hazor (MT). Hazor is a common name for cities in Palestine (e.g. Josh. 11.1; 12.19; 15.23, 25; 19.36), but in this context it either refers to an Arabian locality in the eastern desert or should be translated as the 'unwalled villages' (cf. v. 31b) of that area (cf. G). The bedouin settlements of the desert are to be swept away by the onslaught of the Babylonian emperor. Exegetes differ in their analysis of the limits of the poem (e.g. vv. 28*, 29, 31, 32 [Bardtke]; vv. 28a, 30–32 [Rudolph]), but vv. 28a, 33 may be recognized as secondary.

The oracle against Kedar is the only one in the collection to contain an identifying reference to the destroyer, but that line in v. 30 may well be secondary. It does, however, indicate how the generality of the poems in the OAN may be identified with the Babylonian domination of the ancient Near East (cf. the redactional notes in 46.2, 13; 49.28, 34). The poems themselves do not identify the foe but use conventional terms to describe invasion and defeat, flight and panic. Behind the plight of each nation is Yahweh rather than the Babylonian emperor, but Nebuchadrezzar may be regarded as a convenient historical point of reference for poems belonging to Judaean cultic life. Kedar's destruction is facilitated by the unprotected nature of bedouin settlements and their unawareness of danger which renders them complacent (v. 31). The shout 'terror on every side' (v. 29b) is a characteristic shocked response to invasion and destruction, and echoes through a number of different places in the book of Jeremiah (cf. the development of it in MT 20.3). As in so many other parts of the tradition, the desert settlements will become an uninhabited place where no one will live again, a haunt of jackals (cf. 10.22; 51.37). No reason is given for Kedar's destruction, and the poem may be an echo of Assyrian campaigns in the mid-seventh century or a reference to Nebuchadrezzar's attack on the Arabs in 599–8 (cf. Wiseman 1956, 31–2). As with all the poems in 46–51, if there is a historical setting behind the poem it cannot be detected.

49.34

34 The word of the Lord that came to Jeremiah the prophet concerning Elam, in the beginning of the reign of Zedekiah king of Judah.

[MT 49.34] = G 26.1. **[34]** G lacks this redactional title to the oracle on Elam but concludes that piece (G 25.14–19) with part of it: *en archē basileuontos Sedekiou basileōs egeneto ho logos outos peri Ailam*, 'in the beginning of the reign of king Zedekiah, there came this word concerning Elam'. The different order of the oracles against the nations in G has Elam as the first piece, and because it starts the collection G uses MT 25.13b as a title – *ha eprophēteusen Ieremias epi ta ethnē ta Ailam*, 'which Jeremiah prophesied against the nations: against Elam'. MT *'ᵃšer hāyāh dᵉbar-yhwh 'el-yirmᵉyāhû hannābî',el-'ēlām*, 'what came (as) the word of Yahweh to Jeremiah the prophet concerning Elam': cf. 1.2; 14.1; 46.1; 47.1 for this fractured form of the reception of the divine word formula. MT *bᵉrē'šît malᵉkût ṣidᵉqiyyāh*, 'in the beginning of the reign of Zedekiah': i.e. his accession year; the period between the deportation of Jehoiachin and 1 Nisan 597 (cf. 26.1; 52.28; Rudolph, 295; Bright, 336). Cf. v. 35, where *rē'šît*, 'beginning, first, chief', also occurs.

Elam

An editorial introduction prefaces the piece on Elam (vv. 35–38) and attributes it to an oracular utterance of Jeremiah *the prophet* *c*. 597 at the beginning of Zedekiah's reign (contrast 46.2, 'the fourth year of Jehoiakim'). Rudolph uses these two dating points to divide the oracles against the nations into two parts: 46.2 – 49.33 belong to the fourth year of Jehoiakim and 50.1 – 51.64 are to be assigned to the fourth year of Zedekiah. 49.34–38 would therefore represent a transition between the two sets of oracles. Symmetrical though this division may be, it is scarcely warranted by the text. *If* the redactional notices are to be taken at face value then they may be applied only to the nations named in each note (i.e. Egypt and Elam) and may not be extended indefinitely to cover every oracle within either set (cf. 46.13).

Why Elam should be identified with the beginning of Zedekiah's reign is beyond our knowledge (Bardtke 1936, 257, deletes this element of the notice), though there may have been conflict between the Elamites and the Babylonians *c*. 596–5 (cf. Wiseman 1956, 36, 72–3). After a long history of conflict with the Assyrians Elam was conquered by Assyria under Asshurbanipal in 640. It appears to have regained independence *c*. 625 (cf. Wiseman 1956, 8–10, 50–1) and contributed to the defeat of Babylon in 540–39. The Elam oracle is like all the others in 46–51 in that it contains no specific historical information and its vague, stereotypical phrases are capable of an a-historical explanation. Whether vv. 35–38 are poetry or prose is difficult to determine, though the prosaic nature of some of the elements in them are recognized by most exegetes. RSV and JPSB treat them as prose, but many commentators regard the oracle as being essentially poetic (e.g. NEB, Rudolph, Bardtke, Christensen).

49.35–39

35 Thus says the LORD of hosts: 'Behold I will break the bow of Elam, the mainstay of their might; 36 and I will bring upon Elam the four winds from the four quarters of heaven; and I will scatter them to all those winds, and there shall be no nation to which those driven out of Elam shall not come. 37 I will terrify Elam before their enemies, and before those who seek their life; I will bring evil upon them, my fierce anger, says the LORD. I will send the sword after them, until I have consumed them; 38 and I will set my throne in Elam, and destroy their king and princes, says the LORD.'

39 'But in the latter days I will restore the fortunes of Elam, says the LORD.'

[MT 49.35–39] = G 25.14–19. **[35]** G lacks 'of hosts'. Cf. Isa. 22.6 for Elam's association with archery. MT *rēʾšît gᵉbûrātām*, lit. 'first of their strength': i.e. chief (weapon) of their power (NEB); the occurrence of *rēʾšît* here may account for the dating of the editorial note in v. 34 (*bᵉrēʾšît*, 'in the beginning of . . .'). **[36]** The second part of v. 36 is regarded as a prosaic addition by many exegetes (e.g. Rudolph, Bright, Christensen but not Bardtke). MT *haggōy*, '*the* nation': *ha* due to dittography (lacking in G, T). Some mss and Vrs read *yābōʾū*, '*they* shall come,' for MT *yābōʾ*, 'it shall come'. K *ʿwlm*; Q *ʿêlām*, 'Elam': K 'permanently', perhaps influenced by v. 13b. **[37]** G *kai ptoēsō autous*, 'I will put them in fear': lacking 'Elam'. Cf. 21.7; 44.30; 46.26 for the motif 'those who seek (their) life'. G lacks *nᵉʾum-yhwh*, 'says Yahweh'. Cf. 9.15 (EV 16) for v. 37c. **[38]** MT *wᵉhaʾᵃbadtî miššām*, 'and I will destroy from there': G *kai exapostelō ekeithen*, 'and I will send forth thence', i.e. expel; G may be a corruption of *exapolesō* 'I will destroy utterly', (cf. BHS). G lacks *nᵉʾum-yhwh*, 'says Yahweh'. **[39]** Cf. 48.47. K *ʾšwb ʾt šbyt*, Q *ʾāšîb ʾet-šᵉbût* 'I will restore the fortunes': probable reading should combine K and Q as *ʾāšûb ʾet-šᵉbût* (cf. Rudolph, 294); but Q = 49.6.

The oracle asserts Yahweh's campaign against Elam's power characterized by the bow (cf. Isa. 22.6). Elam will be scattered to the four winds by some great force which is not identified, but v. 37 hints at invasion (though G's 'my sword' may continue the motif of divine power exercised against the Elamites, cf. Ezek. 32.24–25). Scattering and slaughtering are two rather different fates, but the language of vv. 35–38 is too stereotyped to afford precise identification of meaning. Elam will be annihilated by Yahweh and the divine throne will be placed there (cf. 3.17; 17.12 where the throne motif has different meanings). The destruction of the Elamite leadership and its replacement by Yahweh's throne reflect the belief that in the future Yahweh's suzerainty will displace the power of the foreign nations and Judah's god will rule over the empires (cf. Zech. 14.16–19). A new realm of 'history' is envisaged – what some exegetes would call 'eschatological' (cf. Christensen 1975, 223). The oracular assertion of Elam's annihilation is reversed to some extent by the addition of a brief oracle in v. 39 which recognizes a revival of Elamite fortunes in the future (cf. 46.26b; 48.47; 49.6). Such an appendix indicates how rhetorical the language of vv. 35–38 is.

50.1

58 [1] The word which the LORD spoke concerning Babylon, concerning the land of the Chaldeans, by Jeremiah the prophet:

[MT 50] = G 27. **[1]** MT *haddābār ʾᵃšer dibber yhwh ʾel-bābel*, 'the word which Yahweh spoke to (concerning) Babylon': cf. 46.13 (45.1 with Jeremiah as speaker; 37.2 with variations) for this formal introduction; G *logos kuriou, hon elalēsen epi Babulōna*, 'word of Yahweh which he spoke against Babylon', cf. 51.1. MT develops the introduction 'and (with many mss, Vrs) concerning the land of the Chaldaeans, by means of (*bᵉyad*) Jeremiah the prophet'; cf. 37.2.

Babylon

The final section of the OAN consists of two very lengthy chapters of oracular utterances against Babylon. These are almost as long (110 verses) as the material against the other nations in 46–49 (121 verses). Their length indicates the obsessional antagonism felt towards Babylon as the national enemy which had destroyed Jerusalem and ruined the nation (cf. Isa. 13–14; 21.1–10; 47; Ps. 137). Two themes dominate the poems: the fall of Babylon and the restoration of the exiles to their own land (cf. the similar themes in Isa. 40–55) and these are interwoven together without any marked degree of progress of thought. Within a framework of Babylon's fall (50.2–3; 51.54–58) many poetic and prosaic elements depict the downfall of the enemy intercut with pieces about Judah-Israel (cf. analysis in Fohrer 1981, 50–1).

The structural analysis of 50–51 is the most difficult problem in the exegesis of the text and few commentators agree on how to divide the poems into units. From the one extreme of about fifty oracles and fragments (e.g. Robinson 1918) to the other extreme of 'a well-ordered complex of structurally related elements' (e.g. Aitken 1984, 26), exegetes have puzzled over how best to treat the text. The problem may be avoided by a continuous verse-by-verse commentary (e.g. Cornill, Duhm, Giesebrecht, Hyatt) or more realistically side-stepped by dividing the material into units for exegetical convenience (e.g. Bright, Thompson). Other commentators more confidently discern a varying number of poems in the collection: three (Christensen 50; 51.1–40, 41–58), four (Condamin 50.2–20, 21–46; 51.1–37, 38–58), five (Volz 50.2–16, 21–32, 35–38; 51.1–26, 27–58 with additions and citations), six movements (Aitken 50.4–20, 21–32, 33–46; 51.1–33, 34–44, 45–53), fifteen units (Rudolph 50.2–7, 8–20, 21–28, 29–32, 33–40, 41–46; 51.1–19, 20–26, 27–33, 34–40, 41–43, 44–46, 47–48, 49–57, 58) and even more units (cf. Fohrer, Weiser). Whatever their disagreement about unit division, many of these exegetes would agree on the poorly organized state of the collection, its thematic poverty and exorbitant length. It is regarded as a purely artificial literary production, more interested in quantity than quality and monotonous to the point that only a commentator could read it through (Duhm, 360). Dismissive judgments such as '. . . a prolix, disjointed, vacuous literary exercise . . . this inane poem . . .' (Pfeiffer 1941, 507) convey well the opinions of many commentators of the older schools of thought on biblical literature. More recent approaches to the Bible are less caustic and more prepared to detect structure and coherence where once all was thought to be shapeless and incoherent (cf. Aitken, Christensen). The repetitiveness of the thematic material may be attributable to the emotions aroused by Babylon and to circles which celebrated the downfall of the great enemy in terms of its potential for the return of the exiles to their homeland (cf. the hymns of Second Isaiah, where so few ideas are repeated in so many units). Aitken postulates a deep structure for the poem consisting of the matrix 'situation – intervention – outcome' (1984, 28), and these three ground-elements may be found throughout 50–51 in various pairings. Although tending to abstraction, this approach has the advantage of descrying unifying features in the poem which may account for the final form of the text redaction. However many units make up the poem, the creative hand of the editors must be allowed a shaping influence.

In MT the oracular utterance against Babylon is attributed to Jeremiah *the prophet* (contrast G). As part of the redactional framework this attribution cannot be regarded as historically reliable, though from the viewpoint of the holistic approach to the book of Jeremiah the created persona of Jeremiah may be viewed as the speaker of this lengthy poem against Babylon. In such an approach fundamental contradictions are less important than they are for historical reconstructions. If such a poem were to be attributed to the 'historical Jeremiah', it would raise the insuperable problem of reconciling the speaker of this anti-Babylonian outburst with the image of Jeremiah as the friend of Babylon portrayed in 27–29, 39–40. Babylon would not have trusted a man who could utter such things *against* Babylon, even if on other occasions he was credited with the view that Nebuchadrezzar was the servant of Yahweh (25.9; 27.6). Emperors may be very susceptible to flattery, but they are not at all impervious to criticism. Utterances of the calibre of 50–51 lead to death sentences rather than honourable treatment under the patronage of the empire (39.12–14; 40.4–6). It is difficult to see how Jeremiah could have been advocating submission (27) or surrender (38) to the Babylonians and yet *at the same time* (cf. 51.59) have been proclaiming 51.1–14 or 51.25–40 (these oracles are dated to *c.* 590–580 by Christensen 1975, 278–9, and attributed to Jeremiah). The mental reservations required to hold both views together (never mind the problems of confusing the people!) are hardly eased by proposing a sequential aspect to the beliefs (cf. 25.11–14). 50–51 present a very different view of Judah from that given in 2–20 or Parts III and IV, and to attempt to reconcile all these aspects of the tradition is to produce a chimerical Jeremiah.

A better approach to the contradictory elements in the tradition is to recognize that inconsistency is a major feature of the editing of the book of Jeremiah and to accept that the various strands present irreconcilable images of Jeremiah *the prophet*. It is as a prophet that he is represented as a speaker to the nations (cf. 1.5), and this role comes to the fore in MT's presentation of the oracles against the nations (46.1, 13; 49.34; 50.1). As a prophet Jeremiah combines all the disparate attitudes incorporated into the tradition and thus he represents the Jews of Palestine and even Babylon in their quarrels with the Jewish communities in Egypt and also the pro- and anti-Babylon parties of the sixth century. Real, historical people cannot be such representative figures, nor can they speak for every party in the community, but the cumulative effect of the many discrete traditions making up the book of Jeremiah is to produce a figure who transcends all the limitations of history and society and becomes a paradigmatic prophet to the nations. Nowhere is this transcendence of all human limitations so clearly seen as in the material on Babylon. In 27–29 the pro-Babylonian stance is taken by Jeremiah and the anti-Babylonian prophet Hananiah is dismissed (a case of premature anti-Babylonism?). Co-existence with Babylon and even settlement in Babylon is advocated (29), and the well-being of both Jews and Babylonians is bound up together in the religious activity of the Jews in Babylon (29.7). After 597 and especially in view of the destruction of Jerusalem in 587, Babylon becomes the target of great hostility as well as the place where many Jews lived. So in 50–51 the voice of that hostility is given full range – needless to say that voice is Jeremiah's! In his capacity as prophet Jeremiah articulates the great hatred of Babylon felt by its many victims and gives expression to the feelings of countless Judaeans who saw Babylon only as the destroyer of Jerusalem, temple and people.

50.2–3

2 'Declare among the nations and proclaim,
set up a banner and proclaim,
conceal it not, and say:
"Babylon is taken,
Bel is put to shame,
Merodach is dismayed.
Her images are put to shame,
her idols are dismayed."
3 For out of the north a nation has come up against her, which shall make her land a desolation, and none shall dwell in it; both man and beast shall flee away.'

---

[2] Cf. 51.54–58. MT *uśᵉ'ū-nēs hašᵉmīʿū*, 'and raise the signal, proclaim': cf. 4.6; Isa. 13.2; lacking in G. 'Bel . . . Merodach': Bel (= *baʿal*) was originally the patron god of Nippur but became an epithet of the patron god of Babylon, Marduk (cf. Rudolph, 300); hence these are not two gods but different names of the one god (cf. 51.44; Isa. 46.1). G *katēschunthē (Bēl) hē aptoētos, hē truphera (pareluthē Marōdach)*, 'confounded (Bel) the fearless, the voluptuous (Marodach is destroyed)': an inner Greek doublet (cf. Janzen 1973, 20, 28; Ziegler 1958, 96) with later correction to MT (in brackets). MT variant 'shamed are her images, shattered her idols' is lacking in G: *gillūlīm* may be translated 'godlets' (Bright), 'fetishes' (JPSB) or 'godlings' – lit. 'balls of dung', it is a scatological reference to foreign gods/idols frequently used in Ezekiel but only here in Jeremiah. **[3]** MT *mē'ādām we'ad behēmāh nādū hālākū*, lit. 'from man and to beast they have fled, they have gone': i.e. both man and beast have fled and gone away. G lacks the two verbs; they appear together in 9.9 (EV 10) which may have influenced 50.3bβ or they may be variants here.

The poems and prose pieces constituting 50–51 are enclosed in a framework of 50.2–3; 51.54–58. This framework announces the destruction of the great enemy Babylon and reflects (though according to some exegetes it may anticipate) the defeat of Babylon in 539. The gap between the historical reality of the power shift from Babylonian to Persian forces without the destruction of the city of Babylon and the depiction of the overthrow of Babylon in terms of destruction and desolation (e.g. 50.13, 15, 23, 30, 39–40; 51.2–4, 26, 29, 32, 37, 43, 58) has led many exegetes to argue that the poems must belong to the period before the actual defeat of Babylon. Whatever force this argument may have, it is not necessarily a persuasive one. The language of the poems is conventional and influenced by other parts of the book of Jeremiah; it may not therefore be a description of what actually happened but a celebration of Babylon's defeat. Emotion is the key here rather than historical accuracy. For those living in Palestine the defeat of Babylon would have been a great joy, and the details of the event could be supplied from traditional songs of triumph over the enemy. Taunt songs furnish their own emotional charge independent of the actual course of events and, like the folk songs of so many cultures, often are a preferred surrogate to the more mundane reality they celebrate. A different argument detects in the dissonance arousing gap between expectation and reality as constituted by the fall of Babylon evidence for reading 50–51 as an 'eschatological poem' (cf. Christensen 1975, 263, for the phrase and 249–80 for the connections between 50–51 and early apocalyptic; my argument here is not Christensen's). By that weasel-word description (i.e. 'eschatological') is meant a poem in which Babylon is less the historical city-enemy of the sixth century and more the epitome of the antagonist of Yahweh's people in all subsequent ages. As such the fall of Babylon in 539 is the starting point for the development of the belief in a catastrophic overthrow of all the forces believed to be arranged against Jerusalem and the people of Israel (cf. Ezek. 38–39; Isa. 24–27; Joel 3.1–21 [MT

4.1–21]; Zech. 14). The mythic roots of this belief may belong to the temple cult of the pre-587 period but the defeat of Babylon in 539 gave it the boost necesssary to remove it from the sphere of ancient myth to that of potential historical reality. That defeat may not have been as grandiose as expected but in the future there would be a mighty devastation of Babylon (or whatever it stood for) which would dwarf the changeover of power in the time of Cyrus.

The preface to the collection sets out the theme of 50–51: 'Babylon is taken' (*nilkᵉdāh bābel*). This slogan links all the poems and comments in the collection and underwrites its significance. The alternation between Babylon (vv. 2–3, 8–15, 21–27, 29–32, 35–38) and Israel (vv. 4–7, 17–20, 28, 33–34) demonstrates the twin themes arising from this announcement: Babylon's defeat as *punishment* and the restoration of Israel. These themes are also to be found in Second Isaiah which suggests the period (*c*. 550–539?) when the poems were edited, but the language of 50–51 reflects the Jeremiah tradition and must be attributed to the redaction of Jeremiah rather than associated directly with the circles which produced Isa. 40–55. Arising out of the same period the two traditions developed quite distinctive responses to the (impending?) fall of Babylon and the prospects for the exiles emerging from that catastrophe (cf. Isa.47; also sa. 40.1–2; 44.24–28; 48.17–21; 49.24–26; 51.17–23; 52.1–2, 11–12). The primary consequence of the capture of Babylon drawn by the preface is the humiliation of the Babylonian deity Marduk (Bel; cf. Isa.46.1). The defeat of Babylon is the defeat of the god and the triumph of Yahweh – a logic not used in the tradition with reference to Jerusalem's defeat in 587 but mooted in the lament psalms (e.g. 44.23–26; 74.18–23; 79; 89.38–48) within the constraints of the chauvinistic theology of the national cult (cf. the Moabite Stone for the theologization of defeat and victory). In effect the defeat of the god Marduk means the humiliation of the cult's idols (cf. Isa. 44.9–20; 46.1–2), though Cyrus's praise of Marduk (cf. Pritchard 1969, 315–16) should lend perspective to this pro-Judaean understanding of the fall of Babylon (cf. v. 38b for the view of Babylon as 'a land of images'). In v. 3 the universal proclamation of v. 2 is explained in more prosaic terms (many exegetes, NEB, JPSB treat v. 3 as poetry). Out of the north has come up against her a nation which shall destroy her and render her land uninhabited. How ironic this assertion is in the light of the proclamation of the very same motif against Jerusalem in 6.22 (cf. 1.14; 4.6; 10.22)! The tradition has come full circle with this announcement that the destroyer is the destroyed.

50.4–20

4 'In those days and in that time, says the LORD, the people of Israel and the people of Judah shall come together, weeping as they come; and they shall seek the LORD their God. 5 They shall ask the way to Zion, with faces turned toward it, saying, "Come, let us join ourselves to the LORD in an everlasting covenant which will never be forgotten." '

6 'My people have been lost sheep; their shepherds have led them astray, turning them away on the mountains; from mountain to hill they have gone, they have forgotten their fold. 7 All who found them have devoured them, and their enemies have said, "We are not guilty, for they have sinned against the Lord, their true habitation, the LORD, the hope of their fathers." '

8 'Flee from the midst of Babylon, and go out of the land of the Chaldeans, and be as he-goats before the flock. 9 For behold, I am stirring up and bringing against Babylon a company of great nations, from the north country; and they shall array themselves against her; from there she shall be taken. Their arrows are like a skilled warrior who does not return empty-handed. 10 Chaldea shall be plundered; all who plunder her shall be sated, says the LORD.'

11 'Though you rejoice, though you exult,
O plunderers of my heritage,
though you are wanton as a heifer at grass,
and neigh like stallions,
12 your mother shall be utterly shamed,
and she who bore you shall be disgraced.
Lo, she shall be the last of the nations,
a wilderness dry and desert.
13 Because of the wrath of the LORD she shall not be inhabited,
but shall be an utter desolation;
every one who passes by Babylon shall be appalled,
and hiss because of all her wounds.'
14 'Set yourselves in array against Babylon round about,
all you that bend the bow;
shoot at her, spare no arrows,
for she has sinned against the LORD.
15 Raise a shout against her round about,
she has surrendered;
her bulwarks have fallen,
her walls are thrown down.

For this is the vengeance of the LORD:
take vengeance on her,
do to her as she has done.
16 Cut off from Babylon the sower,
and the one who handles the sickle in time of harvest;
because of the sword of the oppressor,
every one shall turn to his own people,
and every one shall flee to his own land.'
17 'Israel is a hunted sheep driven away by lions. First the king of Assyria
devoured him, and now at last Nebuchadrezzar king of Babylon has gnawed
his bones. 18 Therefore, thus says the LORD of hosts, the God of Israel:
Behold, I am bringing punishment on the king of Babylon and his land, as
I punished the king of Assyria. 19 I will restore Israel to his pasture, and
he shall feed on Carmel and in Bashan, and his desire shall be satisfied on
the hills of Ephraim and in Gilead. 20 In those days and in that time, says
the LORD, iniquity shall be sought in Israel, and there shall be none; and
sin in Judah, and none shall be found; for I will pardon those whom I leave
as a remnant.'

---

[4] G lacks *nᵉ'um yhwh*, 'says Yahweh': 4QJerᵇ agrees with MT in reading it (cf. Janzen 1973, 184). Rudolph, 298, treats *ubᵉnē-yᵉhūdāh yaḥdāw*, 'and the people of Judah together', as an addition to the text; it is an unnecessary gloss on *bᵉnē-yiśrā'ēl*, 'people of Israel', which includes Israel *and* Judah (cf. vv. 17, 19). Cf. v. 20; 33.15 for the double phrase *bayyāmīm hāhēmmāh ūbā'ēt hahī'*, 'in those days and in that time' (parallel but separate in 3.17, 18). **[5]** MT *ṣiyyōn yiš'ālū derek hēnnāh pᵉnēhem*, lit. 'Zion they shall ask (the) way hither their faces': i.e. they ask the way to Zion with their faces turned hither. MT *bō'u wᵉnilᵉwū*, 'they came and they shall cleave': G *kai hēxousi kai katapheuxontai*, 'and they shall come and flee for refuge'; many exegetes read *wᵉnillāweh*, 'and let us cleave' with S (cf. BHS) and some read *ūbā'ū*, 'and they shall come', with G (cf. Bright, 340, retaining MT; Rudolph). Cf. 32.40; Ezek. 37.26 for the motif *bᵉrīt 'ōlām*, 'a permanent *bᵉrīt*', i.e. an everlasting covenant (or obligation). **[6]** K *hyh*; Q *hāyū*, 'they have been': K treats *'ammī*, 'my people', as a collective requiring a sing. verb; cf. Gen. 30.43 for Q. MT *hārīm šōbᵉbūm* (Q; K *šōbēbīm*), lit. 'mountains recusant': i.e. (on the) mountains they wander (apostatize); G *epi ta orē*, 'upon the mountains' = *'al-hārīm* (Driver 1937–38, 126, prefers *behārīm*). Christensen 1975, 250, reads *šwbbw* with the next line. Duhm, 361, detects a playful use of 3.23 here. Cf. 23.1–2 for the motif of shepherds (i.e. rulers) who scatter the flock; BHS suggests *mōrēhem*, 'their leaders' (teachers) as a possible reading of *hārīm* (*m* lost by haplography; cf. Rudolph, 298). **[7]** MT *lō' neᵉšām*, 'we are not guilty': cf. 2.3 for *'šm*, 'acquire guilt'; G *mē anōmen autous*, 'let us not leave them alone' = *lō' niššā'ēm*. G lacks *yhwh* at end of v. 7; cf. 14.8 (G); 17.13 for Yahweh as

Israel's hope (*miqwēh*). The true habitation (*nᵉwēh-ṣedeq*) here is Yahweh, but in 31.23 the phrase refers to the sacred hill of the temple. **[8]** Volz, 421, reads MT *yhwh* at end of v. 7 as *hōy* at the beginning of v. 8 (cf. BHS); cf. Zech.2.10–11 (EV 6–7) for this use of *hōy* as a prefix to a command to flee (translated as 'listen' by Petersen 1985, 172–3). K *yṣ'w*, 'they go out'; Q *ṣᵉ'ū*, 'go forth': MT places *atnah* here but many exegetes transpose it to *kaśdīm*, 'Chaldaeans', cf. NEB, BHS. MT *kᵉ'attūdīm*, 'like he-goats': i.e. like the sheep which lead the flock; 'bellwethers' (Bright, 340). G *hōsper drakontes*, 'like dragons, serpents': perhaps a corruption of *archontes*, 'rulers' (cf. *arxantes* = *'attūdē*, Isa. 14.9; BHS) or *tragoi*, 'he-goats' (Streane 1896, 288; cf. *eriphoi* = *'attūdīm*, 'he-goats', in 28.40; MT 51.40). **[9]** G lacks *ūma'ᵃleh*, 'and bringing up', and *gᵉdōlīm*, 'great (nations)': both words may be MT dittographies (cf. BHS). MT *kᵉgibbōr maškīl*, 'like a bereaving warrior': i.e. a soldier who makes childless, cf. JPSB margin; many mss, A, T, V read *maśkīl*, 'successful', i.e. skilful warrior, cf. RSV, NEB. **[10]** MT *kaśdīm*, 'Chaldaeans': here it must refer to the land (hence fem. *hāyᵉtāh*, 'shall be') as in 51.24, 35 (*yōšᵉbē kaśdīm*, 'inhabitants of Chaldaea'). G lacks *nᵉ'um yhwh*, 'says Yahweh'. **[11]** K *tśmḥy . . . t'lzy*, fem.sing.; Q *tiśᵉmᵉḥu . . . ta'ᵃlᵉzū*, masc.plur., 'you rejoice . . . you exult': both are possible in Heb., as is the case for K *tpwšy . . . wtṣhly*; Q *tāpūšū . . . wᵉtiṣᵉhᵃlū*, 'you spring about . . . and you neigh'. MT *kᵉ'eglāh dāšāh*, 'like a cow threshing': G *hōs boidia en botanē*, 'like calves in grass' = *kᵉ'eglē baddeše'*, cf. Mal. 3.20 (EV 4.2). **[12]** MT *ḥāpᵉrāh yōladtᵉkem*, 'ashamed is she who bore you': G *mētēr ep' agatha*, 'mother for good', i.e. (the one who bore you) for good. G lacks *hinnēh*, 'look': BHS suggests *hī*, 'that is (the end of the nations)', cf. Rudolph, 300; cf. NEB 'the mere rump of the nations' as the meaning of *'aḥᵃrīt gōyim*. G only has *erēmos*, 'desert', for MT's three synonyms *midbār ṣiyyāh wa'ᵃrābāh*, 'wilderness dry land and desert', cf. 2.6. **[13]** Cf. 19.8; 49.17. **[14]** MT *yᵉdū*, 'shoot': a few mss *yᵉrū*, 'shoot'; both variations convey the same idea. G lacks 'for against Yahweh she has sinned': a pious gloss. **[15]** G lacks *sābīb*, 'round about'. MT *nātᵉnāh yādāh*, lit. 'she has given her hand': i.e. a gesture signalling surrender (cf. I Chron. 29.24; II Chron.30.8; Latin *manum dare*); G *parelu-thēsan hai cheires autēs*, 'her hands are weakened', cf. v. 43. T 'she is given into their hand' (BHS). MT *'āšyōteyhā*, 'her bulwarks': hapax legom. Q presupposes a noun *'āšyāh*; K *'šwytyh* is uncertain (cf. BHS); G *hai epalxeis autēs*, 'her battlements'. Cf. Aram. *'uššayyā'*, 'the foundations' (Ezra 4.12). **[16]** Rudolph, 302, prefers Hiphil form *hakritū* (*h* lost due to haplography) to Qal *kirtū*, 'cut off', as better linguistic usage (cf. G *exolethreusate*, 'completely destroy'). MT *zōrē'a*, 'sower': G *sperma*, 'seed' = *zera'*. Cf. 46.16 for the phrase *mippᵉnē ḥereb hayyōnāh*, 'because of the sword of the oppressor', and see Notes there for G reading of 'Grecian sword'; cf. 25.38 for a similar phrase. 16bβγ = Isa. 13.14b. **[17]** MT *'ᵃrāyōt hiddīḥū*, 'lions have driven away'; a suffix is required, perhaps *hiddīḥūhū*, 'have driven *him* away'; cf. G *leontes exōsan auton*, 'lions have driven *him* out'. G lacks 'Nebuchadrezzar'. MT *'iṣṣ^emō*, lit. 'he has boned him': the verb is a denominative from *'eṣem*, 'bone', and only occurs here, presumably with the sense 'gnaw off bones' (cf. KB, 727; EVV). **[18]** G lacks 'of hosts, god of Israel'. **[19]** G lacks 'and Bashan'. **[20]** G lacks *n^e'um-yhwh* 'says Yahweh'.

The first section of 50 consists of at least six units (vv. 4–5, 6–7, 8–10, 11–13, 14–16, 17–20), which are here treated together because vv. 4 and 20 form a closure. Within vv. 4–20 the attack on Babylon is celebrated in three poems and the fate of Israel encloses these poems. At the time of Babylon's fall (cf. vv. 2–3) the people of Israel will return to their own land and seek Yahweh in Zion. This weeping procession presents the return in liturgical terms as a pilgrimage back to Jerusalem *and to Yahweh* (cf. 3.21–23). Israel (i.e. Judah, cf. v. 17, though the larger diaspora may be envisaged here) will return to Yahweh in a permanent *b^erīt*. This motif links the view of Judah-Israel in 50–51 with that of 30–31 and their expansion in 32–33. In both collections the restoration of the people to their homeland includes notes about the renewal of the community's relationship with Yahweh as a permanent arrangement. Where the collections differ is in the emphasis put solely on Judah-Israel in 30–33, whereas the central feature of 50–51 is Babylon the enemy, and Judah's restoration is but a concomitant of the Babylonian defeat. Included in the introductory pieces about Yahweh's people is the recognition that the nation has been served poorly by leaders (v. 6, cf. 23.1–2), but that is the most critical the collection ever becomes of Judah. All the other pieces present Israel as the innocent victim of vicious opponents, and 50–51 breathe a very different atmosphere from the trenchant critique of Judah and Jerusalem presented in 2–20. Verses 6–7 present the nation, under the figure of sheep, as wandering aimlessly across the mountains and being savaged by their enemies. These enemies hide behind the excuse that their victims sinned against Yahweh (MT). Such a belittling of Judah's offences is indicative of the attitude taken towards the nation's past in 50–51. 'More sinned against than sinning' is the cliché which well summarizes the presentation of Judah-Israel in the OAN, and it makes a very interesting contrast with other strands incorporated into the book of Jeremiah.

The flock metaphor reappears in v. 8 in a brief poem (prose in RSV, but apart from v. 9a the piece would appear to be poetic) as a figure of the fugitives (exiles?) fleeing from doomed Babylon like he-goats prancing at the head of the flock. Ironically Babylon's enemy comes from the north, that fateful direction from whence came Jerusalem's doom. If the first Babylon poem addresses those who must flee from the ill-fated city, the second one (vv. 11–13) denounces Babylon herself and explains why she will become a complete desolation. Mother Babylon (cf. 10.20; 15.10; 31.15 for the maternal metaphor) will be disgraced because her children plundered Yahweh's territory. That pillaging of the land of Judah is represented in further animal terms as a cow gambolling in the fields and stallions neighing. In v. 13 the cause of Babylon's downfall is identified as Yahweh's wrath (cf. the gloss in v. 14, 'because she has sinned against Yahweh'), though elsewhere in the poems the more specific charge of attacking Israel is stated as Babylon's crime (cf. vv. 17bβ, 28; 51.11, 24, 49). The striking feature of this element in 50–51 is its ignorance of the tradition's claim in other strands that *Yahweh himself* destroyed Judah by means of his servant Nebuchadrezzar and the Babylonians as a punishment for their gross sins, apostasy, oppression and idolatry. 50–51 clearly represent a radically different theological perspective on the exile which cannot be integrated with some of the other perspectives in the book of Jeremiah. Such diversity of opinion on the causes and theologization of 587 is not a problem in the interpretation of the Jeremiah tradition, but it is a serious obstacle to a holistic reading of the book because any holistic approach entails a trimming process whereby the integrity of each individual tradition in the book is seriously diminished. From the perspective of 50–51 Judah was hunted down and destroyed by the king of Babylon (cf. 50.17) and for that outrageous campaign Yahweh will destroy Babylon – 'Babylon must fall for the slain of Israel' (51.49; cf. 50.15, 29 'do to her as she has done').

The poem of vv. 14–16 addresses the attackers of Babylon and stresses the cause of the attack as Yahweh's vengeance against the one who has sinned against himself. The great enemy of so many nations must now face the poetic justice of falling before her own enemy (v. 15a, cf. 51.44). With her destruction all the exiles are freed to flee to their own lands and the section returns to the position of the Judaean exiles (cf. vv. 8, 16). This motif allows the section to conclude with some observations on Israel's past and future (vv. 17–20: a mixture of poetry and prose with vv. 17b–19 as a prose commentary on v. 17a). In the most general way v. 17 summarizes

Israel's history over the previous two centuries under the figure of a scattered sheep (*śeh pᵉzūrāh*) driven away by lions. These lions are then identified as the king of Assyria and the king of Babylon, and the effects of their campaigns against Israel as the devouring of the sheep followed by the gnawing of its bones. Between them Assyria and Babylon have destroyed Israel and *therefore* (v. 18) must be punished. Assyria had been punished already (cf. Isa. 10.5–19; ironically Babylon had had a hand in Assyria's downfall), so now it is Babylon's turn. The corollary of Babylon's defeat is the restoration of Israel to its own land. This return to the old territories – the fertile land of Carmel and Bashan (MT) and the hills of Ephraim (cf. 31.6) and Gilead – will satisfy the nation's appetite (*nepeš*). Here is the same dream as is delineated in 31.2–14; it represents the natural longings of any exiled group or people dominated by foreign powers to find satisfaction once more in their own land, free of the unwelcome attention of foreigners. The idyllic nature of v. 19 is of a piece with the dreams of 30–31, and the prerequisite for their achievement is the destruction of Babylon. Beyond Babylon's fall lies a glorious future. A further note adds the observation that in such a future in their own land the sins (past, present or future?) of Israel and Judah will be undetectable because the deity will have pardoned them (cf. 31.34b). Even here there is no concentration on the sins of the people; the subject is only raised in order to emphasize the prospect of Yahweh's forgiveness in the future. Thus the past with its sinfulness and the present with Babylon the arch-enemy will be transformed in the future when the remnant (for that is all the lions left!) settle down in their own land.

50.21–40

21 'Go up against the land of Merathaim,
    and against the inhabitants of Pekod.
  Slay, and utterly destroy after them,
                                    says the LORD,
    and do all that I have commanded you.
22 The noise of battle is in the land,
    and great destruction!
23 How the hammer of the whole earth
    is cut down and broken!

How Babylon has become
 a horror among the nations!
24 I set a snare for you and you were taken, O Babylon,
 and you did not know it;
you were found and caught,
 because you strove against the LORD.
25 The LORD has opened his armoury,
 and brought out the weapons of his wrath,
for the Lord GOD of hosts has a work to do
 in the land of the Chaldeans.
26 Come against her from every quarter;
 open her granaries;
pile her up like heaps of grain, and destroy her utterly;
 let nothing be left of her.
27 Slay all her bulls,
 let them go down to the slaughter.
Woe to them, for their day has come,
 the time of their punishment.'

28 'Hark! they flee and escape from the land of Babylon, to declare in
Zion the vengeance of the LORD our God, vengeance for his temple.'

29 'Summon archers against Babylon, all those who bend the bow.
Encamp round about her; let no one escape. Requite her according to her
deeds, do to her according to all that she has done; for she has proudly
defied the LORD, the Holy One of Israel. 30 Therefore her young men shall
fall in her squares, and all her soldiers shall be destroyed on that day, says
the LORD.'

31 'Behold, I am against you, O proud one,
 says the Lord GOD of hosts;
for your day has come,
 the time when I will punish you.
32 The proud one shall stumble and fall,
 with none to raise him up,
and I will kindle a fire in his cities,
 and it will devour all that is round about him.'

33 'Thus says the LORD of hosts: The people of Israel are oppressed, and
the people of Judah with them; all who took them captive have held them
fast, they refuse to let them go. 34 Their Redeemer is strong; the LORD of
hosts is his name. He will surely plead their cause, that he may give rest to
the earth, but unrest to the inhabitants of Babylon.'

35 'A sword upon the Chaldeans, says the LORD,
 and upon the inhabitants of Babylon,
 and upon her princes and her wise men!

36 A sword upon the diviners,
that they may become fools!
A sword upon her warriors,
that they may be destroyed!
37 A sword upon her horses and upon her chariots,
and upon all the foreign troops in her midst,
that they may become women!
A sword upon all her treasures,
that they may be plundered!
38 A drought upon her waters,
that they may be dried up!
For it is a land of images,
and they are mad over idols.'
39 'Therefore wild beasts shall dwell with hyenas in Babylon, and ostriches
shall dwell in her; she shall be peopled no more for ever, nor inhabited for
all generations. 40 As when God overthrew Sodom and Gomorrah and their
neighbour cities, says the LORD, so no man shall dwell there, and no son of
man shall sojourn in her.'

---

[21] MT *'al-hā'āreṣ m^erātāyīm ^{a}lēh 'ālеyhā*, 'against the land, Merathaim, go up against her': many exegetes (but not Christensen) read *^{a}lēh ('al) 'ereṣ* . . ., 'go up (against) the land of . . .'. The command is addressed to the sword rather than to an invading people (Nötscher, 337). Rudolph, 302, reads *r^edōp*, 'pursue', after *p^eqōd*, 'Pekod', and transposes *'aḥ^arēhem*, 'after them', to follow it: 'and against the inhabitants of Pekod pursue after them'. Word-play may be detected in the use of the names Merathaim (the district of *marratim* at the head of the Persian Gulf), 'double rebellion' (*mrh*, 'rebel'), and Pekod (*puqudu*, a people in East Babylonia), 'doom' (*pqd*, 'punish'), cf. Bright, 354. MT *ḥ^arōb*, lit. 'put to the sword': a denominative verb from *ḥereb*, 'sword', cf. v. 27; G *machaira*, 'sword': G reads *pqd* with *ḥrb* and translates 'avenge, O sword . . .'. MT *w^ehaḥ^arēm*, 'and utterly destroy': i.e. put to the sacred ban by annihilation, cf. v. 26. **[22]** Cf. 4.6; 6.1; 48.3 for the phrase *w^ešeber gādōl*, 'and great destruction'; G 'in the land of the Chaldaeans', cf. v. 25. **[23]** Cf. 51.41 for v. 23b. The metaphor of hammer (*paṭṭīš*), here used to describe Babylon's domination of the land, appears in 23.29 as a figure of the equally destructive power of Yahweh's word. **[24]** MT *yāqōštī lāk*, 'I have set a snare for you': lacking in G; as Yahweh is spoken of in the third person in v. 24b (*bayhwh* 'against Yahweh'), *yāqōštī* should be read as a second person fem. form, '*you* set a snare (for yourself)'; cf. the forms in 2.20, 33. The nature of the trap is not easily discerned but, avoiding an Aulenesque theologization of v. 24, it is probably just a figure of speech for Babylon's defeat. S lacks 'you were found and also seized' (BHS). MT *kī bayhwh hitgārīt*, 'for against Yahweh you engaged in strife':

whether this refers to Babylon's hubristic campaign of world domination or its attack on Jerusalem is a moot point (cf. Volz, 424; Nötscher, 338, who favour the first view, which fits the context of vv. 23–27; the other possibility is indicated by the notes in the poems attacking Babylon for its treatment of Jerusalem). [25] G lacks 'of hosts': its *tō kuriō theō* may represent *yhwh ʾᵉlōhīm* rather than MT's *ʾᵃdōnāy yhwh*, i.e. 'Yahweh god' instead of 'lord Yahweh', cf. Christensen 1975, 252. Cf. v. 13 for the wrath theme. [26] MT *bōʾū-lāh miqqēṣ*, 'come against her without end': read with 51.31, Symm, and many exegetes (e.g. Giesebrecht, Rudolph, Christensen) *miqqāṣeh*, 'from all sides'; cf. G *hoi kairoi autēs*, 'her times (have come)'. MT *kᵉmō-ʿᵃrēmīm*, 'like heaps': i.e. like heaps of grain (cf *maʾᵃbusīm*, 'granaries') or of rubbish or even of ruins; cf. v. 16a for the harvesting motif. G *hōs spēlaion*, '(search her) as a cave' = *kᵉmō-mᵉʿārāh*; Rudolph reads *bᵉmō-* 'in . . .' (cf. BHS); Christensen 1975, 252, 256, conjectures *km ʿ(mr)ym*, 'as a swath of grain' (cf. A *hōsper sōreountes*, 'like those heaping up' = *kamᵉʿammᵉrīm*). Cf. Isa. 14.22 for the cutting off of Babylon's remnant (*šᵉʾār*); *šᵉʾērīt*, 'remnant, is used here. [27] MT *ḥirᵉbū kol-pāreyhā*, 'put to the sword all her bulls': i.e. slay her warriors, cf. NEB; G *anaxēranate pantas tous karpous autēs*, 'dry up all her fruits' = *ḥārᵉbū kol*, continuing the harvesting motif of laying waste the agricultural products of v. 26 (taken by Christensen with v. 26 and following G). Cf. 48.15 for the motif of going down (*yrd*) to slaughter; *ʿēt pᵉquddātām*, 'the time of their punishment', appears in 6.15 (see Notes); 8.12; 10.15; 46.21; 51.18; cf *šᵉnat pᵉquddātām*, 'the year of their punishment', 11.23; 23.12; 48.44. [28] G lacks *niqᵉmat hēkālō*, 'vengeance of his temple': possibly a gloss from 51.11 defining Yahweh's vengeance in terms of Zion's ideology; cf. Ps. 79.1. [29] MT *rabbīm*, 'crowd, host': many exegetes read *rōbīm*, 'archers', cf. Gen. 49.23; G *pollois* = MT. K *ʾl-yhy*; Q *ʾal-yᵉhī-lāh*, 'let there not be to her': cf. G *mē estō autēs*; v. 26. Cf. v. 15 for the notion of retaliatory behaviour; also Lev. 24.19b; Judg. 1.7, where the talionic principle is similarly expressed (cf. Miller 1982, 94). MT *kī ʾel-yhwh zādāh*, 'for against Yahweh she has acted insolently': cf. the insolent men (*zēdīm*) in 43.2; the insolent one (*zādōn*) of vv. 31, 32; and Edom's insolence of mind (*zᵉdōn lēb*). It is difficult to determine the precise connotation of *zūd* here: whether insolence (i.e. insult NEB), presumption, arrogance or hubris (cf. the accusation against Moab in 48.26, 42); perhaps simple defiance of Yahweh (a concomitant of being a foreign nation) is intended, cf. G *autestē*, 'opposed'. The designation of Yahweh as 'the holy one of Israel' (*qᵉdōš yiśrāʾēl*) is a particular feature of the Isaiah tradition and only occurs here and in 51.5 in Jeremiah. [30] = 40.26 minus *ṣᵉbāʾōt*, 'of hosts'; G lacks 'in that day'. [31] MT *zādōn*, 'O Insolence': G *tēn hubristian*, 'the overbearing one', cf. the similar charge of hubris against Moab in 48.29 (G 31.29). G lacks *ʾᵃdōnāy . . . ṣᵉbāʾōt*, 'lord . . . of hosts'. MT *ʿēt pᵉqadtīkā*, 'the time when I punish you': cf. 6.15 for this form; a few mss, Vrs *pᵉquddātekā*, 'your punishment' = the standard form of this cliché, cf.

v. 27 (Notes). **[32]** In vv. 31–32 masc. forms are used, but throughout the poems Babylon, as a city, is personified in fem. terms (normal Hebrew usage). V. 32b = 21.14b except that *bᵉyaʿrāh*, 'in her forest', is used instead of *hᵉʿārāyw*, 'in his cities'; G *en tō drumō autēs*, 'in his forest' = *bᵉyaʿᵃrō*, cf. 21.14b. MT *sᵉbībōtāyw*, 'his environs': a few mss, 21.14b read *sᵉbībāyw*. **[33]** G lacks *ṣᵉbāʾōt*, 'of hosts'. **[34]** MT *gōʾᵃlām*, 'their redeemer': Yahweh as *gōʾēl* is the kinsman obligated to act on behalf of Israel his kin (cf. 31.11); this designation of Yahweh is a dominant epithet in Second Isaiah (41.14; 43.14; 44.6, 24; 47.4; 48.17; 49.7, 26; 54.5, 8) and later strands of Isaiah (e.g. 59.20; 60.16; 63.16). G *kai ho lutroumenos autous* = *wᵉgōʾᵃlām*, '*but* their redeemer', makes a better contrast with v. 33. MT *rīb yārīb ʾet-rībām*, 'he will surely plead their cause': cf. Isa. 34.8; the punning assonance of MT cannot be captured in English. Christensen 1975, 253, deletes *ʾet-* and translates *rībām* as 'their Champion'. **[35]** G lacks *nᵉʾum-yhwh*, 'says Yahweh'. **[36]** G lacks v. 36a, perhaps due to homoiarkton. MT *ʾel-habbaddīm*, 'upon the empty talkers': i.e. windbags, cf. 48.30; Isa. 44.25; NEB 'false prophets'. Vrs 'her empty talkers' = *baddeyhā* (cf. BHS). Bright, 355, thinks *baddīm* is meant to be a pun on *bārīm* (i.e. the *bāru* priests who practised divination in Babylonian culture). **[37]** MT *ʾel-sūsāyw wᵉʾel-rikbō*, 'upon *his* horses and upon his chariot': possibly a gloss from 51.21a (the suffixes are wrong, though corrected by RSV, NEB, cf. JPSB; G *autōn*, 'their'). MT *wᵉhāyū lᵉnāšīm*, 'and they shall become as women': cf. 30.6; 48.41; 49.22 for the motif of warriors turning into women as a figure of fear and devastation caused by invasion and defeat. MT *wᵉʾel-kol-hāʿereb*, 'and upon all the rabble': cf. 25.20; 46.16; a heterogeneous body of mercenaries and auxiliary troops most prone to weakening against fierce opposition. **[38]** MT *ḥōreb*, 'drought': lacking in G but *ḥereb*, 'sword', is better read here with G^{OL}, S; with the sword (i.e. invasion) will come neglect of the Babylonian irrigation system and drought will ensue. MT *ūbāʾēmīm yithōlālū*, 'and they behave like madmen over terrors': i.e. dreadful gods, numina which frighten (cf. the Emim of ancient folklore, Gen. 14.5; Deut. 2.10–11), V *portenta*; 'bogeymen', cf. Bright's 'hoodoos', 'bogies'. MT Hitpolel *hll*, 'behave like madmen over': Vrs *hll*, 'boast', cf. NEB. Rudolph, 304, treats v. 38b as an addition to the text because the context makes Babylon the sword's target for its treatment of the exiles (vv. 33–34) rather than because of its iconic religion. **[39]** MT *ṣiyyīm ʾet-ʾiyyīm*, 'desert-dwellers with inhabitants of the desert': EVV treat as desert animals: 'wild beasts with hyenas' (RSV), 'marmots and jackals' (NEB), 'wildcats and with hyenas' (JPSB); as usual word-play (cf. Cornill, 505–6) sacrifices meaning to cleverness and obscures the semantic force of the phrase. Perhaps animals are not meant but uncanny or demonic beings associated with the desert (cf. Bright, 355, 'goblins and ghouls'); this would match v. 38b quite well. Both terms appear in Isa. 34.14, and each one appears respectively in Isa. 13.21, 22. Isa. 13.20a = v. 39b (plus *ʿōd*, 'no more'); for vv. 39–40 cf. Isa. 13.19–22. The use of *yšb* three times in MT may not be original; *škn*, 'dwell', probably should be read for the second occurrence of *yšb* (cf. BHS). **[40]** Cf. 49.18; Isa. 13.19 for the Sodom and Gomorrah allusion. 40b = 49.33b.

The second section of 50 consists of a number of units (at least seven: vv. 21–27, 28, 29–30, 31–32, 33–34, 35–38a, 39–40) enclosed by the motif of utter destruction (vv. 21, 40), though vv. 39–40 are essentially an appendix to v. 38b. The invasion and defeat of Babylon are the central elements, and Israel only appear infrequently (e.g. vv. 28, 33–34). Yahweh is the one who attacks Babylon, the one who releases the sword against the hammer of the whole earth (vv. 21, 35–38a). Yet the invading forces can be discerned at certain points as also commanded by Yahweh to destroy Babylon (e.g. vv. 26–27, 29). Babylon's role as devastator of so many countries is reversed in these poems and her overweening arrogance (like Moab, hubris is the flaw in her make-up) is such that she has been trapped into striving against Yahweh. This hubristic attitude of Babylon's is not developed in 50–51, though it is repeatedly referred to, but in Isa. 14.12–20 it gives rise to the splendid satire on Helel ben Shachar (the morning star which via V becomes Lucifer and then is transformed into the devil in gothic theology). Throughout this section the view of Babylon reflects that of all the states devastated by the tyrannical imperium – now it is her turn to experience what she herself has imposed on others (cf. vv. 15, 29). Now it is Yahweh who opens his arsenal, brings forth the weapons of his wrath, and lays waste the land of the Chaldaeans. In brilliant images the poet makes the deity summon up the invading forces to tear apart the enemy Babylon. The metaphors are derived from the harvesting process (vv. 26–27a; cf. v. 16a) and represent Babylon as a land replete with its ingathered harvest. Granaries bursting with produce are to be torn open and the precious grain spilled out in heaps. Gathered fruit is to be ruined (G) or, to vary the image, her bulls are to be slaughtered (MT). Such a reversal of the harvest is the death of a culture (rather different images of the *failure* of the harvest make the same point against Jerusalem in 8.13, 20). Yet how well the images of destroyed granaries convey the idea of a powerful and politically sated empire such as Babylon being overrun and devastated by invaders!

As a dramatic counterpoint to this picture of the reversal of the fortunes of Babylon, v. 28 depicts refugees fleeing from the fallen city and defeated land to announce in Zion the unfolding of Yahweh's vengeance. A glossator anticipates 51.11 by spelling out the nature of that vengeance – it is the vindication of Zion's temple. How bitterly painful had been that perfidious destruction of the sacred house of Yahweh in 587, and now, fifty years later, sweet revenge is gained by Yahweh's defeat of the blasphemers. The sentiment, gloss though it may be, is in keeping with the view of the temple expressed throughout the Jeremiah tradition (e.g. 3.17; 17.12; 31.40; implicit in the placing of Jeremiah in the temple as the centre of his work 7.2; 19.14; 22.1; 26.2; 35.2; it is likely that 7.12–15 represents not so much a denigration of the temple as a criticism of the people who use it). Babylon's crimes may be many, but her destruction of the temple is singled out here in order to define Yahweh's vengeance. A more general account is given in v. 29, where all Babylon's actions are made the grounds of her defeat (cf. v. 15). But these are seen as constituting opposition to Yahweh, the holy one of Israel (an echo of the Isaiah tradition). How different this accusation is from the presentation of Babylon as Yahweh's servant in 27–29, 39–40! And how more realistic it is also from the viewpoint of all those oppressed by the imperial power (cf. Ps. 109; 137).

An independent poem in vv. 31–32 (the gender is different from the standard presentation of city and country as feminine forms) attacks one whose hubris is such that he may be addressed 'O insolent one' (*zādōn*). Babylon is not named here, and the anonymity of the target indicates the conventionality of the poem (vv. 31b, 32b use forms found elsewhere in Jeremiah). But in the context of the edited vv. 21–40 Babylon may be regarded as the hubristic one intended here (cf. Isa. 13–14; 47.7–10; in OAN Babylon is not the only nation guilty of hubris, cf. 48.29 for Moab; Isa. 10.7–14 for Assyria; Ezek. 27–28 for Tyre). Against the hubris of nations and individuals (cf. 17.5–6; Isa. 2.12–17) Yahweh is the implacable opponent, and thus Babylon the great must fall before his wrath.

The exiled Israelites appear for the first time directly in this section (v. 28 is an oblique reference to them) in vv. 33–34 and are represented as being held fast by their captors who refuse to let them go. To this state of affairs Yahweh responds and is thus justly described as their kinsman (redeemer is conventional English). As kinsman he meets his obligations to act on behalf of his kinsfolk by taking up their quarrel (*rīb*, 'case, suit') and vindicating them. This vindication will bring rest to the earth but turmoil to Babylon (contrast 25.31, where Yahweh's *rīb* is directed against the nations and all flesh). Attached to this oracular proclamation of Yahweh's activity on behalf of the exiles is a fine poem about the sword against Babylon, which may be understood as the means whereby the captives will be liberated. The sword motif appears in vv. 21, 27 (used as a verb), but in vv. 35–38a the noun *ḥereb*, 'sword', is used five or six times (cf. Notes) in brief statements delineating the classes of its Babylonian victims. Whether the sword stands for Yahweh's uncanny defeat of Babylon or for the invading (Persian) forces or both is unclear from the text, but the sword's crusade against the Chaldaeans effectively ruins people and land.

38b offers a different explanation for the destruction of Babylon from vv. 33–34: it is a land of images (*pᵉsilīm*, cf. 10.2–5, 8–9, 14–15), and the people behave like madmen over dreadful gods. Appropriately then the land of such wild, superstitious behaviour will be depopulated and become the haunt of wild animals (EVV) or, more likely, the place of 'ghouls and ghosties' (Bright). What the people have worshipped will take over the uninhabited territory, and Babylon will become an unsalubrious place forever (v. 39). So great will be Babylon's devastation that the fate of Sodom and Gomorrah (Gen. 19.24–25, 28) comes to mind as the best analogy of it (v. 40; cf. Isa. 13.19). Here Babylon has a mythical status and its annihilation is so complete that never again will the land (or is it the city only?) be inhabited. Apart from the rhetoric of these poems and comments, the depiction of Babylon's fall is given in such grandiloquent terms that the actual changeover of power between the Babylonians and the Persians is dwarfed into insignificance. This is hardly evidence of a pre-539 setting for 50 (cf. v. 28; or 51), though elements may belong to that period, but indicates the development of Babylon as the symbol of hubristic opposition to Yahweh. After 539 such a symbol became independent of the actual Babylonia where people continued to live, even to this day (i.e. modern Iraq).

50.41–46

41 'Behold, a people comes from the north;
a mighty nation and many kings
are stirring from the farthest parts of the earth.

42 They lay hold of bow and spear;
    they are cruel, and have no mercy.
  The sound of them is like the roaring of the sea;
    they ride upon horses,
  arrayed as a man for battle
    against you, O daughter of Babylon!
43 The king of Babylon heard the report of them,
    and his hands fell helpless;
  anguish seized him,
    pain as of a woman in travail.'
44 'Behold, like a lion coming up from the jungle of the Jordan against a
strong sheepfold, I will suddenly make them run away from her; and I will
appoint over her whomever I choose. For who is like me? Who will summon
me? What shepherd can stand before me? 45 Therefore hear the plan which
the LORD has made against Babylon, and the purposes which he has formed
against the land of the Chaldeans: Surely the little ones of their flock shall
be dragged away; surely their fold shall be appalled at their fate. 46 At the
sound of the capture of Babylon the earth shall tremble, and her cry shall
be heard among the nations.'

[50.41–43] = 6.22–24 with minor variations: in v. 42 the target is daughter Babylon whereas in 6.23 it is daughter Zion; in v. 43 it is the king of Babylon who responds to the invasion as a helpless, pregnant woman but in 6.24 it is the citizens of Jerusalem who respond in this fashion. **[50.44–46]** = 40.19–21 with the necessary changes made for Babylon rather than Edom (see Notes on 49.19–21) and minor variations: v. 44 K *'rwṣm*; Q *'arīṣēm*, 'I will make them run away'; v. 45 the divine plan is against *Babylon* rather than Edom (49.20) and the land of the Chaldaeans instead of the inhabitants of Teman: v. 46 the nations hear the outcry of Babylon, whereas in 49.21 the cry of Edom is heard at the sea of reeds. Cf. BHS for further minor variations between both sets of texts and MT-G variations in 50.41–46.

Two common pieces conclude this part of the collection of material against Babylon with v. 46 forming a closure with 50.2. The interchangeability of material in the book of Jeremiah indicates the conventional nature of the poetry used to construct the tradition (see on 6.22–26). Jerusalem-Babylon or Edom-Babylon or Jerusalem community-the Jewish communities in Egypt may all be the recipients of the same poem, indictment or saying. Material is freely created and applied to different groups, with the necessary adjustments for identification. Hence the tradition has a high degree of formal construction and a correspondingly low degree of semantic content. The enemy in 4–6 and 46–51 is therefore anonymous, the language rhetorical, and the semantics difficult to determine. Yet a glimpse of irony (unintentional perhaps) may be discerned in the interpretation of 6.22–26 as a statement about the Babylonian attack on Jerusalem and the recognition that in 50.41–43 Babylon herself becomes the victim of that very process she implemented against Zion. Thus is it done to her as she has done to others (vv. 15,29). The revenge afforded to the Jews by the downfall of Babylon must have been very sweet and a good liturgy of the events of the sixth century would read 50–51 *after* the reading of the book of Lamentations.

The destruction of Babylon is described in vv. 44–46 using a piece also used in the denunciations of Edom (49.19–21). It is a mixture of prose and poetry (cf. EVV, BHS, various exegetes) and illustrates the variations with which the same material may be applied to different nations. Echoes of the incomparability of Yahweh theme (v. 44b) appear in it, and this motif works well in 50 with its emphasis on the hubristic nature of Babylon's domination of the world. Against the incomparable one even the hammer of the earth cannot prevail, and Babylon is like a flock of sheep against which a lion comes up from the jungle of Jordan. *Among the nations* is heard the outcry of her devastation, and this motif (v. 46) provides a fine conclusion (or midpoint) to the poem's prefatory exclamation 'declare *among the nations* . . . Babylon is taken!' (50.2). 'So perish all thine enemies, O LORD!' (Judg. 5.31a).

51.1–33

51 1 Thus says the LORD:
'Behold, I will stir up the spirit of a destroyer
against Babylon,
against the inhabitants of Chaldea;
2 and I will send to Babylon winnowers,
and they shall winnow her,
and they shall empty her land,
when they come against her from every side
on the day of trouble.
3 Let not the archer bend his bow,
and let him not stand up in his coat of mail.

Spare not her young men;
utterly destroy all her host.
4 They shall fall down slain in the land of the Chaldeans,
and wounded in her streets.
5 For Israel and Judah have not been forsaken
by their God, the LORD of hosts;
but the land of the Chaldeans is full of guilt
against the Holy One of Israel.'
6 'Flee from the midst of Babylon,
let every man save his life!
Be not cut off in her punishment,
for this is the time of the LORD's vengeance,
the requital he is rendering her.
7 Babylon was a golden cup in the LORD's hand,
making all the earth drunken;
the nations drank of her wine,
therefore the nations went mad.
8 Suddenly Babylon has fallen and been broken;
wail for her!
Take balm for her pain;
perhaps she may be healed.
9 We would have healed Babylon,
but she was not healed.
Forsake her, and let us go
each to his own country;
for her judgment has reached up to heaven
and has been lifted up even to the skies.
10 The LORD has brought forth our vindication;
come, let us declare in Zion
the work of the LORD our God.'
11 'Sharpen the arrows!
Take up the shields!
The LORD has stirred up the spirit of the kings of the Medes,
because his purpose concerning Babylon is to destroy it, for that
is the vengeance of the LORD, the vengeance for his temple.
12 Set up a standard against the walls of Babylon;
make the watch strong;
set up watchmen;
prepare the ambushes;
for the LORD has both planned and done
what he spoke concerning the inhabitants of Babylon.
13 O you who dwell by many waters,
rich in treasures,

your end has come,
the thread of your life is cut.
14 The LORD of hosts has sworn by himself:
Surely I will fill you with men, as many as locusts,
and they shall raise the shout of victory over you.'
15 'It is he who made the earth by his power,
who established the word by his wisdom,
and by his understanding
stretched out the heavens.
16 When he utters his voice there is a tumult of waters in the heavens,
and he makes the mist rise from the ends of the earth.
He makes lightnings for the rain,
and he brings forth the wind from his storehouses.
17 Every man is stupid and without knowledge;
every goldsmith is put to shame by his idols;
for his images are false,
and there is no breath in them.
18 They are worthless, a work of delusion;
at the time of their punishment they shall perish.
19 Not like these is he who is the portion of Jacob,
for he is the one who formed all things,
and Israel is the tribe of his inheritance;
the LORD of hosts is his name.'
20 'You are my hammer and weapon of war:
with you I break nations in pieces;
with you I destroy kingdoms;
21 with you I break in pieces the horse and his rider;
with you I break in pieces the chariot and the charioteer;
22 with you I break in pieces man and woman;
with you I break in pieces the old man and the youth;
with you I break in pieces the young man and the maiden;
23 with you I break in pieces the shepherd and his flock;
with you I break in pieces the farmer and his team;
with you I break in pieces governors and commanders.'
24 'I will requite Babylon and all the inhabitants of Chaldea before
your very eyes for all the evil that they have done in Zion, says
the LORD.'
25 'Behold, I am against you, O destroying mountain,
says the LORD,
which destroys the whole earth;
I will stretch out my hand against you,
and roll you down from the crags,
and make you a burnt mountain.

26 No stone shall be taken from you for a corner
and no stone for a foundation,
but you shall be a perpetual waste,
says the LORD.'
27 'Set up a standard on the earth,
blow the trumpet among the nations;
prepare the nations for war against her,
summon against her the kingdoms,
Ararat, Minni, and Ashkenaz;
appoint a marshal against her,
bring up horses like bristling locusts.
28 Prepare the nations for war against her,
the kings of the Medes, with their governors and deputies,
and every land under their dominion.
29 The land trembles and writhes in pain,
for the LORD's purposes against Babylon stand,
to make the land of Babylon a desolation,
without inhabitant.
30 The warriors of Babylon have ceased fighting,
they remain in their strongholds;
their strength has failed,
they have become women;
her dwellings are on fire,
her bars are broken.
31 One runner runs to meet another,
and one messenger to meet another,
to tell the king of Babylon
that his city is taken on every side.
32 The fords have been seized,
the bulwarks are burned with fire,
and the soldiers are in panic.
33 For thus says the LORD of hosts, the God of Israel:
The daughter of Babylon is like a threshing floor
at the time when it is trodden;
yet a little while
and the time of her harvest will come.'

[MT 51] = G 28. **[1]** MT *w^e'el-yōš^{e}bē lēb qāmāy*, lit. 'and against the inhabitants of the heart of those who rise up against me': or perhaps the territory of Leb-Qamay, i.e. Kambul (NEB) or an allusion to Gambuli (cf. Rudolph, 306). Many exegetes treat it as an athbash (see Notes on 25.26) or cipher for Chaldaea (*lb qmy* = *kśdym*): G *Chaldaious*, 'Chaldaeans', cf. T. Rudolph deletes 'against Babylon and' because it ruins the metre: a cipher is hardly needed if Babylon is named in 1a, though such ciphers (cf. v. 41) may be no more than a vestige of incantatory practices directed against the enemy using poems such as make up 50–51. MT *rûaḥ mašḥît*, 'spirit of destruction/destroyer': Heb. is ambiguous cf. vv. 11 (destroyer addressed), 25 (mountain of destruction/destroyer); cf. G *anemon kausōna diaphtheironta*, 'a destructive burning wind'. **[2]** MT *zārîm*, 'strangers': vocalize as *zōrîm*, 'winnowers', with A, Symm, V. MT *kî-hāyû 'āleyhā missābîb*, 'and they shall be against her round about': some exegetes follow Volz, 428, *kî yaḥ^a nû*, 'for they will encamp (against her round about)', cf. BHS; G *ouai epi Babulōna kuklothen*, 'woe to Babylon round about'. Cf. 4.11–12 for a different use of the winnowing image; 19.7 for the emptying (*bqq*) of the plans of Jerusalem, a motif used more literally here for the emptying (*bqq*) of the land of inhabitants. **[3]** K *'l ydrk ydrk hdrk qštw*; Q *'el-yidrōp haddōrēk qaštō*, 'to let bend (let bend K) the bowman his bow': unintelligible; G lacks *'l*; many mss, Vrs read *'al*, 'not . . .'; G^L *ep' autēs 'eleyhā* = 'against her'. These corrections yield 'let the bowman bend his bow against her', cf. JPSB or 'let not the bowman bend his bow', cf. RSV, NEB (with reference to Babylon's inability to defend herself). MT *w^e 'el-yit'al b^e siryōnō*, 'and to let him rise up in his armour': some mss, Vrs *w^e 'al*, 'and not . . .'; Rudolph, 306, reads *'al-yiyga' l^e buš siryōnō*, 'let him not be weary of wearing his armour' (to balance his reading of *'al-yerep haddorēk qaštō*, 'let him not cease from wielding his bow'), cf. BHS. Christensen 1975, 263, 268, treats *'l* as El, 'god' (cf. v. 56; 32.18) in both places (and emends *hyw* in v. 2 to *yhwh*, 'Yahweh'), so that it is El who treads down (*drk*) and rises up wearing armour. Cf. 50.21, 26 for the motif of total war (*ḥrm*). **[5]** MT *kî lō'-'almān yiśrā'ēl wîhûdāh*, lit. 'for Israel and Judah have not been *widowed*': i.e. Yahweh has not killed the husbands of Israel and Judah; a figure of desolation and abandonment. This is a curious image which suggests that the verse is intrusive here (cf. Bright, 356). MT *kî 'arṣām māl'āh 'āšām*, 'for *their* land is full of guilt': whose land? If the land of Babylon is intended, then v. 5b should precede 5a (cf. Cornill, 508–9; Nötscher, 342; Rudolph, 306–7); cf. 50.29 for the holy one of Israel as the one offended by Babylon. 51.5 and 50.7 provide an antithesis: the nations regard Israel as guilty (*'āšām*), but it is their own land (i.e. Babylon's) which is really guilty; cf. 2.3. Isa. 47.8–9 presents the fall of Babylon in terms of widowhood; the assertion that Israel and Judah have not been widowed is strange in view of 721 and 587, when the kingdoms fell to external forces. **[6]** Cf. 50.8. The phrase *ûmall^e ṭû 'îš napšō*, 'and let each man save his life', occurs in v. 45 (cf. 48.6) and may be an addition here (cf. Cornill, 509; Rudolph, 307). **[7]** Cf. 25.15–17 for the cup metaphor; the metaphor is used differently here and some exegetes delete 'in Yahweh's hand' as a gloss from 25.15ff. (e.g. Duhm, Giesebrecht, Cornill, Rudolph). Vrs lack the second occurrence of *gōyîm*, 'nations'. **[9]** K *rp 'nw*; Q *rippinû*, 'we treated' (K *rp'*, original form; for Q cf. 3.22). MT *'iz^e bûhā*, 'abandon her': in this context 'let us abandon her'; cf. G *egkatalipōmen autēn.* **[10]** MT *hôṣî yhwh 'et-ṣidᵉqōtēnû*, 'Yahweh has brought forth *our* vindication': the defeat of Babylon from the perspective of Zion cf. v. 11; 50.28; G . . . *to krima autou*, '. . . *his* judgment'. **[11]** MT *mil'û haššᵉlāṭîm*, lit. 'fill the shields/quivers': meaning of *šeleṭ* uncertain; EVV favour 'quiver', modern exegetes 'shield' (e.g. Rudolph, Christensen); cf. II Sam. 8.7; II Kings 11.10; Ezek. 27.11; G *plēroute tas pharetras*, 'fill the quivers' (translation or interpretative gloss?). The sense of *ml'* appears to be 'make ready' (cf. Rudolph, 308); Driver 1937–38, 127, understands it as 'make full ready the shields'. Cf. Thomas 1952a on *ml'* as a military term; Zech. 9.13 for *ml'* with *qešet*, 'bow'. 11a is continued in v. 12 and 11b should be regarded as an additional comment explaining the battle against Babylon as Yahweh's vengeance (*niqmat hêkālô*, 'vengeance of his temple', cf. 50.28); cf. Fohrer 1981, 50–1, who treats all the references to Zion, Israel, temple and cult as redactional. G has *basileōs*, 'king of' for *malᵉkê*, 'kings of'. **[12]** MT *kî gam-zāmam yhwh gam-'āśāh*, 'for Yahweh has both planned and done': cf. Lam. 2.17: *'āśāh yhwh 'ᵃšer zāmam*, 'Yahweh has done what he planned'; the destruction of both Jerusalem and Babylon are divine acts of the same type. **[13]** K *šknty*; Q *šōkantᵉ*, 'you who dwell': cf. 22.23 (K old fem. ending). MT *'al-mayim rabbîm*, 'by many waters'; reference to the Euphrates and the irrigation canals of Babylon, with a possible allusion to the mythological waters which undergird the earth (cf. May 1955). MT *'ammat biṣ'ēk*, lit. 'the cubit of your unjust gain': uncertain meaning; possibly a metaphor from the weaving trade (cf. Isa. 38.12), 'the cubit of your cutting off', i.e. your cubit (thread of life cf. RSV) is cut off; cf. NEB 'your destiny is certain'. G *hēkei to peras sou alēthōs eis to splagchna, sou* 'your end is truly come to your bowels' = . . . *'ᵉmet bᵉmē'āyik*. The obscurity of MT (partly caused by *bṣ'* as noun, 'unjust gain', or infinitive, 'cut off') would appear to have a simple meaning: 'your end has come' (cf. *bā' qiṣṣēk*), your length of cloth is cut off. **[14]** MT *nišba' yhwh ṣᵉbā'ôt bᵉnapšô*, 'Yahweh of hosts has sworn by himself': for the unusual use of *šb' bnpš* with Yahweh as subject cf. Amos 6.8; the normal forms of self-swearing by Yahweh appear in 22.5; 44.26; 49.13. G *hoti ōmose kurios kata tou brachionos autou*, 'for the lord has sworn by his arm': cf. Isa. 62.8 for this idiom; Rudolph inserts *'ᵉlōhê yiśrā'ēl*, 'the god of Israel' before 'by himself' for metrical reasons (cf. BHS). MT *'ādām kayyeleq*, lit. 'mankind as locusts': perhaps 'men like locusts', i.e. countless men (EVV); Rudolph substitutes *'ōyᵉbîm*, 'foes', for *'ādām* because 'men' is too universal. Cf. II Kings 5.20 for the positive use of *kî 'im*; Nahum 3.15–17 for the locust imagery. It is possible to read the Hebrew as *kî 'ᵃmallē' 'ōtāk*, 'for I *will* fill you', thus resolving the problem of MT's 'I *have* filled you' (Giesebrecht, 256; cf. Cornill, 511); or to translate the line as 'even if you were filled with people (*kᵉ'ādām*) as with locusts, yet would they (i.e. the invaders) chant the triumph shout over you'. **[15–19]** = 10.12–16 with minor variations (cf. Notes there; BHS). **[20]** MT *mappēṣ*, lit. 'shatterer':

variously translated as 'hammer' (RSV; contrast 50.23 *paṭṭīš*, 'hammer': a figure of Babylon), 'battle-axe' (NEB), 'war club' (JPSB), 'mace' (Bright); derived from *npṣ*, 'shatter' (cf. Ps. 137.9), a figure used in 13.14 for the shattering of the inhabitants of Jerusalem. G *diaskorpizeis su moi*, 'you scatter for me': treating Heb. as a verbal form from *pūṣ*, 'scatter'. MT *kᵉlē*, 'weapons of': read sing. *kᵉlī*, 'weapon of (war)', as *bᵉkā*, 'with you', in vv. 20–23 indicates. **[21]** MT repeats *wᵉrōkᵉbō*, 'and its rider': Duhm, 369, changes the second occurrence to *rakkābō*, 'his charioteer', followed by Rudolph, 310, for variety (BHS); also Bright, 348. **[22]** MT may have one clause too many: G lacks 'with you I break in pieces the old man and the youth' (deleted by BHS); Christensen 1975, 269, deletes 'with you I break in pieces the young man and the maiden' as a variant reading; Rudolph also omits this clause. **[23]** Rudolph deletes the third clause as an addition from v. 28 (BHS); whereas Christensen adds 'with you I shatter princes and wise men' as a conjectural emendation from 51.57 to balance the third colon. **[24]** MT *ʾᵃšer-ʿāśū bᵉṣiyyōn lᵉʿênêkem*, 'which they did in Zion in your sight': i.e. those who saw the destruction of Jerusalem in 587 will witness Babylon's defeat in 539; those addressed are the defeated of 587. However, some exegetes link 'in your sight' to 'I will requite' (e.g. RSV, Rudolph, Bright), thus limiting the reference to the witnesses of Babylon's destruction. Cf. v. 11; 50.28 for the same explanation of 587 as the cause of Babylon's punishment. **[25]** MT *har hammašḥīt*, 'mountain of destruction': G *to oros to diephtharmenon*, 'the destroyed mountain' = *har hammāšḥāt*. Bright, 357, translates MT as 'mountain of raiders', cf. I Sam. 13.17; 14.15. The phrase 'the destroyer of the whole earth' may be an explanatory gloss (cf. BHS). G lacks *nᵉʾum-yhwh*, 'says Yahweh'. The metaphor of rolling a mountain from the rocks is a mixed one and 'from the rocks' is deleted by Rudolph, who translates *wᵉgilgaltīkā* as 'and make you a heap of stones'. Rudolph reads *lᵉtannur*, 'fire-pot, stove', for *lᵉhar*, 'mountain (of burning)'. The transformation of the mountain into a fireplace will render its stones useless for building purposes (v. 26). **[26]** Contrast Isa. 28.16. **[27]** 'Ararat, Minni, and Ashkenaz': territories (in modern Armenia) under the control of the Medes (v. 28); probably an explanatory gloss here (cf. Rudolph). MT *qaddᵉšū*, 'prepare for war': lit. 'sanctify'; perhaps begin war with a sacred ritual, cf. 6.4; 22.7. MT *ṭipsār*, 'scribe, marshal': Akk *tupšarru*, 'tablet writer'; a high ranking officer, cf. Nahum 3.17, where it occurs also in a context of locust imagery. MT *kᵉyeleq sāmār*, 'like bristling locusts': G *hōs akridōn plēthos*, 'like a multitude of locusts', reading *mispār* for *sāmār* (a word of uncertain meaning and used only here). **[28]** Cf. v. 11; G 'king of the Medes' for MT 'kings of the Medes'. MT *memᵉšaltō*, 'its dominion': *-tām*, 'their (dominion)', cf. BHS. A gloss on v. 27 reflecting the Median control of territory at some stage in the sixth century. **[29]** MT *qāmāh . . . maḥšᵉbōt*, 'the purposes of . . . stand': sing. verb with plur. noun; a few mss, G, S read 'purpose of . . .'; Q^Or *qāmū* makes number agree. **[30]** MT *hayū l^enāšîm*, 'they have become women': cf. 30.6; 48.41; 49.22; 50.37 for this motif. **[32]** MT *w^e'et-hā'^agammîm*, lit. 'and the swamp-reeds': i.e. the marshes where fugitives might hide (cf. Bright, 357); RSV, Rudolph 'bulwarks'; NEB 'guard-towers'. Christensen 1975, 269, follows G in reading *miqqāṣeh* (v. 32, 'on every side') with v. 33 as qualifying the fords, i.e. 'remote fords'. MT *nibhālū*, 'are terrified': G *exerchontai*, 'are going forth' = *hāl^ekū*. **[33]** G lacks 'of hosts, the god of Israel' and has *oikoi basileōs Babylōnos*, 'the houses of the king of Babylon', for MT *bat-bābel*, 'daughter Babylon'. In preparation for harvesting the threshing floor was tamped to make it hard. The personification of Babylon as a woman here in conjunction with images drawn from agricultural techniques of stomping and threshing may have sexual overtones of rape and pillage (cf. Job 31.10 for a similar use of *ṯḥn*, 'grind'). The savage rape of a young woman is a universal image of the depradations of war which reduce a land and its cities to a bloody, bowed mess. Vrs lack second occurrence of *'ēt*, 'time of . . .'; *qāṣîr*, 'harvest', is a common metaphor of destruction, whether military or otherwise (cf. Hos. 6.11; Joel 4.13 [EV 3.13]).

The first section of 51 is made up of a number of units (e.g. vv. 1–5, 6–10, 11–14, 15–19, 20–23, 24, 25–26, 27–33) and, although few exegetes agree on how to divide the chapter intosections, would appear to consist of vv. 1–33 because vv. 2, 33 form a closure using harvesting motifs. The mixture of motifs and pieces is similar to 50 and there are elements in 51 which may not have originally applied to Babylon's destruction (e.g. vv. 15–19 belong more appropriately to 10.1–16, and vv. 20–23 may have been spoken of Babylon as the destroyer rather than the victim). However, the central theme of the section is unmistakably the defeat of Babylon: a defeat either celebrated (v. 8) or imminently anticipated (vv. 6, 33). Glosses within the poems identify some of the military action against Babylon as Median (e.g. vv. 11b, 27bY, 28; cf. Isa. 13.17), but whether these indicate a period before 550 for the editing of the poem is difficult to determine. The section must be considered independent of such glosses, and therefore pre-Cyrus opposition to Babylon is hardly a feature of the poems. Yet like all the poetry sections of the book of Jeremiah, 51 is too general to be pinned down to a specific time before or after the fall of Babylon in 539. Only a few fragments deal with Zion in this section (vv. 10, 11b, 24), and these simply equate Babylon's defeat with the vindication of Zion. Retribution has come to Babylon – 'let us declare in Zion the work of Yahweh our god' (v. 10). That retribution is Yahweh's vengeance for what happened in Zion, in particular the destruction of the temple (vv. 24, 11b). There is in 50–51 no sense of the justifications offered throughout the book of Jeremiah for the fall of Jerusalem or even of the temple sermon with its analogy between Shiloh and the cult centre in Jerusalem (7.12–14). These are quite foreign to the spirit of the anti-Babylonian material (v. 5 can be read as an acknowledgment of the sinfulness of the land of Israel and Judah, but such a reading depends upon the ambiguity of the Hebrew text; cf. 50.7). Clearly the producers and editors of 50–51 did not share the belief that Babylon had been the servant of the living god when it massacred the people of Judah and destroyed both city and temple in 588–7. Babylon was the enemy, and remained so throughout the decades after the catastrophe, and its defeat is celebrated in poem after poem in 50–51.

The residual incantatory cipher in v. 1 (MT) indicates something of the magical function of the collection of poems in 50–51. Babylon is denounced by various means, including special words which conceal the name of the enemy (cf. 25.26 *Sheshak* for Babylon), and therefore render the spells incapable of being counteracted. Repetitive chantings of these poems (note how little development is achieved from 50.2–3 to 51.54–57) may have been intended to bring about the fate of the enemy celebrated or, in conjunction with various military campaigns against the foe, to encourage every sign of opposition to the Babylonian empire. The agricultural metaphors which enclose the section (vv. 2, 33; cf. 50.26) represent the destruction of Babylon as a great harvesting operation which will empty the land. Within this representation various voices (defined as oracular by v. 1) are heard encouraging the exiles to flee, bemoaning the defeat of Babylon (vv. 8–9), summoning the enemy to attack (vv. 11–12, 27–28), praising Yahweh as the incomparable portion of Jacob, addressing an unidentified power (vv. 20–23), speaking against the mountain of destruction (v. 25 only identifiable as Babylon by virtue of the context of 50–51), and describing the panic induced in the Babylonians by their defeat (vv. 30–32). Such a comprehensive defeat of the great enemy reflects the earlier destruction of Jerusalem (cf. 4–6, 8–10) and must be judged as compensation for that disaster. Total war (vv. 3, 13, 25–26) against Babylon is the theme of the section, and the extermination of the violator of Jerusalem becomes the vindication of Zion and temple.

Interpretative questions arise from the ambiguity of certain verses: e.g. vv. 5, 7, 14, 20–23. The assertion that Israel and Judah have not been widowed is difficult to understand in the light of 587, but given the chauvinism of 50–51 may reflect an optimism arising out of the defeat of Babylon (cf. the similar spirit of Second Isaiah). It is intrusive here, and the ambiguity of '*their* land' may indicate a displaced polemic about the status of Israel and the land (cf. 50.7; Isa. 50.1). Babylon as a golden cup in Yahweh's hand with which he made the nations mad (cf. 25.15–17, where the cup imagery is used differently to represent Jeremiah as the dispenser of the poisonous brew) is a metaphor out of place in a poem about Babylon's destruction. The notion of Babylon as Yahweh's instrument *and* the object of his wrath for behaving as such an instrument raises theological problems (cf. the similar set of motifs in Isa. 10.5–15, but there Assyria is blamed for over-reaching its commission by excessive zeal in conquering nations; here no such charge is made against Babylon). The inconsistency of the two motifs may be resolved by a sharp separation of the different strands which use them: Babylon as the servant of Yahweh and Babylon as the violator of Zion and the nations. But the theological problems of Yahweh using an *idolatrous* nation to do his bidding against another *idolatrous* nation (Judah) remain. How can Babylon's idolatry be overlooked in order to punish Judah for religious deviations? Is this not to strain at a gnat and to swallow a camel on the deity's part? The use of 10.12–16 in 51.15–19 indicates an awareness of Babylon's idolatrous status (cf. 50.2c, 38b–39; 51.47, 52), but the incongruity of the matter is not grasped by the text. For Yahweh to use an idolatrous power so blithely is a serious problem of theological integrity in the tradition and, although diversity of sources in the book may explain why the problem is not recognized, the fundamental incoherence of the belief should be noted. The beginnings of a critique are attempted in a different context in II Chron. 28.9–11, where the prophet Oded berates the invading Israelites for their savage treatment of the Judaeans with the pertinent question: 'Have you not sins of your own against Yahweh your god?'. How much more rigorously might the question be posed to idolatrous nations invading Judaean territory: 'Are not your own idols an affront to Yahweh?'. It would appear to be the case that the notions of Judah as idolatrous (a feature of Part I) and the idolatrous Babylon as the enemy of Judah are quite separate elements in the tradition. Reading the book holistically raises serious problems such as this, but if its redactional history is stressed the difficulties may be modified.

The sympathetic attitude towards Babylon hinted at in vv. 8–9 must be regarded as purely rhetorical, perhaps even satirical. It hardly implies an attempt on the part of the Judaean exiles to save their enemy from destruction, but represents conventional expressions of concern over the wounded (cf. 8.22; 46.11). The sick woman cannot be healed, and the only practical course of action is to abandon her to her fate and flee to the homeland. Just as Zion was once stricken without healing, so Babylon is now mortally wounded. The divine oath in v. 14 is ambiguous in that it is not clear whether the deity will fill the city with the very men who will shout the victory song over it or whether in spite of the city being filled with men like locusts (a figure of troops or number?) the invaders will still chant the shout of triumph over it (cf. Notes). The ambiguity is hardly a significant one. It is not obvious what the shattering imagery of vv. 20–23 refers to: 'with you' could be Babylon (cf. 50.23), Babylon's enemy, or something mythical (cf. Yahweh's weapons, 50.25, or the sword of 50.35–38a). Elements of holy war terminology in 50–51 and the mythical dimensions of Babylon as the hubristic opponent of Yahweh suggest that the poem of vv. 20–23 may be an expression of Yahweh's direct attack on Babylon without the use of intermediaries. The poem would then be a parallel to the song of the sword in 50.35–38a. In a series of ten statements (MT) the weapon of war is unleashed against an unnamed enemy and shatters it. A prose note in v. 24 identifies the victim of this shattering defeat as Babylon and the inhabitants of Chaldaea and explains why Yahweh behaves in such a fashion. It is because of the evil done in Zion that Babylon is destroyed. Again the text is ambiguous because the phrase 'before your eyes' qualifies 'in Zion'. This might mean that those who saw the tragic events of 587 would see Babylon's destruction (though not necessarily in 539) or those who are witnesses of the present state of Jerusalem (the result of Babylonian activity) will see the defeat of the national enemy or, perhaps more likely, those to whom these poems were recited would see Yahweh's requital (*šillam*) of Zion's evil (cf. RSV). It is a minor point, but 'before your eyes' may indicate that v. 24 is a fragment from a liturgy of revenge against Babylon used by the worshipping community during the sixth century (cf. Ps. 137).

51.34–44

34 'Nebuchadrezzar the king of Babylon has devoured me,
he has crushed me;
he has made me an empty vessel,
he has swallowed me like a monster;
he has filled his belly with my delicacies,
he has rinsed me out.
35 The violence done to me and to my kinsmen be upon Babylon,'
let the inhabitant of Zion say.
'My blood be upon the inhabitants of Chaldea,'
let Jerusalem say.
36 Therefore thus says the LORD:
'Behold, I will plead your cause
and take vengeance for you.
I will dry up her sea
and make her fountain dry;
37 and Babylon shall become a heap of ruins,
the haunt of jackals,
a horror and a hissing,
without inhabitant.'
38 'They shall roar together like lions;
they shall growl like lions' whelps.
39 While they are inflamed I will prepare them a feast
and make them drunk, till they swoon away
and sleep a perpetual sleep
and not wake, says the LORD.
40 I will bring them down like lambs to the slaughter,
like rams and he-goats.'
41 'How Babylon is taken,
the praise of the whole earth seized!
How Babylon has become
a horror among the nations!
42 The sea has come up on Babylon;
she is covered with its tumultuous waves.
43 Her cities have become a horror,
a land of drought and a desert,
a land in which no one dwells,
and through which no son of man passes.
44 And I will punish Bel in Babylon,
and take out of his mouth what he has swallowed.
The nations shall no longer flow to him;
the wall of Babylon has fallen.'

[34] K *'klnw hmmnw*; Q *'ekālanī hamāmanī*, 'he has devoured me he has vexed *me*' (K '. . . *us* . . . *us*'): *hmm*, 'discomfit, confuse', cf. Aramaic *hmm*, 'exhaust, debilitate'; G *emerisato me*, 'he divided me'. Rudolph, 312, deletes 'Nebuchadrezzar', because it spoils the rhythm (BHS). K *hṣygnw* . . . *bl'nw* . . . *hdyḥnw*; Q *hiṣṣīganī* . . . *belā'anī* . . . *hedīḥānī*, 'he has set *me* aside as . . . he has swallowed *me* up . . . he has rinsed *me* out' (K '*us*'). A slight change of pointing (*hedīḥānī* to *hiddīḥānī*) would yield 'he has driven me from my Eden (*mē'adānāy*)', i.e. from Palestine (cf. Rudolph, 312). For the mythical connotations behind the swallowing up motif (*bl'*) cf. the Jonah legend; Day 1985, 109–11: *kattannīn*, 'like the dragon or sea-monster': cf. Isa.27.1; 51.9; Ezek.29.3; 32.2 (mostly of Egypt); Job 7.12; Ps.74.13; G *hōs drakōn*, 'as a dragon'. **[35]** MT *ḥamāsī ūše'ērī 'al-bābel*, lit. 'my violence and my flesh upon Babylon': meaning uncertain, but it may have the sense of 'let my violated flesh be on Babylon' (cf. Bright, 358), i.e. Babylon is to be held responsible for the violence done to Zion's flesh. RSV, JPSB treat *še'ēr*, 'flesh', as blood-relation, i.e. 'kinsmen, kindred' (cf. Lev. 18.12, 13, 17; 20.19 for this use of *še'ēr*). G puzzled by the Hebrew reads *exōsan me hoi mochthoi mou kai hai talaipōriai mou eis Babulōna*, 'my hardships and my afflictions have driven me out to Babylon'. Rudolph, 312, reads *šō'ātī*, 'my devastation', for *še'ērī* (cf. BHS). Cf. 50.10; 51.24 for the motif of retribution against the Chaldaeans, here given a liturgical style (cf. Weiser, 436; Ps. 118.2–4; 124.1; 129.1). **[36]** Cf. 50.34. The term 'sea' (*yam*) may refer to the Euphrates (cf. Isa. 18.2; 19.5, where *yam* refers to the Nile), though a mythological allusion cannot be ruled out. **[37]** Cf. 9.11 (MT 10); 10.22. G much shorter, lacking 'the haunt of jackals, a horror and a hissing'. **[38]** G lacks 'they shall roar' and reads *nā'arū*, 'they growl', as *exegerthēsan*, 'they rose up' = *nē'ōrū*. Cf. 49.19; 50.44 for different use of lion imagery. **[39]** MT *lema'an ya'alōzū*, 'in order that they may rejoice': read *ye'ullāpū*, 'they may be stupefied', with Vrs (cf. G *methusō*). Rudolph transposes v. 40 to follow *ya'alōzū* and treats *ne'um yhwh*, 'says Yahweh', as the formal ending of the unit; Driver 1937–38, 127–8, understands *'lz* as 'to have colic'. **[41]** Cf. 50.23. MT *šēšak*, 'Sheshak': a cipher (athbash) for Babylon, cf. 25.26; lacking in G. It is unnecessary as a cipher because Babylon is specified in vv. 41, 42, 44 and it may represent traces of the use of magical spells against Babylon in MT. **[43]** Cf. 2.6c. MT *'ereṣ lō'-yēšēb bāhēn kol-'īš*, 'a land *in them* no man dwells': G lacks 'a land'; MT erroneously repeats *'ereṣ*, 'land', and, as *bāhēn*, 'in them', indicates, the cities should be understood as the places lacking inhabitants. **[44]** G lacks 'Bel in' and vv 44bβ-49a (from *gam* . . . to *gam*); cf. 50.2 for Bel. MT *welō'-yinharū 'ēlāyw 'ōd gōyim*, 'and the nations shall no longer flow to him': cf. Isa.2.2 for the motif of the nations flowing (*nhr*) to a specific place (Zion). This treatment of *nhr 'l* as an idiom derived from *nhr* I, 'flow', is disputed by a number of exegetes who prefer to relate it to *nhr* II, 'shine, radiate with joy', cf. JPSB 'And nations shall no more gaze on him with joy'; Ehrlich

1912, 10, 320; Wiklander 1978, 61–3; 31.12. The fall of Babylon's wall is referred to in v. 58; 50.15.

Wiklander 1978

A shorter section, enclosed by the motifs of gorging and disgorging (vv. 34, 44), is composed of vv. 34–35 with a divine response in vv. 36–37 and further units in vv. 38–40, 41–43, 44. Jerusalem is the speaker in the first instance and laments her experiences at the hands of Nebuchadrezzar, king of Babylon. Like a dragon Babylon has swallowed her, gorging itself on her (flesh) as one might empty a container or devour delicacies. Zion has been wiped off the face of the earth (the final image of v. 34 is less than clear). The sea-monster image (cf. Gen. 1.21) is one derived from ancient mythology (Babylonian and Canaanite; cf. Day 1985) and used to described different things in the biblical traditions: cosmic forces (e.g. Ps. 74.13; Isa. 51.9) controlled by Yahweh in the past or in the future (Isa. 27.1) or as a figure of the national enemy (e.g. Egypt in Ezek. 29.3; 32.2). Babylon warrants the epithet 'dragon' (*tannīn*) because of its cruel destruction of land, city and people in the period 597–582. The image is not only a fitting description of the imperial bully but echoes the imagery of the section which uses a variety of water metaphors (e.g. vv. 36, 42, 44). A liturgical-style (Weiser) response to this outrageous behaviour occurs in v. 35, where Zion encourages her people to chant their curse on Babylon in order to bring about its downfall. To this call for retribution the deity himself responds with asseverations of Babylon's destruction. Its water supplies will be cut off (thereby destroying the sea-monster's habitat?) and the land will be depopulated. Just as Zion's territory had been evacuated of people, so will Babylon become a haunt of jackals (cf. 9.11; 10.22). Poetic justice as well as rhetorical symmetry links the fates of Jerusalem and Babylon (analysis of section in Wiklander, 50–6).

Very different images are used in vv. 38–40 to depict the complete destruction of the people of Babylon. Raging like lions the people (cf. 12.8, or are these images of warriors cf. 49.19–20; 50.44–45?) will be treated to a banquet of Yahweh's (cf. the banquet of death in 9.15; 25.15–17) and, in a drunken stupor, they shall sleep a permanent sleep from which they shall never wake (cf. v. 57). A change of images in v. 40 makes the same point (cf. 50.27).

In vv.41–43 a lament is the response to Babylon's downfall. The world-famous and much-envied Babylon has been transmogrified by the turn of events. Swamped by the sea and lapped by the heavy waves, she is destroyed. Chants (v. 35) and incantations (v. 41 'Sheshak') have had their effect and the imperial enemy is reduced to the very state to which she had brought so many other nations. That the sea images are metaphors is made clear by the drought and desert figures of v. 43. The section ends in v. 44 (Lundbom 1975, 92–5, concludes it with v. 45) with a return to the images of v. 34, but reverses them: what Babylon has gorged herself on she must now disgorge (i.e. the exiled nations and Zion in particular, cf. vv. 34–35; v. 45 of next section). No longer shall the nations flow to (as a river: *nhr*, cf. Isa. 2.2; Micah 4.1) or rejoice in him (i.e. Bel the Babylonian god, but G 'her' refers to Babylon) because the city's walls are down. In v. 45 the flow is reversed as the people flee *from* the doomed city. Thus the monster Babylon represented by its king Nebuchadrezzar (v. 34) yields up its prey (Zion's exiles) to Yahweh.

The reference to Bel in MT v. 44 hints at an ideological interpretation of the destruction of Babylon. In the downfall of Zion the god Bel had defeated the god Yahweh; now in the fall of Babylon Yahweh reasserts himself and demonstrates his superiority by retrieving from the mouth of the monster that which it had swallowed. G lacks this theomachy element, but at some stage in the development of the second edition the theological significance of the downfall of Babylon appears as the triumph of Yahweh over Bel – the reversal of 587. Bel ceases to be an attraction for the nations because Babylon's wall has fallen and the god is clearly no longer able to protect his property. That would appear to be the meaning of v. 44:

> Bel, the god of Babylon, worshipped by its inhabitants and the supreme representative of the city, has taken dominion over the world including Zion-Jerusalem; the nations praise him and cheer him as supreme god. Thus he has committed an offence against YHWH, the Lord of the universe who bestowed world power on Babylon. What is more, Babylon has oppressed Zion-Jerusalem, i.e. the place where YHWH is worshipped and the people who worship him. Therefore YHWH shall take vengeance for Bel-Babylon's haughtiness; he shall take away his power and glory and then the nations will no longer cheer him as supreme god nor praise Babylon's glory (Wiklander, 61).

51.45–53

45 'Go out of the midst of her, my people!
Let every man save his life
from the fierce anger of the LORD!
46 Let not your heart faint, and be not fearful
at the report heard in the land,
when a report comes in one year
and afterward a report in another year,
and violence is in the land,
and ruler is against ruler.'
47 'Therefore, behold, the days are coming
when I will punish the images of Babylon;
her whole land shall be put to shame,
and all her slain shall fall in the midst of her.
48 Then the heavens and the earth,
and all that is in them,
shall sing for joy over Babylon;
for the destroyers shall come against them out of the north,
says the LORD.
49 Babylon must fall for the slain of Israel,
as for Babylon have fallen the slain of all the earth.'
50 'You that have escaped from the sword,
go, stand not still!
Remember the LORD from afar,
and let Jerusalem come into your mind:
51 "We are put to shame, for we have heard reproach;
dishonour has covered our face,
for aliens have come
into the holy places of the LORD's house." '
52 'Therefore, behold, the days are coming, says the LORD,
when I will execute judgment upon her images,
and through all her land
the wounded shall groan.
53 Though Babylon should mount up to heaven,
and though she should fortify her strong height,
yet destroyers would come from me upon her,
says the LORD.'

The lack of vv. 44β–49a in G may be due to haplography (the translator's eye skipping from the first *gam* to the third *gam*), though the similarity of language between vv. 44b–49a and 49b–53 suggests that they are variants conflated in MT (cf. Janzen 1973, 119). **[45]** Cf. 50. 8; 51.6; Isa. 52.11–12.

[46] A prose transition from the exhortation of v. 45 to the oracle of vv. 47–48 (Bright), though understood by some exegetes as an eschatological, rather than historical, statement (e.g. Rudolph, 313; Volz, 433). **[47]** Cf. v. 52; 50.38 for the attack on Babylonian images (*pᵉsîlîm*). **[48]** Cf. 50.3, 41 for the motif of the foe from the north coming against Babylon; Isa. 49.13 for the idea of the heavens and the earth singing because of the release of the exiles. **[49]** MT *ḥallê yiśrā'ēl*, 'the slain of Israel': read with many exegetes *lᵉḥlly* . . . '*for* the slain . . .' (cf. BHS). **[50]** MT *mēḥereb hilᵉkû*, 'from the sword, go': unusual imperatival form (*lᵉkû* is normal form); a redivision of the words yields *mēḥarbāh lᵉkû*, 'from *her* sword, go', cf. G *ek gēs, poreuesthe*, 'from the land, you who escape'. MT *mērāḥōq*, 'from afar': remembering Yahweh from afar indicates the exilic context of the refugees (cf. 30.10) and the Zion orientation of the exhortation. **[51]** Cf. 3.24–25 for the confession of shame and covering with dishonour. MT *'al-miqdᵉšê bêt yhwh*, 'to the sanctuaries of the house of Yahweh': G *eis ta hagia hēmōn, eis oikon kuriou*, 'into our sanctuary, into (the) house of the lord'; read *miqdašēnû*, 'our sanctuary', as the plur. form is unusual for referring to the temple (*miqdāš*). It is possible that Heb. *mqdšy* represents *miqdaš y(hwh)*, 'sanctuary of Yahweh', and *byt yhwh* is a variant or explanatory gloss (cf. Bright, 352 n.). Cf. 50.28; 51.11 for the temple motif in 50–51; Ps. 74.1–8 for the invasion of the sanctuary by Yahweh's foes. **[52]** MT *ye'ᵉnōq*, 'shall groan': G *pesountai*, 'shall fall' = vv. 4, 49; here MT refers *ḥll* to the wounded, whereas G consistently relates it to the dead. Cf. v. 47; 50.38 for the polemic against images.

A number of brief elements constitutes the final section before the framework conclusion of vv. 54–58. Exhortations (vv. 45, 46, 50), a confession (v. 51), two variant oracles on Babylon's destruction (vv. 47–48, 52–53), and an assertion of the necessity for Babylon to suffer the same fate as it imposed on Israel and the slain of all the earth (v. 49) bring together a number of themes to be found throughout 50–51. As a result of the divine punishment of Babylon the Judaean exiles ('my people', v. 45) must flee from Yahweh's anger. A variant exhortation encourages the people to flee from the invading forces and to return to Jerusalem (v. 50). The confession in v. 51 represents a view of the Babylonian conquest of the temple as an occasion of great shame for the worshippers of Yahweh, but lacks any of the sense of responsibility for the event which characterizes other parts of the Jeremiah tradition (contrast the confession in 3.24–25). It does, however, identify the humiliation of Yahweh's house as one of the central charges against Babylon (cf. 50.28; 51.11), and the appearance of this motif in 50–51 indicates a temple orientation in the editing of the poems. The two oracles (introduced by the editorial 'days are coming') about the punishment of Babylon focus on the idols used in Babylonian worship (cf. 50.38b) and may be read as a contrastive comment on the cultic practices of both nations (i.e. Jerusalem's sanctuary and Babylon's images). This is closer to the polemic against other national cults in 10.1–16 than to the discourses on syncretistic worship in 2–3.

Other elements in the section include the encouragement of the exiles in a time of rumours and political intrigue (v. 46: a prose reference to the steady disintegration of Babylonian society after the death of Nebuchadrezzar in 562?) and the universal rejoicing caused by the overthrow of Babylon by the destroyers from the north (v. 48). This note of joy brings the movement of the tradition full circle from the enemy out of the north which destroys Jerusalem (1.13–15?; 4.5–8; 6.22–26) to the enemy from the north which devastates Babylon (50.3, 9, 41; 51.48b). Such symmetry is explicitly expressed in v. 49, where Babylon's fate is sealed by its treatment of Israel and the other nations. As Babylon has done, so it shall be done to her (cf. 50.15, 29) – small wonder that the heavens and the earth sing for joy over her fall!

51.54–58

54 'Hark! a cry from Babylon!
    The noise of great destruction from the land of the Chaldeans!
55 For the LORD is laying Babylon waste,
    and stilling her mighty voice.
  Their waves roar like many waters,
    the noise of their voice is raised;
56 for a destroyer has come upon her,
    upon Babylon;
  her warriors are taken,
    their bows are broken in pieces;
  for the LORD is a God of recompense,
    he will surely requite.
57 I will make drunk her princes and her wise men,
    her governors, her commanders, and her warriors;
  they shall sleep a perpetual sleep and not wake,
    says the King, whose name is the LORD of hosts.'

58 'Thus says the LORD of hosts:
The broad wall of Babylon
shall be levelled to the ground
and her high gates
shall be burned with fire.
The peoples labour for naught,
and the nations weary themselves only for fire.'

---

[55] MT *gallēhem k^emayim rabbīm*, '*their* waves like many waters': i.e. the invading army (cf. v. 53) roars like crashing billows; some exegetes favour reading *galleyhā*, '*her* waves' (cf. G°, A, Symm), i.e. the din of Babylon is destroyed by Yahweh (cf. G; BHS). **[56]** Rudolph, 314, deletes the first line as a marginal comment on v. 55a (BHS); G *talaipōriai*, 'hardship', suggests *šōd*, 'destruction', rather than MT *šōdēd*, 'destroyer' (cf. Bright, 353). MT *ḥitt^etāh qašš^etōtām*, 'their bows are shattered': intransitive Piel should perhaps be read as Qal *ḥattāh qaštām*, 'their bow is broken' (Giesebrecht, 260; cf. BHS; G *to toxon autōn*, 'their bow'). Cf. Isa. 59.18 for the sentiments of v. 56b. **[57]** A prose variation on v. 39 with a list of the high-ranking victims of Yahweh's campaign against Babylon. **[58]** MT *ḥōmōt bābel hār^eḥabāh*, 'the broad walls of Babylon': many mss, G, V *ḥōmat*, 'wall of . . .'. MT *'ar'ēr tit'ar'ār*, lit. 'stripped utterly bare': i.e. razed to the ground. **[58b]** = Hab. 2.13b (with the order of *b^edē-rīq*, 'for naught', and *b^edē-'ēš*, 'for fire', reversed); MT *w^eyā'ēpū*, 'and they weary themselves': read by many exegetes as *yī'āpū*, 'will weary themselves' (MT is repeated by error in v. 64). G negates the force of MT by reading *kai ou kopiasousi laoi eis kenon*, 'and the people shall *not* be exhausted in vain'; it also reads *b^edē-'ēš* as *en archē*, 'in dominion' = *b^erō'š* (*d-r* confusion). Bright, 207n., 359, reads here 'thus far the words of Jeremiah' from v. 64 which, according to him, has been displaced by the insertion of vv. 59–64.

The collection of material against Babylon is concluded by vv. 54–58 forming a framework with 50.2–3. A cry is heard from Babylon which indicates great destruction in the land of the Chaldaeans. The noise is Yahweh laying waste the great enemy and stilling her voice for ever (so G; MT represents a slightly different sense of v. 58: much of the noise is caused by the invading forces). This reversal of Babylon's great prowess is the work of Yahweh who is a god of retributions (*'ēl g^emulōt*, v. 46; cf. Isa. 59.18) and the compensation or recompense he will surely extract (*šallēm y^ešallēm*) from Babylon is the avenging of the defeat of his people by the hubristic foe (cf. vv. 6, 11, 24, 35–37, 49, 53; cf. 25.14b). It is because Yahweh is a god of such recompenses that the catastrophe of 587 is balanced in these poems by the exultation caused by Babylon's defeat (whether imagined, anticipated or celebrated). Her officials, warriors and important people will all sleep a permanent sleep (of death) brought about by Yahweh making them drunk (vv. 39, 57; cf. Isa. 49.26; 51.22–23). It is the king, i.e. Yahweh not Nebuchadrezzar (cf. v. 34), who pronounces this verdict on the enemy (cf. 8.19; 10.7,10; 46.18; 48.15 for the motif of Yahweh as king). A final oracular note in v. 58 declares that Babylon's wall will be razed to the ground and her massive gates burned (cf. 50.2, 'Babylon is taken'). The meaning of v. 58b is ambiguous: it is either a citation from Hab. 2.13b or, more likely, the use of a saying from a common source used by both traditions. It appears to mean that people weary themselves in vain opposing Yahweh or pursuing different goals from his (cf. Hab. 2.12–14), but in its present context other meanings are possible. The destruction of Babylon renders the activity of the nations otiose – over Babylon, which is no more, the people wearied themselves pointlessly (ie a great fuss about nothing!). If the understanding of G is followed, then the negative reading means that the attack on Babylon by the nations has not been in vain. Whatever its precise meaning it is essentially an observation on the futility of the activities of the nations which end in fire, i.e. destruction, in particular Babylon the mighty with its great wall and high gates (cf. Ps. 2.1 for such futility). Hubris has met with nemesis!

All empires disintegrate, collapse and perish – the Assyrian, Persian, Greek, Roman, Holy Roman and British – and Babylon is no exception to this general principle of the fate of large conglomerates of political power and organization. The songs, chants, incantations, poems, diatribes and observations collected together in 50–51 represent Judaean responses to the experience of Babylonian rule in the sixth century. It is not possible to determine the precise relationship of the collection to historical events of the period. Like so much in the book of Jeremiah, parts of 50–51 may be related to the period before the Persian takeover of power in 539, but the poems need not be read in this manner. There is a fair degree of fantasy and stereotypical language in 50–51 and it is not necessarily the case that the poems *must* be derived from before the changeover of power because the fall of Babylon was, in fact, nothing like the descriptions given of razed walls and burning gates. These are clichéd accounts of the fall of Jerusalem and, in positing them of Babylon, the poets have maintained a symmetry of justice against the great enemy for its sacrilegious treatment of the sacred city. Emotionally Babylon was destroyed in this manner – of what importance could the mere details of what happened so many hundreds of miles away be to those who knew at first hand the ruins of Jerusalem! Beyond the political events of the sixth century it is possible to discern in these poems the emergence of Babylon as a mythical entity standing for the hubristic enemy of Yahweh and his people (cf. Rev. 18–19). The outrage generated by Babylon with regard to the sacking of Jerusalem outlived the passing of the Babylonian empire, and 'Babylon' became a catchword for describing *the enemy*.

51.59–64

59 The word which Jeremiah the prophet commanded Seraiah the son of
Neriah, son of Mahseiah, when he went with Zedekiah king of Judah to
Babylon, in the fourth year of his reign. Seraiah was the quartermaster. 60
Jeremiah wrote in a book all the evil that should come upon Babylon, all
these words that are written concerning Babylon. 61 And Jeremiah said to
Seraiah: 'When you come to Babylon, see that you read all these words, 62
and say, "O LORD, thou hast said concerning this place that thou wilt cut
it off, so that nothing shall dwell in it, neither man nor beast, and it shall
be desolate for ever." 63 When you finish reading this book, bind a stone
to it, and cast it into the midst of the Euphrates, 64 and say, "Thus shall
Babylon sink, to rise no more, because of the evil that I am bringing upon
her." '

Thus far are the words of Jeremiah.

---

[59] MT *haddābār '^{a}šer-ṣiwwāh yirm^{e}yāhū hannābī' 'et-ś^{e}rāyāh*, 'the word which Jeremiah the prophet commanded Seraiah': cf. 46.13; 50.1 for this introductory formula (*dbr*, 'spoke', for *ṣwh*, 'commanded'; Yahweh for Jeremiah); G *ho logos hon eneteilato kurios Ieremia tō prophētē eipein tō Saraia*, 'the word which the lord commanded Jeremiah the prophet to speak to Saraia'. Cf. 32.12 for the family of Seraiah, brother of Baruch. MT *b^{e}lektō 'et-ṣidqiyyāhū*, 'when he went *with* Zedekiah': G *hote eporeueto para Sedekiou*, 'when he went *from* Sedekia' (*'et = mē'ēt*); in MT Seraiah accompanies Zedekiah, in G he is sent by him (as a delegate). MT *śar m^{e}nūḥāh*, lit. 'official of (the) resting place': i.e. the one in charge of the bivouacking of troops, etc.; G *archōn dōrōn*, 'chief of gifts' = *m^{e}nāḥōt*, i.e. the one in charge of tribute (to the foreign overlord). **[60]** Cf. 25.13. The motif of Jeremiah writing appears in 29.1; 30.2 and is implied by 25.13; in 36.2 it is combined with the motif of delegation (Jeremiah is commanded to write but delegates the writing to

Baruch). Here the book (*sēper 'eḥād*, '*one* book'; in contradistinction to other books written by him or the indefinite 'a book'?) is a book of ill omen (*kol-hārā'āh*, 'all the evil') spoken against Babylon (cf. 25.13, where the words in the book may be those spoken against *all* the nations, but see Comm.). 60b may be an attempt to link the delegation process of vv. 59–64 with the material in 50.1–51.58 (cf. Bright, 210); 59b–60 are essentially parenthetical and v. 61 resumes v. 59a (cf. Rudolph, 316). **[62]** MT *kī-šimmōt 'ōlām tihyeh*, 'for it shall be permanent ruin*s*': Vrs sing., 'a ruin'. Note how the conventional phrase *hammāqōm hazzeh*, 'this place', so characteristic of the prose of Jeremiah, here refers to Babylon (normally it indicates the temple or Jerusalem [e.g. 7.3, 7; 16.2, 3, 9; 19.3, 4, 6, 7, 12]). G *kurie kurie*, 'lord, lord', for MT *yhwh*. **[63]** MT *'et-hassēper hazzeh*, 'this book': cf. 25.13 *bassēper hazzeh*, 'in this book'. **[64]** MT *kākāh*, 'thus': the standard formula accompanying special actions, cf. 13.9; 19.11; 28.11. MT adds *w*e*yā'ēpū*, 'and they shall weary themselves', after 'the evil that I am bringing upon her': lacking in G; it is repeated from the end of v. 58. MT *'ad-hēnnāh dibrē yirm*e*yāhū*, 'thus far the words of Jeremiah': cf. 48.47 for the formulaic termination of a lengthy section – i.e. 46–51 the OAN and here (cf. Duhm, 377); Job 31.40 uses a similar device to indicate the end of of Job's speeches. The statement would be better after v. 58 (Rudolph, Bright), as Jeremiah hardly stopped speaking in the fourth year of Zedekiah! It is lacking in G because the oracles against Babylon (G 27–28) are not at the end of the collection of OAN; its present position in MT, though displaced, may be due to the addition of 52 to the book of Jeremiah and thus it indicates a separation of Jeremiah's work from what follows.

———

The collection of anti-Babylonian materials in 50–51 is terminated by the report of a magical act of Jeremiah's dated to the fourth year of king Zedekiah (*c.* 594–3). This act is more appropriately associated with the period depicted in 27–29 (cf. Bright's treatment of it after 29.32) than with the post-587 responses to Babylon. However, it is placed here in order to attribute 50–51 to Jeremiah (cf. 50.1) and to demonstrate how the prophet conveyed the words of ill omen to the land of Babylon. Thus he who advocates submission to Babylon in 27–29 here reverses the act of wearing yoke-bars and by his delegated act dooms Babylon to eternal destruction. The question of treason mooted in the treatment of 27–29, 37–40 is balanced by this magical act of speaking, writing, sending and disposing of Babylon. Normally the evil word spoken against the foreign opponent was simply uttered and allowed to take effect accordingly, but in the case of the arch-enemy Babylon more than the spoken word would appear to have been required. Hence the words uttered are written down by Jeremiah (cf. 25.13) in *one* of the books he wrote (cf. 30.2), transported to Babylon by a delegated official (Baruch's brother) who may have been travelling there with the vassal king's tribute to his suzerain lord (cf. G; how ironic that the diplomatic bag which carried such wealth also contained the book of curses!), read out over the land, and then destroyed as an act whereby Babylon is annihilated and the ill omens placed beyond retrieval. Nothing can now prevent Babylon's defeat – just as the smashing of the ceramic vessel outside Jerusalem's gates had destroyed that city (19.1–2, 10–11). The delegated authority of Jeremiah carries the same power as his spoken word (cf. Schmidt 1982), and the magic behind the act of drowning the book is just as effective for Seraiah ben Neriah as for Jeremiah. With this displaced report Babylon's fate is sealed.

51.59–64 should be read in parallel with 36 where there is also a case of Jeremiah delegating a task to another person (i.e. Baruch the brother of Seraiah). Jeremiah speaks the words, has them written down (a unique element in the tradition, because in all other instances Jeremiah does his own writing), and they are delivered by Baruch orally to the people, the princes and the king. At the end of Baruch's mission the scroll is destroyed by the king, but Jeremiah dictates it again and Baruch inscribes it once more. The word cannot be destroyed so easily, though those who oppose it are set aside with ease. In 51.59–64 a similar process is intended to lead to the destruction of the written word and, on this occasion, there is no need for the word to be rewritten. Since its destruction is intentional, nothing can preserve it. It is perhaps too subtle a reading of the text to see in the survival of Baruch's scroll through rewriting and the destruction of Seraiah's book of ill omen the relative difference between Judah and Babylon. One survives; the other does not: the word to Judah can be rewritten, reshaped, even reformulated (cf. 1.10; 29.11); but there is only one word for Babylon – destruction – and that requires no restatement. When the book sinks beneath the waters of the river Euphrates, Babylon sinks with it – never to rise again. Underlining this point is the fact that MT represents Jeremiah as playing Yahweh to Seraiah (e.g. 'the word which Jeremiah *commanded*'; see on 1.10) and speaking from a position (*the prophet*) of established power in the tradition. It is his last word (MT), and it carries the doom of Judah's enemy.

EPILOGUE 52.1–34

52.1–3a

52[1] Zedekiah was twenty-one years old when he became king; and he reigned eleven years in Jerusalem. His mother's name was Hamutal the daughter of Jeremiah of Libnah. 2 And he did what was evil in the sight of the LORD, according to all that Jehoiakim had done. 3 Surely because of the anger of the LORD things came to such a pass in Jerusalem and Judah that he cast them out from his presence.

[MT 52] = G 52. **[52.1–3a]** = II Kings 24.18–20a; G lacks vv. 2–3. **[1]** K *ḥmyṭl*; Q *ḥ^a^mûṭal*, 'Hamutal': cf. II Kings 23.31; I Chron. 3.15–16. 'Jeremiah from Libnah' (*yirm^e^yāhû millibnāh*): the third Jeremiah mentioned in the tradition (cf. 1.1; 35.3). **[2]** A stereotypical Deuteronomistic phrase which indicates the editorial disapproval of the king more than it specifies his faults; in that Zedekiah was a vassal of the Babylonians he can hardly be said to have behaved in the same fashion as Jehoiakim the vassal of Egypt. Cf. 37.1–2 for a similar sweeping rejection of Zedekiah; 15.4 for the identification of Jerusalem's fate with the dealings of a former king (Manasseh). **[3]** MT *kî 'al-'ap yhwh hāy^e^tāh bîrûsalaim wîhûdāh 'ad-hišlîkô 'ōtām mē'al pānāyw*, lit. 'for upon the anger of Yahweh was against Jerusalem and Judah until he cast them from his presence': cf. 32.31 for similarly awkward syntax; this statement makes Yahweh's anger the cause of the deportation, but this was hardly the opinion the Deuteronomists wished to convey (cf. Rudolph, 318); Gray 1977, 762, however, views II Kings 24.20a as meaning that Yahweh consented to Zedekiah's sin because he had already doomed Israel for earlier sins.

The book of Jeremiah does not end with words or actions of Jeremiah (hence the note at the end of MT 51.64), but with an appendix taken from the Deuteronomistic history of the kings of Israel and Judah (i.e. II Kings 24.18 – 25.30). Why this should be the case is not known – the rabbinic view which credited Jeremiah with having written Kings as well as the book of Jeremiah is not an explanation but a deduction from the shared material and the common Deuteronomistic style. 52 and II Kings 25 are not exactly the same: 52 omits the section on the assassination of Gedaliah (II Kings 25.22–26) and has an additional extract from a register of the numbers of people deported to Babylon (vv. 28–30). A similar sharing of material is to be found in the Isaiah tradition, where Isa. 36–39 form a conclusion to Isa. 1–35 drawn from II Kings 18–20. But in this common material the prophet Isaiah is one of the dominant figures, whereas Jeremiah is completely absent in Jer. 52 and II Kings 24.18–25.30. The effect of concluding Jeremiah with an appendix from II Kings is to form a closure with the Deuteronomistic history and reflects the editorial history of the book of Jeremiah. This closure feature is somewhat obscured by the subsequent development of Hebrew Bibles whereby the book of Isaiah now stands at the head of the prophetic collection (replacing Jeremiah, the largest volume in that collection). The editors may have wished to conclude their work with an appendix emphasizing the fall of Jerusalem as the vindication of the work of the prophet Jeremiah and the confirmation of his vision of the overturned pot signalling the northern invasion (1.14–16; but see Comm.). In the tradition's end is its beginning!

The first part of the appendix sets the background to the fall of Jerusalem with a few details about the accession to the Judaean throne of Zedekiah (cf. 37.1). These consist of Zedekiah's age when he became king, the length of his reign, and his mother's name (Hamutal or Hamital, cf. Q–K). A brief homily follows which, in characteristically Deuteronomistic fashion, condemns Zedekiah out of hand without specific reasons. The allusion to the evil he did in terms of 'according to all that Jehoiakim had done' is a mark of the Deuteronomistic concern to underline the continuity of evil maintained by the kings of Judah (esp. Manasseh) which led to the destruction of Jerusalem. Even the details of Zedekiah's reign are modelled on those provided for Jehoiakim (cf. II Kings 23.36–37). Whether the similarity between the reigns of the two vassal kings should be extended to include their rebellion against Nebuchadrezzar their overlord (cf. II Kings 24.1, 20b) is difficult to determine, but both kings are presented as suffering the consequences of the actions of former kings in Jerusalem (Jehoiakim for Manasseh – Zedekiah for Jehoiakim, II Kings 24.3, 19). The syntax of v. 3 is difficult and the meaning far from clear: the fate of Jerusalem is determined by

Yahweh's anger rather than Zedekiah's activities. That would appear to be the most sensible understanding of MT, though the EVV differ considerably in the way they translate it (JPSB at least acknowledges the uncertain meaning of the Hebrew). It is as a consequence of Yahweh's anger that Zedekiah behaves so foolhardily against Babylon (v. 3b). Such an account of his reign is rather different from the presentation of the interviews between him and Jeremiah in 37–38 (where the prophet attempts to persuade him to change his mind but does not denounce him for evil practices), though the end-result is the same in both traditions.

52.3b–11

3b And Zedekiah rebelled against the king of Babylon. 4 And in the ninth year of his reign, in the tenth month, on the tenth day of the month, Nebuchadrezzar king of Babylon came with all his army against Jerusalem, and they laid siege to it and built siegeworks against it round about. 5 So the city was besieged till the eleventh year of King Zedekiah. 6 On the ninth day of the fourth month the famine was so severe in the city, that there was no food for the people of the land. 7 Then a breach was made in the city; and all the men of war fled and went out from the city by night by the way of a gate between the two walls, by the king's garden, while the Chaldeans were round about the city. And they went in the direction of the Arabah. 8 But the army of the Chaldeans pursued the king, and overtook Zedekiah in the plains of Jericho; and all his army was scattered from him. 9 Then they captured the king, and brought him up to the king of Babylon at Riblah in the land of Hamath, and he passed sentence upon him. 10 The king of Babylon slew the sons of Zedekiah before his eyes, and also slew all the princes of Judah at Riblah. 11 He put out the eyes of Zedekiah, and bound him in fetters, and the king of Babylon took him to Babylon, and put him in prison till the day of his death.

[52.3b–11] = II Kings 24.20b – 25.7 (with minor variations); cf. 39.1–2, 4–7 (see Notes and Comm. there). **[4]** G^{BS} *enatō*, 'ninth'; G^{A} *hebdomō*, 'seventh', for MT, G 'tenth (month)'. MT *wayyibᵉnū ʿāleyhā dāyēq sābīb*, 'and they built against it siegeworks round about': *dāyēq* occurs here and in II Kings 25.1; Ezek.4.2; 17.17; 21.27 (EV 22); 26.8; it may be translated as 'siegeworks', 'siege wall', 'siege towers', cf. NEB watch-towers, JPSB towers; Gray 1977, 763–4, 'a wall of circumvallation' cf. Aramaic *zāqa, yāzīq* ('to put a collar on to a shirt'), i.e. a rampart (like a collar) round the city. In spite of the explicit statement here, Nebuchadrezzar did not himself besiege

Jerusalem but remained at his headquarters at Riblah on the Orontes (cf. vv. 9–10, 26–27; 39.5–6). **[6]** G, II Kings 25.3 lack 'in the fourth month'. MT *'am hā'āreṣ*, 'the people of the land': here this term refers to the general populace (cf. 37.2; 44.21) rather than the landed gentry (cf. 34.19; see on 1.18). **[7]** 39.4 reads 'and when *Zedekiah* . . . and all the men of war *saw* . . .': Rudolph, 320, supplies *wayyar' hammelek*, 'and the king saw', from there because some such reference is required to account for the king being among the fugitives of v. 8 (cf. Bright, 363). G lacks 'they fled' and 'from the city'. MT *bēn-haḥōmōtayim*, 'between the two walls': cf. Isa. 22.11, where the term indicates a reservoir area at the convergence of two of the city's walls (for possible location, cf. Gray 1977, 765). A more graphic depiction of this escape by night is given in Ezek. 12.12–14. **[8]** MT 'pursued the king and overtook Zedekiah': cf. 39.5 'pursued them and overtook Zedekiah'; but G, II Kings 25.5, 'pursued the king and overtook him'. MT *b*^e*'ar*^e*bōt y*^e*rēhō*, 'in the plains of Jericho': i.e. the arid, semi-desert plains south of Jericho; G *en tō peran Ierichō*, 'in the (area) beyond (= *b*^e*'ēber*) Jericho'. MT *w*^e*kol-ḥēlō nāpōṣū mē'ālāyw*, 'and all his troops were scattered from him': whether they abandoned him (cf. Gray) or fled when the Chaldaean troops arrived (cf. Bright) is difficult to determine; G *pantes hoi paides autou*, 'all his servants' (= *kol-*^a*bādāyw*), suggests that his personal retinue was dispersed. **[9]** MT *riblātāh b*^e*'ereṣ h*^a*māt*, 'to Riblah in the land of Hamath': G, II Kings 25.6 lack 'in the land of Hamath'; see Notes on 39.5 for Riblah and the idiom *dibbēr . . . mišpāṭīm* (G, II Kings 25.6 *mišpāṭ*), 'to pass . . . sentence', or 'to put on trial' (cf. Gray 'he took process with him'); cf. 1.16. **[10]** Cf. 39.6 'nobles' (*ḥōrē*) for 'princes' (*śārē*) here; 'all' need only govern the princes taken to Riblah rather than all the princes of the realm (cf. Bright, 367, 'various of the princes'); II Kings 25.7 lacks any reference to the slaying of the princes. **[11]** K *bbyt*, '*in* the house of', Q *bēt*, 'the house of': *happ*^e*quddōt*, 'punishments', i.e. prison; G *eis oikian mulōnos*, 'in the mill-house'.

The summary of the siege and fall of Jerusalem (cf. 39.1–2, 4–7) is brief and partial. It picks out a few details of the eighteen-month campaign by the Babylonians to penetrate the city and seize the rebellious vassals. That the siege took such a length of time may be attributed to the unwelcome attentions of the Egyptians elsewhere (cf. 37.5–7) rather than to the skill of the Judaeans or the effectiveness of the city's fortifications. The brief account (cf. II Kings 25.1–7) is less interested in the events of the siege (causes and course) than in the fall of the city and the consequences of that for its rulers and citizens. Hence the story of the breach of the city wall is told from the viewpoint of the besieged rather than the besiegers and the impression is given that the starving citizens broke down the wall rather than the Babylonians (less the case in 39.2–3). Instead of the attacking army pouring into the breached city the Judaean soldiers and the royal party fled through the broken wall *by night* (the dominant escape motif). They successfully eluded the Babylonian army but were overtaken in the plains of Jericho. From there they were taken to Nebuchadrezzar's headquarters in Syria and king Zedekiah faced trial for disloyalty to his overlord. His sons and his princes were executed and he was treated cruelly before being deported to Babylon where he was imprisoned until his death. It is not clear why he was not executed at Riblah along with his family and counsellors, but Nebuchadrezzar may have had political motives for not killing his rebel vassal. Zedekiah's imprisonment in Babylon meant that two Judaean kings were detained there during the same time, and a striking contrast is afforded between the treatment of both kings in this chapter (cf. vv. 31–34). Whatever may have been Jehoiachin's experience of confinement, it cannot have been as wretched as the blinded Zedekiah's. As presented in this epilogue Zedekiah's fate is blinding, imprisonment and death, whereas eventually Jehoiachin is released from prison and enjoys a royal pension until his death in exile. The contrast may be only structural (i.e. part of the story-telling process) but it is possible that the fate of each king represents an observation on the consequences of a life lived in opposition to the prophet's warnings. Although Jeremiah is conspicuously absent in this epilogue, the appending of it to the book of the words of Jeremiah may reflect the wish to underline the fate of king, people and city which did not listen to those words. Jehoiachin could hardly be accused of rejecting the prophet's advice (though 22.24–30 hardly flatter that king), hence he is the only one spoken kindly to in this appendix. That may be an oversubtle reading of the contrast between the kings, but it is not an unreasonable inference from the similar but distinctive fates of the last two monarchs of the city of Jerusalem.

52.12–16

12 In the fifth month, on the tenth day of the month – which was the nineteenth year of king Nebuchadrezzar, king of Babylon – Nebuzaradan the captain of the bodyguard who served the king of Babylon, entered Jerusalem. 13 And he burned the house of the LORD, and the king's house

and all the houses of Jerusalem; every great house he burned down. 14 And all the army of the Chaldeans, who were with the captain of the guard, broke down all the walls round about Jerusalem. 15 And Nebuzaradan the captain of the guard carried away captive some of the poorest of the people and the rest of the people who were left in the city and the deserters who had deserted to the king of Babylon, together with the rest of the artisans. 16 But Nebuzaradan the captain of the guard left some of the poorest of the land to be vinedressers and ploughmen.

[52.12–16] = II Kings 25.8–12 (with minor variations); cf. 39.8–10. **[12]** MT 'tenth day': II Kings 25.8 'seventh day'. G lacks 'which was the nineteenth year of king Nebuchadrezzar, king of Babylon'. The nineteenth year of Nebuchadrezzar was 587, counting from 605 the year when he came to power (II Kings style); v. 28 gives the year of the deportation after the fall of Jerusalem as Nebuchadrezzar's *eighteenth* year! This may follow the Babylonian style of reckoning (cf. Bright, 369), but the Bible is notoriously unreliable in matters of dating and numbers, so the two verses may simply illustrate the complexity of chronological issues and the discrepancies which can appear even within the same chapter. MT *'āmad lip̄nē melek-bābel bīrūšālāim*, lit. 'he stood before the king of Babylon in Jerusalem': this is quite ambiguous, and gives the impression that Nebuzaradan arrived (*bā'*) and stood before Nebuchadrezzar in Jerusalem. As the king was at Riblah this can hardly be the sense of the statement, and it may be intended to qualify Nebuzaradan's special status as one who stands (revocalized *'ōmēd* cf. G) before the great king (cf. 15.19; I Kings 10.8; 17.1 for the idiom); II Kings 25.8 makes Nebuzaradan the 'servant' (*'ebed*) of the king of Babylon and lacks 'in' (Jerusalem). **[13]** The phrase 'and every great house he burned down' may be an addition to the text (cf. BHS); it is unnecessary in view of the previous statement. **[14]** 39.8; II Kings 25.10 lack 'all' (the walls); G lacks 'all' (the army). **[15]** G lacks v. 15: perhaps due to haplography, as vv. 15–16 both begin with *ūmiddallōt* (*hā'ām*?, cf. 39.10), 'and some of the poor (of the people)'; cf. Janzen 1973, 20–1. This phrase may not be original to v. 15, as it is lacking in 39.9; II Kings 25.11; it belongs to v. 16 and its deletion here makes v. 15 virtually equivalent to 39.9 (with the addition of *wᵉ'ēt yeter hā'āmōn*, 'and the remainder of the master-workmen'). MT *hā'āmōn*, 'master-workmen': cf. Prov. 8.30; EVV 'artisans', JPSB 'craftsmen'; yet according to II Kings 24.14 all the craftsmen were deported in 597! II Kings 25.11 has *hehāmōn*, 'the multitude'; 39.9 *hā'ām*, 'the people'; some exegetes favour reading *hā'ommān* (cf. Akkadian *ummānu*; S. of Sol.7.2), 'skilled artisans' (e.g. Rudolph, Bright). **[16]** G *kai tous kataloipous tou laou*, 'and the remnant of the people', for MT 'and some of the poorest of the land'. G, II Kings 25.12 lack 'Nebuzaradan'. MT *ūlᵉyōgᵉbīm*, 'and for ploughmen': meaning of Hebrew uncertain (see on 39.10); G *kai eis geōrgous*, 'and to be labourers, tillers of the ground'.

A month after the breach made in the city wall Nebuzaradan the commander of the Babylonian troops enters Jerusalem and razes the city to the ground. Why a month should pass between the breach being made and the penetration of the city is unknown. Perhaps the troops waited for their commander to arrive (cf. Bright) or they waited to see who else would dare to venture forth through the breach and be slaughtered. These possibilities are derived from the storyteller's presentation of the breach as something made by the besieged rather than by the besiegers. If the Babylonians made the breach (cf. 39.2) they would hardly have waited another month before entering the beleaguered city. Furthermore, the association in v. 6 of the severity of the starvation in the city with the breach made in v. 7 does not really allow a further month for the citizens to linger in a state of such hunger (unless the Babylonians were sadists and the inhabitants of Jerusalem a peculiar form of masochists). However the delay of a month is explained it remains a curious feature of the story.

The variations in the stories told about the Babylonian penetration and destruction of Jerusalem (39.2–10; 52.6–16; II Kings 25.3–12) indicate the lack of a detailed account of what really happened when the city fell to the onslaught of the Babylonians. Dates and figures vary, even though one basic account appears to be the source of the stories, but these variations are typical of biblical narratives which are unreliable in matters of precise dates or numbers. The destruction of the city is followed by the deportation of various groups of people (details are far from clear) and the leaving behind of the poorest to work the land. This arrangement would appear to have emptied the land of people – vv. 15–16 refer to the city and the land but the story is essentially about the fate of Jerusalem rather than the land of Judah (otherwise 40.7 – 41.18 would be inconceivable). However, the figures given in vv. 28–30 for the various deportations of the Jews to Babylon made in the reign of Nebuchadrezzar do not warrant the claim that the land was emptied of its population apart from those of the poor left behind to till the land (cf. Lam. 5). The myth of an empty land is part of the ideology of the Chronicler and others (cf. II Chron. 36.20–21), developed in a period when it became necessary to distinguish sharply between the returning exiles and those who were outside the pale (i.e. the people of the land, cf. Ezra 4.1–5). Such a differentiation belongs to the power politics of the fifth century, when the reestablishment of city and temple polarized various factions in Judaean territory. The account of Nebuzaradan leaving only the dregs of Judaean society behind after the burning of Jerusalem and the deportation of all the important people (though MT v. 15 even includes some of the poorest elements in the deportation!) provides a warrant, however unfounded in reality, for the ideological conflict of the fifth century. One final curiosity in the story may be noted in passing: those who remained in the city were deported by Nebuzaradan and those who fled from the city were executed (v. 10). Yet in the preaching of Jeremiah the potential fate of the different groups appears to be the reversal of this experience (cf. 21.9; 38.2, 17–18). It is an unimportant point and may be modified by stressing the survival of those who did surrender (v. 15). But ironically those who survived the hardships of the siege and did *not* surrender to the Chaldaeans would appear to have gained their lives as prizes of war, even though they may have been deported. Thus even in the best constructed stories prophets do not predict the future with any degree of reliability!

52.17–23

17 And the pillars of bronze that were in the house of the LORD, and the
stands and the bronze sea that were in the house of the LORD, the Chaldeans
broke in pieces, and carried all the bronze to Babylon. 18 And they took
away the pots, and the shovels, and the snuffers, and the basins, and the
dishes for incense, and all the vessels of bronze used in the temple sevice;
19 also the small bowls, and the firepans, and the basins, and the pots, and
the lampstands, and the dishes for incense, and the bowls for libation. What
was of gold the captain of the guard took away as gold, and what was of
silver, as silver. 20 As for the two pillars, the one sea, the twelve bronze
bulls which were under the sea, and the stands, which Solomon the king
had made for the house of the LORD, the bronze of all these things was
beyond weight. 21 As for the pillars, the height of the one pillar was eighteen
cubits, its circumference was twelve cubits, and its thickness was four
fingers, and it was hollow. 22 Upon it was a capital of bronze; the height of
the one capital was five cubits; a network and pomegranates, all of bronze,
were upon the capital round about. And the second pillar had the like, with

pomegranates. 23 There were ninety-six pomegranates on the sides; all the pomegranates were a hundred upon the network round about.

[52.17–23] = II Kings 25.13–17 (a briefer version). An account of the construction of the temple furnishings is to be found in I Kings 7.15–50. **[17]** MT *wayyiśᵉʼû' et-kol-nᵉḥuštām bābelāh*, 'and they carried all *their* bronze to Babylon': II Kings 25.13, G lack 'all'. **[18–19]** G, II Kings 25.14–15 are briefer; cf. BHS for variations between MT and G in v. 19. **[20]** II Kings 25.16 lacks 'the twelve bronze bulls which were under (the sea)'; cf. II Kings 16.8, 17, where king Ahaz removed these in order to pay the Assyrians to attack his enemies – the editor of Jer. 52 may have forgotten this point (so Gray 1977, 767; cf. Rudolph, 320). G lacks 'all these furnishings (*hakkēlîm*)' at the end of v. 20. I Kings 7.27 has *ten* stands: added here by some exegetes (cf. BHS). **[21]** II Kings 25.17 lacks 'and the pillars'. G *triakonta pente pēchōn*, 'thirty-five cubits' (cf. II Chron. 3.15), for MT 'eighteen cubits'. K *qwmh*; Q *qōmat*, 'height' (both mean the same). II Kings 25.17 lacks 'its circumference was twelve cubits, and its thickness was four fingers, and it was hollow'. MT *wᵉḥûṭ šᵉttēm-ʻeśrēh 'ammāh yᵉsubbennû*, lit. 'and a line of twelve cubits surrounded it'. **[22]** II Kings 25.17 gives the height of the capital as 'three cubits'; here it is 'five cubits'. The last word in MT *wᵉrimmōnîm*, 'and pomegranates', is odd in that such a motif is included in the phrase 'and the second pillar (had) the like of these (*kā'ēlleh*)', i.e. the same; II Kings 25.17, 'upon the network'. G *oktō rhoai to pēchei tois dōdeka pēchesi*, 'eight pomegranates to a cubit for the twelve cubits'. **[23]** II Kings 25 lacks the equivalent of v. 23. MT *rûḥah*?, 'windwards': perhaps *rwḥ*, 'spaced', i.e. at intervals, should be read here, cf. *rewaḥ*, 'a space', in Gen.32.17 (EV 16); Bright, 365n. According to I Kings 7.20, 42, each capital had *two* hundred pomegranates, in two rows.

The executions and deportations of vv. 9–16 might appear to be the end of the story, but 52 is derived from the summarizing account of the Deuteronomistic historians and there remain a number of itemized observations on the fall of Jerusalem. The Deuteronomistic interest in the temple provides a list of the valuable furnishings which the Babylonians took as loot to Babylon. II Kings 24.13 and 25.13–17 give accounts of the two lootings of the temple in 597 and 587. Now it may be thought that the Babylonians would have done a thorough job of ransacking the temple the first time and have left very little for subsequent invasions (see on 27.19–21), but the historians appear to work with an idealized notion of the temple. Each time a foreign power attacked Jerusalem the Judaean king would buy it off by using the temple furnishings of gold and silver as tribute or Danegeld.

Perhaps only the movable items were ever taken and then replaced at a later time, ready to be used to buy protection for the city when necessary. Yet each invasion would appear to have successfully plundered the temple without seriously depleting its contents. Hence in 597 *and* 587 the Babylonians could raid it *twice*. However these accounts are to be rationalized, they reflect quite different themes melded together: in some cases the Babylonians break up the furnishings because they are valuable and these must cease to function as sacral utensils. In other cases the furnishings are transported wholesale and these become the source of legends about their return or their misuse (cf. 27.22; 28.3; II Chron. 36.18; Ezra 1.7; Dan. 1.2; 5.2–4). Apart from an additional note to 27.22 the Jeremiah tradition has no interest in the temple furnishings – their loss is simply the judgment of Yahweh against a corrupt nation. The temple is important and respected in the tradition (e.g. 7.11; 17.12), but 52.17–23 reflect the interests of the Deuteronomistic historians rather than those of the other levels in the book of Jeremiah.

52.24–27

24 And the captain of the guard took Seraiah the chief priest, and Zephaniah the second priest, and the three keepers of the threshold; 25 and from the city he took an officer who had been in command of the men of war, and seven men of the king's council, who were found in the city; and the secretary of the commander of the army who mustered the people of the land; and sixty men of the people of the land, who were found in the midst of the city. 26 And Nebuzaradan the captain of the guard took them, and brought them to the king of Babylon at Riblah. 27 And the king of Babylon smote them, and put them to death at Riblah in the land of Hamath. So Judah was carried captive out of its land.

[52.24–27] = II Kings 25.18–21. **[24]** G lacks the personal names of the officials: cf. I Chron. 5.39–41 (EV 6.13–15) for Seraiah the grandson of Josiah's high priest Hilkiah; Zephaniah may be the priest of the same name referred to in 29.24–29; 37.3. MT *šōmᵉrē hassap*, 'keepers of the threshold': i.e. door-keepers, an important temple function (cf. 35.4); G *tous phulassontas tēn hodon*, 'keepers of the way'. **[25]** G lacks 'and from the city'. MT *sārīs 'eḥād*, 'one official': i.e. a certain official; as in 29.2; 34.19; 38.7; 39.3, 13; 41.16 *sārīs* means 'official' and not necessarily 'eunuch'; here it denotes a military officer. II Kings 25.19 has 'five men', whereas here 'seven men':

such discrepancies are typical of the two accounts but hardly significant degrees of error warranting analytical investigation. MT *sōpēr śar haṣṣābā'*, 'a secretary of the commander of the army': II Kings 25.19 *hassōpēr*, '*the* secretary . . .'; G lacks *śar*, 'commander'; cf. 36.12 for the association of the two terms. NEB makes *sōpēr* 'adjutant-general' and treats *śar haṣṣābā'*, 'commander-in-chief', as an addition to the text. MT *w*ᵉ*šiššīm 'īš mē'am hā'āreṣ*, 'and sixty men of the people of the land': *'am hā'āreṣ* is a technical phrase which may mean 'the ordinary peasantry of the country' or 'the landed gentry'; it is ambiguous here and may refer to the conscripted peasants or the landowners forming part of the army. **[27]** MT *wayyakkeh 'ōtām . . . way*ᵉ*mitēm*, 'and he smote them . . . and he put them to death': i.e. had them flogged and then executed (cf. NEB; Rudolph, 322); Nebuchadrezzar will not have carried out this treatment himself but will have given orders for the beatings and executions. G lacks 'and he put them to death' and 'so Judah was carried captive out of its land'.

The impression given by vv. 7–16 is that all the various strata of Judaean society had been punished by the Babylonians, but vv. 24–27 single out a number of specific officials for execution. This may be an alternative account to vv. 8–10 or, perhaps on balance more likely, a supplementary story accounting for the fate of those considered to have been responsible for the events leading up to the siege and for its maintenance over a long period. Again it is noteworthy that the accounts know nothing of Jeremiah – hence the stories told about him in 39.11–14; 40.1–6. He is not part of the official records made of the period and his role in the siege must be presumed to be a part of the fiction of the tradition. A list of 'guilty men' is drawn up: *two* very senior priests, *three* important temple officials, *one* officer who organized the army, *seven* men who had had immediate access to the king (his inner cabinet?), a secretary to the army commander, and *sixty* men found in the city (whether important officers or conscripts or even non-combatants is not clear from the text). These seventy-four men are then taken by Nebuzaradan to Riblah (on the same trip as v. 9?). There they encounter the wrath of king Nebuchadrezzar, are beaten, and then executed. That there were so many executions at Riblah increases the sense of wonderment that king Zedekiah was not also summarily executed there. He was, after all, the one most responsible as king for the policy pursued by Judah, though he may have found his imprisonment a crueller fate than death. The executions and the cruel treatment of the king will have served *pour encourager les autres* and will also have removed the threat of resistance from those deported. All who had escaped during or after the siege (the seventy-four men were probably those important officials who had *not* escaped) were another matter, but the Babylonians do not appear to have taken them seriously (cf. 40.7 – 41.18). In crushing the revolt Nebuchadrezzar effectively exiled Judah, and the section ends with a note making that point. Here may well be 'the climax and conclusion of the theme of the Deuteronomic redactor's continuation of the historical narrative of the Deuteronomic compiler of Kings' (Gray 1977, 769). What follow are two appendices which bring up to date the story of Jerusalem's destruction and the exile of Judah.

52.28–30

28 This is the number of the people whom Nebuchadrezzar carried away captive: in the seventh year, three thousand and twenty-three Jews; 29 in the eighteenth year of Nebuchadrezzar he carried away captive from Jerusalem eight hundred and thirty-two persons; 30 In the twenty-third year of Nebuchadrezzar, Nebuzaradan the captain of the guard carried away captive of the Jews seven hundred and forty-five persons; all the persons were four thousand and six hundred.

G, II Kings 25 lack 52.28–30. **[28]** Rudolph, 322–5, inserts *'eśrēh*, 'ten', i.e. the seventeenth year, and thus makes v. 28 refer to the deportation of Judaeans and v. 29 to the exiling of the citizens of Jerusalem: cf. 34.7. MT refers to 598–7; cf. II Kings 24.10–16, where the figures given are 18, 000 for the number of deported people. **[29]** Cf. v. 12, where the year is given as Nebuchadrezzar's nineteenth. Some mss and Vrs supply *hegᵉlāh*, 'exiled, took captive' (as in vv. 28, 30). **[30]** MT *kol-nepeš 'arba'at 'ᵃlāpīm wᵉšēš mē'ōt*, 'all the persons (were) four thousand and six hundred': it is unlikely that *nepeš*, 'person', should be restricted to male Jews, in spite of *yᵉhūdīm*, 'Judaeans, Jews' being masculine (e.g. would the one hundred and twenty thousand persons of Nineveh in Jonah 4.11 necessarily be male because they are described as *'ādām*, 'human'?). The discrepancy between the total here and II Kings 24. 14, 16 can hardly be resolved by distinguishing between males and others (*contra* Bright, 369), though Rudolph's proposal dissolves the problem by relating the figures to different events and periods.

The only information available for the numbers deported by the Babylonians appears in vv. 28–30 (II Kings 24–25 only record figures for 597). The source of this register is not known and the accuracy of its information cannot be vouched for. As with all statistical accounts in the Bible there are discrepancies between it and the relevant parallel material in II Kings 24.14, 16 (cf. discussion in Ackroyd 1968a, 23). Such discrepancies are better not harmonized but accepted as evidence for the lack of definitive information available to the editors of the biblical stories. The impression given by v. 30 is that the total refers to *all* the persons (*nepeš*) who were exiled to Babylon, rather than just to the males (Bright). The point could be argued, but probably only for the purpose of harmonizing the different accounts, and that would entail some dubious exegesis (Rudolph's solution depends upon interfering with the text), without necessarily resolving the problems.

The deportation of four thousand and six hundred persons over a sixteen year period does not represent a drastic shift in population, though considerable social changes will have been effected by the loss of the landed gentry, the priests, officials and important citizens of the territory (general assessment in Ackroyd 1968a, 20–31). Without knowing the general population figures of Judah and Jerusalem in the early sixth century it is impossible to determine the proportion of deported people or the extent to which the land was populated after 582. The onslaught of the Babylonians certainly devastated the population in many different ways: starvation from the famine caused by invasion and siege, disease as a concomitant product of war and siege, slaughter and executions, deportations and emigration (40.11–12). All these factors changed the face of life in Judah for those who remained after the Babylonians had returned home from their spoliations of the cities and the land. But the deportations were probably only a small part of the changes brought about in social organization in the sixth century, and the impression given by Jer. 52 and II Kings 25 of a radical, large-scale depopulation of Judah (e.g. 52.27b) should be regarded as a distortion of the facts for ideological reasons.

The reference in v. 30 to a third deportation dated to the year 582 is enigmatic, but may refer to the Babylonian reprisals for the assassination of Gedaliah. Too much remains unknown about this period (587–582) for such an interpretation to be anything other than speculation. If the Gedaliah story (40.7 – 41.18) reflects historical events in any sense, then Babylon must have responded in a retaliatory fashion and a further deportation (after slaughter) would have been characteristic of their foreign policy. The fact that, according to vv. 29–30, the numbers of deportees are so similar for 587 and 582 (i.e. a difference of only eighty-seven) should lend perspective to the dimensions of the 587 deportation (taking the text as it stands). However, the similarity of the two sets of figures for two very different events (siege and punishment of land and city in revolt as opposed to retribution for a small-scale assassination) lends weight to Rudolph's reading of v. 28 as a reference to the deportation of the inhabitants of the Judaean territory in 588–7 (cf. 34.7).

52.31–34

31 And in the thirty-seventh year of the captivity of Jehoiachin king of
Judah, in the twelfth month, on the twenty-fifth day of the month, Evil-merodach king of Babylon, in the year that he became king, lifted up the head of Jehoiachin king of Judah and brought him out of prison; 32 and he
spoke kindly to him, and gave him a seat above the seats of the kings who were with him in Babylon. 33 So Jehoiachin put off his prison garments. And every day of his life he dined regularly at the king's table; 34 as for his
allowance, a regular allowance was given him by the king according to his daily need, until the day of his death as long as he lived.

[52.31–34] = II Kings 25.27–30 (with minor variations). **[31]** G has *Iōakim*, 'Ioakim' (= Jehoakim?) for MT's Jehoiachin. II Kings 25.27 'twenty-seventh day' for 'twenty-fifth day' here; G 'twenty-fourth'. MT *'ᵉwīl mᵉrōdak*, 'Evil-merodach': a corruption (deliberate?) of Awel (Amēl)-marduk, 'man of Marduk', Nebuchadrezzar's son (ruled 561–560); *'ᵉwīl*, 'foolish, stupid', suggests Judaean mockery of the Babylonian king. MT *bišᵉnat malᵉkutō*, 'in the year of his reign': i.e. when he became king (II Kings 25.27, *malᵉkō*); the amnesty for Jehoiachin may have been due to the accession of the new king when such acts of kindness were appropriate. G^B *kai ekeiren auton*, 'and shaved him', after the raising of his head (cf. Gen. 41.14). K *hkly'*; Q *hakkᵉlū'*, '(house of) restraint', i.e. prison; cf. 37.4. **[32]** K *mlkym*, 'kings'; Q *hammᵉlākīm*, '*the* kings': i.e. the other kings also detained in Babylon. **[33]** MT *wᵉ'ākal leḥem lᵉpānāyw tāmīd kol-yᵉmē ḥayyāw*, 'and he ate bread (i.e. dined) in his presence continually all the days of his life': this is ambiguous in that it is not clear whether 'all the days of *his* life' refers to Jehoiachin or Amel-Marduk; as the king died *c.* 560 (whether naturally or by intrigue is not known, cf. Wiseman 1956, 38) the phrase should refer to him (Cornill, 529; Rudolph, 322), though it is possible Jehoiachin predeceased his overlord (cf. Gray 1977, 773), or the biblical writer, being only concerned with Jehoiachin, refers to the Judaean 'king-in-exile'. **[34]** Pritchard 1969, 308, gives details of the Babylonian allowance to Jehoiachin (cf. Gray 1977, 774–5), but vv. 31–34 represent a rather different story from that suggested by the Babylonian administrative documents, where Jehoiachin is the recipient of a state pension. MT *mēʾēt melek-bābel*, 'by the king of Babylon': RSV, II Kings 25.30 lack 'of Babylon' (= *mēʾēt hammelek*). II Kings 25.30 lacks 'until the day of his death'; G lacks 'all the days of his life': MT represents a combination of two variants. Cf. 40.5 for the motif of a special allowance (*ʾaruḥāh*).

The appendix does not conclude with the stark listing of the number of deportees but closes the book of Jeremiah (and Kings) on a happier note. A story is told about the release of the exiled king Jehoiachin from prison and the kindness shown to him by Nebuchadrezzar's successor Amel-Marduk. This touching story reverses the treatment handed out to Jehoiachin's successor Zedekiah (vv. 9–11) and suggests that, with the death of Nebuchadrezzar, things may have changed for the better for the Judaean exiles (cf. the opposite reversal for the people of Israel when the king who knew Joseph died and a new king arose over Egypt 'who did not know Joseph', Ex. 1.8–10). In v. 9 Nebuchadrezzar speaks judgments (*dbr mšpṭym*, i.e. passes sentence) on Zedekiah, but in v. 32 Amel-Marduk speaks kindly (*wayᵉdabbēr ʾittō ṭōbōt*, lit. 'and he spoke with him good things') to Jehoiachin. Zedekiah is treated in the most vicious manner and imprisoned until his death (v. 11). Whereas whatever harsh treatment Jehoiachin may have suffered in the past (implicit in the story of his imprisonment) is now ended with his release, his elevated status above the other 'kings-in-exile', his kind reception by the king and the permanent allowance he receives until his death. The contrast between the two kings is almost symmetrical, and in their respective fates it may be possible to detect a subtle statement about the different futures of their family line. Zedekiah's immediate family is cut down before his eyes, so the blinded, imprisoned king brings to an end with his own death any hopes of a dynasty arising from his family. Nothing is said about Jehoiachin's family, but his emergence from prison into the king's favour bodes well for their future. This may be an over-subtle reading of the contrasting stories, but the implicit note of hope makes a better ending to an appendix so full of woeful tales than yet a further word of doom. It also provides a postscript to the tradition which expresses an attitude towards

Jehoiachin which is singularly lacking in the Jeremiah tradition proper (cf. 22.24–30). The hostility with which Jehoiachin is dismissed in the material attributed to Jeremiah is absent in this note from a different tradition appended to the book. Furthermore, the great cruelty of Nebuchadrezzar towards Judah appears to die with his death and his successor behaves in a much more humane fashion towards a deposed monarch who has suffered a very long imprisonment.

Excavations of Babylon have yielded cuneiform tablets which set out, among other things, the allocations for Jehoiachin and his sons (Weidner 1939; Pritchard 1969, 308; cf. Oded 1977, 481) and these may be regarded as confirming v. 34 (cf. Gray 1977, 774–5). However, such discoveries do not confirm the status of Jehoiachin as a prisoner nor do they present him in terms parallel to the story in vv. 31–34. He and his sons receive an allowance from the Babylonian authorities, and this provision (which in no sense singles them out as important or different) may be said to lie behind the story developed by the Deuteronomists. For them Jehoiachin had been incarcerated (*throughout* Nebuchadrezzar's reign?) but released during an amnesty associated with Amel-Marduk's accession year, and this liberation is presented in glowing terms. Questions about how the 'king-in-exile' came to be in jail or how such an exile could behave in such a fashion without being executed can be raised but not answered because they presuppose a real history behind the story. However, the story must be considered in terms of the editors' purpose in shaping their account along the lines of an imprisonment followed by a release at a specific juncture of Babylonian history. Are vv. 31–34 designed to make a statement about the Judaean royal house with which to conclude the Deuteronomistic history of the kings of Israel and Judah?

There are two dominant views of the significance of the release of king Jehoiachin from prison: it is simply the alleviation of the unpleasant lot of the captive king (e.g. Gray 1977, 773–5), or it is a Deuteronomistic statement that Jehoiachin's rehabilitation bears on the fate of the whole house of David as presented throughout the books of Kings (cf. Zenger 1968). The difference between the two views is determined by reading vv. 31–34 as a simple observation of a change in Jehoiachin's fortunes in order to end the book of Kings on an auspicious note rather than to blight the future under the evil influence of a despondent ending (Gray). Alternatively, the story may be read in conjunction with the Deuteronomistic theology of kingship running through the history, of which II Sam. 7 may be regarded as the linchpin. Either reading may be supported from the text but one depends upon a wider reading of the books of Kings in a holistic manner. The Deuteronomistic history of the royal house demonstrates the failure of the monarchy to maintain fidelity to Yahweh, a failure which culminated in the deportation of the king in 597 and the destruction of city, palace and temple in 587. The Deuteronomistic theme epitomized by II Sam. 7 represents a different word active in history, namely that of salvation anchored in the promise to David of a permanent throne and dynasty (cf. von Rad 1962, 343–4). In the light of 587 what had happened to this word? Did the humiliation of king Zedekiah and the massacre of his family extinguish for ever the hope vested in the house of David? Perhaps by ending the history of the royal house with a story about Jehoiachin, rather than Zedekiah, the Deuteronomists wished to leave open the question of the fate of David. The door closed by Zedekiah's tragic end is reopened by a story in which the alternative 'king-in-exile' is made the recipient of Babylonian kindness. Thus the future of the royal house becomes a vital question rather than a dead letter.

If an optimistic reading of vv. 31–34 is to be entertained, it must be done in modest terms. The transformation of Jehoiachin's allowance into a story of his release from prison and his elevation *above* the other 'kings-in-exile' indicates a preparedness to read too much into the king's new status among the exiles in Babylon. But this willingness goes no further than to present Jehoiachin as enjoying some degree of comfort in his declining years. No direct statement is made about the future of his family or the prospects for the dynasty of David. That silence may indicate realistic modesty or cautious optimism; but the Deuteronomists do not show their hand. All that may be said with certitude is that, 'The last verses of Kings announce, in a cautious, nuanced way, that a scion of David, king of Israel, is yet alive and well' (Levenson 1984a, 361). The future is left pregnant with possibility, yet nothing is said or implied which could expose the Deuteronomists to the charge of speaking presumptuously or prophesying falsely. The wise reader of vv. 31–34 may prefer to understand the story as simply the alleviation of Jehoiachin's circumstances, but as the last statement in the lengthy story of the adventures of the house of David it is open to being read as a word to the wise and a nod in the direction of the future.

Thus the book of Jeremiah *as we now have it* ends on an ambiguous note. The original ending represented by the second edition (MT) anticipates the utter destruction of Babylon and, therefore, implicitly asserts the restoration of Judah. The first edition (G) ends with the more modest word of hope to Baruch which represents the possibility of survival for individuals in a time of evil inflicted on all flesh. With the addition of the appendix from the Deuteronomistic history the book of Jeremiah, so characterized by anger, destruction, horror and pain, ends on a kindlier note. So all three endings (or stages in the ending) of the book of Jeremiah reverse the dominant trend of the tradition which rants and rages against the communities of Jews in Palestine and Egypt. Do these endings constitute the prelude to the building and planting of the community in its own land – motifs used throughout the tradition, but related to the nations in the prologue of 1.5, 10? Perhaps they are symptomatic of those elements which form a minor aspect of the book (e.g. 24.4–7; 29.10–14; 30–33) and reflect the more positive outlook of the post-catastrophe period. Whatever they represent, the final element in the appendix closes the book on a brief note of quietness and, dare one say, grace (human, of course). 'Calm of mind all passion spent' – the book ends with a touching depiction of human kindness enacted between human beings. It may even be a beginning . . .

CPSIA information can be obtained
at www.ICGtesting.com
Printed in the USA
LVOW04s0233110216
474635LV00008B/192/P

9 781905 04864